DIRECTING

FILM TECHNIQUES AND AESTHETICS

Fourth Edition

Michael Rabiger

AMSTERDAM • BOSTON • HEIDELBERG • LONDON • NEW YORK • OXFORD •
PARIS • SAN DIEGO • SAN FRANCISCO • SINGAPORE • SYDNEY • TOKYO

Focal Press is an imprint of Elsevier

Publisher: Elinor Actipis
Publishing Services Manager: George Morrison
Senior Project Manager: Brandy Lilly
Developmental Editor: Cara Anderson
Assistant Editor: Robin Weston
Marketing Manager: Becky Pease
Cover Design: Wendy Simpson

Focal Press is an imprint of Elsevier
30 Corporate Drive, Suite 400, Burlington, MA 01803, USA
Linacre House, Jordan Hill, Oxford OX2 8DP, UK

 Recognizing the importance of preserving what has been written, Elsevier prints its books on acid-free paper whenever possible.

Library of Congress Cataloging-in-Publication Data
Rabiger, Michael.
  Directing : film techniques and aesthetics / by Michael Rabiger. — 4th ed.
    p. cm.
  Includes bibliographical references and index.
  ISBN 978-0-240-80882-6 (pbk. : alk. paper) 1. Motion pictures—Production and direction.
2. Motion pictures—Aesthetics. I. Title.
  PN1995.9.P7R26 2008
    791.43′ 0233—dc22

                                                                    2007017582

British Library Cataloguing-in-Publication Data
A catalogue record for this book is available from the British Library.

ISBN: 978-0-240-80882-6

For information on all Focal Press publications
visit our website at www.books.elsevier.com

07 08 09 10 11 5 4 3 2 1

Printed in the United States of America

For Lewis, Netta, Alma,
Lauren, Freya, and Olivia
with much love.

CONTENTS

INTRODUCTION

Here is a practical, comprehensive film directing manual. It will prepare you like no other for the methods, thought processes, feelings, and judgments that a director must use throughout the fascinating experience of creating a film. By talking to you directly and respectfully as a colleague, and by offering hands-on projects as learning tools, it recognizes that you learn best from doing.

Making films that speak with your own voice and identity will engage your head, your hands, and your heart, and enhance every aspect of your waking life.

Film makes extreme demands on its makers so this book makes an ideal companion for the self-taught or for anyone going to film school. There, coursework of necessity focuses on surmounting technological hurdles, and courses will always leave significant gaps in the conceptual and authorial side of filmmaking. These the student must bridge alone. Commonly he or she can get no clear sight of the pathway from beginning to end of the artistic process, and find nobody to give help at moments when it's most needed. This book makes accessible the context, explanations, and mentorship that everyone needs.

FILM'S ARTISTIC PROCESS ENHANCED

Digital technology has massively accelerated the film student's learning experience. Low cost shooting permits a fully professional shooting experience. The novice director can now experiment, improvise, solve problems collaboratively with cast and crew, revise earlier solutions, and treat crises as disguised opportunities. A guerilla approach like this—normal enough in documentary but alien to the cost-driven traditions of the features industry—empowers the low-budget independent to produce cutting-edge creativity. Even seasoned professionals are turning to digital filmmaking: George Lucas made his *Star Wars: Episode II Attack of the Clones* using high definition (HD) digital camcorders. Shooting the equivalent of 2 million feet of film in a third less time, he saved $2.5 million in stock and became an enthusiastic convert. You see the fruits of this liberation in the digitally-enabled work of Mike Figgis, Steven Soderbergh, Wim Wenders, Spike Lee, Michael Winterbottom, Gary Winock, Rick Linklater, as well as the leading lights in the Danish Dogme Group and many, many others.

WHAT'S NEW IN THIS EDITION

This book's organization suggests an ideally linear process for film production, but it's laid out that way so you can find information in a hurry. In practice, everything is connected to everything else, and nothing done early ever seems finished or fore-closed. Filmmaking being more circular than linear, earlier editions of this book evolved into something like an encyclopedia. By the third edition, trying to provide information wherever it was needed was making the book repetitive and too long. This new edition is lighter by about a sixth. Information has been consolidated, there is more internal signposting, and the advice is more concisely prescriptive. Compression notwithstanding, the book is once more expanded in scope and reflects some of the huge increase of information available on all aspects of film-making. Highlights are:

- Part 1 Artistic Identity (Chapters 1–3) includes more about the director's job and characteristics, and, since a film director is really a dramatist, more about dramatic analysis and dramatic construction.

- Part 2 Screencraft (Chapters 4–6) includes a revised and expanded screen grammar. This is not the conventional kind but an original and practical guide to using the hidden origins of film language. By closely observing the actuality around him or her, the director can role-play a figure called the Concerned Observer. Then, by proactively biassing the tale, the director can surpass mere technical proficiency to become a storyteller with a distinctive voice and style.

- Part 3 The Story and Its Development (Chapters 7–11) concentrates on hon-ing a given screenplay rather than laboring to produce original writing. Good manuals exist for this already.

- Part 4 Aesthetics and Authorship (Chapters 12–16) provides an extensive questionnaire to spotlight a developing film's aesthetic needs and potential. Each question links to particular chapters, making solutions easier to locate.

- Part 5 Preproduction (Chapters 17–27) offers a revised and expanded group-ing of information on: the fundamentals of acting; communicating with and directing actors; casting; and the all-important rehearsal and development process. Thirty exercises offer acting experience and experience at directing actors, either with a text or through improvisation. New tables list the acting principles that each exercise explores.

- Part 6 Production reflects the growing use of digital technology as well as an enhanced discussion of crew roles, and of directing actors during the produc-tion cycle.

- Part 7 Postproduction reflects developments in the digital domain, and includes the use of both original and previously recorded music. The postpro-duction phase determines much of the fluency and impact of the final film, and reflects the author's many years as an editor.

- Part 8 Career Track is more clearly structured and starts with a vocational self-assessment questionnaire to help the user identify where his or her strengths lie.

NOW AVAILABLE ON THE BOOK'S WEB SITE

To enhance the book's portability, some material has been shifted to the book's web site (www.focalpress.com/9780240808826), notably the checklists and project assessment forms. Having them downloadable lets you edit or augment them at will. The web site also contains a casting form, a short budget form, and information specific to 16 mm and 35 mm film. For the convenience of teachers (and self-teachers), the web site also contains suggestions for using this book to support different classes and syllabus levels.

PREPARATION VERSUS EXECUTION

You may wonder why a film production book devotes sixteen chapters to the thought and activities prior to the preproduction phase. Most beginners assume that a director mainly needs to know screen techniques and filmmaking technology, but this is like assuming that calligraphy will equip a would-be novelist. In fact, audiences seldom reject original screen works on grounds of shaky presentation. Werner Herzog's earliest films, for instance, were frankly amateurish, but the vision and intention behind them is strong and audiences responded accordingly. When beginners' screen fiction falls short it usually does so because it lacks:

- Credibility in the story's world and its characters. The director needs better understanding of actors and acting, dramatic structure, and the processes of human perception that underlie film language.
- Unity, individuality, and force of conviction in the story concept. The story needs greater originality, greater momentum in the narrative, and something worthwhile and deeply felt to say.
- Design in the film's dramatic, visual, and aural form that would make it cinematic rather than theatrical.

In simple, direct language this book addresses these abiding concerns, for which no amount of new technology can substitute. Most of those aiming to become screen authors, knowing no better, will concentrate on the material, technical side of filmmaking. Though this prepares them usefully to practice a craft, most are making a journey toward a directing career that is purely imaginary. This need not be so, and this book takes the bull by the horns from its first pages. For every phase of fiction filmmaking it tells you clearly and unequivocally what you must know, what you must do, to put moving stories on the screen.

LOCATING THE HELP YOU NEED

You can find information by going to:

- The Table of Contents for the Part covering the filmmaking stage you're at. There you'll find a breakdown of the chapter contents that handle it.
- The Index.
- The Glossary.
- The Bibliography.

- The web site guide. Since web sites die and resurrect with bewildering speed, be prepared to flush out further sources of information using a search engine. Cross-check all important information with other sources before you bet your shirt on it.

THANKS

Anyone writing a book like this does so on behalf of all the communities to which they belong. Many ideas in this book grew from teaching relationships with students at Columbia College Chicago and New York University—students now so numerous that their descriptions would halfway fill this book. I benefited inestimably from help, advice, and criticism from many esteemed colleagues, most recently in Columbia's Film/Video Department. Help with this and previous editions came from Doreen Bartoni, Robert Buchar, Judd Chesler, Gina Chorak, Dan Dinello, Chap Freeman, Paul Hettel, T.W. Li, Emily Reible, Joe Steiff, and Diego Trejo, Jr., Thanks also to Wenhwa Ts'ao, Chris Peppey, T.W. Li, Joan McGrath, and Sandy Cuprisin for help in finding pictorial matter.

I learned much from all the impassioned teaching colleagues I encountered in the many countries where I have taught, and from all the good work done by those who organize and attend the conferences at CILECT (the International Film Schools Association) and UFVA (University Film & Video Association of North America). I think all of us feel we are slowly coming to grips with the Gordian knot of issues involved in teaching young people how to make films.

For extensive and invaluable criticism of this edition I offer grateful thanks to Mark Freeman (San Diego State University), Charles Merzbacher (Boston University), Quinn Saunders (Quinnipiac University), Andrew Shea (University of Texas at Austin), and Eric Swelstad (Los Angeles Valley College). Their detailed criticisms and suggestions motivated me to go many an extra mile.

Enduring thanks go to my publishers at Focal Press; in particular Elinor Actipis, Cara Anderson, and Robin Weston for their unfailing support, good humor, and great work.

Among friends and family, thanks to: Tod Lending for teaching me more about dramatic form; Milos Stehlik of Facets Multimedia for pictorial assistance; my son Paul Rabiger of Cologne, Germany for our regular phone discussions and his advice on music for film; to my daughters Joanna Rabiger of Austin, Texas and Penelope Rabiger of Jerusalem for our far-ranging conversations on film, education, and so much else. Over four decades their mother Sigrid Rabiger has also influenced my beliefs through her writings and practice in art therapy and education.

Lastly, my deep appreciation to my wife and closest friend Nancy Mattei, who puts up with the solitary and obsessive behavior by which books get written, and whose humor, values, and advice keep me upright and keep me going. With all this help, the errors are truly mine.

Michael Rabiger,
Chicago, 2007.

PART 1

ARTISTIC IDENTITY AND DRAMA

Part 1 (Chapters 1 through 3) deals with the film director's role, the current environment for anyone setting out to become one, and what kind of preparatory work it takes to make a mark with audiences. This takes uncovering your intrinsic artistic identity and deciding what kind of stories you are best equipped to handle. Part 1 also explains the fundamentals of drama, and how to use them in filmmaking. It concludes by describing the director's responsibility for storytelling, and what distinguishes those who do it best.

Before you commit time and funds to chasing this alluring prospect, read Part 8: Career Track and start planning out your career strategy. Strangely enough, many people look only a step or two ahead in the belief that they are keeping their options open.

CHAPTER 1

THE WORLD OF THE FILM DIRECTOR

CINEMA ART AND YOU

Cinema is the great art form of our time. It provides popular entertainment and is the preeminent forum for ideas and self-expression. Occupying the place of the theater in Elizabethan times, or the novel in the 19th and early 20th centuries, the cinema is where dreams of every shape and meaning take hold of the contemporary mind. The cinema leaps national and cultural barriers as no medium has ever done before, and the best films excite hearts and minds as only good art can. We each have particular stories to tell, and I shall show you that you do too.

No limit exists to the number of films the world can consume, so if you can direct outstanding screen work, you can make a job for yourself. This won't be simple or easy, and the competition is stiff. But if you can sustain passion for the work, this book will help you succeed no matter whether you've done ten years in the film industry or are just starting out.

Learning to direct films is like learning to conduct an orchestra. Most conductors learn an instrument, master music, and then learn to conduct—which means coordinating an ensemble of top-notch musicians. Most who direct get there by mastering a key craft such as screenwriting, cinematography, or editing. Which one you should choose will emerge as you roll up your sleeves, use this book, and get an all-around immersion. You may do this in film school with fellow students, or outside it working with a few committed friends. Superb, affordable digital technology now makes high-quality filmmaking possible on a tight budget, so learning to direct has never been more accessible.

By the way, when I speak of filmmaking or directing a "film," I include film and digital media together. They draw on a common screen language, use the same directorial approaches, and are different only as screen delivery technologies.

THE DIRECTOR

WHO DIRECTS

People who direct films come in all human types—tall, short, fair, dark, introverted, extroverted, loquacious, taciturn, male, female, gay, straight. Doing it well takes inventiveness and tenacity, getting the best out of a team, having strong ideas about the human condition, and a mountaineering passion for filmmaking's grueling process.

Don't listen either to anyone who says you are (or are not) talented. I've taught thousands, and "talent" can be a flash in the pan. What matters is your quality of effort, dogged persistence, and that you love the work. Nobody can predict who will do well. If entry tests could spot potential, then Britain's National Film and Television School would never have rejected Mike Figgis.

If you really want to direct, find a way to keep at it and do not give up.

RESPONSIBILITIES

A director answers to the producer and is responsible for the details, quality, and meaning of the final film. This requires writing or working with writers; envisioning the film's scope, purpose, identity, and meaning; finding appropriate locations that advance the dramatic meaning and atmosphere of the film; auditioning and casting actors; assembling a crew (though this may be done by the producer or unit production manager, if you have one); developing both cast and script through rehearsals; directing the actors and crew during shooting; and then supervising editing and the finalization of the project. The director is also involved in promoting the production in festivals and other circuits.

The first complete version of a film is called the *director's cut*. Depending on the agreement between producer and director, the producer may supersede the director and demand changes considered essential for the film's commercial success. Releasing the *producer's cut* can cause great bitterness and the end of a working relationship, though the critics do not always favor the director's version. With today's digital storage, we shall increasingly see the director's cut released after the film proves to have a strong following. Little cost is involved in giving the film a second wind. The production company can have its cake and eat it. The additional sales are fuel for the fans' debate over art versus commerce, and end up serving both art and commerce.

PERSONAL TRAITS

Ideally, a director is broadly knowledgeable in the arts; possessed of a lively, inquiring mind; likes delving into people's lives and looking for hypothetical links and explanations; is methodical and organized even if outwardly informal and easygoing; able to scrap prior work if assumptions become obsolete; and possessed of endless tenacity when searching out great ideas and performances. The better directors are able to be articulate and succinct in communication; make instinctive judgments and decisions; get the best out of people without being dictatorial; speak on terms of respectful equality with a range of specialists; and understand technicians' problems and co-opt their best efforts.

If this sounds superhuman, many excellent directors are obstinate, private, awkward, idiosyncratic, and tend to desert actors for crew, or vice versa. During production, most directors sooner or later show signs of insecurity (depression, manic energy, low flash point, panic, irresolution). If that is not enough to puzzle crew members, the director's inflamed mental state will generate superhuman energy that pushes everyone's patience to the limit. They often sink into acute doubt and anxiety during shooting; suffer sensory overload and find choice painful; and, at the end of a production, go into postpartum depression and/or physical illness.

The truth is that giving birth to a story for the screen is an intoxicating business. Whoever does it fully and completely is living existentially—that is, entirely in the present and spending each precious moment as if it were their last. This is especially true after an initial success: thereafter you face artistic and professional extinction every step of the way. Like stage fright, the dread and exhilaration of the chase may never go away. But the sign of any worthwhile experience is that it both attracts and scares you.

COLLABORATION

People think directing must be the ultimate in self-expression, but the cinema earned its preeminent place because it is a collective, not an individualist's, medium. Making a feature film takes writers, dramatists, actors, and computer image and illusion makers. It takes choreographers, stunt specialists, art directors, scene builders, sound designers, and makeup artists—as well as costumers, musicians, editors, artists, and craftspeople of every kind, all working together. To complete the Noah's ark, there are distributors, exhibitors, financiers, and speculators who make filmmaking possible because they insist that it find a paying audience. Each specialist yields the greater part of his or her life to making a contribution, and cinema's strength and appeal come from the collaborative interplay at the core of this process. "As a director," says Christopher Nolan, "I'm a sort of human lens through which everyone's efforts are focused. A big part of my job is making decisions about how all the great talent that I'm working with blends into a single consciousness."[1]

Ingmar Bergman likened it to the great undertakings in the Middle Ages when teams of international craftsmen—specialists who never even bothered to leave their names—gathered in crews to build the great European cathedrals. The cinema, he says, is today's version of such collective endeavor, and from each emerges something greater than the sum of its parts.

LEADERSHIP

Directing means developing the skills and persuasion to make everybody give of their very best. It involves thinking, feeling, and acting like a director from the first idea through to the final cut, which is what this book covers. When shooting's done, the director needs the rigor in the cutting room to work and rework the piece so that its notes merge into a concerto.

[1] Christopher Nolan—director of *Memento, Insomnia, Batman Begins, The Prestige, The Dark Knight*—in *American Cinematographer*, January 2007 (back cover).

For all this, you will have to develop the self-knowledge, humility, humor, and dogged persistence that command respect. You will probably acquire these qualities from endless mistakes, because a lot of learning in filmmaking is negative learning. As you mature as an artist over years, you come to understand better and better how to fulfill the emotional, psychological, and intellectual needs of the common person—that is, your audience. Happily, the members of that audience are a lot like yourself.

FACING TESTS

This book is distilled from a lifetime of shepherding people with your aspirations and midwifing their projects. It is your best friend and has advice, examples, and explanations to answer most predicaments. To begin with, you feel like an inept juggler; but there's no denying that you get better if you work at it. Whatever you shoot will have to be something you thoroughly feel, comprehend, and believe in. And you will have to maintain a huge, wonderful struggle to hold onto your initial vision while you keep everyone going.

THE MEDIUM

FILM OR VIDEO?

Passions, especially among cinematographers, still run high over which medium to use, so let's briefly examine the pros and cons—in particular as they affect the learner. For professional features, 35 mm film is still the preferred camera medium, but digital postproduction is now universal. Film currently records a more detailed image and has a superior look, but this shows up only in a new print projected in a well-equipped, well-run film theater—most being neither. Film's advantages are moot unless writing, acting, and staging are of a very high order. Directing methods are identical, and only the scale of operations and path to completion are different. Thirty-five-millimeter film is special and wonderful, but the digitizing, editing, and matchback processes (in which digital numbers become the sole guide to cutting the negative) are expensive and complex for the beginner, and are prone to ghastly and irreversible mistakes.

Let's look at ground zero, where everyone starts. Shooting fiction on DV or HD video saves 20 to 35 percent of the time, and slashes to near zero the huge budget mandated by film and its laboratory costs. Video lets the filmmaker-in-training shoot ample coverage and edit to the highest standards without regard for expense or compromise. Now that digital storage capacities are up and prices down, you can digitize a whole production in your computer and edit to cinema quality in one process. This is revolutionary and democratizes film production. HD is looking even better now that color correction and image control, formerly done in a lab, can be done in a laptop computer (Figure 1-1).

Film has been necessary for the large, bright, detailed image associated with the cinema, but this, too, is changing. HD digital projection is now as good as 35 mm quality, but comes at a time when Netflix (unlimited DVDs available on subscription and mailed to your home) threatens to empty cinemas. When movies on demand arrive—movies downloadable at 35 mm quality from satellite, cable, or the Internet—the true

FIGURE 1-1

Much of film postproduction can now be handled in a laptop computer (photo courtesy of Avid).

cinema experience will arrive in the living room. Audiences don't know or care if a show was shot on film or HD. What is certain is that more and different films will be needed to feed a worldwide entertainment monster, and they will be made on ever lower budgets by ever more inventive independent production companies. Doing well on a low budget will be the passport to larger productions.

SHORT FILMS OR LONGER?

Serve on a festival jury, and you quickly discover that most films disclose their limitations in the first dozen shots. The screening jury wonders (sometimes testily and aloud) why people don't make films of 5 minutes instead of a mind-numbing 50. The message is clear: short films show in a small compass the full range of production, authorship, and stylistic skills. Their economy lies in shooting costs and editing time, not in brainwork, for you must still establish characters, time, place, and dramatic situation and set tight limits on the subject. These are tough disciplines to acquire, but they pay off handsomely. Poets always do well in longer forms, no matter whether they make plays, novels, or films. And now even short films have a wide audience—among YouTube and iPod users.

It's a puzzle why film schools don't insist more on brevity. Students and teachers alike, I suppose, are drawn into the medium by feature films, so everyone makes zeppelins when they should make kites. But your work must reach audiences if you are to get recognition; two good short films are ten times more likely to get festival screenings than a single long one of similar quality. And when you start looking for work, successful short films are your best calling cards.

DEVELOPING CINEMA ART

Learning to use the cinema is complex because it is all the other arts combined. You'll need to investigate how the other arts contribute to film and how each acts on us. To make your mark, you will need strong, clear, and critical ideas about the condition of your times. To open up interior spaces and existential questions in your audience's imagination, you must aim beyond the ordinary. Good films invite us to dream, to exercise our judgment, and to draw on our feelings and intuitions. Film is still in its infancy, and it needs energetic and original people driving it. The groundwork to begin this is already in you. As I shall show in Chapter 2, you already have an established artistic identity that awaits discovery.

WHY HOLLYWOOD METHODS WON'T WORK

Film schools seem to promise a quick route to the film industry, so let's for a moment compare the professional feature team's process with that of a lean, independent production. The differences are significant to directors-in-training, and show up most in schedules and budgets.

Professional feature film priorities are economically determined. Scriptwriting, though slow, is relatively inexpensive, while actors, equipment, and crew are high cost and used with military precision. Hollywood skills and intelligence are second to none, but the system requires "bankable" stars and highly developed technicians, all able to produce without delay or experiment what is usable and repeatable. During a feature shoot, about 50 to 100 specialists carry forward their particular part of the communal task. Each will have begun as an apprentice in a lowly position and will have worked half a lifetime to earn senior levels of responsibility. Many come from film families and imbibed the necessary mind-set with their orange juice.

A director in the high-budget world is under pressure to shoot a safe, all-purpose camera coverage that can be sorted out in the cutting room. Unless that director is a heavy hitter, he (only rarely she) must fight narrowly for what is achievable in the schedule. Thus, star vehicle films—too profitable to change from within—are often as packaged and formulaic as supermarket novels. Why? Because a box office success can return millions to its backers in a few weeks. Make no mistake, film is a *business*. Producers prefer the standard process over the new or the personal, and if you doubt my words, read a few issues of the film industry's trade journal *Variety*.

The low-budget (or no-budget) independent director can seldom use professional crew or actors, and so must be capable of shaping nonprofessionals into a well-knit, accomplished team. They need extended rehearsals to find empathy with their characters, become comfortable with the filming process, and develop trust in their director. Nothing else will give their performances conviction and authority. Because professional productions dispense with rehearsals, only special, or specially trained, actors do well in the cinema. You, however, must go a different route, and develop the elements of your production before you shoot it. Most people don't know this, and learn a bitter lesson when they come to edit.

If you think nonprofessionals aren't viable, here are fine international cinema examples that draw their casts from villagers, kids, nomadic tribespeople, schoolteachers, doctors, and peasants:

Italy
- Luchino Visconti: *La Terra Trema* (1948)
- Vittorio De Sica: *The Bicycle Thief* (1948, Figure 1-2), *Umberto D* (1952)

FIGURE 1-2

De Sica's neorealist *Bicycle Thief* used untrained actors in its poignant tale of a poor bill-poster trying to recover the bicycle on which his livelihood depends (courtesy Produzione De Sica/The Kobal Collection).

- Francesco Rosi: *Salvatore Giuliano* (1961)

France
- Robert Bresson: *Pickpocket* (1959), *Balthazar* (1966), *Mouchette* (1967)

Great Britain
- Ken Loach: *Kes* (1969)

India
- Satyajit Ray's Apu Trilogy: *Pather Panchali* (1955), *Aparajito* (1957), *The World of Apu* (1959)

Iran
- Abbas Kiarostami: *Where Is the Friend's Home?* (1987), *Taste of Cherry* (1997)

- Bahram Beizai: *Bashu, the Little Stranger* (1991)
- Mohsen Makhmalbaf: *Gabbeh* (1996)
- Jafar Panahi: *The White Balloon* (1995)
- Bahman Ghobadi: *A Time for Drunken Horses* (2000)

These directors saw advantages where others would see only handicaps. They chose a subject and treatment that used ordinary people as actors, and developed significant stories without elaborate events or environments. Today, even established and popular filmmakers are taking this route—for artistic reasons as much as for budgetary ones. None of this may be evident to the newcomer or to the old-timer who grew up in the industry. Each assumes that film skills come from emulating the professional system. Certainly you must learn professional techniques and procedures so you can make a living, but the route to low-budget success lies in a development process long familiar in the theater, as we shall see.

FILMMAKING TOOLS AND FILM EXHIBITION

High-definition (HD) camcorders, digital audio recorders, and computerized editing have massively accelerated the learning process and slashed the outlay and labor of filmmaking. Films produced digitally that are meant for projection in cinemas must presently be transferred at great expense to 35 mm film, but electronic projectors are appearing that improve on many aspects of 35 mm. Sound is phenomenal, there is no weave in the image, colors do not deteriorate, the print does not become scratched, and the show cannot break. There are no botched changeovers between reels, and no leisurely searches for focus by a bleary-eyed projectionist. The entire show can be downloaded to the cinema or home via cable or satellite, saving delay and a fortune in shipping.

Inevitably, digital cinema systems will rival the IMAX experience, which draws crowds to marvel at the cinematic experience, just as they did in the cinema when my great-uncle Sidney Bird was a projectionist in 1909.

Film production is escaping the stranglehold of the studio executive system. Financing and distribution are decentralizing and becoming more like book publishing. Truly diversified distribution is available via DVD, and high-quality movie viewing will soon be available on demand via the Internet or satellite. YouTube is showing what an appetite exists for producing, distributing, and consuming all kinds of eccentric material, and undoubtedly more productions will be "narrowcast" worldwide to audiences of every imaginable specialized interest. They will need savvy directing, so your time has come!

Here, however, we run into the cinema's limitation. The prosaic realism of the camera, showing literally and to the last open pore whatever is placed before it, constantly threatens to drag the experience down into banality. Used unintelligently, the camera conveys a glut of realism and allows nothing to become poetic. This is a handicap, and films that break out of it must work hard at other levels to evoke our feelings. They draw on myths and archetypes, for instance, because we resonate to the whole range of tragic and comic human truths that come down to us from antiquity, and their presence unfailingly triggers our deeper emotions. For instance, Marcel Carné's *The Children of Paradise* (1945, Figure 1-3) will be lovely as long as one print survives and one audience member lives to see it.

FIGURE 1-3

Carné's *Children of Paradise* is a story of unattainable love using the Pierrot and Columbine folktale archetypes (courtesy Museum of Modern Art/Film Stills Archive).

Arletty, who plays Garance, grows beautiful and enigmatic as you watch her, because she is the embodiment of Columbine, the free-spirited, fickle girl of folktales. Poor Pierrot can never hold her because he's too foolishly sincere and earthbound. You don't need to know this, for the lovers evoke the poignancy of your own failed affairs of the heart. Poetic tradition in the arts isn't lumber that holds you back. It's a friend and ally to help you forward.

LEARNING TO DIRECT

ENVIRONMENT

The film industry now accepts that new recruits come from film schools, and that they are more ambitious, educated, versatile, and knowledgeable about the cinema than any generation preceding. The question (for those that can afford it) is not whether to go to film school, but which one might be most suitable. First, however, we must dismantle a common misperception—that all you really need do is learn about equipment and techniques. Certainly there's plenty to learn, and it's fascinating stuff. But tools are just tools, whereas the cinema's lifeblood comes from human feeling and intelligence. And don't believe those who say you must learn the tools before you can have anything to say. To direct intelligently, you'll need:

- A knowledge and love of film language and film history
- A strong grasp of what drama is and how to use it
- A drive to tell stories that comes from passionately held ideas about the human condition

The first two are easy: every aspiring director loves film and enjoys learning about drama. The last, concerning authorship, is harder. Having something original to say about the business of being alive, and telling stories cinematically—those are what face most people when they look beyond equipment. Yet anyone able to use this book can open doors in their own psyche and find a fully formed artistic identity, ready to guide your directing.

FILM SCHOOL

Compared with schools for painting, theater, or dance, those for film are recent. Most teach film history, aesthetics, and production techniques well, and the best lead their students toward expressing critical perceptions of the world around them. They often hire practicing professionals as teachers, and place their best students as interns in professional production. For a discussion of film schools in relation to building a career, see Part 8: Career Track (Chapters 45 through 47).

But supposing you don't have the time or resources to go to film school. Can you learn with friends, develop a style and a film unit without attending film school? Yes, you can. It's not easy, but novices with digital equipment are in the same position as musicians making use of new recording methods in the 1960s. From them came a revolution in popular music—and profound social changes in consequence. Something similar is under way with the screen.

DEVELOPING A CAREER IN INDEPENDENT FILMMAKING

THE GOOD NEWS

The number of "indie" (independently financed and produced) feature-length productions keeps rising, and the Sundance Film Festival is their Mecca in the United States. They outpace studio productions in number and sometimes quality, originality, and awards. Increasingly they use digital production for its lower costs and greater flexibility. Notable digital productions of the past decade include Thomas Vinterberg's *The Celebration* (1998, Figure 1-4), Lars von Trier's *The Idiots* (1998), Mike Figgis' *Time Code* (2000) and *Hotel* (2001), Spike Lee's *The Original Kings of Comedy* (2000), Rick Linklater's *Waking Life* (2001), Steven Soderbergh's *Full Frontal* (2002), and George Lucas' *Star Wars: Episode II—Attack of the Clones* (2002). Lucas used Sony CineAlta high-definition video cameras and pronounced them not only trouble-free, but so liberating that he could not imagine returning to shooting film (Figure 1-5). David Lynch personally used a Sony PD150 camcorder and Apple Final Cut Pro digital technology for *Inland Empire* (2006). The difference while shooting was welcome to its cast. "We were shooting constantly," said Laura Dern. "There were no large lights to put up, and

FIGURE 1-4 ────────────────────────────────

Vinterberg's *The Celebration*, a feature film shot using handheld digital cameras (courtesy Nimbus Film/The Kobal Collection).

FIGURE 1-5 ────────────────────────────────

The Sony CineAlta HDCAM® that convinced George Lucas to give up film and shoot digitally (photo courtesy of Sony).

we had no need to wait between setups for coverage, because David was holding the camcorder—he would cover an entire scene in 20 minutes or an hour. The luxury was an incredible shorthand on the set. There was never any down-time." (*American Cinematographer,* April 2007). For who's doing what in independent filmmaking, see Independent Film Channel (www.ifctv.com)

THE BAD NEWS

Technically proficient as they may be, most independent features are unwatchable and never find a distributor. They suffer from poor writing, poor dramatic structure, poor acting, poor directing—and they sink without a trace. Open access to screen tools has produced a karaoke situation where anyone can stand up and sing—but the public won't stay to listen. So you and I squarely face the problems that follow any liberation: How to use the new freedom effectively? How best to develop one's potential? How not to run over the cliff with the herd?

The Duplass brothers' engaging *The Puffy Chair* (2005), well received at Sundance, epitomizes the strengths and handicaps of the best low-budget indie films, and few can have garnered such contradictory reviews (see www.rottentomatoes.com/m/10005108-puffy_chair/). The film is significant because it shows just how much you can achieve with a main cast of three, a $10,000 budget, a miniDV camera, and well-defined dramatic ideas. A road movie combining comedy and bittersweet lovers' scenes, it involves the confused, well-meaning Josh and his girlfriend, Emily, who yearns for commitment from him. Meaning to salvage their waning relationship, they take a long journey to pick up the puffy armchair that Josh has bought on eBay as a present for his dad's birthday. Then things start going wrong: Josh's self-involved filmmaker brother, Rhett, tags along; the deal turns out to be a scam; and the couple's relationship, vastly aggravated by Rhett's presence, runs on the rocks.

The film doesn't quite live up to the high promise of its opening scenes, reshot at the end of shooting. Its techniques are quite basic, but it has strong dramatic ideas, a clear developmental arc, and well-defined character types. It has a neat and funny setup, but the actors play their characters below their own natural intelligence, and every scene is slowed by improvised dialogue. The deficiencies lie in lack of acting and directing skills at the scene level. There's a brief, candid, and quite inspiring interview with the Duplass brothers about their homegrown career at www.thefilmlot.com/interviews/INTduplassbros.php. Do read it. You'll see that the Duplass brothers are learning fast and that their next work is likely to be a quantum leap.

WITH LOW BUDGETS IN MIND

Most people using this book will work with modest equipment and slender budgets. Take this as a badge of honor, for original and even revolutionary films can come from the intelligent use of simple equipment and minimal production values. Happily, now that most films are available on DVD, I have been able to draw examples from all periods of international cinema history.

THE AUTEUR AND AUTHORIAL CONTROL

This book may seem to offer many encouragements to the auteur. This term emerged at the time of the French New Wave in the 1950s. It refers to the writer/director controlling the whole screen realization process. In filmmaking of any complexity, the auteur concept just isn't a reality. Though we've all grown up with the idea of the artist as an isolated individualist, such total control in film is simply impossible.

So how does a director develop? A typical evolution starts, in film school or alone, by writing, shooting, and editing one's own small films. Then, ready to produce more sophisticated work, he or she uses several people who are each beginning to specialize in one of the contributory crafts. The director might handle the editing, and this or one of the other crafts becomes his or her passport to paid work on leaving film school. By establishing skills, trust, and creative persistence over time in the film industry, and by investing in his or her own artistic development, the craftsperson leverages opportunities to direct ever larger projects.

Early directing is often cautious and commercially oriented, for death at the box office means doing a Humpty Dumpty. Even when constrained by survival instincts to mainstream work, the astute director can still flex artistic muscle and learn about the medium. Gradually becoming known and established, our director has one or two modest successes. Like someone standing up in a small boat, he or she expands cautiously into work that is ever more personally meaningful. As our director gains a mature command of the medium, and gains conviction about the meaning to his or her own life, audiences begin to thrill to an exciting authorial identity at work.

Now something very curious happens: the filmmaker who in film school had total control over a tiny film is now perceived to control an immensely expensive and popular medium. The auteur seems to have reemerged, driving a much better car. In fact, this same person is humbled from years of teamwork, and those teary-eyed thanks to the team during Academy Awards are no empty ritual. They acknowledge where creativity lies in a collaborative art form.

CHAPTER 2

IDENTIFYING YOUR THEMES

This chapter concerns the choice of subject you make when you direct, how you assess its meaning, and how you can unite these with your deepest interests. The clarity that comes from this will help in everything you do.

STORIES YOU CARE DEEPLY ABOUT

Whether you write your own stories, work from someone else's script, or choose something to adapt, you will always face these central questions:

- How am I going to use my developing skills in the world?
- What kind of subjects should I tackle?
- What can I be good at?
- What is my artistic identity?

Each new film project should be about something meaningful to you, not just an exercise in basic skills. If it isn't, you'll be deferring authorship in pursuit of technical excellence—which is a common mistake. Human beings are by nature seekers, and though everyone's quest is different, everyone seeks fresh chapters of meaning during their journey through life. The stronger and more articulate you are in committing to this quest, the more intense your work is likely to be. Those with dramatic life experience (say, of warfare, survival in labor camps, or of being orphaned) seldom doubt what subject to tackle next. But for anyone whose life seems ordinary, finding the keys to your undoubted sense of mission can be baffling. You face a conundrum: you can't make art without a sense of identity, yet it is identity you seek by making art.

ART, IDENTITY, AND COMPETITIVENESS

Some enter the arts in search of self-expression or self-affirmation. This is treacherous ground, for it suggests that art and therapy are synonymous. They overlap, but have different purposes. Art does work in and for the world, whereas therapy is self-directed and seeks relief from doubt or unhappiness. Self-affirmation in the guise of art leads down the slippery slope of self-display. Living as we do in a celebrity culture, we have a great need to be special and different. Hindu belief is interesting here, for Self in their philosophy is *that which you share with all creation*. A Hindu shares his or her identity with a tree, a mountain, a bird, a crippled child. The Western idea of Self is by contrast very isolating. Most people trying to create films actually subscribe to both ends of the spectrum. They want to be individual and recognized, but also to create something universal and useful to others.

If you are asking, "Does all this philosophy and psychology stuff really matter?" then I have to answer, yes, I think it does, because what you believe will determine whether you are happy and productive working in a collective medium like film. When film students fail, it's seldom because they can't handle the work or the technology. It's usually because they can't work as equals with others. Problems arise from control issues, competitiveness, or a refusal to make or keep commitments. Anyone can modify their asocial habits if it matters enough, and some of the group work in film schools exists to sort through and conquer these problems, and to help students locate their best partners. George Tillman, Jr. and Bob Teitel, the writer/producer/director team responsible for *Men of Honor* (2000) and the *Barbershop* films (2002, 2004), were a black student and a white student who met in my college's second-level production course (Figure 2-1). After leaving college, they began their professional output with *Soul Food* (1997) and have worked successfully together ever since. Countless working relationships that come from

FIGURE 2-1

Bob Teitel and George Tillman, Jr., a producer/writer/director team who established their partnership in film school (photo courtesy of State Street Pictures).

similar beginnings persist over decades. People find whom they need and make the relationship that works.[1]

IDENTITY, BELIEF, AND VISION

Film students, asked if they really have stories to tell, are apt to find the question insulting. Surely, to direct, you just need to learn the tools of cinema, and the rest follows! A year or two later, they are anxiously casting around for a decent project.

From your first efforts, I believe you must *tell stories expressing ideas and values about the lives around you*, or your films will be hollow and give audiences nothing to which they can respond. No matter how competently you handle the tools and the medium, your storytelling will be colorless and meaningless.

How, then, can you prepare to make compelling screen fiction? Actually, your options already exist and simply need uncovering. Here's the secret: your life has marked you in unique ways, and these marks—whether you know it or not—will determine how you live your life, what quests you pursue, and what you are equipped to say with passion and authority through a story.

So what are these marks, and how do you recognize them? Everyone has had the experience of suddenly discovering a pattern to some part of their life, and thus feeling the rush of relief and excitement that comes from seeing what has been driving them. Once upon a time, when most people lived in small settlements, everyone saw how you acted over time, and could connect this with your temperament and history. This is still true in farming communities. Lacking those reflections from others, we see our own tendencies only with effort and difficulty. Yet to a large degree, those marks make our destiny, for as Heracleitus said, "a man's character is his fate."[2]

I did not stumble over this truth until I was in my 30s. As part of a study program, I was required to watch all my documentary films and write a self-assessment. My films were about very different topics, so I was astonished to discover there was a common theme linking them all. It was that "most people feel imprisoned, but the inventive can adapt, rebel, and escape." How can you make 20 films and not be aware of such a constant theme? Rather easily, I have to say. And where did the theme come from? The answers came sailing in like homing pigeons. During World War II, my middle-class family relocated to an English agricultural village. For several years, my father, a foreigner, was away serving on merchant ships, and my mother found nothing in common with her rural neighbors. At a local school, I had to contend with kids jeering at the way I spoke. I was derided, my possessions envied, and sometimes I was ambushed. Never doubting that we were "better" than the local people, I had to accept that I was different, unacceptable to the majority, and that fear would be a constant in life. This is something I would have to handle alone because adults were too busy. At home, I was one person; outside it,

---

[1] I am indebted to my Buddhist colleague Dean Doreen Bartoni for enlightening conversations around this subject, as well as to her example of egoless leadership at Columbia College Chicago.

[2] Heracleitus (c.540–c.480 BC).

I was another. I found I could evade tight spots by making people laugh. Later in life, reading about English rural misery and exploitation, I began to understand the innate hostility my type represented. Losing my fear, relationships with fellow conscripts in the Royal Air Force—where the whole thing might easily have been repeated—were quite different and very gratifying.

The common thread in my films came from my character, and my character came from having lived on both sides of a social barrier and empathizing with those in similar predicaments: the black person in a white neighborhood, the Jew among Gentiles, the child among adults. Any story with these trace elements quickens my pulse. But I'd survived into my 30s *unaware that I carried a vision of life*. This vision was of life as a succession of imprisonments, each of which, given determination and friends, one can overcome. Perhaps there's a mark of Cain in my family, for each generation seems to migrate abroad.

The stories you tell always arise from a core of belief, which is your *philosophy*. Mine, had I noted it before starting each film, would have read: "When alone in hostile territory, look for others like yourself, then together search for the right way out, because one always exists."

Each person who creates with originality carries a mark. A biography by Paul Michaud about the late François Truffaut links such films as *The 400 Blows* (1959), *Jules and Jim* (1961), *The Wild Child* (1969), and *The Story of Adèle H.* (1975) with pain Truffaut suffered as a child upon being estranged from his mother (Figure 2-2). His characters' rootless lives, their naive impracticality, and Adèle Hugo's neurotic, self-destructive hunger for love all reflect aspects of the Truffaut known to his friends. This does not reduce or "explain" Truffaut; rather, it points to an energizing self-recognition that he turned outward to develop stories of universal appeal.

Is it helpful or is it destructive to "understand" your own experience too well? Should one seek professional help in doing so? There is a different answer for each person here, but psychotherapy is hard work, and those who pursue it usually do so only to get relief from unhappiness. Making art is a little different, for it arises from burning curiosity and the need to create order and suggest meaning. You should do whatever prepares you best for this. Below are techniques for clarifying your sense of direction and the imprint your life has made on you. If this is interesting, you can explore it in greater depth in my book *Developing Story Ideas*, 2nd ed. (Focal Press, 2006).

Films appear to look resolutely outward and not inward at their makers, so many who work in film do not seek what really drives them. But if drama is to have a spark of individuality, it must come from a strenuous inner dialogue. And whatever starts with yourself and your time becomes ultimately a dialogue with your audience.

FIND YOUR LIFE ISSUES

The marks you carry come from a few central issues in your formative experiences. Reminders of them unfailingly arouse you to strongly partisan feelings. This is your savings bank of deepest experience, and finding how to explore and use it in your work—even if your experiences seem few and personal—can keep you creatively occupied for life. I am talking not about autobiography, but about a core of deeply felt experiences whose themes apply to endless situations outside yourself.

FIGURE 2-2

The desperate search for love by so many of Truffaut's main characters is said to be a heightened version of his own during youth (courtesy The Kobal Collection).

Ideation—the business of defining dramatically charged ideas—begins when you set aside some quiet, self-reflective time away from the hubbub of normal life.

Then,

- Examine without judgment the marks your life has made on you.
- Write briefly how these experiences have shaped you.
- From these reflections, list:
  o The kinds of stories you are best qualified to tell
  o The kinds of characters that particularly attract you
  o The situations you find especially intriguing

     ○ The genre(s) you want to work in (comedy, tragedy, history, biography, film noir, etc.)

- Now go over your answers, and substitute something better for everything that is glib, superficial, or clichéd. Make everything sharply particular. Never settle for fuzzy generalizations. "Generalization," said the acting theorist Stanislavsky, "is the enemy of art."

Quick, reflex answers usually jump out of the pool of clichés we all carry. Consider them a starting point from which to refine and sharpen what you are reaching for. Little by little, something that is itself, something you don't have to reject, will emerge. Work quietly and persistently. Stay open to surprises and changes of direction. Good ideas are not ordered into existence, they are beckoned, and the better ones hide behind a facade of stereotypes. Your job is to find them and lure them out.

At first, it seems that nothing dramatic has happened in your life to draw upon. Perhaps the tensions you have witnessed or experienced never matured into any action. But the writer's gratification—and it may even be the chief reward of authorship—is to make happen what should have happened, but didn't. Any event or situation that is sharply etched in your consciousness awaits shaping into something that expresses emotion and a theme or vision of life. Depending on your tastes and temperament, this may be tragic, comic, satiric, realistic, surreal, or melodramatic. By sending the original characters and events into the confrontations and changes that might have happened, you can follow the road not taken and investigate the originals' unused potential.

Any real-life situation containing characters, events, situations, and conflicts has the elements of drama, and thus the potential to become a full-blown story. Change one or two of the main elements in this borrowed framework, develop your own characters, and the meaning and impact of the entire work will begin to evolve in their own special direction. You can digress imaginatively from a biographical structure or dare to stick more closely to it, as these films did:

- John Boorman's *Hope and Glory* (1987, Figure 2-3) is modeled on the lives and emotional evolution of his family during his boyhood in World War II. With imagination and sympathy, Boorman explores his mother's unfulfilled love for his father's best friend.
- Michael Radford's *Il Postino* (1994) charts the mutually enlightening relationship that developed between a postman and the Chilean poet Pablo Neruda while Neruda was exiled to a Mediterranean island.
- Michael Haneke's *The Piano Teacher* (2001). Isabelle Huppert plays a repressed and sexually perverted piano teacher who falls for a charming student. The script is based on a novel by Elfriede Jelinek, formerly a pianist and teacher herself.

These films make biography dramatic by developing ideas about the underlying causes of their characters' dilemmas. Anyone who studies real lives knows that nothing is more mysterious than the actual.

FIGURE 2-3

Boorman's *Hope and Glory* explores a wartime childhood and a love affair that the boy's mother could not allow to flower (courtesy Columbia/The Kobal Collection).

SUBJECTS TO AVOID

Many subjects that come to mind do so because they are being pumped up by the media or lend themselves to moral propaganda. You'd also be wise to avoid:

- Worlds you haven't experienced or cannot closely research
- Any ongoing, inhibiting problem in your own life (find a therapist—you are unlikely to solve anything while directing a film unit)
- Anything or anyone "typical" (nothing real is typical, so nothing typical will ever be interesting or credible)
- Preaching or moral instruction of any kind
- Films about problems to which you have the answer (so does your audience)

Aim to reach audiences outside your peer group, and you will be making films accessible to a wide audience. For films of a few minutes, try taking something small that you learned the hard way, apply it to a character quite *un*like yourself, and make a modest comment on the human condition. By so doing, you can avoid the self-indulgence afflicting most student films. After all, your work is going to be your portfolio, your precious reel that tells future employers what you can do. You don't want to seem a perpetual student.

DISPLACE AND TRANSFORM

For your first short films, work from events and personalities in your own life, but displace the screen version away from the originals. Fictionalizing frees you from self-consciousness and allows you to tell underlying truths that might offend the originals. Most importantly, it allows you to concentrate on developing dramatic and thematic truths instead of getting tangled in questions of taste and biographical accuracy. You can further liberate your imagination and obscure your sources by:

- Giving characters alternative attributes and work
- Making them composites or amalgamating the attributes of two life models
- Placing the story in a different place or epoch
- Altering the gender of protagonists

One student director whose script told his own story—about abandoning a suburban marriage and well-paying job to become a film student—inverted the gender of his main characters and made the rebel a woman. To give her credible motivations, he had to inhabit both husband's and wife's positions, and so came to more deeply investigate what people trapped in such roles expect out of life. Using the *displacement principle* forced the director into a more empathic relationship with all of them and raised the level of his thematic discourse.

Here are some exercises that you should find helpful.

PROJECTS

PROJECT 2-1: THE SELF-INVENTORY

To uncover your real issues and themes, and thus what you have to say to others, make a nonjudgmental inventory of your most moving experiences. This is not difficult, for the human memory jettisons the mundane and retains only what it finds significant. You can do it this way:

1. Go somewhere private and make rapid, short notes of each major experience just as it comes to mind. Keep going until you have at least 10 or 12 experiences by which you were deeply moved (to joy, to rage, to panic, to fear, to disgust, to anguish, to love, etc.).
2. Organize them into groups, giving a name to each group and the relationships it deals with. Some moving experiences will be positive (with feelings of joy, relief, discovery, laughter), but most will be painful. Make no distinction, for there is no such thing as a negative or positive truth. To discriminate like this is to censor, which is just another way to prolong the endless and wasteful search for acceptability. Truth is truth—period!
3. Now try looking objectively, as though what you wrote were someone else's record. What kind of expressive work should come from someone marked by such experiences? You should be able to place yourself in a different light and find trends, even a certain vision of the world, clustering around these experiences. Don't be afraid to be imaginative, as though developing a fictional character. Your object is to find a storytelling role that you can play with all your heart. If you find nothing is taking shape, explain your notes and groupings to a friend. It's quite strange, but the mere act of telling another person will reorganize how you see your own formation.

Sincerely tried, this examination will confirm which life events have formed your quest, and bring into focus the underlying issues they represent. Almost certainly you'll see that you have resonated all along to these issues in your choice of music, literature, and films, not to mention in your friendships, love affairs, and family relationships.

PROJECT 2-2: ALTER EGOS

Here's a more oblique approach to your deeper aspirations and identifications. Particular characters or situations in films, plays, or books trigger a special response in us, so they offer useful clues to our underlying makeup. This project takes another route to finding how you resonate.

1. List six or eight characters from literature or fiction with whom you have a special affinity. Arrange them by their importance to you. An affinity can be hero worship, but becomes more interesting when you respond to darker or more complex qualities.

2. Do the same thing for public figures like actors, politicians, sports figures, etc.

3. Make a third list of people you know or have known, but leave out immediate family if they complicate the exercise.

4. Take the top two or three in each list and write a brief description of what, in human or even mythical qualities, each person represents, and what dilemma seems to typify them. If, for instance, O.J. Simpson were on your list, he might represent an Othello whose jealous passion destroys what he most loves.

5. Now write a self-profile based on what the resonances suggest. Don't hesitate to imaginatively round out the portrait as though it were about a fictional character. The aim is not to define who you are (you'll never succeed), but to build a provocative and active picture of what you are looking for and how you see the world.

PROJECT 2-3: USING DREAMS TO FIND YOUR PREOCCUPATION

Keep a log of your dreams, for in dreams the mind expresses itself unguardedly using surreal and symbolic imagery. Unless you have a period of intense dream activity, you will have to keep a record over many months before common denominators and motifs become clear. To do this, keep a notebook next to your bed, and awake gently so you hold on to the dream long enough to write it down. If you get really interested in this work, you will spontaneously awake in the night after a good dream to write it down. Needless to say, this won't be very popular with a bedroom partner.

Often dreams project tantalizing images that are symbolically charged with meaning. The British novelist John Fowles started both *The French Lieutenant's Woman* and *A Maggot* from single images—one of a woman gazing out to sea toward France, and the other of a mysterious group of horsemen crossing a hillside accompanying a lone woman. Whole complex novels developed from investigating the characters "seen" in these alluring glimpses. You, too, have hidden patterns and propitious images waiting in the wings to be recognized and developed.

THE ARTISTIC PROCESS

All artists and craftspeople agree that there is an artistic process, and that living it means traveling the most significant and exhilarating journey of your life. At the beginning, you get clues, clues lead to discoveries, discoveries lead to movement in your work, and movement leads to new clues. It never stops opening new doors to meaning, and keeps revealing connections to an ever larger whole.

It will happen if you find that special element that fascinates you. It might be expressed through mountaineering, the rescue of animals, something involving water and boats, or love between school friends. You explore it by producing something external to your own thoughts: the piece of expressive work. What begins as a circumscribed personal quest soon leads outward. You might take two opposing parts of your own character during a trying period of your life and make them into two sparring characters, perhaps making imaginative use of two well-known political or historical characters to do so.

This search for the truths underlying your formation and patterns starts feeding itself once you make a commitment to expressing something about it. A piece of work—whether a painting, a short story, or a film script—is both the evidence of movement and the engine of progress during the search for meanings. Your work becomes the trail of your own evolution and a reflection of your times.

Profiling favorite historical personalities, social assumptions, political events, or the temperaments of the people most influential in your life will help shape and sharpen your consciousness. By doing such things well, you can entertain and excite your audience. Whether they know it or not, they, too, are pursuing a quest and starving to join a journey of exploration like yours.

HOW WRITERS WORK

Whether you write screenplays, or work with a writer, it's useful to know that writing is not an orderly, linear process, but one that is organic and circular. Accomplished writers switch rapidly between different types of thinking, and change hats as a matter of course. To get all the way from an idea to a shooting script, expect to move irregularly through these stages:

- *Ideation* or *idea development* means defining a promising idea and theme as the kernel for a screen story, which can be expressed as a *premise* (example: A soldier returning from constant danger in Iraq tries to reenter his small-town life in rural New England. Can his girlfriend help him make the transition?). The premise is revisited periodically to see how the core idea has evolved.

- *Story development* is the expansion of the core idea into characters, situations, and events. To stay light and mobile, this is often done in outline form with dialogue exchanges briefly summarized (example: they discuss whether Jim should tell Bella's father that he is haunted by the death of an innocent bystander in Baghdad).

- *Story editing* involves revision, restructuring, pruning, shaping, and compressing the overall piece, often while still in outline form.

- *Pitching* the story entails three to four minutes describing the basics of a film to an audience of one or many. This elicits an audience response before you have even made the film, and tells you whether a new version has cured the ills of the old.

- *Writing the screenplay* involves expanding the thoroughly reworked and tested outline into standard screenplay form. A screenplay needs between 10 and 20 drafts before it's ready for filming.
- *Developing the shooting script* means breaking the screenplay down into shots and angles in association with the cinematographer and script (or continuity) supervisor.

Ideation and story development call on taste and instincts. At this stage, the writer may freely follow inspiration, intuition, and emotional memory rather than objectivity and logic. Story editing, on the other hand, employs analytic and dramaturgic skills. These take the objectivity to see the work as an audience sees it, and judge how best to structure and cadence the work for maximal impact on a first-time audience. For this, the writer needs a strong interest in how others assimilate and react to his or her work. Changes in one scene or act can affect what seemed stable in the others, so writing is always a circular activity.

CHAPTER 3

DRAMATURGY ESSENTIALS

Once you know what truly interests you, the next stage is to begin putting it into a shape that has dramatic tension and can grip an audience.

DUALITY AND CONFLICT

Have you received this kind of family newsletter during the holiday season?

> **The Russell News for the Year**
> Betty has completely redecorated the dining room (with an avocado theme!) after successfully completing her interior decorator course at Mallory School of the Arts. Terry spent the summer camping and canoeing, and thoroughly enjoyed being a camp counselor. In the fall, he learned he had a place at Hillshire University to study molecular biology. In spite of what the doctor said, Joanne has successfully adapted to contact lenses. David received his promotion to area manager, but now has a longer drive to work.

What makes this so tedious? Surely it's because Russell life is presented as a series of happy, logical steps with nothing candid, spontaneous, or disturbing. It's not untrue—it's just a selection method that renders the family lifeless, especially if you happen to know that David's drinking is getting worse. Family life is like a pond—calm on the surface, but containing all the forces of warring nature below the surface. So, too, is an interesting individual. This inner contradiction is our *duality*, and every active individual houses contradictions and conflicts.

By avoiding all *conflict*, the newsletter suppresses the dissent, doubt, and eccentricity that give every family dramatic tension. The human psyche is like a raft with rowers working on all four sides so that it moves irregularly under the will of conflicting passions. Some row peaceably in one direction, but others struggle each in their own direction. If an individual is like this, imagine what goes on in a family, a business, or an institution!

Conflict is essential to drama. It can be internal or external; that is, it may be:

- Person versus person
- Person versus environment
- Inner conflict between one part of a person and another

Until you can state confidently the nature of the conflict that a scene or a whole piece handles, you have not mastered it. That conflict can be large (a soldier wants to obey orders, but finds his conscience forbidding it) or something minor (a toddler struggles to get her little wooden chair upright). Each faces some important *issue* that they are trying to solve.

A drama with several characters will have lesser conflicts that, like tributaries to a river, feed into the drama's main conflict. The main conflict a piece handles is its dramatic focus. Othello's conflict is whether to believe in his beautiful wife's fidelity or whether to believe the jealous doubts implanted in his heart by Iago.

IDENTIFYING A CHARACTER'S CONFLICT

Human beings become fully alive only when they have something meaningful to push against. To identify an individual's conflict, we ask: *What is this character trying to get, do, or accomplish?* An insightful answer reveals what the character deeply wants, and what prevents him or her from succeeding. We then look to see if he or she changes tactics to overcome the immediate obstacles. Eventually, we hope the character will come to grips with their *problem* and struggle directly with whatever they need to overcome. This is called the *confrontation*.

REPRESENTATION

Drama can take the elements in a conflicted individual like Othello and, by expanding aspects of his personality into separate characters, set each in conflict with the others. Thus, an internal struggle is transformed into the visible action so necessary to the stage or screen.

Drama can also take the stresses in a whole culture and demonstrate them through events that befall representative individuals. This allows a diffuse and complex situation to be presented coherently through an Everyman simplification. Oliver Stone's prescient *Wall Street* (1988) turns predatory stockbroking into a parable about a young stockbroker seduced into illegal practices by the charisma of a powerful and amoral mentor. Counterbalancing this is the influence for good exerted by his pragmatic, working-class father. A similar configuration of influences vie for the hero's soul in Stone's Vietnam film, *Platoon* (1987), drawn from the director's own experience as an infantryman. Every new recruit, says the film, is inevitably brutalized by warfare. Each must choose between moral alternatives that are represented in its two sergeants. Barnes, physically scarred and psychically dehumanized, represents the cold brutality of experience, whereas Elias is no less brave, but fights with shreds of his humanity still alive (Figure 3-1).

When you make a character a torchbearer for a human quality, take care not to let him or her become monolithic and flat. It is not enough for one quality to predominate: main characters need to be complex and face inner conflicts, or they won't be credible.

FIGURE 3-1

Platoon is about surviving during warfare. Moral choices for the enlisted man are epitomized by the platoon's two sergeants (courtesy Orion/The Kobal Collection).

TEMPERAMENT AFFECTS VISION

Temperament and cultural factors influence how a filmmaker sees. A political historian sees a naval battle as the interplay of inevitable forces, with victory or defeat resulting from the technology in use and the strengths and weaknesses of the leaders. This vision leads to a film that aims to be detached and objective. A more empathic personality, who sees history growing grassroots fashion from the action of individuals, will see a battle quite differently. Her film goes below decks and seeks out the conflicts in both the great and the humble. She places us in the heat of battle—not to show the constants in human history or the eternal repetition of human error, but to highlight the potential inherent in moral choice.

Your temperament and the story you want to tell will decide whether yours is a deterministic world or one in which individuals steer their own destinies and that, collectively, of their society. This comes from the marks your life has left on you and from the stories those marks want you to tell.

CHARACTER-DRIVEN AND PLOT-DRIVEN DRAMA

When a piece is *character-driven*, the storyteller's vision will be made through the experience of the point of view (POV) character or characters. When the piece is *plot-driven*, the storyteller's vision will probably hinge more on settings, situations, and the idiosyncrasies of the plot—that is, the framework that organizes the telling of events.

DRAMA AND PROPAGANDA ARE DIFFERENT

Drama and propaganda handle human duality differently: drama sees the sea battle like a live organism, whereas propaganda puts its characters through token situations that converge on a foregone conclusion. The story does not explore so much as manipulate the spectator into accepting a predetermined view. The dramatist, valuing the integrity and organic nature of struggle, treats the audience with respect and genuinely explores something. You can tell because the piece moves toward an uncertain destination. The absence of quest and uncertainty in most educational and corporate products makes them stultifyingly boring. The viewer is not seen as an equal taking a voyage of discovery, but as a consumer to be programmed.

MORE TYPES OF DRAMA

Ideologically driven work is perfectly possible, but it must be artfully presented to make it stylish, witty, futuristic, or deliciously frightening—otherwise audiences will wearily reject it from their long experience of inept salesmanship.

Morality plays: Drama in medieval times used a polemical approach, and would show the life of a saint dealing with temptation as the struggle between

FIGURE 3-2

Jared Hess' *Napoleon Dynamite* finds comedy and drama in the ordeals of high school (courtesy Access Films/MTV Films/The Kobal Collection).

good and evil. Today's epic morality plays in the cinema, such as George Lucas' *Star Wars* (1977) or Peter Jackson's adaptations of Tolkien's *Lord of the Rings* (2001–2003), rely on spectacle and a strong plot. Their worlds involve journeys in space, androids, puppets, creature costumes, or computer animation—all of which deflect our attention from the elementary nature of the underlying messages. By making epic fables, and by using *distancing devices* (story aspects that make the events remote from our everyday lives), the plots allow us to contemplate courage, loyalty, power, evil, and all the other grand abstractions that perennially haunt human imagination.

Drama on a low budget: The low-budget filmmaker faces some rather crucial problems. Having no access to intergalactic space, unable to afford even a spadeful of Middle Earth, he or she must look for drama in the familiar and accessible. Jared Hess did this in *Napoleon Dynamite* (2004, Figure 3-2), an endearing and funny coming-of-age film about a catatonic high schooler. Hess developed the film from his prizewinning Brigham Young University short, *Peluca*. Finding comedy in the personalities of Napoleon's dysfunctional family and the social round of small-town teenagers, Hess has woven them into the arc of a story with a meaning and a philosophy. Plainly, his film's benevolent and hopeful vision comes from his Mormon background, and from being able to see life as a moral and spiritual journey. Most of us, living in a world impoverished of metaphor and spiritual optimism, lack such a hopeful outlook.

THE DRAMATIC UNIT AND THE SCENE

BEATS

We must look first at the *dramatic unit* and its key component, the *beat*. This is widely misunderstood, for it has nothing to do with rhythm, nor is it a unit of pause or rest, as screenplay usage suggests. A dramatic beat follows mounting pressures that culminate in an irreversible change. This moment of change is when a character experiences the success or failure of an important objective. That is, *a beat is a moment of changed awareness in one of the characters*, and is thus a dramatic fulcrum point. This heartbeat of drama is something few outside the theater grasp. Once film students understand what a beat really is, their directing and editing take a quantum leap.

INTRODUCING THE GOBLIN TEASMADE™

We can understand better what a beat is from looking at the Goblin Teasmade™, an iconic gadget still found in British bed-and-breakfast establishments (Figure 3-3). Invented in 1902 by an enterprising gunsmith, this automatic tea-maker illustrates rather well how a dramatic unit culminates in a beat. Here's how it works:

1. Before bed, fill the metal canister with water, put tea bags into the china teapot, place them side by side, and set the clock for wake-up time.

2. At the appointed hour, the clock silently turns on a heater. Initial rumbles soon turn to hissing as the water comes to a thunderous boil.

FIGURE 3-3

The 1936 Goblin Teasmade™ (© Bruce Hudson and Teasmade.com/Teawaker.com).

3. Steam pressure causes the water to decant from the metal canister to the teapot. The weight of water shifting from one vessel to the other causes a support platform to tilt, turning off the current, and brewing the tea.

4. As the storm subsides, you venture from under the covers to enjoy a fresh pot of tea.

The dramatic beat is not when the current switches on, nor when the water heats up, for these are the pressure-building preliminaries. It comes in Item 3, at the moment of maximum threat, when the shifting weight of water switches the appliance off. As a moment of quite literal fulcrum, it is also a moment of irreversible change. Item 4, when the machine has become harmless and the user feels safe to enjoy another day, is the *resolution*. The full Goblin Teasmade™ story can be found at www.teasmade.com/models.htm/, and yes, people collect them.

A CHARACTER'S AGENDA

Dramatic scenes center on a person with an *agenda*. This is a plan for something that the character wants to *get, do, or accomplish*. An agenda comes alive when a *problem* emerges that must be solved. At age six, I had such a problem when walking out of my English village every day to school. Without fail, an angry terrier would come hurtling out of a row of tumbledown cottages. Though it never actually bit me, the terrier would snarl, dart at my legs, and bark like a maniac. Every day I dreaded this encounter, and getting up the courage to pass this wretched dog was an ordeal. As I slid past, my back to the wall, the animal would eventually decide it had won, would turn back, and would then trot importantly back to its lair.

In dramatic terms, my *agenda* was to get to school, and my obstacle or *problem* was overcoming my fear of a hostile dog. This was a *test* I had to pass every day. The *beat* took place at the point where I knew I had made it and was safe. The *resolution* was the dog going his way, and me going mine. Once again I'd made it past the Singing Dog (my father tried giving it a benign name, but I wasn't fooled).

Any character's major, irreversible change of consciousness is a beat, and you should characterize it with a tag description. Here, the beat is, "The boy realizes he has safely passed the threatening dog." A beat can be subtle, comic, or melo-dramatically extreme, but it always involves a step forward. In the Teasmade scenario, the beat comes at the moment when the user realizes that the threat of being blown apart in his pajamas has passed and tea is served.

The dramatic arc in Figure 3-4 represents a dramatic unit, which includes:

- The *inciting moment* that initiates a new issue
- *Complications* that raise the pressure, otherwise known as the *rising action*
- The *apex* or the *confrontation* (think of me and the dog)
- The *beat*—an irreversible change of consciousness in at least one character

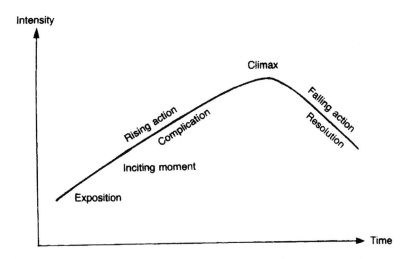

FIGURE 3-4

The dramatic arc can be applied to help analyze a beat, a dramatic unit, a scene, or a whole film.

- The *resolution* or *falling action,* which leads to a new inciting moment, a new issue
- The *outcome*—the abstract meaning of the unit, a whole scene, or a complete drama (for instance, that life has an inexhaustible supply of Singing Dogs to test a person's courage and resolve)

John Howard Lawson, in his *Theory and Technique of Playwriting* (New York: Hill & Wang, 1960), has usefully likened the dramatic unit's action to the cycles of an internal combustion engine.

1. The engine's piston draws in explosive gases (exposition, setting the scene)
2. Compression stage and building of pressure inside the cylinder (rising action)
3. Ignition and explosion at maximum pressure (beat, or climax if it's a scene)
4. Piston is forced downward, initiating a new cycle of intake, compression, and explosion (resolution leading to next dramatic unit or scene).

For an animation of this, go to http://auto.howstuffworks.com/engine.htm. The analogy to the internal combustion engine is nice because its cycles deliver power. Each scene may have several dramatic units or only one. Practice finding dramatic units by looking analytically at the life going on around you. The ability to see dramatic action as it takes place is the preeminent skill for actors and for directors in both fiction and documentary.

A successful progression of beats develops *dramatic tension* by setting up questions, anticipations, hopes, and fears in the audience. These should be extended as long as possible. As Wilkie Collins, the father of the mystery novel, said, "Make them laugh, make them cry, but make them wait."

Try identifying the beats and dramatic units in this little narrative:

> Two bleary and unshaven men, George and Phil, sprawl in a rusty Dodge full of empty beer cans as they drive across a hot, empty landscape. They notice that the car is running on empty, and hope to make it to a gas station they can see in the distance. But the old clunker coughs to a halt before they get there.
>
> Excitable George curses fate and pounds the steering wheel, but phlegmatic Phil steps into the blinding sunlight and walks to the gas station, where he asks for a can of gas.
>
> Don, the sleepy youth on duty, says they don't keep cans. So Phil and George, sweating and cursing, have to push the creaking behemoth to the pumps, where they fill up and then drive away exhausted.

What is their *agenda,* what is *the problem,* and where do the major changes of consciousness, or *beats,* occur? (Remember: there can be one or several.)

Their *agenda* is simply to get wherever they are going. Their first *problem* is that George and Phil are running out of gas and must find more. One *beat* happens when the car dies short of the gas station. This intensifies their *problem* and changes its nature. No longer can they get the car to the gas—they must now bring gas to the car. George howls at the gods, but Phil *adapts* to the new *obstacle,* and puts a new plan into action—to walk to the gas station and get a little gas in a can so they can drive the last few hundred yards. The second *beat* comes when

Phil learns from Don that the garage has no cans. His plan has failed. He cannot bring gas to the car. This raises the question, "What will they do now?" It is answered when the narrative cuts forward to their solution, which is to physically push the jalopy to the gas pump.

What is the *conflict* in this scene? Surely it's two shiftless dudes facing the heavy, inert weight of their dead chariot. We see it played out as a Herculean struggle. Their *confrontations* are first with each other concerning who or what is responsible, secondly with the lethargic attendant, and thirdly with the dead weight of the lifeless car. You spot the confrontation in a scene, or in the larger dimension of a whole work, by deciding at what point each protagonist wins or loses against his main oppositional force. The *resolution*, which is how the major struggle gets resolved, comes when George and Phil arrive panting at the pump. Once they figure out how to fill their tank, they can resume their *agenda*.

DRAMA MAKES US ASK QUESTIONS

Drama is seeing special people in special situations that make us keep asking questions. In the Phil and George story, we have four dramatic units, each posing questions in the spectator's mind.

Unit 1 establishes that as they drive, their car is running out of gas. **Q:** *Will they make it?* **A:** No, they won't, and the problem escalates when the car dies. This dramatic unit ends at the first beat when they realize this. **Q:** *How will they solve the problem?*

Unit 2 deals with the answer, how they adapt to the new circumstances. After some heated discussion that involves mutual blaming, Phil steps out into the roasting heat and walks to the gas station. The next beat comes after a brief discussion during which Phil realizes that this plan won't work either. **Q:** *What he will do?*

Unit 3 jumps forward in time to show their answer: pushing the heavy car in stages into the gas station, where they can fill it up. **Q:** *Do they even have money to fill the tank?*

Unit 4 is the answer, or *resolution*, to the scene as they drive away with the problem solved. **Q:** *What will they do next?*

Notice how much question-and-answer takes place in the minds of the audience. Making this happen is the mark of good storytelling, and lets the audience know it is in professional hands.

INTERROGATING A SCENE

Use the following questions to bare the dramatic components of any scene. I have applied them to our feckless travelers, Phil and George:

Main character(s)?	Phil, because he takes the main action and *develops* most
Agenda?	To complete their journey

Problem or issue?	How to get more fuel after George's failure in foresight
Conflict?	Between men and machine; between fallible, imperfect human beings and the unforgiving demands of their journey
Complicating factors?	Car dies far from gas station, nobody can bring gas, and no help is available
Beats?	See previous discussion
Confrontation?	With each other, with Don, then with the inert car
Resolution?	They refill tank and can now drive on
How many dramatic units?	Four, as in discussion above

THE DRAMATIC ARC

Each dramatic unit follows a developmental arc leading to its completion (see Figure 3-4). In Mike Newell's romantic comedy *Four Weddings and a Funeral* (1994, Figure 3-5), an example is when Charles realizes that Carrie has abandoned him by marrying her wealthy fiancé. The buildup of forces—establishing the situation, complications that augment the situation's pressure, and then the irrevocable change embodied in the wedding ceremony—leads to change and a resolution. It is that Charles, having missed the boat, enters a phase of depression and conflict.

FIGURE 3-5

A major turning point for Charles in *Four Weddings and a Funeral* as the woman he loves marries another man (courtesy Polygram/Channel 4/Working Title/The Kobal Collection).

LEVELS OF ACTION

Drama is modular, each module nesting inside a larger one, like Russian dolls. These different modules are called *levels of action*:

- The interactions between characters are called moments.
- Moments combine into beats, each having its own crisis and resolution.
- Beats often combine to form a dramatic unit.
- Dramatic units combine into compound action to form a scene, which in turn has its own *obligatory moment*, or crisis point (Figure 3-6).
- Scenes combine to form acts.
- Acts combine to form a whole dramatic work.

THE THREE-ACT STRUCTURE

The concept of the dramatic arc applies to a beat, a dramatic unit, or even a whole story. Draw the dramatic arc's undulations for a complete work, and you are on your way to finding the three-act structure for your particular story. Here are the units of division:

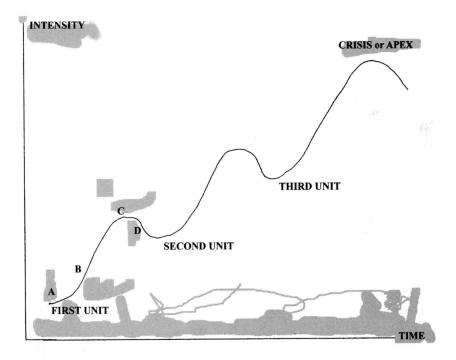

FIGURE 3-6

Graph of rising and falling intensity for a scene having three dramatic units. Each contains an inciting moment *(A)*, complication and rising action *(B)*, a beat *(C)*, and a resolution or falling action *(D)*. The scene apex (or crisis) comes on the third beat. An arc of similar appearance might be drawn for a three-scene act, or a three-act film.

Act I establishes the setup (characters, relationships, and situation and dominant problem faced by the central character or characters).

Act II escalates the complications in relationships as the central character struggles with the obstacles that prevent him or her from solving the main problem.

Act III intensifies the situation to a point of confrontation, and then resolves it, often in a climactic way that is emotionally satisfying.

Take any event you know about and divide it into acts. You can do so because the three-act structure is fundamental to all aspects of life, and thus a vital tool for organizing a tale about life. You'll use it in telling a joke about a psychiatrist changing a lightbulb or in organizing historical footage of the war machine setting out to save the world from weapons of mass destruction.

BUILDING A WORLD AROUND THE CONCERNED OBSERVER

In Wim Wenders' *Wings of Desire* (1987, Figure 3-7), kindly angels keep Berliners under empathic observation. This film serves our purpose well because cinema itself is like one of these angels, following and observing characters as they live their lives. Let's call this scrutiny the work of the Concerned Observer, because he is involved, invisible, and weightless like a spirit. Feeling for the characters, the Observer leaves the periphery to fly into the center of things, always searching for greater significance and larger patterns of meaning.

FIGURE 3-7

In *Wings of Desire*, everyone has a guardian angel looking over his shoulder (courtesy Road Movies/Argos Films/The Kobal Collection).

Developing empathy with the characters and knowledge of them, the Concerned Observer passes through a series of experiences. He or she identifies with the characters, tries to understand them, and feels for them in their unfolding difficulties. It is a part we all have played in life, so it feels familiar, and it is something we shall use hugely in making films. The Concerned Observer, like Wenders' angels, can see, hear, and empathize with the characters, but cannot intercede or express an opinion. This is a handicap.

OBSERVER INTO STORYTELLER

The Storyteller goes several steps further, and arranges the events for the entertainment and instruction of an audience. The Concerned Observer and the Storyteller roles are explored in greater depth in Chapter 4, but here we should note a single curious fact: that a literary storyteller tells a story that has already happened in the past, whereas the film storyteller beckons us into a story happening here and now in the present. Screen language is peculiar in this regard, for we seem to experience stories directly and unmediated by an author. What we see on the screen is not free-functioning, autonomous truth such as we'd see on any street corner, but a show filtered through a temperament.

You wouldn't know this from most cinema or television, which is perfectly professional and absolutely without individuality. This signifies that you can work hard to make your film look professional, but it will be faceless. David Mamet thinks of such work "as a supposed record of what real people really did," as if they were newsreel reports.

If you want to direct screen work with a distinctive voice, you need to take action in at least three areas:

1. **Definition:** Make your priorities telling a good story in a special way and in a particular genre. You'll need clear definitions of all these, ones that enthuse other people. You can go only where you aim to go. This is why a film writer is important—he or she attends only to the nature of the story, not the cinematic translation of it.

2. **Take control:** You must direct the filmmaking process, not become controlled by it. For this, you'll need a strongly visualized design and the sheer obstinacy to get it realized during production. If you don't lead, the crew and the actors will take over and the tail wags the dog.

3. **Create a definite Storyteller:** Impose a strong storytelling "voice" on your film, the kind that lends enchantment to all effective storytelling. This character is not you—that, after all, needs no effort or understanding—but a character that you alone define and that you alone play privately and to the hilt. This character's eyes, ears, mind, and movement are a sparkling stream of consciousness made manifest in your film. In the next chapter, an unconventional film grammar, we'll see how this can be done.

PART 2

SCREENCRAFT

Part 2 (Chapters 4 through 6) contains a detailed workout in the concepts behind filmmaking, beginning with how screen language parallels human perceptual processes. It shows how film techniques approximate human attention interacting with reality. There is a film analysis project, which yields very different insights from a mere viewing. Another study project compares a film's screenplay with how the director interpreted and transformed it. This allows you to peer speculatively into the complicated act of making a film. There is practice at naming and identifying types of lighting, which contributes so much to mood and the way that time and place register with us emotionally. Finally, there are shooting projects, many of which can yield more than one version. Here, you can practice shading and developing point of view in the editing stage, where a film finds its ultimate voice.

This is a lot of work, but even if you do a third of it, you'll emerge with skills that take years to acquire by other routes. Before undertaking projects in Chapter 6 onward, check their Assessment Forms on the web site (www.focalpress.com/9780240808826). These not only help you rate outcomes, they help focus your work. Figure 6–1 provides a specimen.

CHAPTER 4

A DIRECTOR'S SCREEN GRAMMAR

FILM LANGUAGE

As children, we learn to speak because language is a tool to accomplish things. My elder daughter's first sentence was, "Meat, I like it." Effective, if a little shaky in syntax. All languages operate under conventions, and screen language began developing in the 1890s when camera operators and actors competed to get elementary stories before paying audiences. Soon movies became big business, and the actors and camera operators were joined by directors and editors. A production line had evolved needing greater division of labor.

Most of today's screen language emerged in the first two decades of silent cinema.

Separately, through trial and error in each world film center, filmmakers felt their way toward the same movie grammar. In postrevolutionary Russia of the 1920s, filmmakers needed an efficient common language to communicate with a vast, multilingual, and mostly illiterate population, so they made a concerted effort to formulate screen language. Their theories make uphill reading. Even today, theory among working filmmakers is conspicuously absent—not surprising if you consider that sophisticated languages predate philologists. Film, like any language, is evolving to facilitate the stories we want in forms that are novel and striking. It uses the full arsenal of human perception—that is, the juxtaposition of images, actions, and sounds, as well as spoken and written language.

WHAT WORKS

Film is universally accessible because all humans are hardwired for similar processes of perception and emotion. This allows those making a film to discuss it in terms of "what works." Be it an action, rhythm, shot, character's motivation, or dialogue line—everything hinges on "what works." Each person aiding in a critique calls on his or her bank of life experience to recognize what is authentic and organic to the story and its characters, and what is off-kilter. Without this innate ability to recognize authenticity in a stream of events on the screen, neither the cinema nor drama itself could exist.

Film language that relies on something so common should be easy to use, and using it superficially is not difficult. But making it move an audience takes a special grasp. Film grammar is therefore not something academic—it makes or breaks the identity of what you put on the screen. What makes this tricky is that we don't normally pay attention to our perceptual and emotional processes. They work automatically from birth to feed our feelings, and our feelings fuel our actions, so we need know nothing about how all this works—never, that is, until we try to make an effective film.

THE NEED FOR A HUMANE VOICE

Because filmmaking depends on technology, beginners see technology as the major obstacle. Unless enlightened teaching draws attention to larger issues, technology is what film students learn. Most start directing by modeling themselves on admired filmmakers. This is natural and necessary, but holds the same dangers as when actors study other actors. The great acting teacher Stanislavsky warned that actors must learn from life, not from other actors.

Acquiring your own screen "voice"—one with the force of simplicity and truth—takes two things: understanding how your consciousness works to move you, and making short films that embody this understanding.

HUMAN VANTAGE

Human experience and human communication always involve a vantage or point of view, so what you put on the screen should do so too. By this, I mean more than a political outlook or philosophy that can be learned or copied. Your point of view on, say, authority figures cannot be copied because it is too individual and too much the product of complex experience. Potentially fascinating, it implies individual convictions, loyalties, and contradictions. Point of view is not a manifesto or teaching strategy, and does not need to educate or improve others. It is instead the awareness of a living, breathing soul, and it's always present in work loved by audiences and critics. In comparison, run-of-the-mill films are soulless.

Our work here is to arm you against being overwhelmed by the routines of the technology and its high priests. The best starting point is to pick subjects that hold special meaning for you, and to design your storytelling around an integrated human consciousness. Paradoxically, this is often present in students' naive first works, but disappears as they acquire glossier skills. To avoid this dehumanization, here is an unconventional screen glossary that connects each aspect of film language to human perception and behavior.

FILM LANGUAGE AND HUMAN PERCEPTION

The camera's verisimilitude can make events unfold on the screen as inevitably as perfectly judged music. Newcomers assume that cinema's equipment and processes are the alchemy that does this. But cameras and projectors simply frame and magnify. Truth looks truer, and untruth phonier. By delivering a sophisticated or clumsy version of human consciousness, a film makes us see its events through the true or distorted lens of a human mind.

Beginning to use the screen intelligently means recognizing that the elemental units of film language correspond to glancing, reacting, studying, walking, looking around, whirling about, stepping back, rising, sinking, scanning, running, gliding, and a host of other expressive human interactions. Let's review the details by moving from the simple to the complex.

FIXED CAMERA POSITION

A shot is a framed image "taken by" (revealing words) someone for whom it had meaning. Shots evoke more than their subject, for they prompt us to speculate about what, how, and why we are seeing. A fixed camera position reproduces the feeling you get when you stand still and look around. Depending on the context, it can variously convey being secure, fixed, trapped, contemplative, wise, or just plain stuck. Yasujiro Ozu's famous *Tokyo Story* (1953, Figure 4-1), about an elderly couple discovering that none of their married children can make time for their visit, is shot from a single camera height and contains just one movement, a gentle pan, throughout the movie. The film makes you realize that movement is often overused and that camera stasis can be utterly natural.

Brief shots are like the cursory glance that ends immediately after we have conceptualized what we are seeing. We do this to orient ourselves in a new situation or to look in many places in search of something.

Held shots are like the long looks we sometimes take. Maybe we watch a store customer we suspect of shoplifting. Maybe it's a friend leaving on a long

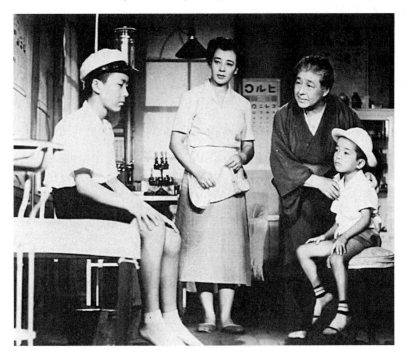

FIGURE 4-1

Techical minimalism and a slow pace concentrate attention on the tragedy of two old people in Ozu's *Tokyo Story* (1953, courtesy New Yorker Films).

journey whose last smile we want to commit to memory. Long looks break into two classifications: resting looks and studying looks.

Close shots mimic intensive observation, maybe of something small like a watch face, or something large like a great weathered rock. There are psychologically driven reasons to look closely at something. Imagine a person who hovers by a phone in a large room, waiting for the results of a medical test. Nothing else exists for that person but the phone and its terrifying aura of power. Here, the close shot reproduces an intense emotional focus that leaves us blind to everything else.

Wide shots convey the way we scan anything large, busy, or distant. We look only long enough to know the object's shape or to locate some aspect we prefer to study in detail. Coming out of a quiet, dark church into a busy street, for instance, takes adapting to the new circumstances while we work out the direction home. Often we must establish the nature of our new surroundings, hence the term *establishing shot*.

MOVING CAMERA

Authentic camera movements, like their human-movement equivalents, never happen without a stimulus or *motivation*. Camera movements divide into three kinds of motivation, which resemble active and passive ways of attention to an event:

- *Subject-motivated*, where the camera follows a moving subject or adapts to a changing composition. Relatively passively, it adapts to keeping a subject in view.

- *Search-motivated*, in which the camera's "mind" actively pursues a logic of inquiry or expectation. This mode probes, anticipates, hypothesizes, interrogates, and even goes ahead of the action.

- *Refreshment-motivated*, in which the camera simulates the human tendency to look around when we run out of stimuli.

Camera movements generally have three phases:

- *Initial composition* (static hold making an initial statement before the camera begins movement).

- *Movement* (with its particular direction, speed, and even its subject to follow, such as a moving vehicle).

- *Concluding composition* (static hold after the movement, making a concluding statement).

CAMERA MOVEMENTS FROM A STATIC POSITION

These include turning, looking up and down, and looking more closely.

Pan (short for *panoramic*) shots occur when the camera pivots horizontally, mimicking the way we turn our head to scan a horizontal subject like a landscape or bridge. Direction of travel is indicated as "pan left" or "pan right."
Tilt shots are similar, but the camera pivots vertically to reproduce the action of looking up or down the length of a vertical subject like a tree or tall building. Direction of travel is indicated as "tilt up" or "tilt down."

Zoom in or out is made with a lens of adjustable focal length. Zooming gives a forward or backward impression of movement, but picture perspective actually remains identical. This is because the size proportion between foreground and background objects stays the same. For perspective to change, the camera itself must move (see "Choosing Lens Type" in Chapter 29).

TRAVELING CAMERA MOVEMENTS

These occur when the camera moves through space—up, down, forward, sideways, backward, or in a combination. Traveling camera movements impart a range of kinesthetic feelings associated with walking, running, approaching, climbing, ascending, descending, retreating, and so on.

Craning (up or down) is a movement in which the camera is raised or lowered in relation to the subject. The movement corresponds with the feeling of sitting down or standing up—sometimes as an act of conclusion, sometimes to "rise above," sometimes to acquire a better sight line.

Dollying, tracking, or trucking are interchangeable names for any horizontal camera movement through space. In life, our thoughts or feelings often motivate us to move closer to or farther away from that which commands our attention. We move sideways to see better or to avoid an obstacle in our sight line. Associations with this sort of camera movement include walking, running, riding a bike, riding in a car, gliding, skating, sliding, sailing, flying, floating, or drifting. **Crab dollying** is when the camera travels sideways like a crab. The equivalent is accompanying someone and looking at them sideways as you walk.

SHOTS AND SUBJECTS IN JUXTAPOSITION

When any two shots are juxtaposed, we look for meaning between their relationship. A + B does not equal AB, but rather, C—a new meaning. This can in fact be done within a single composition: in the 2002 documentary *9/11* by Jules and Gédéon Naudet, a single shot reveals how a crumpled aircraft engine cowling has landed next to an equally crumpled waste bin whose sign says, "Do Not Litter." Juxtaposed within a single shot, these objects comment on the irony of fate. Juxtaposing—in a composition or between shots edited together—aims to implant associations and is used blatantly in advertising: the richly attired couple next to the Mercedes; the bag of fertilizer standing amid a rich green lawn; the bride in her wedding dress running barefoot on the beach outside a Caribbean hotel. A comic strip, however, juxtaposes key frames (specially significant moments) to compress a lengthy process and convey its essence. Each chosen moment makes us imagine (that is, cocreate) the progression from the previous one.

Film's favorite form of juxtaposing is the cut from one image to another. Juxtaposing scene against scene enables the cinema to fly through space and time. By now, we are trained to infer the narrative intention. Figure 4-2 and the remainder of this section show some examples with explanations, and illustrate an engaging disagreement between two early Russian editing theorists.

Continuity and expository editing: Examples 1 through 5 in Figure 4-2 illustrate Pudovkin's categories of juxtaposition in which exposition (building the information of a story line) and continuity of action from shot to shot are

	Shot A	Shot B	Shot B in relation to shot A	Type of cut
1	Woman descends interior stairway	Same woman walking in street	Narrates her progress	Structural (builds scene logic)
2	Man runs across busy street	Close shot of his shoelace coming undone	Makes us anticipate his falling in front of a vehicle	Structural (directs our attention to significant detail)
3	Hungry street person begging from doorway	Wealthy man eating oysters in expensive restaurant	Places one person's fate next to another's	Relational (creates contrast)
4	Bath filling up	Teenager in bathrobe on phone in bedroom	Shows two events happening at the same time	Relational (parallelism)
5	Exhausted boxer takes knockout punch	Bullock killed with stun gun in an abattoir	Suggests boxer is a sacrificial victim	Relational (symbolism)
6	Police waiting at roadblock	Shabby van driving erratically at high speed	Driver doesn't know what he's going to soon meet	Conflictual (still vs. the dynamic)
7	Giant earthmoving machine at work	Ant moving between blades of grass	Microcosm and macrocosm coexist	Conflictual (conflict of scale)
8	Geese flying across frame	Water plummeting at Niagara Falls	Forces flowing in different directions	Conflictual (conflict of graphic direction)
9	Screen-filling close-up of face, teeth clenched	Huge Olympic stadium, line of runners poised for pistol start	The one among the many	Conflictual (conflict of scale)
10	Dark moth resting on white curtains	Flashlight emerging out of dark forest	Opposite elements	Conflictual (dark vs. light)
11	Girl walks into amusement park	Distorted face appears in amusement park mirror	The original and its reflection	Conflictual (original vs. distorted version)
12	Driver sees cyclist in his path	In slow motion, driver screams and swings steering wheel	Event and its perception	Conflictual (real time vs. perceived time)
13	Driver gets out of disabled car	Same image, car in foreground, driver walking as a tiny figure in distance	Transition—some time has gone by	Jump cut

FIGURE 4-2

Examples of juxtaposed shots or cuts.

important. When sound arrived, it became important to maintain the illusion of continuity during multiangle dialogue scenes, and editing had to work harder at creating continuity.

Dialectical editing: Examples 6 through 12 (see Figure 4-2) show the preferred methods of Eisenstein, for whom the essence of narrative art lay in dialectical conflict. His juxtapositions therefore highlight contrast and contradiction, and while they inform us, they argue by creating contrasts and irony.

Action match editing: Editing that is intrusive draws unwelcome attention to authorial manipulation. Early filmmakers discovered that you could edit from a tight shot to a wide shot, or vice versa, by placing the cut, not in the static part of the action, but right in the most dynamic. Like a pickpocket who strikes during a flurry of activity, the action match cut allows an image change to pass unnoticed under cover of compelling action.

Ear and eye together: The mind has only so much processing power, so you can take our attention away from sound by distracting the eye with some compelling action (during an unnatural sound atmosphere change, for instance). You can mask a bad picture cut by introducing an arresting new sound element. In each case, you have directed our critical faculties away from the area of fault.

Sound juxtaposing: Sound effects, music, and language will also be juxtaposed against picture to create, not an imitation of reality, but a composite set of impressions for the audience to interpret. Director Robert Altman became famous for developing dense picture and sound counterpoint in his films.

POINT OF VIEW

Using film effectively depends on maintaining the unspoken collusion between audience and communicator by using film conventions that are neither clichéd and beneath the audience, nor so private that they go over the audience's head. Ethnographers who projected edited footage to isolated tribespeople noticed, for instance, that their subjects understood the "story" until the film cut to a close-up. The tribespeople lost concentration because they could not understand why the camera eye "jumped close." They were unaware of the convention that a close-up signifies not physical closeness, but a stripping away of surplus detail to intensify attention. Meaning and signification are a cultural work in progress—that is, both film audiences and film language are in slow, inexorable evolution.

Perception by humans is different from the mechanical perception of a camera because we develop an intellectual and emotional framework within which to organize what our senses record. The convention of *internal monologue* (also called *voice-over*) verbalizes this process.

THE CONCERNED OBSERVER AND THE STORYTELLER

LITERARY AND FILM STORYTELLING COMPARED

The literary or oral storyteller seeks to affect the listener by a selective presentation of bygone events. Think of how a comedian might describe a wedding. Through the telling, he aims to evoke in the reader's imagination a funny event that has already happened.

Storytelling by a camera, however, is always "now," and appears to show us an unmediated, ongoing present. Unless you temporarily force the past tense into what the audience sees and hears, film always settles back into the present tense. Yet how can you retell something that seems to be happening right now? This is film's paradox, its sleight of hand. It is an artfully constructed "now" in which the camera observes, reacts, and navigates the events as they seem to happen. In reality, of course, a selective intelligence is silently guiding our eyes and ears as much as any literary mediator could. This is the film storyteller at work.

> **Witnessing:** In a court case, a witness often reports having taken no action in response to what he or she saw and heard. But witnessing is not a value-neutral reception of oral and visual information: it includes an inner dialogue of ideas, feelings, memories, expectations, and judgments.
>
> **The Concerned Observer:** The word "observe" has such scientific associations that I am appending "concerned" to imply the observer's feelings, associations, and ideas, which all lead to involvement. The Concerned Observer is a notional figure who forms ideas and anticipations. As an example, imagine an undercover detective at a significant gathering: she would move around, picking and choosing whom to watch. She would decide whom to approach based on prior knowledge, on suspicions about each type and individual, and on what she sees happening. She would also try to discover the purpose of the gathering and what to expect next.
>
> **The Storyteller:** Reporting back at headquarters, our Concerned Observer detective changes from being an informed witness to an opinionated Storyteller. The significance here is that filmed drama can be mechanically reproduced, or it can palpably come to us through an engaging human intelligence. A film Storyteller is seldom an identifiable person delivering a retrospective in voice-over: usually he or she is an *unseen presence through whose creative intelligence we perceive unfolding events and who is palpably alert to their significances and ironies.*

Creating the narrative wit and emotional involvement of a Storyteller is central to evolved film directing. For this to happen, a film's stream of perception must be modeled on how and why someone witty and perceptive experiences events. Here, to begin with, are a few essentials of technique that help keep spatial relationships straight for the audience.

SCENE AXIS ESSENTIALS

In filmmaking, you have to deal with more than one kind of axis, and the obliging presence of our Concerned Observer will demonstrate how this works.

LINES OF TENSION AND THE SCENE AXIS

> **Subject-to-subject axis:** When two people have an animated conversation in your presence, your attention shifts back and forth between them. Figure 4-3 represents Person A and Person B being watched by Observer O, who might be yourself as a child. As O, your sight line plays back and forth between A and B as they talk. Your eye follows an invisible line of tension between them, the active pathway of their words, looks, awareness, and will. Filmmakers call this the *subject-to-subject axis*, or, alternatively, the *scene axis*.
>
> **Observer-to-subject axis:** A two-person scene witnessed by a third person has an additional axis. In my example, it's at right angles to the scene axis (the line of tension between A and B—see Figure 4-3). This is the observer-to-subject axis.

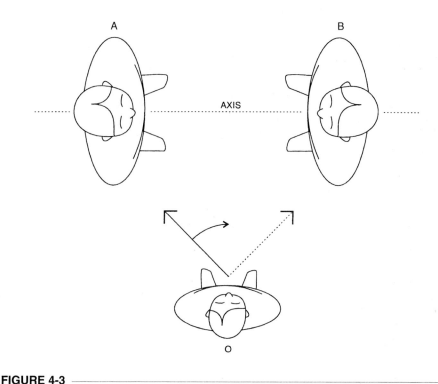

FIGURE 4-3 ————————————————————————————————

The observer watching a conversation.

The word "axis" makes the whole matter sound technical when it is really very human, for the Observer (yourself) develops feelings and ideas toward each person and what passes between them. That makes you the Concerned Observer, who is such an important figure in this book.

Camera-to-subject axis: In turning to look from person to person, the Observer can be replaced by a camera panning (that is, moving horizontally) between the two speakers. In Figure 4–4, the Observer has moved closer to A and B's axis.

Cuts instead of pans: Anxious not to miss any of the action, the Observer now switches rapidly between A and B. You naturally do this by blinking your eyes to avoid the unpleasant blur when your eye swishes between widely separated subjects. To the human brain, momentarily shutting your eyes produces two static images with no "black" period of transition between them. And there you have it—the cut! Historically, the cut must have emerged when someone removed a nauseatingly fast pan between two subjects. It "worked" because its counterpart was already embedded in human experience. Cutting between two camera angles taken from the same camera position reproduces this familiar experience.

I find it fascinating that two angles cut together in this way imply O, that human presence watching from a particular point in space. O is evoked even when we do not see him or her.

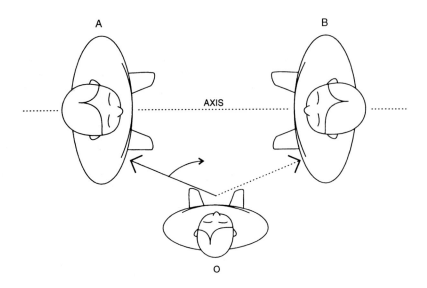

FIGURE 4-4

The Observer moves close to the characters' axis.

CROSSING THE LINE OR SCENE AXIS

Observing events from a fixed place, as O does to A and B, is habitual. The camera generally mimics that experience by staying to one side of a scene axis. Why? Because so long as O stays on one side, A will always be looking left to right (L-R) in the frame, and B always right to left (R-L). In Chapter 30, Figures 30-3A and 30–3B are a ground plan and storyboard to show what happens if you "cross the line"—that is, cross the scene axis. If intercut shots are taken from both sides of the line, the results on-screen are immediately disorienting. If, however, you follow observational logic, you won't transgress the rule.

For a type of shot that allows you to cross the line, see "Changing Screen Direction" below. Let's meanwhile continue with those figures at either end of the scene axis.

THE ACTOR AND THE ACTED-UPON

Consider how you follow a conversation. Sometimes you merely look toward whoever speaks next. Other times, when the talk becomes heated, you find yourself looking at the listener, not the speaker. What's going on?

> **The tennis analogy:** A human interaction is like a tennis game. At any given moment, one player acts (serves the ball), and the other is acted upon (receives it). When we see a player prepare to make an aggressive serve, our eye runs ahead of the ball to see how the recipient will deal with it. We see her run, jump, swing her racquet, and intercept the ball. Certain she's going to succeed, our eye flicks back to see how the first player is placed to handle the return. The cycle of actor and acted-upon has now been reversed because our eye jumps ahead of the ball back to the original player.

This is how we monitor all significant human interactions. We know instinctively that *every human being is trying forever to get, do, or accomplish something*. A game ritualizes this interchange as a competition, but every conversation to the aware filmmaker is equally complex and structured.

Dramatic characters are active: We picture ourselves as patient, tolerant victims being worked on by a greedy and selfish world, and we hate to see ourselves making any demands. So we seldom see how we act on others. But the fact is— and you must take this to heart if you intend to work in drama—that *everyone acts upon those around him*, even when he uses the strategy of passivity.

Anytime one person acts on another, there is always an actor and an acted-upon. Usually, but not always, the situation alternates rapidly, and it is through actions and reactions that we assess another's character, mood, and motives.

Shooting and editing follow the concerned observer's needs: Sit in a café and notice how you watch two people conversing. Your sight line switches according to your notion of who is acting upon whom. As soon as you've decided how A has begun acting on B, your eye switches in mid-sentence to see how B is taking it. Depending on how B adapts and acts back, you soon find yourself returning to A. Once you grasp this, most shooting and editing decisions become no-brainers. You simply use your expectations at each moment to decide where next to look. Editing is therefore visceral, your instincts dictating where the camera eye should look.

AUTHORSHIP ESSENTIALS: TEXT AND SUBTEXT

The text is what is in the screenplay that determines the characters' speech and actions. But while you absorb this, you are also searching for the behavioral clues that unlock the *subtext*.

The subtext is the situation's hidden meaning that lies beneath the visible and audible surface of the text. Each character's hidden agenda—whatever it is they are trying to get, do, or accomplish—is developed by the director and the actors, and goes on developing throughout rehearsal, shooting, and even editing. It is the editor's job, while putting the film together, to liberate or even manufacture other possibilities. Lengthening reaction time before a character speaks often hints at more complex inner processes and yields a more interesting idea of her interior action and motivation.

Shot point of view is the *intention* behind the combination of a shot's content and form. At a photo exhibition, you are guessing what the photographers were thinking and feeling as they chose each shot. You assess this from what each shot includes, and also from what it excludes or implies. For instance, a shot of a man staring offscreen focuses our attention on how, rather than what, he sees. Shot point of view is also used more prosaically to imply where the shot was taken from, such as from a high building down into a plaza.

Image denotation and connotation refer to how we register the meaning of an image. If we see a bus, a pair of worn-out shoes, and a man in a wheelchair, we may see only what those images "are"; that is, what they *denote*. If their context encourages us to ascribe special meanings to them—such as vacation, poverty, and power brought low—then we are reacting to the associations those images trigger; that is, what they *connote*. Denotation is what an image is; connotation is what it seems to mean.

Meaning arises from cultural associations that direct the spectator along a particular path of speculation. For example, when we see carefully framed shots of a flower or of a hand lighting a candle, they denote a flower and a hand lighting a candle. But a flower on a battlefield might connote a single, fragile life; natural beauty; devotion; or a host of other ideas. When audiences respond to connotations in art, it means they go beyond what is literally there and search for deeper meanings.

AUTHORIAL POINT OF VIEW

Image connotations and juxtapositions also cause us to infer the human sensibility that chose to notice the flower or the hand lighting the candle, each in its particular context. This, along with the choice of subject and the treatment it is given, becomes the authorial point of view, the Storyteller's sense of what matters.

MAKE METAPHORS AND SYMBOLS ORGANIC

The flower and lighting candle images mentioned previously are acceptable because they are *organic* to the battlefield situation. If instead you plant a naked baby on the battlefield to symbolize how vulnerable humanity is, you will look obvious and heavy-handed. That's because babies, naked or dressed for dinner, are not organic to trench warfare. Metaphors and symbols need to be fresh and inventive, and organic to the scene.

CONSTRUCTING MEANING

Authorship is making a construct: Present-day footage of familiar scenes may seem objective and value free, but representations, whether of actuality or of life enacted or reenacted, are always constructs. This means they are subjectively involved in a triangular relationship among content, Storyteller, and viewer. As a director, you must be able to articulate what points of view are implied, decide what biases they incorporate, and assess their overall credibility. Travis Bickle in Scorsese's *Taxi Driver* (1976, Figure 4-5) is so crazed that he becomes what literary theory calls an *unreliable narrator*. Usually a point of view, especially when established through camerawork alone, is more subtle and difficult to pin down.

Imagine you are hunting through archival World War II shots in a film library, as I once did at the Imperial War Museum in London. After you recover from the atmosphere of a place so packed with sad ghosts, you notice that by today's standards, the cameras and film stock from this era were less developed. Even so, each shot testifies, in addition to its subject, to different kinds of involvement from its makers—that is, different emotions, emphases, and agendas.

You run a shot that some librarian has neatly labeled "Russian soldiers, vicinity of Warsaw, running into sniper fire." From the first frame, you notice how emotionally loaded everything seems: it's shot in high-contrast black and white that accentuates the mood, and the air is smoky because lighting comes from behind the subjects. Here as elsewhere, filming is undeniably a mechanical process of reproduction, but everything has been polarized by the interrelationship among human choice, technology, subject, and environment. All these things contribute to the powerful feelings you are getting. The camera enters the soldiers' world

FIGURE 4-5

Travis Bickle in *Taxi Driver* may be the ultimate unreliable narrator (courtesy Columbia/The Kobal Collection).

because it runs jerkily with them instead of shooting from a sheltered tripod. You catch your breath when a soldier falls because the cameraman almost trips over his fallen comrade. The camera recovers and continues onward, leaving the wounded soldier to his fate. Then, suddenly, it plunges to the ground. Framing some out-of-focus mud, the camera motor runs out.

   With slow horror, you realize you have just accompanied a cameraman in his last seconds of work. Desolated, you replay his shot several times. As you stop on particular frames, it seems as though time and destiny can be replayed, reentered, and relived. Even when you replay something and know full well what's going to happen, film is always and forever in the present tense. Film permits destiny to be played and replayed.

Now the library produces a photo of a dead cameraman lying face down on the battlefield, his camera fallen from his hands. You recognize the knob of mud from his last seconds of film. It's him, your poor cameraman. Left alone with him, you ponder what made him willing to gamble his life to do his work. You wonder whom he left behind and whether they ever learned how he died. Now you are his witness because you died with him. Somewhere inside you, his work, his good intentions, his gamble that ended in death, will always be with you. You are aching with sadness, but he has given you something and you have grown. Now you carry him in the recesses of yourself. You have become him. There can be a world of meaning in a single shot. Here, authorship and the author's fate converge.

SCREEN DIRECTION AND ANGLES

The term *screen direction* describes a subject's direction or movement (Figure 4-6), and becomes crucial if that movement flows through multiple shots, as in a chase. An important screen convention is that characters and their movements are generally observed from only one side of that movement. Let's imagine that you ignored this and intercut one part of a parade moving across the screen L-R with another going R-L. The audience would expect the two factions to collide, as when police form up to block a demonstration.

Now suppose you run ahead of the parade to watch it file past a landmark. In the new position, you would see marchers entering an empty street from the same screen direction. But in life, you might cross the parade's path to watch it from the other side. This would be unremarkable because you knew about the relocation of your viewpoint. But in film, cutting to a camera position across *the axis* of

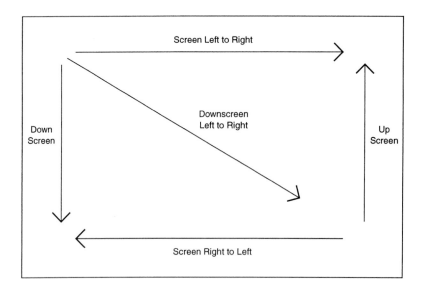

FIGURE 4-6

A range of screen directions and their descriptions.

movement must be specially set up, or it reverses some screen directions and causes disorientation for the audience.

CHANGING SCREEN DIRECTION

You can make a parade change screen direction by filming at an angle to a corner (Figure 4-7). The marchers enter in the background going screen right to screen left (R-L), turn the corner in the foreground, and exit L-R. In essence, they have changed screen direction. If subsequent shots are to match, their action will also have to be L-R.

Another solution to changing screen direction is to dolly during a gap in the parade so the camera *visibly crosses the subject's axis of movement* (Figure 4-8). Remember that any change of observing camera orientation to the action must be shown on-screen. Putting this differently, *you can always change screen direction without trouble if we see the change on-screen.*

DIFFERENT ANGLES ON THE SAME ACTION

So far, we have found everyday human examples for every aspect of film language. But can there be one to justify using very different angles to cover the same action? Earlier, we said that cutting together long and close shots taken along a single axis suggests, by excluding the irrelevant, an observer's changed degree of concentration. But now imagine covering the scene of a tense family meal from several very different angles. It's a familiar enough screen convention, but does it match what happens in life? In literature, it is clear that multiple points of view

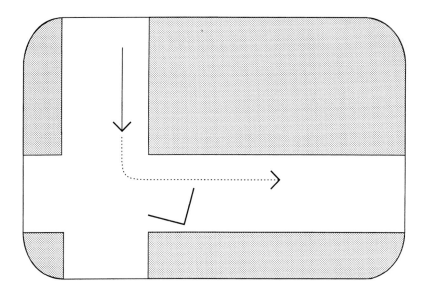

FIGURE 4-7

By shooting at a corner, a parade or moving object can be made to change screen direction.

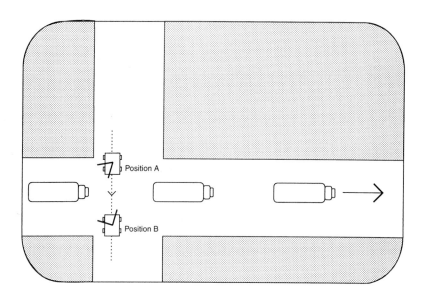

FIGURE 4-8 ————————————————————————————————

Dollying sideways between floats in a parade changes the parade's effective screen direction, but the dollying movement must be shown.

are not physical changes of vantage point, but shifts in psychological and emotional points of view. The same is true when this strategy is used on-screen. But film is misleading because, unlike literature, it seems to give us "real" events and a "real" vantage point. As filmmakers, we must keep in mind that film gives a *perception* of events, a "seeming" that, despite appearances, is not the events themselves.

> **Privileged views:** As a bystander during a major disagreement between two friends, you get so absorbed that you forget all about yourself. Instead, you internally debate a series of internal agreements and disagreements, seeing first one person's point, then the other's, so that you virtually experience each protagonist's realities. By using physically shifting viewpoints, screen language mimics this heightened subjectivity, and signals that they are really psychological. In fact, the shifting viewpoints suggest how an observer identifies with different individual viewpoints as time progresses. Whenever we give such close attention, our sympathy and fascination migrate from person to person.

Such empathic shifts should be rooted in an identifiable point of view—either one of the characters or the Storyteller—if they are to pass as natural and integrated. By the way, nobody maintains this state of heightened and all-encompassing concentration for long, so a film should not do so either.

ABSTRACTION

> **Movement from whole to part, or part to whole:** Watch the shifts in your attention. They often take you to a private realm where you speculate, contemplate, remember, or imagine. While doing this, we often alter our examination from the whole to a part, or from a part to the whole—whatever suffices to occupy our reverie.

Meaningful detail: A detail registered during a period of abstraction often turns out to have symbolic meaning, or is a part that stands for the whole. Thus, a car door immersed up to the door handle in swirling water can stand for the New Orleans disaster. This oft-used filmic principle is called synecdoche (pronounced sin-ECK-doh-kee). It arises when our eye alights on something symbolic in an otherwise naturalistic scene—that is, something conventionally representative much as a scale represents justice, or a handbag lying in an empty lot might represent abandonment.

Contemplation: We enter a state of abstraction for good reason. We may be taking refuge or making an inward journey to interpret something that has just happened. Selective focus is a cinema device used to suggest this state. An object isolated on the screen, with its foreground and background thrown out of focus, strongly suggests abstracted vision. Another device is abnormal motion—either slow or fast—which has rather the same effect. In these ways, we distance ourselves and contemplate an event by dismantling reality. We may be searching for meaning, hiding from pain, or simply regenerating ourselves through imaginative play.

SUBJECTIVITY AND OBJECTIVITY

The world is full of dualities, oppositions, and ironic contrasts. You drive your car very fast at night, and then, stopping to look at the stars, think about your own insignificance under a light that has taken millions of years to reach your eye. Human attention shifts from subjectivity to objectivity, from past to present and back again, from looking at a crowd as a phenomenon to looking a woman's profile as she turns away into the crowd.

There is screen language to replicate every aspect of the Observer's attention. Make the shifts in the image stream of your film consistent with human consciousness, and your audience will experience an integrated being's presence—that of our invisible, thinking, all-seeing Concerned Observer.

DURATION, RHYTHM, AND CONCENTRATION

Human beings are directed by rhythms that begin in the brain and control heartbeat and breathing. We tap our feet to music or jump up to dance when the music grabs us. Everything we do is measured by the beat, duration, and capacity of our minds and bodies. The duration of a shot, for instance, is determined by how much attention it demands, just as the decision to cross the road is governed by how long we take to scope out the traffic. The speed of a movement on the screen is judged by its context, where it is going, and why.

Speech has inherently powerful rhythms. The Czech composer Leoš Janáček became fascinated by language rhythms, and his late compositions draw on the pacing and tonal patterns of people talking. Films—particularly those with long dialogue scenes—are intricately composed around the speech and movement rhythms of the characters. Complex dialogue scenes are always the most difficult to get right in editing because subtextual consistency depends on so many delicate nuances.

That rhythm should play an important role in helping us assimilate film comes from a principle established in antiquity. Old narratives like Homer's

Odyssey, the Arthurian legends, and the Norse sagas were composed in strict rhythmic patterns because the troubadours who recited them from court to court found memorization easier. They must have discovered, too, that rhythmically structured language helps audiences maintain concentration over longer periods.

Film language makes use of every possible rhythm, not only those of speech. Many sounds from everyday life—birdsong, traffic, the noise from a building site, or the wheels of a train—contain strong rhythms that help to orchestrate a sequence. Even static pictorial compositions contain visual rhythms derived from the sensations of symmetry, balance, repetition, opposition, and patterns that intrigue the eye.

SEQUENCE AND MEMORY

You are always surrounded by an everlasting flow of events, but only some are memorable. A biography takes the significant parts of a life and jumps them together. The building blocks are segments of time (the hero's visit to the hospital emergency room after a road accident), the events at a location (the high points of his residency in Rome), or of a developing idea (as he builds their home, his partner loses patience with the slowness of the process). Because changes of time and space are involved, there are junctures between the narrative building blocks that must either be indicated or hidden as the story demands. These junctures are *transitions*, to be emphasized or elided (glided over).

Elision is faithful to human experience because our memory routinely jettisons whatever lacks significance. Think back on the sensations during an accident, and you'll find that recall has kept only the significant parts, virtually a shot list for a film sequence. The memory is a fine editor.

Once, at New York University, I was asked to advise Danae Elon and Pierre Chainet, students feeling defeated by their 70 hours of documentary dailies. They were astonished when I suggested they put away their laborious documentation and simply write down the sequences they remembered. What they listed was, of course, the minority of the footage that "had something." This became the core of their *Never, Again, Forever* (1997), a film on the roots of the settler movement in Israel that gained the dubious distinction of starting fistfights in cinemas.

When we have a dream, or tell an experience, we recall only the peaks of what happened, seldom the troughs. The art of storytelling makes use of this trait to compress a narrative into a short compass.

TRANSITIONS AND TRANSITIONAL DEVICES

The transitions we make in life—from place to place, or from time to time—are either imperceptible because we are preoccupied, or come as a surprise or shock. Stories replicate this by either hiding the seams between sequences or by indicating and even emphasizing them. An action match between a woman drinking her morning fruit juice and a beer drinker raising his glass in a smoky dive contrasts the scene shift by drawing attention to the act of drinking. A dissolve from one scene to another would signal, in rather creaky language, "and time passed." A simple cut from one place to the next leaves the audience to fill in the blank.

However, imagine the scene of a teenager singing with the car radio on a long, boring drive, followed by flash images of a truck, screeching tires, and the youngster yanking desperately at the steering wheel. The transition from comfort to panic is intentionally a shock transition, and reproduces the violent change we undergo when taken nastily by surprise.

Sound can be used as a transitional device. Hearing a conversation over an empty landscape can draw us forward into the next scene (of two campers shivering in their tent). Cutting to a shot of a cityscape while we still hear the campsite birdsong gives the feeling of being confronted with a change of location while the mind and heart lag behind in the great outdoors. Transitional devices used in this way imply an emotional point of view.

Each film transition, like the literary phrase, "and then . . . ," is a narrative device that signals the progression between discontinuous story segments. Each transition's style implies an attitude or point of view emanating from either the characters or the Storyteller.

SCREEN LANGUAGE IN SUMMARY

Screen language when treated like professional packaging robs its subject of soul by making life seem mechanical and banal. But when it follows a Concerned Observer's psychology, and is told with panache by a Storyteller, we sense the sympathy and integrity of a questing human intelligence at work. We see with eyes that are human, critical, and compelling. If, for instance, you went to your high school reunion, then saw what another participant filmed with his video camera, you see what his eyes and ears cared to notice, and *you would see a mind and heart at work*. The industrial process of filmmaking easily destroys this.

Intelligently made fiction film implies an overarching heart and mind governing the flow of perception. The auteur theory of filmmaking calls this "the director's vision." But controlling how a film crew and company of actors create this is not a simple matter, and is scarcely within individual control. We have personified the native intelligence behind a film's point of view as that of the Storyteller. This is not the robust "I" of the director, but a fictional entity arising from the collective inventiveness of everyone involved. What you see on the screen is a collective construct, which is equally true for documentary and other nonfiction forms. Screen language at its most magical always implies the feeling of an intelligence grappling with the meaning of the events it shows us. People who work successfully in the medium seem to understand this instinctively, yet you never hear this or see it explained.

RESEARCHING TO BE A STORYTELLER

If all this seems beyond you, simply pattern your filmmaking around the natural processes of human perception, action, and reaction. See how you process events in life, and are moved to action by what you see and feel. Make film techniques approximate this, and you won't go far wrong. Do it consistently, and your film will take on a narrative identity all its own. And as you see this emerge, your film will let you know where to go next. That's an astounding aspect of the artistic process—that once you embark, films and other artworks use you to make themselves.

HOW MAKING DOCUMENTARY CAN HELP YOU

Those wedded to fiction often think that documentary is a lesser form. Not so. Making a documentary is eye-opening for fiction filmmakers. Direct cinema (also known as observational documentary) demands that the camera be subservient to the action and not intrude its needs on what it films. John Cassavetes' earliest films—such as *Shadows* (1959), *Faces* (1968), and *Husbands* (1970), which were improvised using this style of coverage—remain powerful and disturbing to this day.

For the beginner, seeing what actors are really doing, and assisting them to create between themselves, is extraordinarily demanding. To help you, I strongly advocate in later chapters that you shoot continuous-take, documentary-style coverage of your rehearsals. Shooting live coverage of your rehearsals helps you with the following:

- Discovering the best camera positions
- Practicing camera framing and movements as something subservient to actors' needs, rather than vice versa
- Revealing performance inequities on the screen
- Demystifing the relationship between live performance and its results on the screen
- Seeing the need for rewrites based on the screen results
- Getting experience in working with nonactors or actors only marginally experienced
- Spotting clichés, bad acting habits, and areas that are forced or false
- Preparing actors for the presence of the camera—and thus lowering the regression that normally follows the introduction of a camera as shooting begins
- Helping you face problems of adapting to a here-and-now actuality

You can expect to discover from making one or two documentaries:

For ideation:

- Experience at finding human stories around you and telling them on the screen
- A way to improvise and spontaneously create with your crew
- An ability to see human action as the all-important *evidence* by which we judge whether a story idea is dramatic

For your confidence and intuition:

- Proof of your abilities
- More confidence in your intuition and ability to adapt to the actual

For directing actors:

- An eye for a focused and truthful human presence
- Proof that risk, confrontation, and the chemistry of the moment are vital to both documentary and fiction. Ask any good actor.

- Knowing when subjects are simply *being* instead of signifying. Knowing whether your actors are reaching this state is vital
- Experience at catalyzing truth from documentary participants, so you can do something similar as a fiction director with actors
- Experience of characters revealing themselves through action
- Experience at capturing evidence of character-making decisions. Gripping observational documentary deals with people trying to accomplish things, and the best work is great drama because it reveals these principles at work in life
- Evidence how actions flow from decisions made by active characters, and of how decisions and actions create new issues

For editing:

- Making documentary means fast shooting and slow editing, whereas fiction is often shot slowly, but edited too quickly and superficially
- In documentary, brevity, compression, and rhythm come from editing. This helps you build it into the writing stage of fiction

For film language:

- Documentary provides a complete workout in the language of film
- Documentary is usually character-driven drama, and making it helps you to conceptualize character-driven fiction

For sound:

- Experience at shooting sound inventively. Location inequities teach the pre-eminence of good microphone choice and positioning. Sound design in documentary can be intensely creative

Taking a documentary approach to human truth will put you with those modern masters of the cinema who want to move cinema away from its beginnings in theatrical presentation. If this sounds interesting, this book's sister volume will take you further (Michael Rabiger, *Directing the Documentary* [Burlington, MA: Focal Press, 2004]).

CHAPTER 5

SEEING WITH A MOVIEMAKER'S EYE

The four study projects in this chapter will make you familiar with the essentials of image composition, editing, script analysis, and lighting. Collectively, they yield the basics of seeing with a moviemaker's eye, and will be immensely useful to your confidence when you begin directing. Even if you don't do them, read them through carefully because you'll still pick up some important knowledge.

PROJECTS

PROJECT 5-1: PICTURE COMPOSITION ANALYSIS

A stimulating and highly productive way to investigate composition is to do so with several other people or as a class. Though what follows is written for a study group, you can do it solo if circumstances so dictate.

Equipment required: For static composition, a slide projector and/or an overhead projector to enlarge graphics are best but not indispensable. For dynamic composition, you will need a video or DVD player.

Object: To learn the composition of visual elements by studying how the eye reacts to a static composition and then how it handles dynamic composition; that is, composition during movement.

Study materials: For static composition, a book of figurative painting reproductions (best used under an overhead projector so you have a big image to scan), or better, a dozen or more 35 mm art slides, also projected as large images. Slides of Impressionist paintings are good, but the more eclectic your collection, the better. For dynamic composition, use any visually interesting sequences from a favorite movie, though any Eisenstein movie would be ideal.

Analysis Format

In a class setting it's important to keep a discussion going, but if you are working alone, notes or sketches are a good way to log what you discover. Help from books on composition is not easily gained because many texts make composition seem intimidating or formulaic and may be difficult to apply to the moving image. Sometimes rules prevent seeing rather than promoting it, so trust your eye to see what is really there, and use your own nonspecialist vocabulary to describe it.

Strategy for Study

If you are leading a group, you will need to explain what is wanted, something like this: We're doing this to discover how each person's visual perception actually works. I'll put a picture up on the screen. In the composition, notice where your eye first goes, and then what course your eye takes as you examine the rest of the picture. After about 15 seconds, I'll ask someone to describe what path his eye followed. You don't need any special jargon; just let your responses come from the specifics of each picture. Please avoid the temptation to look for a story in the picture or to guess what the picture is "about," even when it suggests a story.

With each new image, pick a new person to comment. Because not everyone's eye responds the same way, there will be interesting discussions about the variations. There will usually be a great deal of agreement, so everyone is led to formulate ideas about visual reflexes and about what compositional components the eye finds attractive and engrossing. It is good to start simply and graduate to more abstract images, and then even to completely abstract ones. Many people, relieved of the burden of deciding a picture's "subject," can begin to enjoy a Kandinsky, a Mondrian, or a Pollock for itself, without fuming over whether or not it is really art. After about an hour of pictures and discussion, encourage your group to frame their own guidelines for composing images.

After the group has formed some ideas and gained confidence from analyzing paintings, I usually show both good and bad photos. Photography, less obviously contrived than painting, tends to be accepted less critically. This is a good moment to uncover in striking photography just how many classical elements arise from what first appeared to be a straight record of life.

Here are questions to help you discover ways to see more critically. They can be applied after seeing a number of paintings or photos, or you could direct the group's attention to each question's area as it becomes relevant.

Static Composition

1. After your eye has taken in the whole, review its starting point. Why did your eye go to that point in the picture? (Common reasons: brightest point in composition, darkest place in an otherwise light composition, single area of an arresting color, significant junction of lines creating a focal point.)

2. When your eye moved away from its point of first attraction, what did it follow? (Commonly: lines, perhaps actual ones like the line of a fence or an outstretched arm, or inferred lines such as the sight line from one character looking at another. Sometimes the eye simply moves to another significant area in the composition, going from one organized area to another and jumping skittishly across the intervening disorganization.)

3. How much movement did your eye make before returning to its starting point?

4. What specifically drew your eye to each new place?

5. If you trace an imaginary line over the painting to show the route your eye took, what shape do you have? (Sometimes this is a circular pattern, and sometimes a triangle or ellipse, but it can be many shapes. Any shape at all can reveal an alternative organization that helps you see beyond the wretched and dominating idea that every picture tells a story.)

6. Are there any places along your imaginary line that seem specially charged with energy? (These are often sight lines: between the Virgin's eyes and her baby's, between a guitarist's eyes and his hand on the strings, between two field workers, one of whom is facing away.)

7. How would you characterize the compositional movement? (For example, geometric, repetitive textures, swirling, falling inward, symmetrically divided down the middle, flowing diagonally, etc. Making a translation from one medium to another—in this case from the visual to the verbal—always helps you discover what is truly there.)

8. What parts, if any, do the following play in a particular picture?
   • Repetition
   • Parallels
   • Convergence
   • Divergence
   • Curves
   • Straight lines
   • Strong verticals
   • Strong horizontals
   • Strong diagonals
   • Textures
   • Nonnaturalistic coloring
   • Light and shade
   • Human figures

9. How is depth suggested? (This is an ever-present problem for the director of photography [DP], who, if inexperienced, is liable to take what I think of as the firing squad approach: that is, placing the human subjects against a flat background and shooting them. Unless there is something to create different planes, like a wall angling away from the foreground to suggest a receding space, the screen is like a painter's canvas and looks what it really is— two-dimensional.)

10. How are the individuality and mood of the human subjects expressed? (This is commonly through facial expression and body language, of course. But more interesting are the juxtapositions the painter makes of person to person, person to surroundings, or people inside a total design.)

11. How is space arranged on either side of a human subject, particularly in portraits? (Usually in profiles there is lead space—that is, more space in front of the person than behind them, as if in response to our need to see what the person sees.)

12. How much headroom is given above a person, particularly in a close-up? (Sometimes the edge of a frame cuts off the top of a head, or may not show one head at all in a group shot.)

13. How often and how deliberately are people and objects placed at the margins of the picture so you have to imagine what is cut off? (By demonstrating the frame's restriction, you can make the viewer's imagination supply what is beyond the edges of the "window.")

Visual Rhythm: How Duration Affects Perception

So far, I have stressed the idea of an immediate, instinctual response to the organization of an image. When you show a series of slides without comment, you move to a new image after sufficient time for the eye to absorb each picture. Some pictures require longer than others. This is how an audience must deal with each new shot in a film.

Unlike responding to a photograph or painting, which can be studied thoughtfully and at leisure, the film spectator must interpret the image within an unremitting and preordained forward movement in time. It is like reading a poster on the side of a moving bus: if the words and images cannot be assimilated in the given time, the inscription goes past without being understood. If, however, the bus is crawling in a traffic jam, you have time to absorb, to become critical, or even to become rejecting of the poster.

This tells us that there is an optimum duration for each shot to stay on the screen. It depends on the complexity of a shot's content and form, and how hard the viewer must work to extract its significance and intended meaning. An invisible third factor also affects ideal shot duration—that of expectation. The audience may work fast at interpreting each new image, or slowly, depending on how much time the film has allowed for interpreting preceding shots.

The principle by which a shot's duration is determined according to content, form, significance, and expectation is called visual rhythm. A filmmaker, like a musician, can either relax or intensify a visual rhythm, and this has consequences for the cutting rate and the ideal tempo of camera movements.

Ideal films for studying compositional relationships in film and visual rhythm are classics by the Russian director Sergei Eisenstein, such as *The Battleship Potemkin* (1925), *Que Viva Mexico!* (1931–1932), *Alexander Nevsky* (1938, Figure 5-1), and *Ivan the Terrible* (1944–1946). Eisenstein's origins as a theater designer made him very aware of the impact upon an audience of musical and visual design. His sketchbooks show how carefully he designed everything in each shot, down to the costumes. More recent films with a strong sense of design are Ingmar Bergman's *The Seventh Seal* (1956), Stanley Kubrick's *A Clockwork Orange* (1971, Figure 5-2), and David Lynch's *Blue Velvet* (1986). Designer's sketches and the comic strip are the precursor of the storyboard (see example in Figure 6-3 in the next chapter), which is much used by ad agencies and conservative elements in the film industry to lock down what each new frame will convey. Storyboarding is particularly helpful for the inexperienced, even when your artistry is as lousy as mine and doesn't run much beyond stick figures.

Dynamic Composition

With moving images, more compositional principles come into play. A balanced composition can become disturbingly unbalanced should someone cross the frame, or leave it altogether. Even the turn of a figure's head in the foreground

FIGURE 5-1 ————————————————————————————————

Eisenstein developed his striking sense of composition while working as a theater designer. Using images dialectically became his hallmark as a film director, as shown in this still from *Alexander Nevsky* (courtesy MOSFILM/The Kobal Collection).

FIGURE 5-2 ————————————————————————————————

The stylization of *A Clockwork Orange* accentuates the grotesque brutality of the characters (courtesy Warner Bros./The Kobal Collection).

may posit a new eye line (subject-to-subject axis), which in turn demands a compositional rebalancing. Then again, zooming from wide to close shot, or vice versa, demands reframing because the composition changes drastically, even though the subject remains the same.

To study dynamic composition, find a visually interesting sequence of a few minutes, such as the chase in John Ford's *Stagecoach* (1939), William Friedkin's *The French Connection* (1971), or almost any part of Andrew Davis' *The Fugitive* (1993). Here, your DVD player's slow-scan function will be useful. Make a shot list and then see how many of these aspects you can note against the picture descriptions:

1. Reframing,

    a. because the subject moved (look for a variety of camera adjustments).

    b. as a consequence of something or someone entering the frame.

    c. in anticipation of something or someone entering the frame.

2. A change in the point of focus to move attention from background to foreground or vice versa. (This changes the texture of significant areas of the composition from hard focus to soft.)

3. Strong movement within an otherwise static composition. (How many can you find? Across frame, diagonally, from background to foreground, from foreground to background, up frame, down frame, etc. Eisenstein films are full of these compositions.)

In addition, try to assess the following:

4. How much do you feel identified with each kind of subject movement? (This is a tricky issue, but in general the nearer you are to the axis of a movement, the more subjective is your sense of involvement.)

5. How quickly does the camera adjust to a figure who gets up and moves to another place in frame? (Often camera movements are motivated by, even mirror, changes within the composition. Subject and camera move synchronously, with no clumsy lag or anticipation. When documentary covers spontaneous events, inaccuracies are normal and signal that nothing is contrived.)

6. How often are the camera or the characters blocked (that is, choreographed) to isolate one character? What is the dramatic justification?

7. How often is the camera moved or the characters blocked so as to bring two characters back into frame? (Good camerawork, composition, and blocking are always trying to show relatedness. This helps to intensify meanings and ironies, and reduces the need to manufacture relationship through editing.)

8. How often is composition

    a. angled down sight lines and seeing in depth?

    b. without depth and rendering space as flat (point of view often shifts at these junctures from subjective to objective)?

9. What do changes of angle and composition make you feel about (or toward) the characters?

10. Find several compositions that successfully create depth and define what visual element is responsible. (Perhaps the camera is next to a railroad line as a train rushes up and past. Both the perspective revealed by the rails and the movement

of the train create depth. In deep shots, different zones of lighting at varying distances from the camera, or zones of hard and soft focus, can also achieve this.)

11. Can you find shots where the camera changes position to include more (or different) background detail in order to comment on the foreground subject?

Internal and External Composition

So far, we have been looking at *internal composition*, or composition that is internal to each shot. Another form of compositional relationship is the momentary relationship between an outgoing shot and the next, incoming shot. This relationship, called *external composition*, is a hidden part of film language. It is unseen because we are unaware how it influences our judgments and expectations.

A common usage for external composition is when a character leaving the frame in the outgoing shot (A) leads the spectator's eye to the very place in Shot B where an assassin will emerge in a large and restless crowd. The eye is conducted to the right place in a busy composition.

Another example might be the framing of two complementary close shots in which two characters have an intense conversation. The compositions are similar but symmetrically opposed. In Figure 5-3, the two-shot (A) gives a good overall feel of the scene, but man and child are too far away. The close shots, (B) and (C),

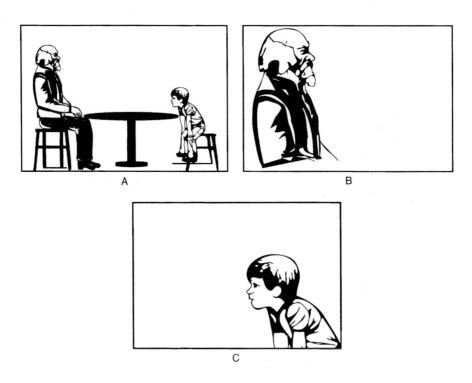

A

B

C

FIGURE 5-3 ————————————————————————————————

Wide shot and two complementary close-ups (CUs). Notice the lead space in front of each CU character, and how the height and placing in the frame of each replicates the composition of the master shot.

retain the feel of the scene, but effectively cut out the dead space between them. Note that the heads are not centered: each person has lead (rhyming with "feed") space in front of his face that echoes his positioning in the two-shot. The man is high in the frame and looking downward, and the child lower in the frame and looking up—just as in the matching two-shot.

Other aspects will emerge if you apply the questions below to the film sequences you review. Use the slow-scan function to examine compositional relationships at the cutting point. Go backward and forward several times over each cut to be sure you miss nothing. Try these for yourself:

1. Where was your point of concentration at the end of the shot? (You can trace where your eye goes by moving your finger around the screen of the monitor. Your last point in the outgoing shot is where your eye enters the composition of the incoming shot. Notice how shot duration determines the distance the eye travels in exploring the shot. This means that on top of what we have already established about shot length, it is also a factor in external composition.)

2. What kinds of symmetry exist between complementary shots (that is, between shots designed to be intercut)?

3. What is the relationship between two different-sized shots of the same subject that are designed to cut together? (This is a revealing one; the inexperienced camera operator will produce medium shots and close shots that cut poorly because the placements of the subject are incompatible.)

4. Examine a match cut very slowly and see if there is any overlap. (Especially where there is relatively fast action, a match cut, to look smooth, needs about four frames of the action repeated on the incoming shot. This is because the eye does not register the first three or four frames of any new image. This built-in perceptual lag means that when you cut to the beat of music, the only way to make the cuts look in sync with the beat is to make each cut around three or four frames before the actual beat point.)

5. Find visual comparisons in external composition that make a Storyteller's comment (for instance, cut from a pair of eyes to car headlights approaching at night, from a dockside crane to a man feeding birds with arm outstretched, etc.).

COMPOSITION, FORM, AND FUNCTION

Form is the manner in which content is presented, and its composition component is a vital element in communication. Good composition becomes an important organizing force when used to project ideas and to dramatize relativity and relationship. It makes not only the subject (content) accessible, but heightens the viewer's perceptions and stimulates his or her imaginative involvement, like language from the pen of a good poet.

If form follows function, involve yourself with content and then look for the form that best communicates it. You can also decide on a form and then look for an appropriate subject. The difference is one of purpose and temperament. Content, form, structure, and style are analyzed in greater detail in Chapters 12 through 16.

We have looked critically at pictorial composition, but the composition of a film's sound track is just as important to a film's impact. The study of sound is included in the next editing study project.

PROJECT 5-2: EDITING ANALYSIS

Equipment required: DVD player as in Project 5-1.

Objective: To produce a detailed analysis of a portion of film using standard abbreviations and terminology; to analyze the way a film is constructed; and to distinguish the conventions of film language so they can be used confidently.

Study materials: Any well-made feature film containing dialogue scenes and processes that have clear beginnings, middles, and ends will do, but I recommend these films for their excellent development of characters and settings:

- Terrence Malick's *Days of Heaven* (1978) for its awe-inspiring cinematography of the Texas landscape, its exploration of space and loneliness, and its unusual and effective pacing. The film uses the younger sister, Linda, as a narrator.
- Peter Weir's *Witness* (1985) for its classically shot dialogue scenes, its exploration of love between mismatched cultures, and the superb Amish work sequences.
- Stephen Daldry's *Billy Elliot* (2000, Figure 5-4) has strong character studies, dynamic dance sequences, and a strong sense of working-class England.

First Viewing

Before you attempt any analysis, see the whole film at least twice without stopping. Then write down all the strong feelings the film evoked, paying no attention

FIGURE 5-4 ——————————————————————————————

In *Billy Elliot*, a boy braves the mockery of his contemporaries to become a dancer. Characters show us most about themselves by what they do (courtesy Tiger Aspect Pics/ The Kobal Collection/Keyte, Giles).

to order. Note from memory which sequences sparked those feelings. You may have an additional sequence or two that intrigued you as a piece of virtuoso storytelling. Note these down, too, but whatever you study should be something that hits you at an emotional, rather than a merely intellectual, level.

Analysis Format

What you write down will be displayed on paper in *split-page format*, also known as *TV script format* (see Figure 5-5). Visuals occupy the left half of the page; all

TB Sanatorium Sequence

ACTION	SOUND
Fade in LS ruins of sanatorium. Camera pans left around buildings, stops with two small figures walking slowly.	Bird song, distant jet, sounds of distant softball players.
Cut to two pairs of feet walking on brick path, weeds growing up.	Fade in sound of elderly man coughing.
2S Sylvia and Aaron in profile.	Young Man's Voice: "Dad? Dad?"
POV shot residential building, windows broken.	Aaron: "This is where I came to see him ...
Telephoto shot of gutter with ferns growing against skyline.	... last. You know what he missed the most?"
	Sylvia: "Your mother?"
LS through ruined greenhouse, Sylvia and Aaron in BG.	Aaron: "No, his garden. His damned garden."
POV shot sapling growing up through broken glass roof.	Aaron: "Why did they let this place go? It used to be so beautiful."
CS Aaron's hand opening creaky gate.	Sylvia: "How long did you come here?"
WS enclosure with vegetable plots, one old man working in BG. Sylvia and Aaron enter shot from camera right.	Aaron: "Just over a year. He had a vegetable plot here. Towards the end I had to do everything for him."
	Sylvia: "That's how you became such a gardener?"
2S, Aaron looks off camera left, Sylvia follows his gaze.	Aaron: "I used to see that thing all the time while I was digging ...
POV shot, high chimney next to large building.	... It seemed to be waiting for him to die."
Neglected rock garden, pond dry with weeds growing out of cracks.	Aaron: "When I was a kid and Dad had left us, I used to try and hate him, but I never could. (Pause) Sylvie, it was a mistake to come back here."
Frontal 2S, Sylvia puts her arm around Aaron, who has become very sad.	

FIGURE 5-5 —————————————————————————————

Split-page format, also known as TV script format. Picture is always on the left, sound on the right. (LS = long shot, MS = medium shot, CS = close shot, 2S = two-shot [shot containing two people], POV = point-of-view shot.)

sound occupies the right. For an extended overview, see "Standard Script Forms" in Chapter 7. First, transcribe the picture and dialogue—shot by shot and word by word—as they relate to each other. Use wide line spacing for your draft so you can insert more information on subsequent passes. Once this basic information is on paper, you can turn to such things as shot transitions, internal and external composition of shots, screen direction, camera movements, opticals (such as titles, fades, dissolves, superimpositions), sound effects, and the use of music.

Your objective is to extract the most information about an interesting passage of film language, so it is better to do a short sequence (two to four minutes) very thoroughly than a long one superficially. Script formats, whether split-page or screenplay, show only what can be seen and heard. Some of your notes (for example, on the mood a shot evokes) will clutter the functional simplicity of your transcript, so keep them separately, or put them in a third column (see "Split-Page with Third Column" in Chapter 7).

Making and Using a Floor Plan

For a sequence containing a dialogue exchange, make a *floor plan* sketch (Figure 5-6). In the example, the character Eric enters, stands in front of William, goes to the phone, picks up a book from the table, looks out the window, and then sits on the couch. The whole action has been covered by three camera positions. Making a floor plan for a sequence allows you to re-create what a whole room or location layout looks like, record how the characters move around, and decide how the camera is placed. This will help you decide where to place your own camera in the future, and it reveals how little of an environment needs to be shown for the audience to create the rest in their imaginations. This is the cocreation discussed earlier in Chapter 1.

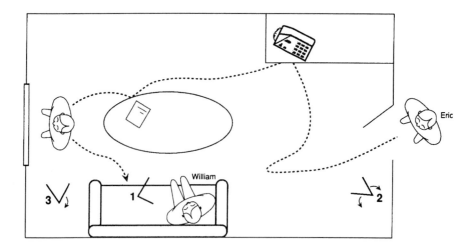

FIGURE 5-6

Floor or ground plan showing entry and movement of character Eric and the camera positions necessary to cover his action.

Strategy for Study

Your split-page script should contain:

Action-side descriptions of:

- Each shot (who, what, when, where)
- Its action content
- Camera movements
- Optical effects (fades, dissolves, etc.)

Sound-side descriptions of:

- Dialogue, word for word
- Positioning of dialogue relative to the action
- Music starting and stopping points
- Featured sound effects (that is, other than synchronous, or "sync," sound)

Very important: read from the film rather than reading into it. Film is a complex and deceptive medium; like a glib and clever acquaintance, it can make you uneasy about your perceptions and too ready to accept what should be seen or should be felt. Recognize what the film made you feel, then trace your impressions to what can actually be seen and heard in the film. To avoid overload, scrutinize the sequence during each pass on just a few of the aspects listed below. Try to find at least one example of everything so you understand the concepts at work.

1. First Impressions
   a. What was the progression of feelings you had watching the sequence?
2. Definition and Statistics
   a. How long is the sequence (minutes and seconds)?
   b. What determines the sequence's beginning and ending points?
   c. How many picture cuts does it contain?
   d. Is its span determined by:
      i. Being at one location?
      ii. Being a continuous segment of time?
      iii. A particular mood?
      iv. The stages of a process?
      v. Something else?

The duration of each shot and how often the camera angle is changed may be aspects of the genre (what type or family of film it is) or a director's particular style, or may be suggested by the sequence's content. Try to decide whether the content or its treatment is determining the frequency of cutting.

3. Use of Camera
   a. How many different motivations can you find for the camera to make a movement?
   b. Does the camera follow the movement of a character?
   c. Does a car or other moving object permit the camera to pan the length of the street so that camera movement seems to arise from action in the frame?

d. How does the camera lay out a landscape or a scene's geography for the audience?

e. When does the camera move in closer to intensify our relationship with someone or something?

f. When does the camera move away from someone or something so we see more objectively?

g. Does the camera reveal other significant information by moving?

h. Is the move really a reframing to accommodate a rearrangement of characters?

i. Is the move a reaction—panning to a new speaker, for instance?

j. What else might be responsible for motivating this particular camera move?

k. When is the camera used subjectively?

l. When do we directly experience a character's point of view?

m. Are there special signs that the camera is seeing subjectively? (For example, an unsteady handheld camera used in a combat film to create a running soldier's point of view.)

n. What is the dramatic justification for this?

o. Are there changes in camera height?

p. Are they made to accommodate subject matter?

q. Do they make you see in a certain way?

r. Are they done for other reasons?

4. Use of Sound: Sound native to the location and heard by the characters is called *diegetic sound*. Sound applied authorially as a counterpoint—for example, panic music and the sound of a loud heartbeat placed over a man trapped in an elevator—is called *nondiegetic sound*.

a. What sound perspectives are used?

b. Do they complement camera position? (Use a near microphone for close shots, and a far microphone for longer shots, thus replicating camera perspective.)

c. Do they counterpoint camera perspective? (Robert Altman's films often give us the intimate conversation of two characters seen distantly traversing a large landscape.)

d. Are sound perspectives uniformly intimate (as with a narration, or with voice-over and voiced thoughts that function as a character's interior monologue) or are they varied?

e. How are particular sound effects used?

   i. To build atmosphere and mood?

   ii. As punctuation?

   iii. To motivate a cut (next sequence's sound rises until we cut to it)?

   iv. As a narrative device (horn honks, so woman gets up and goes to window, where she discovers her sister is making a surprise visit)?

   v. To build, sustain, or diffuse tension?

   vi. To provide rhythm (meal prepared in a montage of brief shots to the rhythmic sound of a man splitting logs; last shot, man and woman sit down to meal)?

   vii. To create uncertainty?

   viii. Other situations?

5. Editing

a. What motivates each cut?

   i. Is there an action match to carry the cut?

      ii. Is there a compositional relationship between the two shots that makes the cut interesting and worthwhile?

      iii. Is there a movement relationship that carries the cut (for example, cut from car moving left to right to boat moving left to right)?

      iv. Does someone or something leave the frame (making us expect a new frame)?

      v. Does someone or something fill the frame, blanking it out and permitting a cut to another frame that starts blanked and then clears?

      vi. Does someone or something enter the frame and demand closer attention?

      vii. Are we cutting to follow someone's eye line to see what they see?

      viii. Is there a sound, or a line, that demands that we see the source?

      ix. Are we cutting to show the effect on a listener? What defines the right moment to cut?

      x. Are we cutting to a speaker at a particular moment that is visually revealing? What defines that moment?

      xi. If the cut intensifies our attention, what justifies that?

      xii. If the cut relaxes and objectifies our attention, what justifies that?

      xiii. Is the cut to a parallel activity (that is, something going on simultaneously)?

      xiv. Is there some sort of comparison or irony being set up through juxtaposition?

      xv. Are we cutting to a rhythm (perhaps to an effect, music, or the cadences of speech)?

      xvi. Other reasons?

  b. What is the relationship of words to images?

      i. Does what is shown illustrate what is said?

      ii. Is there a difference, and therefore a counterpoint, between what is shown and what is heard?

      iii. Is there a meaningful contradiction between what is said and what is shown?

      iv. Does what is said come from another time frame (for example, a character's memory or a comment on something in the past)?

      v. Is there a point at which words are used to move us forward or backward in time? (That is, can you pinpoint a change of tense in the film's grammar? This might be done visually, as in the old cliché of autumn leaves falling after we have seen summer scenes.)

      vi. Any others?

  c. When a line overlaps a picture cut, what impact does the first strong word on the new image create?

      i. Does it help identify the new image?

      ii. Does it give the image a particular emphasis or interpretation?

      iii. Is the effect expected (satisfying, perhaps) or unexpected (maybe a shock)?

      iv. Is there a deliberate contradiction?

      v. Other effects?

6. Music: examine at least three music sections.

  a. Where and how is it used?

b. How is it initiated (often when characters or story begin some kind of motion)?
c. What does the music suggest by its texture, instrumentation, etc.?
d. How is it used in association with featured sound effects?
e. How is it finished (often when characters or story arrive at a new location)?
f. What comment is it making? (Ironic? Sympathetic? Lyrical? Revealing the inner state of a character or situation? Other?)
g. From what other sound (if any) does it emerge or *segue* into? (Segue is pronounced "SEG-way.")
h. What other sound does it segue into as its close?

POINT OF VIEW AND BLOCKING

Blocking is a term for the way actors and camera move in relation to each other and to the set. Point of view seldom means whose literal eye lines the audience shares. More often it refers to whose reality the viewer most identifies with at any given time. As you'll see in greater detail in Chapter 12, "Point of View," a film's underlying statement is achieved largely through the handling of point of view (POV), but how this is achieved is complex, and can be specified with any confidence only after you've considered the aims and tone of the whole film. How the camera is used, the frequency with which one character's feelings are revealed, the amount of development he or she goes through, the vibrancy of the acting—all these factors and more play a part in enlisting our sympathy and interest.

A film, like a novel, can have a main point of view associated with a main point-of-view character, but also can expose us to multiple, conflicting points of view anchored in other characters.

There may be one central character, and one ruling point of view, like the extraordinary portrait of mentally disabled Karl in Billy Bob Thornton's *Sling Blade* (1997, Figure 5-7). Or it may concern a couple whose relationship is at issue, as in Woody Allen's *Annie Hall* (1977), in which successive scenes establish alternate characters' dilemmas and conflicts. Robert Altman's *Nashville* (1975), with nearly two dozen central characters, takes the music town of Nashville as their point of convergence and confrontation with change. Here, the characters are part of a pattern that itself represents an authorial point of view that questions how people subscribe to their own destiny. Quentin Tarantino's *Pulp Fiction* (1994) and Altman's *Short Cuts* (1993) both have large casts and serpentine story lines in which each sequence may have a different point-of-view character. Both films deal with the style and texture of groups in their particular time and place.

Following are some ways to dig into a sequence to establish how it covertly structures the way we see and react to its characters.

1. To whom, at different times, is the dialogue or narration addressed?
    a. By one character to another?
    b. By one character to himself (thinking aloud, reading diary or letter)?
    c. Directly to the audience (narration, interview, prepared statement)?
    d. Other situations?

FIGURE 5-7

Sling Blade masterfully builds the world of its mentally disabled central character, Karl (courtesy Miramax/The Kobal Collection).

2. How many camera positions are used? (Use your floor plan.)

a. Show basic camera positions and label them A, B, C, etc.

b. Show camera dollying movements with dotted line leading to new position.

c. Mark shots in your log with the appropriate A, B, C camera angles. Notice how the camera stays to one side of the subject-to-subject axis (an imaginary line between characters that the camera usually avoids crossing) to keep characters facing in the same screen direction from shot to shot. When this principle is broken, it is called crossing the line, crossing the axis, or breaking the 180-degree rule, and it has the effect of temporarily disrupting the audience's sense of spatial relationships.

d. How often is the camera close to the crucial axis between characters?

e. How often does the camera subjectively share a character's eye line?

f. When and why does it take an objective stance to the situation (that is, either a distanced viewpoint or one independent of eye lines)?

CHARACTER AND CAMERA BLOCKING

How did the characters and camera move in the scene? To the location and camera movement sketch you have made, add dotted lines to show the characters' movements (called blocking). Use different colors for clarity.

1. What points of view did the author engage us in?
2. Whose story is this sequence, if you go by gut reaction?
3. Considering the camera angles on each character, with whose point of view were you led to sympathize?
4. How many psychological viewpoints did you share? (Some may have been momentary or fragmentary, and perhaps in contradiction to what you were seeing.)
5. Are the audience's sympathies structured by camera and editing, or more by acting or the situation itself?

FICTION AND DOCUMENTARY

Most of these analytic questions apply equally to fiction and the documentary because they have much in common. Some of the questions, however, won't elicit answers when applied to most nature, travelogue, industrial, or educational films. These nonfiction forms generally lack what distinguishes the fictional and documentary forms—a Storyteller perspective. That is, they lack a point of view, a varying dramatic pressure, and a critical perspective on the human condition. Such perspectives can show us a familiar world through new eyes.

PROJECTS

PROJECT 5-3: A SCRIPTED SCENE COMPARED WITH THE FILMED OUTCOME

Objective: To study the relationship between the blueprint script and the filmed product.

Study materials: A film script and the finished film made from it on DVD. Don't look at the film until you have planned your own version from the text. The script must be the original screenplay, and not a release script (that is, not a transcript made from a finished film). A suitable script can be found in Pauline Kael's *The Citizen Kane Book: Raising Kane* (Amadeus Press, 1984). Another is Harold Pinter's *The French Lieutenant's Woman: A Screenplay* (Methuen, 1985). The latter has an absorbing foreword by John Fowles, the author of the original novel. It tells the story of the adaptation and describes, from a novelist's point of view, what is involved when your novel makes the transition to the screen.

If obtaining an original script is a problem, an interesting variation is to use a film adapted from a stage play and study an obligatory scene—that is, one so dramatically necessary that it cannot be missing from the film version. Good titles are:

Arthur Miller's *Death of a Salesman*

- Laslo Benedek's 1951 film version with Fredric March
- Wim Wenders' 1987 TV version with Dustin Hoffman (interesting for its Expressionist sets and because a theatrical flavor is retained).

Edward Albee's *Who's Afraid of Virginia Woolf?*

- Mike Nichols' 1966 film version.

Peter Shaffer's *Equus*

- Sidney Lumet's 1977 film version.

Tennessee Williams' *A Streetcar Named Desire*

- Elia Kazan's 1951 film version.

Strategy for Study

Studying the original: Try to select an unfamiliar work and read the whole script (or stage play). Choose a scene of four or five pages, then:

- Imagine the location and draw a floor plan (see Figure 5-6 for an example).
- Make your own shooting script adaptation, substituting action for dialogue wherever feasible and making use of your location environment. (See Figure 7-2 in Chapter 7 for standard screenplay layout.)
- Mark characters' movements on floor plan.
- Mark camera positions (A, B, C, etc., and indicate camera movements) and refer to these in your shooting script.
- Write a brief statement about (a) what major themes you think the entire script or play is dealing with, and (b) how your chosen scene functions in the whole.

Studying the film version: First see the entire film without stopping. Then run your chosen scene two or three times, stopping and rerunning sections as you wish. Carry out the following:

1. Make notes on film's choice of location (Imaginative? Metaphoric?).
2. Make a floor plan and mark camera positions and movements of characters.
3. Using a photocopy of the scene, pencil in annotations to show what dialogue has been cut, added, or altered.
4. Note actions, both large and small, that add significantly to the impact of the scene. Ignore those specified in the original, because the object is to find what the film version has added to or substituted for the writer's version.
5. Note camera usage as follows:
    a. Any abnormal perspective (that is, when a nonstandard lens is used—a standard lens is one that reproduces the perspective of the human eye; telescopic and wide-angle lenses compress or magnify perspective respectively)?
    b. Any camera position above or below eye level?

c. Any camera movement (track, pan, tilt, zoom, crane)? Note what you think motivated the camera movement (character's movement, eye line, Storyteller's revelation, etc.).

d. Note what the thematic focus of the film seems to be, and how your chosen scene functions in the film.

Comparison: Compare your scripting with the film's handling and describe the following:

1. How did the film establish time and place?

2. How effectively did the film compress the original and substitute behavior for dialogue?

3. How, using camerawork and editing, is the audience drawn into identifying with one or more characters?

4. Whose scene was it, and why?

5. How were any rhythms (speech, movements, sound effects, music, etc.) used to pace out the scene, particularly to speed it up or slow it down?

6. What were the major changes of interpretation in the film and in the chosen scene?

7. Provide any further valuations of the film you think worth making (acting, characterization, use of music or sound effects, etc.).

Assess your performance: How well did you do? What aspects of filmmaking are you least aware of and need to develop? What did you accomplish?

PROJECT 5-4: LIGHTING ANALYSIS

Though directors do not have to understand techniques of lighting, they must be able to ask for particular lighting effects and discuss lighting using the terminology a DP understands. The fundamentals of lighting are well explained in Alan J. Ritsko's *Lighting for Location Motion Pictures* (Simon & Schuster, 1980) and Kris Malkiewicz's *Film Lighting* (Fireside, 1986). See www.abebooks.com for used copies at excellent prices.

Equipment required: Video player as in previous projects. Turn down the color saturation of your monitor so that initially you see a black-and-white picture. Adjust the monitor's brightness and contrast controls so the greatest possible range of gray tones is visible between video white and video black. Unless you do this, you simply won't see all that is present.

Objective: To analyze common lighting situations and understand what goes into creating a lighting mood.

Study materials: Same as in previous project (a film script and the finished film made from it on videotape), only this time it will be an advantage to search out particular lighting situations rather than sequences of special dramatic appeal. The same sequences may fulfill both purposes.

Lighting Terminology

Here, the task is to recognize different types and combinations of lighting situations and to apply standard terminology. Every aspect of lighting carries strong emotional associations that can be employed in drama to great effect. The technique and the terminology describing it are therefore powerful tools in the right hands. Here are some basic terms:

Types of Lighting Style

High-key picture: The shot looks bright overall with small areas of shadow. The shot in Figure 5-8 is exterior day, and the lamppost shadow in the foreground shows that there is indeed deep shadow in the picture. Where shadow is sharp, as here, the light source is called *specular*. A high-key picture can be virtually shadowless, so long as the frame is bright overall.

Low-key picture: The shot looks dark overall with few highlight areas. These are often interiors or night shots, but in Figure 5-9 we have a backlit day interior that ends up being low-key; that is, having a large area of the frame in deep shadow.

Graduated tonality: The shot has neither bright highlights nor deep shadows, but consists of an even, restricted range of midtones. This might be a flat-lit interior, like a supermarket, or a misty morning landscape as in Figure 5-10. In that example, an overcast sky diffuses the lighting source, and the disorganized light rays scatter into every possible shadow area so there are neither highlights nor shadow.

Contrast

High-contrast picture: The shot may be lit either high- or low-key, but there must be a big difference in illumination levels between highlight and shadow area, as in

FIGURE 5-8 ————————————————————————————————————

High-key scene, hard or specular lighting, high contrast. Notice compositional depth in this shot compared with the flatness of Figure 5-9.

FIGURE 5-9 —————————————————————————————

Backlit low-key scene, subject silhouetted against the flare of backlit smoke.

FIGURE 5-10 —————————————————————————————

Graduated tonality scene, low-contrast because key light is diffused through morning mist.

Figure 5-11, which has a soot-and-whitewash starkness. Figures 5-8 and 5-9 are also high-contrast images, even though the area of shadow in each is drastically different.

Low-contrast picture: The shot can either be high- or low-key, but with a shadow area illumination level near that of the highlight levels. Figure 5-11 is high-key, low-contrast.

FIGURE 5-11 ——

High-contrast image with very few midtones owing to backlighting and no fill.

Light Quality

Hard lighting: This is any specular light source (one creating hard-edged shadows), such as sun, studio spotlight, or candle flame. These are all effectively small light sources because a small source gives hard-edged shadows. Figure 5-8 is lit by hard light (the sun), whereas the shadow under the chair in Figure 5-11 is so soft as to be hardly discernible.

Soft lighting: Any light source is soft when it creates soft-edged shadows or a shadowless image, as in Figure 5-10. Soft light sources are, for example, fluorescent tubes, sunlight reflecting off a matte-finish wall, light from overcast sky, or a studio soft light. Do not confuse soft lighting with lighting of low power. A candle is a low-power, hard-lighting source.

Names of Lighting Sources

Key light: This is not necessarily an artificial source, for it can be the sun. The key is the light that creates intended shadows in the shot, and these in turn reveal the angle and position of the supposed light source, often relatively hard or specular (shadow-producing) light. In Figure 5-8, the key light is sunlight coming from the rear left and above the camera. In Figure 5-9, it is streaming in toward the camera.

Fill light: This is the light used to raise illumination in shadow areas. For interiors, it will probably be soft light thrown from the direction of the camera, because this avoids creating additional visible shadows. There are shadows, of course, but the subject hides them from the camera's view. Especially in interiors, fill light is often provided from matte white reflectors or through diffusion material such as heat-resistant fiberglass. Fill light can also be derived from bounce light, which is hard light bounced from walls or ceilings to soften it.

FIGURE 5-12 ——

Practicals are any lights seen in frame, like these birthday candles. Strong set light prevents the background from going dark.

Backlight: This is light thrown upon a subject from behind—and often from above as well as behind, as in Figure 5-9. A favorite technique in portraiture is to put a rim of backlight around a subject's head and shoulders to separate them from the background. Rain, fog, dust, and smoke (as in this case of garage barbecuing) all show up best when backlight.

Practical: This is any light appearing in the frame as part of the scene; for example, table lamp, overhead fluorescent, or, as in Figure 5-12, the candles on a birthday cake. Practicals generally provide little or no real source of illumination, but here the candles light up the faces but not the background. This shot illustrates several lighting points. The girl in the middle is lit from below, a style called monster lighting, which is decidedly eerie for a birthday shot. The subject on the left, having no backlight or background lighting, disappears into the shadows, whereas the one on the right is outlined by set light or light falling on the set. The same light source shines on her hair as a backlight source, and gives it highlights and texture.

Types of Lighting Setup

In this section, the illustrations are of the same model lit in various ways. As a result, the effect and the mood in each portrait vary greatly. The diagrams show the positioning of the key and fill lights. A floor plan can show the angle of throw relative to the camera-to-subject axis, but not the height of light sources. These can be judged from the screen image by assessing the positioning of highlight and shadow patterns.

Frontally lit: The fill light used as a key in Figure 5-13 is so close to the camera-to-subject axis that shadows are thrown behind the subject and out of the

FIGURE 5-13 ───

Frontal lighting flattens the subject and removes much of the face's interest. Most flash photography is frontal and correspondingly dull.

FIGURE 5-14 ───

Broad lighting illuminates a broad area of the face, and shows the head as round and having angularities. Revelation becomes interesting because lighting is selective.

camera's view. Very slight shadows are visible in the folds of the subject's shirt, showing how the key was just to the right of camera. Notice how flat and lacking in dimensionality or tension this shot is compared with Figures 5-14 and 5-15.

Broad lit: In Figure 5-14, the key light is some way to the side, so a broad area of the subject's face and body is highlighted. Key light skimming the subject lengthens his face, revealing angles and undulations. There are areas of deep shadow, especially in the eye sockets, but their effect could be reduced by increasing the amount of soft fill light.

Narrow lit: The key light in Figure 5-15 is to the side of the subject and beyond him so that only a narrow portion of his face receives highlight. The majority of his face is in shadow, but lit by fill light, or we would see nothing. You calculate *lighting ratio* by measuring light reflected from the highlight area and comparing it with that reflected from the fill area. When taking measurements, remember that fill light spills into highlight areas, but not vice versa, so reliable readings can be taken only when all lights are on.

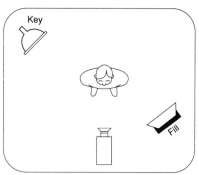

FIGURE 5-15 ——

Narrow lighting illuminates only a narrow area of the face. More fill used here than in Figure 5-12. The effect is decidedly dramatic.

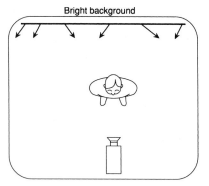

FIGURE 5-16 ——

Silhouette: All light is from the background, and none reaches the subject's face.

Silhouette: In Figure 5-16, the subject reflects no light at all, and shows up only as an outline against raw light. This lighting is sometimes used in documentaries when the subject's identity is being withheld. Here, it produces the ominous effect of someone unknown confronting us through a bright doorway.

Day for night: Shooting exteriors using daylight (day for day) presents few problems, but direct shooting at night or in moonlight is virtually impossible because neither film stocks nor video cameras approach the human eye's sensitivity. One solution is to shoot night for night by carefully modeling bluish artificial light to cast long, hard-edged shadows that simulate those cast by the light of the moon. Day-for-night shooting is easiest in black and white, because you can use early morning or late afternoon sunlight when shadows are long, underexpose by several stops, and use a red or yellow filter to turn blue skies black and increase all-round contrast. Day for night in color uses a similar lighting and exposure strategy, and a graduated filter to darken the sky, but seldom looks very convincing. A more effective color day-for-night effect results from using the so-called "magic hour," a period of little more than 10–20 minutes just before there is too little light to shoot. In urban scenes, streetlights and car headlights are on, and the whole landscape is still visible under what is often a gorgeous reddish sky. Dialogue scenes of more than a line or two must be taken later in close-up with artificial lighting and backgrounds lit to match the long shots.

Lighting temperature: Common light sources in moviemaking contain a different mix of color biases. The particular mix of color in different "white" light sources is expressed in degrees Kelvin (K). This is a scale based on a theoretical black body being progressively heated so that it gives off different colors of light (starting from the cool end: infrared, red, orange, green, blue, indigo, violet, ultraviolet). A tungsten lightbulb gives an orange-biased light of around 2,800 K. Noon daylight is "cooler" (that is, has more blue) and is rated around 5,400 K, whereas the light on mountaintops is very cool indeed and might be 10,000 K. The human eye adapts effortlessly to these changes and generally sees a white object as white. But film and video cameras (or lighting instruments) must be adjusted to the prevailing color temperature if white objects are to accurately reproduce on-screen. Filmmaking has a common problem: if you try to mix 5,400 K daylight coming through a window with studio lights (3,200 K), you get very unnatural lighting effects. The cure is to filter the minority source to make it match the majority, and to adjust white balance, or camera filtering, to that color temperature. Only then will all colors be rendered faithfully.

During your studies, look for mixed-light scenes to see where different sources may have been balanced in this way. In exteriors lit by sunlight, a common telltale situation is to find that faces have blue shadow areas. Though highlights come from sunlight, the blue shadow is reflected fill light from a blue sky.

Strategy for Study

Locate two or three sequences with quite different lighting moods and, using the previously discussed definitions, classify them as follows:

Style:	High-key/low-key/graduated tonality?
Contrast:	High- or low-contrast?
Scene:	Intended to look like natural light or artificial lighting?
Setup:	Frontal/broad/narrow/backlighting setup?
Angles:	High/low angle of key light?
Key quality:	Hard/soft edges to shadows?
Key source:	Source in scene is intended to be _____
Fill light:	Fill source is where?
Practicals:	Practicals in the scene are _____
Time:	Day for day/night for night/dusk for night/day for night?
Mood:	Mood conveyed by lighting is _____
Continuity:	Any discernible differences of lighting between complementary angles that show lighting has been handled differently?

After making some analysis in black and white, turn up the color and see if you can spot further patterns. This often reveals how the DP and art director have

FIGURE 5-17 ――――――――――――――――――――――――――――――――――――――

Citizen Kane is famous for Gregg Toland's revolutionary deep-focus cinematography (courtesy RKO/The Kobal Collection).

employed the emotional associations of the location, costuming, and decor in the service of the script. Predominant hues and color saturation level (meaning whether a color is pure or desaturated with an admixture of white) have a great deal to do with a scene's effect on the viewer. For instance, David Lynch's *Blue Velvet* (1986) portrays its Lumberton in stark, bright toy-town colors as a surreal setting for sadistic sex and loneliness. Robert Altman's *Gosford Park* (2001) uses the low-key interiors and crowded furnishings of a Victorian country mansion as the setting for his convoluted family tale. The predominant tones are dark red and brown.

Two classically lit black-and-white films are Orson Welles' *Citizen Kane* (1941, Figure 5-17), with deep-focus cinematography by the revolutionary Gregg Toland, and Jean Cocteau's *Beauty and the Beast* (1946, whose lighted interiors Henri Alekan modeled after Dutch paintings). A more recent Alekan black-and-white film is Wim Wenders' lyrical *Wings of Desire* (1987).

CHAPTER 6

SHOOTING PROJECTS

If you've dipped into this book and want to jump right into the "doing" part, its design should encourage you to do this. Start production here if you wish, and use the rest of the book to solve problems as you encounter them. Some like to read, understand, and be thoroughly prepared before entering practical work, whereas others (myself included) learn best by doing things in order to discover what's involved. That, after all, is how film history evolved.

Need coaching on the technical and creative details of film or DV production? Excellent at explaining filmmaking technology is Kris Malkiewicz and M. David Mullen's *Cinematography*, 3rd ed. (Fireside, 2005). Also excellent is Mick Hurbis-Cherrier's *Voice and Vision: A Creative Approach to Narrative Film and DV Production* (Focal Press, 2007).

The projects below explore different techniques of expression, but try to make each a vehicle for your own ideas and tastes. I have included a list of skills you can expect to learn, discussion suggestions, and questions to elicit your work's aspects, strengths, and weaknesses. These projects and their variations represent a huge filmmaking workout. Pick and choose to build the particular skills you want—there are far too many otherwise. Use them particularly to explore building a character, a situation, and the audience's involvement through nonverbal, behavioral means. When you can develop the disparate perspectives of the characters and build a Storyteller's point of view, you are doing advanced work.

HOW BEST TO EXPLORE THE BASICS

Production, the seat of learning in the school of hard knocks, teaches teamwork and the advantages of being organized. As a director, your first priority should be creating a gripping human presence on the screen. For this, you will need to develop experience with actors (trained or untrained), the ability to see what is or isn't credible, and the ability to solve problems that actors encounter. Good screen fiction requires multidimensional characters striving visibly after their own goals in truthful and interesting ways. So easy and natural-looking in the cinema, it takes mature skills to produce.

OUTCOMES ASSESSMENT

Outcomes assessment is a tool that helps both teacher and learner—for it rates not what students know in their heads, but what they can put on the screen. Note that criteria expect conceptual and creative outcomes, and not just the usual technical ones. Students appreciate that it focuses on desirable and positive outcomes (see Figure 6-1).

ASSESSMENT 6-1A, B (EDITING)		
Editing	Action match cuts are smooth and natural-looking.	0 1 2 3 4 5
	Uses match cuts on major moments of action to bridge shots wherever possible.	0 1 2 3 4 5
	Match cuts between two sizes of same action, use an image size change large enough to make a natural-looking cut. (If size change is too small, it looks like a messy jump cut.)	0 1 2 3 4 5
	Rhythm of footsteps is perfectly matched.	0 1 2 3 4 5
	Cutting from angle to angle feels natural and motivated.	0 1 2 3 4 5
	Overall editing rhythm feels natural.	0 1 2 3 4 5
Camera operating	Camera movements are so smooth they seem entirely motivated by the subject's movements.	0 1 2 3 4 5
	Pans and tilts sync with motivating action, neither ahead nor behind.	0 1 2 3 4 5
Composition	Camera height is varied to create interesting angles.	0 1 2 3 4 5
	Framing and composition on static shots is excellent.	0 1 2 3 4 5
	Compositions create maximum perspective and depth.	0 1 2 3 4 5
	Lead space ahead of subject is well judged.	0 1 2 3 4 5
	Compositional proportions around subject are maintained between images of different sizes.	0 1 2 3 4 5
Blocking	Screen direction of subject remains logical.	0 1 2 3 4 5
	Camera does not cross the line.	0 1 2 3 4 5
Human presence and continuity	Actor looks so unself-conscious that footage could pass for documentary.	0 1 2 3 4 5
	Nature and speed of actions are consistent from angle to angle.	0 1 2 3 4 5
	Mood changes and development make a character of compelling interest.	0 1 2 3 4 5
	Where actors come from and where they are going are interestingly suggested by acting, props, costuming, etc.	0 1 2 3 4 5
Dramaturgy	Sequence has a natural and satisfying arc of development and conclusion.	0 1 2 3 4 5
	TOTAL	_____

FIGURE 6-1 ────────────────────────────────────

Specimen Outcomes Assessment form for Projects 6-1A and B. The forms for the rest of the book's projects can be downloaded from www.focalpress.com/9780240808826.

By stating a full range of criteria, the teacher sets a broad ground for discussion. If you are working without a mentor, use the assessments to rate yourself on each aspect of your work.

Over several months, scan your project assessments to see how your skills are developing. The circled scores make this easy because they represent a bar graph. Rejoice in your accomplishments, and focus on lifting your deficiencies. Many teachers like students to get practice at scoring each other's work because it helps the scorers become more realistic at evaluating their own work.

SCORING METHOD

Each Outcomes Assessment Form contains a list of desirable facets for you or your group to assess according to agreement. Circle the appropriate score. Numbers aren't in themselves useful, but having to make decisions about relative quality is. The five-point scale of agreement is:

Not true or not applicable	0
Only minimally true	1
Somewhat so	2
Average and acceptably so	3
Considerably so	4
Unusually and strikingly so	5

ON DEVELOPING YOUR ABILITIES

Techniques: The projects that follow will help you develop a broad and representative range of directing and editing skills. Experimental films are sometimes about film technique, but in more mainstream fiction, technique is seldom an end in itself. "Art," said Thomas Hardy, "is the secret of how to produce by a false thing the effect of a true." This could be said about the artifice that goes into most screen narrative. Good technique is transparent, and goes unnoticed by the audience because the film grips the viewer's imagination. Poor technique or virtuosity misapplied is technique that intrudes itself and confounds the film's purpose—unless, of course, the film is a formalist one about filming.

The first projects explore basic technique and embody modest subject matter, but do not be deceived into thinking they are beneath you. I have supplied requirements, procedures, and hints, but I leave much of the problem solving—always the most rewarding area of learning—to your ingenuity and resourcefulness. Where a project requires lighting, keep it simple so you avoid getting sidetracked by the delights of cinematography.

Critique sessions: Assess finished projects in a group or class if you can, so you get used to working with collaborators, and to giving and taking critique. If a project has many assessment criteria, have each person watch for a few particular facets. This ensures a discussion in depth from which everyone learns. The maker's job it is to listen, take notes about the audience reaction, and say nothing. Never explain what the audience should have understood; your "say" is your film, and you must correct it in the light of what your audience missed.

Further help: For additional information, use the table of contents at the front of the part dealing with the appropriate production phase, or the glossary and index at the book's end.

PROJECTS

PROJECT 6-1: BASIC TECHNIQUES—"GOING AND RETURNING"

This project is without dialogue, and asks you to establish the character and situation of a woman who looks forward to arriving at a building, but discovers she has lost her keys. During the discovery and returning to her car to look for them, she can go through a range of subtle emotions—irritation, anxiety, relief, perhaps even amusement. Expect a workout in film grammar basics such as preserving the screen direction of characters and action, and of making action match cuts work. (See "Making an action match cut" and "Match cut guide" subheadings in Project 6-1A.)

Skills to develop:

- Maintaining relevant screen direction
- Panning and tilting to follow action
- Picture framing and composition to suggest depth
- Editing: action match cutting, cutting together different sizes of similar images using action as a bridge, cutting together complementary angles on the same action
- Telling a story through action and behavior, not words
- Ellipsis (compressing real time into cinematic shorthand)
- Editing to music
- Making a long, loose version (first assembly) and a tight, short version (fine cut)

6-1A: Plan, Shoot, and Edit the Long Version

Assessment: Use Assessment 6-1A/B (Editing) from Figure 6-1.

Action: A car draws up. Mary, its occupant, gets out and approaches a house, looking up at a window in anticipation. She mounts a flight of steps to the front door, where she finds she does not have her keys. Perplexed, she returns to her car, expecting it to be open. Finding the door locked, she reacts in alarm, thinking her keys are locked in. But looking with difficulty inside, she sees the ignition is empty. Patting her pockets and looking around in consternation, she spots her keys lying in the gutter. She picks them up, relieved, and returns to the house.

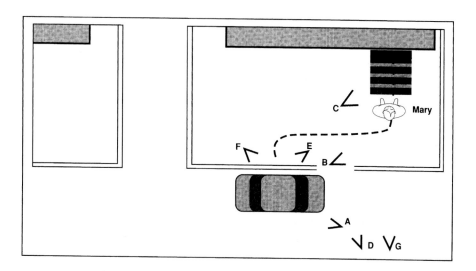

FIGURE 6-2 ───

Specimen floor plan for the "Mary Sequence." Camera positions are marked as A through G.

Figure 6-2 is a specimen floor plan. Adapt yours to your location (mine is a one-way street to allow the driver to drop her keys in the nearside gutter). The floor plan shows Mary's walk and the basic camera positions to cover the various parts of the action. No sound is necessary.

Figure 6-3 is a storyboard of representative frames for each camera position. For your coverage, make your own ground plan and show camera positions and storyboard key frames. Here is a sample shot list related to the ground plan and key frames A through G:

- Establishing shot of locale from camera position A with car arriving as in Frame A.

- Medium shot (MS) panning with Mary left to right (L-R). When she turns the corner in the path, she changes her effective screen direction, ending up as in Frame B.

- Medium close shot (MCS) of Mary's feet walking R-L and L-R on sidewalk and up steps as an all-purpose cut-in (also called insert) shot as in Frame D1.

- Big close-up (BCU) panning, telephoto shot of Mary's head as she walks, looking up at window as in D2.

- Feet enter shot descending steps, camera tilts down to follow action, Frame G.

- Overshoulder (OS) shot of empty ignition, F1.

- Point-of-view (POV) shot, F2.

- BCU keys in gutter, hand reaches into frame and takes them, F3.

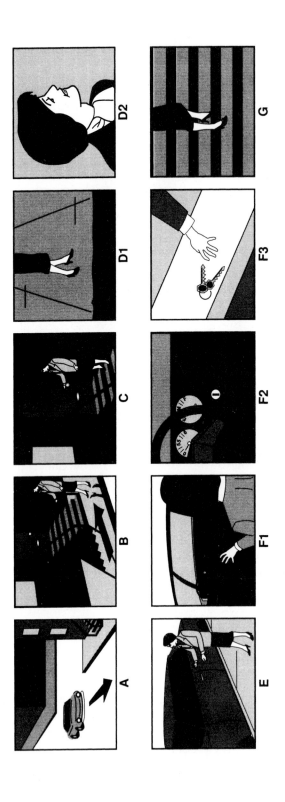

FIGURE 6-3

Storyboard frames showing setups for the various camera angles in Figure 6-2.

In its simplest edited form, the abbreviated sequence might look something like this:

Camera Position	Shot #	Action
A	1	Car arrives, Mary gets out, slams door, exits bottom right of frame.
B	2a	Mary enters L-R, begins crossing frame.
D2	3	CU Mary looks up at window.
B	2b	This is the rest of Shot 2a. Mary continues L-R, turns corner of path, walks R-L toward steps and up them.
C	3	Mary rises into frame from R-L, fumbles for keys, can't find them, looks back at car, turns back out of frame.
B	4	Mary descending steps across frame L-R, turns corner, crosses frame R-L.
E	5a	Mary arrives from screen R, walking R-L toward car, fails to open door, curses.
F1	6	She crosses frame, repositions herself looking R-L to see if key is in ignition, peers inside.
F2	7	Her POV of empty ignition.
E	5b	Mary straightens up, pats pockets, sees something out of frame on the ground.
F3	8a	CU keys lying in gutter from Mary's POV.
E	5c	Mary reacts, stoops down.
F3	8b	CU of keys, hand enters frame, takes them back up.
E	5d	Mary straightens up, looking relieved, and exits into camera, making frame go black. End of sequence.

Notice that Shot 2 is intercut with a CU, whereas the action in Shot 5 has been intercut three times. When directing for intercutting like this, don't waste time shooting individual reactions; instead, shoot a larger section or even the whole action in the two different sizes of shot. Afterward, during editing, select the fragments you require from the continuous take. The more sustained the acting, the more your actors will stay in *focus*; that is, stay unself-consciously lost in their characters' realities.

Notice how, at the end of Shot 5, when Mary returns with the keys, her movement is used to black out the screen by walking right up to the camera lens. To continue the transition in the following shot, back the actor up against the lens and, on "Action," have her walk away from the camera. In the transition, the screen goes from action to black, then from black to a new scene. This is one of many transitional devices; the simplest being the humble cut. Overuse the fancy ones and you run the risk of being tricksy.

- Cut this first, long version together, taking into account cutting from Shot 2a to Shot 3.

- Maintain Mary's walking rhythm across cuts, and be careful you don't make the poor woman take two steps on the same foot. You need rhythm consciousness to edit walking shots, and indeed for anything where rhythms are involved.
- When cutting from Shot 5a to Shot 6, there will probably be an action match. Here are some of the few rules in filmmaking.

Making an action match cut: A cut during action is always preferable to one during stasis. When action flows across a cut, the eye hardly notices the changes of composition or subject. Action matches work best *when the outgoing shot does no more than initiate the movement, and the incoming shot takes over and completes* most of the action.

Match cut guide: For the best action match, follow these steps:

Step 1: Let the outgoing shot run until the start of the action is established. Use no more of the action than we need to recognize the nature of action (standing up, reaching for doorknob, combing hair, etc.). This is important because the eye stops being critical whenever we know what is happening next.

Step 2: Complete the majority of the action with the incoming (closer or longer) shot, but be aware that *if the action flowing across the cut is at all fast, you must repeat three or four frames of the action at the head of the incoming shot*. This overlap is necessary because the eye does not register the first three or four frames of any new image. Of course, a frame-by-frame analysis shows a slight action repeat, but shown at normal speed, the action will appear smooth and continuous.

Cutting from Shot 5c to Shot 8b, use the same principle. Let Mary just begin to stoop, and then cut to keys with hand entering at top of frame shortly afterward. If you leave too much footage before the incoming hand appears, you will imply that Mary is 8 feet tall.

Criteria: Run your cut version. Make an exact minutes-and-seconds count of its length. Rate the criteria in Assessment 6-1A/B (Editing) in Figure 6–1. The scores show where your technique is strong and where it needs improvement.

6-1B: Editing a More Compressed Version

Assessment: Use Assessment 6-1A/B (Editing). Run your cut and consider which moments in the action are vital and which are link material. Surely a lot of the walking is of secondary importance. If, for instance, Mary turns to look back in the direction of the car, we don't need to see her cover every inch of ground to arrive there. Amend the first cut by making a compressed version. The unused bridging close-ups will now be useful. In this new, abbreviated list, they are printed in bold:

Camera Position	Shot #	Action
A	1	Car arrives, Mary gets out, slams door, exits bottom right of frame.
B	2a	Mary enters L-R, begins crossing frame.
D2	3	CU Mary looks up at window.

(*continued*)

Camera Position	Shot #	Action
B	2b	This is the rest of Shot 2a. Mary continues L-R, turns corner of path, walks R-L toward steps and up them.
C	3	Mary rises into frame from R-L, fumbles for keys, can't find them, looks back at car, and turns.
G		**Feet descending a couple of steps.**
D1		**CS feet walking on sidewalk R-L.**
B	4	Mary descending steps across frame L-R, turns corner, crosses frame R-L.
E	5a	Mary arrives from screen R, walking R-L toward car, fails to open door, curses.
F1	6	She crosses frame, repositions herself looking R-L to see if key is in ignition, peers inside.
F2	7	Her POV of empty ignition.
E	5b	Mary straightens up, pats pockets, sees something out of frame on the ground.
F3	8a	CU keys lying in gutter from Mary's POV.
E	5c	Mary reacts, stoops down.
F3	8b	CU of keys, hand enters frame, takes them back up.
E	5d	Mary straightens up looking relieved and exits into camera, making frame go black. End of sequence.

Discussion: How long is the sequence now? It should lose nothing of narrative importance, yet be 30 to 50 percent shorter. See if you can cut it to perhaps as little as 30 to 60 seconds overall. Run and rerun your film until you see shots or parts of shots that can be eliminated. Set the audience up to infer whatever you can, so the audience actively uses its imagination to fill in points of elision. Treat your audience as active, intelligent collaborators rather than passive vessels needing exhaustive information.

6-1C: Setting It to Music

Having discovered how much leeway there is to many shots' length, you can now turn Mary into a musical star. Find a piece of music with a strong beat that enhances the mood of the sequence. Reedit the materials, placing your cuts and major pieces of action on the beat or on the music's instrumental changes. Be aware that *for any cut to appear on the beat, it must occur three or four frames before the actual beat point.* This is owing to the perceptual lag inherent when you cut to a new image. The only nonnegotiable aspects of your earlier cut are the action match cuts. There will be only one optimal cutting place.

Assessment: Use Assessment 6-1C (Music) (download from web site).

Discussion:

- How tightly does the action fit the music?
- Does cutting on the beat become predictable? If so, try cutting on a musical subdivision.

- How much compromise did you have to make with the tight version to adjust the action to fit the music?
- What does the music add to the earlier version's impact?

PROJECT 6-2: CHARACTER STUDY

Skills to develop:

- Revealing a character through action
- Using mobile *cinéma vérité* handheld coverage
- Blocking camera and actor for mutual accommodation
- Developing counterpoint between words and action
- Imposing a second point of view

6-2A: Plan, Rehearse, and Shoot Long Take of Character-Revealing Action

Alan makes breakfast alone in his own unique way. Depending on your actor, this is an opportunity to show someone amusingly smart, dreamy, pressured, ultra-methodical, or slovenly who makes his breakfast in a particular state of mind and emotion. Develop your ideas in rehearsal:

- First decide what Alan's character is going to be.
- Then decide on his situation.
- Then figure out how to externalize these as action without telegraphing what the audience is meant to notice. Put the accent on credibility as though this were reality being shot by a hidden camera.

Camera coverage should adapt to what director and actor develop, and blocking evolves from mutual accommodation between camera and actor. Fast actions, those shot close, won't look normal on the screen unless slowed down by up to a third.

You may need to reblock the action—that is, have the actor turn some actions into the camera or have him move away from a close position to a marked point so the whole of the action is visible without the camera having to move or make choices. You may need some lighting. For this semidocumentary approach, try placing light stands in a tight group against the least interesting wall so your camera has maximum freedom to move around without picking up telltale stands and supply wires. Bounce the light off a white ceiling or reflector so you work relatively shadowlessly under soft light.

Have fun with this shoot, and in your coverage incorporate:

- Action of about four minutes that is emotionally revealing of Alan's basic character, particular mood, and immediate past and future
- Idiosyncratic interaction with objects (no other people, no phone conversations)
- A single, nonstop, handheld take using wide-angle lens only
- Camera movement (pan, tilt, handheld tracking shot, etc.) to follow or reveal as necessary
- Close and long shots produced by altering subject-to-camera distance as necessary. This may be done by moving the camera in and out, or by blocking Alan to move closer or farther from a static camera

- Thorough exploitation of the domestic setting
- Lots of rehearsal with camera, so that all the above look smooth and natural
- Safety cutaways, point-of-view shots, and inserts

The difference between an insert, cutaway, and point-of-view shot is that:

- *An insert* takes detail already inside the main shot and magnifies it usefully.
- *A cutaway* shows something outside the main shot's framing.
- *A point-of-view (POV) shot* replicates what a character sees from his or her eye line.

If they are not to look arbitrary and contrived, cutaways, insert shots, and POV shots must be *motivated* by a character's actions or through a consistent logic of storytelling. If, for instance, Alan glances up and out of the frame in wide shot, you can use this glance to motivate cutting to his point of view (and a cutaway shot) of a bird alighting on the windowsill.

Assessment: Use Assessment 6-2A (Blocking, Acting, and Camerawork) (download from web site).

Discussion: Try to extract findings from the specifics of your work.

- What in general can make fluid camerawork intrusive or objectionable?
- What is the drawback of long-take coverage?
- What are its advantages?
- What is the difference in feeling when the action takes place across the frame instead of back and forth in its depth?
- What are the consequences of framing and camera movement?
- When can the camera look away from Alan and take its own initiative, make its own revelations? (It might, for instance, show that while Alan is searching for eggs, the frying pan is smoking ominously.)
- When is it legitimate for the camera to be caught by surprise or to show it knows what is going to happen next?
- Does the audience feel it is spying on Alan unawares, or is there guidance, a feeling that the camera has its own ideas about him and is deliberately showing particular aspects of him?
- What might determine which storytelling mode to use?
- How much of the take is dramatically interesting, and where are the flat spots of dead or link material?

6-2B: Adding an Interior Monologue

Going further: Now add an interior monologue track as a voice-over (VO) in which we hear Alan's thought process. In planning this, you will need to consider the following:

- Which actions does he do automatically from long habit?
- Which actions require thought?

- On what grounds is each decision made?
- At what points are a character's thoughts in the present?
- At what points do they fly away elsewhere, and why?
- When do we consciously note what we are doing, and why?

Do not forget to shoot monologue "presence track" or atmosphere (also known as buzz track or room tone) to serve as a necessary "sound spacer" should you want to extend pauses in the VO. Room tone (also known as buzz track or presence track) is a simple recording of the set at prior recording level, when no action or dialogue is happening. Every sound location has its own relative silence; you can't extend a track with a silence from another place or even microphone position because they will sound different.

Assessment: Use Assessment 6-2BC (Interior Monologue) (download from web site). When you have completed the assignment, assess or discuss the following:

- Where the interior monologue voice may be overinforming the audience
- Where it is under-informing
- Is there redundancy in what you hear because it can be inferred from the action?
- Is VO used skillfully to set up the audience to notice or interpret something that would otherwise be missed? Could it have been?
- Did you show, then tell—or tell, then show? Which is better?
- Are any losses offset by gains in information, humor, or other aspects?
- Did you use too much or too little VO overall?

6-2C: Vocal Counterpoint and Point of View

Going further: Working again with the original piece, now write and record an alternative voice-over (VO) track that, instead of complementing what you see, contrasts revealingly with it. When action suggests one meaning, and Alan's VO another, the conjunction of the two yields a more complex set of possibilities. The aim here is to develop tensions between picture and sound, a series of deliberate ambiguities or even contradictions that invite the audience to develop its own ideas about the discrepancies. Now you impel the audience to actively develop ideas about Alan's character. Suggested voices are:

- Alan telling his psychiatrist how his compulsions are going away, when clearly they aren't
- Alan rehearsing how to convey his efficiency and foresight in an upcoming and important job interview
- Alan's mother telling him how to eat well now that he is on his own
- Alan's wife loyally telling a friend how easy it is to live with him
- A Homeland Security officer interpreting Alan's culpability from his innocuous actions

Unless your character is reading from a diary or letter, you will want to avoid the mechanical sound of an actor reading. Even the most professional actors have trouble making a text sound like spontaneous thought. Happily, there is an easy way around this. Show the actor the ideas and discuss them, then interview him while recording as he improvises his thoughts. Do several versions and redirect your actor between takes. Edit them to the action. This reliably produces spontaneity. Do not forget to shoot room tone as the necessary sound spacer should you want to extend pauses in the VO.

Of course there is ample scope for comedy here, but did you create sympathy for your central character, or does he come off as a buffoon? The VO has to be carefully developed and rehearsed. Be aware that though the first two options are apparently Alan's view of himself, they should allow the audience to develop an independent sense of Alan that might confirm what a psychiatrist or job interviewer suspected. The remaining three suggestions are perspectives that might better serve to profile the speaker than to profile Alan.

Assessment: Use Assessment 6-2BC (Interior Monologue) (download from web site).

Discussion:

- Did VO lift interest in periods of bridging action? (Use VO to raise the dull parts; let eloquent actions speak for themselves.)
- Did you leave interesting sound effects in the clear (say, Alan dropping his shoes)? Lay in VO as a secondary track, leaving salient portions of the sync or original "in the clear." Raise sync track levels between blocks of VO. The *foregrounded track* may either be VO, featured dialogue, sound effects, or action from the sync track.

PROJECT 6-3: EXPLOITING A LOCATION

Skills to develop:

- Developing a mood
- Shifting the mood from objective to subjective
- Making use of cause and effect
- Capitalizing upon inherent rhythms
- Implying both a point of view and a state of mind
- Suggesting a development
- Using sync sound as effects
- Using music to heighten or interpret the environment

6-3A: Dramatizing an Environment

This assignment has strong research aspects, and you will need to spend some hours just observing with a notebook in hand. Select an interesting location such as a harbor, motorcyclists' café, farmyard, fairground, bookstore, or airport lounge. You want a physical entity rather than a human event. Work your observations into a script incorporating your best material. You can even work in an acted POV character so long as he or she is a credible presence. With no speaking characters, develop a mood sequence of about two minutes that has a structure organic to the location's daily life and that changes and intensifies. In planning your sequence, consider the following:

- What is inherently present that might structure the sequence? (Passengers arriving in an airport, then leaving at the departure gate? Time progression? Increasing complexity in the action? Forward exploratory movement of camera?)
- What cause-and-effect shots can you group together into subsequences? (Within a winter forest scene, you establish icicles melting, drops of water falling past a shack's window, drops falling in a pool, rivulet of water flowing through ice, etc.)
- Are there inherent rhythms to be exploited (water dripping, cars passing, a street vendor's repeated cry, dog barking, etc.)?
- Do the sequences move from micro to macro view, or the reverse? (Start with BCU water droplets, and develop to view of entire forest; or conversely, start with an aerial view of the city, and end on a single, overfilled trash can.)
- Can you create a turning point that marks the onset of a heightened or altered sensibility? (For instance, in a deserted sandy cove, the camera discovers a single, smoking cigarette butt. Thereafter, coverage suggests an uneasy awareness of a lurking human presence.)

Here, fiction merges with documentary; the environment has become a character studied and relished by the Storyteller. We make the same dramaturgic demands, asking that the view of the location grow and change so it draws us into reacting and becoming involved. The classic three-act structure (see Chapter 1) was developed in theater, but can, as we said, be applied to the contents of a single sequence, a short film, or even a full-length fiction film.

As always, contrasts and contradictions are the richest stimulant to awareness. In a seaside scene, it might be the juxtaposition of frenetic game players with corpulent sun worshippers that provides the astringent comparisons, or the waves compared with the stillness of the rocks. Every setting, like every character, contains *dialectical tensions* whose oppositions define the subject's scope, and subjective meaning to whoever is watching.

Depending on your storytelling Observer (a child, an old man, a foreigner, a cat, an explorer, someone revisiting his past, etc.), the environment can be interpreted very differently. Through what you show, you can suggest the observing consciousness of a particular person in a particular mood, even though that person is seldom or never seen.

Assessment: Use Assessment 6-3A (Dramatizing an Environment) (download from web site).

Discussion:

- Did the sequence depend on images and activities or on a central human subject?
- Were inherent rhythms well exploited?

- Was there a symphonic beginning, middle, and end? (Ideally, developments come from the rhythms and activities inherent in the setting.)
- Was the sequence mainly a response to, or an imposition on, the location?

6-3B: Adding Music

Going further: Now add music, but no songs. Aim to work with emotional associations and behavioral narration, not a verbal one. Audition different pieces against your scene before choosing the best and adjusting your film around it. When you lay music:

- Let special sounds bleed through the music in appropriate places.
- Decide where and why you want pure music, with no diegetic sound at all. Making these decisions raises important points about when music needs to be "pure," and when its impact and meaning are enhanced by sounds from the "real" world.
- Be ready to adjust shot lengths and cutting points to accommodate the structure of the music you've chosen. Music is never just applied; there should always be mutual responsiveness between visuals, diegetic sound (where used), and music.

Music can do the following:

- Augment what has been created pictorially and act illustratively
- Suggest something hidden that the audience must hunt for (example: a peaceful harvest scene accompanied by an ominous marching tune, or abandoned houses in a blighted urban area seen against an impassioned Bach chorale)
- Suggest what is subjective either to a character in the film or to the Storyteller (example: that young farm workers go off to die on foreign battlefields, or that poverty and failure are somehow part of God's plan for mankind)

Music is easy to begin and a lot less easy to conclude. The start and stop of a camera movement or subject movement can motivate music in-points and out-points, as can the ending or beginning of a strong diegetic sound effect. Study feature films for further guidance.

Assessment: Reuse Assessment 6-1C (Music).

Discussion:

- When is it legitimate to use music, when not?
- When is music being used creatively rather than programmatically (that is, as mere illustration)?
- What should music's relationship be to dialogue?
- How should music relate to diegetic sound effects (that is, effects natural to the scene)?
- When should music belong to the world of the characters, and when can it come from beyond their world?
- Can music be motivated by the storytelling "voice" of the film?

- Can you mix periods (use modern music on a historic subject, for instance)?
- What determines the texture and instrumentation of a music piece?

PROJECT 6-4: EDITED TWO-CHARACTER DIALOGUE SCENE

Skills to develop:

- Planning and shooting dialogue exchanges
- Camera placement
- Using verbal rhythms and operative words in editing
- Controlling the scene's point of view

6-4A: Multiple Coverage

Overview: This project, though short, covers a lot of ground and will take invention and organization. If you can, read ahead all the way to the Production phase (Chapters 26 through 31). You can learn much from making plans, carrying them out, and then deciding what you'd do differently next time.

1. Write a short dialogue scene (approximately three minutes) that makes use of an active indoor game. One character must realize that the other is bluffing and doesn't know how to play. Justify how this situation has arisen, and develop what it means to each person.
2. Mark the shooting script with your intended pattern of cutting. During shooting, you can overlook portions of shots that you don't intend to use, and can call for another take on important matters.
3. Shoot the whole scene from at least three angles. This style of coverage was once the Hollywood norm. The editor would find a point of view later from multiple coverage. Today, this is considered decisionless coverage that wastes actors' energies, crew time, and film stock. Broad coverage is useful here because it lets you experiment in editing.

Pacing a scene: If it is to look right on the screen, comedy should be paced about a third faster than things would happen in real life. Conversely, serious scenes often must be slowed, particularly at beat points, so that pauses, silences, eye line shifts, or an exchange of glances can be fully exploited. Experienced directors know where the truly high points are in a scene, and how to alter the pacing to their advantage. Beginners often reverse these priorities, and strive to ensure that no silence, or silent action, ever threatens to "bore" the audience. Nothing could be further from the truth.

Stretching or compressing time: Having double coverage in the cutting room lets you double a pregnant moment when it isn't pregnant enough. To do this, use all of the moment in the outgoing shot, then cut to the matching, incoming one at the beginning of the moment. That way, you can double its screen duration, a key technique for stretching time at strategic points. Conversely, if the moment was held overlong in a shot, you can abbreviate it by cutting tight to the matching angles and using editing as an elision device.

Actions, reactions, and subtexts: Although editors cannot speed up or slow down the way words in a sentence emerge, they can control the rhythm and balance of action and reaction, which is a huge part of implying a subtext. Sure-footed editing can make a vast difference to the degree of thought and feeling the audience attributes to each character, and can greatly improve the sense of integration and consistency in the acting.

Steps:

- Cast the actors.
- Decide the location.
- Write a script that implies the characters' backstory (where they have come from) and where they might be going next.
- Mark one script copy with the beats.
- Rehearse the scene and develop the accompanying action, going beyond what the script calls for.
- Make a floor plan showing characters' moves and intended camera positions (see Figure 5-4 as an example).
- Define what the scene should accomplish and whose POV the audience is to (a) mainly and (b) partially share and understand.
- Using another script copy and a color for each camera position, mark up the script with your intended editing plan (see Figure 6-4).
- Use major subject movements as action match cutting places so cuts disappear behind compelling action.
- Shoot the whole scene through in each major angle to allow experiment during editing.
- Edit strictly according to plan and solicit audience critique.
- Reedit according to what you now feel should be done and solicit new critique.
- Write guidelines for your next project based on what you learned.

Assessment: Use Assessment 6-4AB (download from web site).

Discussion: Directing and editing a convincing dialogue scene is one of the most challenging tasks a director faces. How did you do?

- How difficult was it to achieve consistent success throughout a take?
- How right was the pacing of the scene?
- Were the significant moments effectively exploited, and if not, why not?
- How did your writing sound in the mouths of your actors?
- Would the acting in this scene pass as documentary shot with a hidden camera?
- What did you learn about directing actors from this experience?
- What did you learn about directing from a text?

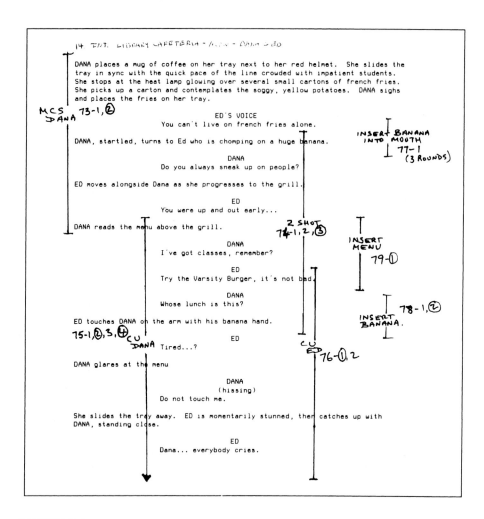

FIGURE 6-4

Marked-up script showing intended cut and generous overlaps to allow action matches and other kinds of alternatives in editing.

6-4B: Editing for an Alternative Point of View

Use your generous coverage to reedit and make the audience identify with a different POV, such as a secondary character's or omniscient Storyteller's POV.

Assessment: Use Assessment 6-4AB (download from web site). See if you did better the second time around.

PROJECT 6-5: AUTHORSHIP THROUGH IMPROVISATION

Skills to develop:

- Involving actors in script idea development
- Spontaneous and creative interaction between actors and director

- Directing an event where actors must merge (for example, with an uncontrollable public event)
- Editing documentary-style coverage
- Script development from taped improvisations
- Stylistic decision making
- Working intuitively and thinking on your feet

6-5A: Developing a Short Scene

Authorial goals: Set up guidelines for a three- to four-minute improvised scene between two people that incorporates an emotional transition in one character from cheerful to angry. The goal is not to produce great drama, but to experiment with camera coverage and editing. Should you need guidance in directing an "improv," read the introductory part of Chapter 21, then follow the instructions for Exercise 19-15: Bridging Emotions. Once your scene has become reasonably stable and secure, cover the scene handheld. Do this at least three times, favoring Character A, Character B, then both in two-shot. This, by the way, is how Larry David's comedy television series *Curb Your Enthusiasm* (2000) is shot.

The goal is to obtain sufficient coverage so you can cut the scene together and then cope with the variations inherent in improvised work. Bring your camera operator in early, because you rely on him or her during improv for the quality of the coverage. In direct cinema documentary, also known as observational camera coverage, the director cannot line up each shot, so creative initiative passes to the camera operator, who must have the mind of a dramatist, not just that of a technician or still photographer. A director quickly finds out whether the operator sees only composition through the viewfinder, or whether he or she is finding dramatic meaning and focus within a scene. Some do and some can learn, but beware—some camera operators will remain detached visual designers.

Camera use: With the advance of Steadicam use, and with high-definition (HD) video being used increasingly in feature films, handheld coverage is increasingly common. Stylistically, it usually projects a strong feeling of spontaneous human observation, as opposed to the godlike omniscience implied by the tripod's perfect composition and rock steadiness. It also injects an interesting sense of fallibility and subjectivity into the coverage. Sometimes, of course, this is intrusively wrong—for instance, during a sequence of misty mountain landscape shots at daybreak when nobody is supposed to be about. In that case, tripod shots are a must.

Sound coverage: Here it's catch-as-catch-can, and a real challenge for the mike operator. While the camera adapts to the action, the microphone operator must stay out of frame and pick up good sound in a swiftly changing, unpredictable situation. Pay attention to sound balance before you show your work to an audience, or discrepancies will make them misread the piece's inherent qualities. One solution is to use a DAT multitrack recorder and put a wireless microphone on everyone who speaks, recording each on a separate channel.

Editing: Edit together a complete version, keeping to the form and length of the original.

Assessment: Use Assessment 6-5ABC (Improvised Scene) (download from web site).

Discussion:
Exposition:

- Was expository detail included so the audience understands the situation? (It is fatally easy in improv to overlook something vital.)
- Was each new piece of expository information concealed artfully enough?
- Did the information come too early or too late in the edited piece?

Camera coverage:

- When was mobile, handheld footage stylistically appropriate, and when not?
- What guidelines can you draw for the future?
- Was spontaneous coverage good, or was the operator caught by surprise?
- What effect do these moments have?
- How much were you able to feature the characters' environment?
- Does composition reveal relationship between people (crestfallen son, for instance, in foreground, angry mother in background)?
- How can you construct a more integrated point of view?
- Did you manage to grab enough close detail?

Sound:

- How acceptable is the dialogue track?
- How hard was it to cover speakers whose movements are spontaneous?

Point of view:

- Whose scene is it?
- Does POV arise mainly from performance or from camera treatment? (Hard to pinpoint, but too important to neglect.)

Improvising:

- What did you gain, what did you lose, from improvising a scene?
- What did you gain, what did you lose, from handheld coverage?
- How credible were the characters?
- How well did the scene "problem" develop, and how well did it resolve?
- How consistent was pacing, and how much do you need to edit around plateaus in the pacing or development?

Time your first cut for comparison with the next assignment.

6-5B: Editing a Shorter Version

Going further: Now edit down your initial cut, trying to make it tighter and more functional by eliminating verbal and behavioral padding. Feel free to restructure the piece should repositioning exposition or other elements improve the dramatic curve. You must decide the necessity of much that is said and done on the screen, and find ways to eliminate whatever doesn't deserve to be there.

Assessment: Use Assessment 6-5ABC (Improvised Scene) again.

Discussion:

- What percentage of the original length did you eliminate?
- What is gained, what is lost, in the new cut?
- How consistent is the pace of dramatic development now?
- What did you feel about the acting?
- What would you do differently?

Improvisation's strength is the spontaneity and realism of the acting and the conviction of the characters. Discuss which of the following weaknesses turned up in your work and how they might be eliminated:

- The difficulty of achieving a satisfying development. Improv often suffers from irregularly paced dramatic growth, with long plateaus during which both actors and audience feel the pressure for something to happen.
- The temptation for actors, when desperate, to resort to manipulating moments to get the piece moving again.
- The difficulty of reliably hiding exposition inside ongoing events.

You do not want your audience to feel the presence of an editorializing hand during verbal exchanges, feeding such giveaway lines as, "Isn't it rough being out of work for three months, Ted?" and, "The last time we met—you remember—it was at the supermarket. You got mad because I couldn't give you back the money you lent me in September."

Even if no clumsy authorial hand comes occasionally crashing through the backdrop, you will probably be dissatisfied with the dialogue. At times, it is skimpy and overcompressed; at other times, prolix and flaccid. Though editing can usually remove padding, it may also reveal inadequate joints and structural problems. However, if things go reasonably well, you end up with interestingly developed characters and a story line. Whatever you have by now is the basis for the next stage.

6-5C: From Improv to Script

Transcribe the previous exercise and rewrite it, keeping the flavor of the dialogue, but compressing verbiage into pithy lines. Distribute and camouflage any expository information, and wherever possible, transform dialogue into actions that do not require accompanying words—that way, characters can show their feelings instead of narrating them to each other. Now, using the same cast and location, rehearse and shoot the scene as in Project 6-6.

Assessment: Use Assessment 6-5ABC (Improvised Scene) again.

Discussion: Compare the two versions of the same scene.

- What was lost, what was gained, by turning an improvised performance into a scripted and more formally controlled scene?
- How did your cast handle their lines and action this time?
- What have you learned about authorship and directing from this project?

PROJECT 6-6: PARALLEL STORYTELLING

Skills to develop:

- Advancing two story lines concurrently so each acts as a cutaway for the other and both are kept to brief essentials.
- Counterpointing two moods or activities to imply a storytelling commentary.
- Making separate, concurrent events develop toward convergence.

6-6A: Seeing the Scenes as Separate Entities

Either write or improvise two whole scenes with content that will intercut meaningfully and provoke the audience to see a connection. Suggested pairs of subjects:

- Man getting ready for a date/woman in very different mood getting ready for the same date
- Burglars getting ready to rob a house/detectives making preparations to trap them
- Man rehearsing how he will ask for a raise/two managers discussing how they will fire him

Write each as a complete, three-minute, stand-alone scene. Cast, shoot, and edit each scene separately, and assemble them so that one whole scene follows the other. Do a reasonably tight edit on each sequence, and then consider them as in the discussion below.

Assessment: Use Assessment 6-6ABCD (Parallel Storytelling), but omit the last section, Parallel Stories.

Discussion:

- What difference is there in implication when you run the sequences as AB or BA? (The detectives, for example, may have arrived too late, and the firing may follow the request for a raise, instead of precede it.)
- How long is each sequence?
- What do you gain in dramatic buildup by staying with each unbroken sequence?

6-6B: Long Intercut Version

Going further: Intercut the two sequences, losing nothing of the original material.

Assessment: Use Assessment 6-6ABCD (Parallel Storytelling), this time including the last section, Parallel Stories.

Discussion:

- What ironies were you able to create? (Say, the woman preparing for the date has a new dress, whereas the man forgets to clean his shoes.)

- What meaningful comparisons do you create? (Both the man asking for a raise and his managers think he is underpaid.)

- What causes and effects does the audience link together? (Both detectives and burglars have radios.)

- Do both sequences appear to be happening at the same time, or is one retrospective in comparison with the other? (For instance, a son from abroad searching for his parents finds that his father is already dead. His father's death is intercut with his mother's account of it, which is softened to spare the son's feelings.)

- Does one sequence foretell the outcome of the other? (In Nicolas Roeg's *Don't Look Now*, 1973, the lovemaking scene is poignantly intercut with the couple getting dressed afterward.)

6-6C: Short Version

Going further: Now reassess the cut. Because it is no longer necessary to maintain the illusion of continuous time, you can pare away anything the audience can infer and that is thus nonessential. You will probably see new and improved points at which to cut between the parallel stories.

Assessment: Use Assessment 6-6ABCD (Parallel Storytelling) with the last section, Parallel Stories.

Discussion:

- How much shorter is the new version?
- How many of the ideas for your new cut arose from the shooting, blocking, and playing of the scene?
- How many of your intercutting ideas were germinated while writing, and how many came afterward?
- What dramatic capital was gained, and what lost, through intercutting?
- How might a writer plan raw materials for such sequences?

6-6D: Discontinuity and Using Jump Cuts

Going further: Experimentally reassemble each sequence in chronological order, retaining only the pieces you chose for the intercut version as a discontinuity version using jump cuts. A *jump cut* is any discontinuous edit that signals that a significant piece of time has been discarded between the scenes and that we have jumped forward in time. By doing this, you are moving from continuity narrative to an episodic narrative using discontinuous time.

Assessment: Use Assessment 6-6ABCD (Parallel Storytelling), but not the last section, Parallel Stories.

Discussion: What are the effects of eliminating the slack material between the high points? Surely this accelerates the story, and by discarding objective time, it probably accentuates an authorial attitude toward what moments matter. Flat-footed realism and linear, continuous time have given way to something more impressionistic and subjective.

If you hate this version of your sequences, it may be because the jump cuts make ugly visual leaps. How true would this be had you designed each jump cut's composition with this in mind? Here are some options to consider:

Similarity of frame: You might, for instance, have cut from a bed with two people reading, to the same bed with them asleep, to a morning shot with one still there and the other dressing in the background. Older convention would dictate a long, slow dissolve between the three setups (which should be taken with the camera locked down in the exact same position so each composition is exactly the same), but the same narrative content can be conveyed in a fraction of the time by jump cutting. This makes the jump cut a formal storytelling device of great agility.

Difference of frame: With a bold difference of composition, you can simply jump-cut elsewhere in space and possibly in time as well. During a wide shot of people preparing to fire a piece of pottery, you can cut to a close shot of the oven. Somebody opens it, and the pot is already fired. We understand that time has been eliminated, even though dialogue continues with an unbroken sentence across the cut into the new time plane. The TV commercial has familiarized audiences with cinematic shorthand like this.

Freed from the literalness and "objectivity" of present-tense realism, discontinuity allows a wealth of possibilities for a fleeter and more staccato storytelling style. These developments are very significant if you want to co-opt the audience's imagination by using a cinematic language of greater flexibility. In *Breathless* (1959), Jean-Luc Godard was the first director to use this style intensively.

PART 3

THE STORY AND ITS DEVELOPMENT

Part 3 (Chapters 7 through 10) deals with the director's relationship to the script—or screenplay, as it's often called—whose job is to present the bones of a film in a standard, shareable form. Whether written by yourself or by your writer, the story is very far from being ready to film. A great deal of development lies ahead.

To create something—whether boat, chair, song, or film—you must first envision the finished article in your head. By all means, write your earliest shorts yourself because experience is the best teacher. Each will face you with a bewildering array of options in point of view, genre, plot, and style—all to be treated in coming chapters.

Once you turn to more ambitious works, you become responsible for sustained performances just as the larger operation becomes onerous. Many overestimate their ability to carry the burden, and they cling to being the auteur—that is, directing their own writing because nobody else's is good enough. Wearing so many hats is like joining the circus and setting out to juggle while riding a bike on a high wire. Sure, acrobats can do it, but you are gambling with your very survival. Wiser would be to develop in measured stages. Do some research, and you'll see that virtually nobody goes to Hollywood (or its local equivalent) as a director. Yes, Robert Rodriguez did so with his first film, *El Mariachi* (1993, Figure 7-1), but he was already an accomplished graphic artist, as you'll learn from the DVD extras that come with his film.

Be kind to yourself: start talent-spotting for your natural collaborators in writing, cinematography, sound, and editing. You can direct, and direct really well—but only if you assemble the best available talents around you, *including a writer*. Give yourself the pleasure and education of collaborating with the best you can find. Now put all your creative energies into making the best film you can. Only then will you learn what to do differently so you will direct better next time.

FIGURE 7-1 ——

Robert Rodriguez' short *El Mariachi* launched his directing career (courtesy Los Hooligans/Columbia/The Kobal Collection).

CHAPTER 7

RECOGNIZING THE SUPERIOR SCREENPLAY

Most fiction films start with a screenplay (also called a *property*). It should be original, well written, and make good use of the cinema. As its director, you must be fascinated with the world it creates and with the ideas that it puts forward, because you are going to be married to it for a long, long time.

Chapter 10, "Alternative Story Sources," shows that scripts can be generated in nontraditional ways. For the time being, however, let's concentrate on the normal source—a screenplay written by a screenwriter.

CHOOSING WHAT IS RIGHT FOR YOU

Whether your film is comedy, tragedy, horror, fantasy, or a piece for children, it should embody issues you find compelling. Even as you learn basic film techniques and grammar, you should choose subjects you care about, because each will give you ideas and energy rather than fatigue. Avoid scripts that preach, debate problems, or demonstrate solutions. Aim to deal, in a suitably disguised and displaced way, with whatever is unresolved and engraved in your psyche. It might be racial or class alienation, a reputation for clumsiness, fear of the dark (horror films!), rejection, a phobia, a period of intense happiness, or a brief love affair. It might be a stigma such as illegitimacy, being foreign, or being unjustly favored.

Make use of the scars you bear from living and the unfinished business that awaits exploration. By working with themes and situations that stir you to strong and, especially, contradictory feelings, your works will explore a corner of existence about which you are knowledgeable but *want to learn more*. If your audience is to leave satisfied, *your main character should learn and grow*, however minimal or even negative that learning may be.

WHY READING SCRIPTS IS HARD

Film schools suffer from the same shortage of distinguished writing as the film industry, so start scouting for exceptional writers and help them to grow. As a fiction director, you do not exist without the screenplay. The professionally written screenplay consists of dialogue; sparse or nonexistent stage directions; and equally brief remarks on character, locations, and behavior. It contains no directions for camerawork or editing, and none of the author's thematic intentions. The reader must supply from imagination whatever is missing, which makes for very demanding work. Inexperienced directors tend to delay or avoid this toil.

SIGNS OF A GOOD SCREENPLAY

The professional screenplay is minimal because it aims to seed a visual, nonliterary, organic, and experiential process. A well-written one:

- Includes no author's thoughts, instructions, or comments.
- Uses few qualifying comments and adjectives (overdescribing kills what the reader imagines).
- Leaves most behavior to the reader's imagination, and instead describes its effect (for example, "he looks nervous"—instead of, "he nervously runs a forefinger round the inside of his collar and then flicks dust off his dark serge pants").
- Underinstructs actors unless a line or action would be unintelligible without guidance.
- Contains no camera or editing instructions.
- Isn't written on the nose (that is, overexplicitly instead of leaving the viewer with interpretive work to do).
- Uses brief, evocative language whenever the body copy wants the reader to visualize something.

Overwriting is dangerous because anything that is detailed ends up conditioning its readers (money sources, actors, crew) to anticipate particular, hard-edged results. The director is then locked into trying to fulfill a vision that disallows variables, including those that contribute positively. In addition, actors get important messages from how a script is written. The overprescribed, closed screenplay tells them they must conform to minutely specified actions and mannerisms, whereas the open screenplay encourages an active process of search between the cast and their director.

The screenplay format itself is treacherous because its appearance and proportions suggest that films are built around dialogue. This may be true for soap opera, but it's quite wrong for good screen drama, which aims to be visual and behavioral.

STANDARD SCRIPT FORMS

The industry standards for layouts are simple and effective and have evolved as the ultimate in convenience. Do not invent your own.

SCREENPLAY FORMAT

The sample page in Figure 7-2 illustrates the following rules for screenplay form:

Typeface: Screenplays use the old-fashioned typewriter font called 12-point Courier. The industry has kept this because in this format, one page runs approximately a minute on-screen.

Scene heading: Each scene begins with a flush-left, capitalized scene heading that lists:

- Number of the scene
- Interior or exterior
- Location
- Time of day or night

```
11. INT. LIBRARY CAFETERIA.  NOON.  DANA & ED

DANA places a mug of coffee on her tray next to her crash helmet. She slides
the tray in sync with the quick pace of the line crowded with impatient
students. She stops at the heat lamp glowing over several small cartons of
french fries. She picks up a carton and contemplates the soggy yellow
potatoes. DANA sighs and places the fries on her tray.

                           ED'S VOICE
                You can't live on French fries alone.

DANA turns startled to find ED next to her chomping on a huge banana.

                             DANA
                Do you always sneak up on people?

ED moves alongside DANA as she progresses to the grill.

                              ED
                You were up and out so early ...

DANA reads the menu above the grill.

                             DANA
                I've got classes, remember?

                              ED
                Try the Varsity Burger, it's not bad.

                             DANA
                Whose lunch is this?

ED touches DANA on the arm with his banana hand.

                              ED
                Tired?

DANA glares at the menu.

                          DANA (hissing)
                Do not touch me.

She slides the tray away. ED is momentarily stunned, then catches up with
her again, standing close.

                              ED
                Dana ... everybody cries.
```

FIGURE 7-2 ───────────────────────────────────

Sample page of screenplay (from an unproduced screenplay, *A Night So Long* by Lynise Pion).

Body copy or **stage directions**: Single-spaced and running the width of the page; this includes action description, mood setting, and stage directions, and is double-spaced away from scene headings and dialogue.

Character names: Outside the dialogue, these should appear in all capitals.

Dialogue sections should be:

- Headed by the speaker's name, centered, and in all capitals
- Block indented and set between reduced margins (left 3.0 inches, right 2.5 inches)
- Preceded and followed by a double space
- Accompanied when strictly necessary by a stage direction inside brackets

Shot transitions: Used only when unavoidable to the script's making sense. Terms like *Cut to* or *Dissolve to* are placed flush right.

Figure 7-2 is a page in pure screenplay form. Notice that there are no camera or editing directions. True, industry practices vary, and some commercial scripts are hybrid creatures that dramatize their contents by moving closer to a shooting script. This may help to sell a particular script in a particular quarter, but in most places it has no practical value. From the beginning, you should do what is mainstream.

SPLIT-PAGE OR TV SCREENPLAY FORMAT

The *split-page format* (see Chapter 5, Figure 5-4), sometimes called a *television* or *TV format* script, is frequently used in multicamera television studio shooting when a complex drama must be enacted in real time. In multicamera television, all production elements have to be preenvisioned and present because there is no postproduction. In cinema-style shooting, each shot is created discretely, and the final version is composed meticulously afterward in the cutting room, so the detail a split-page script affords is usually irrelevant.

Split-page format is, however, the best layout for logging and analyzing a finished movie, for it allows clear representation of the relationship between images and sound elements. Notice that the picture column contains only what you would see, and the sound column contains only what you would hear. Keep this distinction clear, or the point of having a standard is lost.

Chapter 5, "Seeing with a Moviemaker's Eye," strongly recommended that you make a split-page transcript of a few sequences from your favorite contemporary movies. If you did so, you will have seen how truly dense film language is, and how only the split-page format can toggle the reader's attention among dialogue, image, and action.

SPLIT-PAGE WITH THIRD COLUMN

As part of drafting initial ideas, you can use the step outline or split-page format and add an important extra column, as in Figure 7-3. Here, you can work out, scene by scene, what you want your audience to think, feel, question, decide (rightly or wrongly), or remember from earlier in the film. It's instructive to read through your script scanning only this column. By doing this, you are concentrating on the intended experience for the audience.

Picture	Sound	Observer notices ...
Wide shot car graveyard.	Bird song, turns into the regular breathing of someone sleeping.	A mood of decayed hulks, family cars worn out and cast aside
Shots of cars, their headlights making them look like faces.	Mumbling, as of a dreamer	Do cars have ghosts?
Grass and ferns growing up through floors. Glass splintered in black sedan.	Male group making businessman conversation. Sound diminishes to silence	Did important people once use this car?
Executive at head of boardroom table waits for respectful silence.	Child's voice begins nursery song, then ...	What does all this have to do with abandoned automobiles?
Bangs his hand down on table. Everyone jumps.	Bang!!	Why is he angry?
Car graveyard again. A pair of gloves on a dusty seat. A plane passes through top of frame.	Pigeon wings flapping, a voice in a large room says, "Are we all ready?"	Someone has left a pair of gloves ... another voice from another time ... what's going to happen?
A muffled figure rises from backseat, stretches, yawns.	Sync sound	Ah, someone lives here. A new character. Is this street person connected with those boardroom types?

FIGURE 7-3 ————————————————————————

A screenplay draft in split-page form shows precise relationship between images and their accompanying sound. Adding a third column allows you to articulate the Observer's stream of consciousness while following the story.

SCRIPT-FORM CONFUSIONS

Publishers cause confusion by making no distinction between the original screenplay and continuity (sometimes called reader's) scripts. The latter is a transcription of the finished product, not the all-important blueprint that initiated the film. Make sure you know which you are reading; otherwise you may form the appalling idea that films are written and made by omniscient beings.

FIRST ASSESSMENT

After the first reading, examine what imprint the screenplay left on you:

- What did it make you feel?
- Whom did you care about?
- Whom did you find interesting?
- What does the piece seem to be dealing with behind the surface events?

Note your impressions and read the screenplay once or twice again, looking for hard evidence of what you felt. Next, ask yourself the following:

- What is the screenplay trying to accomplish?
- What special means does it use to accomplish its intentions?
- Is what the screenplay calls for within my budget and capabilities?

DETERMINE THE GIVENS

Now carefully determine the *givens*, the hard information directly specified in the screenplay that includes:

- Epoch
- Time of day
- Locations
- Character details revealed by their words and actions
- Clues to backstory (events prior to the period covered by the film)
- Words and actions used by characters

For each actor, all hard knowledge about his or her character's past and future is in the script. A character, after all, is like the proverbial iceberg, with four-fifths out of sight. What is in the script allows the actor to infer and develop what is below the "waterline"—which is the character's backstory or biography, motives, volition, fears, ambitions, vulnerabilities, and so on. The givens will be interpreted by director, cast, art department, and crew, and the inferences that each draws must harmonize or the film won't be consistent. Much else in the film is left unspecified, such as the movements and physical appearance of the characters, camera treatment, and sound and editing details.

MAKING A SCENE-BY-SCENE CONTENT LIST

Make a list of scenes, giving each a brief, functional description (example: *Scene 15: Ricky, seeing Angelo's car again, realizes he's being watched*). Now you can see the flow of the story and begin inhabiting the script as thoroughly as you must. Its underlying dramatic logic, so hard to focus any other way, begins to show. Often you find more going on than screenwriter was aware of. Directors and writers often work together closely on further drafts at this stage, acting as checks and balances to each other's ideas.

ASSESSING CINEMATIC QUALITIES

Use dialogue only when truly necessary, never as a substitute for action. Dialogue should itself *be* action; that is, it should be how characters act on each other, and never a way to narrate thoughts and feelings, or to editorialize. A simple but deadly test of a script's potential is to imagine shutting off the sound to see just how much an audience would understand from what remains. What is told through behavior, and what through dialogue used as narration?

STORYTELLING THROUGH BEHAVIOR

Early cowboy films made a strong impact because the American cinema recognized the power of behavioral melodrama. The strong screenplay is still concerned predominantly with behavior, action, and reaction. It avoids static scenes in which people verbalize their thoughts and feelings.

A character's actions become compelling the moment we see that he or she is trying to get, do, or accomplish something—minute by minute, day by day, year by year. Good drama is about *doing*. Good screenplays are peppered with *doing* words; that is, with verbs.

ESTABLISHING CHARACTERS AND MOTIVES

Prove your script's integrity by tracing each event and character backward to ascertain that the requisite groundwork has been laid. If a cousin arrives to show off a new car, and in so doing, reveals his uncle's plan to sell the family business, that cousin needs to be established earlier, and so does the family's dependence on the business. Drama that uses coincidence or that rolls out a character purely for plot requirements looks shoddy and contrived. Like threads in cloth, you want your tapestry to appear seamless and untailored.

AMBIVALENCE OR BEHAVIORAL CONTRADICTIONS

Intelligent drama exploits the way each character consciously or otherwise tries to control the situation—either to hide underlying intentions and concerns, or, should the occasion demand it, to draw attention to them. Once both director and actors know the subtexts, they can develop behaviors to manifest the tensions between inner and outer worlds, between what the characters want and what impedes them showing or acting on it.

Ambivalences like these are clues to the audience about a character's hidden life and underlying conflicts. When actors begin to act on (not merely think about) their characters' conflicts and locked energies, scenes move beyond an illustrative notion of human interaction and begin to manifest their characters' tensions. The acting begins to imply the pressurized emotion below the aridly logical top surface. This underlying tension may demand that the main character preserve the appearance of being rational, mannerly, and inscrutable. This is all part of how a person keeps their agendas hidden. We all do it, and most of the time.

METAPHORS AND SYMBOLS

Screen characters' inner experiences can also be expressed through artfully chosen settings, objects, and moods. These function metaphorically or symbolically as keys to deeper issues. Is your script using these?

Symbols and symbolic action should be artfully designed, because your audience will gag on the manipulative symbol or the overearnest metaphor. Above all, as we've said earlier, they must be organic to the world in which the characters live, or else they will pop up as contrived, editorial comments. Here, cinematography can serve profound purposes. The parched, bleached settings in Wim Wenders' *Paris, Texas* (1984, Figure 7-4) emblematize the emotional aridity of a man searching for his lost wife and child. Jane Campion's *The Piano* (1993, Figure 7-5) makes an equally breathtaking integration of metaphor into screen drama, and it sweeps the viewer up in its earliest scenes. The film's power speaks through the briefest summary: Ada, a young immigrant Scot who won't or can't speak, arrives with her illegitimate daughter and her piano on the wild New Zealand seashore of the 19th century. She is there to marry a man she neither knows nor loves. But he refuses to bring home her piano, so instead it goes to another man's home. He, not her husband, listens to her music, so it is to him that Ada gives her body and soul.

FIGURE 7-4

In *Paris, Texas*, the desert landscape counterpoints Travis's lost and arid inner state (courtesy Road/Argos/Channel 4/The Kobal Collection).

We are at a time and place where nature is savage, love denied by decorum, and subtlety beyond the reach of language. The soul reaches out by way of music and suppressed eroticism. Who could ask for a more potent canvas?

CHECKING THE EMBEDDED VALUES

All storytelling begins from assumptions about what will be familiar and normal to the audience. Making films is expensive, so those who do so come from the affluent classes and tend to represent as normal only what the privileged see as such. Consider how gender roles and relationships were represented in movies just a few decades back. Women were secretaries, nurses, teachers, mothers, or seductresses. People of color were servants, vagrants, or objects of pity with little to say for themselves. Criminals or gangsters were ethnic types, and so on.

Stereotypes arise from *embedded values;* that is, values so familiar to the makers of a film that they pass below the radar of awareness. An excellent book written by three USC faculty members, *Creative Filmmaking from the Inside Out: Five Keys to the Art of Making Inspired Movies and Television*, offers useful tools to expose unintended stereotyping.[1] I have adapted them below. You might want to apply these tools to any script you are considering.

[1] Jed Dannenbaum, Carroll Hodge, and Doe Mayer. *Creative Filmmaking from the Inside Out: Five Keys to the Art of Making Inspired Movies and Television* (New York: Simon & Schuster, 2003).

FIGURE 7-5

In *The Piano*'s bold premise, a mute woman and her child arrive in 19th-century New Zealand with little more than a piano (courtesy The Kobal Collection/Jan Chapman Prods/CIBY 2000).

Characters:

Class: What class of society do they come from? How are differences handled? How are other classes represented?

Wealth: Do they have money? How is it regarded? How do they handle it? What is taken for granted? Are things as they should be, and if not, how well does the film express this?

Appearances: Are appearances reliable or misleading? How important are appearances? Do the characters have difficulty reading each other's appearances?

Background: Is there any diversity of race or other background, and if so, how is this handled? Do other races or ethnicities have minor or major parts?

Belongings and work: Do we know what the characters do to sustain their lifestyle? Do their clothes, appliances, and cars belong with their characters' breadwinning ability? What do their belongings say about their tastes and values? Is anyone in the film critical of this?

Talismans: Are there important objects, and if so, what is their significance?

Valuation: For what are characters valued by other characters? Does the film question this or cast doubt on the intercharacter values?

Speech: What do you learn from the vocabulary of each? What makes the way each thinks and talks different from the others? What does it betray?

Roles: What roles do characters fall into, and do they emerge as complex enough to challenge any stereotypes?

Sexuality and gender roles: How are gender roles apportioned? If gay or transgender characters appear, how are they portrayed? If the script deals with sexuality, does it contain a range of expression, and how is it portrayed? Is it allied with affection, tenderness, and love? Or is it shown as disembodied lust? Is it true to your experience?

Volition: Who is able to change his or her situation, and who seems unable to take action? What are the patterns behind this?

Competence: Who is competent, and who is not? What determines this?

Environment:

Place: Do we know where characters come from and what values are associated with their birthplace or other origins?

Settings: Will they look credible and add to what we know about the characters?

Time: What values are associated with the period chosen for the setting?

Home: Do the characters seem at home? What do they have around them to signify any journeys or accomplishments they have made?

Work: Do the characters seem to belong there, and how is the workplace portrayed? What does it say about the characters?

Family Dynamics:

Structure: What structure emerges? Do characters treat it as normal or abnormal? Is anyone critical of the family structure?

Relationships: How are relationships between members and between generations portrayed?

Roles: Are roles in the family fixed or do they develop? Are they healthy or unhealthy? Who in the family is critical? Who is branded as "good" or "successful" by the family, and who "bad" or "failed"?

Power: Could there be another structure? Is power handled in a healthy or unhealthy way? What is the relationship of earning money to power in the family?

Authority:

Gender: Which gender is shown to have the most authority? Does one gender dominate, and if so, why?

Initiation: Who initiates the events in the film, and why? Who resolves them?

Respect: How are figures with power depicted? How are institutions and institutional power depicted? Are they simple or complex, and does the script reflect your experience of the real thing?

Conflict: How are conflicts negotiated? What does the film say about conflict and its resolution? Who wins, and why?

Violence: Who is violent, and why? Is violence a dramatic crutch for resolving differences, or is it justified? What does it say about your values when violence is gratuitous? Can differences be negotiated in another and more artistically interesting way?

In Total:

Criticism: How critical is the film toward what its characters do or don't do? How much does it tell us about what's wrong? Can we hope to see one of the characters coming to grips with this?

Approval/Disapproval: What does the film approve of, and is there anything risky and unusual in what it defends? Is the film challenging its audience's assumptions and expectations, or just feeding into them?

World View: If this is a microcosm, what does it say about the balance of forces in the larger world, or macrocosm, of which it is a fragment?

Moral Stance: What shape does the film's belief system take in relation to privilege, willpower, tradition, inheritance, power, initiative, God, luck, coincidence, and so on? Is this what you want?

This is not about being politically correct, which leads to another kind of suffocation, but about avoiding whatever is "normal" and just shouldn't be. To make fiction is to propose reality, and this is as true for fantasy as it is for realism. Do the elements you intend to work with mean what you intend? Do they align with what you'd like your audience to think about? Such considerations are at the core of screen authorship, and *Creative Filmmaking from the Inside Out* asks that you take steps to be fully aware of the ethical and moral implications in your work.

CHAPTER 8

ANALYZING A SCREENPLAY

After making an initial assessment and breakdown of the screenplay in hand, you can analyze in greater depth how it functions, beginning with the plot of the story.

PLOT

Plot is the logic and energy that drive the story forward, and plot is closely allied to the story's structure. Its job is to generate questions in the audience's mind and to keep interest and tension high. Every step the characters take should feel inevitable. Anything unsupported, arbitrary, or coincidental weakens the causal chain on which the feeling of forward momentum depends. Once you describe how the plot works, you need only common sense and a little inspiration to make improvements. For more help, read Part 4: Aesthetics and Authorship—in particular, Chapter 14, "Time, Structure, and Plot," because these elements are interdependent.

In a *plot-driven story*, the sheer movement of events usually compensates for any lack of depth or complexity in the characters. In a *character-driven story*, the momentum comes from the needs and imperatives of the main characters. By strengthening the plot, you can raise the audience's sense of involvement and appreciably improve the whole.

OBSTACLES AND PREDICAMENTS

With each new predicament, the characters face tests of courage and strength, either physical or moral. Here, Chapter 13, "Subtext, Genre, and Archetypes," will be helpful. The characters should face situations and environments that escalate and test them as each tries to accomplish his or her aims. What a person does when backed into a corner can modify or subvert all that hitherto appeared true.

In heroic drama, good characters usually fight evil ones, but main characters will probably need inner conflicts as well as outer ones, or they will seem insubstantial. A character with conflicting feelings and contradictory actions is radically different from the illustrative portrayal that reeks of "message."

PLOT POINTS

A plot point is a moment in which a story, moving in one direction, suddenly goes off at a tangent. If, during a comedy about a happy young couple taking their first holiday together, the man suddenly freezes on the steps of the airplane, we have an unpredictable turn of events. He has been hiding his claustrophobia, and now they must somehow go abroad by sea instead. On the steps of the boat, the young woman clings to the rail on the quay: she for her part has been concealing her agoraphobia. Another plot point.

What will they do now? we ask ourselves.

Tangents and the unexpected are necessary to shake things up and demolish the predictability that any story will fall into. If you are to keep dramatic tension high in your film, plot points should occur when the story needs them.

CHARACTERS: CONFLICT, GROWTH, AND CHANGE

INITIAL IMPRESSIONS

We judge people by the clues in their physical appearance, their body language, and their clothes and how they wear them. Looking at a person's belongings, surroundings, and associates, we wonder which they chose and which were thrust upon them. Their actions help us interpret their temperament, formative pressures, assumptions, and goals. How a character deals with the unexpected or threatening tells us more again. All this helps establish everyone's goals, makeup, and history. Never forget that character is destiny.

STATIC CHARACTER DEFINITION

You first assess the script's characters by their *givens* (age, sex, appearance, work, situation, eccentricities, etc.), but these lead only to a static summation. Characters stuck at this level of conception feel like figures in a photomontage in which each has a single role and attitude. You see this in the TV commercial, which has to sell something in 30 seconds. Each character is typical: a typical mother, a typical washing machine repairman, a typical holiday couple on a typical romantic beach. Homes, streets, meals, and family relations are all typical—which is to say, stereotyped. Actors faced with static characterizations struggle in vain to breathe life into their parts.

DYNAMIC CHARACTER DEFINITION

The dynamic approach moves beyond what a character "is," to focus instead on what challenges and mobilizes him or her. For this, you must *discover what each character is really trying to get, do, or accomplish.* Trained actors know how to look for this, but not all directors do. Yet above all, actors need the help of their director to find the clues embedded in their characters' words and actions and to breathe life into their characters. A director is therefore a midwife to truth, not its final creator.

Intelligent drama pits each main character's will against obstacles. An analogy is watching ants moving through gravel. You can see where each ant is trying to go and what it faces, and you get involved with how each creature solves the obstructions in its path while maintaining its overall intention.

To uncover a character's volition in a screenplay, take a key scene and apply the following questions:

1. What is this character moving toward, and moving away from?
2. What is this character trying to get or do, long term?
3. What is this character trying to get or do, right now?
4. What new situation is this character facing?
5. What does the character want next?
6. What are the obstacles that obstruct him or her?
7. How does the character try to overcome the obstacles?
8. How well does he/she adapt to the obstacles?
9. What new situation does he/she face after adaptation?
10. How does this change his/her goals?

By uncovering immediate goals, these ten questions elicit the character's development, moment by moment. When the answers are consistent, you sense that you are completing a join-the-dots puzzle. Over the whole piece, you should begin to see long-term goals that dominate each character's existence. As the evidence mounts, characters come to struggle for consistent ends and gain the touching qualities of living human beings.

The job of analysis is to find weaknesses and use creative intelligence to address them—this is all part of the director's job. By doing this, you will soon know how deeply the story has been thought through, and what areas need work. If you find confusion, think carefully before taking on the script. You want to find a really good foundation with plenty of challenge for cast, director, and cinematographer.

The director John Cassavetes believed that Freudian psychological keys to character are bogus, and that a person's character is not something fixed, but negotiated in the heat of human interaction. Ray Carney in *The Films of John Cassavetes* (Cambridge University Press, 1994) shows with rare insight how Cassavetes' characters discover themselves from plunging into experience:

> . . . the openness of Cassavetes' characters is much more radical than their merely being open to change or defying prediction, and that leads to the second difference between Cassavetes' characters and those in virtually all other American feature films. The Cassavetean self is open in the sense of pulling down the walls that normally separate one character from another. Like onstage performers, characters such as Lelia, Mabel, and Gloria make themselves up and revise themselves in a continuous process of dramatic improvisation in response to the different audiences before which they appear. Their identities are relational; they are, at least in part, negotiated with others. Cassavetes' leading characters figure an extreme degree of awareness of, sensitivity to, and responsiveness to others; yet that is not to put it strongly enough. Cassavetes' characters are so open to external influences and so willing to make adjustments in their positions that it would be better to say that it is as if their identities are not theirs alone, but shared with

others. They are not in complete control of their selves, but turn over part of the control to others. Their selves are not solid and bounded, but soft and permeable; others reach into them, affect them, change them, and at times even inhabit them. . . . Their identities are supremely vulnerable—continuously susceptible to violation or deformation. (Introduction, pp. 21–22)

An experienced and passionately committed actor himself, Cassavetes came to understand how limited the stock forms of illustrative characterization really are, and found his own way to catalyze characters with an astonishingly truthful degree of volatility. As with Robert Altman, actors longed to work with Cassavetes, as they do with other actor-centered directors.

DEVELOPMENT

No story will move us much unless its main character has to struggle, grow in awareness, and change. This is called a character's *development*. You will need at least one character showing some degree of development, or the story will feel pointless. The development of a short film's main character may be only minor and symbolic, but the fact that it exists is the sign of mature storytelling. A feature film, being longer, will have far more complex architecture.

Stories in which a character learns something have always existed. In a world often cruel and heartless, they are a source of hope—something we often need.

DIALOGUE AND VERBAL ACTION

How does one recognize good dialogue? How does a writer create characters that don't all speak in the writer's voice?

Cinema dialogue aims to be vernacular speech. Whether the character is an immigrant waitress, a young hood, or an academic philosopher, each uses their own speech—broken English, street slang, or jargon-laden abstractions. Each needs his or her own dialogue characteristics, so writing dialogue is an art in itself. Vocabulary, syntax, and verbal rhythms for each character have to be special and unlike another's. Dialogue must never replicate what the camera already shows us (such as, "I see you're wearing your heavy coat"). Dialogue in life and dialogue in movies are different: in the cinema, it must sound true to life yet exclude life's verbosity and repetitiousness. The best cinema dialogue is highly succinct, but just as informal and authentically "incorrect."

Getting this right takes exacting research and a special ear. Superb models are everywhere available to anyone armed with a sound recorder. By transcribing everything you eavesdrop—complete with ums, ers, laughs, grunts, and pauses—it is apparent that normal conversation is not normal at all. People converse elliptically, often at cross-purposes and never in the tidy ping-pong of stereotypical drama. In real life, little is denoted (said directly) and much connoted (alluded to in a roundabout way). Silences are often the real "action" during which extraordinary currents flow between the speakers.

By editing the transcripts, you can remove what is redundant, yet retain, or even strengthen, all the individual's sense and idiosyncrasies. Reduced to essence, characters become more strongly defined and their subtexts more vibrant. This is the secret of masters such as Harold Pinter or Samuel Beckett, and also of any good mimic or comedian. By truly listening they capture the keys to other people's behavior and thinking.

TESTING DIALOGUE

The best way to assess dialogue is to read the lines aloud, listening to the sound of your own voice and asking:

- Is every word and every phrase in the character's own vernacular?
- What is this character trying to do or get with these words?
- Does the dialogue carry a compelling subtext (that is, a deeper underlying connotation)?
- Is what it hides interesting?
- Could it be made more subtextual (allusive and indirect) instead of "on the nose" (evident and obvious)?
- Does it make the listener speculate or respond emotionally?
- Is there a better balance of words or sounds?
- Can it be briefer by even one syllable?

It's a good practice to scan through the script, reading the dialogue of only one main character to see how consistently he or she is realized. It also helps you concentrate on the clues this person generates.

VERBAL ACTION

The best dialogue is *verbal action* because the speaker *uses words to get something*. It is pressure applied even as it seeks to deflect pressures the speaker is experiencing. Active and structurally indispensable to the scene, it is never verbal arabesque or an editorial explanation of what is visible. Least of all is it verbal padding.

CHECKING THE FOUNDATIONS

A screenplay hides more than it shows. It specifies situations and dialogue, but offers little about point of view—that is, about the subjective attitudes to be conveyed through acting, camera work, and editing. Still less does it explain the subtexts, ideas, and authorial vantage point we are supposed to infer and that presumably moved the writer in the first place. These are always hidden, and to uncover them, experienced filmmakers generate three different summaries of increasing brevity: the step outline, the treatment, and the premise.

STEP OUTLINE

A step outline aims to extract the essence of the story in a summary form. In a few words, it tells each scene's setting, action, and the overall content of any conversation. It:

- Is told in short-story, third-person, present-tense form.
- Includes only what the audience will see and hear from the screen.

- Allots one numbered paragraph to each sequence (block of time or action in one location).
- Summarizes conversations and never gives them verbatim.

It should read as a stream-of-consciousness summation that never digresses into production details or authorial comments. Stick to what the audience will see and hear, and any dialogue exchanges should be summarized as in the example below.

Step Outline for THE OARSMAN

1. At night, between the high walls of an Amsterdam canal, a murky figure in black tails and top hat rows an ornate coffin in a strange, high boat. In a shaft of light, we see that MORRIE is a man in his late 30s whose expression is set, serene, distant.
2. Looking down on the city at night, we see a panoramic view over black canals glittering with lights and reflections, bridges busy with pedestrian and bike traffic, and streetcars snaking among crooked, leaning, 17th-century buildings. As the view comes to rest on a street, we hear a noisy bar atmosphere where, in the foreground, a Canadian woman and a Dutch man are arguing fiercely.
3. Inside the fairly rough bar with its wooden tables, wooden floor strewn with peanut shells, and wooden bar with a line of old china beer spouts, is JASMINE, a tough but attractive young Canadian in her late 20s. She is trying to leave the bar during a bitter argument with her tattooed and drugged-looking Dutch boyfriend, MARCO. She says she's had enough.

Each numbered sequence is a step in the story's progression. Doing this will produce a bird's-eye view of the balance and progression of the material and alert you to any changes that are necessary.

TREATMENT

A treatment is a narrative version written in present-tense, short-story form that according to its purpose can be any length, from 1 page to 80. It, too, concentrates on rendering what the audience will see and hear, and summarizes dialogue exchanges, though an especially important exchange might be given verbatim inside quotation marks.

Briefer than a screenplay, but longer, more lyrical, and more informative than a step outline, the treatment is the screenwriter's chance to get a script considered by a particular individual or production company. The treatment allows the writer to fully visualize the story; outline the characters and their interactions; explain the conflict and resolution in the plot; and sketch in important subtexts, moods, and other vital aspects of the overall vision. A treatment can also evoke the tone of the film—whether it's gritty and streetwise, melodramatic, nostalgic, urban and edgy, and so on. If your writer has prepared a full treatment of this kind, you will have much to discuss from the outset. A practical, market-oriented resource is Kenneth Atchity and Chi-Li Wong's *Writing Treatments That Sell: How to Create and Market Your Story Ideas to the Motion Picture and TV Industry*, 2nd ed. (Owl Books, 2003).

PREMISE

The screenplay, treatment, and step outline still do not directly articulate the paradigm underpinning the film's dramatic structure and development. This, called the *premise* or *concept*, is a sentence or two that expresses the dramatic idea underlying either a single scene or a whole movie. For Robert Altman's *Gosford Park* (2001), it might be, "A leader or magnate who uses his power corruptly will eventually be toppled, no matter how far-reaching his authority and no matter how cynically he buys off his supporters."

Like so much else in this organic process called filmmaking, the premise often mutates as you develop the material's potential.

ASSESS AND REASSESS

When a screenplay goes through rewrites, always update your step outline, treatment, and premise, or you will not stay on top of the piece as a whole. Quite likely your work is subtly adopting a changing identity and even a new thematic focus. This is a truly magical aspect of narrative art.

WITH THE AUDIENCE IN MIND

You will always need to consider your audience. This means not exploiting them or making cynical compromises, but trying to conceive a work that investigates some contemporary dilemma, prompts pertinent questions and ideas, and challenges conventional thought. When you succeed, it resonates afterward in the hearts and minds of your audience.

CHAPTER 9

DIRECTOR'S DEVELOPMENT STRATEGIES

Screen works are too expensive and inflexible to test and improve as playwrights do with their first audiences, so this must be accomplished during the script development and cast rehearsal periods. It may involve simplifying, cutting, compressing, or expanding the material, or even wholesale rewriting to take advantage of the way players realize the piece. Feature films I worked on delivered new script pages down to the day of shooting. Writers loathe this compulsive rewriting, but their ideas of completion arise from habits of solo creation. Filmmaking is an organic, physical process that must adapt to the unfolding reality of cast and shooting.

Only by sustained and methodical script development can the director fully inhabit every aspect of the story, explore all its potential, and capitalize on the cinema's strengths.

STORY LOGIC

EXPOSITION AND ESTABLISHING

While developing a story, you work from experience, imagination, and intuition, as well as from assumptions stored in the unconscious. Miscommunication begins from assumptions you make that your audience can't share. What you need is timely *exposition;* that is, information vital to understanding each stage of the narrative. It might be important to know that Harry, the man with the red hair, is brother to the blonde woman with two small children, or that Harry would never perjure himself in court. The screenwriter knows that Harry is honest, but her audience knows nothing of the sort. Harry's openness must be *established*—a frequent word in script discussions. To do this, you might make him return to pay for the newspaper he has unthinkingly carried out with his groceries. Now he's shown how honest he is.

DELAYING EXPOSITION

A story is a progression of events that raises questions and offers clues. For instance, a film about a man adopted in childhood who searches for his biological mother won't remain credible if he fails to look for his birth certificate and never questions his foster parents. These are basic steps. You must either show or establish these things some other way, for we need to know that they yielded no satisfactory result. Later, when the adoptee finds his mother, it would be equally illogical for him to become happy and fulfilled. The audience knows that people meeting their biological parents for the first time have very mixed emotions, not least pain and anger. Immediate and lasting euphoria is foreign to human nature. Either the character or the moviemaker is naive—and if it's the latter, the audience, seeing it's a dumb story, moves on.

You must eventually answer all the audience's expectations, but often you will delay revealing their full significance to keep dramatic tension high. Test the design of your story logic by making notes of the underlying assumptions. Add these to your step outline or treatment in a special column reserved for intended audience questions and realizations (see example in Chapter 7, Figure 7-3). This will help you avoid answering issues too quickly, leaving the audience wondering too long, or failing to resolve something at all.

CREDIBILITY, MOOD, AND ENLISTING THE AUDIENCE

The story and its characters must be interesting, representative, and consistent if they are to remain credible. Other genres, such as documentary or folktale, are hardly less free; each is true in some important way to the spirit of reality, and all are governed by what the audience recognizes as "true." Paradoxically, coincidences that occur freely in life become suspect in fiction. Nobody would accept in a fiction film what once happened to me in life: while visiting friends in Belgrade, I ran into the only other Serb I knew. She happened to be visiting from London, and happened to go to the same theater performance that my friends and I did.

Because successful storytelling depends on creating tension and anticipation, adept storytellers withhold whatever they can and as long as possible.

WORK TO CREATE A SUCCESSION OF MOODS

Settings that are bland or unbelievable compel the audience to struggle with unbelief at every scene change. But use locations and sound composition evocatively, and you can hurl the audience into the emotional heart of a situation.

Whenever you are out and about, note down any place or situation that makes an impact. Later, these can be incorporated into what you film. Like actors, good dramatists pay close attention to their surroundings and are constantly observing and researching in pursuit of their work. Memorable art comes from paying closer attention to reality.

CREATING SPACE FOR THE AUDIENCE

The only way to satisfy your audience is to make films for people whose values and intelligence are much like yours. Some entertainers naturally share much with the greater world; some share less. Popularity is nothing you can plan. All you can do is develop your potential, take risks, and be true to your deepest interests.

A story can be told through literature, song, stage, or screen—but in each case, the successful storyteller creates significant spaces that the audience must fill from its own experience. Unlike the reader of a novel, film spectators do not have to visualize the physical world of the story, so it's all the more important that you provide the impetus to speculate about the characters' motives, feelings, values, and morals. Just as a painting implies life beyond the edges of its frame, so dramatic characters and the ideas they engender should suggest more than we see and hear in the movie.

PLANNING ACTION

A script's issues will sometimes be handled verbally when they could be translated into actions. For example, in a breakfast scene, while a father gives his young son a sermon about homework, you could work out "business" (the acting term for characteristic action) in which the boy tries to rearrange and balance the cutlery and cereal boxes. The father, trying to get his full attention, attempts to stop him. Though we don't see the precise subject in dispute, a conflict between them has been externalized as action.

As a matter of craft, try to substitute action for every issue handled verbally. This may require the rewriting that is a director's prerogative (and a screenwriter's notion of crass sabotage). It may need minimal facial action, it may be movement and activities of a revealing metaphorical nature, or it may be movement that an actor will find heightens tension by concealing rather than revealing his character's true feelings. Such suppression is very human; it reveals inner and outer dimensions, the conscious and the unconscious, the public and the private. The antithesis of this principle is the script in which a tide of descriptive verbiage drowns whatever might be alive and at issue, as here:

> ROSE
> Uncle, I thought I'd just look in and see
> how you are doing. It's so miserable to be
> bedridden. You're Dad's only brother, and
> I want to look after you, if only for his sake.

> UNCLE
> You're such a good girl. I always feel
> better when you look in. I thought I heard
> your footsteps, but I wasn't sure it was
> you. It must be cold outside—you're
> wearing your heavy coat.

> ROSE
> You are looking better, but I see you still
> aren't finishing your meals. It makes me
> sad to see you leave an apple as good as
> this when you normally like them so much.

UNCLE
I know, dear, and it makes me feel almost
guilty. But I'm just not myself.

I wrote this to show the worst abominations. Notice the redundancies, how the
writing keeps the characters static, how there is no behavior to signify feelings,
and no private thought that is separate or different from the public utterances.
Neither character signifies any of the feelings or hidden agenda that gives human
interaction its tension and rich undercurrents. Even between people who like each
other, there are always tensions and conflicts. But this writing grips the audience
in a vice of literalness, and lacks even the unspoken understandings that the
observer might infer. Most damning of all, you'd miss nothing by closing your
eyes. It is like bad soap opera.

By reconceiving this scene to include behavior, action, and interaction, you
could prune the dialogue by 80 percent and end up with something animated by
more tensions. If the scene has to reveal that the old man is brother to Rose's
father, there must be a more natural way for this to emerge. At the moment, editorial information issues from her mouth like ticker tape. Perhaps we could make
her stop in her tracks to stare at him. When he looks questioningly back, she
answers, "It must be the light. Sometimes you look so much like Dad." His
reaction—whether of amusement, irritation, or nostalgia—then gives clues to the
relationship between the brothers.

THE DISPLACEMENT PRINCIPLE

In life, people very rarely deal directly with the true source of their tensions. This
is because we seldom know them ourselves, or we keep what we do know hidden
from those around us. What should happen in drama is often thus a displacement
or an alternative to the characters' underlying desires. Two elderly men may be
talking gloomily about the weather, but from what has gone before, or from telltale hints, we realize that one is adjusting to the death of a family member, and the
other is trying to bring up the subject of some money owed to him. What they say
is that the heat and humidity might lead to a storm, but what we infer is that Ted
is enclosed by feelings of guilt and loss, whereas Harry is realizing that once again
he cannot ask for the money he badly needs. This is the scene's subtext, which we
can define as, "Harry realizes he cannot bring himself to intrude his needs upon
Ted at this moment, and his situation is now desperate."

The subtexts here cannot emerge without important knowledge established
in earlier scenes, and thus well-conceived drama builds and interconnects its
subtexts.

INVITING A CRITICAL RESPONSE

Exposing your work at different stages to criticism from listeners, readers, or
screen audiences will help confirm how well you are reaching a first-time audience. Confirming through *pitching* that you are on target isn't difficult; on the
contrary, it is usually energizing.

PITCHING YOUR STORY

When you are looking for cast members, crew, or financial backing, you will have to repeatedly "sell" a current project. The expression "pitching" comes from baseball, and means rapidly and attractively explaining the essentials of a screen story. You may get 10 minutes to convey a feature screenplay in professional situations, and 20 minutes maximum for a pitch to studio executives. You should be able to pitch a 5- to 20-minute film in 3 to 5 minutes.

Pitching is seldom easy or comfortable, but it's always an excellent workout for you and your project. There is no set formula, and part of the challenge is to handle the idea in the way that best suits it. What you must convey is your passion and belief in the special qualities of the story. Here's what you might cover for a short film:

- Title and brief overview (Example: "This story is called *Deliverance,* and is about four urban businessmen celebrating freedom by canoeing through unspoiled Appalachia. When they discover they are the prey of degenerate, vengeful mountain men, each must put notions of manhood to the test as they struggle against the odds to survive.")
- Genre (that is, what type the film is—mystery, horror, domestic comedy, etc.)
- Main character and problems he or she faces in life generally
- Main character's specific problem or predicament
- Obstacles main character must overcome
- Why these obstacles matter, what is at stake, and why an audience should give a damn
- Changes the main character undergoes
- Resolution: how he or she is at the end
- Cinematic qualities that make the film special
- Why this is a film that you can and must make

Pitch to anyone who will listen. From each new listener's face, attitude, and body language, you will quickly know when your idea is gripping and when it fails. When some aspect is not working, keep changing it until you get it right. These are your first audiences; if they light up, you have worked out the basics for a good story. Keep going until your audience reaction confirms that every aspect of your story is masterful.

SEEKING RESPONSES

To shoot an imperfectly developed screenplay is to open a Pandora's box of problems. Trying to cure them later, as they become apparent in the editing stage, is heartbreaking. As with the initial idea for a film, seek responses to the screenplay:

- Find mature readers whose values you share and respect.
- Ask what he or she understands from the script.
- Ask what the characters are like and whom the reader likes.
- Ask what seems to be driving the characters, what they are each trying to achieve.
- Ask which scenes are effective.

- Ask which are not effective.
- Keep your critics on track; you can't get involved in the film the respondent would have made.

From this, you aim to acquire a complete and accurate sense of what your audience knows and feels at each stage of the proposed film. Critical readers will have to be replaced as they become familiar with the material.

TESTING WITH A SCRATCH CAST

Large cities with a theater community often hold very useful screenplay readings and critique each other's work. Actors and theater organizations usually know about such facilities, as do film schools and film cooperatives. So before you lock down your script, assemble a scratch cast to read the script to a small, invited audience that will tell you candidly what they think. Each actor, however inexperienced, will identify with one character and show your script in an unfamiliar light. In discussion with both actors and audience, you should be able to wholeheartedly justify every word of dialogue and every stage direction in the script. Often, of course, you cannot because you discover something new. That's the purpose of the dramatic reading.

INCORPORATING CRITICISM

Act Only After Reflection

In a mass medium, the director must work for understanding by a wide audience, and this begins with your first critics. If you resist all criticisms of your current project, you are probably insecure. If you agree with almost everything and set about a total rewrite—or worse, scrap the project—it means you are very insecure. If, however, you continue to believe in what you are doing, but recognize some truth in what your critics say, you are progressing nicely.

Never make changes hastily or impulsively. Let the criticism lie for a few days, then see what your mind has accepted as valid. If still in doubt, delay changes and don't abandon your intentions. Work on something else until your mind quietly insists on what must be done.

Be cautious about responses from family or intimates. They often want to hide your faults and naïveté from public view. Almost as damaging is their loving, across-the-board praise. Show your work to friends and family only once it's finished, and then only in the company of a general audience, whose responses will lead your friends and family in theirs. Many artists get only resistance and dissuasion from their family until they hear an audience clapping.

DON'T TAKE CRITICISM PERSONALLY

Your work is not you; it is only the work you did at a particular moment in your life, an interim representation. The next piece will show changes; it will be a little stronger and sharper. François Truffaut admitted late in life that it is as hard to make a bad film as a good one, and he became a kinder critic after experiencing the failures that prepare us to succeed. The integrity and perseverance of the explorer is what matters, so keep going, no matter what.

EXPANDING AND COLLAPSING THE SCREENPLAY

Working in screenplay format means the basic structure becomes obscured, particularly from its progenitor. When a screenplay presents problems (and which one doesn't?), making a step outline from it reveals, as we have said, the plot and inherent structure. Doing this and then further reducing the step outline to a ruling premise are vital steps in testing the validity of a story's foundations.

REWRITE, REWRITE, REWRITE!

A script is not an artwork with a final form, but more like invasion plans that need repeatedly altering in light of fresh intelligence. Be willing to keep developing the screenplay right down to the first day of shooting. Rewriting is frequently omitted or resisted by student production groups because nobody wants to threaten the writer's ego.

When a writer delivers a script in the professional world, he or she relinquishes control of it. There is, of course, good reason for this: director and producer may take over the script and alter it as necessary. In any community of unpaid equals, you may need to be considerably more diplomatic. Have compassion for any writers who must relinquish their work—the profession's path is littered with stones, and happy writers are about as common as happy taxpayers.

FUND-RAISING AND WRITING THE PROSPECTUS

The prospectus is a piece of writing that greatly affects your success in arousing interest and finding funds. Space allows just an overview here, but two helpful books in this area are Louise Levison's *Filmmakers and Financing: Business Plans for Independents,* 5th ed. (Focal Press, 2006) and Morrie Warshawski's *Shaking the Money Tree: How to Get Grants and Donations for Film and Television,* 2nd ed. (Michael Wiese Productions, 2003).

The prospectus is a presentation package or portfolio that describes your project, its purposes, and its personnel. The prospectus aims to create enthusiasm through the eloquence of the arguments and detail it presents. It should be as graphic, personable, tasteful, and word perfect as anything that would make you linger in a bookstore. The prospectus should contain:

Cover letter: This succinctly communicates the nature of the film, its budget, the capital you want to raise, and what you want from the addressee. If you are targeting many small investors, this may have to be a general letter, but fashion a specific letter to a specific individual wherever possible.

Title page: Finding a good title usually takes inordinate effort, but does more than anything else to arouse respect and interest. Evocative photos or other professional-looking artwork here can do much to make your presentation exciting and professional.

Logline or *one-liner:* A simple, compact declaration of the project. Some examples:

- A woman in a small New England town discovers that her husband is gay, and thus she must conquer what it means to be alone as she starts a new life.

- Four 12-year-old friends cut school for a day to find a home for a pony they mistakenly think is unwanted.

- A 40-year-old man conspires to leave his possessive mother and marry the woman of his dreams—who is in prison for something she didn't do.

Synopsis: Brief recounting of the story that captures its flavor and style.

History and background: How and why the project evolved and why you feel compelled to make this film. Here is the place to establish your commitment.

Research: Outline what research you've done and what it contributes. Include stills of locations or actors that will help establish the look of your film. This is the opportunity to establish the factual foundation to the film if there is one, as well as its characters and their context. If special cooperation, rights, or permissions are involved, show that you've secured them.

Budget: Summary of main expected expenditures. Don't understate or underestimate—it makes you look amateurish and leaves you asking for too little.

Schedule: Day-by-day plan for shooting period and preferred starting dates. If you want to be taken seriously in professional circles, your budgeting and scheduling must be done using professional software, and presented in industry-standard format (see Chapter 27, "The Preproduction Meeting and Deciding Equipment").

Cast: Pictures and résumés of intended cast members, paying special attention to their prior credits.

Résumés of creative personnel: In brief paragraphs, name the main creative personnel and summarize their qualifications. Append a one-page résumé from each. Your aim is to present the team as professional, committed, exciting, and specially suited.

Copy of screenplay: This is optional because most potential investors don't have the expertise to make sense of a bare-bones screenplay. The fact that it exists and looks fully professional may be a deciding factor for some. If the screenplay is an adaptation, be explicit that you have secured the rights to film it.

Audience and market: Say what particular audience the film is intended for, and outline a distribution plan to show that the film has a waiting audience. Copies of letters of interest from distributors or other interested parties are helpful here.

Financial statement: Outline your financial identity as a company or group and make an estimate of income based on the distribution plan. If you are a not-for-profit company, or are working through one, say so. This may permit investors to claim tax breaks.

Means of transferring funds: To save potential investors from having to compose a letter, enclose a sample letter from an investor to your company that commits funds to your production account.

If you approach foundations or other funding agencies, bear in mind that:

- Each will have its preferred form of presentation. Research the fund's identity and track record to know how best to present your work.

- Every grant application is potentially the beginning of a lengthy relationship, so everything you send should be consistent and professional in tone.

- Though each prospectus is tailored for different addressees, be careful not to promise different things to different people.

- Your prospectus should have professional-looking graphics and typesetting.
- Have everything triple-checked for spelling or other errors. You are what you write, so use the best available stationery and printing equipment.
- When in discussion with a fund, always write to a named individual and include a reminder of your project and your history with them to date.

THE RISE OF THE ENTREPRENEURIAL PRODUCER

Since the cinema's inception, its overwhelming strength, success, and relevance have come from the process's division of labor. This additive process of creation, in which the whole is greater than the sum of its parts, tempers each contribution with checks and balances that are vital in an audience medium. The latest development in film schools is training the entrepreneurial producer. He or she is educated to specialize in the business (yes, it's a business) of getting projects afloat, and is not a frustrated director or a frustrated anything else. Producers in independent filmmaking not only manage money and do the public relations legwork, they also shop for promising scripts, develop creative teams around them, and work out the business model that makes the production a viable venture. This means working at the fund-raising, co-funding, and presales that today make professional filmmaking possible.

The Brussels-based international association of film schools CILECT initiated the Triangle Project expressly to develop the kind of entrepreneurial partnerships that lie behind many successful European films.[1] Their favored model is a three-person team of producer, screenwriter, and director. The Triangle Project aims to cultivate collaborative teams that have several projects in development at any time, rather than the traditional approach, which bets the bank on a single horse. There is wide support for these cultural shifts. For instance, my college has an undergraduate producing program that includes residential study and internship in Los Angeles (see the Semester in LA program via www.filmatcolumbia.com).

1. See Centre International de Liaison des Écoles de Cinéma et de Télévision— www.cilect.org.

CHAPTER 10

ALTERNATIVE STORY SOURCES

First-rate screenplays are forever in short supply, so here are some other sources.

ADAPTING FROM LITERATURE

There is a constantly growing supply of plays, novels, and short stories that might adapt well to the screen. Good literature can, however, be a quicksand if you assume that the story will make an equally fine film. Effective adaptation may actually be impossible if you can find no cinematic equivalent for the author's writing style and literary form. A story that relies on a subtly ironic storytelling voice, for instance, might be a bad choice because there is no such thing as ironic photography or recording.

Most of the criteria for judging material for an adaptation remain the same as those used to assess any script:

- Does it tell its tale through externally visible, behavioral means?
- Does it have interesting, well-developed characters?
- Is it contained and specific in settings?
- Are the situations interesting and realizable?
- Is there an interesting major conflict, and is it externally dramatized rather than internal?
- Does the conflict imply interesting metaphors?
- Does the piece have a strong thematic purpose?
- Can you wholeheartedly identify with its theme?
- Can you invent a cinematic equivalency for the story's literary values?
- Can you afford to do it?
- Is the copyright available?

COPYRIGHT CLEARANCE

If you make an adaptation bearing a likeness to its original, you must procure the legal right to use it. Copyright law changes periodically. In the United States, you can obtain current information from the Copyright Office, Library of Congress, Washington, D.C. 20559 (www.copyright.gov/). Many works published longer than 56 years ago are old enough to be in the public domain, but do not assume this without careful inquiry, preferably through a copyright lawyer. The laws are extremely complicated, especially concerning a literary property's clearance in other countries.

ACTOR-CENTERED FILMS AND THEIR SCRIPTS

To create believable life on the screen and expose contemporary issues, you above all need credible characters. Low-budget filmmakers face a problem right away, for unsophisticated or untrained actors tend to model their performances not on life but on notions of what other admired actors do. So they signify a character's feelings and "perform" at the mass audience they imagine just beyond the camera lens. Your audience is not taken in, for they know the real thing when they see it. So you must work with each actor to break through to something that is true and moving on the screen. Good film acting looks like *being*, not like acting at all. As a matter of survival, you must liberate the potential of each of your actors. Your film can survive indifferent film technique, but nothing can rescue it from lousy acting—not good color, not good music, not good photography, not good editing. None of these—separately or combined—can change the inherent human qualities that your camera puts on the screen.

Even an untrained cast is a potential gold mine, yet seldom do filmmakers make the text respond to the actors who bring it alive. Most maintain the industry's unidirectional assembly-line operation, even though actors as professional as Jessica Lange believe there's something really wrong with Hollywood norms. She deplores the film industry's refusal to invest in rehearsal time so actors can develop the emotional lives of their characters (see *American Film*, June 1987). Your problem will be far worse if your cast know neither each other nor the film process when you begin shooting.

If you are to lower anxiety levels and build an ensemble that can be playful in its seriousness, you need to plan activities through which cast and script can evolve. Through careful and intensive rehearsal, improvisation work, and honest discussion, you can explore the ideas and emotional transitions in the script and liberate that magic quality of spontaneity. Techniques useful for this kind of work appear throughout Part 5: Preproduction, and particularly in Chapter 19, Acting Improvisation Exercises. You may also find inspiration in Per Zetterfalk's *Norén's Drama* (2006), a documentary about the two-year process by which Sweden's premier playwright Lars Norén realizes his 66th play, *Chill*. As an interview with the playwright reveals, the inspiration for the play came from a deeply humiliating bullying incident in his boyhood. The piece is about three menacing skinheads' hate-filled humiliation of an Asian youth who has wandered into their presence in a forest. The film provides rare insight into a director/writer's process of developing a text while working inductively with his excellent actors. The

DVD, subtitled in English, is available through Noble Entertainment at www. cdon.com.

Here are more scripting methods that use human beings as well as the keyboard. Though nontraditional, they are used by significant filmmakers and can yield significant results.

IDEATION: THREE NONTRADITIONAL WAYS TO START A SCRIPT

METHOD #1: A THEMATIC CORE

Suppose you want to make a film about the ordeal of a young man leaving home. Its characters are a close family with a possessive, autocratic father. You find a live-wire cast, and with your central character begin exploring the core idea. Leaving home and—for parents—letting go of children are such universal experiences that many cast members have strong feelings on the subject. You pose the right questions, and draw out their issues and residual experiences. Each actor's ideas and life experience will be engaged in developing your thematic concerns. As you uncover charged situations, your cast can experimentally play them out. As this happens, consistent characters take shape from each player. As they appear, they demand greater clarity and background. You and your cast will turn from ideas to character development, from character development inevitably to situations, and from situations and characters to creating the specific past events—personal, cultural, political—that seeded each character's present. From the tensions and conflicts your cast members carry within, you can form a fictional world that belongs to everyone taking part. Later, you transcribe rehearsals and then use your script editor skills to tighten the results.

The Dogme Group developed films in this actor-centered way, and so did that icon of European cinema, Ingmar Bergman. He had this to say about the traditional screenplay:

> If . . . I were to reproduce in words what happens in the film I have conceived, I would be forced to write a bulky book of little readable value and great nuisance. I have neither the talent nor the patience for a heroic exercise of that kind.
>
> Besides, such a procedure would kill all creative joy for both me and the artists. (Introduction, *Four Stories by Ingmar Bergman* [New York: Doubleday, 1977])

Bergman developed many of his films from annotated short stories. For his unforgettable portrait of four sisters in crisis, *Cries and Whispers* (1972, Figure 10-1), he supplied notes about the artistic approach, intended characters and their situations, settings, and time period. There are also fragments from Agnes' diary, details of a dream, and the dialogue and narrative of the events. Bergman hands these materials to his intended cast, and the developmental work begins from discussion and assimilation of their possibilities. Much of the creation of characters and action then lies with actors whose careers and talents (and children!) Bergman has been instrumental in developing.

FIGURE 10-1 ——

The script for *Cries and Whispers* was developed from director's notes and improvisational work with the cast (courtesy Cinematographs/Svenska Filminstitutet/The Kobal Collection).

In Britain, Mike Leigh uses a similar process. He, too, comes from the theater, and bases his work on particular actors. *High Hopes* (1988, Figure 10-2) and *Life Is Sweet* (1991) are comedies of character. They make a poignant critique of an English working class struggling to adapt and survive at a time when the mainstays of dignity—work and a place in the order of things—were vanishing. From bittersweet comedies, his work developed a darker strain with *Naked* (1993), an apocalyptic vision of characters lost and in torment in a London where the havenots roam the streets like hungry, wounded wolves.

METHOD #2: CHARACTER-BASED CORE

A more open-ended method is to start, not from a social theme or idea, but from a mood or from the personality of individual cast members. If "character is fate," let your characters develop their fates. By first getting each actor to generate an absorbing character, and then by letting situations grow out of the clashes and alliances of these characters, themes and issues inevitably surface. A project like this is good for a theater company used to working together, or as a follow-up film project when the cast and director have come to trust each other and want to go on working together (not always the case!).

In the United States, actor-director John Cassavetes gave primacy to his actors. He had them improvise completely in *Shadows* (1959) and *Faces* (1968), and used a written script and structured improvisations for *A Woman Under the Influence* (1974, Figure 10-3). Cassavetes and his wife—actress Gena Rowlands, who plays the wife—wanted to dramatize what happens in a blue-collar Italian

FIGURE 10-2

High Hopes is a character-driven comedy about people struggling to adapt to reduced circumstances (courtesy Portman/Film 4/The Kobal Collection).

American family when women's liberation ideas break through. The wife sees that her role as wife and mother is preventing her from growing into an autonomous adult. "The emotion was improvised," said Cassevetes, "but the lines were written." Gena Rowlands' performance is powerful and disturbing, but as in many films incorporating improvisation, the film suffers from uneven pacing, bouts of self-consciously bravura acting, and an uncertainty of structure.

A boat with several oarsmen needs a firm hand on the tiller, and directing a project of this nature takes subtlety, patience, and the authority to make binding decisions. Dramatically, the results may be a mixed bag, but the process is certain to build rapport among cast and director. The cast retains what is successful by consensus, and what began as improvisation gradually morphs into a mutually agreed text. What is truly fascinating is that it reinvents how folk drama must have evolved over the centuries.

Characters and their issues might be developed from the nature and resonance of a particular location, such as a deserted gravel pit, waiting room in an underground parking garage, or street market. Very potent is the site of a historical event, such as a field where strikers were gunned down or the house where a woman who had apocalyptic visions grew up. History is a potent source of inspiration.

Experiments of this kind are excellent for building the cast's confidence so they can play scripted parts with unself-conscious abandonment. Once they have the daring to act upon that priceless commodity, intuition, their work generates energy and ideas. When the dramatic output is rounded up and analyzed, a longer work can be structured.

FIGURE 10-3

A Woman Under the Influence—"The emotion was improvised, but the lines were written" (courtesy Faces International/The Kobal Collection/Shaw, Sam).

METHOD #3: EVENT-CENTERED CORE

In 1960s Britain, theater companies turned their backs on cocktail plays in favor of more explosive local issues. In the cinema worldwide, local-issue fiction could similarly emerge as the equivalent of the regional novel. Amber Films has done this in the industrial north of England (www.amber-online.com/html/index.html) with *Eden Valley* (1994) and *Like Father* (2001).

In America as elsewhere, there are a host of obstacles standing in the way of this, but the main one is the sheer lack of proficiency in filmmaking outside the few metropolitan areas where films are produced. Most regional film production remains imitative and third-rate. In Chicago, the world-class company Steppenwolf Theatre is using its nationally recognized cast to move into filmmaking. This has happened before. In England, the Royal Court Theatre and the Free Cinema movement informally combined to produce Karel Reisz' *Saturday Night and Sunday Morning* (1960); Tony Richardson's *A Taste of Honey* (1961), on which I worked as a cutting room assistant; Lindsay Anderson's *This Sporting Life* (1963); and a number of other impassioned films about a society in upheaval.

In Germany, Rainer Werner Fassbinder and the fine actress Hanna Schygulla, who played in his *Marriage of Maria Braun* (1978, Figure 10-4), emerged from the Munich Action-Theater, later to become the Anti-Theater. The company made no fewer than six of Fassbinder's early films. His short, astonishingly prolific film career was rooted in creating instant theater from personal or contemporary political issues.

FIGURE 10-4 ——

In *The Marriage of Maria Braun*, Fassbinder creates a sardonic history of postwar Germany through the opportunistic career of its heroine (courtesy Trio/Albatros/WDR/The Kobal Collection).

If issue-based films can be generated in London and Munich from experienced casts (sometimes with nonactors too), why not elsewhere? Let's imagine how that might be done. In Chicago, where I live, the steel industry has gone silent, and the hardworking ethnic communities that clustered around it have taken a body blow. The Michigan automotive industry is going the same way, and the generations who earned their slice of the American Dream see heavy industry dying in every Western country. What happens when people whose sense of worth is founded in hard, dirty, repetitive labor have no more work? What happens to their sons and daughters? How do they explain their losses? What do some of them gain? What changes between men and women, and between generations?

You read articles and interviews, and visit union leaders, local historians, doctors, and clergymen. You talk to unemployed factory workers and their families, and find that the story has become diffuse and complicated. Some still live on false hope. Some drink too much. Some have found new lives. Others, to satisfy their work ethic, have taken meaningless jobs that pay a fraction of what they earned before. The women may earn as much or more than the men, and the whole family dynamic has changed. Young people stay if they don't have the resources to escape, or go off to college and guiltily abandon friends and family to their decaying neighborhood.

So much is happening in this situation that you will have to decide what or who is really interesting and accessible, and make a dramatic construct to contain it. You begin to imagine a representative family whose members are composites inspired by real people. You make a list of life events spanning years for this family.

Covering half a lifetime is something fiction does rather well. Here are some key events:

- Father loses job.
- Believes his skills will soon be needed elsewhere.
- No job comes; no job can be found.
- Scenes of mounting economic and emotional pressure in the family.
- Mother finds a job as a checkout clerk at a supermarket.
- Daughter begins going to a college downtown.
- Daughter becomes increasingly critical of her family and its assumptions.
- Son drops out of high school and hangs out on street corners, identifying more and more with racist gang messages of revenge and hatred.

We have built up a series of pressures. Now we need ideas about how these pressures will resolve, what kind of contortions this family and this bereaved community are going to suffer, and what "coming out the other side" may mean. A fictionalized treatment of these very real circumstances must, therefore, have an element of prediction to propose to its audience, a prediction about the way human beings handle slow-motion catastrophe.

Becoming a social analyst or prophet is an exciting job to give yourself. Do it well and you will arouse much interest, but you'll need the abilities of a journalist, sociologist, documentarian, and novelist to make it work. But look what is already available: a host of characters to play minor roles; a landscape of windswept,

FIGURE 10-5

In the very successful comedy *The Full Monty*, lumbering factory hands set out to develop a new job for themselves as strippers (courtesy Fox Searchlight/The Kobal Collection).

rusting factories and rows of peeling houses; and a circuit of bars, dance halls, and ethnic churches with their weddings, christenings, and funerals. Sound too depressing? Then go to the amateur comedian contests and cast a dad who in real life is an aspiring stand-up comic. The community where you are going to film has all sorts of regular activities to use as a backdrop, and within the wide bounds of the possible, you can make the characters do and be anything you want.

People who lose their jobs, providing they are resilient, sometimes say afterward when they have found a new life, "That was awful and it hurt—but looking back, it was the best thing that ever happened to me." When telling stories, it's important to offer hope, and this resolution is indeed hopeful. One way to sugar the pill is to use the genre of comedy. Britain has had its share of industrial catastrophe, and many recent British comedies, set in similar surroundings, have used humor as leavening for fairly awful situations. Mike Leigh's *Life Is Sweet* (1990), Mark Herman's *Brassed Off* (1996), Peter Cattaneo's *The Full Monty* (1997, Figure 10-5), and Stephen Daldry's *Billy Elliot* (2000) all profiled small-town local characters in failing industrial settings. *The Full Monty* proved universal enough to be recycled as a musical about steelworkers in upstate New York.

What is happening in your area that needs to be understood? A rash of teenage suicides? A cult? A new and dangerous form of racing?

CHAPTER 11

SETTING CREATIVE LIMITATIONS

Making a dramatic film is unavoidably an expensive process with its many industrialized stages made necessary by the pressing need to work efficiently. With a number of well-respected films under his belt—in particular *Leaving Las Vegas* (1995), *Miss Julie* (2000), *Timecode* (2000), and *Hotel* (2001)—Mike Figgis has greeted the scaled-down nature of digital filmmaking with relief:

> The further that I went into the digital world the more intrigued I became with the possibilities of this new and unexplored technology. What started out as a marriage of convenience turned into a love affair. My dissatisfaction with the mainstream cinema scene stems from a deep frustration with the stranglehold that technology has in the 35mm, studio-based film business. Visit any set and you can observe the bullshit at first hand. Observe the reverence with which the camera is treated. The iconic status of the crane and the Steadicam; the vast armada of trucks and motor homes; the platoons of young men and women carrying clip boards and wearing status clothing with walkie talkies and hi-tech communication devices; the sense of self importance and Godliness that seems to permeate everyone involved with the process of pretence and fabrication; the deadly trios of execs and agents feeding their faces at the food table whilst talking on their mobiles to other execs on other films at other food tables. One year later the results of this "holy" labor can be seen in a multiplex anywhere in the world. Another Hollywood film about nothing in particular. (Unpublished interview with Mike Figgis at the Dramatic Institute, Sweden, courtesy of Göran Gunér)

No system or procedure is sacrosanct, and you must make yours adjust to the needs and scale of your production.

THE DOGME GROUP

Restrictions always help art, and setting well-chosen ones will help you focus on what's important. The Danish founding members of the Dogme 95 Cinema

Group[1] began playfully setting up their own rules of limitation in 1995, meaning to break with some of the self-serving rituals of filmmaking that Figgis finds so intrusive. Thomas Vinterberg had this to say:

> We did the "Vow of Chastity" in half an hour, and we had great fun. Yet, at the same time, we felt that in order to avoid the mediocrity of filmmaking not only in the whole community, but in our own filmmaking as well, we had to do something different. We wanted to undress film, turn it back to where it came from and remove the layers of makeup between the audience and the actors. We felt it was a good idea to concentrate on the moment, on the actors and, of course, on the story that they were acting, which are the only aspects left when everything else is stripped away. Also, artistically it has created a very good place for us to be as artists or filmmakers because having obstacles like these means you have something to play against. It encourages you to actually focus on other approaches instead. (Interview by Elif Cercel for Directors World at stage.directorsworld.com)

By redirecting their energies, some group members, in particular Lars von Trier (Figure 11-1), went on to produce films as distinguished as *Breaking the Waves*

FIGURE 11-1

Lars von Trier, a founding member of the innovative Danish Dogme 95 Cinema Group (courtesy The Kobal Collection).

[1] Thomas Vinterberg, Lars von Trier, Christian Levring, and Søren Kragh-Jacobsen.

(Lars von Trier, 1999), *The Celebration* (Thomas Vinterberg, 1998), and *The Idiots* (Lars von Trier, 1999). Their self-imposed restrictions are strikingly similar to those chosen by the famous f/64 photographers' group in 1932.[2] Tired of a photography still seeking legitimacy by emulating painting, they proclaimed that photography would mature only by seeking its own values and rejecting mimicry of other art forms.

Compare this with the Dogme Group's manifesto (slightly edited to put it into vernacular English):

The Dogme Vow of Chastity

- Shooting must be done on location. Props and sets must not be brought in; shooting must go where that set or prop can be found.
- Sound must never be produced separately from the images or vice versa.
- Music must not be used unless it occurs where the scene is shot.
- The camera must be handheld. Any movement or immobility attainable by handholding is permitted. The action cannot be organized for the camera; instead the camera must go to the action.
- The film must be in color. Special lighting is not acceptable, and if there is too little light for exposure, the scene must be cut or a single lamp may be attached to the camera.
- Camera filters and other optical work are forbidden.
- The film must not contain any superficial action such as murders, weapons, explosions, and so on.
- No displacement is permitted in time or space: The film takes place here and now.
- Genre movies are not acceptable.
- Film format is Academy 35 mm.
- The director must not be credited.

Furthermore, I swear as a director to refrain from personal taste. I am no longer an artist. I swear to refrain from creating a "work," as I regard the instant as more important than the whole. My supreme goal is to force the truth out of my characters and settings. I swear to do so by all the means available and at the cost of any good taste and any aesthetic considerations.

Signed _____

---

[2] Edward Weston, Imogen Cunningham, Ansel Adams, and Willard Van Dyke.

By forgoing a leadership hierarchy and outlawing personal taste, the last clause strikes down the ego of the director, and hands preeminence squarely to the cast. The Dogme Group's rules removed some of the self-absorption of filming in favor of greater attention to the cast, who responded handsomely. In practice, any number of contradictions appeared, but the group's work, and the high praise it called forth from actors, showed that the manifesto's spirit produced exceptional results. For a while, the tiny nation of Denmark was at the forefront of international cinema, and the Danish government even increased state funding.

Reinvigorated cinema, as in any other art form, always seems to come from a group's determined exploration of fundamentals, something that few individuals have the time, energy, or resolve to sustain alone. The message to remember is that *all undertakings profit from limitations*. Some come with your filming situation, but the best are those you choose that will channel and test your powers of invention. Of course, Dogme can always turn into dogma: your limitations must constantly be refreshed if they are not to turn into a stale formula.

MAKE YOUR OWN LIMITATIONS

Here are some suggestions to put your skills under creative pressure:

- Set time limits (for instance, I'll produce a five-minute script in one day, and shoot and edit it in three).
- Show a character's day in only 60 seconds of screen time.
- Get a friend to look in secondhand stores for three intriguing costumes or three weird objects, then develop a short film using them.
- Shoot an improvised event such as a homecoming (happy? disastrous?) in one take using a mobile camera unit.
- Improvise a problem, crisis, and resolution among three given characters, and shoot it documentary-style in a given location.
- Shoot a *photo-roman;* that is, a short film made entirely of stills. It can either be silent or have an accompanying sound track.
- Make a diary film in one day using nondialogue imagery and a voice-over applied later.
- Devise a credible five-minute interaction between two or more people that uses no spoken language and has a build, crisis, and resolution.
- Try integrating a fictional character into one or more situations improvised in real-life circumstances. Haskell Wexler's *Medium Cool* (1969) takes an actor playing a tough news cameraman and puts him into real-life riots going on during the Chicago Democratic Convention. Under pressure, the wall of professional indifference that the character has built between himself and human suffering breaks down.

What specific, creative challenges will you and your partners build into your next project? How about writing your own vow of chastity? How will you assess your limitations' contribution afterward?

PART 4

AESTHETICS AND AUTHORSHIP

Part 4 (Chapters 12 through 16) concerns aesthetics, which determine how a film will look and how its story will be told. New directors tend to concentrate on the immediate hurdle—the screenplay and its dialogue—which is content rather than form. Form, however, is how that content appears on the screen—and to be striking, it must be designed as such.

The designs latent in your screenplay start taking shape as soon as you can separate the interlocking aspects of film discourse and give each a functional name. For this, you'll find Part 2: Screencraft helpful, in particular the film study projects in Chapter 5, "Seeing with a Moviemaker's Eye." An excellently graphic and user-friendly introduction to film aesthetics is David Bordwell and Kristin Thompson's *Film Art: An Introduction*, 8th ed. (McGraw Hill, 2006), which now comes with video clips on a CD-ROM. Like all such analytic texts, it deals with finished work and not how to make a film from scratch, so you will sometimes be swimming upstream.

If you are impatient with aesthetic criteria and ideas, don't wait until you understand what you are doing—jump in and make short films, no matter what. They will become your best teachers, for they will provide imperfect models that you will be motivated to analyze and learn from.

TELLING STORIES

The philosopher and filmmaker Michael Roemer begins his provocative survey of narrative like this:

> Every story is over before it is begun. The novel lies bound in my hands, the actors know all their lines before the curtain rises, and the finished film has been threaded onto the projector when the houselights dim.
>
> Stories appear to move into an open, uncertain future that the figures try to influence, but in fact report a completed past they cannot alter. Their journey into the future—to which we gladly lend ourselves—is an illusion. (Chapter 1, *Telling Stories: Postmodernism and the Invalidation of Traditional Narrative* [Lanham, Md.: Rowman & Littlefield, 1995])

Standing like an authorial puppet master behind these illusory figures is the invisible and little-understood figure of the cinema Storyteller, whose part is yours to play as the director. You determine the aesthetic decisions, which derive from:

- The nature of the story (for instance, whether it is naturalistic or nonnaturalistic)
- The Storyteller's intended impact on the audience
- The nature and purpose of the main characters
- Their changing points of view (such as hope, fear, expectation, boredom, waiting) inside the story

- The plot and how it is presented in time (structure)
- The associations of space, environment, and time period

These aspects relate to each other in a confusingly circular way, but I shall argue that point of view is pivotal, and makes as good a starting point as any.

FORM AND AESTHETICS QUESTIONNAIRE

This is designed to help you uncover your film's aesthetic potential. Two things to notice: one, the questionnaire starts with your major belief, and ends with the effect you intend on your audience. The artistic process is thus a kind of a delivery system. Two, each question has links guiding you to particular chapters, so help is easy to locate. The index will give further context.

Rabiger, *Directing: Film Techniques and Aesthetics* 4th Edition

FORM AND AESTHETICS QUESTIONNAIRE

Production

Working Title _____

1. **Basic Information**. Film's intended length _____ minutes, to be shot on _____(format), should take _____ shooting days, and cost $ _____.

So far I have (check what applies):
☐ Screenplay   ☐ Step outline   ☐ Treatment   ☐ Premise
☐ Cast: ___ out of ___   ☐ Crew: ____out of ____   ☐ Budget raised: $_____

Conceptual

2. **Philosophy** (see Ch. 2, section "Identity, Belief, and Vision").
In life I believe that _____
_____
_____

3. **Premise** (see Ch. 8, section "Checking the Foundations").
This film explores my convictions by showing (your film's premise):_____
_____
_____
_____

4. **Structure** (see Ch. 14 Time, Structure, and Plot, in particular "Planning a Structure").
The film's timeline is _____but the story will be structured
by_____
_____
_____

5. **Place, Genre, Stylization** (see Ch. 15 Space, Stylized Environments and Performances)
The genre (type or family) of this film is _____ and my film only departs from this genre in that it _____
_____
The major settings or locations contribute_____
_____
_____
and the following elements in the handling of time or space depart from ordinary realism
_____
_____
_____
_____

6. **Characters** (see Ch. 1, "Duality and Conflict"; Ch. 3 "Conflict and Situation"; Ch. 6, Project 6-2)
Main characters' (in order of importance) and their wants, dominant traits, major conflicts:
Character A _____ mainly wants _____
_____
Dominant trait_____
Major conflict _____

Page 1

Rabiger, *Directing: Film Techniques and Aesthetics* 4th Edition

Character B _____ mainly wants _____

Dominant trait _____
Major conflict _____

Character C _____ mainly wants _____

Dominant trait _____
Major conflict _____

Character D _____ mainly wants _____

Dominant trait _____
Major conflict _____

Character E _____ mainly wants _____

Dominant trait _____
Major conflict _____

Character F _____ mainly wants _____

Dominant trait _____
Major conflict _____

7. **Situations** (see Ch. 3, "Situation and the Dramatic Arc")
The main character(s) major situation(s) or predicament(s) are _____
_____
_____
_____

8. **Point of View** (see Ch. 12 Point of View)
(a) The point-of-view character(s) is/are _____ and his/her biased way of
seeing means that _____
_____
_____

(b) Subsidiary characters are _____ and their way of
seeing, by contrast means that _____
_____
_____
_____

(c) The Storyteller's characteristics are _____
_____ and this makes
him/her want to make the audience see in this particular way _____
_____
_____
_____

9. **The film's main conflict** (see Ch. 3 Dramaturgy)
The major forces at conflict in this film are between _____
and _____

10. **Forces in confrontation** (see Ch. 3 Dramaturgy)

The story's main conflict is finally played out between_____
and _____ in (scene) _____
_____which mainly shows that _____
_____

11. **Resolution** (see Ch. 3 Dramaturgy)
The main character's struggle resolves as or into _____
_____
_____

Design

12. **Mood Progression** (see Ch. 9 "Work to Create a Succession of Moods" and Ch. 13 Genre, Subtext, and Archetypes)
Moods in the film start with_____
and progress through _____
_____
to _____
_____
_____

13. **Stylization** (see Ch. 15 Space, Stylized Environments and Performances)
Heightened elements in my film are_____
_____
Their justification lies in _____
_____
And the stylization will be accomplished by _____
_____
_____

14. **Symbols, Metaphors** (see Ch. 15 "Naming the Metaphorical and Using Symbols" and Ch. 16 Form and Style)
Metaphors by which I type the characters or situations are _____
_____
Metaphors or symbols on the screen will be _____
_____
_____
_____

15. **Visual design** (see Ch. 16 Form and Style)
Dominant impression the cinematography gives is _____
_____
Color palette and its development are_____
_____
Elements that organize the visual design are_____
_____
_____

Rabiger, *Directing: Film Techniques and Aesthetics* 4ᵗʰ Edition

16. **Sound design** (see Ch. 16 Form and Style)
Most important design elements are _____
_____
_____
_____

Outcome

17. **Intended impact** (see Ch. 3 Dramaturgy Essentials)
After they have seen my film I want my audience to:
Feel_____
_____
_____

Think_____
_____
_____

Recommend that people see the film because_____
_____
_____
_____

Further Notes

_____
_____
_____
_____
_____
_____
_____
_____
_____
_____
_____
_____
_____
_____
_____
_____
_____
_____
_____
_____
_____
_____
_____
_____
_____

CHAPTER 12

POINT OF VIEW

A point-of-view shot is a camera angle taken from a character's physical location in the scene, but cinematic point of view (POV) is less tangible. Like point of view in literature, you know it because something is making you share a character's feelings and predicaments. The effect is easier to describe than to account for. Harder still is to say how to write, direct, and control it. Film language—unlike the printed page, which obligingly stands still as you analyze it—moves in a flow of dynamic images that are subtly modified by words, symbols, sounds, color, movement, and music. However complex it is, POV is nevertheless within its director's sphere of influence, so let's first glance at antecedents in literature, which are more familiar.

POINT OF VIEW IN LITERATURE

In literature, a story's narrating POV has two basic sources. One is *omniscient POV*, and belongs to the Storyteller standing outside the story; the other is *subjective POV*, and belongs to a character within it. For both, the type of person, his or her outlook, and his or her point of view are inextricably linked.

The *omniscient narrator* has unrestricted movement in time and place. Like God, he or she can see into every aspect of the characters' past, present, and future while revealing the story's events. The *self-effacing narrator* is also omniscient, but, by showing the tale neutrally and without comment, leaves us to make our own interpretations.

The *character within the story POV* offers a more partisan, subjective, and limited perspective that is routed through what that character experiences, sees, hears, and (mis)understands. The character within the story can be:

- A *naive narrator* unaware of all the implications in his or her situation
- A *knowing narrator* who may pretend naïveté, but be more acute than he or she cares to show
- An *epic hero*, such as Odysseus or Superman, who is cunning, heroic, or superhuman

The character within the story sometimes addresses the reader directly and can have omniscient powers, as in the "tall tale" convention in which the narrator affects great knowledge and ability.

There are two types of literary narrative: *simple narrative*, which is functional and supplies an exposition of events, usually in chronological order; and *plot-driven narrative*, which entertains by generating suspense. This type of narrative often reorders story chronology to reveal events according to the story's type and plot strategy.

To generate anticipation and involvement in the reader, all storytelling aims to generate *suspense* or *narrative tension*. This arises from predicaments the characters must face, attitudes they take, or by the author's critical attitude toward the characters. Getting us involved, or *identifying*, with the characters makes us buy into the stakes for which they play. Tension is often raised by withholding information or creating disorientation—familiar from the mystery story, where the reader tries to interpret clues and spot the killer.

POINT OF VIEW IN FILM

Compared with literature, the screen has both advantages and handicaps. Cinematography can set up a situation and a gripping mood in seconds, avoiding literature's lengthy tracts of exposition, but its inclusiveness can present a bewildering array of detail. James Monaco says that the "insistently descriptive nature of the film image inundates both subject and subtext with irrelevant detail. Ideas and authorial clarity are therefore harder to achieve." Terrence Malick's *Days of Heaven* (1978) is a beautiful and moving film on a big screen, but only from the reduced image of a TV viewing did I grasp its underlying themes and allusions.

Film must use framing, blocking (choreographing the subject and camera), and editing to keep the eye where it needs to be. In realism, film most often uses an omniscient POV with occasional forays into individual characters' viewpoints. Let's look at the POV variations available to filmmakers, and examine what they offer as authorial tools. We're going to start close on the particularities of the main character, and then back away, ending on the audience's broad, outside perspective.

MAIN CHARACTERS

Single main character: Main characters and their issues are established by exposing the audience to the events that put the characters under revealing pressure. Audience members merge with them through empathy and identification. Tony Richardson's *A Taste of Honey* (1961) focuses like a documentary on a provincial teenager in the grim industrial cityscape of Manchester. She gets pregnant after her mother takes off with a new boyfriend. The teenager must struggle to survive, but being so often led by raw emotion, bears some responsibility for what happens. Lonely when abandoned by the baby's father, she is befriended by a nurturing homosexual boy. Thus, through the interaction of her character, place, and chance, her destiny takes shape. Curiously, the film lost some of its documentary power in transition from the dailies to the edited version. Editing increases the range of what we see, but can fragment the truthfulness of actors' sustained moments.

Highly subjective main character: High subjectivity affects what the character sees, and thus how you show it. That is, it influences both content and form, and shows up in a number of ways:

- Subjectivity may be explicit, in the form of a character who speaks as a narrator to the audience.
- More often it is implicit, as the audience is led to empathize with a particular character or characters.
- Usually artful mise-en-scène (directing, scene design, and blocking) contributes heavily (see Chapter 29, "Mise-en-Scène").
- The film may feature a retrospective POV (the body of the film is perhaps a diary or exploration of memory).
- A character may directly address the audience. (The whole film must support this—it cannot be incidental.)

Dual main characters: The subjects in Jean-Luc Godard's *Pierrot le Fou* (1965), Arthur Penn's *Bonnie and Clyde* (1967), and Malick's *Badlands* (1974) are partnerships involving two equally important POV characters. All three films involve road journeys ending in self-destruction. The two American films explore the couple relations of fugitives, whereas the French picture develops the incompatibilities between men and women. Here, the tensions are between the characters rather than between the outlaw couples and those chasing them.

Wim Wenders' *Alice in the Cities* (1974, Figure 12-1) is also a journey, but the contest is between characters initially quite unequal: a nine-year-old girl and a

FIGURE 12-1 ————————————————————————

In *Alice in the Cities*, a reluctant journalist helps an abandoned nine-year-old search for her grandmother's home (courtesy of Museum of Modern Art/Film Stills Archive).

FIGURE 12-2

Like other Altman films, *Gosford Park* explores relationships and hierarchies in a special corner of society (courtesy USA Films/The Kobal Collection/Tillie, Mark).

reluctant journalist helping the girl search for her grandmother. By creating two lost and uncertain characters of wonderful dignity, it shows how adults and children can achieve trust and emotional equality. Avoiding kitsch sentiment, the film explores the gulf between adults and children.

Multiple characters: Robert Altman's *Nashville* (1975) and *Gosford Park* (2001, Figure 12-2) have casts of characters reaching into double figures, and there is no dominant POV. Each character becomes a thread in a social fabric, and each film focuses on the patterns that emerge out of group situations. This concern with collective life can also be seen in Quentin Tarantino's *Pulp Fiction* (1994) and Paul Thomas Anderson's *Magnolia* (1999), which are both interested in coincidence and irony.

TYPES OF POV

Fallible POV: Many stories revolve around figures who misjudge their antagonists or their surroundings, as happens in two famous Alfred Hitchcock films. In *Rear Window* (1954), an injured photographer confined to his room is compelled to look at the building opposite. So convinced does he become that a murder has taken place that he takes on the guilt of the murderer. In *Psycho* (1960), Marion Crane struggles to deny her instinct that something dangerous is afoot in the Bates Motel. In both films, the audience enters the main character's predicament by having to question what is real and what is only appearance. At the end, Hitchcock provides the famous keys to unlock the suspense.

Narrated POV: A film's ruling POV may come from one of its characters narrating us through the events, and often these are children. In Malick's *Days of*

FIGURE 12-3 ——

The Sixth Sense establishes a powerful world through the eyes of a suffering boy (courtesy Hollywood Pictures/The Kobal Collection).

Heaven (1978), the fugitive's young sister provides voice-over narration. The country lawyer's daughter narrates Robert Mulligan's *To Kill a Mockingbird* (1963), and the boy houseguest writing in his diary narrates Joseph Losey's *The Go-Between* (1971).

Adult characters also occasionally provide first-person voice-over narration to drive the film and locate its focus, as in François Truffaut's *Jules and Jim* (1962), or Alan Pakula's *Sophie's Choice* (1982).

Where no such verbal narration exists, the POV may not be so obvious. Other notable films that establish powerful worlds less explicitly but through the eyes of vulnerable young people are Satyajit Ray's *Pather Panchali* (India, 1954), Truffaut's *400 Blows* (France, 1959), Víctor Erice's *The Spirit of the Beehive* (Spain, 1973), and Ingmar Bergman's *Fanny and Alexander* (Sweden, 1983). More recently, M. Night Shyamalan's *The Sixth Sense* (1999, Figure 12-3) is outstanding for the haunted state of mind of Cole, its nine-year-old central character.

Implied POV: Most films follow the lead of omniscient literature, and imply POV by involving the audience in the concerns and awareness of whoever is at the center of the work. Dorothy as she sets off down the yellow brick road in Victor Fleming's *The Wizard of Oz* (1939) is a good example. As she passes through a bewitched landscape, we share her shocks and insecurities, and rejoice when she overcomes difficulties. Dorothy is joined by the Cowardly Lion, the Tin Woodman, and the Scarecrow, each an alter ego whom she inspires to continue, but who actually represents a threatened aspect of her own psyche. At the end, when she awakens, we understand that Dorothy has been reordering aspects of herself while dreaming, and that her quest has been to reconcile the anxieties of her waking life.

Subsidiary or alternative POVs: Film, like literature, often switches temporarily to another POV whenever the shift augments or refreshes the viewer's perceptions. This could be done through subject matter, or an angle, that makes us see with the alternate character's eyes and emotions, or it could be achieved through parallel action—that is, by cutting to another story strand happening concurrently.

When POV migrates from character to character, we gain access to a range of people's feelings and awarenesses. Shifts of POV between characters are used to give empathic insight into multiple characters' thoughts and feelings. So enigmatic was the historical Oskar Schindler that Steven Spielberg's *Schindler's List* (1993) sees him mostly through the eyes of those around him. Good fiction uses minor characters, and shows that they, too, have lives, feelings, and agendas to fulfill.

Films have freely used the power of a subjective vantage point since German Expressionist times in the 1920s. When we see how a character sees, we intuit what he or she must be feeling and thinking. There is said to be only one purely subjective, or character-within-the-film, POV movie—the actor-director Robert Montgomery's mystery *Lady in the Lake* (1947), in which the camera *is* the detective Philip Marlowe. Characters talking to him address the camera; we see Marlowe only when he looks into a mirror.

STORYTELLER POV

Authorship of films, even though they all have directors, is a collective more than individual effort, like the music that emerges under a conductor. So the source of the Storyteller's viewpoint is never too evident. Storyteller POV has two main polarities that often overlap. There is the personal, or Storyteller, POV by which a film expresses a coherent attitude toward the characters and their story. This often makes a central character stand for human qualities or provocative ideas, as happens in *The Enigma of Kaspar Hauser* (1974, Figure 12-4). Werner Herzog makes Kaspar an uncorrupted innocent trying to make sense of civilization, and he accomplishes this by developing the famous episode in 18th-century Germany of a young man, kept isolated with pigs since childhood, who appeared one day standing helpless and without language in a marketplace. The film examines what happens when a guileless person makes first contact with human society, and shows the tragicomic results through Kaspar's collisions with small-town factions and manners. Boldly and poetically, the film imparts the developing contradictions in Kaspar's inner, moral life. Through juxtaposition of summer beauty and inner despair, Herzog explores what may have torn the actual Kaspar apart and turned him suicidal.

Storytelling POV may also be expressed through using genres and their archetypes, as in film noir or the Western. Such films often seem to make their statements about humanity as a collective phenomenon. Orson Welles' famous *Citizen Kane* (1941, Figure 12-5) teases us with the riddle of a man's true nature by focusing on reporters trying to assemble a portrait of a deceased newspaper magnate. Charles Foster Kane is a great man whose driving motives remain tantalizingly obscure and contradictory to the little people in his shadow. Kane's mood of unassuageable deprivation is a mystery, and Welles holds back to the end the image that reveals the man, and shows it only to the audience. Through the symbol of a

FIGURE 12-4 ——————————————————————————————————————

The Enigma of Kaspar Hauser tells of the frightened man who once appeared in a German marketplace with neither language nor knowledge of other human beings (courtesy Filmverlag Der Autoren/The Kobal Collection).

FIGURE 12-5 ——————————————————————————————————————

Investigators in *Citizen Kane* try to piece together a deceased newspaper magnate's emotional identity (courtesy RKO/The Kobal Collection).

FIGURE 12-6

All About My Mother explores how compassion and loyalty develop between unlikely allies (courtesy El Deseo/Renn/France 2/The Kobal Collection).

sled, epitomizing the loss of Kane's home as a boy, Welles clinches his argument that such driving energy comes from loss and pain.

Many of Pedro Almodóvar's films have in common the qualities of sped-up farce, melodramatic plots, and characters who seem to be parodying themselves. Yet there is a rare humanity among his druggie girls, harried housewives, battling lesbians, and streetwise prostitutes. *All About My Mother* (1999, Figure 12-6) focuses on a mother who loses her beloved teenage son. Driven to trace his father, she finds he is living a rich emotional life as a transvestite prostitute. Amid Almodóvar's customary circus, a clear and touching vision emerges of love between unlikely partners, and the message is that kindness and loyalty remain paramount—particularly for those living at extremes.

Ethan and Joel Coen's *O Brother, Where Art Thou?* (2000), set in Depression-era Mississippi, makes a Homeric journey out of convicts on the run. The focus is on their epic hero ability to overcome every situation, including a memorable encounter with the Ku Klux Klan. Featuring a bluegrass music track, the film calls up every archetype of the period and seems intent on exploring how legends arise.

In their different ways, these four strongly authored films, even *Citizen Kane*, examine patterns of human behavior rather than the idiosyncrasies of individuals. Of course, we must identify with these characters enough to care about the propositions they exemplify.

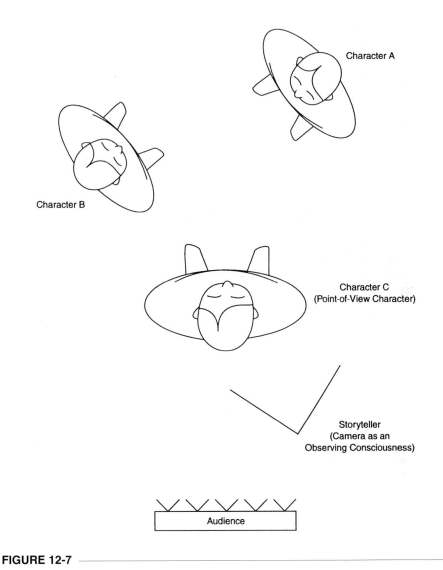

FIGURE 12-7

Diagram of characters, POV character, Storyteller, and audience.

AUDIENCE POV

There is one last POV still to be considered—that of the audience, which assesses the Storyteller, his or her cinematic tale, and whatever the film expresses. Audience POV is always in change. Today, viewing a patriotic World War II film, we experience a gulf between our values and those guiding the film. This means that, individually and collectively, audiences bring their own cultural and histori-cal perspectives to any film. And though you cannot control this, it is something you must be aware of and work with. A story for preteens cannot presume that its audience sees its characters with the same assumptions as an adult audience would. A religiously educated audience won't automatically accept that an anarchist can have powerful and altruistic morals. Western audiences will have difficulty understanding the suicidal agony of an Asian student who must go to his parents with a B grade instead of an A, and so on.

Even the medium or format affects the way we see. Viewing the same one minute of film on television, in the cinema, or via the Internet will make it seem to carry different aims and importance. This means that audience, delivery system, and format create a range of contexts, and that we frame our expectations a little differently in each—even though content remains identical.

POV IS LIKE RUSSIAN DOLLS

Film point of view is diagrammed in Figure 12-7. Its most restricted level of subjectivity is that of a character, whereas its most embracing is that of the audience. In concept, this is a bit like the enclosing and embracing nature of Russian dolls.

- The main character's POV embraces that of the subsidiary characters, but the subsidiary characters also have feelings and views.
- Each character holds up a mirror to the others.
- The Storyteller's POV encloses all the characters' POVs.
- The audience's POV encloses the Storyteller's and characters' points of view.

PLANNING A POINT OF VIEW

Difficult to control but important to influence, POV sets the aesthetic agenda for practically everything. In run-of-the-mill films, it emerges by default from the subject at hand and the idiosyncrasies of the actors and team making the film. You must take a far more deliberate approach. The most practical is to decide what thematic statement you want your story to make, and then to work on developing all the subjectivities you can draw from the characters, their world, and their Storyteller. Each provides a distorting lens through which you can legitimately enhance meaning by using heightened characters in a heightened world.

CHAPTER 13

SUBTEXT, GENRE, AND ARCHETYPES

The fiction film, the documentary, and the short story all are consumed at a sitting, and thus continue the tradition of oral storytelling. In former times, this constituted, along with religion, most of the common person's education. Today, the cinema's preeminence is arguably due to its unparalleled power to make us see and feel from another's point of view. Through the screen, we can temporarily become braver, funnier, stronger, angrier, more beautiful, more vulnerable, or more beset with danger and tragedy. A good movie sends us out energized and refreshed in spirit.

This cathartic contact with the trials of the human spirit is a need as fundamental as eating, breathing, or making love. Art, of which the cinema is but the youngest form, nourishes our spirit by engaging us in surrogate emotional experience and implying underlying patterns.

All art grows out of what went before it, so any film you care to make will veer toward a particular type and aesthetic area, have a prevailing mood, and draw on available language through which to speak to its audience.

SUBTEXT: MAKING THE VISIBLE SIGNIFICANT

Film art is expensive and complex, and its meanings surprisingly difficult to control. Robert Richardson defines the heart of cinema's problem: "Literature often has the problem of making the significant somehow visible, while film often finds itself trying to make the visible significant."[1] Those surfaces rendered so minutely and attractively by the camera actually distract us from seeing *subtexts*, the underlying messages and meanings so fundamental to drama. Put another way: if you don't use film language astutely, your underlying discourse will be swamped and pass unnoticed. One of the aids to communication is working in a *genre*.

---

[1] *Literature and Film* (Bloomington: Indiana University Press, 1973), p. 68.

GENRE OPTIONS

In French, the word *genre* simply means kind or sort, and it describes films that belong to a type that the audience recognizes. Under "genre," James Monaco's *How to Read a Film,* 3rd ed., (New York: Oxford University Press, 2000) lists:

Black film	Detective story
Gangster film	Samurai
Thriller	Film noir
Buddy film	Science fiction
Horror film	
War film	For television, it lists:
Chase	Action shows
Melodrama	Docudrama
Westerns	Soap opera
Comedy (screwball)	Cop shows
Musicals	Families
Youth	Comedy (sitcom)
	Professions shows

Each category contains familiar types of character, role, and situation that are mostly older than the cinema. Each genre promises a world running under familiar rules and limitations. The buddy film category, for instance, promises a film that explores the pleasures and pains of same-sex friendships, and includes works as diverse as Stanley Kramer's *The Defiant Ones* (1958), John Hughes' *Planes, Trains & Automobiles* (1988), and Ridley Scott's *Thelma and Louise* (1991, Figure 13-1).

FIGURE 13-1

As a story of same-sex friendship, *Thelma and Louise* belongs in the buddy film genre (courtesy MGM/Pathé/The Kobal Collection).

The gangster film, the sci-fi film, the Western, and the screwball comedy all embody subjects and approaches that function dependably within preordained limits. Horror and fantasy have been staples throughout cinema's short history because audiences have always craved alternatives to the realistic. They are cinema's continuation of folktales and folk drama, forms through which humankind can indulge its appetite for demons, ogres, wizards, and phantom carriages. Under the guise of futurism, Franklin Schaffner's *Planet of the Apes* (1968) and George Lucas' *Star Wars* episodes (1977–2005) are really traditional morality plays.

Comedy offers its own delightful worlds and constants. Charlie Chaplin, Buster Keaton, Mae West, W.C. Fields, Red Skelton, and Laurel and Hardy—as well as Jacques Tati, Lucille Ball, Woody Allen, John Cleese, and Steve Martin— each play character types from film to film. Each new situation and dilemma puts a new set of comic stresses on a constructed personality. Recent sex comedies in which women take over male preserves, homosexual couples take on parenthood, or men take over women's identities also confirm that comedy functions as a safety valve for anxieties about social change.

Fiction cinema allows vicarious experience of most imaginable types, but until recently there has been a conspicuous silence on nuclear attack and the Holocaust. Steven Spielberg's *Schindler's List* (1994, Figure 13-2) focuses on one of the few uplifting stories to emerge from that period of brutality and shame. Roberto Benigni's weirdly saccharine *Life Is Beautiful* (1997) tackles deportation through humor and nostalgia. Real horror is perhaps nothing we really care to look in the eye.

FIGURE 13-2

Schindler's List, one of the few uplifting stories to emerge from a period of brutality and shame (courtesy Universal/The Kobal Collection/James, David).

Bertolt Brecht's question remains: Is art a mirror to society, or a hammer working on it? Does art reflect actuality, or does it change and therefore create it? The answers will vary with the age and the artist, but we can say with confidence that in every period and in every part of the world, art has supplied a surrogate experience to exercise hearts and minds.

ARCHETYPES

Archetypal characters such as the hero, villain, strongman, demon, avenger, clown, angel, Earth Mother, witch, and wizard appear and reappear in archetypal plots that stretch back to the beginning of recorded history. They often carry out specific functions even in modern drama, where a human force (such as hostility, mercy, justice) is required rather than a complex and fully realized character. Archetypes distill human roles, and appear in Greek plays, Japanese Kabuki and Noh traditions, Italian commedia dell'arte, and other early dramatic forms. More on types and archetypes can be found in Chapter 15 under "The Stylized Performance: Flat and Round Characters."

GENRE AND POINT OF VIEW

A good movie, like any effective artwork, can lead us to experience new conditions and to expand in mind and heart. Because our strong desire is to break out of the imprisoning self and to experience, if only temporarily, the worlds of others, films often project us into a main character's predicament. In a love triangle such as Tolstoy's *Anna Karenina*, multiple worlds are available, because each character sees differently. With the husband, we could view Anna's liaison as a betrayal; with her lover, Vronsky, it's a romantic adventure gone sour; and with Anna, night turns into brightest day and then changes into a long, bloody sunset. Each viewpoint calls for a different story and suggests a different possible genre.

Then again, a story has dimensions beyond those understood by its protagonists. In any Tolstoy novel, we sense Tolstoy the Storyteller sympathetically watching his characters suffer. Alternative Storyteller viewpoints are always possible. A new dramatic interpretation need make no change in the novel's action—all it needs is a new slant, or an altered set of moods, convictions, or motivations. Any of these can propel the basic story into new areas of meaning. For this, you must know your chosen genre and be able to build a convincing world around the characters' new subjectivities. Your audience then decides whether you have succeeded: certainly their will is to believe, because we need stories to help us find new meanings in life. How else could a Shakespeare play set in recent times still resonate in contemporary India?

GENRE AND DRAMATIC ARCHETYPES

How does the poor filmmaker, surrounded by the paraphernalia of scripts, budgets, and technical support, know when to push beyond the realism so generic to photography? I wish there were guidelines to put individual perception into a manageable frame. Instead, we must talk about dialectical worlds animated by oppositions. This tension is usually organized around moral imperatives; that is, the polarity between right and wrong, good and evil. Every film contains a range of oppositions between which its authors are as ambiguously suspended as the main characters. Examining where your work lies should help clarify its genre and even how the film should look. Here are a few sample oppositions, to which you can add those that arise in your own work.

Either	Or
Auteur (personal, authorial stamp)	Genre (film archetype)
Subjective (character's) POV	Objective (Storyteller's) POV
Nonrealistic and stylized	Realistic
Duality requires audience judgment	Conflicts are generic and not analyzed
Conflicts are interpersonal	Conflicts are large-scale and societal
Conflicts are divergent and unresolved	Conflicts are convergent and resolved
Outcome uncertain	Outcome reached via struggle
Subject is an individual hero	Subject is a group
Past	Present
Emotion	Intellect
Humor	Tragedy
Fast	Slow
Dark	Light

No film falls into predominantly one column or the other, and the columns are not prescriptions for good or bad films. They are dialectical oppositions, each gaining strength from the existence of the other. How you decide which to invoke in your particular piece of storytelling is decided by the story itself. Analyze your screenplay, and tease out all the dialectical oppositions you can find. Some are lying there unnoticed, but as soon as you set about magnifying them all, the characters begin to play for higher stakes in a world with greater contrasts and dangers. Keep in mind that *everything or everybody interesting always has contradictions at the center*, and that every story can be routed through one or more of the conflicted intelligences that are experiencing the unfolding events.

A book that demonstrates how useful myth and legend can be to filmmakers is Christopher Vogler's *The Writer's Journey: Mythic Structure for Storytellers and Screenwriters*, 2nd ed. (Michael Wiese Productions, 1998). It shows how the story principles that Joseph Campbell uncovered in world folk stories also apply to innumerable films. A word of warning: use it not as a starting point, but to expand existing ideas during the development of a screenplay.

QUESTION CHECKLIST

Here are some questions to help confirm your screenplay's subtexts and genre:

Genre:
- What genre am I calling on, and how do I fulfill or subvert it?
- What are the origins in other arts of my film's genre, and can I get help from them for my film?

- If a genre permits framing an area of life and seeing it through a particular prism of concerns or values, what predominates in my film?
- How strongly do I use subjectivity in my film's genre?

Subtexts:

- Does my story declare its intentions early enough so the audience knows what to look for?
- How much in my characters requires interpretation and judgment? Could there be more?
- How much in my film carries moral implications, which interest audiences so much?
- Am I juxtaposing events to create irony or humor, events that signify an underlying set of values?
- Is my Storyteller making full use of allegory, analogy, metaphor, or symbol to signify meanings?

CHAPTER 14

TIME, STRUCTURE, AND PLOT

So much about film's appeal is hotly debated, but, "if anything is natural," says Dudley Andrew, "it is the psychic lure of narrative, the drive to hold events in sequence, to traverse them, to come to an end."[1] Every intended film has an optimal structure, one that best conveys its dramatic issues, their working out and outcome. You begin by deciding how to handle time. As with all design problems, less is more, and the simplest solution is usually the strongest. Before you direct something, pause to make a detailed, written analysis of sequences or short films that move you and that parallel your intended project (see Chapter 5, "Seeing with a Moviemaker's Eye"). Then what follows will make more sense.

TIME

Every story, like every sequence of events in life, has its own *chronology*; that is, significant happenings with a beginning, middle, and end. They may not, however, be told in that order, which is just when things get interesting.

TIME COMPRESSED

Transparent cinema, aiming to rid itself of any evident contrivance, gives the illusion of continuous time. But behind the semblance of real time and continuity, the editor is always contracting time and occasionally expanding it. All narratives select, compress, and juxtapose their materials to intensify meaning, reveal ironies, and achieve brevity. This shorthand has become increasingly concise over time as film audiences develop an ever more succinct understanding of filmmakers' intentions. The process was accelerated by that thorn in our flesh, the TV commercial.

The 1960s work of Jean-Luc Godard showed that dissolves used as time transitions were superfluous. The jump cut, familiar from home movies, perfectly well

[1] *Concepts in Film Theory* (Oxford University Press, 1984).

FIGURE 14-1 ————————————————————————————————————

Amélie is both a morality fable and director Jeunet's fond backward glance at the French New Wave cinema (courtesy UGC/Studio Canal+/The Kobal Collection/Calvo, Bruno).

established a time elision between one piece of action and the next, and gave more agility to editing. One caution: overcompression carries the danger of distancing the audience from developing intimacy with personalities, situations, and ideas. Eliminating prosaic details should allow expansion of what is significant—not lead to stuffing ever more into the pint pot. Some genres, especially in comedy, do, however, depend on hectic pacing.

For an entertaining dictionary of editing and stylistic devices, see Jean-Pierre Jeunet's delightful *Amélie* (France, 2002, Figure 14-1), which looks fondly back at the French New Wave cinema and uses every trick in the cinematic book.

TIME EXPANDED

Expanding time on-screen allows the audience to reflect in depth while something significant takes place. Slow-motion cinematography is an easy way to do this, but we have had more than our fill of lovers endlessly floating toward each other's arms. See Hugh Hudson's *Chariots of Fire* (1981) for the overuse of slow motion.

Yasujiro Ozu's *Tokyo Story* (1953) and Michelangelo Antonioni's *L'Avventura* (1959) subverted the action-film stereotype by slowing both the story and its presentation in order to expose the more subtle action within the characters. Both films examine the tenuousness of human relationships, something impossible during a torrent of action. An unattuned audience will find such films boring, and *L'Avventura* was ridiculed at the Cannes Film Festival. Later, it found appreciation in France and became a cornerstone in Antonioni's career.

FIGURE 14-2

In *Hiroshima Mon Amour*, Resnais establishes his enduring fascination with the omissions and distortions of the human memory (courtesy Argos/Como/Pathé/Daiei/The Kobal Collection).

LINEAR PROGRESSION

A linear narrative proceeds in chronological order. This produces a relatively cool, objective film because the narrative flow is not interrupted or redirected by plot interventions. Effect follows cause in a predictable and possibly boring way. Sometimes this does not do a story justice. Volker Schlöndorff's 1975 version of Heinrich Boll's novel *The Lost Honor of Katharina Blum* abandoned as too complex the flash-forward technique of the novel, which early established the murder of a yellow press journalist and then inquired into what pressures could lead a gentle young woman to kill her tormentor. The film concentrated on what she might do rather than why she did it.

NONLINEAR PROGRESSION

Frequently a story's chronology is rearranged according to a character's subjective recall or because the Storyteller has devised a plot that perhaps reorders events to make a better narrative, or to accommodate the past in the film's present.

The past: Alain Resnais, fascinated by the way the human memory edits and distorts time, intercut *Muriel, or the Time of Return* (1963) with 8 mm movie material from the Algerian war to create a series of flashback memory evocations. In his earlier *Hiroshima Mon Amour* (1959, Figure 14-2), the Frenchwoman and her Japanese lover are increasingly invaded by memories of their respective traumas— his, the dropping of the bomb on Hiroshima; hers, punishment for a love affair with a German soldier in occupied France. These memories intrude anguish, and Resnais seems to propose that extreme lives are propelled by extreme trauma. Both films pose questions about the effect of repressed personal history on present behavior.

The future: A scene from the future (as in *The Lost Honor of Katharina Blum*, above) can be a useful foreshadowing device. Jan Troell's *The Flight of the Eagle* (1985) starts with scattered human bones in a deserted Arctic encampment. The film reconstructs a hastily prepared Arctic balloon journey of 1897 that ended in death. It begins with the actual aviators' grisly fate, then fictionally reconstructs their tragic journey.

Flash-forward: Nicolas Roeg's masterly mystery *Don't Look Now* (1974) uses a flash-forward technique in its lovemaking scene, which is intercut with shots of the couple getting dressed later in a state of mental abstraction. The effect is poignant because each act of love, the film seems to be saying, has a banal aftermath waiting to engulf it.

Conditional tense: A favorite device in comedy is to cut to an imagined or projected outcome, as in John Schlesinger's *Billy Liar* (1963), whose hero takes refuge in fantasy from his dreary undertaker's job. This is done altogether more somberly in Resnais' *Last Year at Marienbad* (1961, Figure 14-3), in which a man

FIGURE 14-3

Resnais makes *Last Year at Marienbad* push his obsession with the labyrinth of human consciousness to its farthest point (courtesy Terra/Tamara/Cormoran/The Kobal Collection).

staying in a vast hotel tries to renew an affair with a woman who seems not to know him. Resnais uses film as an expanded, slowed-down model of the human memory trying to reconstitute an event. Note that when you cut to the past, that past quickly becomes a new present. This is why literature is said to speak in the past tense, and cinema in the present.

OTHER WAYS TO HANDLE TIME

Literal time is something seldom tackled by film. Agnès Varda's *Cleo from 5 to 7* (1961) shows exactly two hours in the life of a woman after she learns she has cancer. Jafar Panahi's *The White Balloon* (1996) shows a feisty seven-year-old going through one maneuver after another to get the goldfish she absolutely must have to celebrate the Iranian New Year.

Retrograde time: Christopher Nolan's *Memento* (2001), about a man suffering from memory loss trying to piece his way backward to the moment of his wife's rape, tells its story in time played backward to a source point.

Repeated time: Harold Ramis' very funny *Groundhog Day* (1993, Figure 14-4) features a time loop. A jaded TV weatherman sent to witness whether the groundhog

FIGURE 14-4 ───────────────────────────────────────

In Harold Ramis' highly inventive *Groundhog Day*, a TV weatherman faces a daily replay of the same events (courtesy Columbia/The Kobal Collection/Goldman, Louis).

can see his shadow finds himself returning to the same key moment, each time learning a little more about himself until he can finally escape as a purged and happier man.

Parallel time: Usually called *parallel storytelling*, it was pioneered by D.W. Griffith, who got the idea from Charles Dickens' technique of "cutting" between parallel story lines in his novels long before cinema was thought of.

PLOT

Plot is the design that arranges or patterns the incidents befalling the characters. As the story advances, each event must stand in logical and meaningful relationship to what went before, and must lead with seeming inevitability to what follows. A plot is devised, says Michael Roemer, "to manipulate, entertain, move, and surprise the audience."[2] He argues that it represents the rules of the universe against which the characters struggle. This explains why plot discussions always revolve around whether some event or characteristic is likely or not, and what, morally or ethically speaking, we *expect* to happen.

Thankfully, stories only ever show fractions of their characters' lives. The plot selects significant incidents and actions, and by so doing implies a whole world outside its purview. By concentrating our attention, a plot acts as a frame in which to enact its author's intentions.

The emphasis on plot may be light or heavy. Heavy plotting stresses the logical and deterministic side of life, but plot in character-driven drama tends to be lighter or even invisible. Chance, randomness, and the imperatives of the central characters can play a far larger part. Behind this is an existential question: How much do we determine our own destiny, and how much are we the playthings of the gods?

When you develop an idea for a film, the type and degree of plotting you choose are bound to reflect your own sense of life's causes and effects. Though your film may ardently promote a sense of randomness in life, cause and effect cannot be random in regard to the film language it uses. The relationships among shots, angles, characters, and environments in film language are still governed by cinema precedent, which itself is limited by our common experience of living. Though you have some latitude to modify the expected, there's no more randomness in the basics than with any other language.

PLOT FAILURES

Plot failures are the weaknesses in the chain of events. Such failures disrupt credibility and leave the audience feeling confused or cheated. Common weaknesses include manipulation, excessive reliance on coincidence, or on the *deus ex machina* (the improbable action or incident inserted to make things turn out

---

[2] Michael Roemer, *Telling Stories* (Lanham, Md.: Rowman & Littlefield, 1995), p. 39.

right). Audiences sense when a dramatist is forcing a development or illegitimately wriggling out of a plot difficulty, so you and your collaborators must test your screenplay unmercifully. Each character must be true to his or her nature, and the story must be as tight and functional as good cabinetry.

PLOT SUCCESS: FLOW AND INEVITABILITY

The well-crafted plot flows with an exhilarating sense of inevitability because it includes nothing gratuitous or facile. By respecting the logic of the characters and their situation, the plot generates an energizing sense of excitement at each step, stimulating the spectator to keep asking, "And now what?" This, called *forward momentum* in dramaturgy, is what screenwriters work hardest to accomplish.

STRUCTURE

Structure, the order in which events are told, results from the nature of the story and the intentions of the Storyteller, and nearly always changes during editing. The shape and weight of every sequence is greatly affected by its ultimate content, composition, visual and aural rhythms, context, and so on. Little of this can be more than hazily present in the filmmaker's mind at the outset.

Even for a short film, plan a structure from the outset. Many aspiring directors, resisting the idea of the tightly plotted narrative as too manipulated and airless, head for the hills when they see what screenwriting manuals prescribe— three acts, each of so many pages and with plot points (points at which the story goes off at a tangent) coming at recommended page numbers. These paradigms came from studying cinema audiences, and parallel how the public consumes other time arts (dance, theater, music, radio, and television). But as we shall see, there are other ways to pattern drama.

PLANNING AND TESTING A STRUCTURE

To put any film structure under fine scrutiny:

- Make a step outline, cut up a printout, and gum each sequence to its own index card.
- Briefly title each card with its narrative function (*Albert gets his head stuck in the railings*, or *Engine trouble stops the Aliens from taking off*).
- Lay cards on a table and rehearse summarizing the film's story. Experiment with changing the position of all movable sequences to see if you can tell the story more interestingly. Consider intercutting sequences to create parallel stories.
- With the cards on the table, summarize the story to a willing listener. Ask for critique of the story and for alternative structure suggestions. Your critic can move the cards around as you discuss possibilities.

FIGURE 14-5

The characters' lives in *Slacker* have none of the headlong momentum associated with high-concept plotting (courtesy Detour/The Kobal Collection).

- Keep trying new structures on new listeners until you're satisfied that you've got all you can from the process.
- You can also caption each card with its mood and pacing, then scan them in order to see whether the pacing and flow of changing moods are well cadenced.

NARRATIVE AND NONNARRATIVE APPROACHES

There are narrative and so-called nonnarrative approaches to storytelling, but nonnarrative cinema is not without structure. Consider this from a review of Richard Linklater's *Slacker* (1991, Figure 14-5):

> *Slacker* is a perfectly plotless work that tracks incidental moments in the lives of some one hundred characters who have made the bohemian side of Austin, Texas, their hangout of choice. . . . The two forces that hold the film together are its clear sense of place (specifically Austin, more generally college towns) and its intimate knowledge of a certain character type; the "slacker.". . . . But the film's improvisatory, meandering style is actually carefully constructed. (James Pallot and the editors of *The Movie Guide* [New York: Perigee, 1995])

Artfully fashioned as a vehicle for Linklater's ideas about his characters and their values, *Slacker* has none of the headlong momentum of *high-concept* (strongly plotted) fiction, but it still unfolds its discourse carefully for maximum effect. Minimal plot does not mean minimal structure too.

OPTIONS

Some Bollywood films follow Indian tradition by structuring their stories as a sequence of moods. Peter Greenaway's somnambulistic *A Zed & Two Noughts* (UK, 1985) is structured around an operatic concatenation of events taking place between characters who work in a zoo. It weaves together Greenaway's favorite fascinations: numbers, coincidence, philology, painting, wildlife, decay, and taxonomies—just to mention a few of the topics that give the feeling of a fugue to this utterly bizarre film. Films often order their stories around the Storyteller's priorities. In a mystery or film noir, this aims to test the audience's powers of observation and deduction as long as possible.

THEME AND THEMATIC PURPOSE

The *theme* of a work is the topic of its discourse or representation. For a film about a Nigerian prince who ends up as a New York cabbie, it might be, "Beggars must learn they cannot be choosers." For a film about an unknown actor auditioning for a musical, it might be, "Fake it till you make it." Check to see that everything in your movie serves the film's ultimate thematic purpose and that there is nothing superfluous or omitted.

METAPHYSICS: MEANING BEYOND THE REAL

Some films meant as escapist entertainment employ a realism that leaves little room for anything metaphysical, so audiences feel let down. They like the resonance of deeper meanings, and respond well to drama that offers the seeds of hope and ideas that are provocative. Allegory and parable (from *parabola*, meaning curved plane or comparison) can hit a nerve in audiences very powerfully, as shown by Robert Zemeckis' otherwise predictable *Forrest Gump* (1994, Figure 14-6). Its generous-hearted theme is that the gods protect a man without guile, and that all things eventually come right for the truly innocent.

USING GRAPHICS

To develop your film's thematic purpose, try inventing a graphic image or diagram, one that represents the movement of elements and characters through time in your story. The horizontal axis in Figure 14-7 represents advancing time, whereas the vertical axis represents the degree of pressure experienced by its two characters. Here, you see the development of an initially weak character in relation to a stronger one. You could make the vertical coordinate represent any condition (drunkenness, fear, hope, strength) according to the focus of the story in hand.

FIGURE 14-6 ───

In *Forrest Gump*, the gods seem to protect a man without guile (courtesy Paramount/The Kobal Collection).

FIGURE 14-7 ───

Graphic representation of an initially weak character developing in relation to one stronger.

By making the major dynamics into a graphic, you confront the director's toughest responsibility; that of making the film's underlying thesis palpable. You do this by way of a determined and systematic search—something we all want to avoid.

CHANCE AND CHANGE ALONG THE WAY

A work's full design and meaning emerge only at the end of postproduction. For instance, a problem in editing turns out to be a misjudged scene that subtly disrupts and negates the overall pattern. It must be changed, moved, or eliminated. Often by fixing a problem like this, you establish harmony elsewhere. It's as if by subtracting the false note in a chord, you find what's right. A film is an artwork, and an artwork never stops suggesting changes and improvements to its makers. This makes calling a halt to any stage of development difficult unless there are deadlines to meet.

CHAPTER 15

SPACE, STYLIZED ENVIRONMENTS, AND PERFORMANCES

SPACE

Film abridges space as well as time in the interest of narrative compression. A protagonist suddenly remembering at dinner that he forgot to feed his parking meter might be shown in four brief shots: (a) leaping to his feet, (b) his spoon splashing soup on the tablecloth, (c) his feet running downstairs, and then (d) arguing with a meter maid. Because we can imagine what's left out, only the key actions in different locations are necessary. Likewise, you will need to show only key aspects of a location. You can set three scenes in a baronial hall—one against the fireplace, one by the great stairway, and the last by a doorway flanked with suits of armor—and the audience's imagination will fill in the rest. People may afterward swear you had a shot of the whole hall.

By mentally completing what is suggested by clues, the audience for David Lynch's *Blue Velvet* (1986) cocreates a whole town. Every setup in his small-town America is contrived to be surreal, bespeaking Lynch's origins as a painter. The film's early and brilliant predecessor is Fritz Lang's *Metropolis* (1926), in which the stylized environment is so visionary that it becomes a leading component in the film's discourse. Expressionism creates a subjective, even nightmarish reality. Lynch's first film, *Eraserhead* (1978), about an alienated man learning that his girlfriend is pregnant, takes subjectivity to the limits of imaginable psychosis, and *Eraserhead* makes full and frightening use of the potential of sound. As Bresson said, "The eye sees, but the ear imagines."[1]

---

[1] Robert Bresson, *Notes on the Cinematographer* (Los Angeles: Green Integer, 1997).

STYLIZED WORLDS, CHARACTERS, AND GENRE

A genre, as we've said, is a specialized world in which we expect certain characteristics. Sympathy and involvement with a film character don't automatically arise because you see from a character's location in space; they arise because we have learned to like her from her actions, see what she is made of, and hope she will survive. The stylized (that is, heightened and intensified) camera coverage and editing of a genre do not alone create this, but they do serve it. In a musical, we expect theatricality, whereas the film noir, set in the shadows and at night, has depressed detectives falling in love with their haunted women clients. In a genre, the stylized character and his or her surroundings often come together as a package, and this package affects how we expect characters to behave. Nero in ancient Rome will play his fiddle differently from the fiddler on the roof in a central European shtetl.

DISTANCING AND SUSPENDING DISBELIEF

Any story benefits from being remote. The children's story opening, "Once upon a time . . ." attests how readily we suspend disbelief for anything filtered by time, distance, or memory. Period films fall readily into this category. Victor Fleming's *Gone with the Wind* (1939) was set in the antebellum South. In more recent examples, Anthony Minghella's *The English Patient* (1996) took place during World War II, and Ang Lee's athletic fable *Crouching Tiger, Hidden Dragon* (2000, Figure 15-1) was set in ancient China.

FIGURE 15-1 ————————————————————————————

Because *Crouching Tiger, Hidden Dragon* is remote in time and place, we readily accept its enchanted, operatic world (courtesy Columbia/Sony/The Kobal Collection/Chuen, Chan Kam).

Cinema set in the past continues the oral tradition in which historical events or personages can be freely shaped and embellished so they serve the narrator's artistic, social, or political purpose.

STYLIZATION

Stylizing anything means heightening the characters, settings, or story language beyond normal to accentuate its impact.

Partially stylized: Many of the films listed under single-character POV in previous chapters expose us only sparingly to the POV character's circumscribed vision. Mostly their drama is shown from a more detached and omniscient standpoint. In the famous shower scene in *Psycho* (1960), we temporarily merge with the killer's eye-line after he begins stabbing and POV switches to the last agonized images seen by Marion Crane. This brief foray into immediate, limited perceptions—first of the killer, then of his victim—is reserved for the starkest moment in the film, when Alfred Hitchcock boldly disposes of his heroine. After the killer runs out, we are left with the Storyteller's point of view—alone with the body in the motel room. Thus, Hitchcock makes his audience into privileged collaborators by raising their awareness above that of the characters.

Mainstream, omniscient cinema often uses a stylized POV as a storytelling inflection to indicate, say, a character's temporary imbalance (euphoria, fear, insecurity, etc.), or to share confidential information with the audience as a novelist might do in a literary aside. This information (symbolic objects, foreshadowing devices, special in-frame juxtapositions) is often withheld from the characters, and heightens tension by making us anticipate what the characters do not yet know.

Highly stylized: Robert Wiene's *The Cabinet of Dr. Caligari* (1919, Figure 15-2) borrowed its style from contemporary developments in the graphic arts, which explored a nightmarishly altered reality—a trend that foreshadowed events in Nazi Germany hardly by accident. Characters may have unnatural skin texture or move without shadows in a world of oversized, distorted architecture and machinery. F.W. Murnau's *Nosferatu* (1921) and Lang's *Dr. Mabuse* (1922) sought to create the same unhinged psychology with a more subtle use of the camera. They made their political and satirical comment much as Oskar Kokoschka, George Grosz, and Edvard Munch did through the graphic arts of the 1920s and 1930s.

Some films construct a highly stylized world. Stanley Kubrick's strange, violent *A Clockwork Orange* (1971, Figure 15-3) is a picaresque tale played out by painted grotesques in a series of surreal contemporary settings. Even if you quickly forget what the film is about, the visual effect is unforgettable, and owes its origins to the Expressionism of the German cinema earlier in the century. The band Kiss could almost have taken their visual presentation from the movie.

Expressionist worlds usually run according to inverted or alien rules, and are peopled by characters who neither think nor doubt. Travis Bickle in Martin Scorsese's *Taxi Driver* (1976) insanely misreads an intensified but still familiar world, whereas the hero in Lynch's *Blue Velvet* (1986) is a regular person trying to feel at home in a world that is arbitrary and distorted.

Futurism: No discussion of stylization would be complete without mentioning journeys into the imagined future. Lang's *Metropolis* (1926) is the classic, but there is no shortage of other examples. Charlie Chaplin's *Modern Times* (1936), Jean-Luc

FIGURE 15-2

Robert Wiene's *The Cabinet of Dr. Caligari* drew on experiments in the graphic arts of the period (courtesy Decla-Bioscop/The Kobal Collection).

FIGURE 15-3

A Clockwork Orange owes its origins to early 20th-century German Expressionism (courtesy Warner Bros./The Kobal Collection).

Godard's *Alphaville* (1965), Kubrick's *2001* (1968), François Truffaut's *Fahrenheit 451* (1966), George Lucas' *Star Wars* series (1977–2005), Ridley Scott's *Blade Runner* (1982), and Terry Gilliam's *Brazil* (1986) all hypothesize "what if" worlds of the future. Each shows grave distortions in the social, sexual, or political realms that put characters under duress. Plucked from the familiar and invited to respond as immigrants in a world operating under totalitarian assumptions, we are often shown the fascism of governments made omniscient through technology. In the drive to create a doomsday thesis, secondary characters often emerge as unindividualized, flat characters. Storytelling often explores collective anxieties, and the future seems reserved for nightmares about the individual isolated during a breakdown in collective control.

Stylized environments: Stylization is often derived from the period of a film's setting, as in Laurence Olivier's adaptation of Shakespeare's *Henry V* (1944), whose large figures lean out of small towers in sets inspired by illustrations from a medieval Book of Hours. Pier Paolo Pasolini's *The Gospel According to St. Matthew* (1964) uses cinematography and costuming to make the film redolent of Renaissance painting. Vincente Minnelli's theatrically stylized sets and playfully stereotyped characters in *An American in Paris* (1951, Figure 15-4) allowed Gene Kelly to make Paris into

FIGURE 15-4 —————————————————————————————————

An American in Paris creates a city of romance through unashamedly theatrical sets (courtesy MGM/The Kobal Collection).

FIGURE 15-5

Polanski's *Repulsion* draws us into experiencing the delusions of a mind on the slipway to madness (courtesy Compton-Tekli/Royal/The Kobal Collection).

a dream city of romance. A very different setting distinguishes Spike Jonze's darkly hilarious *Being John Malkovich* (1999), in which an unemployed puppeteer finds a way into the actor John Malkovich's head, and rents out the view from Malkovich's eyes. In Roman Polanski's chilling *Repulsion* (1965, Figure 15-5), the apartment occupied by its paranoid heroine becomes the embodiment of threatening evil. Though you know that events are projections of her deluded mind, the result is a sickeningly unpleasant sense of her psychotic vulnerability.

Stylized environments and music: Though past, future, or distant settings transport us far from the banality of contemporary life, your film can be set in the present, yet make everyday transactions seem heightened and nonrealistic. Music, when you go beyond using it to intensify mood, can impose a formal patterning of emotion on the life on-screen. Jacques Demy's *The Umbrellas of Cherbourg* (1964, Figure 15-6) tells a conventional small-town love story, but uses striking

FIGURE 15-6

Supremely designed and shot, *The Umbrellas of Cherbourg* tells of romance and loss in a small French coastal town. It effortlessly combines dance, story, and sung dialogue (courtesy Parc Films/Madeleine Films/The Kobal Collection).

color schemes and lyrical composition and camera movement. All the dialogue is sung, giving the effect of a realistic operetta (if that isn't an oxymoron). Music can provide historical, social, or emotional context, and can augment something that is inherently strong in emotion, or can counterpoint what we see with a countervailing feeling. It should not be used to illustrate what we can already see.

Music can make us accept an extreme view of human life. Peter Greenaway's use of Michael Nyman's minimalist scores in *The Draughtsman's Contract* (1983), *A Zed & Two Noughts* (1985), and *Drowning by Numbers* (1991) powerfully unites the mood of characters moving like sleepwalkers through worlds dominated by mathematical symmetry and organic decay.

It is better to have no music than bad music. For more on this subject, see Chapter 42, "Working with Music."

THE STYLIZED PERFORMANCE: FLAT AND ROUND CHARACTERS

Most adaptations of Charles Dickens' novels, as in David Lean's *Oliver Twist* (1948), make a young person their POV character and use him as a lens on the adult world. Fagan, Bill Sikes, and their fellow thieves verge on the grotesque, whereas Oliver remains a touching innocent caught in their web. These are what E.M. Forster called flat and round characters—Oliver as the round character is complex and psychologically complete; in contrast, the flat characters are rendered unidimensional by Oliver's limited and susceptible perception.

Whether a secondary character should be played as subjectively flattened can be decided by examining the controlling POV. In Orson Welles' adaptation of Franz Kafka's *The Trial* (1962), it is the character of Joseph K. with whom we identify and through whose psyche all the other, grotesque characters are seen. Likewise in *The Wizard of Oz* (1939), the two witches are flat characters acting in oppositional ways on Dorothy. They represent the opposed forces of good and evil in her life.

In stories where there is a polarization between the POV character and those in the surrounding world, oppositional characters or antagonists often seem like analogues for the warring parts of a divided self. The morality play form, with its melodramatic emphasis on setting the innocent adrift among hostile or confusing forces, is actually a useful way to externalize the flux within an evolving personality. I say "useful" because the cinema, with its emphasis on externals, does not otherwise handle interior reality particularly well.

Flat characters are reminiscent of the early theater's masked, stock characters who each had a dominant characteristic and represented particular types, such as a peasant, landlord, princess, or magician. As bit players, they often function as metaphors for aspects of the round character's predicament, and serve to alert us to a metaphysical subtext we might otherwise miss.

NAMING THE METAPHORICAL AND USING SYMBOLS

It is always revealing to approach every script as though each character has a *metaphorical role* in an allegory. You get at their identity by inventing metaphors to fit each character and then assigning him or her an archetypal identity. The archaeology professor leading an isolated dig with three attractive female graduate students can be the pasha and his harem—until he realizes too late that they are an Amazon warrior cell. These labels are tools to help you develop each cast member's actions and behavior.

Symbols help make the Storyteller's ideas visible and concrete—important because cinematography, as we've said, tends to blur the significant with a torrent of movement and detail. Symbols and metaphors can be built into the world your characters inhabit, but it's important that they are organic and not arbitrary or imposed. For instance, Paul Cox's *Cactus* (1985, Figure 15-7) portrays the developing relationship between an angry, desperate woman losing her sight and a reclusive man blind since birth. She visits him in the inherited cactus house that he tends, to see what she can learn from him about her fate. The dry, spiky cacti, hostile and phallic, aptly represent his predicament, for he survives self-punitively in a place devoid of tenderness or nourishment. In a sexually charged world, he has turned his back on intimacy. "Wounded animals should be left alone," he says.

FIGURE 15-7 ——————————————————————————————————————

Lovers amid encroaching darkness in Cox's *Cactus* (courtesy Spectrafilm).

Having metaphors in hand, and symbols or metaphoric action to shoot, will help focus your film and give it subtexts and subterranean meanings. They will also help you lead your actors toward playing their roles with the meanings you want. This will feature in upcoming chapters on analyzing the script and working with actors.

CHAPTER 16

FORM AND STYLE

FORM

Form is the manner in which content is presented. A film that delivers a memorable and intriguing impact usually has a form special to the story's purpose and nature. Norman McLaren's two shorts *Neighbours* (1952) and *Pas de Deux* (1969) make stunning use of pixilation and optical printing, respectively, to enhance what they have to say about men and territory, and about dance. Chris Marker's unforgettable futuristic fable *La Jetée* (1962) is told entirely in still photos with just a few seconds of movement in a single shot.

Possibilities in form may seem unlimited, but in fact they are limited by story logic and related concerns. From deciding the story's ruling point of view and purpose, you can choose the genre, imagery, and even camera angles that best serve your authorial intentions. Let's see how this might work.

Say you are planning a short film about a holdup in a grocery store. First decide the controlling point of view, which could be that of the store owner, a nearsighted old man out buying a lottery ticket, the off-duty policeman getting a loaf of bread, or the robber himself. The robbery has a different significance for each because every person would be in a different frame of mind and notice different things.

Point of view suggests the choice of lenses and camera positions—all contributing to the cumulative progression of impressions that add up to a particular person's way of seeing. Lighting would flow from the time of day, mood, type of store, and kind of interaction. How the camera is handled (static positions, handheld, mounted on a dolly) would also flow from point of view and the kind of comment the director wants to make. You might additionally choose particular set dressing and a particular film stock or video image characteristics. Then, in the final film, you might place the events in the store in or out of their chronology. That is, the crime need not be shown in chronological order—you might show it in discontinuous portions, as remembered by a survivor, or perhaps in stage-by-stage retrospect in the court case following the arrest of the robber. Different witnesses might have conflicting versions of key actions, and so on.

In fact, screen order is also subservient to the controlling point of view. For the whole film is filtered through the Storyteller, whose agenda and purpose are distinct from any held by the characters. For instance, the Storyteller might concentrate on one character's experience or shift narrative focus among three of the characters, and treat each as equally important.

Good formal choices can be made only from analysis and making decisions. If in doubt, shoot enough coverage so you can delay decision making to the cutting room, where you can experiment.

THE STORYTELLER'S VISION

Audiences know instinctively that *good fiction is not a reproduction of life, but an enactment of ideas about it.* If your topic is robbery, be provocative about what robbery means—socially, culturally, or emotionally. Ask yourself:

- Who carries out robbery, in what way, and why?
- Why am I attracted to this basic situation—does it have roots in an analogous experience of mine?
- How do my characters make their own destiny?
- What moves them to act, and what does the incident say about life and living?
- Where should the moment of robbery lie in the overall development of the film?
- What should it contribute?
- How do I establish who's who before the robbery?
- Who develops during the film's events, and what should the audience learn?
- What do I want my audience to see, consider, wonder about during each phase of my film?

This kind of interrogation, so natural a mental activity while one watches drama, is something you plan during the writing, designing, shooting, and editing stages. Calculating how to reveal the story's events, and what questions the audience will formulate and at what points, are how the Storyteller uses his or her entertainer's power. The following examples highlight the elements of form you can take into consideration.

VISUAL DESIGN

A film gains power when its thematic concerns emerge visually rather than through dialogue exchanges. A striking visual approach is generated by art directing, costuming, set dressing, lighting, choice of lenses, camera height and movements, and by the locations and even the terrain. Ingmar Bergman's *The Seventh Seal* (1956), set in the Middle Ages when people's hearts were ruled by superstition and fear of the plague, tells much of its story amid gloomy forests. The dark figures and low-key, high-contrast black-and-white photography prime us to anticipate the mixture of magic and superstitious terror at the heart of an epoch when life was "nasty, brutish, and short."[1]

[1] Thomas Hobbes (1588–1679).

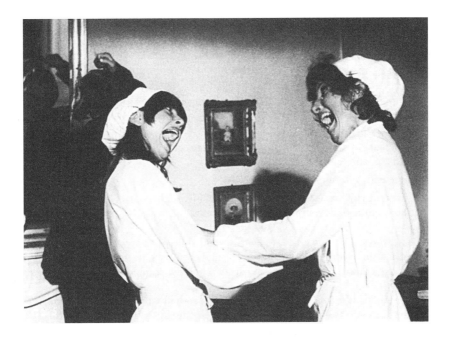

FIGURE 16-1

Two friends discover each is playing the same part in the drama they have infiltrated. Rivette's *Celine and Julie Go Boating* (courtesy New Yorker Films).

Jacques Rivette's *Celine and Julie Go Boating* (1974, Figure 16-1) has a brilliantly original development in its visual style. Two young women break into a shuttered house where a stagy domestic drama is slowly unfolding. Becoming absorbed by the characters, they keep returning in hope of learning the "play's" outcome. One day, they discover they can enter the play's action and affect its course without the characters' noticing. As the piece develops, and as missing links drop into place, the characters and their setting become less and less natural in color. What started as realism gradually becomes surreal, distanced, and artificial—until the main characters have merged into a dynamic genre painting. The film's theme seems to be that living with impassioned active curiosity makes life turn into art.

SOUND DESIGN

Robert Bresson said, "The eye sees, but the ear imagines." Summon for yourself the feelings that go with these sounds: the cooing of doves floating in through a sunny bedroom window, footfalls in a church, children distantly playing hide-and-seek, or muffled weeping in a darkened room. They work miraculously on our imagination and receptivity. Sometimes the sound track can go quiet, presenting us with the shock and tension of silence.

Sound effects should sometimes be a foreground player, not a late cosmetic applied to a stage play. Sound designer Randy Thom complains that he is usually brought into a production just as it has been edited into wall-to-wall dialogue— so he can add nothing. To avert the audience fatigue this produces, he recommends screenwriting for sound. That is, characters should listen, and quiet spaces should exist when the picture is deliberately withholding information so narrative momentum is channeled through sound. David Lynch's films are very sound-sensitive, and make excellent examples of movies that included sound in their original design. Thom's "Designing a Movie for Sound" at www.filmsound.org is a first-rate resource for anyone who wants to use sound inventively.

Sound in feature films is often *diegetic,* so that a traffic scene will have every type of passing vehicle, and every set of pedestrian footsteps. In interiors, every footfall is rendered with correct timbre changes as characters traverse different surfaces. Far from the fidelity it aspires to, the effect is cluttered and suffocating. The Italian neorealist cinema of the 1950s and the French New Wave of the 1960s established that simplified sound tracks augment the characters' emotional focus rather than drowning it in the undifferentiated totality of their environment. When two people talk during a bike ride, you hear just their voices and none of the surrounding ambience. This, you realize, is *what they are aware of*, not what is objectively present. It is very satisfying to watch.

RHYTHMIC DESIGN

The idea of rhythmic design suggests music or sound such as footsteps and clocks ticking, but many other rhythmic elements are present:

- Most natural sound effects
- Speech patterns and breathing patterns
- Scene alternation (long scenes interspersed with short ones, for instance)
- Sound changes
- Picture cuts

There are also visual rhythms present in:

- Shots (affected by content and its movement and its composition)
- Camera movements
- Physical actions
- Particular characters (who vary according to their temperament, mood, time of day, predicament, etc.)
- Pacing of sequences in relation to those before and after

Rhythms important to cinema language emanate from multiple sources at any given time. A good editor and an experienced director are acutely sensitive to their combined effect, and know as instinctively as any musician when their "orchestration" is or isn't working.

An audience's involvement is best sustained by variety. William Shakespeare— who supported a large company of actors by satisfying the tastes of the common people—juxtaposes very different textures and rhythms in the course of elaborating a theme. He switches from action to monologue to comedy, intersperses long scenes and short scenes, group scenes and duologues, duologues and soliloquies. So as you design your narrative, refresh the ear and eye with variations and comparisons, and make us pass through a succession of perspectives and moods. You can also do this as you vary your film's dramatic pressure—increasing or relaxing the tension by bringing rhythmic changes. Bergman says, "Film is mainly rhythm; it is inhalation and exhalation in continuous sequence."[2]

MOTIFS

Motifs are devices placed by the Storyteller to signify thematic aspects. For example, shots of nature and flowing water might in the right context signify that "life goes on no matter what." Any integrated aural or visual element can signify a motif, and one that recurs is called a leitmotif. They help to raise ideas and interpretation above the insistently material world that film throws at us.

VISUAL MOTIFS

The motif in Abraham Polonsky's *Tell Them Willie Boy Is Here* (1969) is the action of running. For the fugitive Indian, running becomes emblematic of his existence—as it once was for Polonsky, who was badly victimized during the McCarthy witchhunt years. In Hiroshi Teshigahara's *Woman in the Dunes* (1964), shots of trickling, invading sand constantly remind us of the woman's threatened situation as sand inundates her beachside house. In Roman Polanski's *Tess* (1979), color itself becomes the motif, just as Thomas Hardy used it in the original novel. The young peasant heroine, moving unconsciously between what society deems innocence and what it deems sin, is repeatedly associated with either white or red (the white dresses in the opening May walk, the red of the strawberry that her seducer, Alec, puts between her unwilling lips, for example). In Nicolas Roeg's *Don't Look Now* (1973), the color red is made to connote incipient danger.

Compositional balance or imbalance, camera vantage (looking through foreground objects, for instance), or the use of sound and silence might all be pressed into service as motifs. Even camera movements can become a motif. The crabbing shots through the trees in Robert Enrico's perfect short film *An Occurrence at Owl Creek Bridge* (1962) communicate the guilty voyeurism of someone helplessly watching a friend meet his end.

AURAL MOTIFS

In John Carpenter's *Halloween* (1978), an ominous, almost subsonic synthesizer sound accompanies the presence of the vengeful escapee. It is a *nondiegetic* sound (meaning it is heard by the audience and not by the characters), and heightens our sense of their incipient danger. Most film music uses the leitmotif principle—that is, a special instrumentation and/or special musical theme running through the film is assigned to a particular character, situation, or sentiment. Sergey Prokofiev's delightful orchestral piece for children, *Peter and the Wolf*, uses leitmotifs for each main character in its fable. It was composed to demonstrate the instruments of the orchestra and their tonal range.

---

[2] Introduction to *Four Screenplays of Ingmar Bergman* (New York: Simon & Schuster, 1960).

BRECHTIAN DISTANCING AND AUDIENCE IDENTIFICATION

Cinema, unlike literature, views characters from the outside, and thus favors action over contemplation. The suspense film and the action thriller go further, for they aim to make you "lose yourself" by identifying with the hero, as the success of the James Bond films testifies. You might think that all films promote audience identification; theater did until Bertolt Brecht (1898–1956) set out to subvert this in a Germany succumbing to the Nazis. Realizing he could not spur his audiences to critical awareness if they willingly sank into the dream state of identifying, Brecht set out to change theater language. By devising a theater of mixed and constantly changing genres, Brecht ensured that his audience could never forget it was watching a show with a purpose, not simulated reality.

Brechtian influence can be found in such different work as Jean-Luc Godard's *My Life to Live* (1962); Mike Nichols' *Catch-22* (1970); Peter Greenaway's *The Cook, the Thief, His Wife & Her Lover* (1989); Baz Luhrman's *Moulin Rouge!* (2001, Figure 16-2); and even in the gloriously loony Monty Python films. Their discourse is essentially postmodern; and may employ authorial narration, titles, songs, musical interludes, or surreal events peopled with bizarre, allegorical, or historical characters. Mass audiences are not yet drawn to Brecht's demanding theater, but the work of those under his influence can be immensely moving, invigorating, and downright hilarious. Keeping an audience thinking and not just feeling is a rare skill that awaits development on a wider scale in mainstream cinema. Wim Wenders' two extraordinary films about angels watching over Berlin—*Wings of Desire* (1988) and *Faraway, So Close* (1993)—point most excitingly in this direction.

FIGURE 16-2 ————————————————————————————————————

Moulin Rouge! owes some of its surreal narrative freedom to Bertolt Brecht's theatrical distancing techniques (courtesy 20th Century Fox/The Kobal Collection).

LONG TAKES VERSUS SHORT TAKES

Rodrigo Garcia's *Nine Lives* (2005), a rare film that plays whole scenes as single long takes, lets you stand back and consider the meaning of the characters' lives rather than pressing you to identify with their emotions. In conventional technique, editing and mobile camerawork inject nervous excitement and enable the point of view to zigzag around a central character—classic techniques for pummeling the spectator into identifying. To eliminate the need for editing, the long take needs astute blocking and rehearsal. Close-ups are produced by blocking (that is, choreographing) characters to move close to the camera. The drawback to this technique is that one cannot intercut takes or cut around problems, so director and cast must maintain a high level and consistency of playing. Actors or technicians may at any time stumble and abort a whole scene.

Somewhere between the extremes—Sergei Eisenstein's fragmentation with its control and exploitation of the spectator's sensibilities at one end of the spectrum, and the unbroken, uninflected presentation of long-take cinema at the other—lies how your Storyteller wants to relay the story to the audience. There is a place for both emotion and intellect in watching any film, though not equally in every single scene it contains. Depending on content and point of view, your film may call for different language at different points.

SHORT FILM FORMS: A NEGLECTED ART

The short film is closest to poetic form because it requires deft characterization, a compressed narrative style, and something fresh and focused to say. It is often overlooked by new directors, who equate length with significance. Here are some classic shorts, compiled with the help of Peter Rea and David K. Irving's excellent *Producing and Directing the Short Film and Video*, 3rd ed. (Boston: Focal Press, 2006). Look for these films via Netflix, the Internet, in specialized collections listed at Facets Multi-Media (www.facets.org), or at Amazon (www.amazon.com). Some of the films have different titles in other languages; I have included alternate titles.

> Block, Mitchell: *No Lies* (USA, 1972; B&W, 16 minutes). It looks like a documentary as the director crudely presses a raped woman for an account of her misfortune, but it's all acted and for a purpose.
>
> Buñuel, Luis: *Un Chien Andalou (An Andalusian Dog)* (France, 1928; B&W, 20 minutes). A surrealist experiment, undertaken with Salvador Dalí, in shocking imagery that consciously avoids any linear story logic.
>
> Davidson, Adam: *The Lunch Date* (USA, 1990; B&W, 12 minutes). A deceptive encounter over a salad between a woman and a homeless man at Grand Central Station.
>
> Deren, Maya, and Alexander Hammid: *Meshes of the Afternoon* (USA, 1943; B&W, 13 minutes). Seminal work in which the mother of American experimental cinema plays a woman driven by loneliness and adversity to dream of suicide.
>
> Enrico, Robert: *An Occurrence at Owl Creek Bridge (La Rivière du Hibou)* (France, 1962; B&W, 27 minutes). An American Civil War soldier makes a miraculous escape from hanging—or does he? A perfect short film that's also a catalog of judiciously used sound and picture film techniques.

Godard, Jean-Luc: *Tous les Garçons s'Appellent Patrick (All the Boys Are Called Patrick)* (France, 1957; B&W, 21 minutes). Two girls find they are dating the same boy.

Lamorisse, Albert: *Le Ballon Rouge (The Red Balloon)* (France, 1956; color, 34 minutes). A lonely boy makes friends in Paris with a balloon, which begins to reciprocate his attentions. No words.

Marker, Chris: *La Jetée (The Pier)* (France, 1962; B&W, 29 minutes). A film almost entirely in stills about a survivor of World War III whose childhood memories allow him to move around at will in time. One shot has motion, and as Georges Sadoul rightly says, "the screen disarmingly bursts into sensuous life."

Metzner, Ernö: *Polizeibericht Überfall (Accident) (Police Report! Assault)* (Germany, 1928; B&W, 21 minutes). A man wins some cash in a beer hall, but it brings him nothing but bad luck. A lexicon of silent cinema and editing techniques.

Polanski, Roman: *Two Men and a Wardrobe (Dwaj Ludzie z Szafa)* (Poland, 1957; B&W, 15 minutes). Two men appear out of the sea, struggling with a bulky wardrobe, unable to solve their problems and avoiding humanity.

Polanski, Roman, and Jean-Pierre Rousseau: *The Fat and the Lean (Le Gros et le Maigre)* (France, 1961; B&W, 15 minutes). An allegory about a fat and a thin man exploring the interdependency between master and servant, and what stops the servant from running away.

Renoir, Jean: *Partie de Campagne (A Day in the Country)* (France, 1936; B&W, 37 minutes). Guy de Maupassant's tale in which a Paris shopkeeper takes his family for a day in the country. His affianced daughter falls in love with another man, but the relationship has no future. Renoir's debt to Impressionism, and to his famous father, emerges.

The dates in these indicate just how few top-notch short films exist. Festivals prefer them to longer films because they are popular with audiences and easier to schedule.

SHORT FILMS AND YOU

To earn recognition, you must win prizes; so please be kind to yourself—save time and money, get invaluable experience, and compete in the less restricted arena. Shorts are inexpensive and place high demand on your control of craft and storytelling essentials. A good short needs:

- A limited but evocative setting
- Characters engaged in a significant struggle to get, do, or accomplish
- One character who develops—however minimally
- A resolution that leaves the audience pondering some aspect of the human condition

Your film can be a farce, a dark comedy, a lyrical love letter, a Chaplinesque allegory, a sitcom—anything. Shorts work you hardest in the ideation area—just where most people are lazy. They send you rapidly through the entire production cycle, are a good learning vehicle, and make perfect "calling card" films (short works that show off your abilities).

Think of it this way: you might make five 8-minute films for the price of one lasting 60-minutes and increase your chances of recognition fivefold. Then, after you've directed five casts and have given life to a host of different characters, you can handle a long film five times as well.

If your best film is well acted, interestingly shot, and tautly edited, it becomes the ultimate advertisement for what you could do with a bigger canvas. Two Chicago wedding videomakers and their composer brother circulated free copies in Hollywood of their deft little 8½-minute comedy *Script Doctor* (1999). Subsequently they were invited to Los Angeles to make a feature. Why not you?

STYLE

Godard said, "Style is just the outside of content, and content the inside of style, like the outside and inside of the human body—both go together, they can't be separated."[3] A film's style evidences its maker's identity, but the distinction is a little messy because film authorship is collective. That said, any Jarmusch, Almodóvar, or Kiarostami film is immediately recognizable. It's not only the content, kind of tale, and forms each tends to choose, but also that their work has the directors' personalities and tastes written all over them. It is this last, virtually uncontrollable element that is properly known as style.

Just as you can't choose your own identity, so you should let your film identity, or style, take care of itself. If you serve each controllable aspect of your film well, people will come to recognize something they will call your style.

---

[3] Richard Roud, *Jean-Luc Godard* (London: Secker & Warburg, 1967), p. 13.

PART 5

PREPRODUCTION

This part (Chapters 17 through 27) covers the crucial project development and self-development that come between choosing a script and beginning the shoot. This includes:

- Breaking down and analyzing the script
- Casting
- The principles of the actor's craft
- Experiencing acting and improvising for yourself
- Working as a director with actors
- Rehearsal and planning camera coverage
- Production design and the logistical planning prior to shooting

Much of this part necessarily concerns acting, which takes great courage to do, and tact and discernment to handle as a director. Acting exercises in improvisation and with a text are vital to any director-in-training. Like nothing else, they reveal the world the actor lives in, and they help you to become knowledgeable, respectful, and fascinated by those who practice this noble craft.

Rehearsal and development are often omitted by professionals and novices alike. Use them wisely, and you can dig deeply into life below the surface of the script. There, you will find those structures and meanings without which a movie is but a hollow facade. I strongly recommend videotaping "off-the-book rehearsals" (those where the actors have learned their lines), and there's a suggested working method that will make this stage fertile and exciting. There are guidelines for actor and director preparing a scene, and then guidance on planning coverage. The roundup of design, logistics, and technical needs comes in the all-important preproduction meetings.

CHAPTER 17

ACTING FUNDAMENTALS

The innate realism of photography leads us to expect psychological realism from film acting, so you will need to understand actors and even become something of a drama coach. Most importantly, you, too, need some exposure to acting. You will need acting skills anyway, to cover your lack of confidence as you play the role of confident film director.

What follows is a brief primer that I hope will launch you into acting and studying books on acting by the master teachers. They provoke very partisan followings, but those I like are Robert Benedetti's concise and accessible *The Actor in You: Sixteen Simple Steps to Understanding the Art of Acting*, 3rd ed. (Allyn & Bacon, 2005), Benedetti's *The Actor at Work*, 9th ed. (Allyn & Bacon, 2004), Uta Hagen and Haskel Frankel's *Respect for Acting* (Wiley, 1973), Charles Marowitz's *The Art of Being: Towards a Theory of Acting* (Taplinger, 1978), and Sanford Meisner's *Sanford Meisner on Acting* (Vintage, 1987). Eric Morris, Joan Hotchkis, and Jack Nicholson's *No Acting Please* (Ermor Enterprises, 1995) is particularly appropriate for film work. Several of these texts are old, and may even be difficult to obtain. Acting is an old craft, however, and some texts explain it more concisely and appropriately for film than others do. Try www.abebooks.com for bargain-priced copies of practically anything.

STANISLAVSKY

The Russian actor Konstantin Stanislavsky (1863–1938) developed the modern explanation of acting from interviewing the best actors of his day. By looking for psychological linkages and extracting common denominators, he developed his groundbreaking explanations. Empty gestures and histrionics do not fool a modern audience, he said, because we are highly expert at recognizing and appreciating the real thing. Actors, he concluded, are called such because they *act upon* each other. Characters become truthful and believable when the actor maintains an interior and exterior life that is authentic for his or her character. Stanislavsky showed how the actor can achieve this by sustaining and disciplining his imagination.

Today, acting is a very well documented craft, so what follows is a brief digest of useful ideas and practices to get you started.

JUSTIFICATION

Every action, every line, should be justifiable according to the *givens;* that is, all the information given in the script. This includes each character's background, history, recent experience, and thought process in relation to the others. A director will frequently review this with the actors, especially when a section seems fuzzy and unmotivated.

IMAGINATION

The doctor and novelist Ethan Canin once said he thought that every act of cruelty starts from a failure of imagination.[1] By this measure, acting is the most generous of professions because it starts from imagining your way into becoming someone else. We did this effortlessly enough as children, but as we grow up to become more self-conscious, it gets more difficult. Techniques exist, however, to encourage and discipline the imagination.

FOCUS AND RELAXATION

Think of how relaxed, concentrated, and boundlessly energetic you feel as you concentrate on something you really love to do. It might be grooming a pet, riding a skateboard, or playing an instrument in an ensemble. People can watch you, come and go, or ignore you—and you stay focused and relaxed. This mental and emotional *focus* allows you to simply *be;* that is, to become completely relaxed in mind and body. Imagine now the opposite condition: you step into a room full of strangers. Under their stare, you feel so awkward, discomposed, and self-conscious that you can barely put words together.

Being focused or self-conscious is the heaven and hell of the actor's existence. Using what Stanislavsky called the *magic "if"* lets the actor find his or her character's mental focus so that the actor can relax, become natural, alert, and present in his or her character's "now." Then the audience sees a character really thinking, planning, remembering, deciding—all those actions that take place inside a living, breathing person. People in documentaries, doing something normal or that consumes all their attention, are effortlessly natural, and this is the gold standard you aim for in fictional characters. Actors cannot will themselves into this, for that makes them try too hard and fear failure. Instead, the actor must let go of tension, ambition, and self-image—all the anxiety-driven mental "noise" that impairs focus and relaxation.

LOSING AND REGAINING FOCUS

The film actor cannot stop thinking his or her character's thoughts or seeing as his or her character sees. That is, the actor cannot afford to *lose focus.* The camera registers everything minutely, so the audience knows when there's any interruption

---

[1] In a National Public Radio interview c. 1998.

in flow. Soldiering on while worrying about his or her loss of effectiveness leaves the poor actor fatally split. This, like drowning to divers, is the actor's occupational hazard.

When actors are focused, then lose it, there's always a reason. Something in the text doesn't sit right, or something has happened to shake them out of character. A misplaced prop, a wrong line from another actor, something happening in their eye line to distract them—all these can cut the flow. Insecurity of all kinds—even the fear of losing focus—leads to loss of focus, and a believable character crumbles in a moment into a beleaguered actor. Unless the actor has learned how to recover, she can feel completely exposed. But the actor trained to regain focus can evade the crippling self-consciousness that sets in.

An effective way to regain focus is for the actor to look closely at something nearby, such as a carpet pattern or the texture of her sleeve. Because it is real and in her character's here and now, the actor's attention is stabilized. Now she can broaden her attention by stages to eventually include her character's larger sphere of awareness. All this can happen with no break during a conversation. Trained actors know how to do this, but untrained ones don't.

THE MIND-BODY CONNECTION

A person's body language, when you know how to read it, subtly expresses what's in his heart and mind. A brother will know whether his sister has had a good or bad day from how she eats a sandwich or sets down her bicycle. From a person's flow of small facial, vocal, and body language, we get a good sense of what he is thinking and feeling, even if he comes from a completely different culture. The truth is that *no inner state exists without outward evidence*. Indeed, there could be no international language of cinema if this were not true.

An actor experiencing her character's thoughts, sensations, and emotions expresses them effortlessly and unconsciously through her physical instrument—that is, through her body, face, actions, and voice. This means that even *interior actions* such as choosing, holding back, or calculating become unexpectedly interesting to watch. I learned this as a teenage editing assistant while watching studio dailies. The best actors remained alive and interesting during reaction shots because you could see their character's interior life continuing. Mediocre actors, on the other hand, looked paralyzed without the cover of lines or action. Having no interior life left them *indicating* during reaction close-ups, which means trying to signal thought and feeling rather than experiencing it.

DEVELOPING THE CHARACTER'S INTERIOR LIFE

An actor can prepare what his character's interior life is likely to be. Working from all the clues in the text, he decides scene by scene what his character wants, thinks, notices, remembers, and imagines. The actor also works out how his character will walk, sit, stand, eat, and do everything else. This helps him imagine how his character feels the weight of cutlery in his hand, smells flowers or freshly dug earth, cries, whispers, eats, or opens a can of food. Every action is unique to his character, to that character's mood, and to the moment—and his or her every action helps convey the character's thoughts and feelings.

INTERIOR MONOLOGUE

Having to develop an inner life compels an actor to articulate the innermost thoughts and feelings that produce whatever he says and does in the script. Then again, everything the other characters do—if the actor is taking this in—helps feed this inner life. Because every relationship (say, with one's parents, teachers, best friend, most hated enemy) evokes a different "me," so characters show a range of selves to each other. A woman, for instance, might show very different selves to her son and to an abusive fellow worker.

Many actors maintain an *interior monologue*, much as you or I do when we talk ourselves through something. This is a reliable way to keep up a focused consciousness, and is especially useful when having to repeat the same scene several times for different camera angles. Fatigue or boredom tempts an actor to cut corners, but keeping up that interior monologue helps the actor stay focused and in the moment.

ISOLATION AND COMMUNION

Preparation can be employed in a counterproductive way when an actor uses it as a protective cocoon. When this happens, it's called *acting in isolation*. The actor neither notices nor reacts to the query in another actor's voice, or to the glance of surprise or slight gesture of submission. He can't—he's visualizing his lines on the printed page and trying to do exactly what he had decided to do, irrespective of the life around him. In fact, that life is subtly different every time the scene is played. True, the scene and its lines are the same, but when everyone reacts to each other's nuances, which vary every time, the scene is fully alive. This is called *communion*.

ACTIONS

Getting on a bike, smiling, or clearing one's throat are plainly *actions*, but it's important to note that dialogue is also a form of action. If you say to a friend, "Do you play tennis here?" you are actively seeking information so you can realize your agenda (to find out whether the place is good, whether you could join him, etc.). Thus, dialogue is often called *verbal action*. It's acting on someone to change something.

OBJECTIVES

Dramatic characters pursue a series of urgent needs, each of which demands satisfaction. An actor therefore must stay physically and mentally busy *in character,* and develop whatever his or her character is trying to get, do, or accomplish in the here and now. These goals, called the character's *objectives*, are discussed as transitive verbs; that is, "doing" words, each denoting an action meant to affect someone. For example, "I'll scream till Dad stops the car." Note that you can't act "being angry," "being hurt," or being anything at all, because it's too general and not playable. The actor who turns on the TV because her character is angry or hurt must know what response her character wants, and if it is not forthcoming, there will be *dramatic tension* as she figures out what course to take next.

In life, we pursue our strategies unconsciously, but actors must consciously construct them. They do this by breaking their parts down into their character's objectives ("I will make him listen and see my side," or, "I will tear open the door and overpower the guard"), and endowing each objective with:

- An active verb (I will charm, *not* I will be charming)
- Someone or something acted upon (my brother's standoffish wife)
- A desired and measurable outcome (so she asks me to stay to dinner)

Applying this formula helps transform every beat into a series of actable goals. The actor-as-character has (a) a motivated action to perform, (b) someone to act on, and (c) a desired outcome by which to assess success or failure. Following an agenda like this gives shape and purpose to his character's every moment, will be fascinating to watch, and will be a joy for other actors to work with.

SUBTEXT

If you say to someone, "So, shall I see you again?" it can mean a number of things. If you have a hidden agenda (hoping to get money back that you lent), then the subtext might be, "Maybe I can get you to finally repay me." The "text" remains the same, but the *subtext* can be very different. ("You never make time for me these days"—"Do you still care for me?") That actors maintain communion is vital, or they won't pick up on each other's subtexts, which carry the hidden life of the scene. If a father and son argue about whether the car needs gas, their words concern the journey, but the subtext may be that the son wants to be an adult in his dad's eyes. Actors arrive at their characters' subtexts through an overall understanding of each one's character, and what that particular character is trying to achieve.

Harold Pinter's plays exploit the tensions between the characters' surface conformity and the dark, groping, private worlds that exist within their psyches. In *The Dumb Waiter*, two hired assassins are left waiting interminably in a disused kitchen for further instructions. The lengthening wait, punctuated with bizarre, unfulfillable messages sent down in the dumbwaiter, acts corrosively on the two men's private fears and distrust. While trying to maintain the faltering normality of their working partnership, each is gnawed by increasing fears so that they regress to feral animosity from sheer insecurity.

The Dumb Waiter's subtexts reveal a world of masters and servants, order and chaos, insecurity and incipient violence. The two characters suggest humankind nervously awaiting God's will. As you can imagine, the piece can flop badly if the actors fail to exploit all the subtextual possibilities.

BUSINESS AND PERSONALIZING

During rehearsal, each actor seeks his character's objectives during every action and line, and all the physical business that accompanies them. Acting is all about verbs, those "doing" words. Those verbs might include *lowering* the eyes, *glancing* out of a window, *searching* for change in a pocket, or *recalling* a birthday kiss from a loving aunt. Interior actions are as important as exterior. It can be entrancing to watch someone deciding to refuse a meal, or put a stop to a phone conversation, when it's done authentically and well. Helen Mirren's stoic, locked-up monarch in Stephen Frears' *The Queen* (2006) faces a series of expectations that she finds intolerable. This requires stillness on the outside, and angry thoughts and feelings pent up within. The result is an empathetic portrait of what a dutiful queen must stomach when her tribe rejects her. Dedicated actors find this kind of challenge irresistible.

An actor *personalizes* by discussing the character's issues and problems in the first, not the third, person. To say, "She's getting really depressed" would signify standing outside one's character, but to say, "I'm getting agitated and blaming myself for the delay" takes full responsibility in the here and now.

ADAPTING AND ANTICIPATING

In life, we frequently meet with obstructions and must find another way forward. Stanislavsky called altering course like this *adaptation*, because dramatic characters with objectives are continuously meeting and adapting to obstacles, which may be external (a locked door) or internal (fear of what the boss will say). Obstacles give the characters something to push against, and how each person adapts gives clues to the workings of their character.

For adaptation between characters, picture something like two people trying to stand up in a small boat. Each must compensate for the changes of balance caused by the movements of the other. This causes many feints, experiments, surprises, and mistakes. A script says nothing about these because it is the actors' work to create whatever adaptations lead to the next line or piece of action. This is less difficult than it sounds because we are all expert at recognizing what is humanly authentic. The actors suggest and demonstrate; the director accepts, rejects, modifies, or asks for a new solution.

An actor's problem is that, knowing what is coming in the text, he *anticipates* what is going to happen. Thus, a vital aspect of an actor's relaxation is to give up trying to look ahead—and to just let the scene happen.

SENSE MEMORY

In life, we build up a bank of memories and associations, and this plays a big part in our capacity to imagine and empathize. Memories and sensory input are intimately linked—the smell of baked potatoes at home, the flapping of one's clothes at the seaside, the rough feel of rope in a gym, the song of a skylark rising ever higher into an azure sky—all these sensory memories are key to a time, place, mood, and special people.

An actor reading a script relates his or her character's experiences to whatever correlates in his memory bank. There, he finds the analogous experiences to help imagine what a pilot does while losing control of an aircraft, what a store clerk does as she wins the lottery, or what a pensioner does on finding that he's lost his door key.

EMOTION AND EMOTIONAL MEMORY

Using sense memory, the actor recovers the specific actions he or she does under particular circumstances. When authentic, these actions evoke particular emotions. For example, practice covering your mouth in the precise way you do when you've spoken out of turn, and you will actually experience some embarrassment. Try it several times!

Any natural, accompanying physical action, which is part of an actor's business, can awaken *emotional memory*. Try several more actions associated with strong feelings, such as shielding your face from a slap, sipping a cold drink on a hot day, stepping back from a sheer drop, walking past a gruesome road accident, or placing your hand tenderly on a child's fevered brow.

Now, without making any physical movement, try just feeling embarrassed—or try summoning any other feeling. You can't do it because *you cannot choose to feel an emotion*. It's humanly impossible. You need business to help you get there, and this is why trained actors must constantly decide what their characters do, moment to moment.

Actions produce emotions, but most people think that emotions produce actions. They do, of course, but the actor's problem is getting to a point from which natural emotion will flow. Actions authentic to the character and moment release authentic emotions in the actor every time he or she performs them, and these communicate to the audience every time too. Recognizing that memory is not in our heads alone, but in our bodies, our actions, and even in smell and feeling, Stanislavsky named this curious reflex *emotional memory*. Unfortunately, it's also the most misunderstood of his discoveries about acting psychology.

You must use the sensory to access the emotional. In Marcel Proust's novel *Remembrance of Things Past*, it was the taste and smell of the little fluted cakes called *petites madeleines* that unlocked the enchanted gate on his childhood.

USING THE ACTOR'S EMOTIONS AS THE CHARACTER'S

What should the actor do when an inappropriate emotion intrudes itself, such as pain from a headache, shock at an unexpected move by a partner, or confusion from a misplaced prop? Well-trained actors, knowing how little remains hidden from an audience, learn to incorporate every genuine emotion into the character's present. The Second City comedy training in Chicago makes it a prerequisite for a comedian's training that they sustain their character under any and every condition.

This means, in effect, embracing and co-opting the invader instead of fighting a losing battle to keep it out. Real emotions are always visible, so struggling to quash the intruder is pointless. You might as well use it.

By using every facet of an actor's consciousness to maintain the character's physical and mental action, and by reacting to every nuance of the other characters' behavior, the actor stays so busy every time the scene is played, and so aware on so many levels, that everything outside the intense, subjective sphere of the character's reality recedes from consciousness. He or she no longer worries about remembering lines or whether anyone is watching.

You can experience this intense state of focus for yourself by trying some of the improvisation work in Chapter 19, "Acting Improvisation Exercises." Maintaining the same focus within the regimen of a text takes more discipline, especially when shooting multiple takes and angles that stretch out into a whole day of movie work. Seeing Rod Steiger's work in dailies during the making of Ken Annakin's film noir *Across the Bridge* (1957) was a revelation—never had I seen acting of such intensity, nor could I imagine anybody maintaining their character and German accent off camera. Steiger did both consummately, and he also did wonderful reaction shots.

THEATER AND FILM ACTING COMPARED

When you see an acclaimed theater production on the screen, some quality in the acting makes the performances ring false. Why are theater and film acting so very different? In fact, it's a psychological matter rather than one of technique, and concerns where actors get support for what they do. The theater actor works symbiotically with the pulse of the audience, but film actors have no such support. They must work wholly from what their character is thinking, feeling, and doing—just as we do in normal life. Directing fiction and documentary film is rather similar, for documentary participants are invariably natural whenever they "lose themselves" in doing whatever is necessary and normal for them. No enlarged action or voice projection is needed, for the camera captures every twitch of an eyebrow and every note in the voice.

For the theater actor to produce this naturalness for an audience seated at a distance, he or she must speak louder and make his or her actions a little bigger. Though theater training is unparalleled, acting on camera for the first time can leave actors feeling alone and self-doubting. It is the same for the untrained actor because all of us in unfamiliar situations depend on the approval of those around us. Crew members cannot become an audience; they remain impersonal and remote as they concentrate on their work, or the actors will start playing for their approbation. And then, all of a sudden, you have a theatrical performance on film!

The film actor's only audience is you, the director. It's your job to draw the actor into an intimate, internalized way of sustaining belief. Clearly, you will need special approaches to support your cast, especially if that cast contains differing levels of experience.

CHAPTER 18

DIRECTING ACTORS

This chapter deals with essentials for directing actors. Procedures for rehearsal follow in Chapter 23, "Actor and Director Prepare a Scene"; Chapter 24, "Initial Meetings with the Cast"; and Chapter 25, "Rehearsals and Planning Coverage." A further resource is Judith Weston's *Directing Actors* (Michael Wiese Productions, 1999), which is usefully prescriptive and never loses sight of the actor's perspective. Theater oriented and concise is Lenore DeKoven's *Changing Direction: A Practical Approach to Directing Actors in Film and Theatre* (Focal Press, 2006). Acting is better understood in the theater, and better respected, so everything you learn there applies also to film. Film people are apt to look for immediate results, whereas theater people know that truthful results come only from the right kind of processes, which nearly always take time and work.

DIRECTOR IN RELATION TO ACTORS

Unlike you and your crew, actors have no equipment to stand behind, and nowhere to hide. Because their work is intense, exposed, and difficult, they are vulnerable, easily discouraged, and quick to compare themselves negatively with other actors. Please do a little acting so you can find out. Actors seldom need challenge or authority—they usually have all that working inside them, and then some. What they work for is recognition, and you, as their director and sole audience, are the only one to confer it. All directions come from you, and you alone. Everyone in the film unit, and every visitor, must be briefed *never* to make critical comments about the actors' work, and no actor may criticize other actors. Any suggestion or comment must be confidentially routed through you, for you to decide whether it should go further.

MAKE CONTACT

Human contact matters most of all to actors. Their handshakes, hugging, and greeting kisses are an important rite having little to do with sexuality. Quite simply, they are sensitive people whose work makes them vulnerable. They depend on each other and they depend on you. The harrowing nature of their work makes them need constant reminders that you like and respect them. Make a point of responding in kind with whatever makes a mutually acceptable expression of warmth and liking. Bear in mind that you are a power figure who must treat all equally and without condescension.

ASK QUESTIONS

Direct inductively through asking questions, and draw your cast into discovering what you may already know. Whatever a person discovers for himself, he or she never forgets. Questioning makes your cast pause to think, and this gives you a grace period in which to think ahead. Avoid reeling off instructions—it can seem authoritarian.

Actors will test you from time to time, so be ready for challenge and resistance, especially if you have to modify or supersede earlier instructions. Along the way, your cast will catch things you missed, because each actor carries responsibility for only one character. This makes learning a two-way street.

DIRECT POSITIVELY AND EQUABLY

The larger the cast, the less time you have for each actor. Getting your feedback is so vital that most actors feel underrecognized most of the time. Be ready to meet with anyone in difficulties and listen carefully to their problems. Not doing so can send them spinning out of control.

Set things up with the cast so that "one-on-ones" are by request, and are known to be problem sessions. Otherwise actors may think you are giving one of their number special attention. As you direct, avoid favoring any one cast member, and never take someone to task in front of his colleagues. Try to remove all fear and comparison from your dealings, and always use positive, constructive phrasing. Rephrase anything like, "Make the next take less wild and rambling," as something resembling, "See if you can keep the intensity in the next take, but try to get her attention by becoming dangerously quiet." Instead of peeling off commands, you should say, "I wonder if you could try . . ." "Maybe you could let me see . . ." Ask for their alternatives, and choose from what they offer. Often you will get back something better than you could imagine.

Say as little as you can to get actors working toward what you want. Don't intellectualize or think aloud—that only clogs the actor's mind with verbiage. Concentrate on giving short, practical, actable directions. That is, give actors things to do, not things to feel or effects to produce. Actors cannot summon feelings or results; they can only do actable things to which feelings come attached. If you specify an effect ("look more contemptuous"), an actor must find an actable way to get there. Out of panic, fatigue, or lack of on-the-spot ideas, you have tempted the actor to short-circuit the search process, and so she winds up "indicating,"; that is, trying to communicate an idea instead of being inside her character.

At the end of work sessions, thank cast members—individually if possible, but collectively if not. Even if things have gone poorly, put an optimistic spin on your comments. People work best for those who expect well of them.

Facing so many unfamiliar pressures, you will be well advised to work with a small cast to begin with, and capitalize on the most successful relationships by using the best of them again in subsequent productions.

COMMON PROBLEMS

Actors seldom need special techniques or arcane information from their director. Rather, they need practical help in casting off the layers of self-consciousness and insecurity in order to simply *be*. Performing, by its nature, is self-conscious and self-judgmental. In adverse conditions, the actor may start to act from the head, signaling ideas, and indicate. This is because he has lost touch with the heart and mind of the character, or has never found them. Your job is to find and undo the tension logjams so that the actor can resume the flow of mental and emotional focus.

LACK OF FOCUS AND RELAXATION

Note the circumstances when an actor loses focus. It will show as a loss of conviction and clarity in their lines and as uncertainty in their body language, but this varies from person to person. Figure out where each actor carries his tension, and whether it shows most in shoulders, face, hands, walk, or voice.

There is always a reason. The actor may have been "thrown" (become uneasy because of what somebody did or said), and now needs your help to remedy the difficulty. Often you can lower anxiety by redirecting an actor's attention or by mentioning something they just did that was effective. Confidence, focus, and relaxation go hand in hand: we regain confidence when someone we respect reminds us of what we do well.

When an actor repeatedly loses focus at the same point in a scene, note it without stopping the scene. Usually the actor knows what is happening and has ideas about the source. Maybe a turn feels wrong, or bending down to pick something up makes costume shoes pinch distractingly. Most often it happens because they doubt the meaning of a line. Through sympathetic questioning, you can locate the cause and address it.

MIND-BODY CONNECTION MISSING

Are you convinced by what you see in the bodily actions, gestures, and tone of what your cast members do? This is a hard one, because you *want* to be convinced, you *want* to feel that the cast is successful. So you, too, must be relaxed enough to let the cast have (or *not* have) an effect on you. Only freedom from tension will allow you to have the same sensations and reactions that an audience has. And you, after all, are the first audience.

Instead of making "either/or" judgments, try keeping an internal barometer going that registers highs and lows through the scene. Use your recall to retrieve the high points of the scene—the places where things were really cooking. By subtraction, you can now turn to what was less successful. Just by reporting where you were convinced and moved, or where your attention lapsed and you felt distanced, you hand initiative to the cast. They will recall their states of consciousness from moment to moment and extract the problems and likely causes. Nearly always, the problem is fuzzy acting objectives, which we'll come to below.

By asking the cast to solve problems, you encourage them to put their artistic process to work, which they will love. Your job is to structure, encourage, and make choices so the process keeps moving.

ANTICIPATING OR NOT ADAPTING

Watch carefully for the quality of each character's adaptation: if the actor has the character's interior life going, if he or she is listening and watching, then adapting to obstacles will be as realistic as it is in life. Some reactions take thought; others should be automatic. After all, you don't stop to think when someone throws a punch at your head.

When a character anticipates or lags, you know the actor is working from prepared ideas. Get him to articulate, line by line, what the other characters are implying, and tell him to work off clues the other characters send off. These allow his character to work at perceiving—correctly or incorrectly—what's around him. A suitor may, for instance, mistake pride and independence as indifference, and to wrongly assume he is rejected. The actor who short-circuits this process will react ahead of time, or, by faking thought, react in a calculated yet dead way. The cure is to get him or her to voice the character's interior processes, and base them on moment-by-moment clues coming from other characters—just as we do in life.

ACTING IN ISOLATION

Someone may not be interacting with the other actors, or may draw attention to himself or herself rather than support the scene. Uptight players preprogram their reactions when in fact they should decide their reactions at the very moment the reactions become necessary. When a player is cocooned inside preconceptions, take him or her aside for a private talk, and see if simply pointing out the effect works. The actor needs to let go, live the moment, and trust that the text will somehow happen. This level of trust and comfort may not come easily, but it's important to find it. Until he feeds into, and receives from, the communal flow, that actor is failing to support the rest of the cast.

You can create this interaction by involving the whole cast in a short and playful improv. Consider those laid out in the Chapter 19 table under "Improv Exercises," especially Projects 19-5 and 19-13. Don't use improv unless you have played in and directed it, and feel confident enough to handle the process. And use it cautiously with players you don't yet know, in case someone feels threatened or thinks it beneath their dignity. Once your cast is relaxed and trusts you, improv can be wonderfully silly, refreshing, and helpful at unlocking phobic anxieties.

Now return to the scripted scene, and ask everyone to (a) feed small, special intentions into their playing; (b) read specifically what is coming from another character; and (c) deliberate before reacting to them. Then (d) try to present an obstacle as a challenge to their fellow player.

Run the scene more than once, asking for changed nuances. The players will have fun trying to really listen and react. Now everyone will see periods of deliberation as highly charged moments rather than dead airtime.

Communion makes a scene become alive and real, and after it's established, simply alert the cast whenever you see people ceasing to play off each other. Is there a particular reason, or are they simply getting fatigued? Is there a hole in someone's understanding that is making him retreat?

MISSING INTERIOR LIFE

Trained actors sometimes let their character's interior life wither, whereas untrained actors haven't encountered the idea, or don't know how to keep one going. I once directed a cast of very mixed experience. Some who had never acted gave lines without conviction, and the timing of their reactions was all over the map. By my taking them aside, showing them how to silently maintain interior monologues, they were able to give transformed performances and consistent timing.

Do this one-on-one or with the untrained actors only—don't risk patronizing your trained players. Take a two-person scene, and ask each actor to improvise the thoughts of his or her character in a low "interior" voice before and after every line. Explore this by using the interior monologue exercises in Chapter 19 (Exercise 19-18: "Blind Date") and Chapter 20 (Excercise 20-3: "Improvising an Interior Monologue"). Coach your actors to find all the dimensions their character can be aware of. When they next play their scene, it will become complex and interesting.

CUING: TREADING ON LINES

How new speakers follow old is called cuing. Actors in the theater overlap and interrupt each other as people do in life. This is usually not desirable in film work because it makes the editor's task nearly impossible. Actors must therefore be directed to play a comedy scene (say) at a fast clip but without overlapping. Then, putting together scenes from separate shots, the film editor creates lifelike overlaps as needed.

MISSING SUBTEXTS

During rehearsal, nail down every part of the text by making sure, especially when anyone loses focus, that the cast can articulate whatever their characters are trying to get, do, or accomplish at any given moment. Each line, each look or glance, each action, must have a defined objective; the actor must know to whom it is addressed and whether his needs are met or not. Each definition should contain (a) a first-person active (not passive) verb, (b) a person (or thing) acted upon, and (c) an intended effect that will either be fulfilled or not. For instance:

- "I mock Evan to take him down a few notches."
- "I menace the prisoner to make him confess."
- "I cradle my child to stop the hurt."

Work to keep improving each objective's definition. Language really matters: the more striking the actors' objectives, the stronger and clearer their performances. It would, for instance, be weak to say, "My objective is to ask my manager to tell me who took money from the till." Stronger would be, "I'll make my manager admit right now who stole from the till." *Make* is stronger and more playable than *ask*, and *admit* is stronger than *tell*. *Stealing* is more loaded than *taking*.

Your characters must know what they want, from whom they want it, and whether they succeed or not. Try to build urgency into their intentions. By sharpening objectives, your actors *raise the stakes* for their characters. He or she then has more to gain and more to lose. Don't be afraid to ask at a weak moment, "Can we raise the stakes here?" and let the cast figure out how.

THE GENERALIZED INTERPRETATION

Clarifying the unfolding action and breaking it into steps, one objective at a time, helps overcome a major problem: actors often try to play all of their character's characteristics all the time. This mind-directed approach muddies and confuses the playing. Applied like a color wash, it produces a scene that is fuzzy and without progression, where instead it should move forward in sharp, forceful increments. Rectify this in two ways. One, ask the actor to speak their character's subtextual thoughts aloud, as in Exercise 20-3: "Improvising an Interior Monologue." If it means humiliating an actor in front of more experienced players, do it one-on-one. Two, make the actor listen to other players. You'll know this is happening when his interior monologue reflects how the others are acting on him. Be careful, by the way, that your role as coach is not appropriated by actors who consider themselves more experienced. This will lead to multiple directors.

DISTANCING AND INDICATING

Actors commonly give too much (voice, actions, movement). Fearing they are not reaching the audience, not "good enough" or "big enough," they drive home their character's intended personality. Watching and grading themselves, they are severed from their character. You can center the actor via work on an interior monologue. You may also need to ask them to withhold their character's feelings from other characters' knowledge, as we do in life. This gives the audience interesting work to do, and lends dramatic tension.

Intellectualizing also causes separating. Insist that your cast personalize: whenever someone speaks of their character as "she," gently insist on using the first person. Speak to her as though she *is* the character, not a technician operating a puppet. Immediately convert anything said in passive voice (*she is being made to look for . . .*) to its active equivalent (*I am looking for . . .*) so the actor has something more immediate and playable to work with.

LACK OF INTENSITY AND INTIMACY

Actors' interactions must be contained, not florid and "actory." You know this is happening when an actor makes unmotivated movements, paces, and flails his arms. Characters gain in power and intensity when gestures and movement are minimal. In Michael Caine's video *Acting in Film* (1989), he demonstrates how much more centered a character seems once the actor overcomes the impulse to blink. In a hilarious "blink count," David Letterman showed Nancy Pelosi, in her first appearance as Speaker of the House, listening to a State of the Union address while standing alongside the basilisk Dick Cheney and blinking no fewer than 29 times to his once.[1]

To be meaningful, actions must be purposeful, minimal, and take place in a small compass. Anyone watching at a distance might imagine that nothing was happening. As a young cutting room assistant in a big film studio, I sneaked onto the set to watch at a respectful distance while the unit shot a close-up. It all

[1] See www.cbs.com/latenight/lateshow/video_player/index/php/904792.phtml.

seemed very static: after some mumbling from the actors and the assistant director calling "Cut," I thought, "Huh, nothing happened—the camera can't have been rolling." Next day on the big screen, I saw a scene electric with tension in which *everything* happened. The scene took place inside an intense bubble of space that the camera had penetrated intimately and completely. Even a whopping Panavision camera is a perfectly intimate voyeur, and reveals the minuscule tightening of a jaw muscle or the waver in a parting glance.

Your cast, particularly when used to the theater, will need a great deal of reassurance over this. Tell them that if they are inside their character, and experience their character's thoughts and feelings, the camera does the rest.

LIMITING AN ACTOR'S SPHERE

Redirect an actor who's playing too large by saying, "Visualize a bubble of space that is large enough only to enclose you and your partner. Talk only to him, here and now. There is no one else, no camera present, just you two." The magnified voices and gestures will stop, and scene intensity will go way up.

TACKLING STUBBORN ARTIFICIALITY

You cast someone for a small part, and then find that their concept of acting comes from TV commercials. Valiantly, your homemaker projects a wacky TV mom personality. Were she playing a stage mom, this might do, but now it's terrible.

Hamming and indicating come from enacting an *idea* of one's part rather than getting inside the character's consciousness. Take your homemaker aside and get her to talk through her character's thoughts and interior monologue. Ask her to recall someone she knows and upon whose image she can model herself. This can be a very successful way to anchor a part. Once she is busy maintaining her character's interior processes, she can no longer stand outside and see herself acting, which is the root of the problem. Now your homemaker fully inhabits her character, speaks and acts from an authentic consciousness, and the difference is like night and day.

When an actor forces feelings and fails to create the character's interior resources, you have a severe problem. As a last resort, videotape some of the unnatural acting, then show it privately in comparison with grabbed footage of the actor having a normal conversation. He will be shocked and depressed to see himself on the screen in this way. Tell him supportively that you want him to *be*, not to act. At desperation's door, he may now open up to your coaching.

With an incurable voice projecter or anyone habitually artificial, the best solution may be to bang yourself over the head and recast. This can badly shake up the rest of the cast, who fear they, too, may be so bad that you will fire them as well.

HOW MUCH REHEARSAL IS ENOUGH?

Actors will express the fear that a scene will be overrehearsed. If it means drilling to a master plan, this is a real enough anxiety. You should not rehearse anything without plans and objectives in mind, or the cast will sense this and resent their time being wasted. During your preparatory work, decide which scenes are pivotal, and use the ensemble's growing ability so you can focus on problem areas and get your actors to discover solutions. Digging deeply for meaning, developing perceptions that flow back and forth between the characters, and creating links and resonances with other parts of the script is tremendously productive. Experimenting like this habituates the cast to change so that later you can ask for changes on the set without fazing them.

"IT'S GETTING STALE"

If an actor becomes convinced that developmental work is spoiling his performance, you as director may have to prove otherwise. Do not, however, extend work beyond the way ahead that you can see. When you reach your threshold, switch to another scene. In any case, many scenes cannot be treated in isolation because of their interrelationship. Take them in rotation—this keeps energies high and actors' attention on the piece as a whole.

SOME DOS AND DON'TS

- *Set limited, positive goals*: Say, "See if you can open the door softly this time"—not, "This time don't make such a racket with that closet."
- *Direct the actor's attention to a particular kind of action*: Say, "I'd like to see you try to figure out what he meant as you turn away." Make the suggestion specific, and locate it in a particular moment. Generalized suggestions could apply anywhere and aren't helpful.
- *Suggest a different subtext*: such as, "Try closing the door on him with finality rather than regret."
- *Remind cast members where their character has just come from.* Wind them up with a reminder: "You've just come from the stock exchange and seen your father's savings vanish." This is vital while directing, because films are shot in small, out-of-order steps, and actors need constant orientation.
- *Remind actors that nobody is present*: Ask actors to ignore the crew's presence, act as they do when alone in real life, and never to look at the camera. This helps them avoid playing to an imagined audience.
- *Never demonstrate how you'd like something played*: This implies you are an actor and want a copy of yourself. But you are not an actor, and what you want is unique to that actor. Ask the cast for *their* solutions.
- *Never say, "Just be yourself"*: This sets actors worrying: "What did he really mean? How does he see me? Which me does he want?" Focus your actor instead on aspects of her character's experience.
- *Never ask for something "smaller"*: An actor takes this as a barbed criticism. Ask for the same intensity but with more intimacy, or for anything else that sounds like development rather than censure.

CHAPTER 19

ACTING IMPROVISATION EXERCISES

Every director needs some firsthand experience of acting, and you can learn the basics most enjoyably by playing "improv" theater games—the subject of this chapter. For books, try John Hodgson and Ernest Richards' *Improvisation* (Grove Press, 1974) and Viola Spolin's *Improvisation for the Theater: A Handbook of Teaching and Directing Techniques,* 3rd ed. (Northwestern University Press, 1999). The latter text was integral to the founding of Second City, the Chicago improvisational school that spawned many actors, comedians, and directors.

Some film directors—notably Ingmar Bergman, John Cassavetes, Ken Loach, and Mike Leigh—use improvisation as a source for drama. Don't assume that this is any easier than working from a script, though. With improvised scenes entirely in the hands of the actors, pacing and development can be fascinating, uncertain, or maddening. Often the players circle a problem repeatedly before breaking through. Sometimes you'll see them, out of frustration or panic, force their character's process to manipulate a solution.

The very same things happen, albeit more subtly, when actors work from a text, so the thrills and spills you experience in improv will set you up to understand all acted situations. You will also see that anyone can act—anyone at all—once the armor is laid down and the actor feels free to play. Once you have done some acting yourself, directing others becomes a matter of diligently and empathically spotting the keys that unlock each individual's difficulties. The exercises in this chapter can establish that:

- Learning that is embedded in shared experience is something you never forget.
- The few major acting principles take repetition to absorb.
- You can't think ahead in improv, so it's very scary at first.
- Players learn to adapt (that is, adjust in a lifelike way to unforeseen obstacles), to take the initiative, and through communion become an ensemble.
- Everything can go hilariously wrong, so people learn without humiliation.

- Like jazz, everyone knows when a piece is "cooking."
- Courageous failures are really successes.

ACTING AND DOING

Acting has a solidly practical theory behind it, but it's something you can learn only through doing, for it requires insight, much concentration, and a certain amount of courage. Wear loose, comfortable clothing that you don't mind getting dirty. Change partners from exercise to exercise so you work with unfamiliar people. Try to play people whose characters, ages, and circumstances are well removed from your own. From improv, expect to learn:

- What it feels like to be closely watched
- How liberating it is to be silly and enjoy it
- Common hang-ups and situations that actors get into
- What being manipulated by another actor feels like (see Chapter 20, "Acting Exercises with a Text")
- That each actor either acts on others or cedes his character's share of input
- That the actor who seizes control is as insecure as the one who relinquishes it
- That improvs often get stuck, and the actors have to unstick the piece so it can develop
- What trust or distrust from other actors feels like
- That each actor must seize opportunities the other actors make available
- That acting with people you trust takes away competitiveness and insecurity
- That failure is the pathway to success
- That anybody can deal with the unexpected once they can relax
- That you feel great getting a round of applause after taking risks

YOUR ROLE AS A DIRECTOR DURING IMPROVS

Most of these exercises need nothing beyond your initial explanation and seeing that the actors understand and keep to the ground rules. The more advanced exercises need a director to select and coordinate cast ideas and take spot decisions, or the piece won't get started in a timely way. Directing an improv may seem like a contradiction in terms, but the director is really the surrogate for an audience. All exercises will benefit from your feedback so the cast can tackle specific problems in subsequent versions.

Good directors know a lot about acting and about each actor in their cast. They learn to sense when an individual isn't living up to potential and how to actively eliminate the blockages. From directing improvs, you can expect to discover:

- How clearly you communicate and what you need to improve
- How each actor needs his own kind of communication
- What it feels like when an actor doesn't trust your judgment or challenges you

- How much actors depend on your feedback in their work
- How actors either accept or avoid responsibility in a scene
- How to challenge a passive actor into becoming an active one
- How to start an interior monologue in an actor whose character lacks interior life
- How divisive personalities function and how to avoid being manipulated by one
- How each actor has limiting habits, mannerisms, and patterns
- What a director can do when actors think they are at their limit
- How guilty you feel when actors give their best and you don't like what you see
- How to best earn the trust of actors and crew (each director does this differently)
- How it feels to take someone over a threshold, and how good you both feel

SEEING BEATS AND DRAMATIC UNITS

The director's major responsibility is to understand the characters' development and changes in relation to the expectations of an improvisation or a text. Throughout the upcoming exercises, the director should work to develop a sensitivity to beats—those special moments when characters change after working toward a goal. To refresh your understanding, refer to "Beats" in Chapter 3. You can go beat-spotting anywhere that people are trying to do something. Standing in a post-office line, you can spot the beats while a clerk and a foreign customer negotiate the postal rate for a parcel.

YOUR ROLE AS AN ACTOR DURING IMPROVISATION

Most of all, have fun and enjoy flying by the seat of your pants. The allure of acting is the call to live dangerously and completely, with nothing held back, and to get audience recognition for it. Most actors are shy people who took up acting in order to make major changes in their lives. Your time has come!

MAKE YOUR AUDIENCE SEE

Use no props; instead, use your imagination to "see" your surroundings and the things you handle. Do it with real conviction, and your audience will see, believe, and be captivated. Once, while serving in the air force during my youth, I sat up in bed, hardly out of a dream I'd been having, and pointed across the barrack with utter conviction. "What's the matter?" those present asked a little nervously. "A spaceship, over there, on the wall," I said with complete belief. They all turned to see it. Afterward, they told me that for a few moments, they had completely believed me. To see is to make others see too.

STAY FOCUSED

The biggest initial challenge will be to achieve and maintain focus; that is, to:

- Think your character's thoughts.
- See your character's physical and mental images.

- Experience your character's feelings.
- See and hear the other characters and react to what they are giving you, here and now.

Improvisation constantly faces the actor with surprises, so you are repeatedly flushed out of your hiding places. It need never cause you to lose focus and fall out of character.

GETTING THE MOST FROM THE EXERCISES

KEEP A JOURNAL

If you are part of a directing class, keep notes in a journal in which you candidly describe your thoughts, observations, and feelings about your assignments and peers. Periodically, the instructor can privately review and report significant trends or observations back to the class as a whole. No writer's confidences or identity should ever be disclosed without his or her prior permission.

The journal functions as a safety valve, a channel for feedback that allows the instructor to be fully aware of personal feelings and triumphs. Through it, the instructor gets to know everyone on his or her own terms and can write confidential replies.

AUDIENCE ETIQUETTE

In a class or shooting situation, there is always an audience of sorts. Etiquette demands that crew and onlookers try to be absolutely still and silent, avoid eye contact with the players, yet contribute every iota of their attention in support of the players. Each person in an ensemble must support and appreciate the others, particularly when it involves pushing limits.

DURATION

Either the instructor can call, "Cut!" or, as confidence develops, audience members give a show of hands as they feel that a piece has run its course. From this, actors get used to satisfying audience demands, and student directors can see how closely their judgments parallel those of an audience.

ASSESSMENT AND DISCUSSION

During an exercise, look for the combination of spontaneity and intensity that comes when actors fully accept the demands of their role. Always reward actors with a round of applause at the end of the piece. After each exercise, brief and concentrated discussion is valuable. Some points are suggested for discussion, but don't hesitate to follow the natural train of conversation. During feedback:

- Describe what was communicated, avoiding all "good" and "bad" valuations.
- Avoid intellectualizing. Academic discussion drains momentum.

- Describe what stages the piece went through (its structure).
- Say what it made you feel at each stage (what it delivered).
- Say what particularly struck you (impact), being as specific as possible.

As an actor or director, listen attentively to feedback, and don't argue or justify what you did. Learn from your audience.

IMPROV EXERCISES

The acting exercises in this chapter and the next sometimes suggest that acting takes place mainly between two people. Of course an actor may act alone or in a large group, but to allow for this range would produce unreadable English, so I have treated the duo as if it were standard. The theater games that follow are good for building skills. Sometimes they incorporate a degree of premeditated structure, and sometimes the actor has no prior guidelines. Some of these exercises will be cited later in the book because they make useful tools when actors get hung up during rehearsal or shooting. The main acting principles explored by the exercises are as follows:

Action, maintaining while speaking	19-11
Adaptation	19-5, 19-12, 19-16, 19-17
Communion	19-5
Conflict, inner	19-19
Conflict, working with	19-8
Emotion, developing toward an	19-14
Emotion, sublimating	19-20
Emotions, bridging between two	19-15
Ensemble, creating within an	19-13
Focus	19-1
Givens, developing character from	19-6, 19-10
Imagination	19-2
Inner life	19-7
Interior monologue	19-18
Observation	19-5
Partnership equality	19-4
Subtext	19-7
Tactile defensiveness	19-4
Trust	19-3, 19-4
Voice and body as expressive instruments	19-9

EXERCISE 19-1: SEE OR BE SEEN

Purpose: Exploring the idea of focus as an antidote to self-consciousness. This exercise lets everyone experience how disturbing it is to have someone watching you when your mind is unoccupied.

Activity: Half the class is the audience and remains seated. The other half, the performers, stand in a row facing the audience looking above their heads. Audience members should carefully study the faces and body language of the performers.

- The instructor tells the performers to empty their minds and concentrate on simply being themselves.
- After a minute or two, the instructor tells the performers to mentally visualize a room they know well and everything in it.
- After another minute or two, the instructor tells the audience and performers to switch roles and repeats Steps 1 and 2 with the other half of the class.

Discussion:

1. Performers: How did it feel to focus on "being yourself"?
2. Audience: How did the performers' feelings show in their behavior and appearance?
3. Audience: What did you see when the performers switched to visualizing?
4. Performers: What kinds of work can an actor legitimately undertake to avoid feeling self-conscious?

EXERCISE 19-2: DOMESTIC APPLIANCE

Purpose: To become in spirit something you are not

Activity: Study a domestic appliance in its full range of action. In class, announce what you have been assigned to do, then give a full impersonation using your whole body and vocalized sound effects. Try to convey the appliance's spirit as well as its shape, actions, and sounds. The class should choose something for the instructor, who breaks the ice by going first (more than once, I have been asked to become a flushing toilet). It is quite normal to feel foolish and painfully self-conscious. Use what you learned from Exercise 19-1 to maintain focus.

Examples that can be assigned:

Coffee percolator	Nutcracker
Overfilled garbage bag removed	Honey pouring
Toilet flushing	Coffee grinder
Cold car engine that will not start	Corkscrew
Electric can opener	Garbage disposal unit
Tomato sauce pouring	Rusty door lock
Rubber plunger opening drain	Steam iron
Dripping faucet	Photocopier
Washing machine cycling	Blender with lumps
Upright vacuum cleaner	Clock radio coming on
Toothbrush at work	Computer printer
Electric toaster	

Discussion:

1. When and why was the actor self-conscious?
2. Where in his or her body could you locate tension from self-consciousness?
3. Did he or she get into focus, and if so, when?
4. Which part of the impersonation made you see the real thing?

EXERCISE 19-3: FLYING BLIND

Purpose: Exploring trust and choosing to be dependent

Activity: The rehearsal space is made into a disordered jumble of obstacles. Divide into pairs. One person is blindfolded and disoriented by spinning him several times. He now walks as fast as he dares—with his partner not touching him, but whispering instructions on which way to move. As a variation, the seeing partner can guide through touch. After a few minutes, switch roles on the instructor's command.

Discussion:

1. Actor: What were your feelings and sensations, being so utterly dependent on another person?
2. Who mostly took the initiative?
3. Instructor/audience: What did body language tell you about different people's reactions to dependency?

EXERCISE 19-4: "TIMBER!"

Purpose: Exploring trust, equal partnership, and tactile defensiveness

Activity: Using pairs (same sex or different), one person is a piece of timber, and the other must try to balance the timber upright. You can use any part of your body—*but not your hands*—to catch and steady the falling timber. After a few minutes, swap roles on command. Actors must be able to make physical contact—and even play love scenes—with people they may neither know nor find attractive. In any acting situation, each must share control equally, being ready to "catch" a partner or be caught, yet neither taking more than momentary initiative. Neither player should fall into a habitually dominant or a submissive acting relationship.

Discussion:

1. What are your thoughts and feelings, being in bodily contact with someone you do not know well?
2. How free and true to gravity was the timber? (How much did he or she protect the two of you by making it easier?)

3. How willing was the timber: To trust you to catch him or her? To fall back-ward and stay rigid?

4. Did one partner tend to control the situation?

EXERCISE 19-5: MIRROR IMAGES

Purpose: Close observation and moment-to-moment adaptation without anticipating

Activity: You arrive in front of the bathroom mirror, come close to its surface, and go through your morning routine. Your partner is your image in the mirror, doing everything you do as you do it, inverted as a mirror image inverts. Swap roles after a few minutes.

Discussion:

1. How successful was the mirror at replicating the actions, without anticipat-ing or lagging?

2. Did the person stay in character?

3. How frank and complete was the person's routine? Who took risks and was therefore self-revealing?

EXERCISE 19-6: WHO, WHAT, WHEN, AND WHERE?

Purpose: Immediate character and situation development from givens and without props

Activity: Instructor designates an actor, then asks successive people to supply a who, what, when, and where. The actor then carries out some appropriate action, in char-acter, for a minute or two. The instructor calls "Cut!" when the action is long enough or if development levels off. The class reports what it saw happening and what was communicated. The actor then says briefly what he or she intended. Example:

> *Who* [is present]? Mary Jo Sorensen, 35
> *Where* [is she]? In an airport lounge
> *When* [is this]? Christmas Eve, late at night
> *What* [is happening]? She is waiting for her parents and must tell them she has lost her job.

Discussion:

1. What seemed to be going on inside the character?

2. What was convincing, and what were false notes?

3. What intentions did not come across as natural?

4. Did the actor carry out all of the assignment?

5. Did he or she remember to interact with the environment?

6. Was there a significant change or development?

Note: From this exercise onward, the class can vote by silently raising their hands. The director stops the piece when most of the audience thinks the dramatic development is past its peak.

EXERCISE 19-7: SOLO, NO WORDS

Purpose: Use unremarkable, everyday action to communicate something of the inner thoughts and feelings of a character whose life is quite unlike that of the actor.

Activity: From an action (the *what*) and using no props, invent a *who*, *where*, and *when* to sustain your character sketch for three minutes. An actor must be able to carry out everyday actions and make them interesting to watch, so avoid storytelling or high drama of any kind. Suggestions:

- Alone in someone's house (whose?), where you explore: (a) the refrigerator, (b) the bathroom, (c) someone else's bedroom that you have been given
- Finding a box of your childhood toys you haven't seen for many years
- Unwrapping a long-awaited parcel
- Waiting in the dentist's office
- Making a grocery list for a meal for special guests
- Trying on a new article of clothing
- Taking medicine
- Caring for a pet
- Taking a bike out after the winter
- Cleaning out your parents' attic
- Wrapping a gift
- Cleaning shoes
- Looking out the window
- Waiting for a phone call
- Dividing up the laundry
- Watching a sport
- Overhearing an interesting conversation in a store

Discussion:

1. In a particular performance, what was interesting, and what did it make you see?
2. Could you see not only the character, but also the environment?
3. When did the player break focus?
4. Why?

EXERCISE 19-8: DUO, NO WORDS

Purpose: To communicate through interaction something of the inner thoughts and feelings of two characters, using an everyday action that involves some element of conflict.

Activity: From an action (the *what*) and using no props, invent a *who, where,* and *when* to sustain your character sketch. Avoid storytelling or high drama, and use action with minimal or no dialogue. Try these:

- Mending a car
- Making a double bed
- Buying a magazine
- Pulling a sliver out of a finger
- Carrying a heavy garbage bag
- Washing the best dishes after a special meal
- Washing a child's hair
- Photographing a model
- Putting up a tent
- Playing pinball
- Maneuvering heavy furniture through a doorway
- Waiting in a doorway for a heavy rainstorm to ease
- Writing out a speeding ticket after the talking is done
- Watching a TV program: one likes it; the other does not.
- A stranger in a plane who is falling asleep against you

Discussion: Did the actors create:

1. Two distinct character identities (who)?
2. A believable and recognizable environment—country, area, city, place, or room—and use it (where)?
3. A distinctive period and time of day (when)?
4. A believable tension?
5. A situation in which speech was not called for?
6. An interaction in which neither was controlling the movement of the sketch?
7. Did you see communion and adaptation?

EXERCISE 19-9: GIBBERISH

Purpose: Using the voice as an expressive nonverbal instrument and using one's body and voice quality as tools of communication. Too often, once actors have lines to speak, they cease to act with the whole body. This exercise simulates speech, but de-emphasizes verbal meaning in favor of underlying intention.

Activity: Using the examples in Exercise 19-8, carry out an activity with a conflict, using gibberish as the characters' language.

Discussion: As in Exercise 19-8

1. How did the actors handle the gibberish conversations?

2. Did they become natural?

EXERCISE 19-10: SOLO, WITH WORDS

Purpose: To create a character, employing *who*, *where*, *when*, and *what*, and using both actions and speech

Activity: In creating your character, remember to develop him or her through actions. Do not sit still and rely on a monologue. Here are some suggestions:

- A difficult phone conversation (maybe with a defective cell phone!)
- Reconstructing a painful conversation
- Writing the opening remarks of an important speech
- Rehearsing in front of the bathroom mirror for a traffic court appearance
- Getting ready to tell someone about a betrayal or infidelity
- Working up to approaching your boss for a raise
- Rehearsing the way you will evict a needy relative who came for a short visit and has long overstayed
- Explaining to your new employer why you must start a new job in a gorilla costume
- Your head is stuck between the railings enclosing a war memorial. Someone has gone to call the fire department, and you are trying to figure out an explanation
- A practical joke has misfired, and you must explain to the irate victim

Discussion: Did the actor:

1. Create a believable character?

2. Keep up a developing action?

3. Make the situation develop?

4. Make you see all the physical objects and surroundings?

EXERCISE 19-11: DUO, WITH WORDS

Purpose: To maintain conversation and a developing action at the same time

Activity: Each of these sketches requires both a conversation and accompanying physical action, which should be purposeful. Do not take it too fast, and do not feel you have to be talking all the time. Examples to try:

- Eating a meal and discussing a prearranged topic
- Demonstrating a kitchen appliance to a family member
- Getting a large piece of furniture through an awkward doorway
- Discussing your son's or daughter's rotten grades

- Asking for some money that you are owed
- Buying something embarrassing from a pharmacist
- Showing someone they have not done a good job of work
- Teaching a friend to drive
- Teaching someone a dance step

Discussion: Did they:

1.   Keep both the topic and the actions going?
2.   Keep the physical world they created consistent?
3.   Listen to and work off each other?
4.   Share the initiative equally?
5.   Allow the piece to develop spontaneously?
6.   Develop interesting characters?

EXERCISE 19-12: MAKE YOUR OWN CHARACTER

Purpose: To place the actor, as a character, in the hands of the audience

Activity: Go before the class, in an item or two of costume, as a character based on someone you know who made a powerful impression on you. The class asks you probing questions about yourself. You answer in character. Each character should be onstage for about ten minutes, and two or three performances per session is the maximum—the interaction can be very intense.

Discussion: This, honestly undertaken, can be really magical, a powerful exercise in portrayal that tells much about the actor's values and influences. There may be little need for discussion if the exercise goes well. Play it by ear.

EXERCISE 19-13: ENSEMBLE SITUATIONS

Purpose: To engage the whole group in a collective creation

Activity: These are situations in which individual characters contribute to a whole. The *where* and *when* will need to be agreed on beforehand. The aim is to keep up your character while contributing to the development of the piece. Sample situations:

- A tug-of-war
- Dealing with an obstreperous drunk
- Someone is hurt in the street
- Surprise party
- A person faints in a crowded train
- Bus driver stops bus because a passenger refuses to pay
- Party is interrupted by protesting neighbor
- Airline clerk announces delay to irate passengers
- Policeman tries to arrest person at demonstration; crowd argues

Discussion:

1. How many subordinate actions were going on during the main action?
2. Did everyone stay in character? (The temptation is to lose focus unless you are important.)
3. How did the piece develop?
4. What compromises did people make to sustain the whole?

EXERCISE 19-14: DEVELOPING AN EMOTION

Purpose: Two or more actors are asked to improvise a scene culminating in a given emotion in one or more of the characters.

Activity: Try this exercise after the class has developed considerable rapport and experience. The players must invent characters and a situation, then develop it to the point where the specified emotion is reached. The class can stop the sketch when the emotion is reached or if the piece is not going anywhere. Emotions one character might feel include Anger, Suspicion, Sympathy, Relief, Jealousy, Condescension, Rejection, Love, Regret, Disbelief, Friendliness, Release, Superiority, Inferiority, Empathy.

Discussion: This asks that actors build to a known conclusion, and it's very tempting to escape by manipulating the situation. All the prior criteria apply, but important considerations here are:

1. Was the interaction credible?
2. Did it arrive at the specified emotion?
3. If not, why not?
4. Was the development even or uneven?
5. Was the initiative shared equally?

EXERCISE 19-15: BRIDGING EMOTIONS

Purpose: To make a credible change from one emotion to another

Activity: Same as Exercise 19-4, except that the players start in the middle of one emotion and find their way to the next. Start with two emotions, and then, if you want to make it truly challenging, specify three.

Discussion: Same as Exercise 19-4

EXERCISE 19-16: SURFING THE CHANNELS

Purpose: To involve a group in immediate and unpremeditated invention

Activity: Divide the class into players and audience. The audience is watching a TV program; the players are actors in TV shows. When the designated situation (facing death, say) is running out of steam, an audience member may seize the "remote control" and "change the channel," announcing what the new program is. The players must now develop "facing death" in the new program format, until someone changes the channel again. After a while, students swap roles. Suggested situations:

- Persuasion
- Confronting authority
- Trapped
- Avoiding commitment
- Returning home
- A life-changing interview
- Facing death
- Cheating on a friend

Discussion:

1. How inventive were the players?
2. How authentic were the situations compared to actual TV programs?
3. How quickly were the players and the audience able to make the change?
4. How equally were roles distributed?
5. Did some actors fall into controlling or passive roles?

EXERCISE 19-17: VIDEO CONVENTION

Purpose: Same as Exercise 19-6

Activity: Same ideas as Exercise 19-6, except that the situation is a huge video dealer's convention offering unsold video programs at big discounts. The audience is composed of potential buyers at a stand where everything imaginable on video is on sale. Because these are videos that have not sold, they probably are obscure or third-rate and full of genre clichés. When the audience decides to see a new sample, an audience member calls out the title of the new video:

- Do-it-yourself kitchen rehab
- Nature films
- 1950s comedies
- Slasher films
- Biology lessons
- Sales motivation
- Teen romances
- Beauty procedures for people over 50

Discussion: Similar to Exercise 19-6. Accent is on spontaneity and speed of adaptation. Did the cast contribute equally?

EXERCISE 19-18: BLIND DATE

Purpose: To work with interior monologue. This exercise takes great concentration from all concerned, but is a lot of fun. It shows what happens when an actor takes time to listen to his character's interior voices. Listening to those voices consistently brings a new richness and ambiguity to any part. Remember, *the real action of any part is interior action*, which goes on behind the character's outward words and physical actions.

Activity: A man and a woman have been set up by friends on a blind date. They meet in a bar and discuss how to spend the evening together. Each of Character A's conflicting personality traits are voiced by class members who sit behind him playing his thoughts. As the conversation between the two slowly proceeds, each of the thoughts-voices chimes in, speaking its biased reaction or tendentious thought. Character A listens and reacts realistically to these "thoughts," acting on those most appropriate in his next words or action. Character B cannot hear the voices, and reacts only to what Character A says or does. Character A may initially get a chorus of "inner voices," or there may initially be none. The voices may overlap and argue with each other. Character A should take all the time needed to assess and react to them, while remaining in character. The personality traits (with a voice for each) could include any four of:

- The need to be liked
- Fear of being manipulated
- Fear of rejection
- Worry about expense
- The need to be unique
- Guilt (feeling bad about something you've done)
- The need to be normal
- Shame (feeling bad about who you are)
- The need to make a conquest
- Pride

Discussion:

1.   How did Character A handle all the input?
2.   What were his or her most noticeable influences?
3.   Where did Character A break character?
4.   Did Character B provide a good foil?
5.   What were the most interesting and convincing interior actions?

Variation: Characters A and B go through the scene again, but Character A internalizes the interior voices by imagining them instead of hearing them spoken aloud. Often the scene will become strikingly different, showing what riches real inner conflict brings to an actor's work.

EXERCISE 19-19: INNER CONFLICT

This exercise was inspired by Richard Nixon's famous "I am not a crook" speech.

Purpose: To portray a character's contradictory tensions, but never directly reveal them.

Activity: The character is anyone prominent in the news who wishes to be correctly understood. He or she begins with the sentence, "Because I think you may have the wrong idea about me, I'm going to tell you what most people don't know." After the character has spoken for a while, the audience is allowed to ask pointed questions.

Discussion:

1. When was the character sincere? When was he or she contrived?
2. When was he/she suppressing the truth?
3. How did you know?
4. What was interesting? What was less so?

EXERCISE 19-20: THROWN TOGETHER

Purpose: To explore the idea that in life, we seldom express what really weighs on our minds; instead, we sublimate our unsolved issues through the situation at hand.

Activity: Put two incompatible characters together in a credible work situation. Within the bounds of ordinary, civilized behavior, each follows his or her usual agenda in relating to other people. The actors should take the time to keep up an interior (and silent) monologue. No issues are ever named; the needs and reactions of the characters must be expressed through the work they are doing together. Whether they finally get along or find mutual accommodation should not be predetermined.

Discussion:

1. Did each character develop?
2. Did each find a way to play out his or her issues through their work?
3. Did each choose a credible path?
4. Did they stay in focus and in character?
5. Did they find a believable way of cooperating?
6. Did you believe the outcome?

7. Did either or both find satisfaction, and did one "win"?

8. What was the obligatory moment in the scene, and what made it so?

Variations: Play the scene again, this time with each actor adding his or her character's thoughts in an undertone. Then play the scene as before, with silent, interior monologues.

Discussion: Did having to improvise thoughts change or improve the scene? Can you see using this method to solve a problem in a scripted scene?

CHAPTER 20

ACTING EXERCISES WITH A TEXT

These exercises, which develop important skills at interpreting texts, work best if you draw scenes from a strong play. Though it won't be cinematically conceived, it will have plenty of potential for your cast. I particularly like Harold Pinter's *The Dumb Waiter* because it maintains a wonderfully dark disparity between what the characters say and what they think. Avoid broad comedy; it begs for a live audience, and you don't want your cast fishing for laughs. Pick shorter scenes so there's time and energy for proper discussion.

SCENE BREAKDOWN

Director and actors should read the whole play and then do a scene breakdown on their own. The object is to determine at every important juncture what each character is trying to get, do, or accomplish in relation to the others. Work from micro toward the macro levels:

- *Lines and action*
  - Give a *tagline* to each line or action that clarifies its subtext. ("I want you to take me seriously.") Taglines should build logically toward the beat.
  - Subtexts can be perceived or unperceived by the characters.

- *Beats*
  - Determine where the *beats* are for each character; that is, at what point each character realizes the success or failure of an objective.
  - In the script margin, bracket each beat's beginning, escalation, and crisis point, and give it a tagline (such as, "I want you to admit that you don't love me").
  - Characterize what *adaptation* the character makes; that is, what he does in adaptation to perceived failure or success. ("Because you won't admit what you did, I'll make this really hurt.")

- *Dramatic units*
  - Divide the scene into dramatic units. If it has three major beats, it probably has three dramatic units.
  - Title each unit with a distinct dramatic function. ("Lynn sends Olivia on an errand so she can get Terry alone.")
  - Decide exactly where the unit's dramatic crisis occurs. ("The game is up when owner and manager make eye contact over the firm's sales chart.")

- *Through-lines.* What is the character driving throughout the scene to get, do, or accomplish? Like objectives, through-lines are expressed in the first person, using an active verb, and have an immediately assessable result in mind. What is each character's goal or objective during:
  - This beat? (Example: "I want you to make space for me in the car.")
  - This dramatic unit?
  - This scene?
  - The whole drama? (Use all the evidence in the piece to draw a through-line between the character's formative experience and what he or she is struggling to get above all else in life. (Example, "Guillermo wants to earn his son's respect," or, "Rosa wants to prove she can support her family alone.")

- *Scene crisis*
  - Designate the scene's apex, or crisis. This is the scene's turning point, or *obligatory moment* (see special section later in this chapter). It can come early or late in the scene, but is usually in the last dramatic unit.

- *Superobjectives*
  - Scene: designate the scene's overall function in the piece. ("Reveals how both brothers are now attracted to Sally and that she encourages it.")
  - Play or screenplay: Designate the dramatic purpose of the entire piece. ("Harold Pinter's *Betrayal* shows how bitterness and isolation result all around when married friends cheat on each other.")

EXAMPLE

Figure 20-1 is the first page of a scene in which husband and wife get lost while driving in a city's outskirts. They argue because Tod, typical male that he is, won't stop the car to look at the map. The page contains a single dramatic unit with its beat typically marked in handwriting. The beat comes at the pivotal moment when Tod realizes that he must act differently because Angela is now seriously upset. Each character takes several steps on the way to this moment, and you decide these by extracting their subtexts. The subtext steps ramping up to the beat are also annotated, each with an interpretative tag.

See if you agree that:

- Angela's first three lines all echo the same subtext, "I'm afraid we're really lost."
- When she realizes they're lost, her subtext changes to, "We've got to get help."
- Tod downplays her anxiety, pitting his will against hers.
- The beat comes when he realizes he's let things go too far.

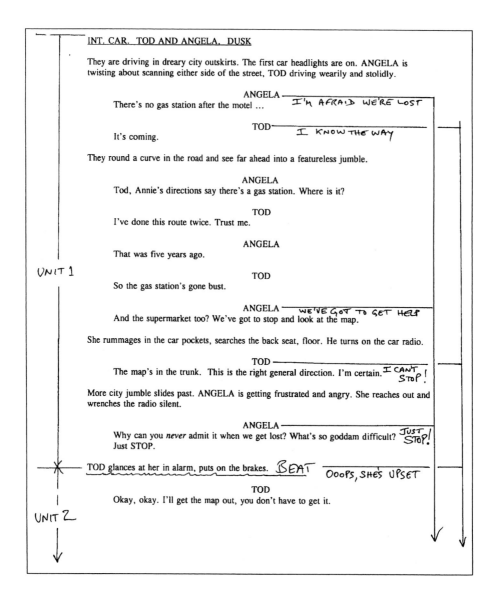

INT. CAR. TOD AND ANGELA. DUSK

They are driving in dreary city outskirts. The first car headlights are on. ANGELA is twisting about scanning either side of the street, TOD driving wearily and stolidly.

ANGELA — *I'M AFRAID WE'RE LOST*
There's no gas station after the motel ...

TOD — *I KNOW THE WAY*
It's coming.

They round a curve in the road and see far ahead into a featureless jumble.

ANGELA
Tod, Annie's directions say there's a gas station. Where is it?

TOD
I've done this route twice. Trust me.

ANGELA
That was five years ago.

TOD
So the gas station's gone bust.

ANGELA — *WE'VE GOT TO GET HELP*
And the supermarket too? We've got to stop and look at the map.

She rummages in the car pockets, searches the back seat, floor. He turns on the car radio.

TOD — *I CAN'T STOP!*
The map's in the trunk. This is the right general direction. I'm certain.

More city jumble slides past. ANGELA is getting frustrated and angry. She reaches out and wrenches the radio silent.

ANGELA — *JUST STOP!*
Why can you *never* admit it when we get lost? What's so goddam difficult? Just STOP.

TOD glances at her in alarm, puts on the brakes. *BEAT* *OoOPS, SHE'S UPSET*

TOD
Okay, okay. I'll get the map out, you don't have to get it.

UNIT 1

UNIT 2

FIGURE 20-1

Script page with taglines delineating a beat and its steps within the first dramatic unit.

- A significant action usually accompanies an obligatory moment. Tod adapts by stopping.
- A new dramatic unit begins.

Trained actors know this work, but the rest of us seldom have the first idea. As a director, work tactfully with your actors until they have planned their character's intentions and adaptations, moment to moment. This work matters because:

- Effective analysis sets you up to direct the action as a set of clear, actable steps.

- Each new dramatic unit is a new course of action fueled by a new volition and emotion.
- The steps in a character's consciousness are like a melody that can extend in time only if the notes are sounded in sequence, not all at once.

READ-THROUGH

Hold a neutral read-through (that is, matter-of-fact and not "acted") of the chosen scene. Allow time for discussions that elicit the actors' ideas about the text. Avoid intellectualizing by stressing the need for motivations and objectives every step of the way and holding to what the text supports. Instruct actors not to learn lines yet so they don't prematurely internalize their understanding of the piece.

DEVELOPMENTAL PROCESS

Allow the exploration process to find its own way. If any of your actors have training and experience, it may be unwise to impose any developmental technique in case they deem it unnecessary or patronizing. Watch, listen, and question. Let your actors get as far as they can with minimal directing. They are getting to know each other and each other's methods. When problems arise, choose whatever technique breaks the logjam.

"USEFUL WHEN"

Each exercise can serve as a resource to help solve common problems during rehearsal or production. Its "medicine chest" utility is provided under the heading "Useful when."

EXERCISES WITH A TEXT

Actors intrinsic characteristics, using	20-1
Beats	20-2
Beats, action at	20-5
Beats, characterizing	20-4
Character's inner life, spot-check for	20-8, 20-3
Dramatic units	20-2
Emotions, overconstrained	20-6
Improvisation, translating scene into	20-10
Indicating	20-7
Interior monologue	20-3, 20-8
Isolation, acting in	20-9
Textual analysis	20-2

EXERCISE 20-1: WHAT THE ACTORS BRING

Useful when: You (as the director) want to fit your thematic intentions closely to the piece by making use of what each individual cast member brings.

Purpose: To make decisions about the special qualities and characteristics of the actors for use in your thematic interpretation.

Activity: After the read-through:

1. Make notes for yourself that capture the intrinsic quality of each actor. This, for example, concerns an actor called Dale:
   Dale has a slow, quiet, repressed quality that masks a certain pain and bitterness. He is watchful, highly intelligent, intense, and his first reaction is often a protective cynicism; really, it matters to him very much that he be liked. He reminds me of a stray cat, cornered and defiant, but hungry and cold too.
2. Develop ideas about how the actors' qualities can legitimately be used to polarize the performances, and how this will affect your thematic interpretation of the piece. For example:
   Dale has the quality of honorable victimhood, and this stacks the cards interestingly against the father, who we assume has practiced subtle or overt violence against his son in the distant past, without the mother caring to know.

EXERCISE 20-2: MARKING BEATS IN A TEXT

Useful when: An actor fails to analyze a text satisfactorily.

Purpose: To fully understand how the script functions and how to act it by locating the characters' beats. These are fulcrum points of emotional change. To find dramatic units, see above and review "Beats" in Chapter 3, under the heading "The Dramatic Unit and the Scene." Beats and dramatic units will also be important to your mise-en-scène (the combination of acting, blocking, camera placement, and editing that produces the dramatic image on film).

Activity: Director and actors should separately study the scene looking for the beats, which are primarily the actor's concern, whereas dramatic units are more yours. A beat may be triggered by dialogue, an action, or incoming information such as a phone call. There may be one beat, or there may be several in a scene. All may belong to one character or to both; some may be simultaneous and mutual. One character may or may not be conscious of shifts in the other, though the audience should be made aware of all important changes.

Discussion: In rehearsal, agree where the beats are and what causes them.

EXERCISE 20-3: IMPROVISING AN INTERIOR MONOLOGUE

When an actor says he's got an interior monologue, but his performance lacks evidence of it, asking for an out-loud inner monologue is a sure way to upgrade a so-so performance. Because it supplies a repeatable interior process, the inner monologue also helps stabilize a performance's timing. This is work that actors tend to evade or forget, but the mere possibility that you may ask for an out-loud version in front of other actors usually keeps them working at it.

Useful when: A text refuses to come alive, and you need a powerful method of getting actors to externalize their understanding. Also good in rehearsal for unlocking intransigent trouble spots. Usually the problem lies with the actor's understanding, but sometimes it's with the writing itself.

Activity: At a troublesome part of the text, have your actors improvise their characters' interior monologues. Ask them to use a full voice for the "out-loud" line, and a soft voice for the "thoughts voice," or interior monologue. The cast may find this hard or baffling at first, and the scene will go at a snail's pace. But having to create publicly and on the spot always yields deeper understandings, and a high degree of commitment is unavoidable.

Discussion:

1.   Do the inner monologues show that your actors are on the same wavelength?
2.   What did you (the director) learn from the actors?
3.   What did you learn about your actors?
4.   What do you think your actors learned about you and your approach?

EXERCISE 20-4: CHARACTERIZING THE BEATS

Useful when: You need to clarify and energize a scene or a passage that is muddy and lifeless.

Purpose: To give each dramatic unit and its beats a clear intention and identity, which in turn sharpens each beat and turning point. Also, to focus attention on subtext and on the actor's body language, movement, and voice range.

Activity:

1.   Ask the actors for their taglines for the steps leading toward each beat. Make sure these tags always express volition. (Examples: "Leave me alone!"; "I need you to notice me"; "You're not going to hoodwink me again.") Be sure each tag is in the active, not passive, voice ("Let me go to sleep"—not, "I am being kept awake") so it expresses active will even when the character is being victimized. Each tagline should contain an element of "I want."

2.   The actors play the actions and movements of the scene, but speak only the tags as their dialogue. A character may have to say, "I need you to notice me" half a dozen times, developing the possibilities of the tag through bodily action and intonation, until they ramp up to the angry or desperate beat point. Where the text used verbal logic, now they must use as instruments of will only action, voice, and body. Abandoning verbal logic for physical and emotional

expressiveness causes interesting developments in the actors' range of expression, with a corresponding increase in power.

3. Now have the actors play the scene as scripted, keeping the body and vocal expression developed previously—and marvel at the difference.

Discussion: What did you learn:

1. About the actors from the movements they used this time?
2. About how they extended their emotional range?
3. About their communion once the exercise had forced it into continuous existence?

EXERCISE 20-5: ACTIONS AT BEAT POINTS

Useful when: A scene seems monotonous, wordy, and cerebral, and actors are playing the scene "in general." This happens because actors are approaching a scene with correct but generally applied ideas. A scene must be built out of behaviorally authentic blocks, each containing a single, clearly defined step in the sequence of human strivings. A scene in which one character shows several emotions will be effective only if he or she builds each separately and sequentially.

Purpose: To focus and physicalize the beats, and differentiate the behavioral phases of the scene. This technique shines a spotlight on turning points.

Activity: When the beat points are located and tagged, ask the actors to devise several possible actions for their character during each beat, or change of awareness. When actors invent from their own emotional range, the action becomes authentic to both actor and character. Actions can start out multiple and exaggerated so the director and actor can locate which feels best, then focus it at an agreed level of subtlety.

Discussion:

1. What is really at stake for each character at each beat?
2. How much interpretational leeway is there at important beats?
3. What is the range of options in terms of behavior that could be appropriate?
4. Of the range presented, did the director choose the most telling? If not, why not?

EXERCISE 20-6: GIVE ME TOO MUCH!

Useful when: One or more of your actors is under an emotional constraint, and the scene is stuck in low gear.

Purpose: To release actors temporarily from restrictive judgments they are imposing and to give them permission to overact.

Activity: Tell the actors that you feel the scene is bottled up, and you want them to reach for the same emotions but exaggerate them. Exaggeration gives actors permission to go to emotional limits they fear would look absurd if produced under normal conditions.

Discussion: You can now tell your cast what to change and at what new levels to pitch their energy and emotions. Often exaggeration alone clears a blockade. When actors switch from dabbling fearfully in the shallows to leaping with abandon off the top diving board, they often find they can let go of a specific fear and do the elegant dive.

EXERCISE 20-7: LET'S BE BRITISH

Useful when: A scene has become overprojected, artificial, and out of hand. Actors are indicating like crazy, and now feel that the scene is jinxed and will never work.

Purpose: To return the actors to playing from character instead of striving for effect.

Activity: Ask your actors to play the scene in a monotone, with emotion barely evident, but fully experiencing their character's bottled-up reality underneath the reticence.

Discussion:

1. Does repressing emotions sometimes heighten them?
2. Did the scene that had turned into sound and fury go back to basics?
3. How did the actors feel about it?

EXERCISE 20-8: SPOT-CHECK

Useful when: A line or an action repeatedly does not ring true.

Purpose: To stick a probe into an actor's process at a particular moment. This exercise is like a Breathalyzer test, jolting the actors into keeping up the inner lives of their characters for fear you will pull them over. Use sparingly.

Activity: Simply stop a reading or an off-book rehearsal at the problem point, and ask each actor what his or her character's thoughts, fears, and mental images were at that moment.

Discussion:

1. Did this flush out a misconception?
2. Was there a forced emotional connection?

3. Did the actors' concentration change afterward?
4. What other effects did this exercise produce?

EXERCISE 20-9: SWITCHING CHARACTERS

Useful when: Two actors seem stalemated and unaware of the other character. This can arise when a defensive actor's overpreparation precludes communion, or when actors distrust or feel incompatible with each other.

Purpose: To place each actor temporarily in the opposite role so later he or she can empathize with another character's predicament and achieve an interesting duality.

Activity: Simply ask actors to exchange parts, without regard for sex, age, or anything else. Then have them return to their own parts to see if the reading changes.

Discussion:

1. Actors: Say briefly what you discovered about the scene from playing the other role.
2. Actors: What revelations did you have about your own part?
3. Director: What did you notice after the actors resumed their own parts?

EXERCISE 20-10: TRANSLATING A SCENE INTO AN IMPROVISATION

Useful when: The cast seems tired and unable to generate emotions the scene calls for. Keep improv scenes up your sleeve for any scene that may give trouble. Actors may initially resist your request, but they usually come to enjoy the refreshment after a scene has become oppressive and immobile. Most will be impressed when you whisk out an alternative approach like this. This exercise can release the malaise built up from repeated failures with the formal text.

Activity: Take the main issue in the scene, or the one causing a problem, and translate it into two or three analogous scene subjects for improvisation. If, for example, you are having trouble in a scene of conflict between a daughter and her suspicious and restrictive father, you might assign analogous improvs on:

- A scene between an officious nurse and a patient who wants to leave the hospital
- A bus driver and a rider who wants to get off the bus before the next stop
- Two customers in a long supermarket checkout line, one of whom, having only two items, wants to cut into the line

Each of these situations has a built-in conflict hinging on rights and authority, and tackling them rapidly one after another will generate a wider emotional vocabulary that will flow back into the original scene. A variation is to let the actors invent analogous scenes. Get further mileage by doing the improvs again with roles reversed.

Discussion:

1. Which improv worked best?
2. What came of switching roles?
3. What were the differences when the cast returned to the text?

CHAPTER 21

CASTING

Your audience, which doesn't care much about screen techniques, knows immediately whether the cast in your film is giving authentic and gripping performances. That's why big-budget pictures pay astronomical salaries to "bankable" actors, and why casting is said to be 75 percent of any film's success.

Beginning directors often cast poorly. Guilty over choosing between fellow aspirants, they settle gratefully for whoever seems right and available. On a BBC film I once edited, the director had cast his wife in the main part and remained touchingly blind to her limitations. The poor man lost his job because of it.

This is an anxious time: you need actors enthusiastic about the character they play, who will work well with you and other cast members, and whose loyalty will be to the project. Acting is an intense and insecure profession, so look for actors keen on building their skills with you. Unless you have considerable budget and worldly achievements, it's unwise to direct players more experienced than you are. Nothing is scarier or riskier than to direct someone out of your league, to have a disagreement, and then find that he or she has spread disaffection and the whole cast doubts your judgment.

Acting is a well-documented craft, so what follows on casting is a brief digest of useful ideas and practices. Supplement what follows with articles on the Internet (for example www.theauditionstudio.com, www.wikihow.com/Audition or www.actingbiz.com/articles/casting_process.php), and read what you can about casting in acting books. Above all, be guided by your intuitions. This is a time when you cannot afford to intellectualize over your choices.

OVERVIEW

In casting, as in all aspects of filmmaking, generate abundance from which you can select. You'll need character descriptions, scenes, and *sides* (selected scenes from your script) as part of searching for actors able to bring something special. If you employ SAG (Screen Actors Guild) actors, you must provide a full script 24 hours before the audition. If you are working in a film-producing area and have a considerable budget, maybe you'll use a *casting director* or *casting agency* to preselect actors.

Main speaking parts are called *principal casting,* whereas *background casting* means finding secondary or background characters such as store clerks, restaurant diners, or nursing staff—those chosen on appearance and often without audition. The knowledge and resources of casting specialists drastically cut the time and labor it takes to find the best.

If you're casting without specialized help, substitute hard work and gumshoe ingenuity, which can still net a brilliant cast. Knowing how to run auditions helps remove the crippling self-consciousness you feel about choosing between likable, hopeful people. Good casting comes from:

- Asserting your right to search far and wide
- Having techniques ready to elicit actors' underlying potential
- Self-knowledge about with whom you should work—and with whom you should not
- Dogged persistence

During the process, you should have your collaborators present to provide a broader spectrum of reaction, but you should use the industry standard process of three or so stages:

1. Locate potential players for an *open,* or *cattle, call,* and audition a lot of people from which to pick out those having the experiential, physical, psychological, and emotional suitability for your parts.

2. Invite back the most promising for *callbacks,* and use procedures that reveal directability, potential under duress, and how each handles a range of representative situations.

3. In semifinal or final rounds, make more stringent demands, and mix and match players before settling on your final choice.

If your talent is trained and professional, follow the theater and film norms outlined here. The procedures are abundantly described on the many web sites concerned with acting and auditions. These address the hopeful actor, and convey much of what auditioning actors experience. If you are casting from inexperienced players, you'll need to approach the task according to where you are and what you can expect. There's plenty of help here to follow.

CAST BREAKDOWN AND CHARACTER DESCRIPTIONS

Generate a cast breakdown with thumbnail character descriptions that you can post or give over the phone. These compress much into few words, allow the reader to infer possible physical appearances, and present an attractive challenge. Typically:

Ken:	15, tall and thin, nervous, curious, intelligent, overcritical, obsessed with science fiction
George:	late 20s, medium height, medical equipment salesman, lives carefully and calls his parents each Friday; husband of Kathy.

Kathy:	early 30s, but has successfully lied about her age; small-town beauty queen gone to seed after a steamy divorce; met George through a dating service.
Ted:	60s, bus inspector, patriot, grower of prize chrysanthemums, disapproving father of George.
Eddie:	40s, washing machine repairman, part-time conjuror and clown at children's parties; too self-involved to be married; likes to spread homespun philosophy.
Angela:	70s, cheerful, resourceful, determined to live forever. Has a veneer of respectability that breaks down raucously after some drinks. In early life, made a fortune in something illicit.

ATTRACTING APPLICANTS

Keep your ad brief, describing the project in a sentence. Give the number, sex, and age of the characters as above, and a phone number or email address to contact. Be sure to specify whether there is any remuneration; if there is none, a DVD of finished work is a must. If you consider union actors, you will have to abide by union rules, which sometimes offer sliding scales for student or nonprofessional productions.

PASSIVE SEARCH FOR ACTORS

If you live in a city, you can spread a large net by advertising in the local theater auditions newspaper, on the Internet, in local newspapers, or by posting flyers on acting school or theater billboards. Be warned that large nets catch some very odd fish—or no fish at all.

ACTIVE SEARCH FOR ACTORS

Apart from the oldest and youngest in the sample cast above, the rest are in an age bracket normally immersed in daily responsibilities. Three of the adults are blue-collar parts, a social class least likely to have done any acting. These generalizations help focus the search, and suggest where to locate the exceptions with the necessary qualities and spare time.

Low-budget filmmakers have to be resourceful, so save time and frustration wherever possible by actively seeking likely participants. Contact key people in theater groups. Locate the casting director, say what you are doing, and ask if he or she can grant you time for a brief chat. This person will have a wealth of information about local talent, but may fear you are poaching in their preserves. The next most knowledgeable people are the producers (who direct in the theater) or other knowledgeable and committed theater workers. Often they will suggest names you can invite to try out. When a theater group uses professional (union) actors, the response may be cautious or even downright hostile. Theaters don't like their actors seduced away by screen parts, and may want to avoid prejudicing their relationship with the actors' union. Don't be surprised by a tight-lipped referral to the actors' union.

If your budget is rock bottom, you will have to work really hard. People well suited to playing specific parts can always be found, but it takes ingenuity and diligence, and whoever you find may need sustained work in rehearsal.

For the character of 15-year-old Ken, I would track down teachers producing drama in local schools and ask them to suggest boys who could play that character well. The teacher can ask the boy—or better, the boy's parents—to get in touch. This allays the nightmare that their child is being stalked by some hollow-eyed pedophile.

The elderly are more of a problem. Because we sideline the old, many become physically and mentally inactive. Your first task in casting Ted and Angela will be to locate older people who keep mentally and physically active. If you are lucky, there may be a senior citizen's theater group, but more likely you will have to track down special individuals. For Ted, I would look among older blue-collar men who have taken an active and extroverted role in life—perhaps in local politics, union organizing, entertainment, teaching, journalism, or salesmanship. These occupations require some flair for interaction and a relish for the fray.

Angela is a hard person to cast, but try looking among retired actresses or vocal women's group members such as citizen's and neighborhood pressure groups—anywhere you could expect to find an elderly woman secure in her life's accomplishments and adventurous enough to play a boozy, earthy woman with a past.

While you cast, remind yourself periodically that hidden among the gray armies of the unremarkable, there always exist a few individuals in any age group whose lives are being lived with wit, intelligence, and individuality. Such people rise to prominence in the often-unlikely worlds to which exigency or eccentricity has taken them. Angela, for instance, might be the president of the Standard Poodle Fanciers Club, and Ted might be a regular entrant in comedian contests or poetry slams.

Werner Herzog's actors include nonprofessionals drawn from around him. The central figures in *The Enigma of Kaspar Hauser* (1974) and *Stroszek* (1977) are played by the endearing Bruno S., a street singer and Berlin transport manager whose surname has remained undisclosed to protect his job (see his portrait in Chapter 12, Figure 12-5).

Robert Bresson, who refused to cast anyone trained to act, chose lawyers in *The Trial of Joan of Arc* (1962) to play Joan's inquisitors. Their lifetimes spent defining details gave them the right punctiliousness for cross-examination. In his *Notes on the Cinematographer*, Bresson gives a compelling rationale, akin to a documentary-making attitude, for using "models" (his word for players) uncorrupted by having performed.[1]

SETTING UP THE FIRST AUDITION

Actors of any experience will ask for your shooting schedule, audition date, callback date, and when casting will be decided. They, or their agents, will supply you with a professional portfolio that includes a résumé and head shots. These are often more glamorous or dramatic than the seemingly nondescript individual who appears before you, but at least they show whether the actor is broadly suitable by age, ethnicity, physical type, and acting experience. Be alert for résumé inflation—it's not a sign of good faith. Anyone of experience should know you can check their claims at prior workplaces.

---

[1] Los Angeles: Green Integer, 1997.

FIELDING PHONE APPLICANTS

Many trying to gain access to a cattle call have little or no experience of acting. You'll encounter a few dreamers looking for stardom, and these should be avoided. First audition those claiming experience, and add the blatantly unskilled to a list of functionary or other undemanding parts. As each person writes or calls, have a strategy ready to politely abort the procedure on grounds of inexperience or other unsuitability. Try informing potential cast in this order:

- *About the project and your experience.* Be direct and realistic, and warn that, even at the highest professional levels, filming is deathly slow. Experienced actors want to know if you are legitimate, so mention what you have produced and any exposure or awards that it garnered.
- *Time commitment and remuneration.* Ask about their experience: if they have screen-acting experience, ask for impressions of the process (it will tell you a lot). Be candid about the time that rehearsal and shooting will take. Cool responses or undue negotiating may result from low interest, high ego, or negative experience with other filmmakers.
- *The role in which the actor is interested.* Determine which role the actor thinks he or she fits, what his or her characteristics are, and be ready to suggest trying for an alternate part.
- *An audition slot*, with clear directions to the audition address if the person sounds appropriate. Confirm the information via email if you can.
- *Say what the audition will demand.* A first call might ask actors to give a table read (sitting at a table reading cold from a script), two contrasting two-minute monologues of their own choosing, or reading from sides. See the discussion below.
- *Written information.* If head shots and résumé are available, ask for them by post or email.

THE ACTORS ARRIVE

Time your audition program so you know whether to schedule arrivals at, say, 10-, 15-, or 20-minute intervals. Arriving actors wait in the holding area, which you place well away from the audition space. Have them individually received by someone lively and pleasant who can answer questions—say, where the bathroom is— and by their understanding manner help allay the extreme anxiety to which actors are subject. This trusted assistant can chat informally and form an impression of each actor's interests, personality, work habits, and punctuality. Your assistant's notes can prove very helpful when it comes to decision time. As actors wait, give each a form (see Figure 21-1 for suggested layout) to complete, so you have on file:

1. Name, street address, email address
2. Home, cellular, and work phone numbers
3. Role for which actor is trying out
4. Acting experience and any references
5. Special interests, skills, volunteer work

```
┌─────────────────────────────────────────────────────────────────────────────┐
│                        AUDITION INFORMATION                                   │
│  Auditioning _____(date) for _____ (Production) │
│                                                                               │
│                          (Please print legibly)                               │
│                                                                               │
│  Name_____ Address_____ │
│  _____ │
│  Phone _____(home) _____(work)   │
│  _____(cell) email:_____  │
│  Role(s) for which you are trying out_____ │
│                                                                               │
│                                                                               │
│                      STAGE OR FILM EXPERIENCE                                 │
│  _____(date)_____│
│  _____(date)_____│
│  _____(date)_____│
│  _____(date)_____│
│  _____(date)_____│
│  _____(date)_____│
│  _____(date)_____│
│                                                                               │
│                                                                               │
│              SPECIAL INTERESTS, SKILLS, VOLUNTARY WORK:                        │
│  _____(date)_____│
│  _____(date)_____│
│  _____(date)_____│
│  _____(date)_____│
│  _____(date)_____│
│  _____(date)_____│
│  _____(date)_____│
│                                                                               │
│                                                                               │
│                      REFERENCES & OTHER NOTES                                 │
│  _____ │
│  _____ │
│  _____ │
│  _____ │
│  _____ │
│  _____ │
│  _____ │
│  _____ │
│  _____ │
│  _____ │
│                                                      Continue on back         │
└─────────────────────────────────────────────────────────────────────────────┘
```

FIGURE 21-1

Suggested layout for audition form.

The last is purely to get a sense of attributes that indicate special energy and initiative. You could also include a section asking the applicant to write a few lines on, say, what acting means to them. From this, you can expect to learn about their values and how committed and realistic they are.

CONDUCTING THE FIRST AUDITION

At the initial call, assess broad characteristics:

- Suitability for a particular part (right age, gender, physical type, coloring, ethnicity, etc.)
- Grasp of acting (experience, concepts of the actor's role in drama, craft knowledge)
- Physical presence (features, body language, movements, voice)
- Innate character (confidence, outlook, reflexes, rhythm, energy, sociability, imprint made by life)
- Type of intelligence (sensitivity to others, perceptiveness of environment, degree of self-exploration, and cultivation of tastes)
- Whether the actor plays up to their intelligence or beneath it
- Directability (interaction with others, flexibility, defenses, self-image)
- Commitment (work habits, motivation to act, reliability)

In this session, you aim to see as many people as practical, so expect much chaff for only a little wheat. Later, you'll hold callbacks for the most promising. If you seek to fill small parts from the community, many people will prove devoid of anything you require or will be unrealistic about their abilities and commitment.

Make a video record of auditions—and try to include close-ups for facial expression, and medium-shot coverage of body expression and movements. If possible, digitize the auditions in an editing program so you can contrast different performers and solicit impressions from key production members.

STARTING THE AUDITION

The actor can now be shown into the audition space where he or she will perform. Most are trying to hide how nervous and apprehensive auditions always make them feel, but a warm, informal greeting and handshake during which you exchange eye contact helps ease the sense of being judged. Being in front of a camera unavoidably increases the pressure, so try to make light of its presence. That an actor is very nervous is not necessarily negative because it means they attach importance to being chosen. Ask for them to give their *slate*, the brief self-identification such as: "Hi, my name is _____, and I'm going to play _____[character's name] from _____ [play]." Later, when you are watching tapes, you will need to know who's who.

Be sure to personally thank each actor for what he or she gives you.

THE DANGER IN IDEALS

Casting means looking for individuals whose age and history fit them for your roles, but you can approach this in two different ways:

1. *Does this actor fit the father in my script?* This contains a built-in bias, for each actor is being held up to an ideal, as though the characters were already formed and each candidate either far or close. This, like searching for the ideal spouse, invites disappointment and misjudgments.

2. *What kind of father would this actor give my film*? This anticipates myriad possibilities in the role, and lets you see the actor's physical and mental being as an active contribution to the process of making drama. Here, casting becomes developmental, not image fulfillment.

MONOLOGUES

You will learn a lot from two brief and very different monologues taken from a play or novel of the actor's choosing. They should show very different characters and moods. If you need to, ask the actor to place his or her point of focus a little above your head. If they fix you in the eye, it becomes disconcerting and blocks you from observing properly. Monologues commonly tell you:

- What material the actor thinks appropriate for himself or herself and for your piece
- What kind of physical presence, rhythm, and energy he or she has
- What his or her voice is like (a good voice is a tremendous asset)
- How different the characters are, and what kind of emotional range he or she can handle

You also see how good they are at:

- Interpreting and memorizing a text
- Acting with the whole body rather than just the face
- *Being* instead of acting. It's very important for film actors to work outward from their character's thoughts and feelings, and not inward from analytic ideas
- Finding the character in themselves rather than imitating a type or version of someone else

Pay attention to your every intuition—they're never unfounded. How well did each actor perform their choice of material? Could you spontaneously "see" the character the actor was playing? The choice and handling of material indicate what they think they do best. It's good when it reflects the actor's research on your production, but may instead indicate an enduring self-image. If an actor trying out for a brash salesman chooses the monologue of an endearing wimp, that actor may already have cast himself in life as a loser, reckoning that his best hope is to be funny. That quality of acquiescence makes him quite unsuitable for the brash salesman's part, though perhaps good for the unlucky boyfriend.

COLD READING

If your first call attracts many entrants, you may not have time for this. Take sides from your script or scenes culled from stage plays, and make several copies. Scene choices should allow you to combine at will two men, two women, a man and a woman, an old person with someone young, and so on. With inexperienced players, you may prefer something from theatrical repertory, and *not* scenes from your film—untrained actors often internalize early impressions. These might be hard to change subsequently. Based on who is waiting, your assistant can decide which piece the available actors might read, giving them copies to study in advance.

In a cold reading, you typically will see:

- Which actors have intelligent questions about their character or about the piece
- Actors having to think on their feet and give life to a part just encountered
- The same scene handled by more than one set of actors, and thus what each brings to the piece
- What quickness, intelligence, and creativity are evoked by the bare words on the page
- How each actor uses their voice
- Whether they understand the importance of their character's problem with other characters, and center on this as essential conflict
- Whether they grasp what their character is fighting for, and the essentials of relationship implied in the scene
- How they modify their performances when you ask for *adjustments* (changes of attitude or behavior from their character). In the next reading, you might, for instance, ask for an attitude of resentment rather than apology.

Different performances and action will affect you differently, and often in ways that pose questions. With two characters of the same sex, try switching the actors to see how well each produces appropriate and different qualities as the new character.

After each actor's audition:

- Thank him or her personally.
- Give a date by which to expect news of the next round or final decision.
- Make a note of whatever was positive about their performance so you can be supportive of everyone you have to reject.

DECISIONS AFTER THE FIRST ROUND

If you have promising applicants, run the tapes of their contributions and brainstorm with coworkers. Discussing their strengths and weaknesses usually reveals further dimensions in the candidates, not to mention insights into your crew members and their values.

Now comes the agonizing part. Call everyone who auditioned and tell them whether they were selected for callback auditions. Telling the bad news to those not selected is hard on both parties; mitigate the disappointment by saying something appreciative and positive about the person's performance. With the people you want to see again, set the place and callback date for further auditioning.

NEGATIVE CHARACTERS AND TYPECASTING

To varying degrees, all actors have some difficulty playing negative characteristics, especially when they fear these are in their own makeup. So be careful. It can be disastrous during shooting if an actor slowly becomes aware that he was cast for his own negative qualities. Villains are easy to play, but playing a stupid or nasty character may be viewed by the actor either as an interesting challenge or as a personal sacrifice. The less secure the individual, the more likely his doubts will fester. A sure sign that this is happening is when an actor wants to upgrade his character's qualities. There are no small parts, said Stanislavsky, just small actors.

All acting is both a departure from self and an exploration of it. People are cast by type, and some hate the type they fall into. Typecasting is both necessary and potentially imprisoning. Acting can be a liberation or a dive into the abyss, all depending on the approaches of the actor and the director.

To protect yourself, ask actors under consideration for their ideas on the cause of their character's negative traits. How do other people regard him? How does he regard himself? What is his function in the world the piece represents? What they say may influence your choice.

LONG- OR SHORT-TERM CHOICES

You may be tempted to cast the person who gave something specially attractive at the audition. This actor may be brilliant or glib but inflexible, developing less than does a partner whose audition was less accomplished. Try to investigate not only what an actor wants to do, but also how willingly he ventures outside customary boundaries. All actors of any experience are fervently committed in principle, but regrettably, practice sometimes reveals something different. Acting involves the whole person, not just ideas: you may find that a genially accomplished personality, coming under the threat of the unexpected, suddenly manifests bizarre forms of self-defense and resistance. The shy but dedicated actor may be the one with the potential to grow and who makes the best candidate. During his first auditions, Marlon Brando mumbled into his shirtfront.

THE DEMANDING PART OF THE CHARACTER WHO DEVELOPS

Small parts usually require little adaptability. To cast a surly gas station attendant for one short scene requires no growth potential, whereas the part of the new wife inexorably realizing how deeply her husband is mother-dominated calls for extended and subtle powers of development. Her character must go through a spectrum of emotions during which she must dig deeply into unpleasant, possibly frightening feelings. You will need an actor with the openness, trust, and emotional reach to undertake a grueling rehearsal and performance process.

FIRST CALLBACK

If you are ready to call back the most promising actors, you will now need some additional testing procedures.

ADDITIONAL MONOLOGUE

Many actors will prepare a further monologue in a different style, to show their range. You can certainly ask ahead of time for another—perhaps making specific suggestions so you can gauge a particular emotion or emotional type.

A READING FROM YOUR SCRIPT

If the callback actors don't have basic information on the story and where the scene fits in, give it now. Be ready in any case to field questions about motivation, prior scenes, and so on. The sides should be demanding dialogue scenes, but limit the material to a couple of minutes' duration if you have many people to audition. You are interested in directability:

- Ask each actor to play his or her character in a specified way. Then give critical feedback and specific directions to develop what you saw.
- Have them play the scene again. Look for who builds on his initial performance, and who holds on to what you praised, yet can alter the areas specified.
- For a further run-through, give each actor a different mood or characteristic to see what he or she can produce from a radically different premise.

IMPROVISATION

If you are auditioning experienced actors, don't set improvs unless you have directed them before and can handle the situation with some confidence. You are putting actors in the most exposed situation, and they must be able to trust your judgment. You must also know what you expect to find. Here's an example of the kind of thing you might ask for: Give two actors brief verbal outlines of characters in the script and a situation from the script that involves them, such as moving a piece of furniture, waiting for officials at a foreign border, or dealing with a car that's run out of gas in a scary neighborhood. Keep expectations low and make it enjoyable:

- Ask your players to improvise their own scene based on the situation in the (unseen) script. The goal is not to see how close they get to the scripted original, but how they handle themselves and interact when much of the creation is spontaneous.
- After they have done a version, give them feedback about aspects you see developing, and ask for a further version, specifying changes you'd like in behavior and mood. Now you can see not only what they can produce from themselves, but how well they incorporate direction.

If you have just one person to audition, test their imaginative resources by asking for an improvised phone conversation based on a situation that you specify. You should feel there's a real person on the other end.

For more improvs, use the guide table under "Improv Exercises" in Chapter 19 to locate what you need to put under test.

SECOND CALLBACK

Depending on the size of the cast and time constraints, the material in this section may be conflated with that in "First Callback," above, or handled separately as a further round.

INTERVIEW

By now, you need to confirm and amplify the impressions you've formed about the individuals you like most. Give your remaining candidates the full script to read.

Tell players *not* to learn any lines, because doing so may fix their performance at an embryonic stage of development. After they have read the script, spend one-on-one time with each actor, encouraging them to ask questions, to talk about their character and the script as a whole, and to talk about themselves. Look for realism, sincerity, self-motivation, and a great interest in drama. A good sign is when an actor is spontaneously excited because the script explores some issue from his or her own experience. You hope to get actors who feel they have something to learn from you and your project.

Be wary of those who flatter or name-drop, seem content with superficial readings, intellectualize, are inflexibly opinionated, or make you feel they are stooping to do you a good turn. Avoid like the plague anyone you suspect will bail out when something better comes up.

MIX AND MATCH ACTORS

When you have multiple candidates for a lead part, assess the personal chemistry that each has with the others. Use mix and match to find the most vivid chemistry. In part, this is to see how they interact with each other, and in part to see what they communicate to an audience. I once had to cast a short film about a man in his 30s who becomes involved with a rebellious teenage girl. We had to reject a more accomplished actor owing to something indefineably sinister in his manner that made the relationship disturbing. Another actor paired with the same actress changed the balance and gave the girl the upper hand, as the story demanded.

Sometimes two actors simply don't communicate well or are temperamentally mismatched. Actors cast to play lovers must at least like each other; if they don't, the result could be a wariness and stiffness in their playing that disables your film. Even when your characters are supposed to be mortal enemies, you want players who are responsive and interested in each other. You may still encounter problems. In *The Middle of the World*, Alain Tanner's 1974 film about a Swiss engineer's doomed affair with an Italian waitress, the director found that Philippe Léotard (Figure 21-2) produced his best work in early takes, whereas Olimpia Carlisi produced hers in late ones. Actors learn and grow at different rates.

MAKING FINAL CHOICES

REVIEW YOUR IMPRESSIONS

Someone who does well may simply be good at auditioning yet unequal to a challenging part. Conversely, someone shy or anxious might develop very well under the right direction. Every person is stamped by their life and by a mass of intangible qualities, to which you must try to respond. Your audience certainly will.

Before making final choices, review your impression of each actor's:

- Physical and temperamental suitability
- Impact
- Imprint on the part in relation to the other actors
- Rhythms of speech and movement
- Quickness of mind and directability

FIGURE 21-2 ————————————————————————————

Actors have different development rates. Philippe Léotard in *The Middle of the World* (courtesy New Yorker Films).

- Ability at mimicry, especially when having to maintain a regional or foreign accent
- Voice quality (its associations are extremely important!)
- Capacity to hold on to both new and old instructions
- Ability to carry out his or her character's development, whether it is quick and intuitive or slower and more graduated
- Commitment to the project
- Long-term commitment to acting as an art and a discipline
- Likely patience with filming's slow and disjunctive progress
- Ability to enter and reenter an emotional condition over several takes and camera angles
- Compatibility with the other actors
- Compatibility with you, the director

Now is the time to confer again with anyone inside or outside your project whose judgment you really respect. Listen carefully to what they say they feel.

CAMERA TEST

To confirm your choices, tape a short scene with the principal actors. Even then, you will probably remain somewhat uncertain. Look for actors to remain in focus and interesting when they are thinking or listening. Show their scenes to your coworkers and thoroughly discuss the impressions each actor makes. If you want to cast someone your intuition says is risky, communicate your reservations tactfully but directly to the actor. You might, for instance, feel uncertain of their commitment, or sense a resistance to authority figures that will make directing them problematic. Candid confrontation at this point shows you how the actor handles uncomfortable criticism, and paves the way should that perception later become an issue or, God forbid, should you need to replace him. Sometimes an actor who seems arrogant and egocentric will, faced with a frank reaction to his characteristics, gratefully admit that he has an unfortunate way of masking uncertainty. Suddenly you both feel closer to each other!

ANNOUNCING CASTING DECISIONS

Make final decisions by the promised date, then personally notify and thank all who have taken part. Give each person whatever appreciative, constructive comments you can. This signals your professionalism and maintains your good standing in the community. If you can, say in what ways they gave a great audition—but add that, unfortunately, your part doesn't fit their type. Needless to say, rejection is painful, and all the more so for those who made it to the threshold. Actors are wearily used to the pain of rejection, but a director who does it sensitively is someone definitely worth approaching in the future. Filmmaking is a village; when you return to the well, your reputation matters.

GIVING AND TAKING

Now that you have your cast, keep this in mind: more than anything else, people in all walks of life crave recognition for who they are and what they can do. Potentially, you can give just as much as you take from your players. When a director liberates an actor's potential, or works responsibly on the deficiencies that mask it, the serious actor responds with love and loyalty. Sharing and honesty is a goal in director-actor and actor-actor relationships, and it's also the very best foundation for a truly creative working relationship. Every committed actor is looking for a director who can lead the way across new thresholds. This means they develop not just in acting, but in living. Perform this function just a little, and your cast will begin to place great faith in you and be your most enthusiastic advocate to other actors.

CHAPTER 22

EXPLORING THE SCRIPT

An additional resource—particularly for script analysis, rehearsal, and directing actors—is Judith Weston's *The Film Director's Intuition* (Michael Wiese Productions, 2003). This expands on her *Directing Actors*, but should be consumed in parallel with practical work if its excellent, always actor-oriented advice is not to seem overwhelming.

ON-SCREEN LENGTH AND MAINTAINING TIMINGS

Films intended for cinema showing have an optimum length based on their audience holding power, but films for a programmed showing like television must fit into a "slot" and be precise to the second. A 30-minute noncommercial TV slot is usually 28 minutes, 30 seconds. Anything for commercial TV has to be written in sections, each ending in cliff-hangers, to accommodate commercials. If you know the market you want your film to enter, plan your project to fulfill a characteristic running time. Be ready to ax parts of the script: a 30-minute film will need a 30-page screenplay, not one of 48 pages. Many length problems come from failing to take timings during rehearsals. Actors developing their characters' business make each scene longer, even though they seem fleeter.

Student directors commonly set out to make the longest film possible, so running times reflect ambition and budget more than audience considerations. Later, the lack of ordinary story compression becomes painfully evident and turns into the hapless editor's major problem.

How to determine a film's ideal running time? Simply decide in advance according to the magnitude of the story. Most people have absorbed 18,000 hours of viewing by age 20, so use your long experience to nominate the *shortest* appropriate screen time. Budget time for each of the story's acts, then for the individual scenes. If scene timings add up to the intended length of the movie, then you have imposed a professional economy on the writing. You can allow no material to be added without subtracting it from somewhere else.

Vow to keep tabs on length during rehearsals, or your 20-minute treasure will self-inflate to a 47-minute toad.

INTERPRETING THE SCRIPT

New directors often underdevelop their scripts, particularly—and this seems para-doxical—those they write themselves. Later, they discover during editing how many possibilities remained latent and unexplored in the screenplay. This chapter offers many tools for development. Taken all together, they are probably excessive, so do as much as you find useful. Short films are a good practice ground: their restricted size lets you experiment in depth to find what works. Later, when you turn to longer forms, you will know what to use.

TWO TYPES OF FILM, TWO KINDS OF PREPARATION

Speech and behavior represent two polarities in fiction filmmaking—each requires a different kind of script interpretation. They can be characterized thus:

- *The theatrical film* tells its story mainly through dialogue scenes. Example: Billy Bob Thornton's *Sling Blade* (1996). Its script came from a stage play Thornton had written and acted in earlier. Mentally and emotionally disabled Karl, discharged after decades of incarceration, returns to the rural community where in childhood he had murdered his mother and her lover. There, he becomes friend and hero to Frank, a young boy whose mother has an abusive boyfriend.
- *The cinematic film* tells its story more through imagery and behavior. Example: Jean-Pierre Jeunet's *Amélie* (2001). A lonely waitress discovers that by carrying out anonymous acts of kindness, she can change people's lives for the better. Eventually, she reaps a reward by changing her own, so that a lover enters her life.

Both films are fully realized cinema, and each has a powerful sense of place: the first uses absorbing and sustained dialogue exchanges, whereas the second uses a montage of short scenes to advance the story through image and behavior rather than dialogue. Neither mode is better or more legitimate than the other—they are simply different stories that use the screen in different ways. Each mode, however, takes a different emphasis during preparation.

The characters in the *dialogue-centered film* pursue their objectives through language and are fulfilled or frustrated at each beat. Dialogue narrates the film and provides its forward movement, and the scene dynamics lie with the players. Let's say quickly that dialogue-centered material does not have to be static and devoid of visual or behavioral interest. Characters can be in movement at work or play, and can be shown doing anything organic to the world they inhabit. With this strongly realistic type of film, the director works as one does with theater actors, digging for the meaning and rhythms of the text and working to build the integrity of the characters.

The *cinematic film* has few sustained dialogue scenes, and builds its dramatic units using a montage technique of images or short action scenes. The characters still need objectives, but the arc of each dramatic unit may be formed from several scene fragments. Like mime, comic strips, or early movies, the story is narrated more by action and images and less by dialogue. The director works at designing action, behavior, composition, and editing juxtapositions—most of which is envisaged at the writing stage. This is a type of film in which the cinematographer's taste and inventiveness are paramount. Much of the film's rhythm and momentum are consolidated during editing, as in a documentary.

PICTURIZATION

Both modes require fully occupied, fully realized characters who pursue their objectives, and both need strong design and *picturization* (the use of visual elements to reinforce intended meanings). Both modes benefit if you initially design your film as though it were going to be silent, for it is easier to bring dialogue to a strongly visualized film than to bring a visual design to a film made of static set pieces.

A film does not find a visual form; you have to actively impose one—and the earlier you start, the better. Start assembling your ideas about your project as a visual entity, making sketches or collecting representative images, so that the film you want forms in your head. Think in terms of particular music, and particular painters or photographers. You should immerse yourself in developing a style for the imagery that accentuates the world in which the characters live, and the way you want us to react to them.

HOMEWORK

Your interpretive work is going to move from the large toward the small. That is, take your large-scale decisions before you begin deciding detail.

BREAK INTO MANAGEABLE UNITS

Read and reread the script, keeping notes as you go. Group and structure your notes so you get the most out of them. Develop a premise and thematic purpose (see Chapter 3, "Dramaturgy Essentials") for your film, and break the script into acts.

Your work will need to stimulate your creative collaborators and represent decisions you can defend, if need be, with spirit and authority. Cast members will each read the script from their own character's point of view, so early readings tend to produce divergent, contradictory interpretations. You cannot have all the answers ready, and you don't want to. This is intensely creative and collaborative work, and your function is to shepherd your ensemble toward a shared understanding of the story's purpose. No matter how much work you put in, probing and intelligent actors will take you into unexamined areas. That's part of the excitement in ensemble work.

SCRIPT BREAKDOWN

Take the script and make a preliminary breakdown (or cross-plot) of characters appearing in each scene, as in Figure 22-1, made for a stage treatment of *Northanger Abbey*. It shows at a glance which characters each scene uses, and what scenes take place in each location. This helps you plan a rehearsal schedule, and lays bare the film's pattern of interactions and underlying structures. A more advanced and detailed version will be essential for planning the shoot. When, for instance, you have three scenes in the same day-care center, you shoot them consecutively to conserve time and energy, even though they are widely spaced in the story.

Scene	Location	Script Pages	Catherine	Isabella	John Thorpe	Henry Tilney	James Morland	Eleanor	Mrs. Allen	General Tilney	Mrs. Thorpe	CHARACTERS PER SCENE
1	The Dance	1-2	✓						✓			2
2	Lower Rooms	2-6	✓			✓						2
3	Pump Room	6-7		✓							✓	2
4	Mrs. Allen's	7-13	✓	✓	✓		✓					4
5	Pump Room	13-20	✓	✓		✓	✓	✓				5
6	Mrs. Allen's	20-24	✓	✓	✓		✓		✓			5
7	On the Journey	24-25	✓		✓		✓					3
8	At the Theater	25-27	✓			✓			✓			3
9	Mrs. Allen's	27-30	✓	✓	✓		✓	✓		✓		6
10	Out Walking	30-35	✓			✓		✓				3
11	Mrs. Allen's	35-37	✓	✓								2
12	In the Street	37-40	✓		✓							2
13	At the Tilneys'	40-41	✓					✓		✓		3
14	Mrs. Allen's	41-43	✓	✓								2
	NUMBER OF SCENES PER CHARACTER		13	7	5	4	5	4	3	2	1	

FIGURE 22-1

Typical scene and character breakdown table showing characters, locations, and script pages necessary for each scene.

Scheduling and budgeting software like the industry favorite Movie Magic™ or Gorilla™ (which offers an upgradable student version) can download from popular screenplay programs like Final Draft® and help you break it down into lists. These are the beginning of the massive scheduling and coordination work that a large production requires if you are to effectively integrate locations, sets, camera and sound requirements, characters, extras, stunts, wardrobe, makeup, properties, special effects, animal handlers, transportation, catering—and anything else the script calls for. There is more on this process in Chapter 27 under "Scheduling the Shoot," and in Chapter 30 under "Script Breakdown"

DEFINE THE SUBTEXTS AND A METAPHOR

Subtexts arise from what each character is trying to get, do, or accomplish. Every part of a well-written screenplay is a skin covering deeper layers of potential meaning. Your success as a director hinges on creating their presence in the audience's mind.

Try moving this time from macro to micro by developing a *logline* (one-sentence summary of the pitch for the production) such as "Rescuing the rescuer," "Finding out where it all started," or "No love as sweet as the first." You also need a guiding metaphor for your production. For Guillermo del Toro's *Pan's Labyrinth* (2006), one might use the metaphor of a laundry. The child Ofelia, an Alice in Francoland, launders the grinding evil of her daytime life in the dream cauldron of her imagination. Her fascist stepfather is the Evil Wizard, her mother the Babe in the Wood, the housekeeper her Guardian Angel, the faun her Taskmaster, and the Pale Man the terrifying Baby Eater of folktale. The fascist army forces are the black knights of evil, and the guerrillas are the decimated powers of light that are fated to become all but extinguished.

By such images, you summon and grasp the essential dynamics of your tale. Such similes and metaphors are a great help when you want to communicate your ideas to others.

TOOLS TO REVEAL DRAMATIC DYNAMICS

Following are some ways to expose the heart and soul of each scene. Bringing to light what would otherwise remain undisturbed and unexamined allows the director to confront the implications of the material. This takes time and energy to implement, but will repay your effort.

BLOCK DIAGRAM

Photocopy the Story Line or Editing Analysis Form in Figure 22-2. With it, make a flowchart of your movie's content, with each sequence as a block. In the box, name the scene, and under "Contributes," write two or three lines to describe what the sequence should contribute to the story line, as in Figure 22-3. This surpasses the step outline because it concerns dramatic effect rather than content. Expect to write descriptive tags concerning:

- Plot points
- Exposition (factual and setup information)

STORY LINE OR EDITING ANALYSIS   Date_____Page#_____
Intended Length_____

Production title_____
=================================   ===========================

Seq   Seq tag title_____   Contributes _____
#____   Action _____   _____
    _____   _____
    _____   _____
    _____   _____

Seq   Seq tag title_____   Contributes _____
#____   Action _____   _____
    _____   _____
    _____   _____
    _____   _____

Seq   Seq tag title_____   Contributes _____
#____   Action _____   _____
    _____   _____
    _____   _____
    _____   _____

Seq   Seq tag title_____   Contributes _____
#____   Action _____   _____
    _____   _____
    _____   _____
    _____   _____

Seq   Seq tag title_____   Contributes _____
#____   Action _____   _____
    _____   _____
    _____   _____
    _____   _____

Seq   Seq tag title_____   Contributes _____
#____   Action _____   _____
    _____   _____
    _____   _____
    _____   _____

Seq   Seq tag title_____   Contributes _____
#____   Action _____   _____
    _____   _____
    _____   _____
    _____   _____

FIGURE 22-2

Form for script or editing analysis.

- Character definition
- Building mood or atmosphere
- Parallel storytelling
- Ironic juxtaposition
- Foreshadowing

STORY LINE OR EDITING ANALYSIS FORM   Page ___1___

Production title __"A Night So Long"__   Length __58__ mins

Editor __Murray Tyndall__   Date __9__ / __01__ /__2002__

Sequence definition (brief line title)	Sequence's contribution to the film's developing "argument."
Seq. # __1__ __BAR SEQ: ED PRESSES HIS COMPANY ON DANA__	Contributes: __ESTABLISHES ED'S & DANA'S CHARACTERISTICS AND THE SPARRING TO COME. HE PROMISES TO KEEP THEIR RELATIONSHIP PLATONIC__ Length __3__ mins __10__ secs
Seq. # __2__ __GARAGE SEQ: DANA SHOWS ED HER MOTORCYCLE. EACH PROBES THE OTHER'S BACKGROUND.__	Contributes: __MORE CHARACTER DETAILS THAT BOTH LOVE COUNTRY MUSIC & THAT EACH CAN BE SENTIMENTAL__ Length __5__ mins __35__ secs
Seq. # __3__ __LEN'S APARTMENT: DANA VISITS OLD BOYFRIEND, MAKES LOVE WITH HIM, REALIZES IT'S A MISTAKE.__	Contributes: __DANA TRIES (AND FAILS) TO HAVE DISCONNECTED SEX, AND REALIZES THAT ED IS A FORCE IN HER LIFE__ Length __4__ mins __15__ secs

FIGURE 22-3

Sample of block diagram analyzing part of a script.

Having to write so compactly makes you find the paradigm for each tag—a brain-straining exercise of the utmost value. Soon you will have the whole screenplay laid out as a flowchart. You will be surprised by how much you learn about its structure, strengths, and weaknesses. Following are common failings you can find, and their likely cures:

GRAPHING TENSION AND BEATS

Once you've read the script many times, graph the changing pressures or temperatures of each scene. Time is the graph's baseline, and tension is the vertical axis.

Fault	Likely cure
Expository scenes release information statically, without tension, and without advancing the action.	Make the scene contribute not just factual information, but action and movement to the story. Consider dropping the scene and burying the exposition in a more functional sequence.
Repetition of information	Cut it out. However, some information may be so vital to the plot that you may want to cover yourself and edit it out only later, when the audience proves not to need it.
Information released early or unnecessarily	Withholding is axiomatic for all drama, so it comes down to deciding how long.
Factual information that comes too late	When an audience is unduly frustrated, they may give up—another judgment call.
Confusions in time progression	This can be disastrous. Better to be conservative in shooting, knowing you can reorder time during editing if experience shows that your story profits by it.
Bunching of similar scenes, events, or actions	You'll spot this only if you force yourself to tag each scene with a premise. The cure is to drop the weaker scenes or give them different purposes.
Characters disappear for long periods until needed.	This can be a sign of having too many characters (amalgamate some?), or of characters who are conveniences and not properly active in their own right.
Characters are invented to serve a limited dramatic purpose.	Amalgamate, thin out cast, or reconsider who does what.
Use of coincidence to solve a dramatic problem ("Guess what, Dad: I've won the lottery!")	Something is drastically wrong with the plotting unless the piece is about the degree to which life is determined by chance.
	Coincidence should never be allowed to carry a major dramatic point.
A lack of alternation in mood or environment	See if you can reconfigure the order or chronology of scenes to produce a more varied progression.

(Continued)

Table (*Continued*)

Fault	Likely cure
Excitement too early, leading to anticlimax	Climaxes in scenes or in whole screenplays are often wrongly placed. You will have to reposition any that undercut the whole.
Similarity (and therefore redundancy) in what some scenes contribute	Remove the weaker of any redundant material.
Multiple endings because of indecision over what (and therefore how) the story must resolve	This is a problem emanating from having an ill-defined premise or multiple and incompatible premises. Sometimes endings depend on the nuance of the playing, and it may be legitimate to shoot more than one ending—even to include them all, depending on the genre of the piece.

Graph the overall scene in black, then try a different color for each main character. If, for instance, you have a comedy scene between a dentist and a nervous patient, graph the rise and fall of the patient's anxiety, then rehearse the action to progressively escalate the patient's fear and link to it the rising irritation of the dentist. Each dramatic unit within the scene culminates in a beat (or moment of decisive realization) for one or the other character. Graphing them forces you to extract essentials from the scene and reveals its hidden contours. The process allows you to survey how many such scenes might be bunched together, and what the predominant mode is in the script as a whole.

As an example, here is a scene based on an experience of my father's in wartime London when food was scarce. You might even want to try rehearsing and shooting this scene for practice. As with all film treatments, it is told in the present tense.

Paul is a sailor from the docks setting out for home across London. On board ship, he has acquired a sack of brown sugar and is taking it home to his family. Food of all kinds is rationed, and what he is doing is very risky. He has the sugar inside a battered old suitcase. The sugar is as heavy as a corpse, but he contrives to walk lightly as though carrying only his service clothing. In a busy street, one lock of the suitcase bursts, and the green canvas sack comes sagging into view. Dropping the suitcase hastily on the sidewalk, he grips it between his knees in a panic while thinking what to do. To his horror, a grim-faced policeman approaches. Paul realizes that the policeman will check what's inside the suitcase, and Paul will go to prison. He's all ready to run away, but the policeman pulls some string out of his pocket and gets down on his knees, his nose within inches of the contraband, to help Paul tie it together. Paul keeps talking until the job's done, then, thanking the policeman profusely, picks up the suitcase as if it contained feathers and hurries away, feeling the cop is going to sadistically call him back. Two streets later, Paul realizes he is free.

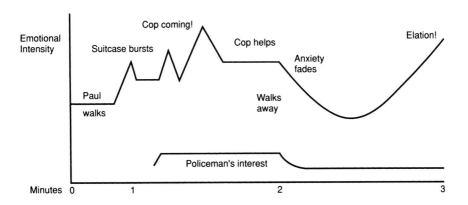

FIGURE 22-4 ———————————————————————————————————

Graph expressing changes of emotional intensity during an interaction between two characters.

Figure 22-4 plots the intensity of each character's dominant emotion against the advance of time. Paul's emotions change, whereas the unaware policeman's emotions are simple and placid by contrast. Paul's stages of development are:

- Trying to walk normally to conceal weighty contraband
- Sense of catastrophe as suitcase bursts
- Assuming policeman is coming to arrest him
- Realizing his guilt is not yet apparent—all is not yet lost
- Tension while trying to keep policeman's attention off contents
- Making escape under policeman's ambiguous gaze
- Sense of joyous release as he realizes he's gotten away with it

The treatment contains some realizations that cannot be explicitly filmed without breaking the sequence into "what if" sequences where Paul imagines himself being arrested, tried, and clapped into prison. A visual like Figure 22-4 brings clarity to where and how changes must take place in dominant emotions. It shows:

- How the actors need to create distinct rising and falling emotional pressures within their characters
- Where characters undergo major transitions, or beats
- Where the cast must externalize beats through action

Actors deal with one objective and its attendant emotion at a time, and have to find credible ways to transition to the next. Your directing must help your actors maintain the specifics of their character's consciousness, one step at a time, one objective at a time.

In the scene above, the policeman feels only a mild, benign interest, which falls away as the sailor with the successfully mended suitcase goes on his way. Not so for Paul. He must pretend he's an innocent man with a luggage problem. Knowing something the policeman doesn't, the audience empathizes with the sailor's anxiety and appreciates his efforts to project petty concerns. Missing from the scene is the knowledge of (1) the nature of the contraband, (2) the family Paul is trying to get it to, and (3) what he risks if he gets caught. For the scene to yield its full potential, this exposition would need establishing. That the sugar is going to Paul's family and not to a crime syndicate alters how the audience views him.

We can underscore Paul's subjectivity and raise the stakes in the scene. By having the policeman appear threatening as he approaches, we could make him test Paul's guilt by pretending to offer help. Late in the scene, we could release the tension by revealing the policeman's motives to have been benign all along. Throughout, compositions juxtaposing the bulging, insecure suitcase against the approaching policeman can visually relay the anxieties uppermost in Paul's mind.

By emphasizing Paul's anxieties, we make the audience identify with his problem. By switching to the policeman's point of view, we show how Paul looks to the policeman, or even how Paul *thinks* he looks to him. This complexity is more interesting than the good versus evil dichotomy in which the main character a rounded portrait and others are all flat.

The audience is being led to participate in Paul's inner experience while seeing how he conceals what he is feeling. Actors and directors of long experience intuitively carry out this duality. For the actor lacking an instinct for this, nothing less than a detailed, moment-to-moment analysis with his director will enable him to effectively mold his character's consciousness, step-by-step, at the core of the scene.

Your breakdown of each dramatic unit for this scene will proceed something like this:

Define the unit's	By asking	Example
Situation	What, when, and where?	During World War II, a young sailor called Paul is leaving London docks with contraband sugar hidden in a suitcase.
Primary point of view	Whose experience are we sharing?	The sailor's
Secondary point(s) of view as resource	Who else's viewpoint might we share?	Bystanders', Policeman's, Hungry seagulls'
Main problem	What is the main character trying to accomplish?	He wants to get it safely home to his family.
Conflict	Where is the main conflict?	Trying to look normal while fearing arrest for contraband.

(Continued)

Table (*Continued*)

Define the unit's	By asking	Example
Obstacle	What is the obstacle that he or she faces?	Just when his suitcase bursts, he encounters a policeman.
Stakes	What is the price of failure?	If he's caught, he may go to jail.
Complications	How do the stakes rise as the situation moves toward the apex, or crisis point?	The policeman may be playing at being helpful, but also playing cat and mouse. He ties up the suitcase while Paul sweats. Paul starts walking away. Has he gotten away with it? He walks jauntily, in dread of hearing, "Hey you! Stop!"
Beat	How does a main character's consciousness change?	Turning into the next street, he realizes that he is free.

FIRST TIMING

For dialogue-centered films, each standard screenplay page should last one minute of screen time. This won't necessarily hold true in practice, for rapid dialogue exchanges or successions of highly detailed images with long, slow camera movements, as you might find in a more cinematic, montage-based film. You can get more reliable figures by reading each scene aloud, acting all the lines, and going through the actions. Time each sequence, then cross your fingers and add up the total. Do this periodically from now onward.

CHAPTER 23

ACTOR AND DIRECTOR PREPARE A SCENE

Actors and their director should thoroughly study the text before coming together. This creates checks and balances so that when actions, motivations, and meanings come under scrutiny, they will draw usefully partisan perceptions from everyone. Each actor sees the world of the text more from the perspective of his or her own character. Thus, the viewpoints of the different actors often spark new ideas. Not all may be compatible, so the director leads the process of coordinating and reconciling them. You will need to be evenhanded, holistic, and speaking for the best interests of the project and its general audience.

Following are the responsibilities that cast members bear at the outset of rehearsal. For inexperienced players, you may want to photocopy this section and hold a supportive discussion before they go to work. This section is addressed directly to cast members.

THE ACTOR PREPARES

Your director is your audience and also the arbiter of all that affects you. Seek feedback from your director alone, and turn a deaf ear to anything being said by crew, onlookers, or other actors.

GIVEN CIRCUMSTANCES

Know at every point in every scene what circumstances and pressures are determining your character's physical and mental state. Your "givens" are the who, what, when, and where of your character. They include physical and psychological traits, social circumstances, special relationships, and your character's values and moral stance.

BACKSTORY AND BIOGRAPHY

Make up a life story for your character that supports the backstory details implied in the script. Everything your character says or does has roots in his or her past, whether near or distant, so you must develop one that is appropriate where none is specified. Your director will sometimes question you during rehearsal about your character's background, always probing when something is not yet coming across clearly.

JUSTIFICATION

Know the specific pressures that motivate your character's every action and line. This extends the process you used to build your character's biography, and helps govern his or her choices and decisions. The script usually contains the relevant clues, but sometimes what motivates your character's actions must be decided between you and your director.

OBJECTIVES

What is my character trying to get, do, or accomplish? He or she is always acting on other characters to get something (a smile, a cup of coffee, a sympathetic reaction, a rejection, a sign of guilt, a glimpse of doubt). As in life, your character is usually aware of immediate, short-term objectives, but long-term ones that emanate from deeply buried needs are likely to be unconscious.

The short-term ones must fit into the long-term ones. Define your character's every goal as:

- An active verb ("I will convince"—*not*, "I will be convincing")
- Someone or something acted upon ("the judge")
- A desired outcome ("to let me off so I can go to my brother in the hospital")

Naturally, your character will often fail to achieve his or her objectives, and this leads to the next objective ("I will plead with my lawyer to intercede so I can reach my brother before his operation").

DEFINING ACTIONS

Giving your actions a descriptive tag helps invest each with identity and meaning. Even common actions like opening a closet door need clear taglines. "He eases the door open," for instance, shows caution and perhaps apprehension. Substitute other active verbs—such as "jerks," "rips," "shoves," "barges," "slides," "elbows," "flings," "dashes," "heaves," or "hurls"—and you open up a range of relationships between person and door. Tag descriptions help you locate playable action and remain consistent from take to take. They also particularize the action and reveal the user's interior life to great effect. Authentic physical and mental actions worked out in advance also tend to liberate genuine feeling as you need it.

HOW DO OTHER CHARACTERS SEE ME? AND HOW DO I SEE MYSELF?

Each character in a drama illuminates our understanding of the others, so:

- How does each of the other characters see you?
- How do you see each of them?
- What do you have in common? What are your most important differences?

- What defenses does your character need in relation to how others see him or her?
- How does he or she rationalize this?

WHAT ARE OTHER CHARACTERS TRYING TO DO TO ME OR GET FROM ME?

During performance, listen acutely to other characters for nuances in their will and intentions, so your character stays fresh and alive. A scene shot in multiple takes and angles can remain vivid because you and your partners are working from the actual, not just from something memorized.

BEATS

As an actor sustaining a single consciousness, you must know where your character's beats are (that is, where his or her consciousness peaks and changes). Play these strongly and be an advocate for your character.

ADAPTATION

As you pursue or defend your character's objectives, you will read either victory or defeat into each turn of events. As obstacles shape up, you make strategic adaptations. Spotting where and how to make these adaptations helps you build a dense and changing texture for your character's consciousness. Because your fellow actors nuance their actions differently each time, you must play to these. Maintaining this work keeps you effortlessly in focus throughout many takes.

KEEP MY CHARACTER'S INTERIOR VOICE AND MIND'S EYE GOING

Summon up mental images from your character's past, remember and imagine in character, silently articulate your character's inner thoughts, and see his or her mental images. This makes you continuously interesting to an audience.

KNOW MY CHARACTER'S FUNCTION

Know what each scene and the whole film are meant to accomplish, and what your character contributes to each. Don't work to inflate or change it. Throughout rehearsal, as you come to know your character more profoundly, you will keep gaining new insights into your character's *superobjective*. This will happen with all the cast, and will deepen your understanding of the film and its potential.

KNOW THE THEMATIC PURPOSE OF THE WHOLE WORK

Each characterization has its dramatic function and must play its part—no more and no less—in the thrust and superobjective of the whole work. In this, you must cooperate, not compete, with the other actors.

THE DIRECTOR PREPARES

You want to be several steps ahead of your cast, so you break down each scene and decide what drives each step forward for each character within each dramatic unit. You will learn more from the work your actors have done on their own, but they will assume that you understand their parts well. From preparation, you derive conviction about what the piece is about, and what you want to do with it. And from all this comes your authority to direct.

Actors seek clarity and decisiveness from their director, as well as short, clear, and detailed feedback on their work. They feel they never get enough of this. The director who is alive to what each actor is giving, who can describe it accurately to the cast, is like the maestro conductor who can tell the fourth cello what wrong note she just played. Nobody is born with this skill—you have to work mightily to acquire it. Doing your homework—studying drama's sources in life, and analyzing the script—lays the foundation.

SUBTEXTS, SCENE ANALYSIS, AND THE AUTHORITY TO DIRECT

Analyzing a play or screenplay—as described in Chapter 20, "Acting Exercises with a Text"—reveals like nothing else how tight or loose its cabinetry is, and what you and your actors must do to fix it.

CONFLICT

The engine of drama is conflict, so you must know how each conflict initiates, develops, comes to a head, and resolves. For conflict to even exist, you must define and heighten the pattern of oppositions so you can orchestrate them well.

Conflict between individuals is like a fencing match—much strategic footwork and mutual adaptation leading to strikes. With each strike, the balance of power changes. That moment of altered consciousness is probably a beat, and thus holds heightened significance for at least one character. Each beat is a moment of "crisis adaptation," and there may be one or several per scene.

HEIGHTENING DRAMATIC TENSION

The cast is inside the drama looking out. You are outside looking in, as the audience will do. You are responsible for dramatic shaping. By relating each beat to plot needs, character attitudes, or characters' feelings, you can focus how it needs to be played for maximum tension. By consolidating the scene's trajectory, clarifying the development of a character's will, you help shape what effect a scene has on the audience. Tag titles help you clarify this and avoid unwanted reiteration. Your aim is to keep the audience involved and guessing all the time.

ACTING "IN GENERAL"

Well-trained actors know that acting is sequencing one clear intention after another, one clear and appropriate action after another, one clear demand after another. The nonactor often acts "in general" because he or she is working from an abstract character description and is trying to indicate that abstraction to the audience. You must help him or her tease the sequence of notes apart and turn them into the steps of a melody.

To strengthen your skills, make a study—in yourself and in others—of how realizations, emotions, and actions happen in life. Once you see a few examples, you will never accept the mishmash rendering.

CHANGES IN A CHARACTER'S RHYTHMS

Rhythmic monotony is symptomatic of an actor performing by rote. The problem has become acute when all the actors in a scene fall into the same mesmerizing rhythm. In life, people have their own rhythms for speech and action. These vary according to mood and the pressures exerted by the situation—whether the person is excited or tired, for instance. Actors can keep their character's rhythms distinctive and varying if they create their character's inner state, which always changes when he or she arrives at a beat point. Make your cast really listen to each other, and use their willpower to act on each other. You'll see the difference in rhythms immediately.

OBLIGATORY MOMENT

One of the beats in a scene will be its *obligatory moment*, the major turning point for which the whole scene exists. Confirm the identity of this moment by subtracting it to see whether the scene could survive without it. Your directing has focus when each scene's obligatory moment is distinct and palpable.

NAMING THE FUNCTION OF EACH SCENE

Like a cog in the gears of a clock, each scene should have its optimal place and function. Defining how the piece gathers power, scene by scene, enables you to interpret each scene confidently and to know what impetus it feeds into its successor. Define your scenes by giving each a tag that names its function and lets you accurately communicate its nature to cast and crew. Charles Dickens' chapter titles from *Bleak House* make good examples: "Covering a Multitude of Sins," "Signs and Tokens," "A Turn of the Screw," "Closing In," "Dutiful Friendship," and "Beginning the World." From charged descriptors like these, ideas about mise-en-scène and scenic design flow effortlessly.

THEMATIC PURPOSE OF THE WHOLE WORK

As director, keep your eye on the authorial thrust, or *superobjective*, of the whole work. Your interpretation must clearly be complementary to the screenplay if your cast is to accept it. Unlike a published play, a screenplay is not a hallowed document, and directors often take considerable liberties with their *property* (what a revealing name for a screenplay that someone purchased!). This occasions much bitterness among screenwriters. But once shooting has begun, you rethink the film's thematic purpose at your peril. Keep in mind the idea that a film is a delivery system for ideas and convictions as much as it is a mirror to particular people and a particular way of life.

CHAPTER 24

INITIAL MEETINGS WITH THE CAST

Plays grow out of rigorous rehearsal, but fiction films are usually denied it. Producers argue that rehearsal may damage spontaneity, and that rehearsing is a waste of money because actors can learn their lines just before shooting. Screen actors as accomplished as Dustin Hoffman, Meryl Streep, and Gary Sinise disagree. They prefer to study and rehearse intensively, and it's no accident that directors famed for building ensemble acting—such as Ingmar Bergman, Robert Altman, and Mike Leigh—have commanded great loyalty and exceptional results from their casts.

If top professionals prefer rehearsal, those using a cast of mixed experience need it even more. Film equipment is not, as many beginners think, an alchemy whose techniques will produce gold, no matter what. Filming merely magnifies: what is good looks better, and what is bad looks worse.

Shaping your ensemble before filming gives your actors a shared history. Your cast has time to embrace the world of the script and its characters, whose relationships become as authentic as those between the actors. The quest for all this is channeled through the sensibility of the director, who becomes coordinator, midwife, and first audience.

SETTING UP THE REHEARSAL SCHEDULE

Once parts are cast, your assistant director (AD) logs everyone's availability and works out a schedule of rehearsal times. Everyone should get a script if they have a major part, or perhaps "sides" (selected scenes) if they play a minor character. The AD should assemble and distribute a list of cast and unit contact information, such as email addresses and cell phone numbers. Ask the whole cast to attend the first meeting with their ideas and a detailed biography (sometimes called backstory) for their character. Be absolutely clear that nobody should learn lines until asked. Lines learned too early can fix the actor's initial understanding, after which it may be difficult to accommodate changes.

Detailed scheduling may best be done after the table reading (below) confirms which scenes need the most work. Aim never to keep anybody waiting around during rehearsals: actors are generally busy people, and using their time well establishes your respect and professionalism.

Plan enough rehearsals for understanding to really evolve; a rule of thumb is to invest one hour of rehearsal for every minute of screen time. A demanding three-minute scene thus needs at least three hours of rehearsal time. For a scene, however, where a utilities man does nothing more than read a meter, no rehearsal is called for. Use your judgment.

Actors tend to lose concentration after about an hour of intense work, so keep sessions short and take breaks. Doing unfamiliar work is particularly tiring for the inexperienced. Mental fatigue will afflict you as much or more than the cast.

After every rehearsal, someone must remind each actor of the date, time, and place of the next meeting, and to make sure they have current schedules.

FIRST MEETING

INTRODUCING THE PROJECT

Actors want to feel they are working on something special, worthwhile, and even beautiful, so aim to start the first meeting by lifting everyone's spirits. Speak of your enthusiasm and love for the project, and say why you chose it and what it means to you. Given the anxiety that everyone feels at first, your commitment and excitement will help raise morale high.

RESEARCH AND VISUALS

When on-site rehearsals are not practical, plan to take the actors for a research exploration, or show them pictures of locations, rooms, furnishings, costumes that you have in mind to give them distinct mental images. This helps to set the atmosphere and trigger associative memories. It also aids the actors in imagining the kind of people they must become.

Director and actors alike benefit from research. Michael Apted, who comes from a documentary background, sends cast members out to research their characters. Before playing a detective in *Blink* (1995, Figure 24-1), Aidan Quinn spent time with Chicago detectives, absorbing the ways they worked and relaxed.

Notice how purposeful actions are in real life compared with those of someone who only signifies using, say, a kitchen. Peter Falk's fine performance as an old Polish baker in Peter Yates' *Roommates* (1995) is a model of focus and clarity. Films that show people doing skilled work or making music are seldom so convincing.

REHEARSAL SPACE

It's good to rehearse in the actual locations, but usually rehearsal takes place in a large, bare space that is borrowed or rented. With tape on the floor, you can indicate the location of walls, key pieces of furniture, doors, and windows. Minimalist rehearsals have the advantage of giving the cast nothing but the text and and its characters to focus on, so there are few distractions.

FIGURE 24-1 ——————————————————————————————————

Aidan Quinn in *Blink* spent time with Chicago detectives before playing one (courtesy New Line/The Kobal Collection/Rudolph, Joyce).

WORK WITH THE BOOK

The first work is with "the book" (reading from the script).

TAKING NOTES

It's tough to retain the mass of fleeting impressions you get during rehearsals, especially as fatigue descends. Late impressions erase earlier ones, and sooner or later, you find yourself with a near-empty mind and facing an expectant cast. Avoid this by carrying a large scratch pad on which to keep notes. You can't take your eyes off actors while they perform, so scribble down a key word or two as a reminder. By momentarily glancing down, you can place your pen ready for the next note. Afterward, the pages of large, wobbly prompts will trigger the necessary recall.

FIRST REHEARSAL: THE TABLE READING

Seat the cast around a table so everyone can see everyone else. Designate the AD to read the stage directions, and ask the ensemble to read their parts in neutral, not "acted," readings. You are looking for meaning at this stage, not who can act best.

Go through the script without stopping, and have a list of fundamental questions to pose during the discussion that follows. Encourage the cast to dig into the piece and explore what kind of person each character is. Now relax and really listen. You begin to see what each cast member brings to the framework that you have set in your motivational opening remarks.

Actors like their director to treat them as partners in problem solving, which is at the heart and soul of creativity. They, not you, must develop what motivates their characters, and so they have a stake in clarifying everything that lies behind the script. Dedicated actors love this approach. Each is an advocate for a single character, and will contribute new insights. Ask cast members to personalize (speak and think in the first person) when they talk about their character. A well-founded disagreement may point to problem areas in the script, so you need this dialogue quite as much as the cast does. If, however, someone ventures an opinion that is off the wall, ask to see where in the script they formed that idea. You want close attention to the script rather than a looser association. If you disagree, don't risk publicly bruising someone's confidence by making it seem like an authority issue. Keep this for the round of one-on-one meetings during the first week.

The table reading establishes how each actor sees the piece and how well the nascent characters are fitting together. Expect to get glimpses of where your biggest problems will lie: in particular scenes, in particular actors, or both. Keep an eye open for anyone who seems unduly insecure and might need special support.

At the end, shake hands with everyone and thank them cordially for their good work. Reiterate that nobody learns any lines yet—not until you feel that interpretations, meanings, and characters have been thoroughly explored and agreed on.

CONSOLIDATING CHARACTERS' FORMATIVE EXPERIENCES

Try making use of Chapter 19, Exercise 19–12: "Make Your Own Character." The ensemble poses difficult, probing questions to one main character at a time. Questioning should concentrate on formative events and avoid the period covered by the film. Answering in character, each actor replies to questions about his or her formative experience, the kind of person that character is, and what he or she may think of the other characters. This challenges each actor to fully inhabit his or her part and to know his or her past. It will also deepen everyone else's sense of the character. Try this with all the major roles.

FIRST SCENE STUDY SESSIONS

Specify what you consider to be key scenes, and ask the players to develop subtexts for each. Ask the cast to review and prioritize the themes of the piece. During this process, press to unify opinion into a coherent whole. If you cannot achieve agreement, agree to differ and let it go. Goodwill disagreements provide a creative tension that spurs closer examination during the next phases of work. By then, actors will probably be too busy with immediate concerns to make it a running fight, and will arrive at a tacit agreement through shared problem solving or, failing all else, simple fatigue.

You are now ready to begin developing the piece and testing your ideas through close readings, one act at a time.

The First Act is very important. Though it probably contains action, its function is primarily expository. It sets up the world of the characters by laying bare their desires, ambitions, fears, and the main problem that will put the principal character or characters to the test. The initial challenge may be something the central character at first denies. In folktales, the hero is often reluctant or initially refuses the call to duty, as the folklorist Joseph Campbell puts it. But refusing only makes the call return more insistently—that's a law of the universe.

The Second Act: Here, the complications arise and pressures on the main character escalate. The piece is no longer expository because we know who the characters are and what they face. Now we see them tackling rising obstacles and tests of strength, ingenuity, and persistence. The main predicament becomes important to solve, so you and your players will be working during this act to focus the characters on their issues and to raise the stakes. What will make the outcome of each situation more pressing and urgent? How can the actors develop their interaction to make each other hope and suffer more?

The Third Act brings the crisis at the apex of the dramatic curve. It's the point where everything for which the main character has struggled comes to a head and the outcome gets decided. The resolution reveals what the central character has learned (or not learned), and indicates—either subtly or obviously—how he or she has developed.

Imagine a film about a demobilized soldier called Tom whose conscience tardily sends him in search of the pregnant girlfriend he abandoned several years ago. Much of the film concerns the search: this shows what kind of man he was, and what he wants to do now with his life (make amends). But the film's crisis, when he finds her, is that she is happily married and that he is too late. Now the film, to make its comment on human nature, must show what he has learned. That he shrugs it off, goes to work in a homeless shelter, or gets drunk all have different implications for how he has (or has not) developed, and you handle the last phase accordingly. A lot of this revolves around how you and the cast see human nature, whether you have met people like Tom. And this informs how you develop Tom, his strengths, and his faults during the first two acts.

WORKING ONE-ON-ONE WITH ACTORS

In the first week, see everyone alone, even minor parts, for maybe half an hour. Much of the part's future direction can take flight from the private relationship set up during this initial session. Again you should mainly listen. Plumb the actor's approach and establish a personal and supportive attitude. The actor may well confide his or her insecurities, which you mentally note so you can give the right support. This is a good time to get any of the actor's further ideas, and to encourage, develop, or redirect. You can also get the actor to discuss how the character sees his past, the other characters, and how they see him. The character will need defenses and justifications to handle these.

FEEDBACK AND ESTABLISHING A WORKING RHYTHM

From now on, try to rehearse collectively. Be sure to tell the cast you are pleased with progress, and as you go, characterize progress any way you can. Be careful about chastising a whole group: the hardworking and blameless will feel particularly hurt by the lash of your tongue. Even when a rehearsal has disappointed you, find positive things to say, such as, "Well, we dealt with some tough stuff today, but it's definitely coming together. Keep up the good work, guys!"

At this stage, the cast is still working with "the book." Actors are searching for their characters' full range of motivations and developing an understanding of how each scene functions in the whole. Film scenes often seem very fragmentary, perfunctory even, to actors from the theater. Allay fears by showing clips from analogous productions.

REHEARSAL ORDER

At first, concentrate on one act at a time, and rehearse scenes in script order. Every actor in every scene must know from moment to moment what his or her character is trying to get, do, or accomplish. This may take hours of work on more complex scenes, but the results will richly reward the effort. Actors must know what their character expects as the outcome of his beat—and when the result is success, failure, or the unexpected, he should know how to form the new objective that starts the next dramatic unit. To this end, you will be working a lot on interior monologues.

When every aspect of the piece becomes thoroughly familiar, you will be able to adopt a plan of convenience, and work around people's schedules. For the time being, give priority to key scenes and those presenting special problems.

CHARACTER COMPLEXITY

It's a cliché, but no less true, that strong people always have an Achilles' heel, the beautiful have an ugly streak, and bright people occasionally do really dumb things. Such faults make them human, fascinating, and contradictory, and this is why acting can be such profound work. Encourage your cast to find the fault lines in their characters, the irregularities that make them special.

DEALING WITH "NEGATIVE" CHARACTERS

Be ready to deal with actors wanting to parlay some unpopular ("negative") trait in their character's makeup into something, well, more likable. Help your actors see that truth is neither positive nor negative, but simply human and part of the job. The Roman dramatist Terence described his artist's responsibility thus: "Nothing human is alien to me." You can tell the actor that unpleasant people, or people who do unpleasant things, don't think of themselves as bad. They always have an explanation, a good reason for their actions, and this lets you work with the actor to create his character's explanation—to himself and to the world—where it may be lacking in the script. Even a villain, in his own eyes, is a good person with unpleasant tasks to perform. Few real-life torturers feel remorse; it was a job the authorities said must be done—for national security.

MISSION CREEP

Actors have problems with all sorts of things, mostly quite justified. Be very careful, however, not to let an actor start rewriting his part. Other actors will see this as a privilege that they should have too. Encourage the actor instead to identify the root of the problem and to suggest several alternative solutions that he can implement. Have him try them out, and select one if you like it. If you don't, say you need to think about it, and could he keep on with the present text for the moment. Chances are, he'll forget it, especially if there's something you can praise in his work elsewhere.

DEAL ONLY WITH TOP-LEVEL PROBLEMS

At each run-through, deal only with major problems, or you burden actors with too much information and blur priorities. A rehearsal will often spiral backward and forward, oscillating between particular details and the more abstract areas of meaning and philosophy. Try to forestall intellectual discussions—they waste time. Ask to see people's ideas, not hear about them.

As major problems get solved, others of secondary significance, such as lines or actions that lack credibility, will move to the top of the heap and claim attention. The rehearsal process is thus an archaeology of continuous discovery and refinement.

FROM BEAT TO BEAT, THE DRAMATIC UNIT

Once a scene's identity and purpose come under control, you should go over everything within each beat, one unit at a time (in Chapter 3, see "The Dramatic Unit and the Scene" and the sections that follow). For this, the players need to understand how to identify their own beats. Make tactful inquiries to find out if anyone needs a little coaching.

Correct but generalized ideas can get applied to a scene and make it muddy and lacking in dynamics. Avoid this by insisting that characters live keenly and restrictedly within their immediate present, experiencing one discovery after another and moving ahead from what they discover. They should develop one thought and feeling after another, and carry out one action after another, never making them become a blend or soup, which results from intellectualizing.

FOCUSING THE THEMATIC PURPOSE

For the film to deliver its theme (overall thrust of meaning), you have to get everyone behind it. For as long as possible, it's wise to avoid committing yourself while you learn from the rehearsal process. Thereafter, you can periodically summarize the steps and focus of the whole piece. Your theme need not encompass universal truth or provide moral uplift. Audiences resent being preached at, especially because most films of global aspiration fall short of their ambitions. Limited, specific, and deeply felt aims have the most impact. "Frankie and Johnny were lovers, but he done her wrong" still raises goose bumps when carried out well.

Your thematic statement will be strongest if it embodies a simple principle that implies profound consequences. Examples: "Sometimes marriage between two good people is not practical and everyone suffers," or, "He is inflexible and dangerous to those that love him." When you can get small truths right, larger truths of wider resonance often follow.

PHYSICAL MOVEMENT

Even though the primary focus is on the meaning of words, encourage your cast to get up and move whenever their character requires it. Holding a script will inhibit this, but the emphasis on movement plants the need to act using the whole body, not just the voice and face. On the other hand, don't let actors pace and flail as a substitute for movement with meaning and purpose. Each cast member should develop the actions that reflect his or her character's internal, psychological movement, especially at the beats.

For example, a man secretly engaged to marry is being questioned by his possessive mother. He decides now may be the time to confess. The text reveals what he says, but how significant the issue actually is will emerge only from what he does—and the screenplay does not specify. Maybe he can start drying the dishes, handing items to his mother so her hands are never empty? Let's try the two of them to see how this works. As she becomes especially probing, he goes silent, so maybe he could let the water out of the sink and watch it drain away. When it has gurgled away, he turns and blurts out his secret. Handing off the family china and letting the water run away combine into credible action for the pressure he feels to act on a "now or never" decision. Spontaneous invention usually produces clichés at first, so you must keep demanding fresh and less predictable action from your cast.

While hampered by the book and unable to fully interact with each other, actors' readings will remain inadequate, so content yourself with rough sketch work at this stage. Once you are satisfied that you've got the character, motivation, and ideas for action right, ask the cast to learn their lines for a scene.

A LONG JOURNEY

The piece will deepen and grow stronger as you and your cast stumble upon yet more meanings and interconnections. This continues even when it seems there can be nothing left to discover. With a little luck, you will have an exhilarating sense of shared discovery and closeness that everyone will recall nostalgically years later.

CHAPTER 25

REHEARSALS AND PLANNING COVERAGE

REHEARSING WITHOUT THE BOOK

When work begins, actors' anxiety about remembering lines will temporarily usurp the physical action. Should an actor keep saying he's unsure of the lines and must have the book just *one* more time, take the book away and ask him to improvise. It's more important in any case to play the meaning and spirit of the scene—lines can always be tightened later.

TURNING THOUGHT AND WILL INTO ACTION

Actors and directors together develop the pressures in the characters that produce physical and verbal action (that is, dialogue). Meaningful dialogue always acts on someone to get something; in return, it energizes action in the person addressed. Is this consistently happening?

Track the psychic ebb and flow of each character's volition. It should be like watching a fencing match in slow motion in which swordsmen parry, thrust, retreat, and advance as they try to get past each other's defenses. This is the actors' responsibility, but the director's job is to spot breakdowns. Something is wrong with the actors' understanding if a character's actions and words fail to grip or move you. Having to will yourself to understand or feel something you know should be there is a sure symptom of a problem to be solved.

Expect discussion and even disagreement over the nuances of motivation behind the action and dialogue. Occasionally you will have to rein in disagreement and decide what the cast must work with. This you try to do firmly and pleasantly. Disagreement is not a subversion of your authority, but the heady and untidy excitements of discovery. The elements of each character are becoming important because their actions should build consistently from scene to scene.

Proof of a scene's success is when an audience senses what is going on without hearing a word. I do a certain amount of international travel, and am forced to watch a lot of insipid movies. I survive by watching without headphones to see what I get nonverbally. Any behaviorally conceived film will show you a lot even without sound.

USING SPACE SIGNIFICANTLY

How characters use space should be significant. Space is territory, and territory denotes who's in command, who's advancing or losing ground, and so on. The space between people tells a lot about their intimacy, whether they feel threatening or threatened, and whether they are isolated or close. If actors know the location, they should be encouraged to use what's in it as part of their space utilization, whether it is a kitchen, library, bike repair shop, or battlefield.

A CHARACTER'S INNER MOVEMENT

Even when characters appear in harmony, one may be buying time—that is, going along verbally while turning the whole matter over in her mind. A colleague with whom I shared an office used to disappear into examining the split ends of her hair. A character in your film might check his cell phone on a pretext, or rub a grass stain off tennis shoes. Inner states always have an outward expression, so you should demand fresh, subtle actions that manifest what each character is experiencing within, particularly at beats.

WHEN A CHARACTER LACKS AN INNER LIFE

When an actor seems unable to show his of her character's inner life, the symptoms are that he or she:

- Seems to have no credible thought process.
- Comes to life only when there is something to say.
- Goes fixed or blank while waiting for the next cue.
- May actually be visualizing the script page—certain death for movie acting.

You can shift an actor out of this mode by requesting an out-loud voicing of thoughts between lines, as in Chapter 20, Exercise 20-3: "Improvising an Interior Monologue." This will probe where an actor repeatedly loses focus, and will dig out skewed understandings.

REACTIONS

Working in the cutting rooms of a big studio, I noticed that only the better actors could bring reaction shots alive. A character can look alive during reaction times only if he or she is keeping their character imaginatively active. When an actor's reaction shots are clichéd and disappointing, help them change what they are doing within. Avoid having the script supervisor feed lines for reactions; try always to have the necessary actor offscreen.

USEFUL MISPERCEPTIONS

As in life, dramatic characters often make errors of judgment—out of nervousness, hope, fear, misplaced confidence, wrong expectations—and read a fellow character's intentions wrongly. This can arise from unfamiliarity with the culture or from personality differences with the antagonist. To this, we could add inattention, preoccupation, partial or distorted information, habit, or inebriation—to name just a few more reasons for myopia. Misunderstanding is a fertile component of both drama and comedy. Just think of Basil Fawlty and his luckless employees in the *Fawlty Towers* series.

EXPRESSING THE SUBTEXT

You can monitor subtexts in two ways: one, deciding whether what you want is there or not; and two, by identifying exactly what arises each time. The latter is more work but more fertile. Actors at this point are both midwife and advocate for their characters, and guided by a growing sense of what feels authentic. They are developing what sustains the flux of their individual character's behavior and words, and will be more sensitive to what doesn't work and thus needs changing. You encourage this with feedback while trying to deal evenhandedly with the whole cast so nobody feels neglected. Stretching your attention simultaneously among your needy cast is exhausting. Staying on top of what is being expressed subliminally is even more demanding.

SPONTANEITY

A scene that reaches the point when it seems to unfold automatically, without strain or anxiety, has arrived at the threshold of spontaneity. The actors are now confident that the scene will always happen, and so can listen and watch each other without worrying about their lines. You can now raise the stakes, ask them to move in particular ways, and they have attention to spare for this. You can feel the intensity and scene tension rising. It's a very satisfying feeling.

BLOCKING

Blocking means moving and positioning actors and camera in relationship to each other. Initially, you encourage the cast to freely develop movement and action. Where and when they move arises from their characters' evolving needs. You assist in this. With repeated work, this organic and experimental development settles into a tacitly agreed pattern expressing the characters' perceptions, thoughts, feelings, and will.

You can begin to explore compositional ideas such as using the politics of space—that is, who's dominant, who is being controlled, who is acting on whom. From first to last, it remains a process of mutual accommodation, and any component may change. Actors should therefore become used to blocking remaining fluid. Lighting, microphone, or set restrictions all tend to dictate organic changes during shooting. You might see that you can save an additional camera angle and all its lighting changes by simply altering a walk from one side of a table to the other. Unless actors are used to this, changes can be irritating or even threatening. Plenty of practice during rehearsal helps them play a scene easily and naturally while hitting all the floor markers without looking down.

CUING AND PACING

As mentioned in the section "Cuing: Treading on Lines" (see Chapter 18), characters' voices in the theater often overlap each other, but must usually remain discrete for film work. Depending on chosen takes, the editor then creates any necessary overlaps, but can do so only if there are no overlaps and if the general pacing supports it. Your job is to set and maintain each scene's dynamics and pacing. With enough coverage (separate shots to intercut), the editor can smooth most ills, but cannot change the basic line pacing. Comedy, for instance, usually needs to be a third faster than straight drama. Taping and editing rehearsals, as described below, will show whether you're on target or not.

USING THE SETTING

Make each setting expressive and integral to the characters' predicament, not a merely logical container for their words and action. The setting can be a character worthy in itself of loving portrayal. Let's say the script specifies a kitchen or a drugstore; these are settings that can easily be visualized. Rehearsing to a hazy, generalized idea of the location and then shooting in an actual kitchen will leave the characters barely connecting with their surroundings. Ideally, you would rehearse in the chosen location, but an advance visit or a set of good stills can substitute. Tape the rehearsal space floor with the positioning of furniture and appliances, and with this detailed advance knowledge, actors can work out how to use the location in telling ways.

THE DIRECTOR AS ACTIVE OBSERVER

Now that interpreting the characters and developing their action are well advanced, it's time to plan their presentation on the screen. Habit makes you want to sit as you observe, but this is dangerous. Unconsciously, you have become a theatergoer who sits in a fixed seat and who naturally choreographs the action for a static camera placement. To counteract this, stay on your feet during rehearsals, move around, and keep adjusting your viewing position. By looking for the Storyteller's best viewpoint for each phase of the scene, you are seeking the camera angles that best reveal it. Your cast will become accustomed to mobile observation and won't form the habit of relating to you as an audience in a known place. They are all the more likely to play to and for each other—just as happens in real-life relationships. When you need to break the action into separate shots, it should all proceed with few conceptual problems.

FORM: SEEING IN AN UNFAMILIAR WAY

During rehearsals, you first occupied the position of the Observer; now, gaining an active storytelling purpose, you are developing the Storyteller's POV. Like an actor playing the Storyteller, you create a distinct outlook separate from yourself.

Your initial ideas came from interrogating the script: What exactly do the story and its times call for? Could it be a comic book style with brightly colored figures? A film noir shot at night in a rainy cityscape? Should the story take place in nightmarishly distorted spaces in the Expressionist style? Should it be fast-paced, or slow and shot in long takes? You answered all those larger questions, but further ideas keep coming as you take a larger view of the story's purpose. How the Storyteller must act on the audience gives you further ideas about how the story should be accentuated.

VIDEOTAPING REHEARSALS

As soon as the cast is off book and reasonably confident, cover rehearsals with a handheld video camera using direct cinema (also known as cinéma verité) documentary style. Read the whole of this section and consider the status and insecurities of your cast before deciding whether it can be fruitful to show them any of the results. You, however, can benefit greatly from contemplating coverage of rehearsals.

Cover each off-book rehearsal with a continuous take using a handheld camera, moving close for close-ups, and backing away, panning, or tracking as the action requires. This treats the rehearsal as a spontaneous happening to be recorded without intervention. It needs no editing because the camera takes pains to be in the right place at the right time. Taping scenes affords particular advantages to the crew and yourself. Together, you can:

- Privately or together review rehearsals.
- Keep a check on running times. The actors' business makes scenes appear faster but run longer.
- Judge what works from seeing it on the screen.
- Get early warning of mannerisms, clichés, and trends, as well as subtleties that would otherwise appear only in dailies or postproduction.

During taping, the actors can:

- Move freely as their characters demand because the camera is so mobile and attentive.
- Know that the camera serves their process, and does not make them puppets by leading it.
- Get to know and trust key crew members.
- Open their action to the camera instead of avoiding it, as sometimes happens.

While taping, the crew can:

- Seek each scene's optimal form in terms of camera angles, movement, lenses, lighting, and sound coverage.
- Discover how to cover more action with fewer angles and longer takes.
- Anticipate sight lines and movements from the imperceptible signs each actor gives when he or she is about to move or speak.
- Begin asking for compromises in actors' speed or destination to overcome a camera or microphone problem.

By the time formal shooting begins:

- Everyone is at ease with each other and their roles.
- Camera placements and movements that show the scene to advantage are known, not theoretical.
- Shooting is based on a living reality, not the static, heroic concepts of the storyboard approach.
- Dealing with the unexpected is easier when everybody knows the foundations.

WHEN NOT TO SHOW ACTORS THEIR WORK

When a group intends to function as a repertory company, as Rainer Werner Fassbinder's did in his early films, the cycle of performance and critical viewing can get actors past the stage of horrid fascination with their own image, and working instead on the places where their resistances and growth lie. This is a long process. It needs a committed, resident cast and a trusted director; it is unlikely to be productive without these conditions. Once you start shooting, it is usually a bad idea to let the cast see themselves until shooting is over. This is because:

- People are normally appalled to see themselves on-screen, and this feeds their insecurities.
- Anticipating the judgment of other cast members makes staying inside their own characters' thoughts and experiences harder.
- Actors who depended on your judgment may now apply their own corrective actions, giving you new problems.
- Untrusting actors—often those who think themselves superior in reputation—can begin to direct not only themselves but each other.

If you tape rehearsals, but decide not to let the cast see the results, explain that:

- Everyone hates the way they look and sound on the screen.
- Feature films bar actors from seeing rushes because it is too unsettling. Say that you will show them their work in a fine cut later.

Taping also helps clarify what you'll need for your mise-en-scène (camera treatment). Without practice, you are making a theoretical fragmentation and will probably overshoot. This may look choppy and lack an integrated point of view. But by documenting your rehearsals and evolving the coverage, you are rehearsing to capture elegantly what your cast produces.

FOLLOWING THE FILM INDUSTRY

The professional film industry, as we have said, forgoes meaningful rehearsal to save costs and preserve spontaneity. Dare to follow this practice only if you have a highly experienced cast and a crew whose professionalism will entirely compensate for lack of rehearsal and development.

CHECK TIMINGS

As rehearsals proceed, keep a running check on scene timings. Everything will look shorter, but run at longer timings. During rehearsal, stay poised to review, edit, or tighten pacing as you go. Axing material always seems impossible, but one shooting script in a thousand has already been pared to its working minimum. If you tape rehearsals, there's another way to spot the redundant—by cobbling together a trial movie.

MAKING A TRIAL MOVIE

A variation on simple, one-take shooting is to cover each scene wholly in wide shot, and then, on subsequent takes, cover it in two continuous closer shots that cover, say, two main characters. Now you can make a roughly edited scene with emphasis on key moments.

Whether you intercut scenes or stay with one continuous shot, assemble the best material so you can show the whole film to a small audience unconnected with the project. Seeing the bones of your film through their eyes will bring startling new perspectives. Suddenly you'll see redundancies, slow areas, expository omissions, wheel spinning, and mannerisms in the performances. You'll also begin to know what you need as final pacing, coverage, and point of view.

When the show is overlong (and it will be), simply watch it over and over on your own until all the necessary cuts in the script scream aloud at you. Go back to the computer and see if the cuts work, then strike the material from the script.

When you think the pacing is about right, try cutting your piece onto the end of a representative television show taped off the air. Watching from one to the next will tell you whether you are on target.

All this, happening before formal shooting, need extend your schedule by no more than a few weeks. At no extra cost, it lets you make your film twice, with the second shoot profiting immeasurably from the first.

CHAPTER 26

PRODUCTION DESIGN

The production designer starts planning the look of a film from the first reading of the script. He or she aims for a design that is visually eloquent about the script's characters, settings, predicaments, and moods. This involves conceiving a complete world with all its characters, costumes, settings, furniture, properties, and color schemes. If your film is set in the present or the recent past, you can produce integrated settings at low cost by working with property and costume masters who are good at finding furniture, clothing, and properties through resale shops and junk stores. The final design is an important part of your Storyteller's point of view.

PRODUCTION DESIGN QUESTIONNAIRE

Make sketches or take digital photos of each setting, and think in terms of its colors. Lighting, of course, will affect very much how sets render on film, and the director of photography (DP) is a major resource during the planning stages. In low-budget filmmaking, you are likely to shoot wholly in locations rather than on a stage. Here are questions to ponder:

- What is the film's theme?
- What are its mood progressions?
- What kind of location should each sequence have? (Use photos to help discussion.)
- What statement should each location make toward the film's premise?
- How should each set be lit?
- What kind of props go with the set?
- What kind of belongings do the characters keep around them?
- What might be present that is deliberately out of key?
- What kind of clothes does each character wear, and what do the clothes tell us?
- How does their wardrobe vary from scene to scene?
- What color palette and progression would promote the film's thematic development?

EXAMPLES FOR DISCUSSION

Take three very different films: Stanley Kubrick's *Barry Lyndon* (1975, Figure 26-1), Sam Mendes' *American Beauty* (1999), and Lasse Hallström's *Chocolat* (2000). Each has a strong design and represents a different milieu.

Kubrick's adaptation of William Thackeray's *Barry Lyndon* tells the story of an 18th-century opportunist rake who, believing he has killed a man in his Irish hometown, goes on the run and encounters a lawless world. He becomes a soldier, then robs, cheats, and lies his way up the social ladder until established in an honorable place as the husband of Lady Lyndon. All this is accomplished with alluring charm and humor.

Kubrick has directed the actors to behave entirely naturally, so there's a welcome absence of the posturing self-consciousness you find in so many period movies—indeed, it feels like a visit to the 18th century. Roy Walker and Ken Adam, art director and production designer, fully re-created the feel of the period. Architecture seems authentic inside and out, and costumes and wigs are worn as naturally as people wear sunglasses and jeans today. The film feels like a lavishly made documentary captured during a bout of time traveling. Much of this comes from John Alcott's photography, which pioneered special lenses to shoot without artificial light. Night interiors, which have a golden glow, were shot using nothing but candlelight. Notice how the characters' behavior, their leisure, their treatment of

FIGURE 26-1

Barry Lyndon is a meticulously re-created period film about an 18th-century rake's progress (courtesy The Kobal Collection/Warner Bros.).

FIGURE 26-2 ————————————————————————————————————

Even the settings, costumes, and props in *American Beauty* make a satirical comment on American suburbia (courtesy Dreamworks LLC/The Kobal Collection/Sebastian, Lorey).

each other, their facilities and resources, all fit together. Candlelit evenings promote storytelling and long meals, and candles and open fires make interiors smoky and grimy. Travel by coach or horseback is a messy, uncertain business and threatened by highwaymen—the muggers of the 18th century. Clothing and wigs are none too clean unless you are wealthy. Animals and people live in close proximity. All this makes a fascinating setting for a story about ambition pursued with good-natured assiduousness.

Sam Mendes' *American Beauty* is a sardonic fable set in suburban America (Figure 26-2). It tells of a marriage gone awry and a middle-aged husband who decides to abandon keeping up with the Joneses. The setting is as wealthy, indulgent, and standardized as only the American suburbs can manage. Depressed that his beliefs have proved hollow, Lester decides it's all because he's had no beauty in his life. He becomes fixated on a cheerleader who is his daughter's best friend.

Naomi Shohan and David S. Lazan, production designer and art director, have made a deadly compendium of everything that wealthy suburbanites cram into their lives. Dress, cars, gadgets, and sexual partners are signifiers by which the characters represent their values and achievements—to themselves and to each other. At first hilarious, their world grows tawdry because of the encroaching spiritual darkness at the edges of everything. Visual design is at the heart of this highly critical film, and the naked girl spinning in the rose petals stands as the enticing, impossible object of Lester's fantasies.

In Lasse Hallström's *Chocolat*, adapted from a Joanne Harris novel, a young woman arrives with her illegitimate daughter in a tightly wound provincial

FIGURE 26-3

In *Chocolat*, Vianne sets up shop in a conservative French town whose upstanding citizens mean to reject them (courtesy Fat Free Ltd./Miramax/The Kobal Collection/Appleby, David).

French town to set up a chocolate shop (Figure 26-3). Facing insular disapproval by its churchgoing population, she wins people over, one by one, with her store's delicious confections. As she goes, she learns their stories, and then, by light-hearted acts of kindness, she makes peace—with each and between each.

The production design team of John Frankish, Louise Marzaroli, and Lucy Richardson produces a quintessential French ambience of stone buildings, dimly intimate old-fashioned interiors, and tiled floors. The townspeople are flat characters (that is, types): peasants living 50 years out-of-date, with a small, insular upper crust bent on keeping up moral standards. Their small town is a dark, sober world unto itself, and an affectionate caricature of French inwardness. The dark palette of the film, all stone interiors and dark wood, invokes the hues of the chocolate that is, after all, the forbidden pleasure that nobody can ultimately resist. The town's social and emotional paralysis is broken by an interloping sorceress, and the film's strong design makes all this credible.

THE IMPORTANCE OF THE PALETTE

The design team puts a large imprint on a film by using a range of colors in their palette. Kubrick's film is rich in golds, browns, and dark reds like an old master painting—and paintings evidently played a large part in the design and lighting of the whole film. Mendes (who comes from a theater background) worked with his design team to use the loud, discordant colors that nouveau riche families typically choose. The palette for *Chocolat* started from the rich browns of Vianne's confections. Matched to it are a range of very saturated (dark-hued) greens, purples, and reds. The chocolate store seems built out of chocolate and cream, so don't see this film while you're hungry.

Allied to the palette is the choice and processing of film stock, or making special use of the digital camera's settings for particular color effects. A close working relationship among art director, cinematographer, and director is vital.

DESIGNING A WORLD

Each of these films delineates the specifics of a way of life. Each by design expresses a point of view on the enclosed world it presents, a vantage reached by the production designers interpreting the script in consultation with director and producer. Everything is involved: locations, casting, lighting design, furnishings, clothes, props, music, sound design, and even the weather. Each film could be represented by a painting or style of painting—Gainsborough, Hopper, and Renoir, say. This is not far from what happens. The cinematographer Guillermo Navarro, writing about *Pan's Labyrinth* (2006), mentions as his influences the painter Francisco Goya; the directors James Whale, George Romero, and David Cronenberg; the cinematographer Mario Bava; and the illustrator Arthur Rackham, whose drawings, redolent of opium dreams, accompanied the 1907 publication of *Alice in Wonderland*.[1]

MOODS

Scan your script solely for its moods. This lets you and your team cadence the movie by color in step with the mood of the story and characters. If you can, alternate interiors and exteriors, day and night, to give a sense of breathing in and out. Each change contributes its own new mode of feeling. Combine these with color and image designs, and a very large statement lies in the hands of the production designers. Jacques Demy's *The Umbrellas of Cherbourg* (1964) chronicles its lovers from their first raptures during the brash 1950s to their final muted encounter, each now married to another. At the beginning, the color schemes contain shocking pinks, violets, blues, and grays—but their last meeting, years later, takes place at dusk in a colorless service station as snow begins to fall. Visually, Demy makes the point that the sober, settled life of their middle years is an inevitable compromise after the misunderstandings, betrayal, and extinguished passions of an overoptimistic youth.

COSTUMES

Consider clothing as a coded projection of its owner's self-image and intentions. Consider what personality and mood each character manifests at different times, and how their clothing contrasts with that of other characters. Think not only of color and design, but of overall tone in relation to surroundings. Very light-toned costumes may be too reflective, whereas dark tones, especially in night exteriors, may disappear altogether. The size and fit of clothes, the way they are worn, the accessories that go with them, can express volumes about the wearer.

Have a fitting session well in advance in case clothing needs adjustment for comfort. Arrange for backup costumes to allow for cleaning and wear and tear.

---

[1] Interview with Navarro, *American Cinematographer*, January 2007.

Shoes should be chosen for their style (and size!), but soled with rubber so they don't clatter during movements or dialogue.

SOUND

Furnishings and props can complicate a dialogue scene. For instance, actors should carry groceries in a quiet plastic bag because unpacking a paper bag sounds thunderous. Man-made fibers should be avoided in clothing because they generate static electricity, which microphones pick up as crackling and popping. Ceilings can constrict lighting and cause a boxy sound quality, so constructed sets should omit them. In conversation with your sound designer, decide what each scene's soundscape might be, and aim to record any tracks during shooting that can assist in building them.

MAKEUP AND HAIRDRESSING

A further step is to design the makeup and hairdressing. In *Barry Lyndon*, some of the most affected characters have a chalk-white makeup, fashionable in the 18th century, which gives them a peculiar corpselike presence. This, too, is part of the design. Always make camera tests to prove that even the most naturalistic makeup will work, the more so when departing from established norms or when you depend on special effects such as wounds, scars, or an appearance of illness.

If actors wear wigs, make sure the hairline is subtle enough to stand close-ups. Research the world of your film, in books, galleries, or in real life. If your central character is a gambler, go to a racetrack and make notes and take photographs of the characters you see there. The real world is far richer than imagination can ever be. What kind of makeup and hairdos will you find among ladies who play bingo once a week? Do lobster fishers really look like the fishermen of your imagination?

WALLS, FURNITURE, PRACTICAL LAMPS

Some common gambits that affect set design:

- When you cluster furniture on a set, raise chairs or tables by putting blocks or boxes under the legs if seated characters end up at mismatched heights.
- Consider redecorating a room that is currently white—an awful proposition for lighting—using a neutral gray or a bamboo color. This allows you to light a foreground without the background burning out. After filming is complete, you can repaint it.
- Move furniture away from walls so shadows cast by high key lights are thrown low and out of sight. This is impossible if characters are blocked near walls.
- When using *practicals* (any table or other prop lamp in sight of the camera), have different size bulbs available so you can control light output. Lower a lamp's brightness by placing neutral density filter around the inside of the shade. A dimmer won't work because it lowers the color temperature, and light output becomes orange.

- Be ready to use dulling spray (available from an art supply store) on anything shiny, like a tubular chair that sends off strong highlight reflections.
- Characters who turn on lights should do it to a countdown so the electrician can fire up the movie lights at the right moment.

PROVING THE DESIGN

The production design team's work may result in storyboards, but it is more likely to be sketches and drawings. If you are building sets, drawings must be as specific as architectural blueprints. Sets must be large enough to accommodate the action and camera equipment, and flexible in construction, with removable walls that allow the camera access to relevant parts of the set.

Try to work with an art director who can sketch the ideas you discuss. Storyboard computer programs typically fall short in their attempts to generate a suitable collection of human images from which you can choose your characters. For creating a collection of the imagery that fires your imagination, there's no substitute for artist's sketches.

Use a digital still camera to record your characters in their costumes against a limbo background or at the proposed locations under varying lighting conditions. Working with Adobe Photoshop™ or other digital imaging program, make a storyboard of sorts, then experiment with changing the image characteristics. By roughly lighting the set and manipulating the contrast, hue, and brightness of the image in your computer, you can produce a set of pictures that relay what you like to the cinematographer and production designer.

BLUE SCREEN OR GREEN SCREEN

If you are shooting digitally, you can, with the right software and by shooting scenes against a special blue or green background, replace any visible blue or green with a background shot that the computer obligingly fills in. Thus, your impoverished student couple can stand outside a Paris church discussing whether they can afford a bistro meal. To the perfect sound you have acquired, you can later add street background, and no passerby will rubberneck from the background. If you want to have an apartment with a view over San Francisco, put the regulation blue or green in the windows, then matte in passing streetcars in postproduction. The art department finds some old furniture to suggest subsistence living, and your starving artist's pad is ready to go.

MODELS

Your art department may also be involved with producing miniatures—an aerial view of a village in the Black Forest or a railway yard at night. This is a fertile area for fantasy or children's films, but a miniature can sometimes look very amateurish. Shoot tests before you place any reliance in it.

MISE-EN-SCÈNE

Production design lays the foundations for shooting the scene, which is covered in Chapter 29, "Mise-en-Scène."

CHAPTER 27

THE PREPRODUCTION MEETING AND DECIDING EQUIPMENT

The final production meeting, really the culmination of many planning sessions, exists to lock down arrangements before shooting. By now, everyone heading a department has visited locations and brings their respective breakdowns. Participants include the producer, unit production manager (UPM), director, script supervisor (also known as continuity supervisor), director of photography (DP), art director, and head of sound. Now it's time to coordinate everyone's efforts and make last-minute corrections.

SCHEDULING THE SHOOT

Scheduling is normally decided by the UPM and the AD (assistant director): it is double-checked by the director and principal crew members, in particular the script supervisor and DP. Higher-budgeted productions may use a line producer who works directly with the day-to-day production details on behalf of the UPM.

Aim to set the shortest practicable schedule because the number of working days translates directly into costs (see below, "Under- or Overscheduling"). Scheduling involves educated guesses because no film is quite like any other. The logistics of travel, time to build and to strike sets, and time allowed for contingencies like bad weather, illness, or equipment breakdowns all must be factored in.

Anyone using the excellent scheduling and budgeting software available can do a thoroughly professional job, as we shall see. Take into account any or all of the following:

- Availability of actors and crew
- Availability of locations

SHORT BUDGET ESTIMATE FORM

1. Production & Personnel Details

Working Title:_____Length_____mins_____secs

*Producer*_____Tel: _____(h)_____(w)
Street Address_____City _____
State/Postcode_____Email_____@_____

Director _____Tel: _____(h)_____(w)
Street Address_____City _____
State/Postcode_____Email_____@_____

*Cinematographer*_____Tel: _____(h)_____(w)
Street Address_____City _____
State/Postcode_____Email_____@_____

*Sound*_____Tel: _____(h)_____(w)
Street Address_____City _____
State/Postcode_____Email_____@_____

*Editor*_____Tel: _____(h)_____(w)
Street Address_____City _____
State/Postcode_____Email_____@_____

Other_____Tel: _____(h)_____(w)
Street Address_____City _____
State/Postcode_____Email_____@_____

Project stage is: Preproduction   Production   Postproduction
Format (circle one): Betacam, Digital Betacam, MiniDV, DVCAM, 16mm, 35mm, Other_____
Premise:_____
_____
_____
_____

Thematic focus:_____
_____
_____
_____
_____

FIGURE 27-1 ——

Short budget-estimate form. Note high- and low-estimate figures. A contingency percentage of the below-the-line costs is added to the total to allow for the unforeseeable.

- Relationship of locations and travel exigencies
- Costs involved at each stage if hiring talent, equipment, crew, or facilities (see
  above concerning scheduling software, or basic budget form in Figure 27-1)
- Scenes involving key dramatic elements that may be affected or delayed by
  weather or other cyclical conditions

2. Above the Line Costs

	High	Low
Screenplay	$_____	$_____
Story rights	$_____	$_____
Producer's fee	$_____	$_____
Director's fee	$_____	$_____
Principle actors' fees	$_____	$_____
Travel	$_____	$_____
Accommodation	$_____	$_____
Phone	$_____	$_____
Rehearsal	$_____	$_____
Hospitality	$_____	$_____
Other (_____)	$_____	$_____
Other (_____)	$_____	$_____
TOTAL	$_____	$_____

3. Below the Line Costs

		High	Low
Art Dept:			
Salaries	_____ days at $_____ per day	$_____	$_____
Sets		$_____	$_____
Props & Costumes		$_____	$_____
Makeup & Hairdresser _____ days at $_____ per day		$_____	$_____
Production Dept:			
Production manager _____ days at $_____ per day		$_____	$_____
Assistant directors _____ days at $_____ per day		$_____	$_____
Camera Dept:			
Director of photography _____ days at $_____ per day		$_____	$_____
Camera assistant 1 _____ days at $_____ per day		$_____	$_____
Camera assistant 2 _____ days at $_____ per day		$_____	$_____
Gaffer _____ days at $_____ per day		$_____	$_____
Electrician _____ days at $_____ per day		$_____	$_____
Other_____ _____ days at $_____ per day		$_____	$_____
Sound Dept:			
Sound recordist _____ days at $_____ per day		$_____	$_____
Boom operator _____ days at $_____ per day		$_____	$_____
Other_____ _____ days at $_____ per day		$_____	$_____
Artistes			
Nonprincipal talent (See 4a below for itemization)		$_____	$_____
Stand-ins ____ for ____ days at $_____ per day		$_____	$_____
Crowd ____ for ____ days at $_____ per day		$_____	$_____
Personnel			
Accommodation		$_____	$_____
Social Security contributions		$_____	$_____
Living expenses ____people for ____days @ $____ per day		$_____	$_____

FIGURE 27-1 ————————————————————————

(Continued)

- Availability and special conditions attaching to rented equipment, including props. Slow-motion scenes, for instance, that require a special camera might be scheduled around its optimal hire period.
- Complexity of each lighting setup and power requirements

Equipment:

	High	Low
Camera equipment (See 5a below for itemization)....................................	$_____	$_____
Lighting equipment (See 5b below for itemization)..................................	$_____	$_____
Sound equipment (See 5c below for itemization)..................................	$_____	$_____
Materials (film & sound stock, cassettes, labs--see 5b itemization below).	$_____	$_____
Power...	$_____	$_____
Studio and location facility rentals...	$_____	$_____
Transport..	$_____	$_____
Catering..	$_____	$_____
Insurances..	$_____	$_____
Other (_____)...............................	$_____	$_____
Other (_____)...............................	$_____	$_____
Other (_____)...............................	$_____	$_____
TOTAL..	$_____	$_____

4. Itemization of Talent and Materials

a) *Talent*

				High	Low
_____x _____days at $_____ per day ....$_____					$_____
_____x _____days at $_____ per day ....$_____					$_____
_____x _____days at $_____ per day ....$_____					$_____
_____x _____days at $_____ per day...............$_____					$_____
_____x _____days at $_____ per day ....$_____					$_____
_____x _____days at $_____ per day ....$_____					$_____
_____x _____days at $_____ per day...............$_____					$_____
_____x _____days at $_____ per day ....$_____					$_____
TOTAL... $_____					$_____

b) *Materials*

		High	Low
Film camera raw stock____ to _____ rolls of type_____ @ $___ per roll	$_____	$_____
Videocassettes ____ to _____ type_____ @ $___ each	$_____	$_____
Videocassettes ____ to _____ type _____ @ $___ each	$_____	$_____
Sound rec. raw stock ____ to _____ rolls of type_____ @ $___ per roll	$_____	$_____
Develop ____ to _____ rolls of type_____ @ $___ per roll	$_____	$_____
Workprint ____ to _____ rolls of type_____ @ $___ per roll	$_____	$_____
Sound transfer ____ to _____ rolls of type_____ @ $___ per roll	$_____	$_____
Video transfer ____ to _____ type cassettes____ @ $___ per hr.	$_____	$_____
Lab digitization ____ to _____ cassettes type____ @ $___ per hr.	$_____	$_____
TOTAL...	$_____	$_____

FIGURE 27-1 ——————————————————————————

(Continued)

- Time of day, so available light comes from the right direction (take a compass when location spotting!)

LOCATION ORDER

Normal practice is to shoot in order of convenience for locations and availability of cast and crew. During a shoot, lighting setups and changes take the most time,

5. Equipment Itemization

			High	Low

a) **Camera** (film or video):

		High	Low
Lenses	type_____ for___ days at $____ per day	$_____	$_____
Filters	type_____ for___ days at $____ per day	$_____	$_____
Tilt head	type_____ for___ days at $____ per day	$_____	$_____
Tripod/Baby legs, etc. type_____ for___ days at $____ per day	$_____	$_____
Dolly & Tracks	type_____ for___ days at $____ per day	$_____	$_____
Magazines	type_____ for___ days at $____ per day	$_____	$_____
Changing bag (film)	type_____ for___ days at $____ per day	$_____	$_____
Clapper board	type_____ for___ days at $____ per day	$_____	$_____
Light meters	type_____ for___ days at $____ per day	$_____	$_____
Batteries	type_____ for___ days at $____ per day	$_____	$_____
Video monitor, etc.	type_____ for___ days at $____ per day	$_____	$_____
Other_____	type_____ for___ days at $____ per day	$_____	$_____
Other_____	type_____ for___ days at $____ per day	$_____	$_____
TOTAL...		$_____	$_____

b) **Lighting**:

		High	Low
Quartz lamps	type_____ for___ days at $____ per day	$_____	$_____
Softlights	type_____ for___ days at $____ per day	$_____	$_____
Spots	type_____ for___ days at $____ per day	$_____	$_____
PARs	type_____ for___ days at $____ per day	$_____	$_____
HMIs	type_____ for___ days at $____ per day	$_____	$_____
Sun guns	type_____ for___ days at $____ per day	$_____	$_____
Stands	type_____ for___ days at $____ per day	$_____	$_____
Tie-in cables	type_____ for___ days at $____ per day	$_____	$_____
Clamps	type_____ for___ days at $____ per day	$_____	$_____
Gaffer equip.	type_____ for___ days at $____ per day	$_____	$_____
Other_____	type_____ for___ days at $____ per day	$_____	$_____
Other_____	type_____ for___ days at $____ per day	$_____	$_____
TOTAL...		$_____	$_____

c) **Sound**:

		High	Low
Sound recorder	type_____ for___ days at $____ per day	$_____	$_____
Mikes: Gun	type_____ for___ days at $____ per day	$_____	$_____
Omni type	type_____ for___ days at $____ per day	$_____	$_____
Cardioid	type_____ for___ days at $____ per day	$_____	$_____
Lavalier	type_____ for___ days at $____ per day	$_____	$_____
Radio	type_____ for___ days at $____ per day	$_____	$_____
Mike cords	type_____ for___ days at $____ per day	$_____	$_____
Mixer board	type_____ for___ days at $____ per day	$_____	$_____
Headphones	type_____ for___ days at $____ per day	$_____	$_____
Mike boom	type_____ for___ days at $____ per day	$_____	$_____

FIGURE 27-1 ———————————————————————

(Continued)

so a compact schedule avoids relighting the same set. Schedule wide shots first, because they may take all the lighting you've got. Closer shots follow because their lighting must match the master shot. For these reasons and more, it is highly unusual to shoot in script order. Scenes from the beginning, middle, and end of a film may all be shot at once because they use the same location. Rehearsal pays off

Other_____ type_____for___ days at $____per day $_____ $_____
Other_____ type_____for___ days at $____per day $_____ $_____
TOTAL.. $_____ $_____

6. Postproduction

		High	Low
		High	Low

Editor _____days at $_____ per day ....$_____ $_____
Assistant editor _____days at $_____ per day ....$_____ $_____
Editing equipment _____days at $_____ per day ....$_____ $_____
Foley studio _____days at $_____ per day ....$_____ $_____
Automatic dialogue replacement _____days at $_____ per day ....$_____ $_____
Composer _____days at $_____ per day ....$_____ $_____
Performers _____ for _____days at $_____ per day ....$_____ $_____
Music rights...$_____ $_____
Sound editor _____days at $_____ per day ....$_____ $_____
Sound mix _____days at $_____ per day ....$_____ $_____
Titles...$_____ $_____
Transfer magnetic master to optical...$_____ $_____
Conform camera original.. $_____ $_____
Make first answer print.. $_____ $_____
Make first release print.. $_____ $_____

7. GRAND TOTAL

Above the line (Section 2)..$_____ $_____

Below the line (Section 3)..$_____ $_____
Below the line (Section 6)..................................... $_____ $_____
Below the line subtotal Section 3 + Section 6......... $_____ $_____
Add 10% of below-the-line costs as **contingency**......$_____ $_____
Subtotal **below-the-line + contingency**.................. $_____ $_____ ➔ $_____ $_____

Legal.. $_____ $_____
Production office expenses... $_____ $_____
Miscellaneous_____ $_____ $_____
Miscellaneous_____ $_____ $_____
Miscellaneous_____ $_____ $_____
Other _____ $_____ $_____
Other _____ $_____ $_____
Other _____ $_____ $_____

GRAND TOTAL.. $_____ $_____

FIGURE 27-1 ————————————————————————

(Continued)

because the director and cast can move confidently between the different script junctures and their associated emotional levels.

The specimen character and location breakdown in Chapter 22, Figure 22-1 shows at a glance which scenes and characters must be shot at each location.

Good scheduling software helps you distill this information from the script, and enables you to schedule actors, props, and other necessities accordingly. This—along with the cost and availability of actors, crew, equipment, and locations—determines the order in which you shoot.

SCRIPT ORDER

Certain types of films may need shooting in script order, particularly if director and cast are inexperienced. Here are examples:

- Those depending on a graduated character development—like the king's decline into insanity in Nicholas Hytner's *The Madness of King George* (1995).
- Films using a high degree of improvisation. You shoot in script order to maintain control over an evolving story line.
- Those taking place entirely in interiors and that have a small, constant cast. Here, there may be little advantage to shooting out of scene order, so you might decide there are benefits to shooting sequentially.

KEY SCENES AND SCHEDULING FOR PERFORMANCES

Some scenes are so important that no film is possible should they fail. Let's say that a key scene in your film requires its young heroine to fall deeply in love with an emotionally unstable man. It would be folly to shoot very much until you know that your actors can make this difficult and pivotal scene work. Key scenes must be filmed neither too early (when the cast is still green) nor too late (when failure might render weeks of work a waste). If the scene works, it will give a lift to everything else you shoot. If the scene bombs, you will want to work out the problems in rehearsal and reshoot in a day or two. But until this problem has been solved, you cannot risk shooting the bulk of the film.

Problems of performance should show up in rehearsals, but when shooting starts, camera nerves often kick in, especially in demanding scenes. Filming is occasionally better than the best rehearsal, but is quite often a little below it at first. The cast may feel more deeply during the first takes of a new scene, but strong feeling is no guarantee of control or character development. As actors realize they must sustain a performance over several takes per angle and several angles per scene, some instinctively conserve energy. You can minimize this by predetermining how you want to edit so that you shoot less extensively. Knowing how much or how little to shoot, drawing a line between adequacy and wastefulness, is hardest for the new director. Err on the side of caution, and give yourself enough coverage.

EMOTIONAL DEMAND ORDER

Take into account the demands some scenes make upon the actors. A nude love scene, for instance, or a scene in which two characters become violently angry, should be delayed until the actors are clearly comfortable with each other and the crew. Schedule such scenes late in the day's work because they are so emotionally draining.

WEATHER AND OTHER CONTINGENCY COVERAGE

Make contingency shooting plans whenever you face major uncertainties. Schedule exteriors early in case they are delayed by unsuitable weather. Have interiors ready as standby alternatives, so you need lose no time.

ALLOCATION OF SHOOTING TIME PER SCENE

Depending on the amount of coverage, the intensity of the scene in question, and the reliability of actors and crew, you might expect to shoot anywhere between two and four minutes of edited screen time per eight-hour day. Traveling between locations, elaborate setups, or relighting the same location will greatly slow the pace. Many directors allot setup time for the mornings, and rehearse the cast while the crew is busy, but this is unlikely to work well outside a studio setting.

UNDER- OR OVERSCHEDULING

A promising film may also be sabotaged by misplaced optimism. Consider the following:

- Work may be alarmingly slow at first because the crew is still figuring out efficient working relationships. Schedule lightly during the first three days of any shoot.
- You can always shorten a long schedule, but it may be impossible to lengthen one that is too short.
- Most nonprofessional (and some professional) units expect to shoot too much screen time in too short a schedule.
- As a dog-tired crew and cast work progressively slower, tempers and morale deteriorate, and artistic intentions evaporate.
- A cast and crew working 14-hour days will settle for merely surviving.

Any shoot can fall seriously behind if the AD and producing team do not keep the unit on schedule. An inexperienced crew tends to start slowly and get little faster without determined progress chasing. Crew responsibilities are detailed in the next chapter.

DRAFT BUDGET

Everything planned must be double-checked for cost, so make a rough budget using the form in Figure 27-1. Take into account the expected schedule, locations, equipment, crew, and cost of the artists. Use pessimistic figures because the total for a film can be a mortal shock. Better face the music while you can still adapt, and be ready to rewrite scenes that incur more expense than they merit.

If you mean to approach anyone in the professional filmmaking world, you must present all of your paperwork using recognized budget and scheduling software. The industry favorite is Movie Magic™, an expensive but all-encompassing software package. Less pricey, and good for the lean independent, is that made by Gorilla™. Either one will help you break down the script, turn it into a schedule, and arrive at a detailed, properly laid out budget based on all the variables that you supply. Most new users will need a lot of training to make full use of their purchase, but the beauty of dedicated relational databases is that any change you enter in rates, coverage, or scheduling shows up immediately everywhere that it matters. Properly used, the software monitors daily cash flow, so there need be no unpleasant surprises hiding in the accounts department. It will support your project from first to last, and even import text from popular screenwriting programs and export to editing software. Programs like these earn their keep by reminding you of everything you might otherwise forget—and then some. See descriptions and reviews at www. writersstore.com, which also sells tutorials and manuals.

ABOVE- AND BELOW-THE-LINE COSTS

Budget issues divide into *above-the-line* and *below-the-line* costs. The line itself is the division between preproduction and beginning production. Thus:

> **Above-the-line** costs:
> Story rights
> Screenplay
> Producer's fee
> Director's fee
> Principal actors' fees
> _____ "The Line"
>
> **Below-the-line** costs:
> Production unit salaries
> Art department
> Salaries
> Sets and models
> Props and costumes
> Artists (other than those above)
> Cast, stand-ins, crowd
> Studio or location facility rentals (with location and police permissions)
> Film or video stock
> Camera, sound, and other equipment
> Laboratories
> Digital intermediate (a DI takes the place of "timing," or color grading)
> Power
> Special effects
> Personnel
> Catering, hotel, and living expenses
> Social Security
> Transportation
> Insurance
> Miscellaneous expenses
> Music
> Postproduction
> Publicity materials
> DVDs
> Festival entry fees and travel to festivals

Indirect costs include finance and legal overhead costs. You should ask:

- How much does the production have in the bank?
- What is still to come?

- What will the film cost using the projected shooting schedule?
- Are there enough funds to cover projected costs?
- Are more funds needed?
- Where can savings be made?
- Can any shooting be delayed until funds have been assembled?

Many factors affect what a film costs. The digital revolution offers new options, new complexity, and new costs. A DI, or *digital intermediate*, is the digital method of "timing," or color grading, film. More sophisticated than the traditional method of filtering and adjusting the three printer lights, DI offers control over selected areas of the image as well as over individual colors within the spectrum. Like all lab work, it is highly skilled and very expensive.

All movie budgets should include a *contingency percentage*, usually 4 percent or more of the total budget. This is your Murphy's Law surcharge; it allows for equipment failure, bad weather, reshooting, and so on.

COST FLOW AND COST REPORTING

The goal of budgeting is to make a cost flow projection, which computer software does nicely so long as the production office enters new information. The object is to complete the project on cost and in the agreed time. During production, the production department prepares a daily cost report:

1. Cost for period
2. Accumulated cost to date
3. Estimated cost to complete
4. Final cost
5. Over or under budget by how much?

INSURANCES

Even some film schools, mindful of the litigiousness of John Q. Public, make their students carry insurance. Depending on the expense and sophistication of a production, it will carry some or all of the following:

Preproduction indemnity: Covers costs if the production is held up due to accident, sickness, or death during or before production.

Film producer's indemnity: Covers extra expenses incurred by problems beyond the producer's control.

Consequential loss: This covers increased production costs due to the loss of or damage to any vital equipment, set, or prop.

Errors and omissions: Covers the kind of intellectual property claim leveled against Ron Howard's *The Da Vinci Code* (2006), and includes copyright, slander, libel, plagiarism, or other oversights.

Negative insurance: Covers reshooting costs due to loss or any damage to film negative.

Employer's liability: Mandatory insurance that may be required for protection of employees.

Public, or third-party, liability: Insures against claims for property damage and personal injuries.

Third-party property damage: Insures against claims brought against film company for damage to property in their care.

Equipment insurance: Covers loss or damage to hired equipment.

Sets, wardrobe, props: Covers costs resulting from their loss or damage.

Vehicles: Coverage for vehicles, particularly specialized vehicles or those carrying costly equipment.

Fidelity guarantee: A financial backer's requirement to guard against infidelity—the budget being embezzled, that is, not bed-hopping on location.

Union and other insurances: Film workers are often union members, and their union stipulates what coverage is necessary when they are hired. Special insurances are often required when working abroad under unusual health or other conditions.

DRAWING UP AN EQUIPMENT LIST

CAUTION: OVERELABORATE EQUIPMENT

Getting overelaborate is a particular temptation for the technician trying to forestall problems by insisting on the "proper" equipment—which, of course, is always the most complicated and expensive. Early in your directing career, you and your crew will be trying to conquer basic conceptual and control difficulties, so you should forswear advanced equipment and the time it takes to master it. Sophisticated equipment in experienced hands, however, may save time and money. Expect the sound department in particular to want a suspiciously large inventory. They may need it to quickly adapt to changed lighting or other circumstances. Within reason, this is legitimate overkill.

CAUTION: EQUIPMENT INCOMPATIBILITY

Whenever a software or camera manufacturer recommends particular associated equipment, follow recommendations assiduously:

- Digital tapes shot on one manufacturer's equipment may not have identical recording specifications or interface properly with other equipment.
- If you shoot in nonnative format (say, PAL in America, or NTSC in Europe), you should run tests to prove that your equipment can meet all likely situations.
- If you edit in PAL in an NTSC country, you may need multistandard players and recorders, and your film lab may not be able to do a 25 fps transfer to film.
- You may have a problem transferring 25fps sound to your 24fps editing rig.
- If you mix and match equipment, manufacturers are apt to say that breakdowns were caused by the other guy's equipment. Whenever possible, stay with a single manufacturer's gear. Then you should get their ear if anything goes wrong.

- For the same reason, have your processing lab conform the film prior to making an *answer print* (first trial film print). If you use an outside service and the negative is scratched, the lab and conformer can blame each other.

Know and understand each stage's process. Get definitive answers before you commit to using particular equipment and methods. Most important of all, *get advice from those who have done what you want to do, and follow their advice to the letter.*

How the film looks, how it is shot, and how it conveys its content all affect your equipment choices. If you are inexperienced, plan to shoot as simply as possible. At the production meeting, make lists as people brainstorm. Remember to include manuals, basic repair and maintenance tools, and first aid. On location, something or someone is bound to need first aid.

Never be discouraged if your equipment is not the best. The first chapters of film history, so rich in creative advances, were shot using hand-cranked cameras made of wood and brass.

DIGITAL ACQUISITION

Digital television has spawned an explosion of competing formats and compression codecs. Googling keywords on your computer will bring up any number of excellent, detailed explanations. For starters, try www.howstuffworks.com/hdtv.htm. Some cameras, such as the Panasonic AG-HVX200, work across a range of formats and dispense with tape in favor of recording onto plug-in solid-state memory cards (Figure 27-2). What's available can be bewildering, so here are some salient features.

Aspect ratio expresses the width of the frame in relation to its height. The aspect ratio and video format you choose will affect equipment and postproduction processes, and even how you shoot, because the wider screen allows you to compose differently. The traditional aspect ratio for cinema and TV was 4:3; that is, a screen of four units wide by three units high. In the 1950s, cinema adopted various widescreen formats (1.85:1, 2.35:1, 2.39:1, 2.55:1). For a short illustrated history, see www.dvdaust.com/aspect.htm. HD video at 16:9 approximates the

FIGURE 27-2 —————————————————————————————————

The versatile Panasonic AG-HVX200 records 16:9 widescreen in 720p and 1080i. It records either DV or HDV formats, and runs at a variable frame rate like a movie camera, using P2 memory cards instead of tape. These can be directly downloaded to a computer without the digitizing process that tape demands.

cinema format of 1.85:1, and is now the preferred aspect ratio for HD television. Low-end camcorders mimic this format by using the middle of the imaging chip, leaving an ugly black band of unused video top and bottom. The picture you get has fewer *pixels* (individual picture cells), more grain, and more *artifacts* (jagged lines in the image where there should be straight, sharp edges). See "Aspect Ratio" in Chapter 29 for a discussion of the aesthetic repercussions.

Frame rates: Because of differing electrical supplies, American NTSC television runs at 30fps (frames per second), and the European PAL at 25fps. Which you use depends on where you live. NTSC constructs each of its 30fps from two "i," or interlaced fields. PAL does the same, but records 25i, which in practice is nicely compatible with film's 24p recording. The "p" stands for "progressive," meaning that each frame is recorded progressively rather than cobbled together from two interlaced frames.

Pixels: More pixels means finer detail. Take standard definition (SD) NTSC 720 × 480 image: it contains 720 pixels per line and 480 horizontal lines per frame. Its HD siblings do far better and rival 35mm film in acuity. Video in American usage currently comes in three main formats:

- *1080/24p HD* records 1,920 pixels × 1,080 lines at 24p, and makes transfer to film straightforward.
- *1080i HD* records 1,920 pixels × 1,080 lines at 30i.
- *720p EDV* (enhanced definition video) records 1,280 pixels × 720 lines at 30i.

EDV is currently favored by cable companies because it makes less stringent demands on their transmission systems. Cameras using 720p and 1080i commonly use widely and cheaply available miniDV tapes.

Picture compression: When each frame has more pixels and more lines, your camera, postproduction equipment, and television transmitters end up having to process a torrent of digital information. However, much of the information in each frame repeats information from the preceding frame. Thus, engineers have invented compression codecs that, like shorthand, reduce what gets "written" to the recording medium. A high-compression, "lossy" codec will, however, visibly intrude its economies onto the screen, particularly during image movement. For examples and further explanation, see www.cybercollege.com/tvp047.htm

Sound: Digital sound recording also uses codecs and varying *sampling rates*. These are the refresh rate used by the system as it draws sound waveforms. For sound fidelity, choose 48k or above (48,000 redraws per second) rather than 32k, and be consistent because some editing software won't let you mix sample rates.

DRAWBACKS OF CONSUMER CAMERAS

A low-end camcorder with its small imaging chips may shoot a terrific image in daylight, but prove to have an unmanageably large depth of field. This produces the characteristic video image where everything from here to eternity is in the same focus. Such cameras often have sloppy lenses that are hard to focus and zoom. Features such as white balance or sound level may become accessible only by laboriously tapping your way through a menu—and the settings, by the way, have a nasty way of changing without anyone noticing.

A serious problem is holding focus on a moving subject in low light. Most video cameras lack the precise manual control of a film camera, so your crew will have to make compromises, or let the automatic focus feature handle it. This usually focuses on whatever is center frame, irrespective of compositional balance or where you want the audience to look in the frame. Manual controls are slowly appearing in lower-priced camcorders.

A professional digital camera is large and has many external setting knobs and switches so the camera assistant can eyeball the settings. Many professional cameras also take a *memory stick*, a solid-state memory the size of a credit card that holds all the camera settings used for a particular scene. Much time can be saved when you have presets for each location.

Timecode: In NTSC, you must make a choice concerning *timecode*, the coding that is given each video frame. In NTSC (apocryphally, "Never The Same Color"), you must choose either *drop frame* or *nondrop frame* timecode. Drop frame removes a digit every so often to keep the recorded timecode in step with clock time. Which one you choose doesn't usually matter so long as you stay consistent throughout production. See "Timecode: NTSC Drop Frame and Nondrop Frame" in Chapter 39 for a fuller description.

FILM ACQUISITION

What camera equipment to use depends on the format you choose, such as 35 mm or Super 16 mm (16 mm widescreen): 35 mm film captures superior image quality, uses lenses with a usefully limited depth of field, can be shown in any cinema in the world, and can be transferred to any video format—at a price. It takes heavy funding up front to buy stock, and is vastly expensive to process and print. Anybody experienced enough to light and shoot in film will probably know where to get the equipment and how much it will cost. A feature completed on a $1 million budget for film acquisition is considered cheap.

Super 16 mm shoot: This widescreen format is a less expensive way to shoot features on film, but get advice from someone who has successfully (and recently) completed your preferred chain of production. Remember that Super 16 runs on different-sized sprockets and that few labs can handle and print it. The eventual blowup from Super 16 to 35 mm is very expensive indeed.

35 mm shoot: If you shoot in 35 mm, especially Panavision (Figure 27-3), you will need the appropriate camera support systems and a dolly on rails. Any hand-held shots intended to give the feeling of unsteady human movement will need either one of the newer shoulder-mounted, short-run 35 mm cameras or, if you intend a more gliding motion, a Steadicam™ operated by someone very strong and experienced at using it.

SOUND

Planning to shoot sound poses a number of questions:

- Will you use the video camera to record sound, or will you use a separate digital recorder?
- What is the most number of channels you will need to record?
- How many sound channels are available on your camera, and will you need a multichannel mixing board?

FIGURE 27-3

Samantha Sanders checking the frame while directing her Columbia College thesis film, *Gypsy Blood*, shot in Panavision 35 mm (photo by Jane Kim).

- How will you mike each different situation?
- If you are using radio mikes, will you carry wired mikes as backup? (You should.)
- What kind of clapper board will you use if you are shooting double system (a camera and sound recorder that are separate)?
- What thought has been given to sound design?
- What effects or atmospheres are not obvious in the script, and must be found or concocted during location shooting?

POSTPRODUCTION

Whatever acquisition medium you use, you will need an appropriate postproduction setup, from a $3,000 Mac computer equipped with $1,300 Final Cut Pro at the low end to a $200,000 Avid|DS HD postproduction rig at the high end. The length of the movie, the amount of coverage, and whether special effects will require extensive rendering (computer processing) all profoundly affect the postproduction schedule. Remember to budget for plentiful hard drive storage and for the audio phase when the final track is mixed using a Pro Tools™ software suite. This may be housed in a studio with a large theater, and cost hundreds or thousands of dollars a day. Also budget for safety copies, burning DVDs, and otherwise making distributable copies. To aim for release either in television, Webcast, DVD, or the cinema, you'll need to survey other people's experiences with the particular combination of camera, video format, editing software, film laboratory (if you're using one), and release medium. Some initial questions:

- Are you going to strike editing work prints, or have the film camera original transferred straight to digital tape?
- Who's going to do it, how quick is the turnaround, and how much will it cost?
- What provisions are you making for *matchback*, the process by which the negative is *conformed* to an edit decision list (EDL) generated by the editing software? (Beware: this is a minefield!)
- How are you going to finalize sound and have it married to the picture in the lab?

Each stage is risky and demanding, and costs megabucks. If you shoot on film but mean to edit digitally, your camera original negative must carry Keykode or your negative cannot be conformed. Get information from:

- Kodak's student program, reachable through www.kodak.com/go/student. Kodak, of course, would very much like you to use film, and its publications and web sites provide superb technical guidance.
- *DV Magazine* at www.dv.com. Thorough reviews on software and hardware, especially cameras.
- Mike Curtis' site HD for Indies (http://hdforindies.com/) is an example of the passionate enthusiast who sets up as a clearinghouse for information, new equipment, and problem solving.
- The Internet via user groups and suchlike. People who have been burned sometimes like to save others from the same fate.

Computer and software concerns: HD's information torrent can easily fill terabytes of hard disk space and clog the beefiest computer. You can find yourself sitting paralyzed during lengthy render times as the computer preprocesses what's on your editing timeline. Consider using a reduced definition codec for editing, and then finalizing later at full definition ("hi res"), and possibly on more advanced equipment. For a discussion of Apple Final Cut Pro HD compression codecs and render times, see http://images.apple.com/finalcutstudio/finalcutpro/pdf/20050627_HDV_FAQ.pdf.

Video to film transfers: Video to film transfers from 30fps video (NTSC system) are very expensive. A time base has to combine the interlaced frames, then do a step-printing operation to render 30fps of video as 24fps of film. Using a 24p or PAL 25p video camera in the first place obviates all this.

Sales and publicity: Remember to include the cost of duplicating DVDs for sale, and of printing publicity kits, posters, and flyers.

HIRING EQUIPMENT

Your crew should never leave the equipment checkout point without putting all the equipment together and proving that absolutely everything functions as it should. There should be spare batteries for everything that uses them, and extra cables, which commonly break down where the cable enters the plug body. Carry basic repair equipment: screwdrivers, socket sets, pliers, wire, solder and soldering iron, and a test meter for continuity and other testing.

PRODUCTION STILLS

Stills should epitomize the subject matter and the film's approach, and be good enough in a poster to draw people. Someone should be ready to shoot 35 mm or digital production stills throughout the high points of the shooting. Give careful prior thought to compositions that will represent the thematic issues in the film, the personalities of the players, and any exotic or alluring situations that might draw audience members into watching.

A good still photographer is the ideal, but you may have to designate someone with intermittent duties and an acceptable eye for composition. The director or DP should re-create the moments and juxtapositions epitomizing the film's main issues. Good stills are vital when you come to prepare a publicity package for festivals and prospective distributors.

When you start shooting, remember to set a policy so everyone knows to freeze on command while a still is being taken.

AGREEING ON BUDGET AND SCHEDULE

By the end of the meeting, everyone should have agreed on equipment and schedule. The PM (production manager) can make a detailed budget, and the first AD can go to work on preparing the call sheets.

CAST AND CREW CONTRACTS

Once all details are decided, the PM sends out letters of engagement to cast and crew members. These describe the job, the salary, working hours, and length of contract. There will be clauses stipulating rights and expectations on either side. Follow union requirements scrupulously if you want to avoid trouble. Unions have vast experience in dealing with producers who cut corners.

AWFUL WARNINGS . . .

Make "test and test again" your true religion. Leave nothing to chance. Make lists, then lists of lists. Pray.

GOLDEN RULE #1: BE PREPARED FOR THE WORST

Optimism and filmmaking are bad bedfellows. One blithe optimist left the master tapes of a feature film in his car trunk overnight. The car happened to be stolen—and there being no copies, a vast amount of work was transformed instantly into so much silent footage. Imagination expended darkly at predicting the worst makes you carry particular spares, special tools, emergency information, first-aid kits, and three kinds of diarrhea medicine. A pessimist never tempts fate and, constantly foreseeing the worst, is tranquilly productive compared with your average optimist.

GOLDEN RULE #2: TEST IT FIRST

Whoever checks out equipment should arrive early, and assemble and test every piece there and then. Nobody should ever assume that because the equipment is coming from a reputable company, everything will be all right. Murphy is waiting to get you. (Murphy's Law: "Anything that can go wrong will go wrong.") Expect him to lurk inside everything that should fit together, slide, turn, lock, roll, light up, make a noise, or work in silence. The whole Murphy family hides out in every wire, plug, box, lens, battery, and alarm clock. Make no mistake; the whole bloody clan means to ruin you.

PRODUCTION PARTY

Once you've engaged crew and actors, throw a production party as an icebreaker. One of the lovely aspects of the film business is that, being an itinerant industry, you work with the same people from time to time throughout your working life. Because everyone is freelance, everyone is happy to work. Production parties are thus festive and optimistic occasions that lower the tensions for when shooting begins.

PART 6

PRODUCTION

Part 6 (Chapters 28 through 37) covers the production period. For anyone using an untried crew, this should involve some trial shooting. The amount and expense of equipment and the degree of technology will vary greatly between those shooting their first works and a more seasoned group making a short or even independent feature, but the basic organization and procedures vary only in scale. The director, who should engage a director of photography (DP) able to effectively lead the crew, should concentrate on directing the action, and never lose sight of the preeminent needs of the cast.

CHAPTER 28

DEVELOPING A CREW

ON CREW AND ACTORS

USING PEOPLE WITH EXPERIENCE

Because crew members affect your actors, they should be cast for personal as well as technical capabilities. This chapter is titled "developing," rather than "choosing," a crew because even when experienced technicians are available, you still need to see their work and do some trial shooting with key members before the main shoot. Expect to continue developing standards and communication all through the production.

"Videotaping Rehearsals" in Chapter 25 strongly advised using a documentary style of spontaneous coverage to record practice sessions. If you haven't yet done so, consider covering some rehearsals. In addition to the benefits already mentioned, you will:

- Find out how well you and your crew understand each other.
- Develop a terse and unambiguous language of communication before you need it.
- Discover what developments (or outright changes) are required in key crew members.
- Confirm that equipment is functioning and determine how expertly the crew handles it.
- Dispense with surprises: one camera operator's close-up, for instance, may be another's medium shot.

Filmmaking is relativistic—framing, composition, speed of camera movements, and microphone positioning are all determined through mutual adjustment. This happens only when crew members are attuned to each other's values and terminology. Shooting rehearsals and test footage can reveal wide initial variations in skill levels, interpretations of standard jargon, and assumptions about solving technical problems. The first step is to agree on terminology and lines of responsibility, and get these locked down before shooting, which brings its own problems.

DEVELOPING YOUR OWN CREW

If you are working with colleagues whose skills are already familiar from film school, some of what follows may seem irrelevant, but cast your eye over it anyway. Let us take the most daunting situation—that you live in a place remote from centers of filmmaking and must start from scratch, work up your own standards, and find and train your own crew. We will assume you have access to an adequate camcorder, a microphone on a short boom, and computerized editing with good sound reproduction. How many and what kind of people will you need? What are their responsibilities?

Commitment: First and foremost, everyone you recruit must understand and accept your commitments to the project and to the significance of drama. Ideally, the people you choose should share your values.

Naturally, this matters more in a DP than in a grip or assistant editor, but a low-budget enterprise needs optimal unity because much will be done by few. Belief, enthusiasm, and morale really matter.

Ideas and identity: Before committing to crew members, assess not only their technical expertise and experience, but also their ideas and values. Of course you must see (or hear) their work, but ask about favorite films, books, plays, hobbies, and interests. Technical acumen is important—but under stress, maturity and values become more so. Technical deficiencies can be remedied, but someone lacking maturity or positive responses to your work can become a liability.

CREW MEMBERS' TEMPERAMENTS

A low-budget film crew is small, perhaps six to ten people. The crew's aura of commitment and optimism can easily be undermined by a single misfit with a bad attitude. Personnel problems come in various forms. You may need to apply some pressure to one member so that he or she maintains focus on the job at hand. More seriously (and usually under pressure and far from home), someone may become unbalanced and regress into bizarre hostilities. You may even have to deal with someone actively subversive or emotionally out of control. Such people are like black holes, swallowing up energy, enthusiasm, and morale. You cannot always foresee such extremes, but they are an appalling liability in something so dependent on good working relationships. François Truffaut's *Day for Night* (1973) dramatizes those tendencies at work in the cast, but crews are susceptible too.

A well-functioning staff, under the benign but watchful leadership of the DP, makes a huge contribution to morale of the actors, some of whom may be acting for the first time. The crew's interest and implied approval is a vital supplement to that of the director. Conversely, any team member's detachment or disapproval will be wounding to actors. Their exposure makes them hypersensitive to judgments, both real and imagined.

While recruiting, speak with key figures in prior workplaces about their experience with the person you intend to use. Filming is intense, and former colleagues will know the candidate's strengths and weaknesses.

Warning: In all cast or crew positions, beware of people who:

- Have only one working speed (usually slow). Faced with pressure, this temperament can slow up in confusion or even go to pieces.

- Forget or modify verbal commitments.
- Talk too much.
- Fail to deliver on time—or at all.
- Habitually overestimate their abilities.
- Have a short attention span.
- Act as though they are doing you a favor (in mid-shooting, they may use your project as a stepping-stone to something better).

In addition to relevant experience, look for:

- Warmth, sociability, and a lively sense of humor
- A nurturing temperament
- A love for their work
- Enthusiasm for films and an appreciation of how painstaking filmmaking is
- Low-key realism toward problems
- Reliability and ability to sustain effort and concentration for long periods

CREW ETIQUETTE

Warn your team members that actors may privately seek their opinions on the quality of the work. This is treacherous ground, and the crew member must react with extreme diplomacy. However flattering this may be, it is probably neurosis. Wrongly handled, it can become dangerously divisive. To avoid such pitfalls, technicians should be generally supportive, which is mainly what actors seek. When actors solicit support for negative attitudes or wish to communicate something to the director, the crew member should remain neutral and afterward discreetly report the situation up the chain of command. Staffers should never voice criticism that can weaken anyone else's authority, either on or off the set. This preserves the all-important working morale.

Take the same precautions when conversing with bystanders on location—they may take it upon themselves to cause trouble or generate unwelcome publicity. Any purposeful questions should be referred to the AD or other staff member delegated to deal with public relations.

Warn inexperienced members of the team that during shooting, each must stand as still as possible, and well out of actors' sight lines so as not to distract them. If the film is a comedy, the crew must remain silent and expressionless, even on the funniest line. It is vital never to behave like an audience—for that would initiate theatrical, rather than cinematic, performances.

CREW ROLES

AREAS OF RESPONSIBILITY

Lines of responsibility: Crews are generally organized according to logical norms, but also according to the particulars of the production. No staff functions well,

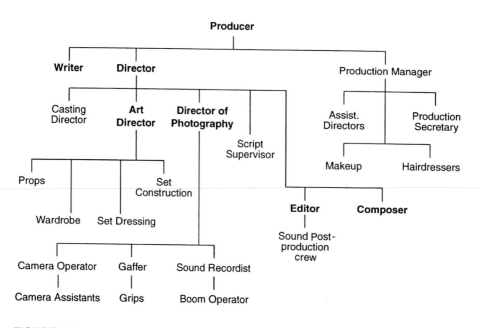

FIGURE 28-1 ——

Lines of responsibility in a small-feature crew, with department heads in bold type. Lines of accountability vary according to actual unit.

however, unless roles and responsibilities are established and each chain of command clearly defined. Contingencies make this all the more important. When the director is occupied with the cast, the DP normally leads the crew and makes necessary decisions. In most cases, team members should take queries first to the DP, not to the director. The line producer, assistant director(s), unit production manager (UPM), and DP are all there to take unnecessary burdens from the director, whose entire energies should go into the craft of directing. For example, the director should not have to deal with whether someone should put another coin into a parking meter.

Start formal: When first working together, and for a long time after, stick to your agreed structure of working relationships. Figure 28-1 shows a typical "genealogical chart," including customary lines of responsibility, for a small film unit. When everyone takes care of their own responsibilities and refrains from getting involved in—or even commenting on—the responsibilities of others, all goes well. As people come to know and trust each other, the formality can be relaxed by cautious and mutual consent.

Other roles: In time, the members of a small film crew fall into additional roles such as prophet, diplomat, visionary, navigator, Earth Mother, scribe, nurse, and strongman. Because every crew develops its own special humor and inside jokes, certain people always assume the role of jester or clown.

Synergy: Working effectively as a group can be the most exhilarating and energizing experience imaginable, especially during times of crisis. A team of determined friends is unstoppable.

ROLE DESCRIPTIONS

Judging from a feature film's end credits, a unit has a bewildering number of roles and an army of people. Paradoxically, low-budget films often have even more names in the titles because many have contributed only a day or two of service.

The role descriptions that follow, organized under the customary department structure for a large feature unit, represent the modest core for a low-budget shoot. I have outlined each crew member's responsibilities and the desirable personality types, backgrounds, strengths, and vulnerabilities you can expect to find—though in real life, the best practitioner may be the exception.

Direction department

Director

For the director's role, responsibilities, and characteristics, see Chapter 1, "The World of the Film Director."

Script Supervisor

Answers to the director.

Responsible for understanding how the film will be edited together and, during shooting, continuously monitoring what words, actions, props, and costumes are in use from shot to shot. The script supervisor, also called continuity supervisor, assists the director by ensuring that there is adequate coverage of each scene, and by pointing out what economies can be made when time or resources run out. Shooting digitally makes checking a shot's contents simple, if time-consuming, but shooting on film leaves no such record visible until the dailies have been processed. If one shot is to reliably match another, you need an eagle-eyed observer who keeps a record of every significant variable no matter what acquisition method you use. If a video assist is used with a film camera, it is a simple matter to back up the script supervisor's notes by rolling a VCR as a running record.

Personality traits: The good script supervisor:

- Has formidable powers of observation and memory.
- Thoroughly understands editing.
- Knows the script and how the film will be constructed inside out.
- Has fierce powers of concentration.
- Produces continuity reports used extensively in features by the editor.
- Is a fast and accurate typist.

On student films when directors are unable to find a script supervisor, I have seen the editor do the job. The motivation is certainly there to do it well.

Production department

In the United States, where the producer's role is primarily fiscal and logistical, he or she heads the production department. With the growth of budgets and an increasing complexity of production, this department has grown in order to maintain control over all the activities and resources in play.

Producer

Answers to executive producer, investors, or studio heads.

Responsible for assembling and administering the necessary funds, and overseeing the project as a whole. Traditionally, the producer has ultimate say in an artistic dispute between, for example, a principal actor and the director. Because each may have status conferred by track record, fame, or success, the power relationship may be delicate, and producers sometimes have to arbitrate. In Europe, the producer may also be an artistic entrepreneur, putting together the creative triangle of writer, director, and producer to initiate a project.

Personality traits: The ideal producer concentrates on being an enabler, supplier, and a firm and authoritative rationer of vital resources. To this end, planning, scheduling, and accounting should be a producer's strengths, but producers of experience and taste are important arbiters of the film's artistic progress, especially because they normally have some distance from day-to-day production. The ideal producer is a cultivated, intelligent, and sensitive businessperson whose goal in life is to nourish good work by unobtrusively supporting the artists and craftspeople hired to produce it.

And here is where it can all go wrong. Because they control money, producers have power—and some producers, especially the inexperienced, assume that because artists and technicians are subordinates, their work and values are subordinate as well. Experienced filmmakers are wearily familiar with the crass philistine who made his money in insurance and now wants to express what he imagines to be his artistic side by producing a film. This type assumes that the creative and organic process of filmmaking can be organized like a property construction project. In the end, much energy is wasted trying to educate this newcomer into trusting his experts. Usually the film suffers as much as its makers.

Probably all producers yearn to control the artistic identity of the work, but the wise ones sublimate their impulses and retain respect for those whose artistry has taken many years to mature. Like anyone else who has been in the business for a long time, an experienced producer has a track record—and you can check out his or her reputation through the grapevine. Never, ever believe from the producer's overtures that you will be treated differently or better than your predecessors were.

With producers of all degrees of experience, look for these danger signs:

- Visceral distrust of everyone's motives
- A drive to personally control everything (micromanagement)
- Inability to listen to or learn from experts' advice
- Great interest in money and status, and great impatience with the filmmaking process

Filmmakers usually lack all flair for venture capitalism, and consequently depend on those who are at ease with financial operations. It is in the filmmaker's interest to educate a producer, and vice versa, but this is sometimes frustrated by the unscrupulous operator's common compulsions:

- Playing people off against each other
- Solving problems by using aggression and fear tactics
- Pretending they are competent when they are not

- Replacing anyone who has seen the producer's ignorance
- Being willing to trash whatever person or arrangement can be bettered
- Taking credit for other people's work

What may pay dividends in the business jungle alienates film crews in record time. Now there is at last real schooling for producers, and an orderly induction into the tightly organized, interdependent world of filmmaking. Still, anyone with access to money can call himself a movie producer and get away with it. In the past five decades, I recall working for producers who were, variously, an insurance man, a real-estate developer, a gentlemanly hood, and a playboy draft dodger. For one or two of them, hell has room reservations. Although the funds these men assembled made production possible, their congenital distrust, crassness, and megalomania made the crews' lives into a tragicomic roller-coaster ride. Using threats, sudden dismissal, and humiliation, such people prosper because filmmakers cannot do without financing.

I also worked under men and women who were principled, educated, restrained, and a source of support and discriminating encouragement to everyone. These were the professionals—true leaders with a long history of deserving survivorship.

Unit Production Manager (UPM)
Answers to the producer.
Responsible for day-to-day logistics and money disbursement. The UPM, an absolute necessity in the smallest crew, is the producer's delegate and closely concerned with preproduction and production. As business manager, he or she is based in an office (with the line producer, if there is one), and manages all the arrangements for the shoot, which include:

- Issuing crew, cast, and other contracts
- Booking rented equipment to the specifications of camera and sound departments
- Locating accommodation, restaurants, and toilet facilities near each location
- Making catering, travel, and hotel arrangements
- Making up (with the AD and director) a shooting schedule
- Arranging for the dailies to get to and from the laboratory or to the cutting room for digitization
- Monitoring cash flow and paying bills
- Incubating contingency plans in case bad weather or other contingencies stymies shooting
- Being the liaison for the outside world
- Hustling and preparing the way ahead

The UPM's work lightens the load for the rest of the crew, and helps them keep up the pace of shooting without distractions.
Personality traits: The good UPM is:

- Organized, methodical, and an able negotiator
- Trained in business practices, as well as computerized scheduling and budgeting

- A compulsive list keeper
- Socially adept and diplomatic
- Able to multitask, delegate, and juggle shifting priorities
- Able to make quick and accurate decisions involving time, effort, and money
- Unintimidated by officialdom

Good UPMs often become producers, especially if they have developed the requisite contacts, cultural interests, and knowledge of the film industry.

Line Producer
Answers to the UPM.
Responsible for being the UPM's mobile arm on location and head of production on the set. Manages day-to-day logistics and budget, negotiates with vendors, and may hire key crew members.
    Personality traits: Same as UPM's.

Assistant Director (AD)
Answers to the UPM, the line producer, or the director, depending on his or her main function.
Responsible for all the legwork and logistical planning of the production. A feature shoot may have first, second, and third ADs. They almost never become directors because their skills are organizational rather than artistic, and lean toward production management. Their jobs include:

- Helping schedule for shoots
- Arranging locations and permits
- Getting the right people to the right place
- Coordinating props, wardrobe, hairdressing, and makeup personnel
- Contacting, reminding, acquiring information
- Calling and managing artists
- Herding or even directing crowds, and barking orders in a big voice for the director

Sometimes, in the director's absence, the first AD will rehearse actors, but only if he or she has a strong grasp of the director's intentions. An experienced AD may direct the second unit, but this more often falls to the editor.
    Personality traits: The main requirements for an AD are to be organized, and to have a good business mind, an encyclopedic knowledge of guild and union working regulations, a nature both firm and diplomatic, and a voice that can wake the dead.

Craft Services
Answers to production department.
Responsible for servicing the other departments, protecting the set, and keeping light refreshments at the ready, especially high-octane coffee. Catering is usually handled by contractors who provide a full meal every six hours or so. Food and drink keep the troops human and even happy, and skimping on this can be a bad mistake.
    Personality traits: Should be watchful, helpful, and take a personal pride in nurturing the army that marches on its stomach.

Personal Assistant (PA)
Answers to whoever employs him or her.
Responsible for tasks delegated by directors, producers, celebrities, overburdened actors, script development departments, agents, and publicity people—all of whom use PAs. This is a good starting position from which to see behind the scenes. The work can be literally anything. On a low-budget production, a PA may carry considerable responsibility and will need the initiative to see where help is needed.

Personality traits: A sunny, can-do temperament (or a good imitation thereof), the loyalty of a Saint Bernard, sealed-lips discretion under all circumstances, and the ability to organize and juggle priorities. Mind reading and clairvoyance are an advantage.

Camera department

Camera Crew Generalities
Personality traits: Camera crew members should be:

- Image-conscious and have a background in photography or fine art
- Good with the theory and practicalities of equipment and techniques
- Observant of details found in people's surroundings
- Team players
- Decisive
- Practical, inventive, and methodical
- Dexterous

Depending on the weight of the equipment, camera crew members may also need to be robust. Hand-holding a 20-pound camera for most of an eight-hour day is not for the delicate, nor is loading equipment boxes in and out of transportation. The job is dirty, grueling, and at times intoxicatingly wonderful. The best camera people seem to be calm individuals who do not ruffle easily. They are knowledgeable and resourceful, and take pride in improvising solutions to intransigent technical and logistical problems. What you hope to find is the perfectionist who still aims for the best and simplest solution when time is short.

Rather alarmingly, some quite experienced camera personnel isolate themselves in the mechanics of their craft at the expense of the director's deeper quest for themes and meanings. Although it can be disastrous to have a crew of would-be directors, it can be equally frustrating to find isolated operatives in your crew. The best crew members comprehend both the details and the totality of a project, and can see how to make the best contribution to it. This is why a narrow technical education is not good enough for anyone in a film crew.

Director of Photography (DP)
Answers to the director.
Responsible for all aspects of cinematography or videography. Also known as lighting camera person, the director of photography (DP) is the most important crew member after the director, and is responsible for the look of the film. That is, he or she collaborates closely with the director and makes all decisions about

camera, lighting, and equipment that contribute to the camerawork. The DP is also:

- Responsible for specifying the lighting and camera equipment, lenses, and film stock, or their video equivalents
- Leader of the crew's work while the director concentrates on the actors
- Responsible for selection (and, on a low-budget film, the testing and adjusting) of the camera and lighting equipment and knowing its working principles
- When the crew is small, responsible for reconnoitering each location in advance with the gaffer to assess electrical supplies and lighting design
- The person who decides and supervises the placement of lighting instruments
- Supervisor of the camera and lighting crews

No important work should ever be done without the DP's running tests as early as possible to forestall Murphy's Law, which is inexorable in filmmaking.

Camera Operator
Answers to the DP.
Responsible for every aspect of handling the camera, which means deciding on camera positioning (in collaboration with the director) and physically controlling framing and all camera movements such as panning, tilting, zooming in and out, and dollying.

The operator should be someone quick to learn the behavioral nuances that reveal when each actor is going to speak or move. In improvised fiction, as in documentary, camera work is often "grab-shooting," so the operator often has to make decisions over what to shoot in a busy scene. Even in a highly controlled shoot, actors going wide of their marks can pose a compositional conflict that the operator must resolve if the take is to remain useful.

Whereas the director sees content happening in three dimensions in front of (or sometimes behind) the camera, the operator sees the action in its framed, cinematic form. The director may redirect the camera to a different area, but without a video assist, the operator alone knows exactly what the action will look like on the screen. Very controlled framing and composition often require immediate and spontaneous reframing, so the director must be able to rely on the operator's discrimination.

Assistant Camera (AC)
Answers to the camera operator.
Responsible for everything concerning the camera. The first AC stays beside the camera and is responsible for keeping the camera optics and the film gate clean, for lens changes and settings, for focus, and for setting camera speed (or frame rate). The second AC maintains the clapper or slate, sets actors' marks in association with the first AC, and may load the camera if there is no third AC to do it. ACs and gaffers manhandle the camera from place to place between setups.

Their main requirements are to be highly organized, reliable, and zealous at maintaining the camera in prime condition, whether it is film or videotape. Because their responsibilities are almost wholly technical, they need to be good and diligent technicians.

Gaffer (also Grips and Best Boys)
Answer to the DP.

Responsible for rigging lighting and knowing how to handle anything (including the camera) that needs to be fixed, mounted, moved, pushed, lifted, or lowered. Gaffers need a good grasp of mechanical and electrical principles, and to be able to improvise solutions for which no special equipment exists. Because a good gaffer (head electrician) must be able to quickly grasp the intentions behind the DP's lighting instructions, he or she understands lighting instruments and the principles and practice of lighting itself. The *best boy* is the gaffer's chief assistant.

Grips should be strong, practical, organized, and willing. The job of the key grip is to rig lighting according to the gaffer's instructions. He or she also has the highly skilled and coordinated job of moving the camera support (dolly, crane, truck, etc.) from mark to mark as the camera takes mobile shots. Under the key grip is the best boy grip. On a minimal crew, grips may double up to help with sound equipment and camera assisting. They may also leave the crew to fetch or deliver during shooting.

Personality traits: Gaffers and grips need patience because their work involves moving and maintaining large varieties of equipment, of which there never seems enough for the job at hand. While they work, production waits; while production is in progress, they wait. When everyone else is finished, they tear down their masses of equipment, stow it, and haul it away, ready to set up again for the next day's shoot. All this must be good for the soul, for they are often highly resourceful and very funny. *Gaffer* is Old English for grandfather, singularly appropriate for one who must know every imaginable way to skin the proverbial cat.

Sound department

Sound Recordist and Boom Operator
Answer to the DP.

Responsible for quality sound, the unfailing casualty in an inexperienced crew. Capturing clear, clean, and consistent sound is very specialized, yet sound recording lacks the glamour that would cause most people to care about it.

The sound recordist is responsible for setting up sound equipment, monitoring levels and quality, and solving problems as they arise. The boom operator's job is to place the microphone as close to sound sources as possible without getting it in the shot or creating shadows. In a complicated dialogue scene, this requires following the script and moving the mike in time to catch each new speaker. In an interior setup, lighting and camera position are determined first, and the sound recordist is expected to somehow position the mikes without their being seen or causing shadows, and without losing sound quality. A shoot, therefore, turns into a series of aggravating compromises that the recordist is all too inclined to take personally. Exterior location shooting is often the most troublesome because background sound levels are uncontrollable, and any hope of getting the best quality is usually compromised by a tight schedule. In the postproduction phase, this requires *Foley* work (voice and sound effects re-creation) and other costly postsynchronization work.

Personality traits: Sound crew members need patience, a good ear, and the maturity to be low man on the totem pole. An alarming number of professionals turn into frustrated mutterers who feel that standards are routinely trampled. But it's the disconnected craftsman more than the whole filmmaker who fails to see the necessity and priority of compromise. Sound can at least be reconstituted by the sound crew later, but camerawork and actors' performances are immutable once shot.

The recordist is often kept inactive for long periods, and then suddenly expected to "fix up the mike" in short order—so you need a person who habitually thinks ahead. The unsatisfactory recordist is the one who comes to life as shooting gets close, and then realizes he needs a lighting change.

Sound recordists listen not to the sense of words but to sound quality, so you need someone able to listen analytically, and who hears all the buzz, rumble, or edginess that the novice will unconsciously screen out. The art of recording has very little to do with recorders, and everything to do with the selection and placement of mikes—and being able to hear the difference. No independent assessment is possible apart from the discerning ear. Only musical interests and, better still, musical training seem to instill this critical discipline.

Sound recording is often left to anyone who says he or she can do it. Yet poor sound disconnects the audience even more fatally than a poor story. Too many student films sound like studies of characters talking through blankets in a bathroom.

When shooting is done with a Steadicam, and sound equipment must be mobile, the sound crew must be ready to work without a conclusive rehearsal. With a cast and camera on the move, it takes skill and agile, quiet footwork to keep the mike close to, but not in the edge of, the camera's field of view. There are always multiple solutions to any sound problem, so knowledge of available equipment and an interest in up-to-date techniques is a great advantage.

Art department

Production Designer
Answers to the director.
Responsible for designing everything in the film's environment so that it effectively interprets the script. This means overseeing props and costumes, as well as designing all aspects of sets and locations. If the film is a period production, the production designer will research the epoch and its social customs to ensure that costumes and decor are accurate and make an impact. Production designers on low-budget movies often do their own sketching and set dressing, whereas, on a larger production, there will be an art director, draftspeople, and set dressers.

Personality traits: A production designer has:

- A design, fine arts, or architecture background
- The ability to sketch or paint fluently
- A lively eye for fashion, tastes, and social distinctions
- A strong interest in the social and historical background of these phenomena
- A strong grasp of the emotional potential of color and its combinations
- Ability to translate the script into a series of settings with costumes, all of which heighten and intensify the underlying intentions of the script
- Managerial abilities and good communication skills, because the art director works as a project manager and oversees painters, carpenters, props, set dressers, and wardrobe personnel.

Construction Specialists

These include the specialists you would find on a large construction site—such as carpenters, plasterers, painters, electricians, and riggers.

Answer to the art director.

Responsible for all aspects of constructing sets with removable walls and ceilings, or for making anything with the built-in flexibility required for convenience in shooting. Construction crews must be able to build a convincing nightclub, cave, subway tunnel, airplane hold, jungle camp, or whatever else. It must be modular and movable—and must not hurt its users.

Personality traits: Each must be a master craftsperson and good at teamwork.

Special Effects

Answer to the art director.

Responsible for making explosions, fires, bridges that collapse, or windows that a stunt artist can safely jump through. (The *Lord of the Rings* cycle is a veritable dictionary of special effects, from Middle Earth rock kingdoms to creatures that crawl, prowl, and fly.) At one time, they provided models for ships sinking or cars blowing up, and process shooting in which a live foreground was married to a preshot background. With the advent of computers and robotics, and a market for exotic spectacle, the special effects purview has expanded to cover everything from dinosaurian life to space travel. If the script says it's wanted, then it's a point of honor for them to make it, using every imaginable principle—electrical, mechanical, computer, robotic, biological—to provide a working answer. They also handle anything that involves danger and stunt people.

Personality traits: Tenacious, inventive, resourceful, with a love of impossible challenges. Stunt people have a Houdini relationship with danger: they are attracted to it and get something out of cheating injury and death. They embody survival of the fittest.

Wardrobe and Props

Answer to the production designer.

Responsible for locating, storing, and maintaining costumes and properties (objects such as ashtrays, baby toys, or grand pianos that dress the set). Must keep master lists and produce the right thing in good working order at the right time. When no wardrobe person is available, each actor becomes responsible for his or her own costumes. The assistant director (AD) should double-check beforehand what clothes each actor must bring for the next scene so today's costume is not still sitting in the actor's laundry basket.

Personality traits: Highly resourceful and able to develop a wealth of contacts among antique, resale, theatrical, and junk shop owners. Very practical—because things borrowed or rented must often be carefully operated, maintained, or even first put into working order. Costumes, especially ones that are elaborate or antique, take expertise to keep clean and functional, and often need temporary alterations to fit the particular wearer. Props and wardrobe departments must be completely organized: each scene has its special requirements, and the right props and costumes must appear on time and in the right place, or shooting becomes a nightmare.

Makeup and Hairdressing

Answer to the production designer.

FIGURE 28-2

Makeup man Paul Rabiger applying the notorious gold paint in *Goldfinger* (courtesy Danjaq/Eon/UA/The Kobal Collection).

Responsible for the appropriate physical appearance in face and hair, often needing careful attention to period details. A hidden part of the job is catering to actors' insecurities by helping them believe in the way they look. Where the character demands negative traits, the makeup artist may have to work against an actor's resistance. Where makeup is tricky, shoot tests to ensure that it is credible and compatible with color stock and any special lighting.

    Personality traits: Diplomacy and endurance. My father, Paul Rabiger, was a makeup man and arrived at work before anyone else, preparing actors hours ahead of shooting when elaborate beards and whiskers were required. Apart from character or glamour preparation, his work included the bizarre, such as putting a black patch over the eye of Fagin's dog in David Lean's *Oliver Twist* (1948), applying gold paint to Shirley Eaton in Guy Hamilton's *Goldfinger* (1964, Figure 28-2), and inventing ghoulish effects for Hammer horror films. One such was flesh melting from a corpse's face to leave eyeballs staring out of bony eye sockets, which he accomplished by building a wax face on a skull and placing an electric iron element underneath. These challenges he enjoyed, but having to placate the neuroses of aging idols or foul-tempered alcoholics at dawn was less pleasant. After the early rush, makeup and hairdressing often have to sit idle on the set, keeping a sharp eye out for when their handiwork needs repair.

POSTPRODUCTION DEPARTMENT

See descriptions of postproduction personnel and their responsibilities in Chapter 38, "Preparing to Edit."

CHAPTER 29

MISE-EN-SCÈNE

The material in this chapter builds on fundamentals established in Chapter 26, "Production Design."

PURPOSE

The French term *mise-en-scène* (literally, "putting into the scene") is usefully holistic and describes the aspects of directing that take place during shooting. It includes:

Blocking, which means planning the positions of:

- Actors in relation to each other (close, far, above, below, etc.)
- Action in relation to set or location
- Camera placement in relation to actors and special set features (close, far, high, low, etc.)

Camera

- Film stock and processing, or color settings (video)
- Choice of lens
- Composition (depth, perspective, treatment of space)
- Movements
- Coverage for editing
- Image design

Use of color

- Lighting mood, and treatment of place and time of day
- Frame design in terms of the scene's dramatic functions

Dramatic content

- Rhythms (action and visual)
- Point of view (whose consciousness the audience should identify with)

- Motifs or leitmotifs
- Visual or aural metaphors
- Foreshadowing

Sound Design

- Whether sound is diegetic (native to the situation) or nondiegetic (added by the Storyteller)
- What part sound plays as a narrative device
- Whether it relays a subjective or objective point of view
- Whose point of view it is

All this must be planned in practical rather than intellectual terms. You will have to make an overall mise-en-scène design for the whole script, and thereafter fit each scene into the intentions of the larger structure. Develop clear ideas about what options exist and how you will discuss them with the director of photography (DP) and sound crew. The DP is the most important collaborator during the shoot, and this is a time when an underprepared director can fall under the spell of a strong-minded DP. *American Cinematographer* contains excellent descriptions by renowned cinematographers of the lighting and camera equipment they used to create specific aesthetic effects for a particular production. (www.theasc.com/magazine). It's surprising how often they have to invent their own solutions.

SURVEYING THE FILM

Make a brief content description of each scene, annotate it with how you want the audience to feel about it, and you have a firm beginning. Turn the list into a colored graph or storyboard to show what the audience should feel from scene to scene, and then you can think about how the Storyteller must tell the tale to make this happen. Once you have an overall strategy, you can design individual scenes.

LONG-TAKE VERSUS SHORT-TAKE COVERAGE

Covering a scene means shooting enough variation in angle and subject so the scene shows to advantage on the screen. This can be done using long, intricately choreographed takes lasting an entire scene, as in Alfred Hitchcock's *Rope* (1948)—or it might call for the flow of rapidly edited images favored by such disparate filmmakers as Sergei Eisenstein in *The Battleship Potemkin* (1925), Baz Luhrmann in *Moulin Rouge!* (2001), or just about any MTV music video.

The **long-take method**: Generally requires a mobile camera and intricate blocking of both camera and actors to avoid a flat, stagy appearance. You cannot cut around any acting or camera problems, so it requires virtuoso control by actors and technicians. Any error consigns an entire take to the trash can. Another risk shows up only in the first assembly: having no control of individual elements within a scene, the editor cannot rebalance the rhythm, performances, or pacing of the story. For a superb example of fluid camera control and blocking in long takes, see Jacques Demy's masterpiece, *The Umbrellas of Cherbourg* (1964,

FIGURE 29-1 ――――――――――――――――――――――――――――――――

Jacques Demy's touching masterwork *The Umbrellas of Cherbourg* uses color, camera movement, and image design to perfection (courtesy Parc Films/Madeleine Films/The Kobal Collection).

Figure 29-1). A story of lovers in a small French town when the upheavals in Algeria took recruits off to war, it is an operetta in which all dialogue is realistic, yet sung, not spoken. Surprisingly, this works very well. Even if you find it sentimental, the film is a model for frame and color design, camera movement, and blocking. Another that uses movement exceptionally well is Wim Wenders' *Faraway, So Close!* (1993). By this time, the Steadicam body mount (Figure 29-2) had been invented, and DP Jürgen Jürges and his Steadicam operator, Jörg Widmer, took full advantage of the extraordinary liberty afforded the normally ponderous handheld 35 mm camera. Just as effortlessly, Wenders' film moves

FIGURE 29-2

The Steadicam camera mount takes skill, practice, and strength to operate, but frees the camera to glide wherever it will.

between a black-and-white world seen by the angels, and the more heated color one seen by human beings.

The short-take method: In short-take coverage generally, shots are edited together to create rhythm, juxtaposition, and tension, but the audience must expend mental energy on interpreting the cuts. The material is more evidently manipulated— and at MTV's frenetic extreme, the viewer is bombarded with fragments of action from which to infer a whole. Rather than rely on overwrought editing, many

FIGURE 29-3 —————————————————————————————————————

Handheld camerawork in *Breaking the Waves* helps us share Bess's emotions as her world skids out of control (courtesy Zentropa/The Kobal Collection).

directors choreograph their mise-en-scène as individual shots containing complex blocking. They shoot safety coverage in case longish takes are flawed or their otherwise inalterable pacing falters.

FIXED VERSUS MOBILE CAMERA

A camera on a tripod is able to zoom in and hold a steady close shot without physically crowding the actor. On the other hand, it cannot move to a better vantage point unless you mount it on a dolly or crane to allow smooth movement through a preplanned cycle. This requires precision from crew and cast, who must hit chalk marks on the floor if composition and focus are to hold up. Here, the casualty is spontaneity in the cast. A dolly and its crew are also apt to make unintended noise—resulting in extra takes where floor creaks obscure dialogue, as well as extra postproduction sound work.

If you need to shoot a semi-improvised performance and shoot fast, then intelligent handheld camerawork may be the best solution. In the right hands, it can solve most problems—but in the hands of someone inexperienced, you can lose hours. Lars von Trier's unsettling *Breaking the Waves* (1996, Figure 29-3) is entirely handheld. Lunging, urgent camerawork complements the way that Bess, a naive young Scot whose husband is paralyzed in an oil-rig accident, sets about blindly remaking her future.

SUBJECTIVE OR OBJECTIVE CAMERA PRESENCE

The two kinds of camera presence—one studied, composed, and controlled; the other mobile, spontaneously reactive, and adaptive to change—convey quite different observing presences. One feels subjective, the other more objective in relation to the action. Camera-handling alone may thus alter the voice of a film to make it more personal and vulnerable or less so. Maintaining either mode may become dull, whereas shifting justifiably between them can be very potent.

RELATEDNESS: SEPARATING OR INTEGRATING BY SHOT

Composition and framing can greatly alter what a scene feels like. Isolating two people, each in their own close shots, then intercutting them, produces a different feeling than intercutting two overshoulder shots would. The close-ups' relationship in space and time is controlled by the filming process, whereas the people in overshoulder shots remain palpably related to each other in space. The Observer relates to two people in the overshoulder shots, but is always alone with one of them in single shots. In cinema, such isolation is the exception: frame limitations usually compel using precious screen space by packing it and showing the spatial relationship between everything and everybody. In scenes that contain multiple characters, plan to shoot alternate angles and plenty of reaction shots. That way, the editor can abridge material that is overlong, or can cut around any problems involving dialogue and simultaneous movement.

HAVE THE COURAGE TO BE SIMPLE

Viewing heavily edited scenes is work that exhausts the audience's critical faculties, so try to block subject and camera in relation to each other and maximize what can be packed into a single shot. Reduce the need for associative editing by making each frame feature the main elements you want to juxtapose. Shooting down the axis instead also helps create perspective. The only depth in the two-dimensional screen image is that deliberately created through using perspective, composition, or lighting (Figure 29-4). Camera movements usually arise from having to reframe when characters move or when you want to reveal what was formerly out of frame. Your master teachers in all this are the best films in your chosen genre. Simple technique can look really good when there's a compelling story, good acting, and inventive blocking. Flashy camerawork is sometimes a substitute for a lack of these.

THE CAMERA AS OBSERVING CONSCIOUSNESS

Treat the camera as a questing Observer, and imagine how you want the audience to experience the scene. If you have a scene in a turbulent flea market, it makes no sense to limit the camera to carefully placed tripod shots. Make the camera into a wandering buyer by going handheld and peering into circles of chattering people, looking closely at the merchandise, and then swinging around when someone

FIGURE 29-4

Space and distance on the screen must be created through composition. Still from Zsolt Kézdi-Kovács' *Forbidden Relations* (1982, courtesy Spectrafilm).

calls out. If you are shooting a church service, with its elaborate rituals, your camera placing should be rock steady because that is how anyone present experiences such a situation. Ask yourself whose point of view the audience is mostly sharing. Where does the majority of the telling action lie? With the newcomer? The priest? The choir or the congregation?

THE HEART OF DIRECTING: THE STORYTELLER'S POINT OF VIEW

David Mamet in *On Directing Film* protests that too much fiction filmmaking consists of following the action like a news service. Do you want to document happenings like an Observer, or tell them like a Storyteller? The first is surveillance, and the second involves inflection; that is, having an active and critical eye for contradictions and ironies, raising questions, and implying a critical mind and heart at work. What identity will you give your Storyteller? What singularities must we notice in your characters and their situations? These are not easy questions, and you certainly won't find answers during shooting or editing.

The key lies in the *attitude* that the storytelling mind, intelligence, and heart take. It should be the lens through which your audience experiences your story. How would you describe the attitude of your Storyteller? What are the ironies and humor in his or her way of seeing? How will you make these evident?

Your Storyteller's attitude must infuse every possible aspect of the movie. This means implying puzzlement, doubts, enjoyment, censure, opprobrium, delight, distrust, regret, or fascination. Whatever grips your Storyteller's heart and mind must be implied through the way the Storyteller displays the tale.

Your ideas have formed while you moved around during rehearsal. If you shot documentary coverage of rehearsals, you watched these newborn characters living salient pieces of their lives on the screen. You watched and identified according to a pattern that began in the intentions behind the writing, and that now arises more completely from the chemistry of personalities and situation. Review your impressions. Use your mind to examine your heart.

To create the Storyteller, you have to bring alive not only the telling, but also the tale—that is, you must give the narrative the integrity of a quirky human mind that sees, weighs, wonders, feels, and supposes while the story unfolds. Do this successfully, and your work will have the humor and intelligence of work with a human character. In the struggle for high-concept plotting, filmmaking's factory processes often trample the humanity out of their work. Few films have the feeling of a human soul, but when they do, audiences universally respond. It takes a director with a clear, strong identity—one not overwhelmed by the people and the procedures.

For an example of this, see Jean-Pierre Jeunet's *Amélie* (2001), a fable about a resourceful but lonely waitress. Finding some old toys in her Paris apartment, she sets out to return them to their owner. By contributing to other people's lives anonymously and from a distance, she discovers new pleasures. Of course, you reap what you sow, and she finds a lover to cherish her. This funny, quirky film, made intimately around the presence of the elfin Audrey Tautou, looks fondly backward to the Paris of the French New Wave.

APPROACHING A SINGLE SCENE

SCRIPT, CONCEPT, AND SCENE DESIGN

A scene's design is based on its intended function in the script, your gut feelings about it, and the limitations built into the filmmaking process. How, for instance, might you show a man who is being watched by the police get into his car and try to start it? Here is a checklist you can apply to any scene:

- What is the scene's special function in the script?
- What does the audience need to know about the scene's setup and spatial content:
  - At the outset of the scene?
  - Later? (How much later?)
- What perspectives and relationships must be indicated through using space?
- What information can be left to the audience's deduction or imagination?
- What elements should be juxtaposed:
  - Visually, within each shot's framing?
  - Conceptually, by editing shots together?
- How much are characters aware of their predicament, and what are each character's expectations:
  - At the start of the scene?
  - At its end?
- Who learns and develops, and how does this affect POV?

- Where is the scene's obligatory moment?
- Is there anything the audience should learn, but not the characters?
- What is the ruling image or motif here?
- Is any foreshadowing called for?
- What visual design is called for in:
  - Amount and distribution of light?
  - Tonality?
  - Hue?
  - Costuming?
  - Set design?
  - Sense of space—or lack of it?
- What is the Storyteller's attitude to this scene compared with others?

Should the audience see our man being watched by police from the policeman's point of view, or from the POV of one more omniscient (that is, the Storyteller)—in which the audience, but not the man, notices the cop? This will probably be decided on plot grounds, but what the characters experience should influence your coverage, just as characters in real life influence whom you choose to watch in any given situation.

Now imagine a more complex scene in which a child witnesses a sustained argument between his parents. How should point of view be handled there? First, what does the argument represent? Is it "child realizing he is a pawn," or is it "parents too bitter to care what their child sees"? It's your choice that matters here—whether we share what the child sees, or whether we feel how the dispute acts upon him.

Issues like this determine whether the scene is really the boy's, the father's, or the mother's. The scene can be shot and edited to polarize our sympathetic interest in any of these directions at any given moment in the scene. Making *no* choice would produce faceless, expressionless filmmaking—technical filmmaking with no heart or soul.

There remains a detached way of observing events, that of the Omniscient Storyteller. This point of view is useful to relieve pressure on the audience before renewing it again. Sustained and unvarying pressure is self-defeating because the audience either becomes armed against it or tunes out. Shakespeare in his tragedies intersperses scenes of comic relief to deal with this very problem.

To summarize: what is salient will vary with the scene depending on its contents, complexity, and what it contributes to the film as a whole. Defining what the Storyteller notices and feels helps you decide how to reveal what matters, and makes everything less arbitrary. Here, you've got to develop instincts and really listen to them.

POINT OF VIEW (POV)

WHOSE?

Controlling point of view may remain an elusive notion. As we said, it is not literally "what so-and-so sees," though this may comprise one or two shots. Rather, POV sets out to convey how a character in the film is experiencing particular events. Top priority will always be to ask whose point of view this scene favors. A great many of your decisions about composition, camera placement, and editing will flow from this.

POV CAN CHANGE

Point of view can mean the way our sympathy and curiosity might migrate between patient and doctor, subject and object—even though finally the film is about the patient. To understand and care for the doctor, we need to share those paradoxical moments when she empathizes with our central character, vacating her own protected reality to enter that of the sick person. Anyone without occasional feeling for others would either be alienated or inhuman.

Decide POV by asking what makes dramatic sense to the Concerned Observer. Answers come from the logic of the script and from your instincts. There may be no overriding determinant, in which case the editor will have to decide later, based on the nuances of the acting and whether you've shot enough alternative coverage.

A reminder: subjective POV shots tend to be close-ups and shots close to the axis, the line of psychic tension between characters. Objective POVs tend to be wider shots and farther from that line (Figure 29-5). These generalizations are no more than a rule of thumb because POV works by oblique means. It impinges on the audience through a subtle combination of action, characters, lighting, mood, events, and context. Your judgment is the final arbiter.

COMPROMISES: SPACE, PERCEPTION, AND LENSES

The art of the screen arises from compromises made to accommodate the fact that the camera sees in two dimensions instead of three, and that its field of view is very limited compared with human visual perception. To compensate for this, we render the spirit of consciousness, not its actuality, by using associative techniques

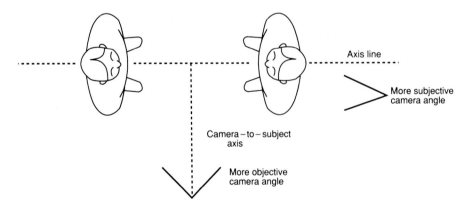

FIGURE 29-5 —————

Camera-to-subject axis can be close to the scene axis or at right angles to it. This controls how subjective or objective the angle feels to the audience.

to counterpoint sound and images; we compress more into the frame and accomplish more in time than happens in real life.

CAMERA EYE AND HUMAN EYE ARE DIFFERENT

The eye of the beholder during rehearsals is misleading, for the human eye takes in a field of almost 180 degrees (Figure 29-6). Although a 16 mm camera lens of 10 mm focal length is called a wide angle when shooting in TV aspect ratio, it still takes in only 54 degrees horizontally and 40 degrees vertically. This means that a reasonably comprehensive wide-angle lens (before gross fairground distortion sets in) has only one-quarter of the human eye's angle of acceptance. This translates to a very restricted field of view indeed, and one with resounding consequences for dramatic composition. Film aspect ratios are described later in this chapter.

We compensate for such limitation by rearranging compositions so they trick the spectator into the sensation of normal distances and spatial relationships. Characters holding a conversation usually have to stand unnaturally close before the camera, but will look normal on-screen; furniture placement and distances between objects are often cheated—that is, they are moved either apart or together

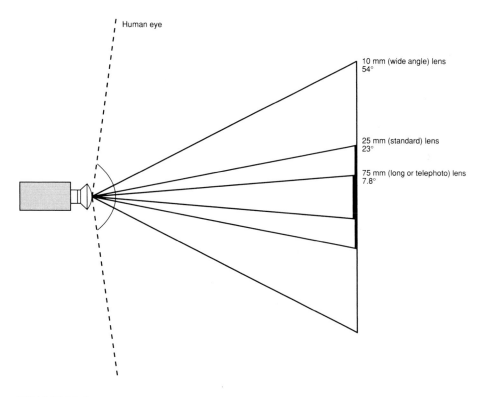

FIGURE 29-6

Human eye's field of vision compared with much more limited angle of acceptance for 16 mm camera lenses. Note that vertical angles of acceptance (not shown) are 25 percent smaller or less, depending on aspect ratio.

to produce the desired appearance on-screen. Ordinary physical movements such as walking past the camera or picking up a glass of milk in close-up may require slowing by a third or more to look natural on-screen. Note, however, that comedy dialogue (though not necessarily movement) often needs faster than normal playing if it is to avoid looking slow on-screen. As always, screen testing helps you make all such decisions.

Packing the frame, achieving the illusion of depth, and arranging for balance and thematic significance in each composition can all compensate for the screen's limited size and its tendency to flatten everything. As Thomas Hardy says, "Art is the secret of how to produce by a false thing the effect of a true."

ASPECT RATIO

Aspect ration refers to projected image proportions in terms of height versus width (Figure 29-7). Early cinema had an aspect ratio of 1.33:1—that is, it was 1.33 units wide to every 1 unit high. Television maintained roughly the same proportions. In the 1950s, widescreen aspect ratios came along, and today's cinema aspect ratios are 1.66:1 (Europe) and 1.85:1 (United States). High-definition television (HDTV) camcorders are designed to shoot widescreen, but less advanced camcorders, if they shoot in widescreen at all, do so by electronically chopping a band off the top and bottom of the image. This means that the recorded image contains fewer pixels (picture cells inherent to the electronic imaging chip) than the standard ratio, and is less

FIGURE 29-7

Common screen aspect ratios. The earliest gives a very cramped view of the canal ahead of the barge.

satisfactory in terms of quality. Television viewers are by now familiar with so-called letterbox format, in which a shrunken image leaves unused black bands, top and bottom.

As HDTV takes over, all film and video will be shot widescreen. Cinema and television screens will share similar aspect ratios, and everyone will compose for widescreen. Inherently wide pictorial matter, such as landscape shots and anything making horizontal movement, fills the screen more satisfactorily. Inherently vertical pictorial matter, such as head shots and tall buildings, is harder to accommodate, but virtually everyone feels that, on balance, widescreen allows for more interesting filming.

CHOOSING LENS TYPE

Some people find this forbidding, but you don't need a physics degree to use lenses intelligently. As the standard reference, we call normal those lenses that give the same sense of perspective as the human eye, whereas the departures to either side of normalcy affect magnification and are called wide angle and telephoto. Analogies from everyday life show the basic differences:

Wide angle of acceptance	Normal angle of acceptance	Narrow (or telephoto) angle of acceptance
Door security spyglass (diminishes sizes, makes foreground seem huge compared with background)	The human eye (gives the sense of perspective we consider normal)	Telescope (magnifies, brings everything closer, but compresses foreground and background together)

These familiar optical devices allow us to pursue a range of dramatic possibilities inherent in different lenses. Compare the telescope image to that of the security spyglass, which allows the cautious householder to see whether the visitor on the other side of the door is friend or foe.

The telescope: brings objects close; squashes together foreground, middle ground, and background; and isolates the middleground object in sharp focus while foreground and background are in soft focus.

The security spyglass: brings in a lot of the hallway outside and keeps all in focus, but produces a reduced and distorted image. If your visitor is leaning with one hand on the door, you are likely to see a huge arm diminishing to a tiny, distorted figure in the distance.

PERSPECTIVE AND NORMALCY

Our sense of perspective comes from knowing the relative sizes of things and judging how far apart they are in near and far planes. In a photo containing a cat and a German shepherd, we judge how far the dog is behind the cat from experience

FIGURE 29-8

Normal lens.

of their relative sizes. Human eye perspective is normal, but other lenses can alter this relationship radically. The focal length of a lens rendering perspective as normal on-screen will vary according to what camera format is being used:

Format	Focal length for normal lens
8 mm	12.5 mm
16 mm	25 mm
35 mm	50 mm

There is a constant ratio between the format (width of film in use) and the lens' focal length. The examples that follow discuss only 16 mm-format lenses, the equivalent of which are found (though seldom calibrated) in many small-format video cameras.

Normal perspective (Figure 29-8) means that the viewer sees an "as is" size relationship between foreground and background trucks, and can accurately judge the distance between them. The same shot taken with a wide-angle lens (Figure 29-9) changes the apparent distance between foreground and background, making it appear greater. A telephoto lens (Figure 29-10) does just the opposite, squeezing foreground and background close together. If someone were to walk from the background truck up to the foreground, the implications of their walk would be dramatically different in the three shots—all would have the same subject, all walks would last the same time, but each shot offers a different dramatic "feel" through the choice of lens.

PERSPECTIVE CHANGES ONLY WHEN CAMERA-TO-SUBJECT DISTANCE CHANGES

By repositioning the camera and using different lenses (as in Figures 29-8, 29-9, and 29-10), we can standardize the apparent size of the foreground truck,

FIGURE 29-9 ───

Wide-angle lens.

FIGURE 29-10 ───

Telephoto lens. Foreground and background distances appear quite different in Figures 29-8 and 29-9.

as shown diagrammatically in Figure 29-11. Ultimately, changes of perspective result only from changing camera-to-subject distance, not from changing the lens itself.

Now examine Figures 29-12, 29-13, and 29-14. Each is taken with a different lens, but from the same camera position. The proportion of the stop sign in relation to the background portico is identical in all three. Perspective—size proportions between planes—has not changed; we simply have three different magnifications. So we have confirmed that, indeed, perspective is the product of camera-to-subject distance. For when this remains constant, proportions between foreground and background also remain constant—even though the image was shot through three different lenses; that is, with three different degrees of magnification.

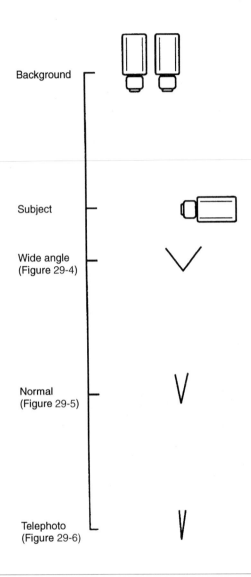

Background

Subject

Wide angle
(Figure 29-4)

Normal
(Figure 29-5)

Telephoto
(Figure 29-6)

FIGURE 29-11

Perspective changes come from altering the camera-to-subject distance in relation to the subject-to-background distance.

MANIPULATING PERSPECTIVE

Using the magnifying or diminishing capacity of different lenses allows us to place the camera differently, and yet produce three similar shots (see Figures 29-9, 29-10, and 29-11); and when camera-to-subject distance changes, we can manipulate perspective. Wide-angle lenses appear to increase distance, whereas telephoto lenses appear to compress distance.

FIGURE 29-12 ──────────────────────────────────────

Wide-angle lens.

FIGURE 29-13 ──────────────────────────────────────

Normal lens.

ZOOMING VERSUS DOLLYING INTO CLOSE-UP

A zoom is a lens having infinite variability between its extremes (say, 10 mm to 100 mm, which is a zoom with a ratio of 10:1). If you keep the camera static and zoom in on a subject, the image is magnified, but perspective does not alter. With a prime (fixed) lens dollying in close, the image is magnified, and you see a perspective change during the move, just as in life. One is movement; the other, magnification.

LENSES AND IMAGE TEXTURE

Compare Figures 29-13 and 29-14. The backgrounds are very different in texture. Although the subject is in focus in both, the telephoto version—by putting the rest

FIGURE 29-14

Telephoto lens. Figures 29-12, 29-13, and 29-14 are taken from a single camera position. Notice that the stop sign remains in the same proportion to its background throughout.

of the image in soft focus—isolates and separates the subject from both its foreground and background. This is because the telephoto lens has a very limited *depth of field*, and only the point of focus is sharp.

Conversely, a wide-angle lens (Figures 29-9 and 29-12) allows deep focus. This is useful if you want to hold focus while someone walks from foreground to background. But deep focus distracts if it drowns its middle-ground subject in a plethora of irrelevantly sharp background and foreground detail.

Telephotos have a soft-textured background, whereas the wide angle has one that is hard. Lens characteristics can be limiting or can have great dramatic utility, depending on what you know and how you use it.

WHY THERE IS A FILM LOOK AND A VIDEO LOOK

Film stocks and video used to yield differing image aesthetics, but with the more sophisticated HD cameras' control over image characteristics, you can closely imitate the look of different film stocks. Considerable control over contrast, gamma (black levels), hue, and color saturation (color intensity) is also available in the latest postproduction software.

Differences between film and video images also derive from the optics that go with a camera's image-collecting area. A film close-up of a man in a park will show his face in sharp focus, but the background and foreground will be agreeably soft. Using selective focus like this indicates the subject by plane as well as by framing. The same close-up shot with a video camera often deluges the eye with detail by having foreground, middle ground, and background all in similar degrees of focus.

At the root of these differences is lens depth of field (DOF). A 35 mm film aperture is much larger than that of most video imaging chips. The larger image size requires more refraction (bending of light through the lens), and this means that less is in acceptable focus behind and in front of the subject at the focus point. If you

FIGURE 29-15 ————————————————————————

The P + S Technik MINI35 adapter, which enables the videographer to realize all the depth of field and other qualities of a 35 mm film lens (courtesy P + S Technik).

look at the image produced by a plate still camera: the negative (imaging) area is huge, the subject is sharp, but the rest of the image is in soft focus. Now look at the family 8 mm film camera, with its tiny image area: refraction is minimal, and most of the image is in focus most of the time.

It would be reasonable to assume that a video camera such as the Canon XL series, which uses interchangeable 35 mm lenses, would behave like its 35 mm film brethren. In fact, the camera's imaging area is smaller than 35 mm film, so it discards much of the given image. True, you get manual lens control and superior acuity, but there's little progress so far as the lens's DOF and angle of acceptance are concerned.

To get the restricted DOF of the 35 mm film camera lens from your camcorder, you can shoot off a tripod and use the telephoto end of your lens. This will isolate the subject from foreground and background planes, but camera movements will be handicapped by the need for extra steadiness. Alternatively, you can use the German optical firm P + S Technik's MINI35 digital adapter (Figure 29-15). Using a two-stage optical operation, the adapter uses interchangeable 35 mm lenses to produce an internal image. This image is then copied and projected into the video camera's imaging path. Now you have the focal length, depth of field, and angle of view of the 35 mm format. At a stroke, the videographer has the lens choice and control of the 35 mm cinematographer. For details on which cameras it fits, see www.pstechnik.de/en/index.php

LENS SPEED

Lens speed is a deceptive term, for it concerns light transmission and has nothing to do with movement. A fast lens is one that transmits much light, making it good for low-light photography. A slow lens is simply one that fails to admit as much light. By their inherent design, wide angles tend to be fast (with a widest aperture, say, of f/1.4), whereas telephotos tend to be slow (perhaps f/2.8). A two-stop difference like this means that the wide-angle is operative at one-quarter the light the telephoto needs for an exposure. With one lens, night shooting is practical; with the other, it's out of the question. Prime (that is, fixed) lenses have few elements, so they tend to be faster than zooms, which are multielement. Primes also tend to have better acuity, or sharpness, because the image passes through fewer optics. Note that zooms have one optimal lens speed over their whole range.

CAMERA HEIGHT

The film-manual adage says that a high camera position suggests domination; and a low angle, subjugation. There are other, less colonial-sounding reasons to vary camera height. A high or low camera angle may accommodate objects or persons in either the background or foreground, or may accommodate a camera movement. This was covered previously in this chapter, in the section "Relatedness: Separating or Integrating by Shot." If you completed Project 5-1: Picture Composition Analysis (see Chapter 5), taking as your subject a film as cinematically inventive as Orson Welles' classic *Citizen Kane* (1941), you saw many occasions when the departure from an eye-level camera position simply feels right. Often there is a dramatic rationale behind the choice, but don't turn such decisions into a filmmaking Ten Commandments.

In his book *On Screen Directing* (Focal Press, 1984), the veteran Hollywood director Edward Dmytryk makes a persuasive case for avoiding shots at characters' eye level simply because such shots are dull. There may also be a psychological reason to avoid them. At eye level, the audience feels itself intruding into the action, just as we would standing in the path of a duel. Being above or below eye-level positions puts us off axis and out of the firing line.

LIMIT CAMERA MOVEMENTS

Camera movements—apart from simple ones such as zooming, panning, and tilting—spell trouble to your schedule unless you have an expensive dolly and tracks, along with a highly experienced team to operate them. Student camera crews yearn for advanced camera support systems because it gives them practice and makes them feel more professional. The consequence may be a production repeatedly paralyzed while someone tries to master a complex move that has only virtuosity to contribute.

ADAPTING TO LOCATION EXIGENCIES

There are no real rules for camera positioning and movement because every situation imposes its own demands and limitations. The latter are usually physical: windows or pillars in an interior that restrict shooting in one direction, or an incongruity to be avoided in an exterior. A wonderful Victorian house turns out to have a background of power lines strung across the sky, and must be framed low when you had wanted to frame high. Filmmaking is always serendipitous, and so often your vision must be shelved and energy redirected to solve the unforeseen. For the rigid, linear personality, this constant adaptation is frustrating; but for others, it poses interesting challenges. Nonetheless, you must plan, and sometimes plans even work out.

BACKGROUNDS

Deciding what part background must play in relation to foreground is a lens-choice and camera-positioning issue. If a character is depressed and hungry, there is a nice irony in showing her being watched by a huge Ronald McDonald at a bus stop. Unobtrusively, the composition highlights her dilemma and suggests she might blow her bus money on an order of large fries. Sometimes the subject is in the middle ground (a prisoner, bars in foreground, cellmate in background at back of cell, for instance). Foreground compositional elements are an important part of creating depth.

CAMERA AS INSTRUMENT OF REVELATION

The camera should reveal not just the subject, but the subject's context. Looking down on the subject, looking up at it, or peering between tree trunks, all suggest different contexts and different ways of seeing—and therefore of experiencing—the action central to the scene. While you can use Eisenstein's dialectical cutting to make us see that riot police are near a nice bed of tulips, how much more subtle and effective to make the point in a single well-chosen frame.

Making the location a meaningful environment and responding to the actions and sight lines of participants in a scene creates a more vivid, spontaneous sense of the scene's dynamics unfolding. Why? Because we are sharing the consciousness of someone intelligent and intuitive who picks up all the underlying tensions and ironies. Too often we get the dull reactions of someone who merely swivels after whatever moves or makes a noise, as dogs do.

COMPROMISES FOR THE CAMERA

When shooting action sequences, especially in close shot, you may need to ask actors to slow their movements. This is because movement within a frame can look 20 to 30 percent faster than in life. Even the best camera operator cannot keep a profile in tight framing if the actor moves too fast. And if the actor strays from the chalk marks on the floor, the operator may lose focus too.

Accommodating the limits of technology raises an important question: How much should you forgo performance spontaneity to achieve a visually and choreographically polished result? This, of course, depends on the values of the story and what you expect of the production. But much else will depend on the expertise of actors and crew, or even the time of day. Tired actors are more likely than fresh ones to feel they are being treated like glove puppets. Politics and expediency do not end here, for the crew can be disappointed and even resentful if you always forgo interesting technical challenges on behalf of the cast.

Sometimes, when panning across a repetitive pattern such as a picket fence, you must vary the speed of the movement to stop the subject from *strobing*. This happens when the frequency of the railings' movement interacts with the camera's frame rate. This is how they won the West with wagon wheels turning backward.

WORK WITHIN YOUR MEANS

Any departure from simple cuts and camera movements must be motivated by the needs of the story, or the audience will not feel they are sharing someone's consciousness. Dollying through the noise and confusion of a newsroom in *All the President's Men* (1976) is dramatically justified, but dollying, craning, and other big-budget visual treatments are seldom necessary for the low-budget filmmaker

FIGURE 29-16 ——————————————————————————————————————

Dirty Dancing—when a dancing couple falls in love, the camera must move with them (courtesy Vestron/The Kobal Collection).

because few impressions cannot be achieved in simpler ways. Whole films have been successfully made with a static camera mainly at eye level or without cuts within a scene. Heavily scored music, rapid editing, and frenetic camera movements are often the nervous stimulation injected to mask a lack of content. Just take a jaunt around the channels on your TV.

Complex camera movement always needs to be justified. In Emile Ardolino's *Dirty Dancing* (1987, Figure 29-16), where a young girl falls in love with her dance instructor, Jeff Jur's camera cannot remain static on the sidelines. It must enter the lovers' dance and accompany them. Can this ever be done inexpensively? Yes. An experienced camera operator, using a wide-angle lens and taking advantage of a moving subject in the foreground that holds the eye, can handhold the camera and dispense with truckloads of shiny hardware. As mentioned, the Steadicam counterweighted body camera support, can, in experienced hands, produce wonderfully fluid camerawork. See Mike Figgis' *Leaving Las Vegas* (1995) for fine examples by DP Declan Quinn, whose first love was documentary.

STUDY THE MASTERS

For ideas on how best to shoot a problem scene, study the way good films have handled similar situations. Learn from them, but be guided most by your knowledge of perception in life. Find the simplest solutions that answer your perceptual needs. In Project 5-2: Editing Analysis (see Chapter 5), there is a film study project to help you assess how a director embodies choices and intentions.

CHAPTER 30

PRODUCING A SHOOTING SCRIPT

If you shot rehearsals documentary-style, you will already have a good sense of the coverage you want, and its optimal camera positions. Final decisions must be taken with your director of photography (DP). Simple poverty may preclude dollying or craning shots, but this, after all, is elegant packaging—its absence should never debilitate a worthwhile film.

Responsibility for the graphic aspects of filmmaking lies variously with the director, cinematographer, and art director. Steven D. Katz's *Cinematic Motion: A Workshop for Staging Scenes (Film Directing)* (Michael Wiese Productions, 2004) does a fine job explaining the staging options for different kinds of scenes. However, many of the book's techniques depend on dollies, cranes, and take-apart sets that are common enough in professional filmmaking but beyond the purse of the low-budget group. Even were you able to afford this equipment, operating adequately when the crew is learning on the job will massively slow the production—slowdowns excruciating for the cast.

Decades of classic cinema were shot with quite limited equipment, and you can do excellent work using the simplest techniques that serve the film's artistic intentions. Resist your crew's desire to experiment with "better" equipment. Fight for simplicity—simple is strong; less is more.

DIAGNOSTIC QUESTIONS

Ask yourself these questions to help you develop a shooting and editing strategy for a scene:

Geography:
- What must the scene show to establish the environment satisfactorily?
- Does this orientation come early, or is it delayed for dramatic reasons?
- What combination of distance and lens will I need to contain the widest angle, and is the location big enough to allow this?
- Will I have enough lighting to shoot the most comprehensive shot?

Movements by characters:

- At which points do characters move from one spot to another, and why?
- How will I show it?
  - Drop back to a wide angle?
  - Move the camera with a character?
  - Show another character's eye line changing as he or she hears the moving character's footsteps?
- What axis does the character follow at each stage of his or her movements?

Point of view:

- At each significant moment, whose point of view (POV) are we sharing?
- Whose global POV predominates in the overall story?
- When and why does POV change?
- Does a POV change become more subjective or more objective, and why?
- What other emotions, thoughts, or preoccupations might additional POVs convey?
- How will I make evident the Storyteller's attitudes to the events in this scene?

Eye lines:

- What are the significant *eye lines* in the scene? (Such changes motivate what the audience wants to see. They can help decide camera placement from shot to shot.)
- Where do eye lines change?
- Where should the camera look along an eye line?

Camera movement:

- When and why should the camera move?
- What feeling does its movement create?
- At what speed should the movement be? (Movements must be paced appropriately if they are to integrate with other aural or visual rhythms in a scene. When panning over repetitive patterns such as railings, be careful of *strobing*. Remember the wagon wheels that seem to revolve *backward*? For further information, see any good camerawork manual on "strobing.")

Compositional relationship:

- When and how to show significant relationship? For instance, you might:
  - Take a sleeping character who is supposed to be catching a plane, and frame him or her with a clock in the background—more effective than laboriously intercutting the clock.
  - Play a whole mother–daughter argument in tight, single shots to emphasize the adversarial, isolated feel of their relationship.

Isolation:

- Who or what might legitimately be isolated from surroundings? For instance:
  - A misfit boy is frequently shown alone, but the gang members who try to recruit him always appear as a pack.

    ◦ A phone silently refusing to ring for someone waiting on tenterhooks for a call might also be shown as a single shot. (In this and the previous case, isolation complements a dominant perception, either of someone within the film or that of the Storyteller.)

Space:

- What is the significance of space between characters? Space between people is charged, and can indicate who is gaining control and who is retreating or hiding.
- Camera position and the choice of lens can alter the audience's perception of space. For instance, a crowded street is often shot with a telescopic lens to compress cars and people into a bobbing sea, whereas someone reaching imploringly through prison bars might be shot with a wide-angle lens so his or her hand comes across a void and becomes enormous in the foreground.

PLANNING COVERAGE

You must now lock down your coverage plans and provide yourself with graphics or verbal reminders so you don't rely on memory while directing. Once a shoot gets under way, sensory overload may render it blank.

CUT TO SEAGULLS

Provide every sequence you shoot with safety coverage such as reaction shots, cutaways, or insert shots that can be used to bridge shots that don't match. The saying in the industry used to be, "When in doubt, cut to seagulls." But please don't use actual seagulls!

    An insert shot, such as the coins a character glances at in his hand, magnifies the detail *inside* an existing shot. A cutaway shows detail *outside* the pertinent shot, and might be of a man who, while crossing the road, catches the attention of our main character as he waits for his bus.

COVER IMPORTANT ASPECTS IN MORE THAN ONE WAY

Be prepared to cover vital story points or important emotional transitions more than one way so you later have a choice and can exercise maximum control over the telling moment. For instance, if, during a family reunion, the mother accidentally breaks a glass from her wedding set, your beat is her moment of realization and grief. You can give it additional poignancy by shooting reactions by others present. Her son shows anger at her clumsiness, her daughter is surprised, her husband is amused because he thinks it's just a minor accident, and her daughter-in-law fears she has cut herself. You would not use all these reactions, but having them allows you to later choose just the right inflection in the scene's finished state. Covering this spectrum of reaction allows for a variable richness in defining the moment, and follows our oft-mentioned principle of generating more than strictly necessary so you have choice and control later. In the same spirit, if a line is so understated that it risks being unintelligible, shoot two or three versions.

This is not compromise but survival; only foolish optimists take a two-day water supply to cross a two-day desert.

THE FLOOR PLAN AND THE STORYBOARD

Draw a floor plan. Figure 30-1 is a scene from a script, and Figure 30-2 is its floor plan. The latter consolidates your intentions for blocking, and helps you plan the fewest and most effective camera angles. On it, show the characters' movements

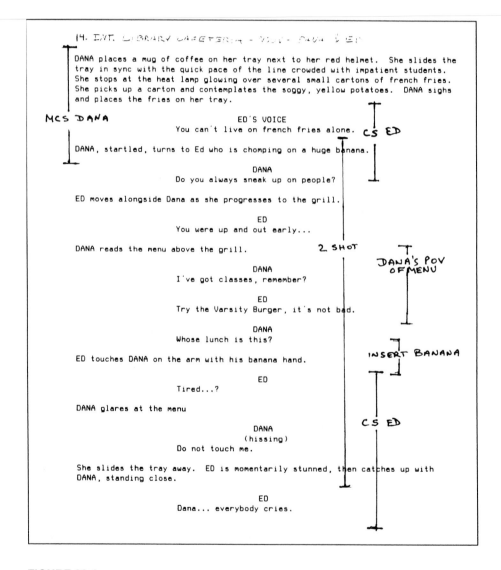

FIGURE 30-1 ————————————————————————————

Script page bracketed with intended shots. Editing options are immediately apparent.

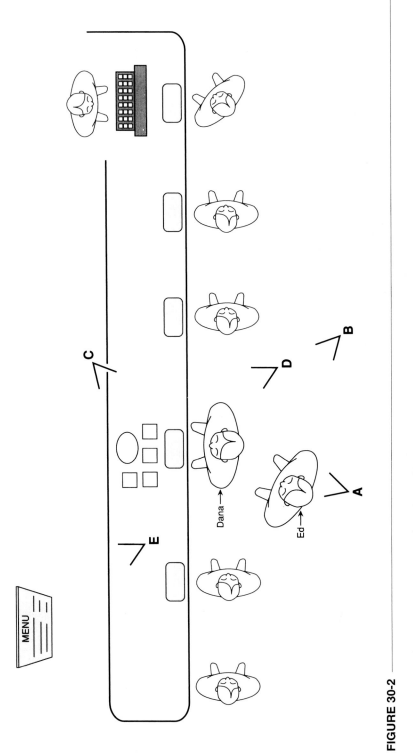

FIGURE 30-2

Floor plan for lunch counter scene scripted in Figure 30-1.

and the camera angles necessary for the edited version you want. This diagram, growing out of the blocking developed during rehearsals and modified by location realities, helps plan the editing and enables the DP to plan lighting placement and camera movements.

On a tightly planned production, the art director may make storyboard sketches for each angle, as in Figure 30-3A. Storyboard software such as FrameForge 3D Studio 2 can help you generate a professional-looking storyboard, but you may feel underwhelmed by its stock characters. Go to http://writersstore.com/public/KillBill42606.html and see what an animated story looks like. Something like this might prove pivotal for an action film during fund-raising, but unless you are experienced and have considerable directing skills, storyboards often go out the window once you shoot. The particularities of a lens's field of view, problems with lighting, the needs of a character's movements, and even the size of the framing may all lead you to recompose the image and block actors differently.

Even inexpert sketches are good enough to work out compositions that are as interesting and relevant as possible. Suggestions from key crew members can also help you develop your ideas. As always in a true collaboration, the whole is greater than the sum of its parts.

SCRIPT BREAKDOWN

Better (as always) than a simple list is a graphic representation to show the intentions and the state of play. Going farther than the floor plan and bracketed script described in Chapter 6 will provide you with a thorough and up-to-date version. It works like this:

1. Floor Plan
   a. *Make a floor plan* of the intended scene showing walls, doors, windows, and furniture, and indicating the characters' movements and stopping points, as in Chapter 5, Figure 5-6.
   b. *Mark the camera positions*, designating them A, B, C, and so forth. Position A will be shot first because the lighting for the widest (master) shot determines all the others. Tighter shots (positions B, C, and so on) follow because closer shots need individual relighting to augment the lighting logic of the master shot.

2. Shooting Script
   a. *Bracket each intended shot* on the shooting script (see Figure 30-1). Remember to give good overlaps between shots so the editor has a range of options for cutting from one to the next. The most useful editing overlaps occur on strong actions (such as rising from a chair or turning to leave the room).
   b. *Designate each bracket as Cam A, Cam B, Cam C,* and so on, to show which camera position it will be shot from.
   c. *Give each bracket a shot description* to avoid ambiguity (example: "CS [close shot] hand lighting fire").

Each bracket, along with its brief identifying description, represents a camera angle, as in Figure 30-1. When you shoot the coverage, you will need to *supply*

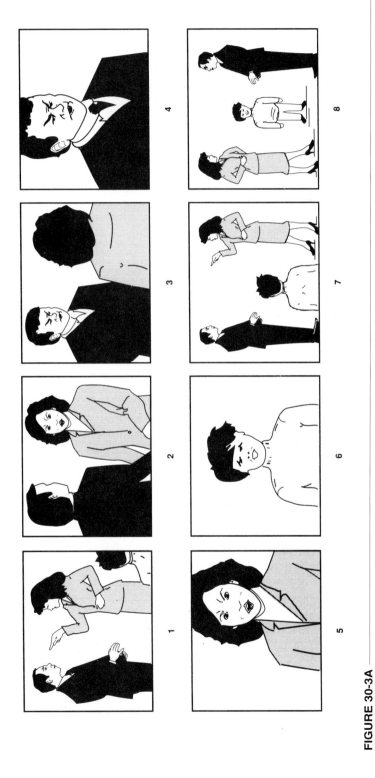

FIGURE 30-3A

Storyboard frames for camera positions 1 through 8 in Figure 30-3B. Note that in position 8, the two figures have reversed screen direction because the camera has crossed the scene axis line.

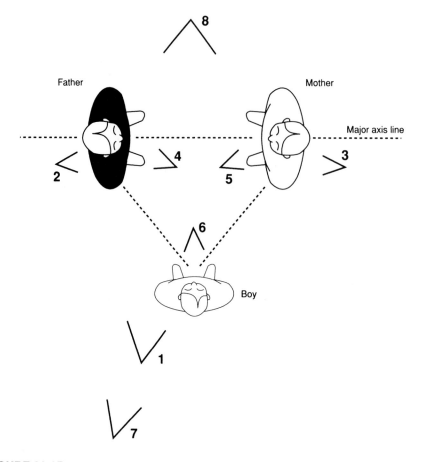

FIGURE 30-3B —————————————————————————————————————

Floor plan showing camera positions to cover child's view of an argument between his parents. Lines of tension are indicated between the characters.

generous action overlaps so your editor has a wide choice of action match cutting points from shot to shot. Make sure you reflect this as you mark up your script.

Once you have a bracketed script, you can see at a glance how you mean to cover the action and what editing alternatives will be possible. Keep in mind that for smooth and seamless editing, *the best place to make a cut is always on a strong physical movement* (for instructions, see "Making an action match cut" in Chapter 6, Exercise 6-1a). To see this principle at work, pick a well-made feature film dialogue scene with plenty of action, make a floor plan, and analyze the coverage and cutting points.

CAMERA PLACEMENT

Placing the camera can seem like an industrial decision based on lighting or other technical considerations. But your work will have no soul unless technique mimics the way human awareness works at an event. Let's see how this works.

USING LINES OF TENSION

Consider the camera's relationship to the scene's axes, or lines of tension. These are the invisible lines of strong feeling you would draw between the most important people and objects in a scene. Often they are also sight lines and have great dramatic potential (changes of eye line, for instance). They justify particular camera angles, and imply the emotional connections (and therefore POVs) associated with particular characters.

Look at the floor plan for child's view of a mother–father argument (Figure 30-3A). The dotted-in sight lines are also the possible lines of psychic tension. The major axis is between the parents, but others exist between each parent and the silent child. Each sight line suggests a camera position. What each camera angle covers is shown in the storyboard sequence (Figure 30-3B). Some angles are close (as in 4, 5, and 6), some in medium two-shot (1, 2, and 3), and there are two master shots—wide angles that take in everything (7 and 8). Positions 1, 2, and 3 are all to some degree omniscient because they are an outsider's view of the characters; that is, seen in pairs and related to each other. Position 7 is even more comprehensive, taking in all three. Positions 4, 5, and 6 are, however, close and subjectively involved, as if viewed by one of the other characters. Position 6 would be useful to show shifts in the child's eye line.

SUBJECTIVE AND OBJECTIVE

No matter whose point of view your film favors, POV will move. Changes in lines of tension and fluctuations in scene intensity are your prime clues. Let's recall how an onlooker's consciousness moves around when observing two people in conversation. The Concerned Observer's view is the average, relatively detached movement of human perception, and we use it as a model for how the camera and editing move our attention around within a scene. Together, camerawork and editing mimic the way an observer's ears, eyes, and psychological focus migrate within an environment, whether quiet or busy.

Angle and shot changes are suggested by stimuli from the scene, but they also arise from a narrative agenda as the Storyteller pursues a line of inquiry. Indeed, perception is often shaped by the predispositions of the Storyteller. Salient observation can be that of a character in the film or of a Storyteller who directs our attention from outside. The mood of observation may start relatively detached, and then grow involved with the predicaments and personal qualities of the characters, or it can happen in reverse order. A film, just as you or I would in any gripping situation, will "breathe" in and out between extremes. The difference can be dramatized by returning to the familiar experience of watching a tennis game (see "The Actor and the Acted-Upon" in Chapter 4).

The closer the camera is to a line of tension, the more subjectively involved the audience will feel. When complementary angles are used, the audience is switched rapidly between each protagonist's subjective experience, so the aggregate effect may be to enter the fray without identifying with one contestant or another. This depends on the balance of editing, as well as, less measurably, the power in each actor's characterization.

We can vary the Observer's relationship to the axes, and vary his or her closeness to what is observed. A close shot is both a magnification of compelling detail (a surprised expression, say) and the psychologically driven exclusion of other, irrelevant detail. You can juxtapose subjects in an antithetical relationship to each other (cat and canary, say) by editing shots of them together—or, more subtly and compellingly, by blocking them together within a single shot.

SHOW RELATEDNESS

How are the protagonists to be spatially related? Showing the couple arguing in the same frame, but the boy separated in a close-up, reinforces his separation from his parents. Relating boy and mother in one frame to father alone in another suggests a different configuration of alliances. There could be other factors—using foreground and background, the sides of the frame, different camera heights, and different levels of lighting—any combination of which might predispose the audience toward interpreting the scene in a particular way or from a particular POV.

THERE ARE NO RULES, ONLY AWARENESS

There are no hard-and-fast rules here because human judgment is made from a multiplicity of clues. What matters is the sensibility and rationale by which each shot is composed, lit, and blocked. Compositionally, you are always showing the specifics of relationship between person and object, object and object, or person and person. By relating them, you imply the relationship of one idea, principle, personality, or judgment to another. You can achieve the same effect through editing or story construction. Using parallel storytelling, for instance, you might intercut a boxing match with a lover's feud. Try out such an idea, and judge from what you see and feel, rather than relying on theory.

AVOID CROSSING THE SCENE AXIS

Because the child in our example remains in a fixed position, camera coverage that replicates his vision of his parents must stay to one side of the A to B axis line. If you cross this axis with your camera, as in position 8, your characters begin to look in the wrong screen direction, as you see in the storyboard sequence. In positions 1 through 7, the father always looks screen left to screen right, and the mother right to left. Even in the big close-ups (4 and 5), the character's eye lines maintain the same screen direction. However, in camera position 8, that consistency disappears because the camera has strayed across the scene axis line. Conventionally, this is avoided. Try shooting an additional shot after crossing the line, and intercut it to see if you really want to break the conventions.

REGROUPING AND RESET TRANSITIONS

In scenes where characters move, they often regroup to face in new screen directions. At the very least, this means that early and late reaction shots cannot be interchanged, and the scene cannot easily be restructured in the cutting room if so desired. *Movements that lead to regrouping must be shown on-screen.* Regard them as *reset transitions*, each of which establishes a new compositional phase of the scene. When designing a scene, you don't want people milling around; you want to choreograph movements and compose group configurations strictly for their new importance. Movements nearly always carry dramatic significance, and so you will want to show them anyway.

PLANNING WHERE TO EDIT

In marking up the script for the scene, you now know what shots you intend to use to cover each part, but you probably feel unsure about how to cut from one angle or one size of shot to another. Here are some guidelines, but remember to leave plenty of overlap between shots so the editor has a choice of cutting place.

EDITING IN MOVEMENT

Plan to use any pronounced movement in the scene as a convenient cutting point between angles. These—as you will recall from Chapter 6, Exercise 6-1a—are called action match cuts, or simply, match cuts. They are useful as transitions because they occur in movement, when the eye is least critical.

EDITING FOR INTENSIFICATION AND RELAXATION

If you made a graph of scene intensity, you will know where you want close-shot coverage and where a longer or group view is more appropriate. If the scene needs to breathe between extremes, you will want to provide the material to move our attention between long and close shots.

EDITING AS REFRESHMENT

Cutting between different angles can also renew and refresh the spectator's perspective, show different POVs, and invoke different feelings. If the angles stay close to the axis, we remain subjectively involved and eventually become desensitized. So for variation, the Storyteller may temporarily take us out of the firing line to review the situation from a more detached perspective. In a political meeting, for instance, this might suggest a stepping back from the maelstrom of personalities to take a longer historical or sociological perspective. This interrupts what has become standard, and pushes us into interpreting from another intellectual or emotional angle. You will, of course, have to foresee this and shoot it.

OVERSIGHT

Plan your coverage, but ensure against surprises. Try to foresee weather changes and scheduling difficulties, and though you intend to show only one character on-screen during an intense exchange, shoot both. This allows you abundance—a fallback alternative if your plans are not fulfilled.

SHOOTING ORDER

A glance at the shooting script and the floor plan shows in what order to shoot. Wide or establishing shots are done first because they take all the lighting resources. They set performance levels, and closer shots must then match both the acting and the lighting. Close-ups and overshoulder shots follow, with reaction shots, inserts, and cutaways done last.

Any changes of approach during the shoot may have an impact on scheduling, so vow to go over the shooting script, before each day's work, with the script supervisor, DP, and assistant director (AD).

CRIB NOTES

When you first direct, make brief crib notes on index cards as reminder lists (Figure 30-4) so you don't forget any of your intentions in the hurly-burly of the set. Defining the beats and story points you must make, and nailing down what you intend for each sequence, means you are directing from a plan instead waiting to recognize success if it should appear. When fatigue sets in and memory and imagination shut down, crib notes become a lifesaver. As you gain in experience and confidence, you may not need shopping lists any longer.

KEEPING TRACK OF PROGRESS

The script supervisor amends the shooting script as each setup is completed, checking off shot material by adding takes and circling those considered best.

```
              Scene 15: TONY RETURNS HOME AFTER 5 YEARS' SILENCE.

   Metaphor: Return of the prodigal son

   Timing:   2 mins 25 secs

        Tony wants to:  avoid showing the love he feels for his father
                        evade specifics of the past
                        signify apology but evade admissions
                        make his father think he's returned out of duty
                        make contact with his childhood again
                        move his father to affection and thus forgiveness
                        retrieve mother's photo
                        convince Dad he's not a failure
                        ask for forgiveness

        Dad wants to:   keep Tony at an emotional distance
                        deny to himself that he's very moved by the boy's return
                        get him to think he's washed his hands of him
                        let him know the whole family disapproves of him
                        not act in the authoritarian way that alienated the boy
                        not let him know his bedroom has been kept unchanged
                        deny that he used the boy to get at his mother
                        signify that he loves him
                        ask for forgiveness

        Scene must convey that:  Tony has grown in confidence through travel
                                 Dad has been ill and sees his own mortality
                                 House is still as Mother left it
```

FIGURE 30-4 ———————————————————————

Example of director's crib notes.

Bracket lines can be amended or colored so that at any point the director, script supervisor, or DP can see at a glance the balance of intended and amended coverage. The unit must always know what it has shot, what remains to be shot, and that it will cut together. Lists remain obstinately abstract, but a graphic representation (the bracketed script, for example) requires no cross-referencing or special knowledge.

Especially during your early projects, your notes will be valuable when you do postmortem sessions and compare the planning against the actual shoot. This is when you make good resolutions for the next time.

CHAPTER 31

BEFORE THE CAMERA
ROLLS

RIGGING THE STAGE

Although you will probably be shooting in authentic locations rather than constructing sets on a stage, we will, for the sake of simplicity, refer to the shooting area as the "stage." The first shot of any scene will be an establishing, or master, shot because:

- Wide shots take the most lighting, and you want to use your light judiciously.
- Closer shots match the wide shot for lighting and continuity.
- You want to work out blocking problems for the whole first and the parts later.
- All continuity matches refer back to the *master shot,* or *establishing shot.*

Rigging the stage therefore means placing lighting instruments and adjusting furniture and objects for a shot wide enough to contain the intended action. This takes into account the *motivating light source* (the apparent source of light, such as a window, lighting fixture, skylight) and deciding a general direction for the camera. It also means placing lighting stands out of shot and hiding cables so there is an unobstructed field of view.

AVOIDING SHADOWS AND "CHEATING"

Move furniture well away from walls so that anyone nearby doesn't immediately cast a shadow. Then, by setting lamps high, shadows are thrown downward and out of sight of the camera. Because walls tend to be bland planes, and films are constructed from edited fragments, the audience is unlikely to notice that you've distanced your cast a little from their background. This is called *cheating* distances, because it's a subterfuge that doesn't register with the audience, and you expect to get away with it.

The sound crew technicians set up their equipment in view of the set, but out of the camera's field of view.

FIRST SETUP AND LINEUP

After rigging the lights, placing props and furniture, and anticipating the action, the crew now asks for the precise setup from the director, who will confirm with the director of photography (DP) what is or isn't in shot. The director will also reiterate what the characters are going to do. The camera is set in place, and the operator can frame what's expected. The actors or their *stand-ins* (people of similar size and build to the actors) will likely be asked to do a walk-through so that stopping points can be chalked on the floor, focus can be set for the different points, and difficulties can be resolved.

BLOCKING AND FIRST REHEARSAL

In a walk-through, actors repeat their lines in a relaxed manner, and move in stages under the director's instruction to points where they will stand or sit during the scene. At each stage, DP and camera operator decide framing and lighting—in particular how to handle the key and fill lighting, and what shadows will be cast to indicate the light source. The intended source might be a table lamp, a window or skylight, or a candle carried by one of the characters. Each of these situations may take elaborate lighting procedures.

At this stage, the crew is focused on getting the environment ready for a performance, not on any aspect of the performance itself. The sound crew takes a close interest in where the lights are going to be, which direction the characters face as they speak, and how to best cover the scene for sound. If coverage presents undue difficulties, the crew may ask for blocking or lighting compromises.

PLACING MARKS

Where a character stops to say something and where he or she next moves and stops will be marked on the floor with tape or chalk by the assistant camera (AC), who must follow focus. To the AC, these distances represent vital focus points. If the camera has a professional lens, the assistant will put tape on the focus ring and mark it with salient points of the action denoted by the floor marks. That way, the lens can be in sharp focus at each important moment. The lower the light on the set, the smaller the lens's depth of field, so it's important for the actor to hit the mark and for the AC to hold focus.

REHEARSAL

The director, cast, and script supervisor now leave the set to do last-minute work on the scene. If an actor is missing, the script supervisor will read his or her lines or provide action cues so the scene can be worked over. This is called *running lines*. Some directors make it a policy to have all cast members present for such scenes.

LIGHTING WITH STAND-INS

Lighting can be a long, slow business, especially if there are two or more characters with elaborate movement paths. This may require multiple key lights and a great deal of planning and adjustment. Any practicals (lights meant to be seen in shot) must be adjusted either in wattage or with scrim or neutral density filter inside the shade so they render as the right intensity and color.

To see the effect of their work, the DP and crew will use stand-ins. As the stand-ins move in increments as directed, the DP can see the lighting's effect at each stage of the scene. In a small crew, a stand-in may simply be a spare crew member of the right height.

The first shots of the production always seem to take an eternity to line up, and the assistant director (AD) must be on hand to supply some pressure and to report as soon as the set is ready.

FIRST WALK-THROUGH

Actors now take the place of stand-ins and are advised of any revisions affecting their path of action or the marks they must hit. They are first walked through, for their benefit and for that of the DP and operator. Their hair and makeup, first attended to in the morning, may need touching up by makeup and hairdressers.

DRESS REHEARSAL

Next comes a dry run if the scene is complex. This is a full rehearsal in costume and makeup, but without running the camera. To conserve energy, the cast will do this at low intensity until the camera is running. The dry run helps internalize what they must think and do to make their lines and action coincide with the precise needs of the camera, its movements, and attendant lighting. Any problems with costumes will show up and can be fixed. At this time, the members of the sound crew are checking their sound coverage and rehearsing what they must do to get on-mike sound without casting shadows or making any movement noise. Wireless mikes give complete mobility, and if they are to be used, they are running at this stage. The script supervisor will take a timing of this scene as a benchmark for other shots to follow.

Everything should now be in order, and everyone is set to roll camera.

CHAPTER 32

ROLL CAMERA

As it comes time to roll camera, the script supervisor makes a last check to see that actors are correctly costumed, that the right props are at hand, and that nothing has been forgotten or misplaced on the set.

The assistant director (AD) marshals everyone to their starting positions, ensures that doors and windows are closed to seal out exterior sounds, and calls for silence on the set. There is a last hair and makeup check, and the director of photography (DP) confirms that all lights are on. If you are using a film camera, the assistant camera (AC) has inspected the film gate for debris, something that must be done regularly and without fail.

Distances have been measured out, and the focus puller is ready to adjust the lens in perfect synchronization with the actors' movements, all according to the marked tape on the lens focus ring. With 35 mm, this is vital because depth of field may be very shallow and focus is critical for viewing on a large screen.

The script supervisor confers with the AC concerning the next slate, or clapper, number, which we will assume is Scene 62, Take 1. Correctly slating every shot is the key to knowing what you have covered, and afterward being able to organize it in the cutting room. This information goes into camera, sound, and continuity logs, and these logs become vital sources of information as the footage proliferates. So vital, in fact, that we must digress for a moment to establish how marking systems work.

SHOT MARKING SYSTEMS

SHOT AND SCENE IDENTIFICATION

Your crew keeps logs of important information as you shoot. These logs serve the same end for both digital production and film, but record keeping and continuity observation are more stringent for film because film allows no instant replay.

CLAPPER BOARD

A *clapper board*, or *slate*, is, at its simplest, a basic information chalkboard with a hinged bar (Figure 32-1). Banging its bar closed creates a visual and aural

FIGURE 32-1

The traditional clapper board.

marker point for syncing picture with sound, and there is only a piece of chalk and a hinge to go wrong. The clapper-board ritual has three main functions:

- Visually, the slate identifies the production, scene, and take number for the film laboratory.
- Aurally, the operator's announcement identifies the track for sound transfer personnel.
- The closing *bang!* of the bar provides an exact picture frame against which to align the bang in the recorded track. This is vital when sound and picture are processed separately and must be synchronized for viewing.

There are fancier, more automatic film-marking systems, such as the "smart slate." This is a clapper board containing a timecode display that comes on when the bar is opened and whose timecode freezes at the point where the clapper bar is closed (Figure 32-2). This makes syncing sound to its timecoded picture easy, and is especially handy for grab-shooting when voice announcements may have been impractical. However, camera and recorder must be compatible. Every morning, technicians must jam-sync (synchronize) the timecode generators because their clocks drift apart over a period of time.

Strictly speaking, you need no clapper board when recording digitally and using single system (that is, sound and picture on the one recording). Having a

FIGURE 32-2 ————————————————————————————————————

The "smart slate" electronic clapper board (photo courtesy of Denecke, Inc.).

clapper as sync reference becomes vital whenever you shoot double system (that is, film or video picture plus sound recorded separately).

Whatever rig you use, you will need a foolproof shot-numbering system to identify setup and take numbers against the script. Then, using the log and time-code (a unique time signature for every frame) that cameras automatically generate as they go, a chosen section can be rapidly located for viewing on the set.

Clapper boards carry not only scene and take numbers, but also reference charts for the image quality-control experts to use in the film labs or video production studios. These include a gray scale, white and black as a contrast reference, and a standard color chart. In video, an electronic color chart called *color bars* is usually generated by the camera, and recorded for reference purposes at the head of every camera original tape.

To summarize:

- For film production, use a clapper board with verbal announcement before filming.
- For single-system (camcorder) digital production, use a number board for the camera with announcement only.
- For double-system video or film, treat the operation like film, and use an announcement and a clapper board.

SETUP AND TAKE NUMBERS

The setup is the apparent position of the camera, and it is usually changed by physically moving the camera to a new position. However, a simple lens change also counts as a new setup. There are two philosophies of slate (that is, clapper board) numbering.

Method 1: The Scene/Setup/Take system is favored in the Hollywood fiction film system. Numbering is based on the script scene number. For example: Scene 104A, Shot 16, Take 3. Hollywood makes big, highly supervised productions, and needs lengthy factory part numbers. For the small, flexible production, this is unnecessary. The more elaborate a system is, the more susceptible it is to breakdown when you depart from the script or when people get tired. Also, by taking longer to announce, you waste precious film stock.

Method 2: The Cumulative Setup/Take system is preferred for documentaries and features in Europe. Shooting simply begins at Slate 1, and each setup gets the next number. For example: Slate 142, Take 2. This system is preferred for the overstretched small crew because it requires no liaison to coordinate numbers with the script, and no adaptation when the inevitable script departures come up. The slight disadvantage is that the script supervisor must record the setup and take number against its scene in the master script or enter these numbers into a database.

SHOOTING LOGS

A film shoot requires various logs:

A **camera log** (Figure 32-3), kept by the AC, records each film magazine's contents by slate, take, and footages. Each magazine, or digital cassette, gets a new camera roll number. This information comes into play during processing and later in editing. A day-for-night scene, for example, would be shot using a blue filter to give it a moonlit look—but without the relevant documentation, the film lab might easily treat the filtering as an error needing color correction in the work print.

A **sound log** (Figure 32-4), kept by the film sound recordist, records slate and take numbers and whether each track is sync or wild (nonsync voice or effects recording). The latter information is important to whoever syncs the rushes.

DOUBLE-SYSTEM RECORDING

When sound is recorded by an independent recorder, its rolls, cassettes, or discs do not stay in numerical step with their equivalent picture roll. This is because stock durations are different, and wild track, sound effects, or atmosphere recordings have been added to the sound master rolls as the production progresses, and so more sound is shot than picture.

FILM

Separate sound and camera logs are necessary because the component parts of film dailies travel to their destination in the cutting room by different routes (Figure 32-5).

Film origination, editing using film: The film laboratory processes the negative and strikes a work print, which they send to the editor. Meanwhile, the magnetic master tape or DAT (digital audiotape) cassette goes separately to a sound transfer suite, where a copy is made onto sprocketed magnetic stock. This, too,

```
FILM CAMERA LOG    Production Title_____ Page_____

Operator_____ Camera #_____ Magazine #_____ Cam. Roll #____
Location_____ Film Type _____ Date ___/___/_____
-----------------------------------------------------------------------------
Setup Take Comments                                                   Footage
_____:____:_____:_____
_____:____:_____:_____
_____:____:_____:_____
_____:____:_____:_____
_____:____:_____:_____
_____:____:_____:_____
_____:____:_____:_____
_____:____:_____:_____
_____:____:_____:_____
_____:____:_____:_____
_____:____:_____:_____
_____:____:_____:_____
_____:____:_____:_____
_____:____:_____:_____
_____:____:_____:_____
_____:____:_____:_____
_____:____:_____:_____
_____:____:_____:_____
_____:____:_____:_____
_____:____:_____:_____
_____:____:_____:_____
_____:____:_____:_____
_____:____:_____:_____
_____:____:_____:_____
_____:____:_____:_____
_____:____:_____:_____
_____:____:_____:_____
_____:____:_____:_____
_____:____:_____:_____
_____:____:_____:_____
_____:____:_____:_____
_____:____:_____:_____
_____:____:_____:_____
_____:____:_____:_____
_____:____:_____:_____
_____:____:_____:_____

Process Normal Yes/No:_____ Total Shot :
-----------------------------------------------------------------:-------
Notes:


_____   Cam. Assistant:_____
```

FIGURE 32-3

Camera log for film production.

is sent to the editor. Sound and picture are thus synced and reunited for the first time under the assistant editor's hand in preparation for editing.

Film, cutting digitally: For low-budget production, the film negative is run through a telecine machine, and sound is synchronized by the lab to produce a

SOUND RECORDER LOG Production Title_____ Page_____
Mike Op. _____ Recorder_#_____ Tape Type_____Roll #_____
Location_____ Date ___/___/_____
Setup Take Comments   Mike(s) Sync?

Notes:

Recordist:

FIGURE 32-4

Sound recorder log for film or video double-system production.

cassette of sync sound takes, which the editor then digitizes into the editing system. Feature films, with more at stake, are fearful of undue negative handling. So they pay for a work print to be struck from the negative, and this is digitized in the labs and sound-synchronized. The editor works from digitized cassettes as in

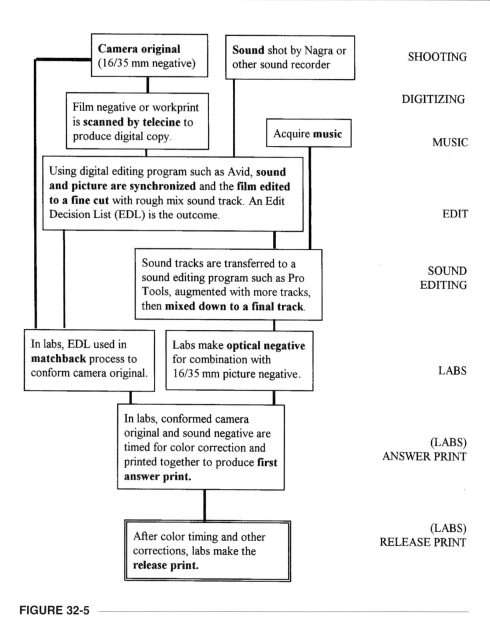

FIGURE 32-5

Flowchart for a production shot on film (double system).

the television method. Direct recording to hard drives is nowadays cutting out the use of cassettes as intermediates.

VIDEO

Single-system recording: When shooting single system with a camcorder, logs (Figure 32-6) can be simpler because sound and picture are recorded side by side

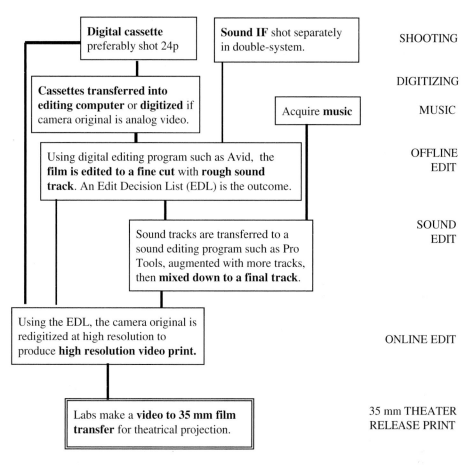

FIGURE 32-7 ——

Flowchart for a production shot on digital video, with single- or double-system sound, resulting in a 35 mm release print for theatrical exhibition.

Double-system recording: When using video, sound is frequently recorded "double system" on a separate recorder for quality reasons (see Figure 32-7), as in a film shoot. The sound is synchronized to the picture by the cutting room assistant after the two have been digitized for editing.

LOGS IN ACTION

Logs help the right material go to the right place. The camera log will inform the labs what to expect as they process and print the work print from the camera original. If a scene looks very blue, they won't try to color-correct the work print because the camera log says in block capitals: DAY FOR NIGHT. Similarly, the sound log acts as an inventory of what the sound transcription service—and later, the editor—can expect. It saves much time when syncing dailies if you know, for instance, that the rest of a cassette contains only wild tracks of trains shunting.

A less obvious function of logs is to record (by serial number) which piece of equipment made which recording. Should a strange hum appear in the sound, or a scratching turn up on a film negative, the offending machine can be quickly withdrawn for examination.

COUNTDOWN TO "MARK IT," THEN "ACTION"

The director, satisfied that all is ready for a take, nods to the AD, and so begins an unvarying ritual that gets everything rolling:

AD (loud voice): "Okay, quiet everybody—we're about to roll."

Silence descends. The clapper operator takes a position holding the clapper board in front of the first actor, at a height where it is clearly visible. On close shots, the operator will sometimes direct its placement to ensure that the all-important number and clapper bar are in shot.

AD: "Roll sound."

The sound mixer turns on the recorder and waits a few moments until able to report that the recorder'ss mechanism has stabilized.

Sound Mixer: "Speed."

The camera operator now turns on the camera, which comes up to speed almost instantaneously.

Camera Operator: "Mark it."
Camera Assistant: "Scene 62, Take 1."

BANG!—the clapper closes, and the camera operator scuttles out of shot and into position next to the camera.

Camera Operator: "Rolling."
Director: "Action."

The magic word "Action!" can be said in a variety of ways, depending on what you want to convey: excitement, mystery, surprise, dread, routine. It's the director's last prod, and as the scene begins, the script supervisor starts the stopwatch.

If, during the scene, a car horn is supposed to sound from Johnnie waiting in the road, the script supervisor will call out, "Beep, beep" at the right place, and a character will respond with, "Aha, there's Johnnie. I gotta go." Other scripted cues, such as a voice calling from the alley below, or a plane going overhead, will be cued in the same way.

STARTING WITHOUT A CLAPPER

Sometimes, when the setup is so tight that the clapper board cannot get into shot, or when you are shooting spontaneous material and don't want to alert everyone, you quietly signal camera and sound recorder to start rolling. After the action is complete, and while the camera is still rolling, the clapper board (also called *clapsticks*) is brought into shot by the AC, but upside down. The AC calls out the scene number and says, "Board on end" or "End clapsticks," then claps the bar, after which the director calls "Cut." In the cutting room, the person syncing the material will have a note in the continuity sheets warning of the end-clapped material—which, if it is film, will have to be end-synced, then wound back to the beginning.

CREW RESPONSIBILITIES

Every crew member has something to monitor:

- The camera operator watches through the viewfinder for focus, composition, framing, movements, and whether the mike is dangling into shot. Film cameras have an oversize viewfinder, so the operator can see anything about to encroach before it enters the filmed area.
- The director of photography is watching the lighting as the actors move from area to area.
- The camera assistants watch for focus, stock running out, and that the camera gate or image chip is clean.
- The script supervisor notes how each physical movement is accomplished, and listens for departures from the scripted dialogue.
- The director watches every aspect of the scene for its emotional truth and intensity. What is being expressed? Is the scene focused? Does it deliver what it's meant to deliver? How was this take different or special?
- The sound recordist listens for dialogue quality, background, any sound intrusions, and whether the actors' lines are on axis and clear of any footsteps or audible body movements.
- Assistant directors watch to see if actors hit their marks, and make sure all is quiet on the set.
- Makeup and hairdressers watch to see if their work is wilting under the lights.
- Electricians are watching to see that all lights stay on.
- Grips are watching to see that the rigging they have done is remaining firm, that lights are staying up, that scenery is firmly anchored, and that the camera hits its marks during tracking shots.

The scene proceeds until the director calls "Cut."

WHO CAN CALL "CUT"

Sometimes you'll let an unsuccessful take run its course to avoid chopping actors short during the middle of a difficult scene. Nobody may call "Cut" unless their right to do so has been first established with the director. Someone else might be allowed to abort the take if:

- The camera operator sees a hopeless framing mistake or that an actor went wide of the mark and veered out of frame.
- The sound mixer may for some reason be getting unusable sound.
- A stunt supervisor sees a situation of imminent danger or failure.
- Very occasionally, a prestigious actor may call "Cut."

Directors never want the cast to decide which aspects of their work are usable. A big-name actor might be accorded that privilege, especially if the director is of lesser status. Ordinary mortals are expected to keep the scene going until released by the director. Even though someone flubs a line, the director may know that this part of the scene is to be covered in another shot, and that a momentary glitch is unimportant.

PICKUP SHOTS

Sometimes a take is excellent except for a couple of lines or a movement. Then and there, the director will reshoot that section, sometimes without even stopping the camera and saying, "Go back and do the section about the storm again." The script supervisor will call a beginning cue, and the scene will resume until the director calls "Cut." At that point, director and script supervisor will confer and decide whether to shoot cutaway shots of listeners so the new section can be edited in. These shots will get appropriate numbers, and their function will be noted in the continuity sheets.

Another way to cover the inserted section would be to move the camera and shoot from another character's angle—and in editing, bounce the section off a close shot of this listening character to make it her point of view.

PRINT IT

In film shooting, the director chooses whether to print a take that has just been shot, or to go for another take. To conserve money, the laboratory does not print every take that the camera shot, but uses the camera reports to select only those marked as a "print." If the take was good, the director will say, "Cut it . . . print that one," and will dictate a note to the script supervisor about what is usable. If the director needs another take, it will be: "Cut, let's go for another take." Then the director will have a quiet word with the actors, saying what she is looking for and from whom. Particularly if a scene is long, there may be two or three takes printed up, with accompanying notes such as "Use the first part of Take 4 and the last part of either Take 6 or 7." With digital shooting, there is no need for such on-the-spot choices because no extra expense is involved in digitizing everything into the editing computer.

COMPLEMENTARY SHOTS

Once the master shot has been achieved, the camera will be moved in to get a variety of closer shots. Each new setup gets a new slate number; each new attempt is a new take. Different camera positions may use different lenses or different camera heights to alter the sense of space and perspective. The backgrounds may be cheated to contain enough of something significant in the frame as a juxtapositional comment. Lighting will also be cheated because lighting for a wide shot only sets the general mood of the scene. Closer shots must often be adjusted for contrast or to achieve a better effect. The key lighting must still come from the same direction, and the shot must still intercut with the master shot, but within these parameters, there is plenty of latitude for poetic license.

KEEPING TRACK

The script supervisor has to monitor how each segment of script is being covered, especially when the director must depart from the original plan. In such a case, the two must confer to ensure there are no ghastly omissions. Usually the script supervisor plans script sections in light pencil, then goes over the script with a heavy line for everything successfully covered. When changes happen, the light original can be left, and a heavier alternative marked in for the new approach.

BLOCKING CHANGES

Sometimes when you change blocking, it's fatally easy to "cross the line," which means the camera has strayed across the scene axis (see "Crossing the Line or Scene Axis" in Chapter 4). This will cause headaches in the cutting room and make an assembled scene look truly awful. Here's where your ground plan is a lifesaver, for it establishes who is supposed to be looking in which direction. No matter where the camera is placed, everyone must consistently look either screen left or screen right if the scene is to cut together correctly. When people change position, you must show the characters taking up their new positions, and then observe the new logic of axes that result from this change.

DIRECTOR, SCRIPT SUPERVISOR, AND CONTINUITY REPORTS

Directing means being wholly occupied with the actors every moment of the shoot. You planned coverage in advance with your script supervisor, and now it would be counterproductive to waste precious energy ensuring that the coverage is being fulfilled. That is your script supervisor's job. He or she must see that the editor is getting enough coverage and that matching shots really match. Which hand a character used to open the suitcase, how much was eaten from his sandwich when he stood by the window, and which direction he turned as he left for the door—all these things must be consistent with adjacent shots.

In the event of changes or economies, the script supervisor must at all times guard against omissions, and must feel confident that the revised footage will edit together.

CONTINUITY SHEETS

For a feature shoot, the script supervisor produces reports that are often masterpieces of observation. Each setup has its own sheet to record the following:

- Production, personnel, and date
- Slate and take number

- Script scene number
- Camera and lens in use
- Action and dialogue variations
- Successes and flaws for each take
- Which takes are to be printed by the film lab (big-budget films use the camera reports to request selective printing)
- Any special instructions from director or script supervisor to the editor

A script supervisor needs fierce powers of concentration and the ability to do huge amounts of typing in spare moments. After a day of location shooting, when everyone else has gone to sleep, you will hear the script supervisor still at work.

You can replay a digital recording, but not undeveloped film, so the script supervisor's work is vital. Its quality later determines how readily the cutting rooms can locate a given shot in their filing system and how well that shot fits together with its complementaries.

IT'S A WRAP

When the materials for a scene have been shot, and the editor has everything needed, it's time to strike (dismantle) the set. But wait, the sound department must first shoot a presence track. A voice yells, *"Everyone stand still!"* In eerie silence, the unit stands like statues, uncomfortably aware of their own breathing and of the little sounds in the room. "Cut," calls the sound recordist (see "Ambient Sound and Presence Tracks" in Chapter 33). Then: "It's a wrap!" yells the AD. Pandemonium breaks out as everyone starts their winding-up responsibilities:

- Electricians lower all the lights and roll up cables while hot lighting fixtures cool.
- Grips strike the set and collect their clamps, stands, and boxes.
- Props collect all the properties and stow them for safety, marking them off an attendance list.
- Camera people take their equipment apart and stow it in its many travel boxes.
- Stuff accumulates in piles on the floor: all the C-clamps here, all the sandbags there, all the cables in that grubby pile.
- Sound equipment goes into its boxes.
- Makeup cleans off the actors, who change into their street clothes.
- Hairdressers collect wigs, mustaches, and sideburns for overnight repairs and cleaning.
- Wardrobe collects costumes for cleaning and repairs.
- The AD hands out call sheets for the next day, plus some script revision sheets photocopied on different-colored paper. Several people groan at the sight of changes still coming in.
- The director is in close conversation with the actors, thanking them. Then, to the unit, the director calls out: "Thanks for a good day's work, everyone."

- The AD or craft services checks that there is no damage to the location and that everything is left clean and tidy.
- The caterer or gofer (the runner, or "go for this, go for that" person) unexpectedly produces coffee and sandwiches, and a low sigh of relief goes up.

Doors open and close as weary, exhilarated people schlep the equipment out to the transport, munching as they go. The camera assistant is checking the lens and camera gate or carefully labeling cassettes or film cans while the recordist and continuity supervisor are finishing reports. The latter is filling out a daily progress report for the line producer or production manager, who will be anxious to know how many pages of script were covered and, if it's film, how much stock was consumed. Engines start up, and the circus moves on its way. Tomorrow, it will reconvene at the next location.

CHAPTER 33

LOCATION SOUND

Particularly in film school filmmaking, sound recording is the neglected stepsister. Because dialogue replacement is usually too expensive for low-budget films to entertain, their effectiveness depends on getting good original dialogue tracks. This takes thought, preparation, skill, and the will on the director's part to accommodate the needs of the location sound crew. Good handbooks are Tomlinson Holman, *Sound for Film and TV*, 2nd ed. (Book and CD-ROM, Focal Press, 2001); and Lewis Yewdall, *Practical Art of Motion Picture Sound*, 2nd ed. (Focal Press, 2003). For an enthusiastic and engagingly eccentric source for everything concerning sound, see the Equipment Emporium in Los Angeles at www.equipmentemporium.com. Its discussion is a mine of information, and deals with the principles and practice of equipment while keeping up-to-date with everything new. The choice in sound equipment is gargantuan: a few equipment items are shown in this chapter, more for flavor than as recommendations.

A costly assumption is that location sound can be skimped because it can somehow be fixed in the cutting room. Though true to a degree, this is damaging when practiced wholesale, for re-creating dialogue later using *automatic dialogue replacement* (ADR), also known as *looping*, is damaging to your drama and expensive in time and effort. See below for explanations.

In a fine article full of information and examples from a raft of feature films, sound designer Randy Thom contends that most directors give no attention to sound design, and relegate location sound recording to lowest priority (see his article in www.filmsound.org—most informative for all sound information).

Following are some basic guidelines for successful sound coverage.

MONITOR ALL RECORDED SOUND

The most common oversight is to record without monitoring through headphones, trusting that all is well. We've all done it: later, you find crackles, dropouts, or no sound at all. The fact is that all sound must be closely monitored through high-quality headphones that enclose the ears and isolate the user from external sound. No exceptions, ever.

SOUND THEORY

Sound reflectivity in different environments is logical enough to anyone who has ever watched a game of billiards. Of course, there's more to sound theory than how sound bounces off surfaces, but even the small amount of the knowledge that follows will help you choose film sound environments wisely.

Sound perspective is the aural sensation of distance that we get from acoustic changes in a voice as someone moves around. Partly it's due to changes of subject-to-mic distance, and partly it's the changing relationship of the voice to its acoustic environment.

Pyschoacoustics: The most potent aspects of sound for film lie in psychoacoustics, which describe an audience's perception of sound and its emotional connotations. The doyen in this area is the French sound expert Michel Chion, whose *Audio-Vision: Sound on Screen* (New York: Columbia University Press, 1994) explains the ideas he has been developing over several decades. His concepts are far from simple, and require learning a specialized vocabulary.

SOUND EXPERTS SHOULD SCOUT EACH LOCATION

The first thing a sound specialist does in a new location is to clap her hands, once and loudly. She listens intently for what follows the "attack" of the hand clap. Ideally, it is an equally rapid decay. If the room is live (reverberant), there is an appreciable comet's tail of sound being reflected and thrown around the room. This concerns her greatly. The composition of surfaces in a location can make the difference between sound that is usefully "dry" (that is, nonreverberant), and that which is unworkably "live" and reverberant.

A reverberant room is one whose hard, facing surfaces reflect and multiply the original, or source, sounds. Because reverberations have traveled farther, they are fractions of a second behind the original—and thus muddy the clarity of their source, or original, sound. You can reduce sound reflections by laying felt or other soft, sound-absorbent material on hard floors, and hanging blankets in front of any walls out of camera sight. To be effective, blankets must be hung about 6 inches away from the wall, not against it.

A resonant room is one that has a "note," within the range of speech, to which the room resonates. You'll know this phenomenon from singing in your shower, and finding one note (or frequency) at which the room joins in, augmenting your song with a resonance of its own. Resonances are bad news to sound recordists, but their effect can to some extent be tuned out in postproduction. If the room is small, your sound crew may recommend mocking up the desired small space within a larger one, to avoid a boxy acoustic quality.

You can reliably assess a sound location in advance by auditioning dubious sound locations and shooting tests. Record sample dialogue from representative microphone positions, then edit the results together. In no time at all, you have the measure of your problem. The sound crew will be concerned with:

- Reflectivity of ceiling, walls, and floor (drapes and carpet greatly reduce this)
- Whether there are, or can be, soft furniture or irregular surfaces to break up the unwanted movement of sound within the space

- Alignment of surfaces likely to cause standing waves (sound bouncing to and fro, tennis-ball fashion, between opposing surfaces, augmenting and cross-modulating the source sound)
- Whether the room has intrusive resonances (this happens mainly in rooms with a lot of concrete or tile surfaces)
- Whether actors can walk and cameras can be dollied without the floorboards letting out a chorus of tortured squeaks
- Ambient sound, and sound penetrating from the outside

Typical intermittent sound intrusions from the surroundings occur when you are:

- In an airport flight path
- Near an expressway, railroad, or subway
- Near refrigeration, air-conditioning, or other sound-generating equipment that runs intermittently and will cause problems unless you can turn it off while shooting
- Near construction sites. You scouted the location on a weekend, not realizing that come Monday morning, a pile driver and four jackhammers greet the dawn. You have no hope of stopping them
- Near schools. Kids spill out during recess and make an uproar

Dialogue shooting must usually be done with all doors and windows closed. Part of checking a location is to ensure that you can get electric power cables under the doors so they can be completely closed during takes. In the heat of summer, this can be trying.

UNWANTED LOCATION AMBIENCE

Locations spring all sorts of other sound problems. Autumn leaves sound like swishing cornflakes when actors walk and talk. Sound from an expressway that was minimal at two in the afternoon rises to a dull roar by five o'clock, when the rush hour begins. Overhead wires turn into aeolian harps, dogs bark maniacally, garbage trucks mysteriously convene for bottle-crushing competitions, and somebody starts practicing scales on the trumpet. Some of these sonic disasters the astute location spotter can anticipate, some not.

Urban locations spring most of the cruel surprises on the sound recordist, yet it's usually sound that makes a film work dramatically. There is no substitute for experience and a good complement of sound gear to create optional ways of covering the situation.

SOUND EQUIPMENT

As with all equipment, never leave the checkout point without putting all of it together and testing that absolutely everything functions as it should. Make sure you have spare batteries and extra cables, which often break down where the cable enters the plug body. Carry basic repair equipment too: screwdrivers, socket sets, pliers, wire, solder and soldering iron, and a test meter for continuity and other testing. Expect to need a full complement of directional and ultradirectional

FIGURE 33-1 ⎯⎯⎯⎯⎯⎯⎯⎯⎯⎯⎯⎯⎯⎯⎯⎯⎯⎯⎯⎯⎯⎯⎯⎯

The Nagra DII four-track digital recorder. Tough and reliable, Nagra has long been the industry standard (photo courtesy of Nagra).

microphones, lavalieres (clip-on body mics), radio mics (for free movement), a mixing desk, and many cables.

RECORDERS

For reliability and highest-quality recording in either analog or digital format, the Nagra range of recorders is unparalleled (see Figure 33-1 or www.nagraaudio.com). On lower-budget productions, a digital audiotape (DAT) recorder with timecode—such as the HD-P2, made by Tascam—is often used (see Figure 33-2 or www.tascam.com). Robert Altman's pioneering sound recordist built a location sound recorder capable of simultaneously recording 16 radio microphones to eliminate the rigmarole of following individuals with mics while shooting. Today, you can do the same thing with multitrack DAT machines, some of which offer up 8 or more tracks. This means you can record up to 8 monophonic microphones, or 4 stereo, and worry about creating a usable master track later.

A recent trend is to record into a portable hard drive. Zaxcom Deva recorders combine ten-track location mixers and recorders that pack many track hours of uncompressed recording into a tough and hermetically sealed hard drive (Figure 33-3 or www.zaxcom.com). Their ten-second sound buffer is useful for spontaneous shooting or the odd missed cue because you always know on start-up that the previous ten seconds come with the recording. The Deva creates DVD backup copies, downloads rapidly in the cutting room, and can even be plugged directly into the

FIGURE 33-2

Tascam HD-P2, a stereo recorder that writes to flash memory (photo courtesy of Tascam).

FIGURE 33-3

Sennheiser ME 66 deluxe shotgun (photo courtesy of Sennheiser).

computer. With no accessible moving parts, the machine is sealed and immune from grit and dust, as well as from extremes of temperature and humidity.

MICROPHONES

Film recording is done with a variety of microphones made by Audio-Technica, Sennheiser, Schoeps, and many others (Figure 33-3). It's useful to know what each mic reception pattern can and cannot do. Contrary to legend, there is no such thing as a zoom microphone, and no way to cheat a microphone's characteristics to make it sound close when it is distant. A close recording can, however, be made to sound distant. This is done in postproduction by adjusting the recording level and subtracting some of the lower frequencies, which fall off more quickly over a distance.

An omnidirectional mic produces the most natural voice recording, but can seldom be used because it picks up so much additional sound from off axis, such as reverberant or ambient sound.

A **cardioid,** or **directional, mic** gets its name from its heart-shaped pickup pattern. Cardioids discriminate against off-axis sound (that is, sound coming from the sides or behind). By suppressing sound from unwanted directions, their signal-to-noise ratio is enhanced. This means that ambient and reflected sound are a little lower in relation to the desired source.

The **hypercardioid,** or **gun, mic** (because of its shape and appearance) does the best job of discriminating against off-axis sound, but at some cost to naturalness of reproduction.

The **lavaliere,** or **body, mic** is an omnidirectional microphone clipped on the actor at chest level and connected to a small personal radio transmitter. These produce a good and constant voice level with a low ratio of ambient sound. They do, however, have some quirks:

- Unless you obtain top-rate wireless systems, radio transmission sometimes fails or unexpectedly pulls in taxi and police messages.

- They pick up digestive sounds and clothing rustles. Clothing made of man-made fibers generates static electricity, which sounds like thunder on a small scale.

- Lavalieres lack sound perspective. By remaining at a constant distance from the speaker and picking up so little reverberant coloration, a lavaliere removes all sense of the speaker's movement or perspective changes. These must be emulated later in the mix. Live now, pay later. Other microphones have various advantages and disadvantages, but basically there is no substitute for a quiet background and a good mic close to each speaker.

BOOM

An overhead microphone boom is a large and specialized piece of mic support equipment that needs plenty of space to operate. Low-budget productions generally use a *hand boom*, or *fishpole*, which has the added advantage of being able to place the mic out of sight below the frame instead of above it.

LOCATION MIXER

Camcorders or location recorders may have no more than two microphone inputs. When several must be combined and balanced, you will need a mixer. The ENG-44 is a modest and serviceable battery-powered portable mixer (see Figure 33-4 and www.signvideo.com/fpamxr.htm). Mackie makes mixers that are much favored by music and film productions (see Figure 33-5 or www.mackie.com). Monitor all sound by using professional, ear-enclosing headphones that isolate you from the surrounding world.

RECORDING REQUIREMENTS

DIRECT AND REFLECTED SOUND

In dialogue sequences, the sound crew aims to get clean sound that is "on mic." This means dialogue spoken near a microphone and into its most receptive axis. They want sound relatively uncolored by reverberant sound reflected off walls,

FIGURE 33-4 ——

Basic ENG-44 battery-powered four-input, two-channel output location mixer (photo courtesy of Sign Video Ltd).

FIGURE 33-5 ——

Mackie 1402-VLZ3 mixer for ten microphone/line inputs and two-channel output (photo courtesy of Mackie).

ceiling, floor, or other hard surfaces such as tables and other furniture. Reflected sound, bouncing off surrounding surfaces before finding its way to the microphone, travels by a longer route and arrives fractionally after its direct, source sound. It can appreciably muddy the clarity of the original, but you probably won't realize this until you edit together different mic positions. These are the mic position changes necessary to any well-covered dialogue sequence. In a reverberant location, each microphone position may have very different acoustic characteristics. This is determined by the different admixtures of reflected sound and differing distances from the speakers. Just when dialogue should sound seamless, editing together different mic positions makes the seams glaringly evident.

AMBIENT SOUND AND PRESENCE TRACKS

Ambient sound is sound inherent to the location, whether interior or exterior. A playground may have a distant traffic accompaniment coming from one particular direction. A riverside location may have the hum of a power station a quarter mile off. Every room you record in will have its own ambient sound that is noticeable only during silences. It may be a faint buzz from fluorescent fixtures, the hum of voices from an adjacent office, or birdsong and trees rustling from outside.

Presence tracks: Before calling for a wrap at any location, interior or exterior, the sound department always records an *atmosphere track* (also known as *room tone*, *presence track*, or *buzz track*). The procedure is simple: on the heels of the last scene, nobody leaves the set or changes anything, and actors and crew freeze. For a couple of minutes, the sound crew makes a recording of the particular quality of silence in the location. This becomes the all-important sound filler for gaps in dialogue tracks. The two minutes can be duplicated to create as much track as needed.

SHADOWS AND MULTIPLE MICS

Getting microphones close enough to actors without causing visible shadows takes cooperation between sound and camera specialists and the director. Quite often this requires placing more than one mic and feeding their inputs into a mixer. Location sound must be recorded carefully because every mic left open records its own share of ambient, source, and reflected sound—and these joined together can produce a chaotic set of problems. If you can, record each microphone input into a different sound channel (by using a multichannel recorder) to keep their contributions discrete. Later, you can audition the various mic contributions and make a mix-down of the best coverage. If mixing must be done on the spot, the sound mixer really must know what he or she is doing, for once mixed, the omelet cannot be unscrambled. Verify your first results before proceeding.

SOURCE-TO-MICROPHONE DISTANCES

Keeping microphones close enough to do a good job of recording actors on the move is a rare skill. The boom operator's main task is to at all times stay just out of frame—but also near the axis of each speaker. Failure to do so means that sound levels plummet as the mic-to-subject distance increases. Ambient sound levels, however, remain constant. Thus, the ratio of source to ambient sound can vary a lot. Raising playback level afterward can bring up the source level to make the speaker's voice consistent from angle to angle, but then you get large changes in ambience levels.

Shooting procedures are optimized for photography: sound recording must fit around the needs of the camera while keeping its microphones out of sight. You can help the sound department by stabilizing speakers during a dialogue sequence, or by getting creative with set dressing so that a nice potted plant on a dining room table conceals a strategically placed microphone.

SOUNDS ON THE SET

Actors should be costumed in soft-soled shoes, and floors should be carpeted, to avoid Frankenstein footsteps. The crew must stay stationary and silent during takes, and the camera cannot make any mechanical noise. Most film-camera sound comes from the hollow metal magazines; these are muffled with a soft, soundproof casing called a *barney*. If the problem persists, vibration is probably passing through tripod legs to become amplified by a resonant floor. To fix this, place carpet under the camera support.

Fluorescents like to buzz, filament lamps hum, and pets come to life at inopportune moments. Sound cables, placed in parallel with power cables, may produce electrical interference through induction. Long mike cables sometimes pull in cheery DJs via radio frequency (RF) interference. A large motor or elevator equipment nearby can generate alternating current (AC) magnetic fields, and the most mysterious hum sometimes proves to come from something on the floor above or below.

SOUND EFFECTS AND WILD TRACKS

A **sound effects** (SFX) **track,** or **atmosphere,** is a nonsynchronous recording of sounds that might be useful to augment the sequence's sound track later. The recordist might get a separate track of that barking dog, as well as other sounds to help create a soundscape. In a woodland location, this might mean getting up early to catch birdcalls, river sounds of water gurgling, ducks dabbling, and wind rustling in reeds. A woodpecker echoing through the trees is probably best found in a wildlife library, because these birds are hard to get close to. Initiative and imagination are important in the sound recordist, plus a high level of tolerance for frustration.

A **wild track** (WT) is any track that is shot independent of picture. When an actor flubs a line or when some extraneous sound punctuates dialogue, the alert sound recordist asks for a wild voice-only recording immediately after the director calls "Cut." The actor then repeats the lost line as he or she just spoke it during the take. By recording in exactly the same acoustic situation, the words can be seamlessly edited in, and a new take avoided.

ATMOSPHERE LOOPS

Often a short original atmosphere is made long by repeating or looping it in audio editing. This can be perfectly acceptable unless recognizably individual sounds return at set intervals. A bus station with the same sneeze or cackling laugh every six seconds is a very strange place indeed. When recording atmospheres, the recordist listens intently to make sure an appreciable amount, clear of such noises, has been recorded so that an effective loop can be made later. By the way, atmospheres in sound libraries often prove to be loops replete with giveaway sounds.

SOUNDSCAPES

The BBC is a great resource for ideas on sound, and they publish an excellent sound library on CDs. For starters, try "Noisy Planet" at www.bbc.co.uk/worldservice/specials/1643_noisyplanet/page2.shtml.

AUTOMATIC DIALOGUE REPLACEMENT

Automatic dialogue replacement (ADR) in postproduction, sometimes called *looping*, is expensive and time-consuming, and tends to kill dramatic potential. Actors must lip-sync their lines to short loops of picture. They loathe doing it, because they can never regain the emotional truth of a scene while recording one line at a time in a sound studio. ADR is misnamed: it is neither automatic nor any real replacement.

CHAPTER 34

CONTINUITY

During shooting, the script (or continuity) supervisor works hardest and longest of anyone. It is many years since I worked with one, so I am indebted for this chapter to the gold mine of procedures and methods in Pat P. Miller's *Script Supervising and Film Continuity*, 3rd ed. (Focal Press, 1998).

COORDINATING AND REPORTING

The script supervisor works closely with the director and editor, and plays a key role in guarding against omissions or mismatches in the production. Going to the "goofs" section of the Internet Movie Database (www.imdb.com/title/tt0371257/goofs) reveals most reassuringly how nobody's perfect. If you lack a continuity supervisor on your project, try using the editor. They have more reason than most to get things right.

Continuity work begins as soon as a finished script exists, but comes into its own during shooting. The script supervisor monitors the continuity of costumes, properties, and characters' words and behavior—something that otherwise falls haphazardly to director, actors, and crew. The professional continuity supervisor's note taking culminates in one or more sheets per camera setup. These records provide guidance during the shoot and are used intensively by the editor.

SCRIPT BREAKDOWN

A close reading of the script yields a list of locations and of people in the first breakdown. Very important are their names, characteristics, physical attributes, overt action (as opposed to action offscreen or implied in the past), and their entries and exits.

CHRONOLOGY

Next, the script supervisor makes a chronology for the story that, at the very least, will have time lapses. If the story is told out of order, or has flashbacks or flash-forwards, this may have profound consequences for the age or condition of the characters, and thus for their makeup and costuming. Continuity must at all times know where the story is, spatially and temporally, as well as what has befallen the characters before we see them and where they go afterward. The chronology is key to keeping track of all this, and will be measured off in minutes, hours, days, or years—whatever the story calls for. If the story is set in four days, the main unit will be Day One, Day Two, Day Three, and Day Four, and each scene will be specified by time within the day. Other key temporal and spatial aspects are day or night, and interior or exterior.

PLANNING THE SHOOT

As coordinator for many important details, the script supervisor gets specifics from wardrobe, props, and makeup, and makes sure the production manager has the right details for each scene. The production office will issue the daily *call sheet*. This list of personnel is handed to everyone who is being called in for the next day's work. The call sheet specifies scenes, actors, costuming, properties, equipment, transport to locations, and any other special provisions.

TYPES OF CONTINUITY

Continuity implies the simple match of details from one scene to the next, but if a chronologically late scene precedes an earlier one, continuity must be back-matched to preserve the logic of compatibility. There is also direct and indirect continuity:

Direct continuity is when one shot or one scene follows another. A character cannot change jackets while stepping from one room to another, for instance.

Indirect continuity is that between scenes separated by time or other scenes. If a man goes carousing and we next see him many hours later, this is indirect continuity. Although he is in the same clothes, they are now rumpled and stained, and his face shadowed with stubble. During parallel storytelling, we might intercut two stories, so indirect continuity must hold good in all the A segments and all the B segments.

The script supervisor's job is to watch for everything that an alert audience will ever notice. Sometimes this takes research—otherwise someone will write in to point out that Slender Willow cigarettes were not produced in China until five years after the period of the film. Further, the Greater Crested Jub-Jub *never* makes its mating call in September.

WARDROBE AND PROPERTIES OVERSIGHT

The script supervisor must know wardrobe details from scene to scene, and keep a hawk eye on costumes, hair, makeup, and properties. There are three classes of property:

Hand props, such as a comb or diary, which the characters handle.

Stage props, such as a lava lamp or princess bed, which are part of an environment and may be related to one of the characters.

Breakaway props, such as a pottery figure or a foam cup, which get broken or used up in some way (and for which replacements must be on hand for subsequent takes).

The continuity supervisor must know which buttons must be done up in which suit, and whether the Cuisinart Mini-Prep food processor has its lid on or off. A cake with two slices taken in one scene cannot appear later with only one piece gone.

CONTINUITY BREAKDOWN

The script supervisor must read, analyze, break down, and reread the script until its every need is committed to memory. He or she makes a breakdown of the type shown in Figure 22-1 (see Chapter 22) to lay out the scenes in order, each with their:

- Location
- Time of day
- Chronological data
- Characters
- Pages in script
- Length

TIMING

How long each scene should last is predicted by a page count. One normal page lasts one minute of screen time. Scene length is specified to the nearest eighth of a page. Naturally, a scene description saying only "A montage of shots in Montana showing the transition from fall through winter and spring" must be interpreted differently.

During shooting, the script supervisor uses a stopwatch to time every take of every shot in every scene. Master scenes yield the first overall timing. Keeping track of script pages shot per day and of screen time completed lets the unit know its progress. The producer thus gets a warning if the film is lagging its schedule or exceeding its length.

MONITORING DIALOGUE

From take to take, the script supervisor logs all the words that the actors use. The supervisor records any variations that will create problems in editing. Plot information is often embedded in dialogue, so it would be disastrous to settle for a take in which the detective gave the suspect's name wrongly. The script supervisor may note the relative pacing, subtext, and feeling from take to take.

PHYSICAL CONTINUITY

If a character picks up a glass of wine with her right hand in the master shot, but her left in closer shots, the editor has a problem. Similarly, if a character rises during a line in a medium shot, but after the line in the long shot, there will be another problem—and much wailing and gnashing of teeth in the cutting room.

Continuity's job is to alert everyone to continuity lapses and to inconsistencies in camera movements or timing, and to know what options exist as alternatives. This means being very prepared and very observant, all the time. Taking digital snaps of characters or sets before and after each take helps keep tabs on what people wore, how they wore it, and how their hair looked. Shooting on video makes this less necessary, but it's amazing how sure an actor can be that his jacket was unbuttoned—until video footage proves otherwise.

COVERAGE

From discussions with the director, the script supervisor knows how a scene should be covered—then, after shooting, how it was actually covered and can be edited. Script supervisors thus need to know editing and dramaturgic structure because both can be in flux during shooting.

BRACKETING THE SCRIPT

Bracketing the master script lightly in pencil (see Chapter 30, Figure 30-1) shows how the scene will be broken down into shots, and heavier penciling can then record the actuality. Color codings for particular characters, or for their entries and exits, may be helpful, but like any system, must be used consistently for it to work.

SCRIPT SUPERVISOR'S POSITIONING

Normally, the script supervisor sits beside the camera in order to see what it sees, but he or she might sometimes watch a video feed. Often the monitor's acuity won't be good enough, or, if it's an exterior scene, the screen will be washed out by daylight. Events also start to happen off camera before they appear in frame, so the wider awareness of sitting next to the camera is preferable.

CHAPTER 35

DIRECTING THE ACTORS

The director must be aware of many people's work simultaneously. A supportive, enthusiastic cast and crew will endure and triumph together, but under the best of conditions, work will be stressful. It's a period of high concentration as everyone tries to do their best work. For you, it is a time of unremitting pursuit of perfection shot through with occasional euphoria or despair.

DAILY ORGANIZATION

The first step toward a happy shoot is that everyone be well prepared. A smoothly running organization signals professionalism to cast and crew. This is particularly vital if low-paid (or unpaid) people are to maintain confidence in your leadership. Your unit keeps the following updated:

- Printed call sheets for cast and crew well in advance
- A map of how to get to the location
- A contact list with everyone's (cell) phone numbers in case of emergency
- Floor plans for camera crew
- A preestablished lighting design
- Tricky camera setups rehearsed in advance
- Correct props and costumes ready to go
- Scene coverage thoroughly worked out with the director of photography (DP) and script supervisor

Your assistant director (AD) should carry lists of everything so that you carry nothing in your head and nothing gets forgotten.

YOUR ROLE

To direct a film means starting out with a detailed movie in your head. You break it into its components, and then manipulate cast and crew into creating each part as you want it. Along the way, obstacles and opportunities intrude on the process, so the movie inside your mind must constantly evolve and adjust. Crew and cast know this, and when they turn to you expectantly after a shot, they are asking, "Did you get what you wanted?" One way or another, you have to be able to answer. And not only answer, but lead.

ACTORS' ANXIETIES AT THE BEGINNING

WARN ACTORS THAT SHOOTING IS SLOW

Warn actors unused to making movies that filming is invariably s-l-o-w. Even a professional feature unit may shoot only one to four minutes of screen time per eight-hour day. Tell them to bring books, playing cards, or crossword puzzles— anything to help them fill the inevitable periods of waiting.

BEFORE SHOOTING

Actors suffer maximum jitters and minimum confidence just prior to first shooting. Take each aside and tell him or her something special and private. It should be sincere and supportive. Thereafter, that actor has a special understanding to maintain with you. Its substance and development will reach out by way of the film to the audience, for whom you are currently the surrogate.

TENSION AND ITS CONSEQUENCES

Whatever level of performance was achieved in rehearsal now comes to the test. Actors feel they are going over Niagara Falls in a barrel, so wise scheduling puts the least demanding material early as a warm-up. In the first day or two, there will be a lot of tension, either frankly admitted or displaced into one of the many behaviors that mask it. Try not to be wounded or angered; if someone is deeply afraid of failing a task, it is forgiveably human to pick quarrels or demote the work's importance. It does not mean, as many film technicians secretly believe, that actors are a childish breed. They are normal, often shy, people who sometimes succumb to agonies of self-doubt. Why filming takes so long is incomprehensible to the uninitiated, and the crew members, enviably busy with their gadgets, seem removed and uncaring. Your appreciation and public recognition given for even small achievements—and your crew's astute diplomacy—will work wonders for morale.

HITTING STRIDE

Anxieties subside as the process establishes its rhythms. As the cast falls in with the pace and demand of shooting, each player begins to take pride at being one of a team. Performances improve so much that you wonder about the usability of the earlier material.

DIRECTING

While the actors are publicly working their way through a labyrinth of strong feelings, the director is meanwhile suffering privately in stoic silence. The cast

FIGURE 35-1

A student unit at work. The director must oversee many interlocking operations and never lose track of the actors' needs (photo by Nancy Platt).

members endow you with their trust, so in return you become the all-caring, supportive, and quietly confident parent figure. Inside, you may be racked with uncertainty about whether you have the authority for the job. How can you, when you feel like a fraud? So you play the role of being confident—a role the whole unit wants to believe. You can help yourself by limiting the area you oversee, by being better prepared than anyone else, and by keeping everyone busy.

Your major responsibility is always to the cast; the actors' respect rests on how accurately and briefly you can reflect what each just did, and where in detail each should go next (Figure 35-1). You are the conductor directing your instrumentalists. That is your central function, so divest yourself of anything else impeding it.

Cast and crew may test your patience and judgment. Leaders usually have their powers challenged, yet behind what seems like a sparring and antagonistic attitude may lurk a growing respect and affection. The unaccustomed parental role—supporting, questioning, challenging—may leave you feeling thoroughly alone and unappreciated. You are Authority, and creative people often maintain their most active and ambivalent relationships with authority figures.

For each member of your cast, "my director" and the other actors are temporarily the most important people in his or her life—allies with whom to play out complex and personal issues that involve love, hate, and everything between. This is a legitimate path of exploration for an actor or any other artist, and you are the arbitrator. Finding a productive working relationship with the subtle personalities of your actors is really discovering how best to harness your temperament and theirs as you create something bigger than all of you together.

With crew and cast, try to separate the roles of friend and director. A friend may be forgiving and understanding, and not hold anyone's feet to the fire. But a director must uphold the purpose of the project, not least because it involves so many people's work and so much money. Standing at the crossroads, you do what it takes to keep everyone intent on the common enterprise. There is no set way to handle this except to demand that everyone concentrate on their own area of responsibility and remain loyal to the project. Your dedication is a model of leadership here. Professionals understand this—the rest do not. Human relationships under stress are always different and evolving, but if you must choose, aim to be respected rather than liked. Later, after things have turned out well, admiration and liking will come.

DIVIDING YOURSELF BETWEEN CREW AND CAST

A student director is often using an untried crew and wants to personally monitor everything the crew does. Desist. You won't be adequate for your cast unless you let the DP and AD lead the crew. Know what you need from your cast, and work unceasingly to get it. This will take all your attention, and then some.

RUN-THROUGH

Run through the shot's action for the camera crew, who must resolve many framing and lighting problems. (For the process as seen by the crew, see "First Setup and Lineup" in Chapter 31, as well as the following text.) The DP may borrow crew members as stand-ins for lighting and movement checks so that, by the time the unit is ready to shoot, cast members aren't unnecessarily fatigued.

BEFORE THE TAKE

As the crew finalizes the setup, take your cast aside and cue each actor on his character's recent past and emotional state as he enters this scene. This is both information and motivation, and needs repeating before every setup—and sometimes before every take. The prior scene may not yet have been shot, so you alone know its emotional content. You alone can judge whether today's scene will graft naturally onto tomorrow's.

Your AD will quietly tell you when the setup is ready so actors can start with the minimum of waiting. Actors now take their positions. The DP makes a last check that all lights are on and everything is ready. Then you call the magic word, "Action." It can be said 50 different ways—urgent, thoughtful, gentle, questioning, challenging, abrasive, singsong, or fearful. "Action!" can be a cue all by itself.

AFTER THE TAKE

Immediately after calling "Cut!":

- Say whether that was a "print" (acceptable take), or whether you are going for another take. This cues the actors whether their work is on target. Good work is best rewarded by moving forward, not by an approving postmortem, which would squander time and momentum.

- If going for another take, briefly give the actors any new, actable goals you want them to go for.
- Shoot before the collective intensity dissipates. Momentum is everything, so avoid unnecessary discussion.

Sometimes a technical flaw in sound or in camera coverage requires another take, but usually you want better or different performances. This may require something different from each actor in a group scene. From one, you want the same good level of performance; from another, a different emotional shading or energy level. Each actor must know what you expect. Avoid asking anyone for the same thing again. Asking for the same thing is baffling because the actor is inside his instrument and doesn't know what you saw that you liked in the previous take. Part of him thinks, "If she liked what I did, why do I have to do it again?" He may understand that you want him to reproduce an effect. So give even the satisfactory players objectives that will keep them building rather than trying to repeat a result.

Actors sometimes feel they can do better, and so they will ask for another take. You must decide whether or not that's necessary. Your competency is under pressure, because either the actor noticed something you missed, or he is blowing something out of proportion. Which is it? The cast should always be allowed to improve, but asking for just one more take can become an anxiety fetish or a manipulation of directorial decisions. If you were paying full attention and saw nothing wrong, you may have to simply say that the last take was fine and that the unit must move on. Actors' insecurity has a thousand faces.

DEMANDS AND FEEDBACK

The director's enemy is a passive and gullible tendency to accept what actors give as the best they can do. As an audience of one, you at first feel a lot of guilt and uncertainty. All these people doing all this . . . for little old me! You want to please them, to thank them, to be loved by them. And you can't even react while they perform, to tell them how grateful you feel. You echo their need for approval with your need to be liked. . . . It's an uncomfortable, squirming kind of experience.

Try to adopt the confident artist's creative dissatisfaction. Treat each scene as a seeming beneath which hide layers of significance that only greater skill and aspiration can lay bare.

Never grade your players with "good" or "bad." Concentrate instead on telling them in a few words what they communicated. This will vary from take to take. Say what you would like in the next shot, and give separate, additional input to individual players. Sometimes you can privately seek confirmation of your impressions from the continuity supervisor, who also monitors performance shadings. But you must place trust in your own instincts, which means clearing the mental and emotional space for your instincts to operate.

Pushing for depth means expecting at the right times to be moved by the actors, and sometimes it happens strongly When your cast members deliver real intensity, you will feel it—no question. You and they are creating as you go, not simply placing a rehearsal on record. Watch out when you feel tempted to *make* yourself feel what you should feel naturally. This comes from guilt: the cast is trying so hard, and you are the hard-to-please pasha. Somehow you must resist this, or you will not be able to react as you should—like an unattached audience member. If the performance works, it works; if it doesn't, it doesn't. Accept it and ask yourself why. Is it fatigue? Repetition? Tell your cast what you felt. Often one actor knows something that can help you sort out what went wrong. Try refreshing the cast objectives or taking a coffee break. Now try anew.

To put tension back into a scene that is sagging into comfortable middle age, see if the cast has stopped listening to each other. Remind your players to listen, or take each aside and privately suggest some small but significant change that will impact other cast members. By building in little stresses and incompatibilities, by making sure cast members are working off each other, you can restore tension when it has languished.

SIDE COACHING WHEN A SCENE IS BECALMED

When a scene goes static and sinks to a premeditated appearance, try side coaching to inject tension. This won't work if your actors are caught by surprise. If they are unfamiliar with side coaching, warn them not to break character should you use it.

To side coach means that you interpolate at a quiet moment in the scene a verbal suggestion or instruction, such as, "Terry, she's asking the impossible—she's laying a trap." Your voice injects a new interior process in the character addressed, and the scene moves off in a new direction.

REACTION SHOTS

Side coaching is most useful when directing simple reaction shots. The director provides a verbal image for the character to spontaneously see or react to, or an idea to consider, and gets an immediacy of reaction.

Usually the best reactions are to something actual. If a character must go through a complex series of emotions while overhearing a whispered conversation, make the other characters do a full version of their scene even though they are off camera. If, however, your character must only look through a window and react to an approaching visitor, her imagination should provide all that is necessary.

Reaction shots are enormously important, because they lead the audience to infer (that is, create) a character's private, inner life. They also provide the vital, legitimate cutaways that allow you to combine the best takes during editing. Never dismiss cast and crew from a set without covering all likely reactions, cutaways, and inserts for each scene.

FOR THE NEW SHOT

As soon as you have an acceptable take, brief the DP about the next shot, then turn to the cast. Give any brief, positive feedback necessary about the last shot and provide preparation for the next. The AD may decide to take the actors aside to rest them if the crew is roaring into action changing the camera, set, lights, everything. Previously, the cast had control—now they slip into obscurity as the crew sets up a new shot. Actors feel their relative insignificance compared with that of the medium and all its technology.

CHALLENGING YOUR CAST

You and your cast are working in a highly allusive medium, so your audience expects metaphorical and metaphysical overtones. To draw us beyond externals and surface banality, and to make us see poetry and conflict beneath the surface, you must challenge your actors in a hundred interesting ways. Your demands should reinforce their own sense of always being capable of something just a little better. This dissatisfaction is as it should be, but you may get back an undertow of complaining. Emphasize the positive, and regard the grumbling as the noise of the rigging in a ship pushed to capacity. Or think of dancers, who so often are in the bodily pain that comes from pushing themselves to make dance look effortless and wonderful. Your cast is in pain, too, so take it for what it is, and don't imagine you can always make everyone feel good.

EVERYONE NEEDS FEEDBACK

Actors learn from their schooling and theater work to depend on audience feedback. Now, during filming, you are their only audience—and anyway cannot signify approval, amusement, or anything else during a take. When the camera stops, your job is to briefly make each actor feel the sense of closure he used to acquire from a live audience.

Actors are not fooled by empty gestures. Your brain has been running out of control trying to factor in all the editing possibilities that might make the last performance usable, and now you must say something intelligent to your trusting players, each of whom is (and must be) self-absorbed and self-aware. You manage to say something approving, and the cast nods intently.

Now your crew needs you, and the actors are asking, "What are we doing next?" The production manager is at your elbow demanding confirmation for the shooting at the warehouse next week. The warehouse people are on the phone, and they sound testy. So there you have it: you wanted to direct, but the true glamour of directing is walking around faint from lack of sleep, feeling that your head is about to explode.

SENSORY OVERLOAD

The director's occupational hazard is sensory overload. In a typical take, while you watch the actors keenly, you will also hear a lamp filament humming and a plane flying nearby. Can the sound recordist hear them? Cocooned inside her headphones, she returns your questioning look with a silently mouthed, "Huh?" Next, you see a doubtful camera movement, and wonder if the operator's brow will wrinkle ominously. Your heroine turned the wrong way when leaving the table, and your mind races to figure out whether you have a cutaway so you can cut to the longer shot. Now, to further boggle your mind, the camera assistant holds up two fingers, signifying only two minutes of film left. At the end of the take, your cast looks at you expectantly. How was it? Of course you hardly know. If you are working on tape or have a video assist, you could replay the actors' work, but that would cast doubt on your competency and double the shooting schedule.

The only way to do well is to be ruthless with how you use your energy. A competent crew will catch all the sound, camera, and action problems, and report anything you need to rectify. If you have a union crew, from a system that produces highly experienced and reliable workers, you can delegate without fear. But if you draw from a casual labor system, you are often using freelancers with little experience. A film school produces some quite brilliant people, but their lack of practice results in a high number of mistakes and omissions. No way around it: you get what you pay for, and when you can't pay, you have to work twice as hard.

DELEGATE

The solution lies in setting priorities and delegating as much as possible of the actual shooting to the DP, who directs the crew. Your AD and UPM (unit production manager) must take most of the logistical work off your shoulders.

CRITICISM AND FEEDBACK

Be prepared for personality problems and other friction during shooting. Any preferences or criticisms expressed by actors during rehearsal may surface more vehemently under duress. There will be favorite scenes—and scenes the actors hate. There will be scenes that involve portraying negative characteristics. There will even be certain lines upon which an actor becomes irrationally fixated. In serious cases, a palliative is to allow a take using the actor's alternative wording. Don't offer this until all other remedies have been exhausted—and do it as a one-time-only concession, or your cast may all want to start writing alternatives.

As knowledge of each other's limitations grows, actors can become critical or even hostile to each other. Occasionally two actors who are supposed to be lovers take a visceral aversion to each other. Here, only loyalty to the project and commitment to their profession can avert disaster.

Filming makes intense demands on people, and a director must be ready to cope with everything human. You will learn hugely about the human psyche under duress, and this will make you a better director—and maybe even a better human being. If this sounds scary, take heart. The chances are good that you and your cast will like each other and that none of these horror stories will happen to you—yet.

FROM THE CAST

The cast members may have criticisms or suggestions concerning the script or the crew—or you, their director. If a criticism or suggestion is justified and constructive, acknowledge it warmly and act upon it diplomatically and without guilt. If you are a wise director, you will try to stimulate and utilize the creativity of all the major figures in the team, aware that organic development and change are inevitable and will always threaten someone's security, especially your own.

Always be ready to take things in, think about them, and delay making changes until you are sure. When critical suggestions are incompatible with the body of work already accumulated, say so as objectively as you can. Remaining open-minded does not mean swinging like a weather vane. You can best deflect impractical suggestions by being so well prepared and so full of interesting demands that everyone is too busy to become critical. This shouldn't deter genuinely thoughtful and constructive ideas.

FROM THE CREW

Student crew members are sometimes unwise enough to let those in earshot know how much better they could direct than the director. This is intolerable and must be immediately squelched. Nothing diminishes your authority faster than actors feeling they are being directed by a committee. Directing a film effectively is not, has not been, and never will be democratic. Improvised drama is the closest you can get.

Guard against anarchy by making sure all territories are clearly demarcated before shooting starts. Anyone who strays must be told, privately and very firmly, to tend his own area and no one else's. A crew member with a legitimate complaint should address it to the DP. It may not even require your attention.

There will be occasions when you have to make a necessary but unpopular decision. Make it, bite the bullet, and do not apologize. Like much else, it is a test of your resolve, and the unpopular decision will probably be the one everyone knows is right.

MORALE, FATIGUE, AND INTENSITY

Morale in both crew and cast tends to be interlocked. Giving appropriate credit and attention to each member of the team is the best way to maintain loyalty to the project and to each other. Everyone works for recognition, and good leadership trickles down. Even so, immature personalities will come unraveled as fatigue sets in or when territory is threatened. Overworking the crew is a key factor here. Under severe fatigue, people lose their cool, and work becomes sloppy.

Keep morale up by taking special care of creature comforts. Your production department must keep people warm, dry, and ensure that they have food and drink, bathrooms to go to, and somewhere to sit between takes. Avoid working longer than four hours without a break, even if it's only a ten-minute coffee break. From these primal attentions, cast and crew infer that "the production" cares about them. Most will go to the ends of the earth for you when they feel valued.

PROTECT THE CAST

Actors find the spectacle of dissent among the crew very disturbing, so warn the crew to keep disagreements completely out of public view. Anything that can disturb the actors should be kept from them. They are vulnerable to emotional currents, and their attention must remain with their work.

YOU AS ROLE MODEL

You are the director, and your seriousness and intensity set the tone for the whole shoot. If you are sloppy and laid back, others will outdo you. If you demand much of yourself and others, but are appreciative and encourage appropriate humor, you will run a tight ship. Convert every negative criticism into a positive request for an alternative. Your vision and how you share it will evoke respect in the entire team. People will follow an organized visionary anywhere.

USING SOCIAL TIMES AND BREAKS

During the shooting period, spend time (outside the actual shooting) with your cast. However exhausted you become, it is a mistake to retreat from the neuroses of your actors to the understanding camaraderie of the crew. Try to keep cast and crew together during meals or at rest periods. Frequently, while lunching or downing a beer after work, you will learn something that significantly complements or changes your ideas. Under good conditions, the process of filmmaking shakes out many new ideas and perceptions during downtime. This generates a shared sense of discovery that binds crew and participants together in an intoxicating feeling of adventure. Conserved and encouraged, this sense of excitement can so awaken everyone's awareness that a profound fellowship and communication develop. Work becomes a joy.

AT DAY'S END

Thank everyone individually at the end of each day for their good work. Respectful appreciation affirms that you take nobody for granted. By implication, you demand that respect in return. Under these conditions, people will gladly cede you the authority to do your job.

DON'T SHOW DAILIES TO THE CAST

Actors want to work with a director of vision whose methods they trust. Their greatest pleasure comes from working with one who gets more from them than they had realized possible. This cannot happen if you let actors see their dailies (see "When Not to Show Actors Their Work" in Chapter 25). Actors are like the rest of us, and hate what they see of themselves on the screen. By trying to cure perceived faults, each begins to self-direct instead of listen to you. Your perfectly good footage becomes part of their struggle with their demons.

SHARE DAILIES WITH THE CREW

The crew must, however, see each day's work. It's an important evolutionary process for everyone. If the cast finds this discriminatory, promise your actors a viewing of the first cut to assuage their natural curiosity. By then, they will have already given their performances, and thus cannot compromise what they do.

CHAPTER 36

DIRECTING THE CREW

Look in a film school's movie credits for any particular period, and you will keep finding the same few names in different capacities. These are the people who so loved filmmaking that they would direct one month and be a friend's writer, gaffer, or production manager the next. This is the kind of person you aim to become, and the kind you want in your crew.

LIMIT YOUR RESPONSIBILITIES

As we have said, beginning directors want to oversee the whole crew's work. Too often neglected is the human presence on the screen, the only aspect the audience really notices. A check of composition, as we shall see, is absolutely necessary, but the director must be willing to give technicians and production personnel control of their areas. For their part, those people must be fully aware at all times, and take the appropriate initiative without waiting for explicit instructions.

INITIATIVE

Finding crew members who take initiative yet work as a team is not easy. Some are too passive to act without instructions. Some in a student shoot, regimented by family and schooling, can produce only from within a punitive, monitoring structure, and cannot act when something in their area needs doing. Others seize initiative so they can exert control for its own sake. Status issues absorb too much of their energy, meaning that they cannot contribute properly in the give-and-take of film teamwork.

COMMUNICATING

Before shooting begins, each crew member should have read and questioned the script and contributed ideas in his or her own area of specialty. A director should, in turn, understand the rudiments of each technician's craft and be able to communicate in the craft's special terms. That's why this book contains so much about the whole production process.

From you or your delegates, the crew needs positive, concise directions with as much advance warning as possible. Your technical team will not rise to cope with genuine crises if things that could have been foreseen go unattended. Avoid thinking out loud, especially when the pace heats up. Instead, arrive at conclusions so you can produce brief, practical instructions that are worded so they cannot be misinterpreted. Without being condescending, get people to repeat instructions of any complexity so you are sure they understand. Anything that needs to be in writing should be.

Wherever possible during shooting, the assistant director (AD) and the director of photography (DP) should deal with all production and technical questions. This frees you to do your job properly, which is to *answer the needs of the actors and concentrate on building the film's dramatic content.* Your script supervisor will be an important ally, although this person cannot always judge performance quality well—their own job requires a fierce concentration on words, actions, and materials. Do not fail to confer over coverage, especially if you make changes.

LOOK THROUGH THE CAMERA

When a new shot has been set up, *you must look through the viewfinder* to ensure that you are satisfied with the framing at the start and at the conclusion, as well as with other key compositions throughout the shot. When there is a lot of moving camera coverage, you will need to agree with your operator on compositions, angle, size of the image, and so on (see Figure 36-1). Walk the actors (or stand-ins)

FIGURE 36-1

When shooting a dynamic scene, the director must place trust in the camera operator's sense of framing and composition (photo by author).

through the take, freezing them at salient points to agree with the operator on what should appear in the frame. To stabilize these decisions, your crew will need to make chalk marks on the floor for both actors and the camera dolly. Everyone may have to hit particular marks at specific moments in the scene.

Precision of this kind separates the experienced from the inexperienced in cast and crew. Trying to impose too much control on an inexperienced ensemble may be an exercise in futility that wrecks cast morale. Because framing, composition, lighting, and sound coverage are the formal structuring that translate a live world into cinema, the director must keep the strongest possible contact with the outcome on the screen. When shooting video (or film with a video assist), you can watch the whole take on the monitor during recording and know immediately what you have. With film and no video assist, the results remain in doubt until the rushes return from the laboratory. This is why dailies (also known as rushes) are rushed daily back to the unit—so reshooting can take place when necessary.

On a film shoot without a video assist, all you can do is to clearly brief the technical crew through the DP, and then stand close to the camera so you know what it sees. With a little practice, you can see from the operator's movements if he or she is in sync with the action. Not doing these things invariably leads to some rude shocks at the dailies viewing, when it may be too late to make changes.

If you are shooting on film, expect the assistant camera (AC) to obsessively check the film gate and periodically conduct a *scratch test*. Film cameras tend to deposit debris in the aperture, where it shows up in outline, ruining the footage and sometimes scratching it as well. A scratch test involves taking a short length of virgin film that has passed through the camera, and examining both sides closely for evidence of scratching.

If you watch the action on a video monitor, the actors may feel abandoned because you are not beside the camera and physically present for them.

MAKING PROGRESS

Shooting is stop-start work, with many holdups for lighting or camera setups. A crew can easily slow down while everyone waits. Nobody can say quite who is holding things up. In fact, everyone is waiting for the notorious and elusive A. N. Other, a Murphy relative who bedevils the tired and disorganized. The good AD is, among other things, a sheepdog constantly looking for bottlenecks and barking everyone into action the moment that shooting can continue.

WHEN YOU AND YOUR CREW ARE ALONE

If you have a fairly small and intimate crew, encourage them, when you are alone, to discuss their impressions of the shoot. Some members—such as grips, electricians, and ADs—do their work before shooting, and then stand observing during the actual take. What they notice may usefully complement your sense of what is really happening. You, after all, have goals from rehearsal to fulfill, but they are seeing the action for the first time and have an audience-like reaction.

The work of other crew members—such as the camera operator, DP, and sound recordist—demands such localized attention to quality that they cannot reliably register the dramatic. You will therefore get a very mixed bag of observations, some of them way offtrack. Encourage all views, but do not feel you must act upon or rebuff ideas that imply criticism of your work. If, however, most members of the crew find fault with a main character, take serious notice.

WRAPPING FOR THE DAY

At the end of a working day, thank each actor and crew member personally, and make sure that everything in a borrowed location has been replaced exactly as found. Attention to someone else's property signifies your concern and appreciation, and helps ensure a welcome should you want to return. Initial reluctance to accept a film crew's presence often arises because people have heard horror stories about cavalier treatment of property.

On a small crew, those with little equipment to wrap up should help those with much (lighting, for instance). Like all human organizations, a film crew can personify divisions of rank. As general of your troops, you must be concerned for the whole army's welfare. You need their affection and loyalty. If it seems appropriate, pitch in and help with the donkeywork.

No wrap is complete without a careful reiteration of the following day's arrangements by the AD and the unit production manager (UPM). If you are shooting exteriors, someone must keep abreast of weather reports and have contingency shooting ready as bad-weather alternatives. Call sheets should be issued to cast and crew, and rented equipment should be returned, batteries charged, and film dailies delivered to wherever they must go.

DAILIES

If you can watch the latest work, now is the time—before dinner being better than after. You are interested in every aspect: the performances, camerawork, lighting, sets, and support organization. This is when trends—good or not so good—can be spotted and congratulations or corrections can be diplomatically handed out.

CHAPTER 37

MONITORING PROGRESS

A director's recurring nightmare is to discover, after crew and cast have departed, that a vital angle or shot has been overlooked. This is most likely to happen in low-budget filmmaking, where too few people cover too many tasks. Working fast and hand to mouth, intentions must often be modified, and crossing intended shots off a list can easily go awry. The checklist may be so rife with changes that the list itself becomes a hazard.

When a film's story proceeds by a series of images, or when the narrative is carried by nonverbal actions, directing and keeping track of what you have covered are relatively simple. Mistakes and omissions occur more frequently when scenes involve several simultaneous actions, such as crowd or fight scenes with many people in frame whose relativity must match from shot to shot.

Even complex dialogue scenes, especially if characters are moving around, can spring unpleasant surprises when shooting crosses the axis or if reaction shots get forgotten. Fatigue and last-minute changes raise the odds of error in all situations. If the script supervisor and the cinematographer really understand editing, their attention or that of the editor (standing in for the script supervisor) can provide vital checks and balances as shooting progresses.

MONITORING YOUR RESOURCES

Many first shoots are liberally covered in the first stages and stretched perilously thin toward the end. Late coverage may be editable only one way, if at all. To counter this, budget your production and monitor its resources as you expend them, or your shoot will be like an expedition that eats steak upon leaving home—and then has to boil its shoes in the wilderness to stay alive.

No matter what order you shoot in, your line producer or production manager (PM) should compute from day to day where the production stands in relation to its projected budget. Modern budgeting software makes this easy. Knowing early that a complicated sequence has consumed more resources than intended will signal that you must either raise more money, economize to get back on track, or be ready to drop the least vital scenes.

DRAMATIC AND TECHNICAL QUALITY

There are various levels of oversight to monitor dramatic quality, which is top of the list so far as your future audience is concerned.

Film without video feed: To see no film dailies until the final wrap (end of shooting) means relying on limited and subjective impressions as you shoot. For a low-budget film unit away on location, this may seem the only practical solution, but the risks are manifold. Without dailies, you have little or no check on the following possible faults:

- Performances (level, credibility, consistency, relativity)
- Action (continuity)
- Camerawork (inaccurate viewfinder, focus problems, negative scratching, unsteady image or inaccurate camera movements, exposure inequities)
- Lighting (inadequacy or mismatches)
- Sound (quality, consistency)

Running film dailies silently on a projector is better than nothing, but you should really see them with sound. A cassette copy of the dailies made via telecine at home base and viewed on a videocassette player at the location is best when no portable double-system projector is available on location. Both camera and sound crews will take a dim view of this representation of their work, but it will provide you with essential feedback on acting, coverage, continuity, camera handling, composition, and so forth. Lighting and sound quality will be harder to judge.

Digital video or film with video feed: A feature unit must see dailies so any reshooting can be done before the set is struck, or before lighting becomes difficult to reconstruct. Even a dog-tired unit can summon enthusiasm for seeing its own work. As we have said, you must politely but firmly exclude the actors by saying it's a technical check for the unit only.

Quality of the edited piece: Because computerized editing is now possible anywhere, the editor can accompany a location unit and digitize taped dailies as cassettes become available. Once material is captured, a day's work can be assembled in an hour or two. The unit then sees its latest work in rough outline before the set is struck. Many mismatches show up only in edited form—such as inconsistencies in acting, lighting, framing, sound, or continuity. These, once known, may be improved or corrected in subsequent shooting. Most importantly, the director can see whether performances are consistent and pitched right and whether stylistic intentions are working out. Because the editor can be continuously assembling and revising the whole film as its parts become available, a rough assembly of the whole movie should be available within days of the end of shooting.

This avoids what used to be a delay of weeks or months as the production scraped together money for a work print (single-light positive print used as the working copy by the editor). Until the camerawork has been viewed in final film form, the camera crew will lack final proof of their work.

FULFILLING YOUR AUTHORSHIP INTENTIONS

Fatigue and the oblivion that comes with it are the director's biggest hazard. It's fatally easy to let your attention ease into the comforting industrial rhythms of production—to the detriment of your prime responsibilities. The big questions, which may seem blindingly obvious, are: Am I fulfilling my authorial intentions? Do I have a film? (See Figure 37-1.) Success is hard to measure except in unreassuringly subjective terms. Make this easier by breaking your intentions into a series of specific goals.

Dramatic clarity: The sign of effective performances is that, standing by the camera, you spontaneously feel what the audience is going to feel. When it's real, it takes you over. If you are searching for what you expect, something is missing, and you must take action.

Directing film actors means getting clear detail from both their interior and exterior lives. You watch like a hawk to see that your cast maintains the detail and clarity of performance you expect. This is extremely taxing, and you can easily become distracted. Any notes you made, transformed into brief crib notes, will help you avoid dropping the ball (see "Crib Notes" in Chapter 30).

An effective human presence on the screen is deceptively simple: when actors truly feel what their character is feeling, you and the audience will feel it too. If, however, the actors fail or fake it, you must take them psychically to a place where they reconnect with their characters' thoughts, actions, and emotions. This is usually different from actor to actor.

FIGURE 37-1 ────────────────────────────

From one's first film onward, the director is haunted by the question: "Do I have a film?" (photo by author).

Subtext: All takes on all angles of all scenes remain unpredictable of outcome, which is why you have to maintain such high concentration and sensitivity if you are to interpret nuances accurately. A director who looks only for the expected, or who allows his or her attention to wander, will miss the boat. After actors play a take, you should be able to immediately describe its subtext. These vary, and in long scenes with multiple angles, they can evolve into something that compromises the scene's integrity once it's all cut together.

The ideal director is really a hypersensitive, uncluttered, and articulate audience member, able to communicate back what he or she just saw and felt. Did he convince me he's lost? Is she fooling when she says she will walk out? This, in few or no words, is what your cast most needs to know. If they felt or did something different, they probably know it, but they don't necessarily know what *you* got. As their first audience, you must be able to extract reliable, coherent impressions from yourself and pass them over in few or no words.

Here are typical internal responses to two takes of a scene set in a bus station. Late at night, two stranded passengers start a desultory conversation. The action and dialogue in each take are identical, yet each take elicits different responses from anyone alert. One suggests two losers unenthusiastically sizing each other up. The other take shows two depressed, disgruntled people wondering whether they can be bothered making conversation. You ask yourself, What truth was played out? The answer offered by one take is that "you despise someone with your own shortcomings." In the other take, the answer is that "alienated people in social situations tend to isolate themselves." You look for an analogy. One is that "two neutered cats circle each other." The other is that "two exhausted convicts decide it's not worth cooperating to break rocks."

The answers reveal that, quite spontaneously, different subtexts emerged in the playing of each take. You catch these differences only if you are alert to the nuance of the moment, which is actual and transient, not theoretical.

Scene dialectics: With repetition, scenes can fall into a mesmerized, singsong state, and you are apt to go along with it. Make sure, therefore, that the dialectics in each scene are well evidenced. By this, I mean the opposing polarities of will and opinion that set person against person, movement against movement, idea against idea, and the parts of a person against himself or herself. These are the insoluble and irresolvable pressures and tensions that stand out like spars in a majestic bridge construction.

Interrogating your psyche is the only way to break into that sealed room where your intuitive self lives, the part of you that knows the scene's underlying qualities and meaning. It will resist unless you are merciless. Once you access what it knows, you can set about remedying any shortfall between intention and execution. Your cast will also know instinctively when you are right, and their respect for you will rise.

MEASURING PROGRESS

Keep nothing in your head that can instead be dumped onto paper as a checklist. Lists save your life when that fatal fog descends during sustained shooting because you are too tired to think or feel. Check your crib notes so you waste no energy ransacking memory for your goals. Check them at the start of the scene, and check them again at its conclusion. Did you cover every item in your notes? Are there fresh consequences for scenes that follow?

At each juncture, assess whether you have won or lost. This is hard and lonely work because what you see taking place before the camera is often underwhelming. Just when you expected to feel creative, you suffer gnawing doubts—doubts that you can share with nobody.

The dailies invariably reveal more on the screen than you saw at the time. There is a negative aspect to this: a bravura performance seen live comes across as hamming it up on the screen. If you suspect this while shooting, call for more takes, and direct the actors to seek more contained and sincere emotion. The less certain your judgment, the more you should shoot alternatives for choices in editing later.

MOVING BEYOND REALISM

When you go beyond the literalness of recorded realism, your work begins linking up with forms pioneered in film's sister arts, such as music, dance, theater, and literature. There is no set formula for achieving this, and unfortunately, you won't know whether your design—worked out in writing, rehearsal, and preproduction—is succeeding until the film is on its way to being fully edited. Your film's inner life ultimately comes from the life and spirit of the players, from the mood of the company's chemistry together, from the juxtaposition of materials, and from orchestrating them. It also emerges through expressive lighting or settings, sound composition, music, or other approaches germane to your piece. Somehow the production achieves this complex identity for itself.

If complete control is what you want, become an animator. But if you are ready to gamble with metaphysics and accommodate the unexpected, you'll like making fiction films. If you really love the idea of serendipity and improvisation as ingredients in story making, do some cinéma verité documentary as a prelude to a more improvisational approach to fiction. Giving priority to your actors and to chance will put you in very distinguished company.

CEDING CONTROL

Artistic control is a paradoxical notion because it requires that somewhere during the postproduction process, or even earlier, you find yourself yielding control to some higher truth that the film begins to emanate. It works like this: First, your assembled piece will begin to make its own insistent demands, dictating to you and to your editor what it wants its final form to be. Then, like a growing child, your work begins to assert its own nature, to have its own imperfections and integrity, and even to start declaring its own autonomous decisions. Finally, with shock and delight, you find you are assisting your film to make itself.

Similar capitulation may be required during shooting. A typical situation is an actor producing an unexpected and arresting quality that affects the character's potential or skews a certain situation you are shooting. Now you must choose: Do I rein it in, or do I acknowledge a new direction and run with it? Whatever you decide will have an impact on the other players, and may put your authority on the line if they don't like what is happening. Yet to deny these emerging, elusive truths would be to choose security over the living, breathing quality of true drama. Directing is never free of moral and ethical dilemmas, or of compromise.

KEEP THE STORYTELLER ALIVE

Authorship was analyzed in some depth in Part 4: Aesthetics and Authorship. Authoring a movie means you are almost certainly seeking to re-create some aspect of your own inmost experience, and vicariously to extend and further that experience. My friend Lois Deacon once said, "Nothing is real until I have written about it." We use our medium to make an earlier journey real—for ourselves, and for our audience. When others are moved, they confer recognition on some aspect of our inmost selves, something we could scarcely believe in alone.

To direct a story with special meaning, you must make the passively observing witness rise up and become the proactive Storyteller. The Storyteller's passion and intelligence take us beyond surface reality to show its underlying meanings. You do this by challenging and provoking your cast. As director, you play the most important role: that of the unseen but ever-present Storyteller. Lose your vision of why the story exists, of what the film could be and should be, and the film loses its way. At each stage of the movie, whose heart should we see into, and whose eyes and intelligence should we see through? Who should make our heart bleed, and at what particular moments? What must the audience know and feel by the end?

Dialogue sequences are the quicksand where the story's identity most easily sinks from sight, which is why so much of this book concentrates on handling the interaction between characters. To guard against this, shoot coverage to allow shaping options in the cutting room. Single-setup coverage for any part of a scene means that no changes in point of view, pacing, or reaction are possible. Shoot alternatives in case your plans don't work out.

COST REPORTS

As the director, you handle the human, the spiritual, and the ineffable. Your decisions all translate into bills, changing costs, rates, and schedules. Every day during production, your production department will be at your heels. Is the production under or over budget? If you've overspent, what will you do? Maybe you can shoot the last scene without the crane. . . .

AT THE END OF THE PRODUCTION

You had an icebreaker party before shooting began—now have a get-together at the end of shooting to thank and congratulate everybody. If money's low, have a potluck in which everyone makes their favorite dish or brings drinks or desserts. Someone should coordinate this, so you don't get five pasta salads and no dessert. Notice how different everyone is together after their shared journey with its battles and fellowships.

When shooting ends, your role at last eases up. The toll on your psyche is far more severe than you yet know. At the end of a demanding shoot, many directors get depressed or even physically ill.

PART 7

POSTPRODUCTION

Postproduction is that phase of filmmaking when sound and picture dailies are transformed into the film seen by the audience. Thus, the editing suite is the crucible of filmmaking. Editing—or being present while your work is edited—will teach you more about your directing than anything else will.

Part 7 (Chapters 38 through 44) covers the vital postproduction phase of filmmaking, when raw materials are fashioned into a seamless tale. Because of the experimenting that digital editing encourages, and because today's editors are so screen literate, this is usually a stage done well even by novices.

My purpose in these chapters is less to discuss editing methodology or software than to lay out the procedural steps of editing, and to discuss what to expect from the artistic process and your work's evolution. This is an important and exciting phase; in documentary, the editor is regarded as the second director—and the fiction editor, if provided with adequate coverage, can have almost as much creative input. Film is an unbelievably malleable medium, and though you can't much improve a poor individual performance, editors regularly perform miracles at the narrative level, where sheer momentum obscures many a passing blemish.

CHAPTER 38

PREPARING TO EDIT

Most operations described in this chapter are the editor's responsibility, but if the director is to get the best film, he or she must know what to expect of postproduction. Editing is not just assembly, as Hitchcock mythology suggests, but more like coaxing a brilliant musical performance from a set of imperfect, overlapping, and incomplete scores. This requires you to see, listen, adapt, think, and imagine as you try to liberate the best from your film's potential.

Because editors deal with the structure and flow of narrative, editing is a common professional path to directing. Some famous directors who also edited (in the A–H range alone) include Altman, Antonioni, Buñuel, Capra, Coppola, Eisenstein, Ford, Godard, Griffith, Hawks, Herzog, Hitchcock, and Huston. These are all men: plainly, the film-going public is ready for some gender equity.[1]

THE POSTPRODUCTION TEAM

Those who make up the whole postproduction team include the editor, assistant editors, sound editor and sound team, composer, music editor, and sound-mix engineers. The composer's work is discussed in Chapter 42, "Working with Music," but the work of the rest of the team begins in this chapter. Heading the team is the editor, whose qualities and focus are representative of the whole postproduction crew.

THE EDITOR

Answers to the director during the director's cut, but to the producer if changes are demanded for the producer's cut. For the differences, see Chapter 1, "The World of the Film Director."

Responsible for making all the practical and aesthetic decisions while building a movie from the dailies. He or she oversees the whole postproduction team,

---

[1] To see the rest of the alphabet, enter "director" and "editor" as keywords in the invaluable www.imdb.com film database.

from first assembly to final lab work or digital postproduction. The materials may, for instance, be inherently entertaining, but lack design—and so are capable of broad possibilities of interpretation. The editor must often make responsible, subjective judgments. On a documentary or improvised fiction film, the editor is regarded as the second director. Even in a tightly scripted fiction film, the editor needs the insight and confidence to know when to alter the original intentions to better serve the film's needs. Editing is thus always far more than following a script, just as jazz is much more than playing notes. Composing is indeed the closest analogy to the editor's work, and many film editors have music among their abiding interests.

Personality traits: The good editor is patient, highly organized, willing to experiment endlessly, and diplomatic about trying to get his or her own way. Assistant editors and sound personnel echo these qualities. The accomplished editor is really someone of authorial caliber who works from given materials. Editors are adept at finding more possibilities in actors' performances or in narrative pacing and structure. Directors are blinkered by their intentions, whereas the editor, not present at shooting, comes on the scene with an unbiased eye similar to that of the audience. Editors are better placed to reveal to the director what possibilities or problems lie dormant in the raw materials. Editors can be private and uncommunicative while at work, obsessed with detail, and unable to leave well enough alone. The nature of their work allows them to think in deep and sustained ways, which is part of their value. Most established directors have a favorite editor who accompanies them, like a marital partner, from film to film.

EDITING FILM AND VIDEO

With film and video nonlinear editing (NLE), any part of an edited version can be substituted, transposed, or adjusted for length. Systems such as Adobe Premiere, Avid, and Final Cut Pro have become ubiquitous. From digital original—or film-camera original material scanned by a telecine machine—the material is digitally recorded in the editing computer's hard drive. Edits are compiled as a series of *clips* (which are actually titled, numerical quotes) arranged on a timeline. As in word processing, you may enter at any point and transpose, lengthen, or contract what is there. With film editing, you carry out a similar operation, but use a splicer to cut and join the work print, and a synchronizer to keep picture and sound in synchronization. When you use a table editing machine such as a Steenbeck or a Moviola, you are really using a motorized synchronizer with sound and viewing capability.

Among NLE systems, Avid was established early in the film industry and remains the front-runner in performance and user-friendliness. It has, however, been legendarily expensive to maintain. Avid has been losing ground to Apple Inc.'s Final Cut Pro (Figure 38-2), which is stable, intuitive, modestly priced, and extremely capable. To compete, Avid has produced Avid Xpress Pro, which has the merit of running on both Mac and PC platforms (Figure 38-1). The Apple, Avid, and Adobe low-end programs are backed by large companies serving worldwide consumer markets, so you can expect them to remain on the scene. If you are a bona fide student or teacher, you should be able to find academic pricing.

FIGURE 38-1 ——

Avid, the film industry's preferred editing software (courtesy Avid).

FIGURE 38-2 ——

Apple Final Cut Pro editing software on a PowerBook laptop computer (courtesy Apple).

Their modest cost and increasing capacities are a wonderful advance for those needing professional features. See the next chapter for web sites and more details.

No matter what system you choose, there is a huge amount to learn. Your learning curve will remain precipitous for a long time, and you'll need a good manual. Following my daughter's advice, I swallowed my pride, headed for the bookstore yellow section, and bought Helmut Kobler's *Final Cut Pro HD For Dummies* (Wiley, 2004). Sure enough, it assumes no prior knowledge, and is graphic, consistent, and (really important) thoroughly indexed. The book knows that you want to edit, not flounder in software architecture.

A POSTPRODUCTION OVERVIEW

Supervised by the editor, **film** and **video** postproduction include a number of tasks. Synchronizing sound with action when film or double-system video recording are used:

1. Syncing sound and picture together so footage can be watched in *dailies* viewings
2. Screening dailies for the crew, and for the director and producer's choices and comments
3. Marking up the editing script strictly according to what was shot
4. Logging material in preparation for editing
5. Making a first assembly
6. Making the rough cut
7. Evolving the rough cut into a fine cut
8. Supervising narration or looping (postsynchronized voice recording)
9. Preparing for and supervising original music recording
10. Finding, recording, and laying component parts of multitrack sound such as atmospheres, backgrounds, and sync effects
11. Supervising mix-down of these tracks into one smooth final track
12. Supervising shooting of titles and necessary graphics
13. Supervising the film lab or video postproduction finalization processes

In **film,** the process also involves the following film laboratory processes:

- *Developing the camera original*, and, for larger-budget films, making a work print to protect the negative from unnecessary further handling
- *Delivering to the cutting room* either a film work print or a tape for digitization made from a telecine scan of the negative

Once editing arrives at a fine cut and sound mix, the **film** lab uses either the edited work print or the edit decision list (EDL) to do the following:

1. *Make film opticals* (optical effects such as dissolves, fades, freeze-frames, titling), some of which cannot be done during the final printing. This is an expensive, highly specialized, and fallible process that nobody should undertake lightly.
2. *Conforming* (or *negative cutting*), in which the original negative is cut to match the work print so that fresh prints may be struck for release. Conforming includes instructing the printing machine to produce fades, superimpositions,

and dissolves. Conforming the traditional film-editing method is simply matching negative to work print in a synchronizer.

3. *Matchback conforming* follows a digitally edited film. An EDL of Keykode numbers compiled during digital editing is the sole guide to cutting the negative. This is a risky business—see Film Aquisition, Digital Postproduction, Release on Film in Chapter 39.

4. *Making a sound optical negative* from:

   a. The sound magnetic master in the case of traditional mixing

   b. The sound program output in the case of a digitally edited film

5. *Timing* (or color grading) the picture negative or the *digital intermediate* (DI) by the lab in association with the director of photography (DP). A DI permits finer control over the color, intensity, contrast, and other image aspects. From it, the lab can make a fully corrected negative for release printing.

6. *Combining sound negative with timed picture* to produce a composite, or "married," print. It is called the first *answer print* (or trial print).

7. *Making release prints* after achieving a satisfactory answer print.

8. *Making dupe (duplicate) negatives* via a fine-grain interpositive process. For films with a large release, too many copies would subject the original negative to too much wear and tear, so dupe negatives are made.

In **digital postproduction,** the camera original material is digitized and stored in its entirety in a computer hard drive, then assembled as segments laid along a timeline. Multiple sound tracks are laid and levels predetermined so you can listen to a layered and sophisticated track even while editing. Many systems are now so fast and have such large storage that you can edit high-definition television (HDTV) on a desktop computer at full resolution. This abolishes the need for the

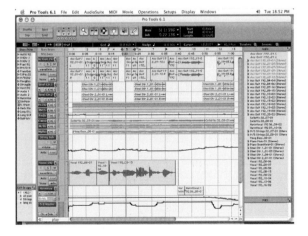

FIGURE 38-3

Digidesign's Pro Tools, the industry standard for sound editing (photo courtesy of Digidesign).

two-pass offline and online processes with the extra time and expense those would take.

Postproduction involves finalizing sound in the audio-sweetening process using sophisticated sound-processing software such as Digidesign's Pro Tools. Beyond simple level setting, such programs enable control over sound dynamics by offering:

1. *Limiting.* Sound dynamics remain linear until a preset ceiling, when they are held to that ceiling level.
2. *Compression.* All sound dynamics are compressed into a narrower range, but remain proportionate to each other.
3. *Equalization* control. Sound frequency components within top, middle, and bottom of sound range can be individually adjusted, or preset programs can be applied.
4. *Filtering.* For speech with prominent "s" sibilants, for instance, you can use a de-essing program.
5. *Pitch changes,* or pitch bending. This can be useful for surreal sound effects or creating naturalistic variations from a single source.
6. *Musical Instrument Digital Interface* (MIDI) integration. This allows you to integrate a keyboard-operated sampler or music setup.

When finalizing, **digital editing**'s ability to find whatever you want in a flash has removed the necessity to search through outtakes and other material. Editors, no longer forced to contemplate unused material in their daily work, say it is fatally easy to miss diamonds in the rough, although excised material of any promise can always be stored in specially marked bins. Editing schedules have also gotten shorter, so the editor must fight to ensure that nothing useful was overlooked on the way to the fine-cut stage.

Producing a **final digital print** includes:

1. Color correction
2. Audio sweetening, as described previously
3. Copy duplication for release prints on DVD or other media

Two good **resources** for current technology information are:

- Kodak's student program (www.kodak.com/go/student), for everything to do with film and filming. Lists student contests and a wealth of other information.
- *DV Magazine* (www.dv.com), for up-to-date information and reviews on everything for digital production and postproduction.

SYNCING DAILIES

It is beyond the scope of this book to describe the procedure of syncing film dailies, other than to say that the picture (marked at the point where the clapperboard bar has just closed) and the sound track (marked at the clapper bar's impact) are aligned in a synchronizer or table editor so that discrete takes can be cumulatively assembled for a sync viewing. The same principle applies when the outputs from double system are synced up in a computer. Every respectable film-making manual covers this process (see this text's bibliography).

KEEPING A DAILIES BOOK

When readying dailies for viewing, make a record of the running order. You can, of course, use the NLE database, though the space for on-screen display may be cramped. If you use a notebook, make a preparatory log divided by sequences and showing slate and take numbers. Leave space for cryptic notes during the dailies viewing. Figure 38-4 shows part of a typical dailies book. An NLE program will allow you to display your material by different priorities, such as ID number, date, description, and so on (Figure 38-5).

CREW VIEWING SESSION

Although the crew has seen the dailies piecemeal, let them view their work in its entirety. Everyone can learn from this, especially because mistakes tend to be sup-

```
                          LAUNDRY SEQUENCE
     1-1   NVG
      -2   End good for David
      -3   Best, but focus change NG (slow)
     2-1   Safety cutaway only
     3-1   NG
      -2   Fair (Liz has interesting dreamy reaction to bad news)
       3   Liz angriest - try to use
       4   Best for consistency - David's reaction best in T2
```

FIGURE 38-4 ————————————————————————————————————

Typical dailies book notes.

```
Scene   | Edge #              |Sync Code # | Cam Roll | Sound Roll | Date
--------|---------------------|------------|----------|------------|--------
29-1-1  |29J6 434114- 158     | 000 - 018  |    14    |     6      |13 Aug 87
     2  |     434159- 207     | 019 - 038  |    "     |     "      |    "
     3  |     434208- 222     | 039 - 050  |    "     |     "      |    "
29-2-1  |34Z7 945781- 879     | 051 - 099  |    15    |     "      |    "
     2  |     945880- 904     | 100 - 151  |    "     |     "      |    "
29-3-1  |     945905- 965     | 153 - 186  |    "     |     7      |    "
     2  |     945966- 971     | 187 - 193  |    "     |     "      |    "
     3  |     945972-6034     | 194 - 224  |    "     |     "      |    "
29-4-1  |21X3 100676- 771     | 225 - 277  |    9     |    MOS     |14 Aug 87
        |                     |            |          |            |
```

FIGURE 38-5 ————————————————————————————————————

Final Cut Pro log layout.

pressed (you hope) in the final edit. Screening may have to be broken up into more than one session because four hours or so of unedited footage is about the longest even the most dedicated can maintain concentration. The editor can be present, but discussion is likely to be a crew-centered postmortem rather than one useful to editing.

TAKING NOTES

If you write during a viewing, try never to let your attention leave the screen, because you will assuredly miss important moments and nuances. This means making large, scribbled notes on many pages of paper. If you have a voice recorder or an assistant, dictate notes without looking away from the screen.

REACTIONS

After the crew or others have seen dailies, there is usually a debate over the effectiveness, meaning, or importance of different aspects of the material. Participants may have differing feelings about the credibility and motivation of the characters. Listen rather than debate, for these represent the possible reactions of a future audience. Keep in mind, however, that crew members are far from objective. They are disproportionately critical of their own discipline and may overestimate its positive or negative effect. They also develop their own subjective relationships with the actors and the filming situations.

THE EDITOR AND DIRECTOR VIEW DAILIES

During shooting and after it, editor and director see the dailies seated next to each other. A marathon viewing in particular will highlight the relativity of the material and expose the problems you face in the piece as a whole. You might discover that certain mannerisms arise repeatedly in one actor and must be cut around during editing if he is not to appear phony. Or you might discover that one of your two principals is more interesting to watch and threatens to unbalance the film. If, during the dailies viewing, you find yourself reacting to a particular character with, "She seems unusually sincere here," write it down. In fact, note any unexpected mood or feeling.

Gut feelings often seem unfounded, so you are tempted to ignore or forget them. However, they are seldom unrepresentative; what triggered them is embedded in the material for any first-time audience to experience. The notes you make will be useful as reminders later when inspiration flags and memory glazes over from overexposure to the material.

Next, view the material a scene at a time. With considerable labor, film dailies can be reassembled for projection in scene order. Dailies that have been digitized can easily be called up in scene order. Run one sequence at a time, then stop to discuss its problems and possibilities. The editor will need the dailies book (see above) to record the director's choices and note any special cutting information.

THE ONLY FILM IS IN THE DAILIES

The sum of the dailies viewing is your fragmentary impressions of the movie's potential and deficiencies, and a notebook full of choices and observations.

Now you must confront the raw material—and change hats. You are no longer the instigator of the material, but (with your editor) the surrogate for your audience.

Empty yourself of prior knowledge and intentions. The only film you can make is hiding in the dailies, and your editor may discern it more quickly than you do. Nothing beyond the dailies has any relevance. The script is a historic relic, like an old map to a rebuilt city. Stow it in the attic for your biographer. Nobody in the cutting room wants to hear about what you intended or what you meant to produce.

MARKING UP THE SCRIPT

When logging the footage is complete, the assistant editor prepares the editing script, each page of which should end up looking like Figure 38-6. To mark up

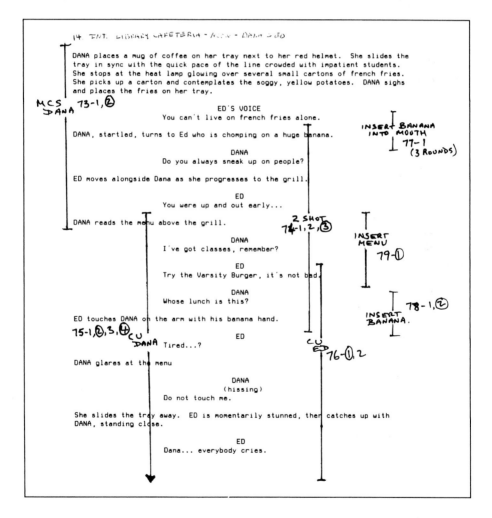

FIGURE 38-6

Editor's script marked up with dailies coverage.

the script, view the material for one scene, looking at one camera setup at a time. Each setup is represented as a line bracketing what the angle covers. Note that a change of lens is treated as a new setup, for although the camera may not have physically moved, the framing and composition will be different. Shots that continue over a page break are indicated by an arrow. Leave a space in the line, and neatly write in the scene number, all its printed takes (circling those chosen), and the briefest possible shot description. More detailed information can now be quickly found in the continuity reports or dailies book.

The editor's markings appear to duplicate the shooting script (see Chapter 30, Figure 30-1), but they are based on actual footage and chosen takes—footage that definitively exists. Now the editor can see at a glance what angles cover every moment of the scene and which are the best moments in each. This makes it easy to find alternative coverage during the lengthy period of refining the cut.

EDITING BEGINS

ASSEMBLY

Low-budget film economics sometimes prevent cutting until everything is shot. This is risky because errors and omissions surface when they can no longer be rectified. For this reason, feature films normally employ the editor from the start of shooting. Dailies are viewed immediately so that reshooting can be scheduled before quitting the location, and an assembly edit of the unit's output is assembled on the spot. The low-budget film shoot may have no such luxury, but dailies can often be synchronized and transferred from the editing machine screen via DVD or the Internet, and viewed at the location at minimal cost.

BEGINNING WORK WITH THE DIRECTOR

Once shooting is over, the editing staff begins full-time work with the director. He or she is usually fatigued, and will be anxious and uncertain until the film begins proving itself. Many directors suffer a sort of postnatal depression following the sustained impetus of shooting, and most, however confident they may appear, are morbidly, even grotesquely, aware of their material's failures. If the editor and director do not know each other well, they will usually be formal and cautious. The editor is taking over the director's baby, and the director often carries mixed and potentially explosive emotions.

PARTNERSHIP

Relationships between directors and editors vary widely according to the chemistry of their status and temperaments. The director will initially discuss the intentions behind each scene and give any necessary special directions. The editor then sets to work making the assembly, which is a first raw version of the film. Wise directors leave the cutting room so they can return with a usefully fresh eye. The obsessive director sits in the cutting room night and day, watching the editor's every action. Whether this is amenable depends on the editor. Some enjoy debating their way through the cutting procedure, but most prefer being left alone to work out the film's initial problems over their logs and equipment in bouts of intense concentration.

In the end, nothing escapes concentrated discussion; every shot and every cut is scrutinized, questioned, weighed, and balanced. The creative relationship is intense, and often draws in all the cutting room staff and the producer. The editor often has to use delicate but sustained leverage against the irrational prejudices and fixations that occasionally close like a trap around the heart of virtually every director. Ralph Rosenblum and Robert Karen's book *When the Shooting Stops . . . the Cutting Begins* (Da Capo Paperback Series, 1986) tells just how crazed the editor/director relationship can become.

DIRECTOR-EDITORS

In low-budget movies, the director is sometimes a director-editor and is called a *hyphenate*. Doing both jobs is risky, especially if sharing control is an issue. Such personalities usually field critical reactions to their work with pain and difficulty, and feel under attack. Even among accomplished feature directors, some of the slackest films come from wearing too many hats. See *Dances with Wolves* (1990) at 183 minutes, then bear in mind that Kevin Costner—star, director, and producer—issued a director's cut of 224 minutes.

Every film is created for an audience, so during its creation yours will need the steadying and detached point of view of an editor as an audience proxy. Lacking the tension of this partnership, directors seldom get the necessary distance from their intentions and their actual material. Commonly, hyphenates fall prey to love or hate, axing in disgust what may work perfectly well, and clinging obsessively to "darlings," those unjustly favored moments or scenes that film folklore says you must kill. A good editor's cool advocacy does more to produce a tough, balanced, and effective film than anyone can deliver alone. Because editing is now universally digital, the notes for making a film log and organizing film rushes have been moved to this book's web site www.focalpress.com/9780240808826.

CHAPTER 39

GETTING STARTED
ON THE FIRST ASSEMBLY

HARDWARE AND SOFTWARE

Ever since computers have replaced the cumbersome business of editing film, film and digital technology have joined forces. Whatever production path you take, these notes will alert you to some of the relevant issues. Use the bibliography to seek more comprehensive manuals. Conduct conclusive tests and, unless you are using a thoroughly established combination of equipment and method, trawl the Internet for cautionary tales. There is a lot that can go wrong.

Editing software accepts or applies different standards of compression. High-end rigs are expensive because they process extremely high resolution footage with minimal degradation. The industry standard is the Avid range of editing software, which runs on either the PC or Mac platform (see www.avid.com). The competing software, increasingly favored by professionals, is Apple's Final Cut Pro (see www.apple.com/finalcutpro/). With a beefy enough computer, it can handle the most demanding HD formats. The Mac OS platform is regarded as more user-friendly, more stable, and better integrated than the PC range, which depends on the quirky and overloaded Microsoft platform. The next most popular software, also modestly priced and striving to match the capability of the others, is Adobe Premiere for PC (see www.adobe/motion/main).

The editing process is a bridge that links the acquisition medium on one side (which may be film or digital video) with the release medium on the other (which may be film, digital tape, or digital disc.). Even when when working with film alone, you will still need to create DVDs. The different production paths bring different interface problems at the entry and exit points of the bridge. Each production method represents different degrees of hazard and expense, so we'll look at them briefly in ascending order of complexity and cost.

PRODUCTION VARIATIONS

ALL-DIGITAL ACQUISITION, POSTPRODUCTION, AND RELEASE

This is the least expensive, least hazardous path for the newcomer. All you need is a camcorder with a FireWire link to a computer that has editing software capable of digitizing and storing the camcorder's footage. Apart from the NTSC (National Television Standards Committee) or PAL (Phase Alternate Line) divide, there is now a proliferation of proprietary high-definition (HD) camcorders, recording media, and *codecs* (video compression standards). There are now also several screen *aspect ratios* (see descriptions in Chapter 27). This leaves plenty of room for error, but if your editing software can handle your camera's codec, you are up and running.

DIGITAL ACQUISITION AND POSTPRODUCTION, RELEASE ON FILM

You can transfer your edited digital production to film for cinema projection. For it to be done well and not break the bank, there is a small matter of frame rates to consider. Standard cinema frame rate, set at 24 fps in the early days of sound, is likely to remain a worldwide standard because it embraces the entire history of 35 mm sound film. NTSC standard-definition (SD) video has never been easy to transfer because its frame rate is 30 fps—with each frame made up of first odd, then even, lines in a two-pass, interlaced solution. Video acquired and edited in this way transfers awkwardly and expensively to 24 fps film. The European standard, PAL, is easier because the frame rate is 25 fps. By ignoring the slight speed mismatch, this format can be transferred straight to film, then played at 24 fps with only a slight increase in running time.

Many NTSC cameras using MiniDV cassettes now record in high definition at 24 p (24 fps progressive scan). This means that each frame is "written" at 24 fps in a one-progressive (that is, single) pass instead of using two interlaced passes of odd and even lines. The great merit of 24 p is that it transfers to standard 24 fps film without problem.

Because video projection is so much better today, almost all festivals now accept videotapes or DVDs. If you win the lottery, or if distributors clamor for your film, then it's time to consider sinking a fortune into making a 35 mm transfer.

FILM ACQUISITION, DIGITAL POSTPRODUCTION, RELEASE ON FILM

When a production is originated on film, edited digitally, and then destined for a film release, you must proceed very, very cautiously. Each day of the shoot, the film lab sends the newly developed negative (or a safety print struck from the negative) through a telecine machine to produce a tape copy. This includes the Keykode information from the edge of the camera original negative. The tape copy is then digitized, synchronized with its accompanying sound, and edited using software that can prepare a Keykode *edit decision list* (EDL). Very important: the program should bar you from using adjacent pieces of film without a minimum of three frames gap between them. One and a half frames minimum of "handle" is required at each end of the negative section in order to physically make overlap cement splices.

So far, so good. Now we come to the *matchback* process, when Keykode numbers guide the physical cutting of the negative, which is still required for the A and B roll film printing process. From the dawn of cinema, film negatives were conformed by cutting them shot by shot against the edited work print running alongside in a set of sprocketed wheels called a synchronizer. You see what you are doing, and in the hands of a professional, negative cutting is unfailingly accurate. (There is more on the conforming process in the book's web site, www.focalpress.com/9780240808826) But now—enter the digital age—your irreplaceable negative is conformed by numbers alone, with no more picture matching. This is like putting your liver transplant into the care of a computer-driven robot! Errors don't show up until the first answer print, when the negative has been been cut and there is no way back. And then, because sound is prepared and mixed digitally, there is also a risk that it won't be in sync. So now, at answer print time, you sweat bullets.

EDITING MECHANICS

Much as governments identify their citizens by Social Security numbers, video editing finds and handles its materials by timecode or Keykode numbers, about which there is more below. You will need a good logging database to keep track of your materials, and one comes with your editing software. As you decide on the content and length of clips, and arrange them in sequences and bins before placing them on the timeline, all your decisions to produce a fully effective film are stored as a table of numbers, the EDL.

Nonlinear, or digital, editing (NLE) is a fantastic advance for speed of execution and for the sophisticated manipulation of imagery and sound tracks. Optical effects, such as slow or fast motion, freeze-frames, compositing (layered imaging), titling, fades, or dissolves—all of which are so expensive and difficult to specify in film—are immediately accessible in video. Once you know your program, any imaginable experiment with your footage can be tried in seconds. Though the best editors are said to have learned their aesthetics from editing film, all approve of nonlinear's advantages.

SOUND CONSIDERATIONS

NLE programs allow multiple sound tracks, which you split and lay on parallel timeline tracks according to their origin and purpose in the movie. Movie sound postproduction has always included provisions for mixing multiple tracks together, but once upon a time, they were rolls of film, each played on a dubber 6 feet high. Now they are tracks originating from a diagram on the monitor screen. You can even vary their levels and set lengths for fade-ins or fade-outs.

Sound, which should mostly appear to be seamless, takes a lot of postproduction work. This is because location recording conditions produce sound of varied quality and backgrounds, and this sound simply doesn't cut together smoothly. Even interiors present problems: in a dialogue scene, for instance, there may be four different microphone positions, one for each camera position. Each has a slightly different level, acoustic coloration, and room resonance. Played cut to cut without any adjustments except level, they sound truly awful—and worse, they fragment the scene for the audience. Plainly, they must all come to sound like one track. This is done by placing all the close shots on one track in the sound timeline, all the two-shots on another, all the long shots on a third, and so on. Then you can set levels, sound filtering, and equalization for each mic position to make all the tracks sound acceptably similar. Because you can seldom subtract *ambient sound* from a sound track, you will have to add specially shot *presence track* (a.k.a., *room tone*, or *buzz track*) to the quieter tracks to bring their ambience up to match those tracks with the most ambient sound. Of course, you must allow for perspective changes because we expect sound to vary according to how close or distant we are from its source. Truly, a good sound track takes an immense amount of specialized work.

Now you can view the film under optimal sound conditions and make final dramatic and other decisions based on a close knowledge of their potential. Having multiple tracks available allows you to lay in *wild tracks* (that is, nonsync sound)—such as doorbells, car horns, or various atmospheres—exactly where they belong. They, too, can now play their part in the story. Often a sound effect helps narrate a step in the story, and editing pace will be affected by its presence.

If you have the right music at hand while editing, or *scratch music* that can serve as an interim guide, this, too, can be laid in. Now you can make compositional decisions concerning scene rhythm and duration that would be quite uncertain if taken on a theoretical basis.

TIMECODE: NTSC DROP FRAME AND NONDROP FRAME

Timecode provides every frame of picture and sound with its own time identity in elapsed hours, minutes, seconds, and frames. Video editing operation utterly depends on it. However, because of the primeval nature of American 525-line television running on a 60 Hz electrical supply, there is an anomaly. Although NTSC appears to have a frame rate of 30 fps, it really runs at 29.97. Cumulatively, this becomes significant over time, so a solution was devised called *drop frame* timecode. This arrangement drops a frame every so often to yank the displayed timecode back into sync with clock time. For this reason, camcorders and editing software menus offer a choice between DF (drop frame) and NDF (nondrop frame recording). Remember to stay consistent, and you should have no problems.

EDITING CONCEPTS

You can learn basic editing using common sense, but you can reach for more sophistication if you first make a detailed analysis of one or two complex feature film scenes (in Chapter 5, see Project 5-2: Editing Analysis). Most people, having ingested an average of 18,000 hours of television while growing up, take to editing like ducks to water. If you carry out the hands-on shooting and editing projects (Chapter 6, "Shooting Projects"), you will learn quite a bit about editing and shooting—and well before you need them for projects determining your professional survival.

All editing programs come with instructional projects of some kind, but they always seem geared to teaching the software rather than to showing how to accomplish particular editing tasks. Most film education is, in any case,

"Yow Learning"—as in "Yow! Why didn't I shoot a [fill in the blank] shot?" How the chickens come home to roost!

The chapters that follow give an overview of the conceptual and artistic processes, as you can expect to encounter them, stage by stage.

THE FIRST ASSEMBLY

Making the first assembly is exciting. Don't worry about length or balance at this stage. Work on one scene at a time, and put the film together in whatever order is convenient. To get there, you should:

- Run all the material for the scene so you commit it to memory. Sit through everything—outtakes, false starts, aborted takes—because there is always something that you'll need later.

- Bracket the content of each setup in your script so it shows how the scene is covered and what options you have. Place slate numbers and take numbers against each bracket, and circle the chosen takes.

- Figure out how the coverage might be initially assembled. At this stage, use mostly master shots, and leave until later any close-ups or double-cutting (repeatedly cutting between, say, two speakers when a single angle would adequately relay the action). At this stage, don't use any lap (overlap) cutting (for example, a speaker's outgoing dialogue overlaps a shot of the listener before the listener replies).

- Assemble the simplest version that is faithful to the script. Don't bother trying to cure anything questionable, such as changes in actors' pacing.

- Include two versions of anything if both seem equally viable. You can choose later in the widest possible context.

Of course, you will be longing to go to work on favorite sequences, but to fix nagging details would be to avoid confronting the film's overall identity and purpose. View the whole film as soon as possible in long, loose form.

FIRST ASSEMBLY VIEWING

NO INTERRUPTIONS

Run the first assembly without interruption of any kind. Make no notes, because this will take your attention from the screen. You want to take in the film as any superattentive audience would.

WHAT DO YOU HAVE?

The assembly viewing will yield important realizations about the character, dramatic shape, and best length of the film. You will get a handle on all the performances and know what overall control you need exert. Fundamental issues are now out of the closet. The film is slow. Some scenes include unnecessary exposition, start slowly, or hang on beyond a good ending point. You may have two endings, one false and one intended, or one character who is unexpectedly stronger than another. A sequence you shot in miserably cold conditions by a river at night turns out to stall the story's advance and needs to be dropped. Kill your darlings, but keep them in a special bin in case you need to resurrect one.

The first assembly is the departure point for the denser and more complex film to come. As a show, it is long and crude, yet despite its artlessness, it can be affecting and exciting.

RUN THE FILM A SECOND TIME

Now run your movie again to see how your original impressions stand up. Following further discussion with your editor, make a list together of major aims for each sequence, arranging them strictly by priority.

DIAGNOSTIC QUESTIONING

To question the imprint your story has made and to predict a likely audience response, you must always try to view the film as if seeing it for the first time. Right now, your project is in its crudest form, so aim to elicit only dominant reactions.

After seeing an assembly, list memorable material. Look at the script and see what left no particular impression. The human memory discards what it does not find meaningful, so all that good stuff you forgot simply did not contribute. This does not mean it never can, simply that it's not doing so at present. Here are some common problems and their solutions.

Problem	Possible Solutions
The writing is poor in comparison with other sequences.	Cut the whole scene? Shorten? Rewrite and reshoot?
Acting is at fault. Dramatic rhythms are too predictable, or actors are not in character or in focus.	Help, but not a cure, is available in further editing. Very often, reaction times are wrong and convey the wrong (or no) subtext. Rebalancing these can help.
Scene outcome is predictable.	Scene structure is at fault? Too long or too slow? Maybe the scene is in the wrong place?
Two or more sequences make a similar point.	Repetition does not advance a film's argument unless there is escalation in dramatic pressure, so make choices and ditch the redundant.
Dramatic intensity plummets. A useful analogy is the idea of a rising or falling emotional temperature. To see material in its context is to see correct relative temperatures more clearly.	If your film is raising the temperature, then inadvertently lowering it before the intended peak, the viewer's response is seriously impaired. Perhaps you can transpose one or two sequences. Sometimes this works wonders.
The viewer is somehow set up by the preceding material to expect something different.	We read film by its context; if the context gives misleading signals or fails to focus awareness in the right area, the material can fall unaccountably flat.

These are only a few areas of dramatic analysis. Just as a playwright routinely rewrites and adjusts a work based on audience feedback, so the filmmaker makes a vast number of adjustments, large and small, before admitting that a work may be finished.

First, you dig into your instincts by feeling the dramatic outcome of your material. Later, when you have a fine cut and the material becomes showable, you will call in a few people whose reactions and tastes you respect. You will probably find quite a bit of unanimity in what they tell you. Because a filmmaker has only trial audiences until the work is finished, assessments are hard to make and are certainly not objective.

While still in this assembly stage, you and your editor begin asking basic questions:

- Does the film feel dramatically balanced? If you have a very moving and exciting sequence in the middle of the story, the rest of the movie may seem anticlimactic.
- Does the film seem to circle around for a long while before you feel it start to move?
- When is there a definite feeling of a story unfolding, and when not? Asking this will help you locate impediments in the project's development.
- Which parts of the film seem to work?
- Which parts drag, and why? Some of the acting may be better than others. Sometimes the problem is that a scene is wrongly placed or repeats the dramatic contours of a previous one.
- Which of the characters most held your attention, and which the least?
- Was there a satisfying alternation of types of material, or was similar material clumped indigestibly together?
- Which were the effective contrasts and juxtapositions? Are there more to be made?
- Sometimes a sequence does not work because the ground has not been properly prepared, or because there is insufficient contrast in mood with the previous sequence. Variety is as important to storytelling as it is to dining.
- What metaphorical allusions did you notice your material making? Could it make them more strongly? That your tale carries a metaphorical charge is as important to your audience as a water table is to pasture.

RESOLUTIONS AFTER SEEING THE FIRST ASSEMBLY

Once you have seen and discussed the whole ungainly epic, you and your editor can make far-reaching resolutions about its future development. These may involve performances, pacing, parallel storytelling, structure, or overall meaning. Remember that your editor is massively uninterested in whatever you originally intended—that's ancient history.

PRIORITIZE

To tackle problems in any cut, arrange them by hierarchy and *deal only with the major issues*. If the story's structure is awry, reorder the scenes and run the film again without making any refinement to individual scenes. If there is a serious problem of imbalance between two characters who are both major parts, go to work on bringing forward the deficient character. Correct only the major problems after each running.

LENGTH

Most beginners' films are agonizingly long and slow, and advice about slashing their running time is painful but necessary. If you can recognize early that your movie should be, say, 20 minutes long at the very most, you can get tough with that 40-minute assembly and make some basic decisions. Films have a natural span according to the richness and significance of their content, so look to the content of your film itself for guidance over length and pacing. The hardest achievement in any art form is having the confidence and ability to say a lot through a little. You and your writer felt you'd cut the script to the bone: now you see all the other places you should have cut. Nonlinear editing can preserve each of your cuts, and during the film's evolution, you can always look back to see whether there's anything in an earlier version that you actually prefer. Commit all these cuts to DVD, perhaps, for your private amusement in later life.

STRUCTURE

Most of all, you need to find the best dramatic structure to make the movie into a well-told tale. A good screenplay does not guarantee the best experience for an audience because the cast, production, and editing all bring new emotional shading and development. These, not the original intentions, are what the audience experiences; and these, as they become apparent, are what you must address. Ironically, the director is always the one most encumbered by the film's history.

LEAVE THE EDITOR TO EDIT

Having decided the next round of changes, leave the cutting room until summoned back. Not all editors or directors can work this way, but it is important to try. The editor loses objectivity while correcting the many problems, and so will any director who remains present. But a director returning with a fresh eye can tell the editor where changes are working.

Everyone working in postproduction must constantly struggle to rid themselves of their expectations and conditioning in order to become the surrogate for a first-time audience. It takes Zen mastery to let go of prior experience and see "what is" rather than "what was" or "what should be."

CHAPTER 40

EDITING PRINCIPLES

Once you know the finer points of your editing software, you can take one sequence at a time and make each sequence and all its coverage yield what it's capable of giving. Here are some general principles that can help your editing seem natural and inevitable.

EDITING MIMICS AN OBSERVING CONSCIOUSNESS

As we established in Chapter 4, "A Director's Screen Grammar," we cut between speakers in a dialogue scene based on whatever would make an observer shift his attention. Watch how eye contact and eye-line shifts function in real life, for these are the outward signs of shifting attention. Edit according to eye-line changes, and you'll be working from human behavior rather than disembodied theory. The veteran editor Walter Murch says, "The blink is a momentary and unnoticed cessation of vision, which I believe we use unconsciously to punctuate the phrases of our thoughts."[1] He uses eyeblinks as a key to dialogue editing, as you can read in his *In the Blink of an Eye*, 2nd rev. ed. (Silman-James, 2001).

Counterpointing visual and aural impressions is a variation on what was called "montage" in film's earliest days. Because it was silent, film had to juxtapose two shots and scenes to imply continuity, development, relatedness, or contrast. The audience guessed the relational associations. I think that the audience's enjoyment comes from imagining and hypothesizing as they follow the narrative and compile its subtexts.

Counterpointing sound against action, instead of using sound to accompany or illustrate, came relatively late. It was probably developed by documentary editors trying to compress lengthy materials drawn directly from life. Robert Altman among fiction filmmakers—particularly in *M*A*S*H* (1970), *Nashville* (1975,

---

[1] Interview by Kiran Ganti at the Film and Television Institute of India, Pune, April 2004, www.folkbildning.net/%7Ee-kurs/sound/interview-with-walter-murch.htm. More interviews and articles on Murch can be found via http://filmsound.org/murch/murch.htm.

FIGURE 40-1

In *Nashville*, as in his other films, Robert Altman trusts the audience to make sense of dense, layered sound tracks that convey the feel of lifelike group situations (courtesy Paramount/The Kobal Collection).

Figure 40-1), and *Gosford Park* (2002)—shows great faith in the audience's ability to interpret densely layered dialogue tracks.

EYE CONTACT

Imagine two diners having a romantic conversation across a restaurant table. Inexperienced players gaze soulfully into each other's eyes as they speak. The results are phony because they are playing an *idea* of how people converse, not what happens in life. Do some discreet people-watching at a restaurant. What you'll see is more subtle and interesting: often neither person makes eye contact more than fleetingly. Generally, the intensity of eye contact is reserved for special moments—that is, to:

- Check what effect we have just had.
- Get information from the other person's expression so we know how next to act on him or her.
- Put additional pressure on the other person as we act on him or her.
- See from the person's body language or expression what is meant when he or she is acting on us.

In subtle ways, each speaker is either pressing or being pressed. Only at crucial moments does one search the other for facial or behavioral enlightenment. Much of the time, the listener's gaze rests on isolated or neutral objects while he or she mentally focuses inwardly on what the other person may want or mean.

Hearing is different. It may be totally focused on the other person for the duration of the conversation. But it, too, may wander. Eyes and ears move their attention independently, but are always working in tandem, feeding information to the overworked brain.

Play the Concerned Observer while you watch a couple in conversation, and monitor how and why your eye line shifts between the speakers. Notice how:

- You often followed the shifts in their eye lines, wanting to see what they were looking at, and involuntarily switching your gaze from subject to object.
- Your mind hypothesized a new motivation after each eye-line change.
- There is a rhythm to your eye-line changes (controlled by the shifting contours of the conversation itself).
- You made an instinctive judgment about who and what to look at, often on the basis of something on the periphery demanding a closer look.

WATCHING IS ALSO THINKING

Independently, your center of attention switches back and forth, often following the conversing pair's action and reaction, their changes of eye line, and their physical action, but (and this is very important) you also make directional choices *based on your evolving thoughts and hypothesis* about them. Making a hypothesis is like shining a light ahead in the dark. Unconsciously, the Observer uses his developing insight to search out the most telling information.

HOW CAMERA POSITIONS REVEAL PSYCHOLOGICAL VANTAGE

To reproduce on film what you have just seen, you would need to cover each speaker from the viewpoint of the other, and add a third viewpoint to encompass them both as you, the Observer, see them. For good measure, you'd add complementary overshoulder shots. The Observer's point of view (POV) is outside the enclosed consciousness of the two speakers, and because it shows them in a more detached, observational way, it implies the Storyteller's POV. Now you have a complete model for basic movie coverage.

INNER LIVES

Film, as we have said, has difficulty relaying people's interior life, but where a person looks suggests what she is thinking and feeling, even though she may try to hide it. Editing is thus a powerful tool to imply inner life and inner character contours. This flexibility of viewpoint allows the film to structure what the audience sees, and to structure whose point of view and whose state of mind the audience shares at any given moment. This probing, cinematic way of seeing is modeled on the way we unconsciously delve, visually and imaginatively, into an event that interests us.

OBSERVER INTO STORYTELLER

According to choices made in shooting and editing, the audience will identify with one or other of the characters inside the story or with the more detached perspective of the invisible Storyteller/Observer. While Character A talks, the film might allow the audience to look detachedly at either A or B, to share the perspective of either one upon the other, or to look at both of them in long shot.

The Concerned Observer turns into the Storyteller when faithful, thoughtful watching (much as you'd see in an anthropological documentary) becomes active and critical. This kind of involvement holds distinct expectations of the characters and their agendas. Though observation may be routed through a central character, it can also come from outside the characters. When it does, it implies that the Storyteller is struggling to hypothesize the characters, to guess who they are and what they are trying to get. We recognize this from our struggles to understand such pivotal figures in our lives as parents, employers, and life partners. Any of these would merit a lively and partisan account. That is the Storyteller at work, full of zest to tell tall tales.

EDITING TO INFLUENCE SUBTEXTS

ALTERING PERFORMANCE RHYTHMS

For any scene that was adequately acted and shot, a very significant dramatic control now rests in the cutting room. This concerns not only who or what is shown at any particular moment, but *how much time each character takes to process what he sees or hears.* This timing originated with the actors, but can be altered by the editor whenever there is sufficient coverage. Reaction time—which is the inner action that occurs before outward action—contributes hugely to the power and consistency of a scene's subtext.

THE POWER OF SUBTEXT

Inexperienced film actors, learning lines and repeating them in numerous takes and angles, tend to drop into a set rhythm. This levels out their characters' inner lives into a shared average. This will show up in force in an early cut, and is deadly. The scene rhythms must be adjusted in editing to recover some of the changeableness and unpredictability of spontaneous action. Imagine a two-person, interior scene where a man asks a simple question of a woman who is visiting his apartment for dinner: "Do you think it's cold outside?" Depending on the context and on her nonverbal reaction, this could imply several subtexts. He could be saying:

- "Because we're about to leave, do you think I need warmer clothes?"
- "Let's not go to the party after all."
- "Do you want to stay the night with me?"

What makes the audience choose the most likely subtext? How the lines are said and how the listener reacts to the speaker tell you a lot. An easy and unreflecting "No" is very different from one delivered after a momentary silence or one that is long delayed by apparent internal struggle. Not only do such timing differences and behavioral nuances direct what we imagine, but prior events (if the man visited the doctor) also condition the subtext we supply. Thus, *the order of material in a film and the amount of apparent thought each character devotes to each part of their interaction can imply quite different subtexts*, and lead the audience to generate a whole new set of open questions. You want this because it raises dramatic tension.

MAKING OR ALTERING SUBTEXTS

When performances are not stellar, and particularly when they are uneven, sensitive editing can drive up the stakes in a scene so it acquires more intensity and a more defined point of view. By exerting fine control over the original rhythms of reply, eye-line changes, actions, and reactions, the scene can become a unified entity that nobody could quite have foreseen.

No editor can change a character's rate of speech or reaction times in a single, unbroken take, but much potential opens up when the scene is covered from more than one angle or in more than one image size. Look at Figure 40-2. Diagram A is a representation of the master take, a timing that the actors reproduced in all subsequent takes. The diagram shows picture and sound as separate strands, much as you see them on an editing program timeline.

In Diagram B, the cut to close-up simply preserves the actors' original timing—though merely by using it, the audience begins to expect a greater significance in her reply. Diagram C uses overlap cutting (see following section for extended explanation) to make her reply come as quickly as possible. Diagram D, however, doubles her reaction time by adding together the pauses from both takes. Diagram E goes still further by double-cutting her thinking and his waiting reaction before cutting back to her in thought before she replies. To create this degree of delay, you will need a complementary close-up reaction shot on him and a second take on her from which to steal the extra close-shot reaction.

Intelligent choices of reaction, and careful rebalancing of performance reaction times, can add massively to the credibility of the characters' inner lives. This deepens the choices and reactions that compel each into action or speech, and contributes greatly to the overall impact of the film. New rhythms are now aiding and abetting performances and creating the grounds for us to infer greater thought, feeling, and reaction.

VISUAL AND AURAL EDITING RHYTHMS: AN ANALOGY IN MUSIC

The interplay of editing's rhythmic elements needs further explanation if the possibilities are to be visible. Though everything in editing takes place in minutes, seconds, and frames, dramatic decisions can no more be made from script or stopwatch calculations than music can be composed with a metronome.

```
!2S: Him                                           Her
_____
/   "Do you think it's cold out?"                 "No"
_____
                        <----t------>
```

Example A: Master Two-Shot (actors' timing "t" as played)

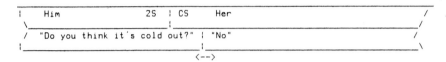

```
\    Him                           2S  ! CS: Her                           !
_____!_____/
/   "Do you think it's cold out?"    !       "No"                          !
!_____!_____\
                        <------t---->
```

Example B: Cut from Two-Shot to CS (still actor's timing as played)

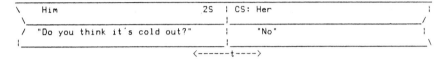

```
!    Him              2S  ! CS   Her                                       /
_____!_____/
/   "Do you think it's cold out?" ! "No"                                   /
!_____!_____\
                        <-->
```

Example C: Reply Now Comes Quickly Using Picture Overlap Reaction

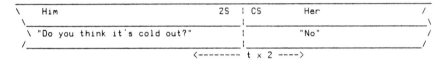

```
\    Him                           2S  ! CS   Her                          /
_____!_____\
/   \ "Do you think it's cold out?"    !       "No"                        /
/_____!_____/
                        <-------- t x 2 ---->
```

Example D: Reply Delayed by Summing Reaction Time from Both Shots

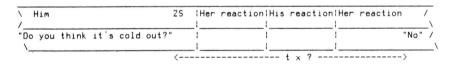

```
\   Him                       2S  !Her reaction!His reaction!Her reaction  /
/_____!_____!_____!_____\
   "Do you think it's cold out?"  !           !           !        "No" /
_____!_____!_____!_____\
                        <----------------- t x ? ---------------->
```

Example E: Double Cutting Reaction Shots Creates Maximum Delay

FIGURE 40-2 ───

How the timing of a pause (t) between lines can be removed or augmented to alter the rhythm of dialogue responses. This can quite change the subtext of the exchange.

RHYTHMIC INTERPLAY

Let's examine an edited version of a conversation between two people. We have two different but interlocked rhythms going. First, there is the rhythmic pattern of their voices in a series of sentences that ebb and flow, speed up, slow down, halt, restart, and continue. Set against this, and often taking a rhythmic cue from vocal rhythms, is the visual tempo set up by the complex shifts of visual choice, outlined previously and evoked in the interplay of cutting, camera composition, and movement. The visual and aural streams proceed independently yet are rhythmically related, like the relation between music and the physical movements of two dancers.

HARMONY

When you hear a speaker and see his face as he talks, sound and vision are allied like a melody with its harmony. We could, however, break the literalness of always hearing and seeing the same thing (harmony) by making the transition from scene to scene into a temporary puzzle.

COUNTERPOINT

We are going to cut from a woman talking about her vanished husband to a shot panning across a view of tawdry seashore hotels. We start with the speaker in picture and sound, and then cut to the panning shot while she is still speaking, letting her remaining words play out over the hotels. The effect is this: while our subject is talking about her now fatherless children and the bitterness she feels toward the absent husband, we glance away and in our mind's eye imagine where he might now be. The film version of this scene can suggest the mental (or even physical) imagery of someone present and listening. The speaker's words are powerfully counterpointed by the image, and the image lets loose our imagination, so we ponder what he is doing and what is happening behind the crumbling facades of the hotels.

Counterpointing a sound against an unrelated image has its variations. One usage is simply to illustrate. We see taking place what the woman's words begin to describe: ". . . and the last I heard, he was in Florida. . . ."

Many an elegant contrapuntal sequence in a feature film is the work of an editor trained in documentary and who is now trying to raise the movie above a pedestrian script, as Ralph Rosenblum relates in *When the Shooting Stops . . . the Cutting Begins* (Da Capo Paperback Series, 1986). Directing and editing documentaries has contributed importantly to the screen fluency of Robert Altman, Michael Apted, Lindsay Anderson, Carroll Ballard, Werner Herzog, Krzysztof Kieslowski, Ken Loach, Louis Malle, Alain Resnais, Martin Scorsese, and Haskell Wexler, to name but a few of the better-known fiction directors.

DISSONANCE

Another editing gambit exploits discrepancies. For instance, while we hear a salesman telling his new assistant his theory of dynamic customer persuasion, we see the same man listing the virtues of a hideaway bed in a monotone so dreary that his customer is bored into a trance. This discrepancy, if we pursue the musical allusion, is a dissonance. It spurs the viewer to create a resolution. Comparing the man's beliefs (heard) with his practice (seen), the viewer is driven to conclude, "Here is someone who does not know himself." This technique of ambiguous revelation is equally viable in documentary film, where it may have originated. Documentary has a big problem getting the audience to look critically at reality. People think documentary is just a record—when, in fact, it, too, is a construct like fiction, and must use all the devices at its disposal to alert the audience to critical subtexts and hidden dimensions.

THE OVERLAP CUT AND TRANSITIONS

DIALOGUE SEQUENCES

The *overlap cut*, also known as a *lap cut* or *L cut*, is a contrapuntal editing device useful for blurring the unnatural seams between shots. It works by bringing a speaker's voice in before his picture, or vice versa, and this removes the level cuts that reduce editing to staid and predictable blocks of action.

Figure 40-3 is a straight-cut version of a conversation between A and B. Whoever speaks is shown on the screen, and before long this becomes predictable. You could alleviate this by slugging in some reaction shots (not shown).

Now look at the same conversation using overlap cuts (also called lap cuts or L cuts). Person A starts speaking, but then we hear B's voice (during Overlap x). We wait a sentence before cutting to him. B is interrupted by A (during Overlap y), and this time we hold on B's frustrated expression before cutting to A driving his point home. Before A has finished, because we are now interested in B's rising anger, we cut back to him shaking his head (during Overlap z). When A has finished, B—whom we have seen waiting—caps the discussion, and this ends the sequence.

How do you decide when you should make overlap cuts? Let's return to our trusty editing model: human consciousness at work. Imagine you are witnessing a conversation between two people; you have to turn your head from one to the other. Seldom will you turn at the right moment to catch the next speaker beginning; only an omniscient being could be so accurate. Editors who make neat, level cuts between speakers tend to give a prepackaged, premeditated look to their work. Such omniscience destroys the illusion of watching something develop spontaneously. In real life, you can seldom predict who will speak next—it is hearing a new voice that tells you where to look. If a film is to convince us that a

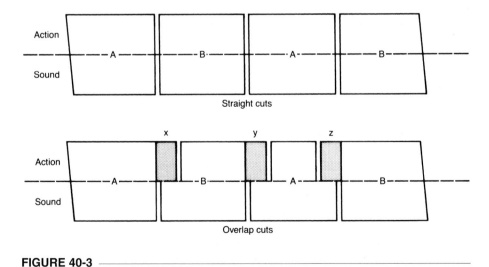

FIGURE 40-3

Straight-cut dialogue sequence compared with its overlap-cut version.

dialogue sequence comes spontaneously from real life, its editor must replicate the disjunctive shifts when our eyes follow our hearing, or our hearing (that is, concentration) catches up late with something we have just seen.

Effective editing begins with the unfolding consciousness of the story's characters. Added to this is what the involved and opinionated Storyteller wants us to notice. This spectator and guide is not only engaged in hearing and seeing each speaker as he speaks (which would be boring), but *in guessing at what is happening inside each protagonist* through clues embedded in their actions and reactions. A Concerned Observer notices evidence, but the Storyteller goes further by developing attitudes from hypothesizing the characters, their significance, their contradictions, and even their place and time.

A film that truly entertains makes you feel you are in the company of an astute, witty onlooker who savors human nature. This critical and privileged guide shares every special observation and lets you see as much as possible about the characters.

For filmmaking and editing in particular, the message is clear. To take the audience along with the astute subjectivity of the Storyteller, the editor often makes sound and picture changeover points as staggered cuts, for these replicate moving consciousness at its best.

SEQUENCE TRANSITIONS

In the least cinematic scene transition, a character exits the frame leaving an empty set, and the film cuts to another empty frame before he moves into the scene. This is really proscenium arch theater, a kind of clumsy scene shifting that puts a huge hiccup in a film's momentum. Inexperienced directors often engineer scenes to start and stop this way, but a savvy editor quickly looks for ways to ax the dead footage.

Just as there are dialogue overlap cuts, so there are live transitions from one sequence to another by using the lap cut. Imagine a scene with a boy and girl talking about going out together. The boy says he thinks her mother will try and stop them. The girl says, "Oh don't worry about her; I can talk her round." Cut to the next scene, where the girl asks the question of her mother, who closes the refrigerator with a bang and says firmly, "Absolutely not!"

First, it is redundant to restate the girl's situation in this way. A level cut would take us instantly from the boy/girl sequence to the mother/girl scene where the mother answers, "Absolutely not!" A more interesting way of leaving the boy/girl scene would be to cut to the mother at the refrigerator while the girl is still saying, ". . . I can talk her round." As she finishes, the mother slams the fridge door and says, "Absolutely not!" as the camera pans to show the girl already in the scene.

Another way to create an elision instead of a creaky scene change would be to hold on the boy and girl and have the mother's angry voice say, "Absolutely not!" over the tail end of their shot. You would use the surprise of the new voice to motivate lap cutting to the mother in picture as the new scene continues.

Either of these devices (sound trailing picture, or sound leading picture) diminishes the evidence of coupling between one sequence and the next. Though you sometimes want to bring a scene to a slow closure, perhaps with a fade-out, more often you want to keep up momentum. Filmmakers used to interpose dissolves because a level cut jerks the viewer too rudely into a new place and time, but the dissolve inserts a rest period between scenes and dissipates your precious onward momentum.

SOUND EFFECTS AS SCENE ELISION

You have seen this overlap technique done with sound effects. It might look like this: The schoolteacher rolls reluctantly out of her bed, and as she ties up her hair, we hear the increasingly loud sound of a playground until we cut to her on duty at the school door. Because our curiosity demands an answer to the riddle of children's voices in a woman's bedroom, we do not find the location switch arbitrary or theatrical. Anticipatory sound dragged our attention forward to the next sequence.

Another type of overlap cut makes sound work another way; we cut from the teacher leading kids chanting their multiplication tables to her getting food out of her refrigerator at home. The dreary class sound subsides slowly while she exhaustedly eats some leftovers. In the first example, anticipatory sound draws her forward out of her bedroom, while in the second, holdover sound persists even after she gets home. Because the Storyteller shows how the din exists in her mind, the implication in both cases is that she finds her workplace burdensome. So overlap cutting does more than soften transitions between scenes; it here implies what dominates our schoolteacher's inner consciousness. We could suggest something quite different by playing it another way and letting the silence of her home trail out into the workplace.

In this scenario, she is seen at work with her bedroom radio still playing softly before its sound is swamped by the rising uproar of feet echoing in a corridor. At the end of the day, her TV sitcom could displace her voice giving out the dictation, and we cut to her relaxing at home.

By using sound and picture transitions creatively, we can transport the viewer forward without cumbersome optical effects such as dissolves, fades, or worse such intrusions. We are also able to scatter important clues about the characters' subjective lives and inner imaginings, something film cannot otherwise easily do.

THE PROBLEM OF ACHIEVING A FLOW

After you run your evolving cut a few times, it will strike you more and more as a series of clunky blocks of material, with a distressing lack of flow. Dialogue scenes, centered as they are upon showing each speaker, seem especially cumbersome. First, there is a block of this speaker, then a block of that speaker, then a block of both, and so on. Even sequences seem to change from one to the next in a blocky way, like watching train boxcars pass, each discrete and hitched to its fellows with a plain link device. I think of this kind of editing as boxcar cutting.

How to achieve the effortless flow seen in the cinema? To move in this direction, we must return to how human perception functions at points of transition.

COUNTERPOINT IN PRACTICE: UNIFYING MATERIAL INTO A FLOW

In practice, this means bringing together the sound from one shot with the image from another, as we have said. To return to my example of a salesman with a great self-image who proved to have a poor performance, you could show this on the screen by merging two sets of materials: one of him talking to his assistant over a coffee break (Sequence A), and the other of him in the salesroom making a pitch to clients (Sequence B).

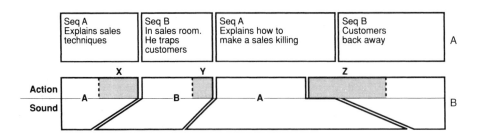

FIGURE 40-4

Counterpointing the content of one sequence against another. Sequence A assembles material in blocks with straight-cut sound, whereas Sequence B takes advantage of overlap editing and counterpoint.

We can edit the materials into juxtaposition. The conservative, first-assembly method would alternate segments as in Figure 40-4A: a block of explanation, then a block of sales talk, then another block of explanation and another of sales, and so on until the point had been made. This is a common, though clumsy, way to accomplish the objective, and after a few cuts, both the technique and the message become as predictable as a boxer slugging a punching bag.

Instead of crudely alternating the sequences, let's integrate the two sets of materials as in Figure 40-4B. Start Harold explaining his sales philosophy (Sequence A) during the salesmen's coffee break. While he's showing off to the younger men, we begin fading up the sound from the salesroom (Sequence B) in which we hear Harold's aggressive greetings. As he reaches full volume, we cut to the salesroom picture (Sequence B) to see that he has trapped a reluctant customer and is launching into his sales pitch. After this is established, we fade up the coffee break conversation again (Sequence A). We hear the salesman say how he first fascinates the customer. We cut to Sequence A's picture, and see that Harold has moved uncomfortably close to his juniors. He tells them how you must first make the customers admit they like the merchandise. While the voices continue, we cut back to the salesroom (Sequence B) picture, only to see the customer backing away angrily. We bring up Sequence B's sound as the customer says she came only to buy a pillow.

Notice that in the overlap areas (X, Y, and Z) of Figure 40-4B, picture from one sequence is counterpointed against sound from another. Instead of having description and practice separated as discrete blocks of material, description is now laid against practice, and ideas against reality, to make a much harder-hitting juxtaposition.

The benefits are multiple. Talking-head conversation is kept minimal, whereas the behavioral material—the salesroom evidence against which we measure his ideas—now predominates. There is a closer and more telling juxtaposition between his idea of himself and his sales performance, so the audience is challenged to reconcile the gap between the man's ideas and what he is actually doing. Counterpointing the essentials allows you to pare the combination of materials to a muscular, spare version that you never get when film writing is conceived as theatrical dialogue.

Counterpoint editing cannot really be worked out in scripting, because entry and exit points depend on the nuances of playing or camerawork. But if both scenes are shot in their entirety, one becomes a parallel action to the other. The resulting sequence can be worked out from the materials themselves, and will reliably and effectively compress the two.

There is a shooting/editing project to practice these skills in Chapter 6, "Shooting Projects." Look for Project 6-2C: Vocal Counterpoint and Point of View. This adds a vocal counterpoint to action, but you might want to try improvising the salesman scene from the earlier example, using one scene as parallel action to the other and fusing the two in counterpoint.

THE ROUGH-CUT VIEWING

The next cut after the assembly is called the rough cut. Here, the full range of material is deployed toward goals that were decided after seeing the assembly. No sequence is yet fine-tuned, but the editor tries to make each sequence occupy its right place and be dramatically successful. The scrutiny you give this new cut is similar to the previous versions, and it remains important to deal with the large-scale dimensions first:
Exposition:

- Is there adequate, too little, or too much expository detail?
- Is exposition integrated with the action, or does the film pause to inform the audience?
- What exposition, if removed, could the audience still infer?
- What exposition could be delayed (always better to make the audience wonder and wait if you can)?

Momentum:

- Does momentum keep up throughout?
- Where does momentum falter, and why?

Duration:

- What sequences feel long, and what material feels redundant?
- How does the film duration feel as a whole—long, short, or right?

Characters:

- How logical and satisfying is the development of each major character?
- Is anything misleading or alienating about the characters?
- Do they appear (as they should) before becoming dramatically necessary?

Balance:

- Does the film breathe so that, like music, each movement feels balanced and inevitable, or is there a misshapen, unbalanced feel to some parts?
- Is there a satisfying balance between interiors and exteriors? (This often means dealing with claustrophobia the film generates. Well-constructed films alternate between intensity and release, much as a person must alternate intimacy with solitude, indoors with outdoors, family with work, day with night, and so on.)

Theme and Meaning:

- What is the film's present thematic impact?
- Who or what is delivering it?
- Where is the intended impact failing?

After seeing the rough cut a second or third time, you might ask more localized questions, such as:

- Which sequences would benefit from later in-points and/or earlier out-points? (Most scenes are better entered or left in action rather than opened and closed on static action like stage curtains).
- What needs to be done for each character to exert maximum impact, and in which sequences?
- Which sequences cry out for special attention to rhythm and pacing?
- How effective is the ending?
- Are there still false endings before (or worse, after) the true one?

Again, ask the editor to fix only the glaring faults before you schedule another viewing.

SEE THE WHOLE FILM

Even if work has been done on only two sequences, run the whole movie, for a film is like a tent: change the height of one pole or the length of one guy rope, and new stresses course through the whole structure. Always review changes in the context of the whole work. At each new viewing, you will be struggling to see your film empty of foreknowledge and as if for the very first time—just as your audience does.

THE AUDIENCE

DRAMA TAKES PLACE IN THE AUDIENCE'S IMAGINATION

By creating a texture of sound and picture requiring interpretation, a film juxtaposes antithetical elements with great economy, and kindles the audience's involvement in developing ideas that might resolve the story's dialectical tensions. Now the audience is no longer passively identifying and submitting to the controlling will of the movie, but is living an imaginative, critical inner life in response to the film's suggestions. Such critical awareness was what Bertolt Brecht, striving to arrest the audience habit of identifying, set out to accomplish in the theater.

THE AUDIENCE AS ACTIVE RATHER THAN PASSIVE PARTICIPANTS

This more demanding texture of word and image thrusts the spectator into a critical relationship and encourages active rather than passive participation. The Storyteller has developed an understanding with the audience that promises not just diversion but a challenge to interpret, a chance to weigh what is seen against what is heard and to balance an idea against its contrary. The film will now sometimes confirm and other times contradict what had seemed true. As in life, the viewer must use critical judgment when, as in our example of the salesman, a man's self-image turns out to be unreliable.

More interesting ways to use juxtaposition and counterpoint emerge when the basic coupling of sound and picture is broken. For instance, you might show an interior with a bored teenage girl looking out a store window at people in the street. A radio somewhere offscreen is broadcasting the report of a dog show as she watches a boy and his mother having a violent argument outside. The girl is too abstracted to notice the counterpoint. Though we see the mother and child, we hear the commentator detailing the breeds and their traits. There is an ironic contrast between all the different planes of consciousness: an argument is raised to the level of a public spectacle, yet our main character is too naive or too inward-looking to notice. Very succinctly and with not a little humor, both her unconsciousness and a satirical view of mother and child relationships have been compressed into a 30-second shot. Now that's economy!

SUMMARY

In these examples, we have established that our consciousness can probe our surroundings, either:

- Monodirectionally (eyes and ears on the same information source)
- Bidirectionally (eyes and ears on different sources)
- Ears pull eyes forward to see a new setting.
- Eyes pull ears forward to hear a new setting.

With these techniques, film can impart the sensations of a character's shifting planes of consciousness and association. A welcome result from creative overlap cutting is that you can completely dispense with optical transitions such as the fade or dissolve.

HELP, I CAN'T UNDERSTAND!

These cutting techniques are hard to grasp from a book, even though they closely mimic the way our awareness shifts a hundred times a day. If this is getting beyond you, do not worry. The best way to understand editing is to take a complex and interesting sequence in a feature film and, by running a shot or two at a time, make a precise log of the relationship between the track elements and the visuals.

Chapter 5, Project 5-2: Editing Analysis is a self-education in editing, with a list of techniques for you to locate and analyze. Try shooting and editing your own sequences from the directions in Chapter 6, "Shooting Projects," Projects 6-1 through 6-6. After some hands-on experience, return to this section and it should all be much clearer.

CHAPTER 41

USING ANALYSIS AND FEEDBACK

After weeks or months of sustained editing, a debilitating familiarity sets in. You lose objectivity and the ability to make judgments on behalf of an audience. Every version begins to look the same, and all look too long. You become obsessed with particular faults in your footage, and curing them grows to an overwhelming task. Not unusually, you want to hang on to a sequence or a minor character that the editor and others think is redundant. These are your darlings, and you must kill them if the film is to be consistent and work well.

This disabling condition is particularly likely to overwhelm the hyphenate, the director-editor, who has lived closely with the intentions and the footage since their inception. But it also afflicts whole editing crews. This is why you call on outsiders' reactions to the piece. First, though, you need to do some preparation.

DIAGNOSTICS

MAKING A FLOWCHART

Before showing the cut to outsiders, make an abstract of your film in the form of a block diagram so that you can spot anomalies. A useful dual-purpose form that speeds up the job of analysis can be photocopied from Chapter 22, Figure 22-2. Some problems you will easily fix because diagramming alone brings revelations and new ideas.

To better understand anything, translate it into another form. Statisticians make the meaning of their figures evident through a graph, pie chart, or other proportional image. Film is a slippery, deceptive medium whose mesmerizing present-tense detail inhibits much sense of overview. But a flowchart can give you a fresh and more detached perspective on your work. Run your film a sequence at a time and:

1.   Make a brief note of each new sequence's content in a box (characters and main action).

2. Next to the box, write what the sequence contributes to the development of the film as a whole. This might be factual information; it might introduce a setting, a character, or a relationship to be developed later in the film; or it might exist to create a special mood or feeling.

3. Now look at the flowchart for your film. Like any representation, it has limitations because film sequences are not like a succession of soloists, each singing a self-contained song, but more like the delayed entry of several parts in a choral work. Each entering voice joins and cross-modulates with those preceding. Some foreshadow or set up references that will make sense only later.

4. Draw and annotate lines indicating any special relationship existing between each new sequence and those preceding. This might show that in parallel storytelling, for instance, one sequence is too far away from its counterpart.

5. Examine how much time each sequence takes, and give each an impact rating so you can assess how the film's dramatic pressures evolve.

Do this work from the life on the screen, not from memory or the script, if you want to dispassionately see what is there for an audience. Analyzing your work like this forces you to acknowledge what actually comes from the screen, and to translate amorphous sensations into hard-edged statements.

What does the progression add up to? As with the first assembly, you will find some of the following:

- The film lacks early impact or has an unnecessarily pedestrian opening that makes it a late developer (fine for 19th-century Russian novels, but fatal for a film that may live or die on TV).

- The main issues are unclear or take too long to emerge (a writing problem, but you may be able to reposition a scene earlier, even ahead of titles, to commit the film to an interesting line of development).

- The type and frequency of impact is poorly distributed over the film's length (feast or famine in dramatic development and progression).

- There is a nonlinear development of basic, necessary information about characters, backstory, and environment, including:
  o Omissions
  o Duplication
  o Back doubles (going back to something that should have been dealt with earlier)
  o Redundancy
  o Expository information positioned too early so audience forgets it
  o Insufficient expository information or information placed too late

- The film makes the same dramatic contribution in several ways. (Three consecutive scenes reveal that the hero has a low flash point. Choose the best, and reposition or dump the others.)

- A favorite sequence or character does not contribute to the thrust of the film. (Another darling. Close your eyes and swing the ax.)

- The film's resolution emerges early, leaving the remainder of the story tediously inevitable. (Rebalance or withdraw indicators in the movie to keep resolution in doubt, so the audience stays interested and working.)
- The film appears to end before it actually does. (False or multiple endings are a common problem.)

Naming each ailment leads to its cure. When you have put these remedies into effect, you will sense the improvement rather than see it. It is like resetting a boat sail; everything looks the same, but she surges under new power.

USING THE FLOWCHART AGAIN

Film practices unending deceit on its makers, so after a few rounds of alteration, make a new flowchart to ensure that housecleaning has not introduced new problems. Even when making a new flowchart seems utterly unnecessary, you will find another round of anomalies that have grown up like weeds. Filmmakers of long standing know this, and subject their work to intensive formal scrutiny. Most of the discussion during the cutting of a feature film is during the last phases, and centers on the film's dramatic shape and effectiveness.

A TRIAL SHOWING

Preparing flowcharts brings one more benefit. Knowing now what every brick in your movie's edifice is supposed to uphold, you are excellently prepared to test the film's intentions during a trial show for a small audience.

THE TRIAL AUDIENCE

Your audience should be half a dozen or so people whose tastes and interests you respect. The less they know about your film and your aims, the better.

PREPARATION

Give your movie a working title. It signals the story's purpose and identity, and forms part of the viewer's "contract" with the film. Check sound levels and adjust them in your software, or you will get misleadingly negative responses. Even film professionals can drastically misjudge a movie whose sound elements are inaudible or overbearing. Once you have your audience in its seats, warn that the film is a work in progress and still technically raw. Also warn that you will call out a brief description of any music, sound effects, or titles that are missing.

SURVIVING YOUR CRITICS AND MAKING USE OF WHAT THEY SAY

LISTEN, DO NOT EXPLAIN

Asking for critical feedback must be handled carefully, or it can be a pointless exercise. After the viewing:

- Ask for impressions of the film as a whole.

- Say little; listen much. Your film must stand or fall on its merits, so concentrate on what your audience may be telling you.
- Focus and direct your viewers' attention, or you may find the discussion quite peripheral to your needs.
- Avoid the temptation to explain anything. Explanations confuse and compromise the audience's perceptions, and can even imply that they are inept viewers.

LINES OF INQUIRY

Because you usually need to guide the inquiry into useful channels, here are some open-ended questions that move from the large issues toward the component parts:

- What is the story really about?
- What are the major issues in the film?
- Did the movie feel the right length, or was it too long?
- Were there any parts that were unclear or puzzling? (You can itemize those you suspect fit the description because audiences often forget anything that passed over their heads.)
- Which parts felt slow?
- Which parts were moving or otherwise successful?
- What did you feel about ___ (name of character)?
- What did you end up knowing about ___ (situation or issue)?

Inquiring in this way, you test the effectiveness of the function you had assigned each sequence. Depending on your trial audience's patience, you may be able to survey only dubious areas, or you may get feedback on most of your film's parts and intentions.

BALANCING DIFFERENT VIEWS

Dealing with criticism really means absorbing multiple views, and then, after the dust settles, reviewing the film to see how audience members could get such varying impressions. In the cutting room, you and your editor now see the movie with the eyes of those who never understood that the messenger was the workmate seen in an earlier scene. You find a way to put in an extra line, and, without compromising the film, the problem is solved.

Before rushing to fix anything, take into account the number of people reporting any particular difficulty. Comments from different audience members may in any case cancel each other out, so no action may be called for. Make allowances, too, for the subjectivity and acuity of individual critics.

THE EGOCENTRIC CRITIC

An irritation you must often suffer, especially among those with a little knowledge to flourish, is the person who insists on talking about the film he would have made rather than the film you have just shown. Diplomatically redirect the discussion.

WEAR AND TEAR

Taking in reactions and criticism is an emotionally draining experience. It is quite usual to feel threatened, slighted, and misunderstood, and to come away with a raging headache. You need all the self-discipline you can muster to sit immobile, say little, and listen. Take notes or make an audio recording of the proceedings so that later, in peace, you can go over what the audience said.

MAKE CHANGES CAUTIOUSLY

Make no changes without lengthy and careful reflection. Remember, if you ask for criticism, people try to make their mark on your work. You will never be able to please everyone, nor should you try.

HOLD ON TO YOUR CENTRAL INTENTIONS

Never let your central intentions get lost, and never revise them unless there are overwhelmingly positive reasons to do so. Act only on suggestions that support and further your central intentions. This is a dangerous phase for the filmmaker—indeed, for any artist. If you let go of your work's underlying identity, you will lose your direction. Just try to keep listening and to think deeply about what you hear. Don't let strong emotions make you carve into your film precipitously. You may need a week for contradictory passions to settle.

MEA CULPA

It is quite normal by now to feel that you have failed, that you have a piece of junk on your hands, that all is vanity. If this happens, take heart. You might have felt this during shooting, which would have been a lot worse. Things are never so awful as they seem after the first showings. Keep in mind that the conditions of viewing invite mainly negative feedback. Lay audiences (and even professionals) are often disproportionately affected by a wrong sound balance here, a missed sound dissolve there, a shot or two that needs clipping, or a sequence that belongs earlier. These imbalances and rhythmic ineptitudes massively downgrade a film's impact. The glossy finish you have yet to apply will greatly improve the film's reception.

THE USES OF PROCRASTINATION

Whether you are pleased or depressed by your film, it is always good to stop working on it for a few days, or even a few weeks, and do something else. If this degree of anxiety and depression is new to you, take comfort; you are deep in the throes of the artistic experience. It is the long and painful labor before birth. When you pick up the film again after a lapse, its problems and their solutions will no longer seem overwhelming.

TRY, TRY AGAIN

A film of any substance usually demands a long evolution in the editing room, so expect to make several rounds of alterations and to try the film on several new audiences. You may want to show the last cut to the original trial audience to see what changes they report. Sometimes you can get a real sense of progress made during editing, and sometimes not.

As a director with a lot of editing in my background, I have seen, times without number, how a film really emerges in the editing process. Magic and miracles appear from the footage, yet even film crews seldom appreciate this. That so much can happen goes unguessed by anyone who has never lived through it, and will seem unconscionably slow to the novice. Putting a year of part-time work into a 30-minute film is nothing unusual for new directors wanting to make their work live up to potential.

KNOWING WHEN TO STOP

Avoid setting deadlines for editing. Instead, look for compelling evidence that your film's development is coming to a standstill. Some directors go on fidgeting and fiddling, and some even spoil their work. It comes from the fear of letting go. It's a bit like admitting your child is now a grown-up and doesn't need you anymore.

MAKE A FINAL CHECK OF ALL SOURCE MATERIAL

Before regarding an edited version as approaching finality, the editor should review all shot material to make sure nothing useful has been overlooked. At this point in editing, and especially if there is a lot of coverage, this demand is skull-crackingly tedious and time-consuming, but almost invariably there will be some "Eureka!" discoveries in compensation. If there aren't, you can rest easy that night.

CHAPTER 42

WORKING WITH MUSIC

In extreme youth, I was an assistant editor on a dozen feature films. Each time, music would take us, jaded from living for months with the project, on a whole new journey into the story and its characters. This was always a miracle of revelation.

SPOTTING SESSION

Spotting for music is the process of viewing the fine cut, deciding where it needs music and where that music will come from. Some may be popular music from a time or place that is used for atmosphere. If so, its copyright will have to be acquired. The rest of the music will need a film composer, about which more later.

MUSICAL CHOICE AND USING SCRATCH MUSIC

To decide what type of music you want, try passages of recorded music against key sequences. This is called using *scratch music*. As with so much else, you know what you like only when you see it. Of course, it's easy to be obvious and use Beach Boys for surfboarders, ethnic accordions for European holiday makers, or cancan for anything French. Even quality orchestral music will seem clichéd if it's already too familiar and the audience cannot see it afresh.

Playing against the obvious can yield fresh insights. Better than illustrating, which means duplicating the visual message, is counterpointing the visible with music providing an unexpected emotional offset. Jean-Marie Straub, for instance, used Bach cantatas against shots of bombed-out Berlin. Where you anticipate musical pathos, he gives you spiritual yearning and nobility—and heightens the desolation in an unexpected way. Even an uninspiring sequence may suddenly come to life because music lends it a subtext that deepens the story or boosts its forward movement.

A well-judged score can supply the sense of integrity or melancholy in one character, and the interior impulses directing the actions of another. Music can enhance not just the givens of a character, but indicate invisible motives or foreshadow significant action. Structurally, music can supply needed phrasing to a scene, or help create scene or action demarcations by bracketing transitions in scenes or between acts. Short "stings," or fragments of melody, can also be good if they belong to a larger musical picture.

COPYRIGHT

Never assume that recorded music you would like to use will be available when you get around to inquiring. The very worst time to negotiate with the lawyers representing composers, performers, publishers, and performing rights societies is after your film has come to depend on a particular recording. You are now in the weakest position, and those with a nose for such things will try to suck you dry.

MUSIC LIBRARIES

You can use a royalty-free music library and pay "needle drop" fees (or "laser drop," as it's now called in the CD age) for the precise amount of music used. Because you pay as you go, costs are modest and scaled to your needs. If you want to enhance car chases, high-tension mountaineering, or need general feel-good music, you may be in luck. Otherwise, the chances of finding something suitable for drama of any originality are slim. See for yourself by entering "royalty-free music" or "music library" into a search engine and auditioning the many possibilities.

HIRING A COMPOSER

Commissioning original music obviates the difficulty of getting (and paying for) copyright clearance on recorded music. This is costly, but leaves you free thereafter to use the music as you wish. Closely examine the composer's prior work—in other media, not only film—to assure yourself that he or she works in the idiom you need. To get a rough idea whether their musical identity fits your story, place existing music experimentally against your film. Then, before you commit yourself, talk with whoever has previously worked with your composer to be sure there are no problematic tastes, work habits, or preferences.

HOW LONG DOES IT TAKE?

An experienced composer likes to take more than 6 weeks to compose about 15 minutes of music for a 90-minute feature film—but to be ready for the recording session, she may have to do it in 3, with a flurry of all-night music copyist work at the end.

BEGINNING WORK

Film composers are hired late, and generally have to work under pressure. The more time you can give them, the better. For much of what follows, I am indebted to my son, Paul Rabiger, who makes film music in Cologne, Germany. Like so many, he works largely with synthesizers, using live instrumentalists when the budget allows. The software favored by composers includes Steinberg Cubase (www.steinberg.net) and Emagic Logic Audio, which is now a division of Apple (www.apple.com/support/logic). These programs permit many tracks, integrate Musical Instrument Digital Interface (MIDI) with live recording, and support video in QuickTime format so the composer can build music to an accurate video version of the film.

Ideally, the composer reads the screenplay and sees the first complete cut. He or she avoids coming in with preconceived ideas, and asks what the director wants the music to accomplish. He or she will mull over the film's characters, settings, and overall content, and take time to develop basic melodic themes. Next comes deciding, within the budget, what instrumental texture works best. Particular characters or situations often evoke their own musical treatment, or leitmotif (recurring theme), and this is always best worked out with some time in hand, especially when research is needed because the music must reflect a particular era or ethnicity.

In common with sound designers, composers sometimes get maddeningly cerebral requests. I once heard a sound editor cry out, "He says he wants a thin, *tenuous* sound over the night shot. What the *!*!! does that mean?" So be concrete with your composer by describing what you want the audience to feel at particular points, or what the characters feel. Avoid intellectualizing or thinking out loud, because this can paint a confusing picture. Don't pretend to know more about music than you know. Be ready to say what you feel in response to a musical example, and bring as many recorded exerpts as you need to illustrate whatever can't be put into words—which is usually almost everything. This is a precious time when you and your composer explore each other's minds, and it should be unhurried and relaxed. Often your composer will bring revelations about your film—things you didn't even know were there, and which he or she can now accentuate.

WHEN THERE'S A GUIDE TRACK

The *scratch music* that nobody expected to keep now confronts the composer with a problem. Perhaps it's a stirring passage from Shostakovich's *Leningrad Symphony* or Jimi Hendrix in full cry. Certainly this indicates what you'd like, and what mood, texture, or tempo you'd prefer. But it also raises a barrier, for the hapless composer must extract whatever you find valuable, and then try to outgun the examples with his or her own musical solutions. In short, use scratch tracks to explore musical possibilities, but ask your composer whether or not to include them in musical deliberations.

DEVELOPING A MUSIC CUE LIST

Once the film's content is more or less locked down, it is formally screened by the director, editor, and producer for the composer. Ideally, the screened version has timecode burned into the lower part of the screen, and displays a cumulative timing for the whole movie. You have the story broken down into acts, and know where these occur on the film's timeline. You discuss where music seems desirable and what kind seems most appropriate. Typical questions center on how time is supposed to pass and whether music is meant to shore up a weak scene. The composer finds out (or suggests) where each music section starts and stops, and aims

```
                    "THE WATER-PEOPLE" MUSIC SECTION 4

00:00.0  Music segment begins as Robert jumps in car
00:03.5  Engine starts
00:05.0  Car lurches forward
00:10.5  Cut to Robert checking fuel gauge
00:14.5  Looks in rearview mirror
00:19.0  Frowns, realizing that a motorcycle is behind
00:27.5  Cut to Carl gunning his Harley-Davidson
00:38.0  Cut to Robert staring in mirror, car going off track
00:46.0  Shriek of tyres for 3 seconds as Robert drags car back on to road
00:58.5  Cut to Carl lying forward on motorcycle tank
01:06.5  Cut to BCU Robert's face realizing it's Carl behind
01:08.5  Begin Robert's line: "So you want trouble.  I can give you trouble"
01:12.0  End of line.
01:14.5  Cut to BCU hand opens glove pocket, takes out revolver
01:16.0  Revolver visible
01:17.5  Cut to flashing ambulance light, zoom back and siren drowns out
         music fades to silence and ...
01:29.0  music ends here.
```

FIGURE 42-1 ───

Typical scene measurements for a music cue segment.

to depart with a music cue list in hand and full notes as to function, with beginnings and endings defined as timecode. Start points may begin with visual clues (car door slams, car drives away) or dialogue clues ("If you think I'm happy about this, you've got another think coming" CUE MUSIC).

If the editor generates the music cues (also known as *spotting notes*), sections should be logged in minutes and seconds down to the nearest half second. Figure 42-1 shows a typical composer's cue sheet. Like other addictive substances, music is easy to start but difficult to finish. That is, you'll have no difficulty starting a music segment, but ending one so the audience doesn't feel deprived will take careful planning. A common practice is to conclude or fade out music under the entry of something new and more commanding. For instance, take music out during the first seconds of a noisy street scene or just before the dialogue in a new scene. Develop your own guidelines by studying films that integrate music with the kind of action you have in your film.

The computer-savvy composer then gets a DVD or tape copy to compose to. He or she will either create a traditional score to be performed and recorded, or will work with computers and MIDI-controlled synthesizers to make music sections directly. In the course of hands-on composing like this, music cues are occasionally added, dropped, or renegotiated when initial ideas meet actuality. Poorly placed or unjustifiable music may prove worse than no music at all.

Sometimes a composer will start from simplicity and develop to a complex musical destination. In Joseph Losey's *The Go-Between* (1971), Michel Legrand's superb score starts in the main character's Edwardian boyhood with a simple but slightly ominous Mozart theme. While visiting at an aristocratic home, the boy finds he is being used as a go-between, carrying messages in a forbidden love affair. A terrible conflict develops in his loyalties. Gradually, we realize that the elderly man making present-day inquiries is the boy grown up. As the tragedy unfolds, the theme deepens into a full and tragic voice for its elderly subject—a man atrophied from this emotional trauma in boyhood.

KEYS: DIEGETIC AND NONDIEGETIC MUSIC

An initial planning stage for the composer is deciding what progression of keys to use through the film, based on the emotional logic of the story itself.

Sound that is a part of the characters' world is called diegetic sound. Following it may be a very different kind of music, perhaps a score of massed cello. Of course the characters do not hear or react to this, for it is part of the film's authorial commentary and addressed to the audience. This is called nondiegetic sound. If, for example, nondiegetic music takes over from a diegetic tune whistled by a soldier, the key of one must be related to the other or the transition will be jarring. This holds true for all adjacent music sections, not just original scoring.

WHEN TO USE MUSIC, AND WHEN NOT

Music is commonly a transitional device, a filler, or something to set a mood. Avoid enhancing what's already visible on the screen. Instead, use music to suggest what is invisible, such as a character's withheld expectations, interior mood, or feelings. The classic example is Bernard Herrmann's unforgettable all-violin score for Alfred Hitchcock's *Psycho* (1960), with its jabbing violin screams as the pressure within the outwardly amenable Norman Bates becomes intolerable. Music is natural to melodrama, but perhaps hardest to write tastefully for comedy.

Music effectively foreshadows events and builds tension, but should never give the story away, nor should it ever "picture point" the story by commenting too closely. Walt Disney was infamous for "Mickey Mousing" his films—an industry term for fitting scores closely to the minutiae of action. The first of his true-life adventures, *The Living Desert* (1953), rendered its extraordinary wildlife footage banal by making scorpions square-dance and by sounding notes, trills, or percussion rolls for anything that dared move. Used like this, music becomes controlling and smothering.

A related problem is using too much music, or burdening the film with a musical interpretation that blocks the audience from making its own emotional judgments. Hitchcock's *Suspicion* (1941) and many a film of its vintage are marred in this way. Far from heightening a movie, the score flattens it out by maintaining an exhausting aura of perpetual melodrama. The ubiquitous "horse operas," the TV Westerns of the 1950s and 1960s, once served up unending music punctuated by gunshots, horse whinnies, and snatches of snarling dialogue. Happily, fashions change, and now less is considered more. A rhythm alone, without melody or harmony, can often supply the uncluttered accompaniment a sequence needs.

When its job is to set a mood, the music should do its work and then get out of the way to return and comment later. Sometimes a composer will point out during the screening just how effective, even loaded, a silence becomes at a particular point. The rhythms of action, camera movement, montage, and dialogue are themselves a kind of music, so you need not paint the lily.

An intelligent film often contains scenes whose longitudinal relationships need strengthening, so a composer at work may color-code his cues to longitudinally group scenes, characters, situations, and the like into musically related families. This keeps the composer aware of the logical connections and continuity the music must underpin. In a 40-minute film, there may be 30 music cues—from a sting, or short punctuation, to a passage that is extended and more elaborate. There will be music for a main plot, but there may also be musical identities for two subplots. Keeping these discrete during cross-cutting can be problematic, so their relationship, particularly in key, is important. Many factors are involved in producing an integrated score, so it is important that music cues, once decided, should never be changed without compelling reason.

CONFLICTS AND COMPOSING TO SYNC POINTS

An experienced musician composing for a recording session will write to very precise timings, paying attention to *spot effects* such as a tire screech or a dog barking. The choice of instrumentation must not fight dialogue, nor can the arrangement be too busy during dialogue or effects. Music can, however, substitute for a diegetic sound track that is too thick. Musical punctuation, rather than a welter of naturalistic sound effects, can be effectively impressionistic. If, however, you add music to an already loaded sound track, you force the audience to expend much mental energy interpreting it, especially when poorly reproduced by the television speakers through which most may hear your work.

If the composer is to work around dialogue and spot effects, supply a well-advanced version of the sound track, not the simple dialogue one used during editing. This is particularly true for anything destined for a cinema setting, where the sound system may be powerful and sophisticated, and everything in the track fully exposed.

When a written score is recorded to picture, it is marked with the cumulative timing so that as the music is recorded (normally to picture as a safeguard), the conductor can make a running check that the sync points line up. The composer might put a dramatic sting on the first appearance of the pursuing motorcycle at 27.5 seconds, and on the appearance of the revolver at 01:16, for instance.

Low-budget film scores usually use MIDI computerized composing techniques rather than live musicians. The composer builds the music to a QuickTime scratch version of the film, digitized from a DVD or cassette, so music fitting is done at the source.

THE LIVE MUSIC SESSION

The editor makes the preparations to record live music and attends the recording session. Whether a particular shot can be lengthened or shortened to accommodate slight timing inaccuracies is something only the editor knows. Adjusting the film is easier and more economical than paying musicians to pursue perfect synchronicity.

MUSIC EDITORS AND FITTING MUSIC

After the recording session, the editor fits each music section and makes the necessary shot adjustments. If the music is at all appropriate, the film takes a quantum leap forward in effectiveness. *Music editors* specialize in cutting and fitting music, and may play a large role in finding the period music to create the right atmosphere in, say, a coming-of-age film set in the 1970s. Sometimes they work closely with a composer, making sure during the fluid late stages of editing that the composer's intentions are maintained, and sometimes they work as hatchet man for the director, cutting and splicing to make film and music come together (see Jason Gross's *Online Music Magazine* interview with David Slusser www. furious.com/perfect/slusser.html). They often have formal training in an instrument or in composition, and their expertise is vital to a musical, where much of the film is shot to playback on the set.

THE MIX

The composer will ask to be present at all mix sessions affecting the functionality of the music he or she has composed. When music has been composed on MIDI, it is only a matter of a small delay to return to the musical elements and produce a new version with changes incorporated. An experienced music editor can handle this, whereas a film editor generally cannot.

CHAPTER 43

EDITING FROM FINE CUT TO SOUND MIX

THE FINE CUT

With typical caution, filmmakers call the outcome of the editing process the fine, not final, cut. There may yet be minor changes and accommodations, some from laying sound tracks in preparation to produce a master mixed track.

FINALIZING SOUND

SOUND, PSYCHOACOUSTICS, AND SOUND'S NARRATIVE CONTRIBUTION

Sound is an incomparable stimulant to the audience's imagination, and only rarely gets its due. Ideally, everyone is alert to sound-composition possibilities from the script onward, but often sound is left as a late mop-up operation. To combat this, it's important to note down every idea for sound that anyone has along the way, and not leave it all to an *audio-sweetening* session. (That, by the way, is an expression I detest. It suggests that sound is sour and needs sugaring. Sound design, sound editing, and sound mix are the more direct and respectful terms.)

Finalizing sound is a computer operation, usually using Pro Tools and a first-rate amplifier and speaker system that approaches a cinema sound environment. Though few movie theaters come close to being "state of the art," good sound—as Dolby cinemas have discovered— is good business, so sound may yet get its day.

Any good sound editor will tell you it's not quantity or complexity of sound that makes a good sound track, but rather, the psychological journey that sound leads you on while you watch. This is the art of *psychoacoustics*. Effective sound is usually simple rather than complex, specific and focused rather than generic.

Although film sound is made of different elements—music, dialogue, atmospheres, effects—it is a mistake to put them in a hierarchy and think of them separately at this, the ultimate compositional stage. Walter Murch, the doyen of editors and sound designers, makes a practice of watching a film he is editing without the sound turned on, so he imagines what the sound might properly be. Listed among Randy Thom's "Designing a Movie for Sound" (www. filmsound.org/articles/designing_for_sound.htm) are less-obvious functions of sound, which supply narrative information as well as mood. Sound can:

- Indicate a historical period.
- Indicate changes in time or geographic locale.
- Connect otherwise unconnected ideas, characters, places, images, or moments.
- Heighten ambiguity or diminish it.
- Startle or soothe.

SOUND EFFECTS (SFX) AND THE SOUND SPOTTING SESSION

Before the sound editor goes to work splitting dialogue tracks and laying sound effects, there should be a roundup discussion between editor and director about the sound identity of the whole film and how each sequence fits in. This is sometimes called the *FX spotting session*. Sound-editing software can help you keep inventory by project, reel, scene according to footage or timecode so nothing gets lost or forgotten.

In the spotting session, you decide where the film needs special effects, atmospheres, or music. The session also determines where:

- Dialogue problems may require dialogue replacement (ADR).
- Sound effects are needed. *Spot effects* sync to something on-screen, such as a door closing, a coin placed on a table, or a phone being picked up.
- Foley effects (specially recorded SFX—footsteps, for example) will be needed. Each sound must be appropriate and in the right perspective, and usually needs to be specially shot.

Sound effects, especially tape library or disc effects, often bring problematic backgrounds of their own. As with music, reduce distractions by cutting into the effect immediately before its attack (see Figure 43-1, Arrow A) and immediately after its decay (Arrow B), to minimize unwanted background.

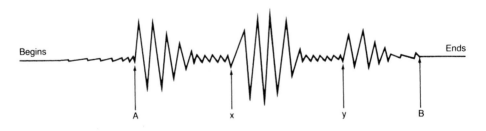

FIGURE 43-1

Sound modulations: attack, three bursts, and decay. Arrows x and y indicate the best cutting points.

Especially if you have monitored and directed the sound treatment throughout, the sound mix will be a special and even exhilarating occasion. But if sound has been given low priority, rough dialogue tracks alone can disrupt the dream-like quality that a good film attains, so sound is worth a lot of attention.

Agree on the known sound problems and on a strategy to handle them. This should be a priority because dialogue reconstruction—if it's needed—is an expensive, specialized, and time-consuming business, and no film of any worth can survive the impact of having it done poorly.

POSTSYNCHRONIZING DIALOGUE (ADR)

Postsynchronizing dialogue means ensuring that each actor creating new speech tracks is in lip sync with an existing picture. This extremely laborious operation is also called dubbing, looping, or automatic dialogue replacement (ADR). Each actor watches himself on the screen and rehearses before getting the okay to record. Long dialogue exchanges will be done perhaps 30 seconds at a time.

Avoid this process like the plague because newly recorded tracks invariably sound flat and dead in contrast to live location recordings. It's not only lack of background presence or sound perspective, or even location acoustics—all of which can be reconstituted. It's the artificial situation in which the actor finds himself. He's reproducing dialogue in snippets and is completely in the hands of whoever is directing each few sentences. However good the whole, the process invariably drags down the actors' performances, so they hate ADR with a passion.

THE FOLEY STAGE AND RE-CREATING SYNC SOUND EFFECTS

Many sound effects shot wild on location, or in a Foley studio, can be fitted to picture and will work just fine. The Foley studio was named after its intrepid inventor, Jack Foley, who in the 1940s discovered that you could mime all the right sounds to picture. A Foley studio has a variety of surfaces (concrete, heavy wood, light wood, carpet, linoleum, gravel, and so on). Foley artists may add sand or paper to modify the sound of footsteps to suit what's on the screen. Baking powder in a plastic bag, for instance, makes the right scrunching sound for footsteps in snow, and a punched cabbage can sound like someone being hit over the head. Part of my job on an extremely forgettable Jayne Mansfield comedy, *The Sheriff of Fractured Jaw* (Raoul Walsh, 1959), was to make horse footsteps with coconuts, and steam engine noises with a modified motorcycle engine. It was great fun.

Sounds to fit a repetitive action—such as knocking on a door, shoveling snow, or footsteps going up a flight of stairs—can be re-created by recording the actions a little slower and then cutting out the requisite frames before each impact's attack, which is easy with a computer. More complex sync effects (two people walking through a quadrangle) will have to be postsynced just like dialogue in a Foley session, paying attention to the different surfaces the feet pass over (grass, gravel, concrete, etc.). A grueling series of postsync sessions makes you understand how vital it is for the location recordist to procure good original recordings. You also see just how good location film sound and editing crews really are.

For the low-budget filmmaker, where and how you record sound effects is not important; what matters is that that they sound authentic and are in sync with the action. Sometimes you will find what you want in sound libraries, but never assume that they will work until you have proved them against picture. To locate libraries, enter "sound effects library" in a search engine. Some will let you listen to or even download effects. Try Sound Ideas at www.sound-ideas.com/bbc.html.

A caution: many sound libraries are top-heavy with stuff shot in the Dark Ages. Effects tracks may come with a heavy ambient background or ineradicable system hiss. Noisy, exotic sounds such as helicopters, Bofors guns, and elephants rampaging through Malaysian undergrowth are easy to use. It's the nitty-gritty stuff—footsteps, door slams, dog growling, and so on—that proves hard to make work. Sound effects can be authentic, but sound nothing like you expect. At one time, there were only six different gunshots used throughout the film industry. When my unit tried recording authentic new ones, they sounded like pitiful cap-gun noises.

SOUND CLICHÉS

Sound effects can easily be overdone. A cat in a kitchen does not automatically call for a cat meow, unless said cat is seen in the next shot demanding its breakfast. At www.filmsound.org/cliche/, there's a hilarious list of sound clichés. All bicycles have bells, car tires always squeal, storms start instantaneously, wind always whistles, doors always squeak . . . and much, much more.

SOUND MIX

WHAT IT CAN DO

After the fine cut, editing culminates by preparing and mixing the component sound tracks. A whole book could be written on this preeminent subject alone. What follows is a list of essentials along with some tips. The mix procedure determines the following:

- Relative sound levels—between a dialogue foreground voice track, say, and a factory scene background (if, and only if, they are on separate tracks).
- Equalization—the filtering and profiling of individual tracks to match others or maximize intelligibility or ear comfort. A voice track with a rumbly traffic background can, for instance, be much improved by *rolling off* the lower frequencies, leaving the voice range intact.
- Consistent quality—two tracks from two angles on the same speaker need careful equalization and level adjustments if they are to sound seamless.
- Level changes—fade-up, fade-down, sound dissolves, and adjustments for new track elements such as narration, music, or interior monologue.
- Sound processing—adding echo, reverberation, telephone effect, and so on.
- Dynamic range—*compression* squeezes the broad dynamic range of a movie into the narrow range favored in TV transmission; *limiting* leaves the main range untouched, but limits peaks to a preset level.
- Perspective—equalization and level manipulation can mimic perspective changes, which helps create a sense of space and dimensionality through sound.

- Multichannel sound distribution—for a stereo or surround-sound track, different elements go to different sound channels to create space and horizontal spread.
- Noise reduction—Dolby and other noise-reduction systems minimize the system hiss that would intrude on quiet passages.

You are ready to mix tracks into one master track only when you have:

- Finalized content of your film
- Fitted music
- Split dialogue tracks, grouping them by their equalization (EQ) needs and level commonality:
  - A separate track for each microphone position in dialogue tracks
  - Sometimes a different track for each speaker, depending on how much EQ is necessary for each mic position on each character
- Filled-in backgrounds (missing sections of background ambience, so there are no dead spaces or abrupt background changes)
- Recorded and laid narration (if there is any)
- Recorded and laid sound effects and mood-setting atmospheres
- Finalized Pro Tools timeline contents

SOUND-MIX PREPARATION

Track elements are presented here in the conventional hierarchy of importance, but this order may vary; music, for instance, might be faded up to the foreground, and dialogue played almost inaudibly low. When cutting and laying sound tracks, be careful not to cut off the barely audible tail of a decaying sound or to clip the "attack," or beginning. Sound editing should be done at high volume so you hear everything that is there—or isn't there when it should be.

Laying nonlinear digital tracks is much easier than in the old manual days because now you follow a logic visible to the eye and can play your work immediately. Modern sound-editing programs allow you to edit with surgical precision—even within a syllable. The equivalent operation in manual film is not impossible, but you never properly heard your work until sound-mix time. Traditional mix theaters are nowadays about as common as steam trains, and there is not much weeping over their demise. Getting dozens of tracks laid for a mix was a monumental task, and watching 30 dubbing players churn them to and fro, slaved to a film projector, was exquisitely stressful (my first job was cement-splicing film in a feature film studio). Twelve people worked a day or more to mix ten minutes of film track. For battle sequences or other complex situations, you could multiply that period several times. Some battles did not stay on the screen, either.

NARRATION OR VOICE-OVER

For actors to make a written narration sound spontaneous is next to impossible, so consider using the improv method in which actors, given a list of particular points to be made, improvise dialogue in character. By judicious side-coaching, or even interviewing the actor, you can get a quantity of entirely spontaneous material. Make a number of passes that can be edited down. Though labor-intensive, the result will be more spontaneous and natural than anything read from a script.

If you lay narration or interior monologue, you will need to fill gaps between sections with "presence" so the track remains "live," particularly during a quiet sequence.

DIALOGUE TRACKS AND THE PROBLEM OF INCONSISTENCIES

A variety of location acoustic environments, different microphones, and different mic working distances will play merry havoc with voice consistencies. Instead of focusing on the characters, the listener suffers strain and irritation from making constant adjustment to unmotivated and irrational changes. Even interiors, once edited, reveal ragged and distracting changes of sound level, perspective, and room acoustics. Suddenly you really appreciate the seamless continuity familiar from feature films. It's available by adjusting sound levels and equalization (EQ) at the mix stage, but only if the tracks are intelligently laid for the sound mix, which is a painstaking and labor-intensive process.

1. **Split dialogue tracks** (lay them by grouping on separate tracks) according to the needs imposed by the coverage's microphone positioning.

    a. In a scene shot from two angles and having two mices positions, put all the close-shot sound on one track, and all the medium-shot sound on another. With four or five mic positions, you would need to lay at least four or five tracks.

    b. Sometimes tracks must additionally be split by character because different voices may need different sound treatments.

2. **Equalization** (EQ) settings can be roughly determined during track laying, but final settings will be determined in the mix. If an intrusive background sound, such as a high-pitched band saw, occupies a narrow band of frequency, you can sometimes effectively lower it using a graphic equalizer. This tunes out the offending frequency, but takes with it all sounds in that frequency band, including that part of your character's voices. The aim with EQ is to bring all tracks into acceptable compatibility, given that the viewer sometimes expects slightly different sound perspectives to match the camera distances.

3. **Inconsistent backgrounds:** The ragged, truncated background is the albatross of the poorly edited film. Now is the time to use those presence tracks you shot on location. Often you must augment the lighter background to match its heavier counterpart.

    a. Clean up background tracks of extraneous noises, creaks, mic-handling sounds—anything that doesn't overlap dialogue and can therefore be removed. If it does overlap dialogue, you must either steal the words from another take or resort to ADR (and prayer).

    b. When backgrounds fail to match, add to the quieter one so you can fade rather than cut between them. Try to make a sound dissolve behind a commanding foreground sound so the audience's attention is distracted from the change. The worst place to make such a background change is in the clear.

Bear in mind that the ear registers a sound cut-in or a cut-out much more acutely than any graduated change. Bring alien background unobtrusively in or out by fading it up or down rather than letting it thump in and out at cuts. Mask an unwanted sound change (in background, for instance) behind a foregrounded sound. Thus, an unfavorable atmosphere change might be cunningly masked by the sound of a passing car.

LAYING MUSIC TRACKS

Laying music is not difficult. Just remember to cut in immediately before the modulations so its arrival isn't heralded by studio atmosphere. Arrow A in Figure 43-1 represents the ideal cut-in point; to its left is unwanted presence, or hiss. To the right of A are three attacks in succession leading to a decay to silence at Arrow B. A similar attack-sustain-decay profile is found for many sound effects (footsteps, for instance), so you can often use the same editing strategy. By removing sound between x and y, we could reduce three drumbeats or footfalls to two.

You may have to rebalance some of your action (cuts, actions, camera movements) to move them into synchronization with the music. If you cannot, then lay the music so that no sync relationship seems intended.

ATMOSPHERES AND BACKGROUND SOUND

Atmospheres are laid for two main reasons: to create a mood (birdsong over a wood, or hammering over the exterior of a carpenter's shop), or to mask inconsistencies with something relevant but distracting. Always obey screen logic by laying atmospheres to cover the entire sequence, not just a part of it. Remember that when a door is opened during an interior shot, the exterior atmosphere (children's playground, for instance) will rise for the duration that the door is open. If you want to create a sound dissolve, remember to lay the requisite amounts to allow for the necessary overlap and check for any inequities in each overlap, such as the recordist quietly calling "Cut."

SOUND-MIX STRATEGY

PREMIXING

In a feature film, a busy exterior may comprise 40 or more sound tracks, and these usually require premixes. Do your premixing in an order that reserves control over the most important elements until last. Intelligibility depends on audible dialogue, so you must retain control over the dialogue-to-everything-else levels until the very last stage of mixing. Were you to premix dialogue and effects right away, adding effects and music would uncontrollably augment and compete with the dialogue. This is particularly true for location sound, often on the cusp of intelligibility from the start.

TAILORING

Many tracks, if played as laid, will enter and exit abruptly, giving an unpleasantly jagged impression to the listener's ear. This can be minimized by tailoring—that is, making a very quick fade-up or fade-down of the noisy track to meet the quiet

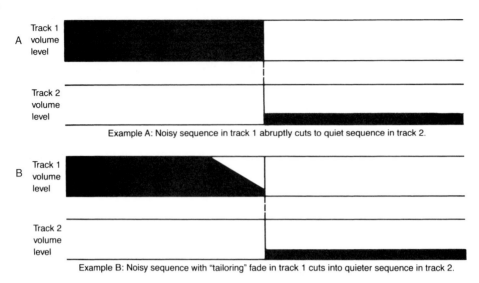

Example A: Noisy sequence in track 1 abruptly cuts to quiet sequence in track 2.

Example B: Noisy sequence with "tailoring" fade in track 1 cuts into quieter sequence in track 2.

FIGURE 43-2

Abrupt sound cut tailored by quick fade in outgoing track so it matches the level of the incoming track.

track on its own terms (Figure 43-2). The effect on-screen is still that of a cut, but one that no longer assaults the ear.

COMPARATIVE LEVELS: ERR ON THE SIDE OF CAUTION

Mix studios sport excellent and expensive speakers. The results can be misleading because filmmakers must expect their work to be seen on domestic TV sets, which have small, cheap speakers. Not only do luckless consumers lose frequency and dynamic ranges, they lose the dynamic separation between loud and soft, so foregrounds nicely separated in the mix studio become swamped by backgrounds.

Err on the conservative side and make a deliberately high separation, keeping traffic low and voices high. A mix suite can usually play your track through a TV set so you can judge what the home viewer will hear.

APPROVE SECTIONS, THEN LISTEN TO THE WHOLE

At the mix, you need not know how to create a particular effect, only how to say what each sequence should sound like. To your requests, and according to what the editor has laid in the sound tracks, the mix engineer will offer alternatives from which to choose. During the mix, you and your editor approve each stage of the process. At the end, listen to the whole mix without stopping. Usually your time will be rewarded by finding an anomaly or two.

MAKE SAFETY COPIES AND STORE THEM IN DIFFERENT LOCATIONS

A sound mix requires a long and painstaking process, so it is professional practice to immediately make safety or backup copies. These are stored in multiple buildings in case of loss or theft. Backups are then available should loss or damage occur. Follow the same principle with film negative and video original cassettes; keep masters, safety copies, negatives, and internegatives (copy negatives) in different places so you won't lose everything should fire, flood, revolution, or act of God (or those claiming to act on His behalf) destroy what otherwise fits so nicely under your bed.

MUSIC AND EFFECTS TRACKS

If there is any chance that your film will make international sales, create a music and effects mix, or M&E track. This allows a foreign-language crew to dub the speakers and mix the new voices in with the original atmosphere, effects, and music tracks.

CHAPTER 44

TITLES, ACKNOWLEDGMENTS, AND PROMOTIONAL MATERIAL

TITLES

Festival programs and TV listings rarely have much space to describe their offerings, so your work's title may be its sole means of drawing an audience. Although every film acquires a working title, the final one is often plucked late and in an agony of indecision. It must be short, special, and epitomize your film's allure.

Title style: Overambitious front titles are a liability if they promise more than the film delivers, so be conservative. For models, see films of comparable length and subject. Artistically ambitious ones often use brief and classically simple white-on-black titles. You could do a lot worse. Make legibility your priority, and decide your titling and its placement according to the background composition.

Overladen titles: A film egocentrically loaded with credits is a sure sign of amateurism. Titles should be brisk, and the same name should not crop up in multiple key capacities. An unknown main actor should never be introduced as "Starring Sherry Mudge." Avoid fancy logos or visionary company names. Let your film, not its packaging, do the talking.

Contractual or other obligations: If you have used union actors, obey the contractual obligations that stipulate size and wording of title credits—or live to regret you were ever born. Many favors are granted filmmakers in return for a screen acknowledgment, so be sure you've left nobody out and honor your debts to the letter. Funding or college degrees may also prescribe special wording, so review and double-check all your commitments.

Font, layout, and size: Many newcomers' titles are illegible, so choose a font not just for its period and associations, but for clarity and size. Avoid anything too small or too fancy—or it will disappear on the television screen. Lettering extended to the screen edges is lettering lost when TV sets are badly adjusted or projection crops the picture.

Spelling: Have spelling checked scrupulously by at least two literate eagles. Double-check names; misspelling connotes indifference to the very people who have given you their all.

Title lengths: Determine the longest a title should remain on-screen by *reading each screenful of titling one and a half times out loud*. Crawl titles, if long, are run really fast, or TV just chops them off.

Titles for film: See Focal Press web site notes.

Titles for video: Most editing provides an array of typefaces with options for drop shadow, movement, crawl, collapse, and other exotic behaviors. Keep yours classically simple—unless, of course, your film's topic and treatment really call for something more. View what you have chosen, and experiment until it's perfect. Superimposed lettering, whether colored or white, is more legible with a drop-shadow or black outline.

SUBTITLES

Foreign festivals may ask for a subtitled version in a particular language. This is now easy (if time-consuming) to do digitally. Guidelines:

Lettering and placement: Superimpose yellow subtitle lettering with a black outline, and place them in the lower part of the frame.

Summarize: Don't just translate the dialogue word for word; give briefest essentials. If the audience is busy reading, they won't see your film.

Native translation: Get the text translated by a literate, native speaker (not that friend who took several Spanish classes), and have it typed up with all the appropriate accents.

Don't straddle: Place every sentence within a continuous shot. If a sentence spills into the following cut, the audience is irritated to find itself reading the same title all over again. When shots are short, break subtitle into short sentences, indicating run-ons with triple periods. For example:

"How are you?"	Shot 1
"I am feeling all right . . .	Shot 2
. . . but I was hoping that you can . . .	Shot 3
. . . give me some advice."	Shot 4

Copyright: At the very end of the titles, remember to include your name, the © symbol, and the year as a claim to the copyright of the material. To file for copyright in the United States, see www.copyright.gov/register/performing.html for information and application forms. If you reside in another country, be sure to check its copyright procedures. If a television channel, cinema, or festival wants to show your film, you will have to document your legal right to use absolutely everything that requires clearances (locations, story adaptation rights, music, etc.). If they get sued for infringement, they make sure it's your head on the block.

PROMOTIONAL MATERIAL

Most filmmakers find promoting themselves odious, but your work is your child, and you must be ready to work hard and enthusiastically so it doesn't starve.

Publicity is the key to getting your work seen and its maker remembered. Bite the bullet.

Publicity: Study other people's promotion, and copy anything you find effective. Most filmmakers hate stepping forward to publicize their work, and so they do a shoddy job. This is like cooking a beautiful meal and then serving it on chipped plates. So hoist up your pants and learn how to launch a publicity blast. You will need large, appealing posters to go up wherever your film will be shown, as well as a publicity folder. Its materials should be on attractive, glossy paper and contain:

- The kind of evocative stills you used for your poster
- Festival awards
- A "teaser" informative description that makes people want to see the film
- Cast names and prior accomplishments
- Contact information, web site, and prices for copies
- Email and phone contact information for you or your distributor
- Your business card

Web site: If you can't do it yourself, pay someone to set up a web site and teach you how to update it. See www.hubertsauper.com/index.html as an example. Web sites allow people to find you, to see what you have been doing, and to contact you easily. Up-and-coming filmmakers' web sites usually contain:

- Filmography
- Professional biography
- News (showings, festivals, conferences, interviews, awards)
- Contact (email address or preaddressed email form)

MAKING FESTIVALS AND SCREENINGS WORK FOR YOU

Festivals: Enter your work in every festival that might further your artistic and commercial identity. Go to them all if you can, because the ultimate rite of passage is seeing your work with a paying audience. Reactions can be thrilling or chastening, and different from place to place. This is your Judgment Day; from its baptism, you will emerge knowing what film to make next.

Personal contacts: Just about everything of value happens through person-to-person contact. Attend festivals and work the crowd. Research who's who, pleasantly introduce yourself by name and film to anyone who matters, look them in the eye, and say sincerely how much you'd like them to see your film (as a target, I know this really works). Give a flyer specifying the screening's time and place.

Filmmaker's comments: Rehearse so you can publicly introduce your film briefly and graciously. Give credit to others, and signify openness to comments of all kinds—in person or via email. If there is a question time afterward, get things started by telling the audience what you'd like to learn from them. In your replies, don't ramble: be brief, informative, modest, and stay in learning mode. You can learn hugely from a random audience, but many will be anxious to move on, so be brief and personable. If anyone asks what film you want to make next, pitch your best one or two ideas in 30 seconds each.

After the screening, shake people's hands by the door and thank them for coming. Give your business card to whoever wants one, and ask for honest comments by email. If there's a bar or social area, hang out till closing time—and stay sober so you can chat people up, collect information, and make new friends. Collaborators, associates, employers, supporters, and backers all seem to materialize through such social occasions.

And now for something completely different . . . So, what *are* your ideas for another movie? Only when you finish a film, and empty yourself out completely does another project begin to form in the vacuum. That's how the artistic process begins all over again.

PART 8

CAREER TRACK

Preparing to become a professional filmmaker is not very different from preparing to make a living as an actor, writer, journalist, photographer, or other professional artist. You will need to plan an individual pathway based on your interests, ambitions, and abilities.

Part 8 (Chapters 45 through 47) outlines the steps you are likely to take while you develop from initial interests into a full career. This breaks into three stages, each covered by a chapter:

- Making a self-assessment, setting goals, and planning an educational path (Chapter 45, "Planning a Career")
- Choosing how to study. Assessing available schools and initiating plans for self-directedness during schooling. Amassing solid experience and proof of your skills to make yourself employable (Chapter 46, "Major Film Schools")
- Using your screen works, work record, and contacts to find paid work after school. Then building a reputation as you work, and directing your own projects as you seek wider recognition (Chapter 47, "Breaking into the Industry")

Revisit Part 8 periodically, and check the Internet to see what other people report as their experience, and what they recommend.

CHAPTER 45

PLANNING A CAREER

The film industry has no formal ladder and no predictable steps for promotion. It's a branch of show business. Where you go, how far you get, and how long it takes you to get there depend on your ability and tenacity—and, to a lesser extent, your connections and luck. This path won't work if your primary loyalties are to family, community, and material prosperity, for the industry is informally structured and unpredictable; it assumes you take initiative and are totally committed 24/7 to every project you join. Actors, musicians, writers, dancers, painters, sculptors—indeed, everyone in the arts—all live with similar conditions.

Many like you aspire to work in the film industry, so getting work is competitive but far from impossible. To make this your way of life will take looking ahead, taking early decisions, and focusing your energies on preparing yourself. What will you be good at? What will you like most? The surest way to find out is to start making short films so you discover your tastes and capacities.

I believe that *everyone* serious about working anywhere in film ought to do some directing during their education, just as they should also experience writing, acting, cinematography, and editing.

Make a self-assessment of your aptitudes right now. Answer the vocational questionnaire below and get a rough indication of where you might fit in. It won't say what you *must* become (only you control that), but it will show what roles align with your temperament and present interests. Whatever profile emerges, you control your destiny. You can remedy weaknesses or build on your strengths, just as you choose.

VOCATIONAL SELF-ASSESSMENT QUESTIONNAIRE

Photocopy these pages, and answer the questions as honestly as you can. Nobody need see the results. Keep what you write—you may find it interesting later in life!

If you had to choose your life's work from among these six film craft areas, how would you rank them?	A. Camera & Lighting	#_____/5 for me
	B. Sound	#_____/5 for me
	C. Directing	#_____/5 for me
	D. Screenwriting	#_____/5 for me
	E. Editing	#_____/5 for me
	F. Producing	#_____/5 for me

Now rate your agreement 0–4 with the statements below. 0 = "completely untrue," and 4 = "very true." Your answers will show how much your innate focus and interests align with your preferred roles in filmmaking.

		0	1	2	3	4
A 1	I go to art exhibitions whenever I can.					
A 2	I get pleasure out of using my camera regularly.					
A 3	I have shot, edited, and printed my own digital photos.					
A 4	I have elected to take one or more art classes by choice.					
A 5	I have taken one or more film, video, or photo classes by choice.					
A 6	I am more aware of imagery and cinematography than most people I know.					
A 7	I am more knowledgeable than most people about lighting.					
A 8	I am more knowledgeable than most about picture composition.					
A 9	I keep a sketchbook and/or use a computer to make visual designs.					
A 10	I have shot four films myself and want to work mainly in cinematography.					
B 11	I have sung in a choir or played a musical instrument.					
B 12	I own a lot of music albums, including nonvocal music.					
B 13	I can identify most instruments of the orchestra by their timbre alone.					
B 14	I can hear the individual elements in film sound tracks most of the time.					
B 15	I am interested in the science and mechanics of sound.					
B 16	I have made a sound composition using a computer.					
B 17	I can list four feature films whose sound tracks are especially interesting.					
B 18	I am interested in the psychological effects of sound.					
B 19	I have used sound recording, reinforcement, or playback equipment.					
B 20	I want to work mainly in sound recording and sound design.					
C 21	I like acting in public performances.					
C 22	I actively probe causes and meanings in life.					
C 23	I have researched the life and vision of four favorite directors.					
C 24	I can adopt someone else's idea in a group activity even when it isn't mine.					
C 25	I have a reputation for being patient, determined, and diplomatic.					
C 26	I am good at finding trustworthy partners to work with.					
C 27	I am fascinated by the lives and viewpoints of others.					

		0	1	2	3	4
C 28	I am unafraid of confrontation and handle human crises effectively.					
C 29	I trust my instincts and can act on them even when others disagree.					
C 30	I want my work in life to be changing hearts and minds as a film director.					
D 31	I write often and for pleasure, I like being alone, and I miss writing when I cannot do it.					
D 32	I have read several short stories or novels in the past four months.					
D 33	I follow local, national, or international news most days.					
D 33	I often discuss writers and writing with friends.					
D 34	I regularly make use of all the writer's aids on my computer (dictionary, thesaurus, synonyms, style & spelling suggestions, etc.).					
D 35	I love several different writers' work, inside and outside my own culture.					
D 36	I am fairly expert in at least one area of contemporary fiction writing.					
D 37	I have a good knowledge of my country's great writers prior to my own era.					
D 38	I own copies of several outstanding screenplays or stage plays.					
D 39	I have at least one good storyteller in my family.					
D 40	As a writer, I want to author works for the screen.					
E 41	I listen to a good deal of music.					
E 42	I am actively interested in four different art forms (painting, literature, etc.).					
E 43	I am interested in how differently stories can be structured.					
E 44	I am interested in sound design and the way sound tracks blend.					
E 45	I like projects that involve an intense partnership.					
E 46	I am by nature orderly and methodical.					
E 47	I am used to redrafting or remaking something many times to get it right.					
E 48	I am really diplomatic when I try to get my own way.					
E 49	I can absorb and act on criticism of my work even when it hurts.					
E 50	As an editor, I want to build and orchestrate film materials.					
F 51	I am good with figures and planning logistics.					
F 52	I would find it fulfilling to bring creative people together as a team.					
F 53	I have a real talent for recognizing good stories.					

(*Continued*)

		0	1	2	3	4
F 54	I can say truthfully that I don't want to write or direct.					
F 55	I am at ease with all kinds of people, and good at talking them into doing things.					
F 56	I am entrepreneurial by nature and come from an entrepreneurial family.					
F 57	I am attracted to management in the arts because the arts are civilizing.					
F 58	I have a flair for salesmanship of all kinds.					
F 59	I can use rules and persuasion to settle conflicts between people.					
F 60	I want to be a producer, or in the management side of filmmaking.					

These questions reflect common crew interests and personality traits as outlined in Chapter 28, "Developing a Crew." In most film schools, your initial training ensures that you do a little of everything. Once you've rotated through all the roles, you'll know what you are good at and can choose as a specialization. By then, you will also know enough about everyone else's job to become a first-rate team member. The key to further interpreting this questionnaire is at the end of this chapter, along with some discussion of its indications.

OPPORTUNITIES

Film, video, and television are now one growing, multifaceted industry. At the low end of the spectrum are web site development, wedding videos, advertising, corporate, educational, and other nonfiction forms, including documentary. Here, over time, the adroit can develop a comfortable income. At the high end are the high-prestige national or international feature films. In the upper-level industry, where budgets are high, the stakes are high, too, so the demand on young entrants is for high skills, commitment, and reliability. Somewhere in the ambitious, low-budget middle ground are independent shorts and features. That's where this book assumes you want to go.

CRAFTS THAT LEAD TO DIRECTING

Becoming successful in any of several craft areas can lead to directing. Editing is a common route because the editor orchestrates acting, directing, camerawork, sound, music, and everything else. Writers and directors of photography, actor-writers, comedians, theater directors—and even the occasional visionary choreographer or painter—have all made the transition. Assistant directors, producers, and production managers seldom if ever do so because they handle logistics and organizational details rather than ones deemed creative.

To set your sights on directing fiction films, you should probably specialize in editing or camerawork. You should also either write, or work intimately with writers, because to make headway, you will need to constantly winnow and propagate film ideas.

To gain experience with actors, work with a theater group of any kind. You could always emulate Rainer Werner Fassbinder by making a short dramatic film with a willing theater ensemble every few weekends. The step from directing well in the theater to directing well in film—providing you engage a first-rate director of photography—is quite a short one. Ingmar Bergman, John Cassavetes, Mike Leigh, Sam Mendes, and Mike Nichols all did that.

DIRECTING DOCUMENTARIES STRAIGHT OUT OF SCHOOL

By studying documentary, you can enter the film industry through nonfiction filmmaking (documentary, educational, travelogue, industrials, corporate, or promotional films). It will get you out into the world, and by working with a small crew, you take on the high degree of control and responsibility that makes people grow. Making a living in documentary is difficult unless you have a nose for sensational subjects. This book's sister publication, *Directing the Documentary* (Boston: Focal Press), will introduce you to making this type of film. Be careful: the work is very addictive!

HAVING PASSION

Keep this in mind: the only things that people get good at are the things that they really love. Liking films and making them are as different as liking to drive cars and building them. If you are passionate about the cinema, you may become equally passionate about making movies, but getting there will be hard, slow, and unglamorous. Yes, unglamorous. A lot of people go to film school to see whether they "have it." It really comes down to whether you love the slow, methodical, painstaking process of film production—most do, but not all.

FILM SCHOOL ADMISSIONS

Most film schools operate selection tests and believe ardently that these tests work. This is a self-fulfilling prophecy because they never teach anyone else. My colleagues and I, teaching for decades in a school that lets any high school graduate enroll in beginning film classes, still cannot predict who will thrive. So, if your choice of film school rejects you, consider yourself in good company. Successful artists are often self-taught and fail to find favor in academe. Keep trying.

WHO SUCCEEDS

Filmmaking is unsuitable for the undisciplined, unreliable, and nonperfectionist. Equally unsuitable are those whose egos, prickly personalities, and insecurities prevent them from working for others, or for a particular gender. The stress of teamwork in film school flushes out all such cultural impediments, but most people manage to overcome their difficulties. Anyway, it's all part of a film school's job to help its students, reared on interpersonal competition, to socialize for collaborative work.

In general, the film industry favors three kinds of people:

1. **The craftsperson.** Everyone working in film is a dedicated craftsperson. This means practicing the highest standards in work, commitment, and diplomacy, and giving one's all to the common endeavor. Most find huge satisfaction in their craft—which may be electrician, grip, sound recordist, colorist, editor, costume designer, or camera assistant. They do not feel in the least compromised because they are not directing.

2. **The craftsperson with an author inside struggling to get out.** These people aim first to become successful writers, editors, cinematographers, screenwriters, or actors. Because they consistently demonstrate authorial reach through their craft area, someone influential notices, and—in the belief that the aspiring director can direct well—gives them an opportunity.

3. **The craftsperson who is a fully realized visionary.** This person is the Mozart or Beatle of film students, and emerges from film school with a masterly short that knocks everyone's socks off. Innate visionaries are as rare as hen's teeth, they direct all through film school, and they continue directing when they leave. Such people often have family or other special circumstances that prime them for the arts. A film school "star" has occasionally taken the comet's path to Hollywood, only to suffer a catastrophic baptism.

Your chances of being a No. 3 are similar to your chances of winning the lottery or being struck by lightning. Prepare instead to move up slowly and carefully. Solid progress in filmmaking, as in everything else worthwhile, is reliably won through growth, hard work, and love for what you do—not through brilliance, "talent," or ruthlessness.

GETTING STARTED

Industry veterans may tell you that only on-the-job experience counts. They value procedural knowledge and professionalism (which often are deficiencies in recent college graduates), and assume on immediate evidence that schooling fails. Certainly no college education can teach consistency, tact, and reliability—nor should it drill students in industrial procedures at the expense of a holistic screen education, which is its real job.

Happily, much has changed now that so many new directors come from film schools (see Figure 45-1). Good schools cut years out of the learning curve, but all are geared to the common denominator and can be frustrating to anyone who is slower, faster, or more motivated than average.

If film school is out of the question, use this book to prepare yourself outside the available educational structures. The best education will always be that which you give yourself. There are, in any case, no sure routes, only intelligent traveling.

FIGURE 45-1 ————————————————————————————————

Students shooting an early project at Columbia College Chicago. Film schools are now the accepted cradle of the film industry (photo by author).

WHAT YOU GET IN FILM SCHOOL

Virtually every entering film student wants to be a director. Film is a very complex language, and you will need time and hard work to develop three essential skills, only the first of which can be taught:

- The human and technical skills to put a well-conceived, well-composed series of shots on the screen and make them tell a story
- Knowing yourself and what you can contribute to the world
- Remaining true to yourself even when you and your work seem under attack

You can, however, expect the educational process to:

- Give you a holistic experience of filmmaking that leaves you less liable to intimidation by other people's expertise and job mystiques.
- Help you determine where your talents, skills, and energies lie—and where not.
- Encourage you to learn through collaborating and experimenting (to over-reach in the professional world spells suicide).
- Prepare you to grasp opportunities as they arise, something terrifying to the underprepared apprentice.
- Help you form resolutions that continue to flower for years to come.

A good film school gives you:

- Cultural, historical, and intellectual perspectives on your chosen medium
- The opportunity to reinvent the medium through a lot of hands-on experience
- Experience of teamwork and of holding many different responsibilities
- The theory and practice of one or several of the contributory crafts
- The ability to use equipment and technical facilities and acquire a holistic sense of the whole production process
- A can-do attitude unfazed by new equipment or technical obstacles
- The opportunity to put work before an audience of peers
- Permission to make films that show who you are (You are what you can put on the screen.)
- How to use mentors and become one yourself
- Aspirations to use your professional life for the widest good
- Marketable skills and a community of peers, some of whom you will work with for the rest of your life

APPRENTICESHIP AS A BEGINNING

Some students eagerly drop out of school if an industry opening comes their way. It seems like a dream come true, but dropping out to take a job is almost always a mistake. The progress of the dropouts is usually slow, and their self-esteem eroded by their seniors' self-serving mystiques. As a scarred survivor of industry apprenticeship myself, I strongly recommend a purposeful education. Students in a 15-week editing class learn techniques and insights that took me 10 years on the job to discover for myself. That I learned slowly and in isolation isn't unusual: in the film world, know-how and experience are earning power, so workers avoid enlightening juniors. How much easier to let schooling prepare you for more complex duties.

SELF-HELP AS A REALISTIC ALTERNATIVE

If you can afford neither the time nor the money to go to school, you can acquire the necessary knowledge and experience by other means. Werner Herzog once said in my hearing that whoever wants to make films should waste no more than a week learning film techniques. This seems a tad brief, but fundamentally, I share his attitude. Filmmaking is a practical subject and can be tackled by any group of zealous do-it-yourselfers. The Internet allows such people to find each other and to explore cooperative projects. This book means to encourage you to learn from making films, to learn through doing, and, if absolutely necessary, through doing in relative isolation. Somewhere along the way, you will need a mentor, someone to give knowledgeable and objective criticism of your work and to help solve the problems that arise. Do not worry if none is in the offing right now, for the beginner has far to go. It is a law of nature, in any case, that the right people come along when you've earned their interest.

KEY TO THE VOCATIONAL APTITUDE TEST

The questionnaire at the beginning of this chapter has six batches of questions, one for each of the six main filmmaking disciplines. The questions are based on the strengths and personality traits associated with each craft: the director's in Chapter 1, "The World of the Film Director"; the rest in Chapter 28, "Developing a Crew"—with the exception of postproduction personnel, whose attributes are described in Chapter 38, "Preparing to Edit."

The disciplines are divided by a bold line in the questionnaire, with the "A" questions for camera, "B" questions for sound, and so on. The maximum score per discipline is 40. Add your totals per discipline, then draw a horizontal line representing each total below. You've created a visual representation of where your strengths lie at present.

Craft area	Question block	Total	Bar graph representing comparative scores 0　　5　10　15　20　25　30　35　40
A. Camera	Questions 1–10	___/40	
B. Sound	Questions 11–20	___/40	
C. Directing	Questions 21–30	___/40	
D. Screenwriting	Questions 31–40	___/40	
E. Editing	Questions 41–50	___/40	
F. Producing	Questions 51–60	___/40	

Now you have totals for your present tastes and aptitudes, one for each of the main filmmaking disciplines. If you:

- Scored highly in one discipline and significantly lower in the rest, then you could build on your strengths and adopt that specialty as your own.

- Got highest marks for directing—*in addition to* screenwriting or camera or editing—then your tastes and interests indicate a good potential to become a director.

- Got similar scores throughout, then only practical work will clarify where your interests and energies lie.

How seriously should you take these results? They indicate where you are right now, but there's nothing to stop you from saying, "This is what I want to become"—and then going on to do the necessary work to become it. That's everyone's choice. The film industry is full of people who lacked credentials but nevertheless acquired the knowledge they needed, and whose passion for their area has taken them forward ever since. You see this happen in film schools too.

CHAPTER 46

MAJOR FILM SCHOOLS

CHOOSING THE RIGHT SCHOOL

Many schools, colleges, and universities now have film courses. No serious study of film is ever wasted, but be careful and critical before committing yourself to any extended course of study.

Mainly film studies: Many film departments are underequipped, underbudgeted, and are committed to film studies, not field production. They are a necessary part of a liberal education and sharpen student perceptions, but these institutions teach social history, analysis, and criticism, not creation. The measure of a film school is what the students and faculty produce. Quite simply, you must study with active filmmakers.

Fine arts filmmaking: Be cautious about film departments in fine arts schools, especially if they undervalue craft control and emphasize exotic form presented as personal vision. Students are sometimes encouraged to see themselves as reclusive soloists, like the painters and sculptors around them. This encourages gimmicky, egocentric production that lacks the teamwork the medium needs. Graduates leaving school with no respectable work under their arm find developing a career next to impossible. Ask where the graduates of these institutions are working in the film industry.

"McFilmmaking": Beware of short-order schools, which advertise themselves through heroic imagery of a stylish young individualist surrounded by state-of-the-art equipment. The fare probably consists of "taster" courses catering to the notion that brief association with professionals and their equipment turns you into a professional filmmaker. Their courses are short, and promise all the secrets known to the giants of the industry.

Holistic education leading to professional specializations: From the previous chapter—indeed, from the whole of this book—you can see that a good film education is like going to medical school, and takes several years. The school balances sound technical education with a strong counterpart of conceptual, aesthetic, and historical coursework. A large school will offer a core of foundation courses, and these in turn lead to specialization tracks in screenwriting, camera, sound, editing, directing, producing, documentary, animation, and critical studies. Only a large institution can offer study in multiple genres and training in the craft specialties.

Equipment holdings, community, and attitudes to the film industry: Students tend to rate schools by equipment, but this is only half the story. Of course there must be some professional-level equipment and plenty of basic cameras and editing equipment to support the fundamental levels. More important is for the campus to be the center of an enthusiastic film-producing community, where students support and crew for each other. The school's attitude toward its students and how they fit into the film industry is also significant. An institution remote from working professionals, or one that focuses on "talent" and rewards individualist stars, cannot prepare the majority of its student body for reality. A campus too much in the shadow of industry moguls may harbor competitiveness that destroys more human potential than it nurtures. Some schools even make their seniors compete to decide whose ideas get produced. You enrolled to study directing, but you may wind up recording sound for the winner. Look before you leap.

Signs of a good school: If a center of learning has been in existence for a while, successful former students give visiting lectures and return as teachers. Often they employ or give vital references to the students who earn their liking and respect. Everywhere the film community operates like a village in which personal recommendation is everything. Through networking like this, the lines separating school from profession are crisscrossed in both directions. Mentors give advice and steer projects, and exemplify the way of life that students are trying to make their own.

A hard-to-get-into, expensive school is not necessarily one that will suit your temperament. A less prestigious institution may fit your educational needs and your purse very well.

A sure way to locate good teaching is by attending student film festivals and noting anywhere that's producing good films. A sure sign of energetic and productive teaching, even in a small and obscure facility, is when student work is receiving recognition in competitions.

Brief immersion schools: Many institutions run brief immersion courses, typically in the summer, when busy people have some time free. I have taught in, and can recommend, the Maine International Film and Television Workshops (www.theworkshops.com/). Brief immersion introduces the basics of a discipline and lets students experience what working professionally might be like. The New York Film Academy (www.nyfa.com/) runs a variety of courses in England and Italy as well as in New York City. In order to survive, these institutions must attract large numbers of students, so their advertising often oversells the goods.

Guidance: Other than Garth Gardner's *Gardner's Guide to Colleges for Multimedia and Animation,* 4th ed. (Fairfax, VA: Garth Gardner Publishing, 2004), there is nothing currently doing the same for live action filmmaking for undergraduates. If you want to study at graduate level, good practical information is available about the major schools from Tom Edgar and Karin Kelly's *Film School Confidential: The Insider's Guide to Film Schools* (New York: Perigee, 1997; updated 2007). Its opinions are, however, formed on small samples, and its occasional compulsion to be flippant sometimes leads to absurdities. For example, the book's glossary definition of "actor" is "a difficult person." The book's web site (www.filmschoolconfidential.net) has comments, updates, and other information. There is really no substitute for doing your own research, for which the Internet is essential. Enter "film schools" in Google, and you'll see how much is on offer. Shop wisely and cross-check everything—there are a lot of storefront operators offering the quick fix.

You can do a top-down study by reading Nicholas Jarecki's *Breaking In: How 20 Movie Directors Got Their First Start* (New York: Broadway Books, 2001), in which directors say how they got started. This reiterates the common values that go with making a film career, but won't show where the rungs of the ladder are. The fact is, the only rungs are those you make for yourself. A director's prime asset is being able to research a situation and to put together a picture from multiple sources of information. As you decide whether a particular film school fulfills your expectations, here are some considerations:

- How extensive is the department, and what does its structure reveal?
- How close is the institution to a thriving film production center? (Some campuses are far from major cities and don't have teachers, actors, or urban filmmaking locations nearby.)
- Number of courses? (Having a greater number of specialized courses is better.)
- Number of students? (In this case, more may not be better, but it does enable course variety.)
- Subjects taught by senior and most influential faculty?
- Average class size? (Very revealing.)
- Length of program? (If less than two years, the program is probably superficial.)
- How much specialization is possible, and what proof is there that upper-level courses approach a professional level of specialization?
- How much equipment is there, what kind, and who gets to use it? (This is a real giveaway.)
- What kind of backgrounds do the faculty members have?
- What films have they made lately? (Another giveaway.)
- How experienced are those who are teaching beginning classes? (Many schools have to use their graduate students.)
- Ratio of full-time to part-time faculty? (Also very revealing, though part-timers may be professionals and excellent in their field.)
- Consider tuition and class fees:
  - How much equipment and materials are supplied?
  - How much is the student expected to bankroll along the way?
- Does the school have competitive funds or scholarships to assist in production costs?
- Who owns the copyright to student work? (Many schools retain the copyright to their students' works.)
- What proportion of students wanting to direct actually do so? (Some schools make students compete for top artistic roles, and then they sideline the losers.)

- What does the department say about its attitudes and philosophy?
- What does the place feel like? (Visit the facilities.)
- How do the students regard the school? (Speak to your choice of senior students.)
- How much are your particular interests treated as a specialty?
- What kind of program do they offer?
  - Do they offer a BS, BA, or BFA? (The latter is marginally longer and probably more specialized.)
  - An MFA is a terminal degree and a good basic qualification for production and teaching. What's the MFA degree emphasis?
  - A Ph.D. is a terminal degree, but signifies a scholarly emphasis that generally precludes production.
- For a BA or BFA, how many hours of general studies are you expected to complete, and how germane are they to your focus in film or video?
- Where are their students in the profession?

There is no special accreditation for film schools, and none even for teachers, so it's buyer beware. The institutions listed in this chapter are affiliated with professional bodies, but you should use all your powers of research to determine a school's reputation and what you can personally expect to get from its education.

Many students start in a small college program and transfer to a larger and better-accredited institution. This may lead to culture shock because the new place often has a highly motivated student body that may prove competitive and even alienating. Give careful thought to the atmosphere in which you best thrive, and whether you might do yourself a disservice by leaving the more nurturing environment. However, if you are determined to work professionally in the top echelon of the film industry, a competitive campus close to the industry in your particular country will almost certainly be your best choice.

The first list is mostly schools affiliated with the University Film and Video Association (UFVA). You can see the most up-to-date version via www.ufva.org/ under "About UFVA." The UFVA Job Listings, which seek teachers, often describe the facilities at a particular institution.

Another way to check reputations is the web site www.filmmaker.com, which includes some lengthy and often sulfurous film school reviews. These are by students, and you should read them gingerly, looking for tendencies and peripheral information. In general, discount anything written by those who can't spell or punctuate. Being free and anonymous, it is a great place for malcontents to unload spleen, but common denominators among the reviews may help you avoid a costly mistake. Avoid trade schools and anything that offers the complete, no-nonsense lowdown in next to no time. Filmmaking takes several years of hard learning, like any demanding profession.

NORTH AMERICAN SCHOOLS

Some are private, some state financed, and all have web sites that you'll find by plugging the school name into a search engine. Academic facilities, expertise, cost, and reputations vary widely. Most colleges offer BA, BS, or BFA undergraduate degrees, and many offer MA or MFA graduate degrees. Be advised that a BS (Bachelor of Science) is going to be technology based, whereas a Ph.D., being a degree in scholarship, will be a film studies degree rather than one that involves making films. Graduate schools sometimes prefer people with undergraduate film degrees, sometimes not. Graduate degree programs, which presume that you are a little older and more sophisticated, are more likely to specialize in directing.

All selective film schools want to see what proof you can produce that you are reliable, self-motivated, collaborative, and tenacious in carrying long projects through to completion. Your résumé and application letter should address these points as best you can, and show that you have a mature understanding of the medium's complexity.

Schools commonly thought to have more prestige, facilities, or connections are in **boldface.**

American Film Institute (Graduate students only)

American University

Boston University

California Institute of the Arts

Chapman University

Columbia College Chicago

Columbia University

Curtin University of Technology

Doane College

Duke University

Eastern Michigan University

Emerson College

Florida Metropolitan University, Melbourne

Florida State University

Gallaudet University

Georgia State University

Grand Valley State University

Hellenic Cinema/TV School (Greece)

Houston Community College Southwest

Ithaca College

Lane Community College

La Salle University

Los Angeles Film Studies Center

Loyola Marymount University

Mills College

Montana State University

Montclair State University

New York Film Academy Ltd.

New York University (Tisch School of the Arts)

North Carolina School of the Arts

Northeastern University

Ohio University

Piedmont Community College

Rochester Institute of Technology

Rowan University

Ryerson Polytechnic Institute

San Antonio College

San Diego State University

San Francisco State University

School of Visual Arts, Inc.

Smith College

Southern Illinois University

Stanford University (documentary only)

Suffolk University

Syracuse University

Texas A&M University, Corpus Christi

Universidad de las Comunicaciones (Santiago, Chile)

Unitec Institute of Technology

University of Arizona

University of California at Los Angeles

University of Central Florida

University of Florida Foundation, Inc.

University of Hartford

University of Kansas

University of Nevada, Las Vegas

University of New Orleans, Lakefront

University of North Carolina

University of South Carolina

University of Southern California

University of Texas at Austin

University of Toledo

University of Toronto

University of Washington, Educational Outreach

University of Windsor

Valencia Community College

Vanderbilt University

Vassar College

Villanova University

Watkins Film School

William Patterson University

York University

STUDY ABROAD

There are major film schools around the world, but be warned that most, especially national entities, are small, elitist, and set very competitive entry requirements. Others may be hand-to-mouth, private institutions that are enthusiastic, and great as a social experience, but use underemployed and possibly undereducated local film workers as part-time teachers. If you are accepted into a foreign school, apply for a student visa early because obtaining one can be a long and uncertain process. This is particularly true for anyone applying from abroad to an American school.

You cannot work or support yourself in another country unless you are a citizen. Most countries' immigration policies exclude foreign workers wherever its own filmmakers are underemployed. That situation changes only if you have special, unusual, and fully accredited skills to offer. Check local conditions with the school's admissions officer and with the country's consulate before committing yourself. Also check the length of time of the visa granted against the average time it takes students to graduate—sometimes these durations are incompatible.

SCHOOLS AFFILIATED WITH CILECT

A list of institutions affiliated with CILECT, the Brussels-based International Association of Flm and Television Schools, can be found organized by country on

CILECT's web site (www.cilect.org/).[1] Clicking on a school's name will give you standard information and a link to the school's web site. The + sign before a phone or fax number means you must first enter your country's overseas telephone code (011 in the United States). The numbers that follow are the country code, the area or city code, and finally the school's phone number—as in +44(0)20 7836 9642 for the London Film School. If you are calling from overseas, don't dial what's in parentheses.

CILECT is an excellent source of international information and technical reviews. Don't overlook Corresponding Members; there may be one available to give local advice in your own country. Spanish speakers willing to study in Latin America should consider the Escuela Internacional de Cine y Televisión international (EICTV) in Cuba. Although spartan and running under perpetual material difficulties, it is modestly priced, idealistic, and consistently gets work of really outstanding authorship from its students.

Many countries now have excellent national and private schools. Some—such as the European Film College in Denmark and the Maurits Binger Film Institute (Binger Filmlab) in Amsterdam—even teach in English. Many European schools teach summer film courses in English, which is another (and very pleasant) way to find out whether you like the work.

PREPARING FOR A CAREER DURING YOUR EDUCATION

Film school will be highly structured, but don't assume the thinking has been done for you. Teaching is project based, and almost every assignment is collaborative. This means that each project offers experience that you largely determine for yourself. Volunteer to work on as many other people's films as possible so you get varied experience and make working contact with many other students. Actively seek the help and advice of your teachers, and whenever possible follow their advice. What I'm saying is, *make use* of the school and interact with everyone you can. Don't simply endure its demands.

Unfortunately many college students are in the last stages of user fatigue. They have ingrained habits of passivity developed to survive their earlier dull and unimaginative schooling. They keep a low profile, avoid undue work, and wait good-naturedly for classes to end. These weary, institutionalized victims will never survive in a way of life that depends on energetic, self-motivating activity. If this is you, then film school is where you must turn your life around and seize the rudder of your destiny.

You will know from the way people receive your finished work which of the three filmmaker categories you belong in (see "Who Succeeds" in Chapter 45). For most, naturally enough, directing professionally is some way off. No matter who or what you are, you must *develop at least one craft specialty to professional entry level*, so you have marketable skills when you seek to make a living. This is the subject of the next chapter.

---

[1] CILECT stands for Centre Internationale de Liaison des Ecoles de Cinéma et de Télévision.

CHAPTER 47

BREAKING INTO THE INDUSTRY

Breaking into the industry actually begins during your education as you work to build a good social network, a sound education, and competent work. When your money or your training period runs out, the transition from learner to freelance crew member will become unavoidable. Prepare for this awful day by establishing proof of your skills. Make original short films and get them into festivals or conferences—which is not as difficult as you might think. Awards give your résumé distinction, establish the foundations of a professional identity, and incline employers to interview you. Whether your work is made in or out of film school is immaterial. A degree on its own does nothing to impress media employers, and may even raise red flags, but is vital if you decide later in life to make lateral career moves requiring more formal education. For now, only festival awards, an attested good reputation, and demonstrable skills will get you taken seriously by professional filmmakers.

Getting employment won't be easy, and often depends on the success of your cohort at school. Work to remain in contact after school ends because the good luck of a cameraperson can mean the good luck of several more unit members whom he or she recommends. These, in any case, are the people with whom you will make your next productions, so it's vital to nurture social and professional networks.

FESTIVALS, CONFERENCES, AND EARNING RECOGNITION

Check festival entry conditions, length and format specifications, fee, and other expectations such as student status and nationality. If your DVD is Region 1, make certain that a festival in Germany accepts all-regions DVD or tape. Pay special attention to language or translation requirements. Some foreign competitions require that you subtitle your film and/or supply an English transcription for a simultaneous translator. To find festivals, use an Internet search engine to look for, say, "short film festival." I brought up 100 web sites; with different search words, you would undoubtedly find even more. Guidance on festivals is also available through these web sites:

1. www.film.queensu.ca/Links/Festivals.html Canadian festivals and their deadlines.
2. www.ufva.org/index.php University Film & Video Association for North America. A good site to check periodically.
3. www.filmfestivals.com/index.shtml Devoted to festivals. Lists them by country and month, as well as by other criteria.
4. www.variety.com/ *Variety* magazine. Look up "Festivals."
5. www.cilect.org International Association of Flm and Television Schools. Links to databases, scholarly articles, and information of all kinds.
6. www.cyberfilmschool.com/ Also known as Film Underground. Has much information for the independent filmmaker, including equipment discussions and many articles on the filmmaking process.
7. www.filmmaking.com/ A cornucopia of filmmaking information. See "Nine Ways to Become a Director."
8. www.withoutabox.com/v2/ Another encyclopedic site for independent filmmakers. It exists to give direct access to film festivals, film buyers, and film audiences throughout the world.

Films meant to compete in festivals should be short and snappy, and you should make sure that every tape or DVD copy runs faultlessly from beginning to end. What you send should have a running order list with timings, and should be professionally packaged with your name and contact information on everything.

Festivals are so numerous, and the entries so dismal, that a competent piece will pick up an award or two without difficulty. If your work is really special, you may well pick up a slew of awards, and the existence of these—more than your work itself—will recommend you as someone out of the ordinary. Everyone everywhere is impressed by prizes.

See Chapter 44 for making the most of social contacts at festivals and festival showings.

INTERNSHIPS

Well-established film schools have internship programs that allow you to work unpaid as a professional and prove yourself. Choose a school with a thriving internship program if you can. My own institution has a program where producing and screenwriting students round out their knowledge under the tutelage of professionals in Hollywood.[1] Other major North American schools have similar programs. National film schools usually have a symbiotic relationship with leading lights in their own industry, and employ them as part-time teachers and mentors.

---

[1] See www.filmatcolumbia.com Under "Special Interest," look up "Semester in LA," which lists Hollywood internships.

WHERE YOU LIVE MATTERS

Many people go off to college and dream of returning to their hometown in glory to start a film or video company in comfort there. If it works at all, there is often a glass ceiling that keeps you perennially making commercials for Joe's Used Cars ("Walk in; drive out—bad credit no problem"). Employment of any regularity can be found only where the moviemaking community resides. Either go to college near such an area, or be ready to move there after you graduate. Established schools usually have alumni in the main film centers who will help new graduates launch their careers, and there may even be an alumni association that puts on regular events and socials, as my college does.

PERSONAL QUALITIES

How fast you advance in the film industry after you get a toehold, and what responsibilities people care to give you, depend on your contacts, luck, social skills, and maturity. Almost certainly you will start as a freelancer, dependent on your contacts.

In the industry, as in film school, you become established by maintaining positive and constructive relationships with others, and by doing good work, on time, and within agreed parameters. Sustain this, over a period and under grueling conditions, and your good reputation will slowly spread through the grapevine until you become a preferred crew member. Any costly mistake will circulate to your detriment, which is why craftsmanlike care and forethought are so important.

COMPROMISE?

Becoming known and fitting into a commercial system may seem like compromise, but need not be. After all, the films on which we were raised were produced for profit, and many were good art by any standard. Almost the entire history of the cinema has its roots in commerce, with each new work predicated upon the ticket sales of the last. If cinema and capitalism go hand in hand, this marriage has a certain cantankerous democracy. Tickets or DVD sales are votes from the wallet that prevent screen works from becoming irrelevant or straying too far from the sensibilities of the common man. Shakespeare and his Globe Theatre company flourished under similar conditions. Then as now, purists got themselves to a monastery.

For a bracing taste of the market forces you aim to join, grit your teeth and immerse yourself in the cinema trade journal *Variety* (www.variety.com). Read whatever you can about recent low-budget productions and their tortuous relationship to distribution. Work your way through the waxing and waning independent filmmaking web sites for a sense of international trends. Explore web-based distribution as it develops. Go to genre festivals and see examples of the work you prefer. That way, you will know what the competition is.

PATHS TO THE DIRECTOR'S CHAIR

Let's suppose you have the equivalent of several years of film school under your belt and have significant knowledge and experience in at least one of the craft areas. The film industry has always been an area for the self-starter, so unless you are accepted somewhere as a full-time employee (most unusual these days), you and your friends must make independent and cooperative efforts to get established. Here's what lies ahead.

Filmmaking is entrepreneurial, so your group will need to assemble entertainment packages, about which much has been written to help the novice (see this text's bibliography). To make money from your work, you must appeal to the tastes of a sizable chunk of the paying public. You can learn these things from trade papers and published accounts, and also from observing how others do it in the film business. How you go about developing your own path to directing depends on your resources and on which of those three categories you belong in.

CRAFTSPERSON

Plenty of people get work straight out of school as a grip, assistant editor, camera assistant, assistant director, or personal assistant—but this happens only if you have developed industry contacts and have proven skills, professional discipline, and great references from film professionals. If you are fortunate enough to get work, you will initially be given very limited responsibilities, and then watched closely to see how you perform. At the outset of your career, keep the faith, work hard to keep body and soul together, and get to know the self that emerges under duress. You will advance because the people you work with like you and respect your work and work ethic. Every so often, someone will be unavailable, and you will be given a chance to do something more advanced. You will probably love your work and wish for nothing better than the community to which you belong.

CRAFTSPERSON WITH A DIRECTOR STRUGGLING TO GET OUT

Your bread-and-butter assignments will be entry-level craft work, but you should continue developing your directing skills after you graduate. If you left school with a body of work that won any national or international awards, you may be able to talk people into letting you direct local commercials, educational films, or industrial projects. This can get you invaluable experience at directing actors. A good resource for self-starters is back issues of *DV Magazine* (www.dv.com/magazine/).

Maintain social and professional contact with colleagues from film school whose values you share. Getting established is long and lonely, and best done with friends. Eventually, you'll feel experienced enough to make a move toward directing. See "Experienced Industry Worker Wanting to Direct" below.

MATURING

Maturing is a tempering process that happens as you navigate the pressures and discoveries associated with career, intimate relationships, marriage, and parenthood. Fire, said Seneca, is the test of gold, and adversity is the test of strong people. To become a first-rate narrative artist means looking deeply into the life you lead, and extracting from it something that you can give to others as a compelling story.

The barriers to your directing may seem to lie with those higher up—but really, they lie within yourself. If your life has been fairly normal, your early professional years will be centered on mundane fundamentals that do not equip you with much out of the ordinary. If and when you have worked beyond this, you will begin to express it. That more mature identity will manifest itself through your judgment and values. It will be sensed by those around you as an aura of authority, and implicitly recognized. When you have it, you'll know it. Until then, keep working at it.

THE VISIONARY: DIRECTING STRAIGHT OUT OF SCHOOL

As mentioned earlier, only rare or remarkably lucky human beings move straight from school into directing—and when they do, they are in peril because success has come dangerously soon. Nevertheless, some people's early work shows unmistakable promise, as Roman Polanski's work did in *Two Men and a Wardrobe* (1958) and *The Fat and the Lean* (1960). Through surreal allegory, these vaudeville sketches express a profoundly skeptical and dreamlike view of human quest and interdependency. Plainly, this came from Polanski's extreme suffering as a child in central Europe during World War II—experiences that nobody would ever choose or want. Some people find vision; others have it thrust upon them.

EXPERIENCED INDUSTRY WORKER WANTING TO DIRECT

Consider setting up a unit of your peers to cooperatively produce independent projects that will benefit you all. From the outset, make sure you are working from a fully developed, professional, and commercially viable script. Film crew associates routinely underestimate what goes into a script, and overestimate the contribution their own disciplines make to a movie's success. Unless they are critically astute, they will often run with something second-rate or unfinished. In consequence, film labs are full of abandoned feature film negatives—the graveyard of poor scripts, inept production, and money wasted by innocents who trusted in beginner's luck.

There is plenty of good advice available on the Internet concerning screenwriting, and plenty of links to get further help. Make *Script Magazine* (www. scriptmag.com) part of your immersion program in the brainwork you need to expend. Your script must be of fully professional quality because you must survive at the box office. The hard work and critical values this takes are not secret or arcane. Learn in depth what you need to do, and do it. Keep *on* doing it until even your toughest critics think you've got something first-rate. If your script is really good, it will win recognition in script contests, which is an inexpensive way to test your goods.

For your independent movie to win recognition, it must create an authentic world, be really well acted, *and have something heartfelt to say* about the human condition. Then you have a really good chance of winning awards, getting the film distributed, and recouping your costs. Above all, work incrementally toward this goal, and accrue the experience, encouragement, and confidence to build on your skills. Do not give way to the big temptation—which is to bet all your credit cards on a single horse.

Do not listen to the wise guys who say, "Never make films with your own money." That's like saying, "Never invest in your own development," which is plain daft. Who will know your potential if you won't take risks and prove it to everyone? You will learn as much from directing a short film as from a long one. The more and better your short films, the more the odds improve that you will make a first-class feature.

LOW-BUDGET AND STRAIGHT-TO-DVD MARKET

This is a growing area of paid work that tests all the skills of both fiction and documentary filmmakers. It includes low-budget work for commercial concerns, social agencies, or nongovernmental organizations (NGOs). They don't pay well, but the work allows you to stretch your skills and travel the world. There is already a big market for "how-to" videos, as well as special-interest material, and it can only grow. If you have any passionate interests—for example, underwater archaeology, energy conservation, or restoring old trains—then you can connect with enthusiasts to see what they or their organization lack by way of films. You can direct actors, fictionalize pieces of history, re-create discoveries, show "typical" situations—and all the while be building your directing, leadership, and film business skills. For ideas, browse the special-interest areas of a large videotheque such as Netflix (www.netflix.com).

FREELANCING

The aspiring director will for a long time have to use his or her craft skills (camera, editing, sound, production management, or writing) to fulfill quite humdrum commercial needs. You may find yourself expending imagination and effort crewing for television; music video; reality TV; educational, industrial, training, or medical films; or even shooting conferences and weddings. Doing this reliably and to high standards will teach you plenty. Commercials are particularly good training for fiction because extraordinary expense and effort are focused on highly specific ends. The superb technical and production knowledge you gain will transfer easily to the features setting—if you can let go of the good living that commercials provide.

Most crew work is freelance, which means feast or famine until demand for your services exceeds supply. As an aspiring director, you must aim to be in the right place at the right time, taking other craft work while you establish your identity as a reliable craftsperson. As you eke out a precarious living as a freelance technician, continue making your own films with the contemporaries who are also struggling to gain experience and recognition. When you have concrete, visible results, you then have something proven to offer an employer or a sponsor. Once you get a little paid directing work, you start building up a directing "voice," a track record, and a reputation. It is this (and festival recognition) that will propel you onward to ever more interesting and demanding work.

TELEVISION AS A ROUTE

American television produces very little drama outside the soaps, reality shows, and sitcoms made in Hollywood, but these, if you can get work there, represent exceptional experience in fast, professional-level production. European television—in particular French, British, Dutch, German, Scandinavian, and Italian—has nurtured many fine directors and actors. Some of these countries, in self-defense against the rapacious attractions of the American product, have schemes to help developing local product get off the ground. The European arts channel ARTE, for instance, supports culturally oriented European projects, and is managed jointly from France and Germany.

DEVELOPMENT INSTITUTES

There are two preeminent development institutions in the USA. One is the AFI (American Film Institute, www.afi.com/), a conservatory with a full program of training courses for beginners onward and a graduate-level directing program. The second is the Sundance Institute (http://institute.sundance.org), which, in addition to its famous annual festival, runs labs in directing, film composing, producing, theater, and documentary. Sundance also sponsors an independent producers' conference and an indigenous filmmaker program to encourage moviemaking by native peoples.

The best way to find out what your own country offers is to trawl the Internet, beginning with independent filmmaker web sites. The Maurits Binger Film Institute (Binger Filmlab, www.binger.ahk.nl/) in Amsterdam teaches in English. As a postacademic training facility for film professionals, Binger Filmlab offers intensive five-month programs that focus on script development and the individuals who create scripts. The lab considers applications from all parts of the world on a competitive basis, provided that the applicant (a) has completed a recognized program of film studies, and (b) has a promising script idea. The institute helps young filmmakers develop scripts to a professional level, and tries to place them with an appropriate European production company. The lab's offerings include scriptwriting, script development, coaching directors, and a creative producing course.

In the United States, film production is concentrated in Los Angeles and New York City. Some regional production takes place in other major cities, but there is a real need for ambitious regional production such as the Amber Group in the north of England (see www.amber-online.com/) or the former Dogme Group in Denmark. The successful British company Working Title Films (http://workingtitlefilms.com/) shows what independent filmmakers can do. Founded by the BBC and co-owned by Universal Studios, Working Title has produced a huge number of television films and features, most notably those by the Coen brothers.

IMPORTANCE OF THE SAMPLE REEL

You are what you can show, so make a good sample DVD for prospective employers or financial backers. Show your range by offering an hors d'oeuvre selection of brief (30 seconds to 2 minutes) highlights, then append complete works as necessary. The items should be numbered and titled, and the clips itemized as a list on the case. Collectively, they should be quick and easy to see, and show your range of work and professionalism. Make yourself look as capable, flexible, and interesting as possible. Key your reel to your résumé and to the kind of work you are seeking. Have a boilerplate letter of self-introduction standing by so you can customize it and fire off an individual letter to anyone you meet.

If you can show lighting, camerawork, production design, editing, or acting in addition to your original directing, supply clips to show the breadth of your accomplishment. A busy employer will dip into several bands of the DVD to get a quick impression, so making the DVD comprehensible and easily navigable is your best sales tool.

From this, you can hope for interviews for feature or other crew work. If your fiction directing attracts real praise, have a script or two on hand in case somebody asks what you'd like to direct if you had the chance. It must be a superb script, and you must be able to pitch it on the spot like a practiced impresario.

PRESENTING YOURSELF FOR EMPLOYMENT

Following are some pointers to help you find employment. Employers expect you to know what they do. They look for strong signs that you would fit well into their environment. This depends on how specific your knowledge of their operation is, whether you have relevant experience, and how committed you are to the kind of work they do.

1. **Résumé.** A good one is vital. Print it on good paper, lay it out professionally (get a book on résumé writing), and present what you have done logically and in the best light. Show evidence of pertinent employment, dependability, good character, and self-motivation. A range of different employment is good. You should have, ready for inspection, letters of recommendation available from past employers. Include any work you did for good causes—selfless commitment to a community is always a good character reference. Be able to explain any employment gaps.

2. **Awards.** Nothing, they say, succeeds like success, and people with judgmental responsibilities often seem most impressed by prizes and honors. Make sure you get yours.

3. **Your reel.** With your résumé, enclose a professionally laid out DVD as described above. Some people put together different DVDs, depending on the type of job or company they are approaching.

4. **Knowledge of your potential employer's business.** Use your research skills to learn everything possible about the business or organization. Write to the appropriate individual by name in the company or group. With your résumé, send a brief, carefully composed, individual cover letter that shows realistically how your work goals will contribute to what the company does.

5. **Follow-up call.** Follow up with a phone call a week after the application arrived. You will probably be told that the company has no positions open. Ask if you might stop by for a brief chat with someone in case a position opens up in the future. Person-to-person contact is vital if you are to be remembered.

6. **Interview.** If you are granted an interview, dress conservatively, be punctual, and have all relevant information at hand. How professionally you conduct yourself is the key to whether the interviewer decides to take matters further.

7. **Let the interviewer ask the questions,** and be brief and to the point when you reply. Be modest, realistic, and optimistic. Enthusiasm, realism, and a great desire to learn are attractive qualities. Then:

   a. Take up no more time than you sense is appropriate.

   b. Be ready to open up if invited to do so.

   c. Say concisely what skills and qualities you have to offer. Don't try to hoodwink or manipulate the interviewer.

   d. Say what you want to do, and show you are willing to do (almost) any kind of work to get there.

   e. Use the interview to demonstrate your knowledge of (and therefore commitment to) the interviewer's business.

   f. Ask if the interviewer can recommend other contacts or avenues of inquiry. If he or she says yes, ask if you can use his or her name.

8. **Be ready to work gratis.** If necessary, volunteer to work without pay for a set period. It will give you experience, a reference, and possibly a paying job after you've proved yourself.

9. **Have questions ready.** Interviewers often finish by asking if you have any questions, so have two or three good ones ready. This is an opportunity to engage your interviewer in discussion about the company's work. Most in a position to hire are proud of what their company does. Through conversation, you may learn something useful.

10. **Extend the contact.** When the interview is over, ask politely if you can keep in touch in case something turns up. Polite persistence over time often makes the deepest impression because it marks you as someone who really wants to join the company.

11. **Leave your résumé and reel.** Bring additional copies of your résumé and DVD reel in case the interviewer offers to pass your materials on.

People accustomed to dealing with a volume of job seekers rapidly distinguish the determined realist from the hopeful naïf adrift in alien seas. The judgment is made not on who you are, but on how you present yourself—on paper, on the screen, and in person. You'll do this best by doing your homework, by resourceful reading, and by networking. You don't know the right people? Write this on your cuff: anyone can get to anyone else in the world through five or fewer contacts (phone calls or emails). This means that anyone can find out a whole lot prior to any important meeting.

DEVELOPING NEW PROJECTS

Reread Chapters 2 and 3 of this book for a full treatment of sources for stories. What follows here places that information in a more commercial perspective.

People who invest in films do so to make money, not films. If they could make $50 million in two weeks by backing horses or making potato chips, then horses and potato chips are where their money would go. Any feature film you propose must have wide audience appeal, and you must equip yourself with all the jargon so you can argue like a pro for your movie's earning power.

FINDING FICTION SUBJECTS

The search for subjects and treatments is really a search for those issues and situations that stir you at the deepest levels. Most of the population has opted to live in pursuit of comfort and happiness, and will never unlock the rooms where those shadowy parts are stored. Maybe because sustained comfort brings a sense of deprivation ("the unexamined life isn't worth living"),[2] they need you and your films so that they can live vicariously by watching other lives unfold on a screen— lives akin to their own. Searching to move a wide audience means searching to connect with and represent the sector of contemporary humanity that resides inside *you*.

Help yourself by plunging into the mainstream of modern awareness. Read omnivorously until you feel that local, political, and international affairs are your responsibility. Assume that the major voices of your time are your equals. Look for your fellow spirits. Some will be on the other side of the grave, their voices still urgent and speaking personally to you through their works. Some will be very much alive, struggling to make sense and to give utterance. Some will become your lifelong friends and collaborators, allies with whom you can face the world and tell what it's like to be alive at this moment in humanity's history.

You have probably noticed a strange omission from my list of recommended sources—other films. Of course you will be seeing movies and will be influenced by them. But cinema subjects and cinema approaches should be developed from life, not from other films; that road leads to derivative and imitative work having no authentic voice.

Find one or more screenwriters whose tastes and interests you share and with whom you can collaborate. Jointly explore subjects and make a commitment to meet regularly. Truly creative partnerships are tougher, more resilient, and more likely to lead to a strong, marketable story idea than anyone trying to go it alone.

FINDING AN AGENT

No commercial film company will read unsolicited scripts. It is too wasteful of their time and too risky. Reputable film companies read scripts forwarded by reputable agents, so your scripts (if you write them) must first find a good agent. This person's job is to advise you and represent your work wherever he or she thinks it will find favor. A good way to get an agent is to win a screenwriting competition. Web sites for screenwriters are full of up-to-date advice on how to work your way up the ladder. The Writers Guild of America's web site (www.wga.org/) lists agents of different degrees of accessibility. Some accept only a letter of inquiry, some accept new writers, and some accept new writers only with a reference from someone known to them.

One thing the whole film industry agrees upon is that there are too few original scripts, so it follows that there are always channels open to original new product.

---

[2] Plato c. 428–348 BC.

FORM AND MARKETABILITY

More than content, a film is a way of seeing. The implication is important: how a movie shows its world may be more important than the movie's plot or subject. There are a limited number of plots, but infinite ways of seeing—as many as there are original characters and original minds. You must be as creative in developing story form as you are at finding story content. Building an artistic identity means not only finding subjects of general interest to an audience, but also stimulating ways of seeing them. Part 4: Aesthetics and Authorship discusses some of the many issues affecting film form.

If shyness is holding you back, don't wait for it to cure itself, or for a benefactor to take pity on you. Be proactive; do something about it—now. If you need assertiveness training, get it. If none is available, join a theater group and force yourself to act. It will be impressive in your résumé, and will do wonders for how you present yourself. Your fingerprints prove you're different, but they won't get you noticed. This you must actively demonstrate through your work and your words. Only you can find what you have that makes you stand out from the others.

Thank you for using this book. If our paths should cross, don't hesitate to tell me whether it helped and how I can make it better.

My very best wishes go with you.

GLOSSARY

For greater detail, try Ira Konigsberg's *Complete Film Dictionary* (Penguin, 1998), Frank Beaver's *Dictionary of Film Terms: the Aesthetic Companion to Film Art* (Peter Lang Publishing, 2006), or Wikipedia online at www.wikipedia.org.

A & B rolls   Two or more rolls of film-camera original or duplicate ("dupe") negative from which release prints are struck. A & B roll printing hides splices, and permits dissolves and title superimpositions.

acetate sheet   Clear plastic sheet used as base for titles or animation "cel" frames. In traditional animation, each frame is painted onto cellulose acetate sheet.

action match cut   Cut made between two different angles of the same action using the subject's movement as the transition.

AD   Assistant director.

adaptation   (a) A film work derived from a play, novel, short story, etc. (b) The way characters adjust to changing obstacles. How they adapt gives strong clues to their conflicts and temperament.

ADR   Automatic dialogue replacement. *See* **postsynchronization.**

aerial shot   Shot taken from the air.

AFI   American Film Institute.

ambience   Sound naturally occurring in any location. No space is truly silent, not even a quiet, empty room.

analog recording   Any sound or picture recorded as proportional voltages rather than waveforms registered through digital numbers, as in the coordinates for a graph.

angle of acceptance   The height and width of a lens's subject matter, expressed in degrees or measurements, accepted by a particular focal length lens at a particular distance. Angles vary according to the image's aspect ratio.

answer print   First print from a film laboratory in which color and other corrections first show up.

anticipating   Term used to describe when an actor speaks or acts earlier than appropriate.

anticipatory sound   Sound introduced ahead of its accompanying picture.

artistic process   The method and manner by which a person makes an artwork, which has common elements of discovery and experiment in all forms of art.

aspect ratio   The size of a screen format expressed as a ratio of units of width to height. Standard TV is 4:3, and high-definition television (HDTV) is 16:9. *See also* **angle of acceptance.**

atmosphere track   Sound suggesting an environment (café, railroad, beach, rain, etc.). *See* **ambience.**

attack (sound)   The beginning portion of any sound.

audio sweetening   Sound level and equalization adjustment process, also called sound mixing.

auteur theory   The concept that one mind controls the creative identity of a film.

AV format   A two-column audiovisual script format that places action in the left column and its accompanying sound in the right. Also called *split-page format*.

axis   *See* **scene axis; sound axis.**

baby legs   A miniature tripod for low-angle shots.

backlighting   Lighting from behind the subject.

backstory   Implied or stated events that happened prior to those we see in a story.

barney   A soft camera cover designed to muffle camera noise.

bars   Standard color bars generated in video systems, usually by the camera.

BCU   Big close-up (also ECU, extra, or extreme, close-up).

beat   Point during a scene where buildup of dramatic pressure causes major realization in one or more characters.

best boy   Assistant to the gaffer.

BFI   British Film Institute.

BG   Background.

blocking   Choreography of actors and camera movements within the set.

body copy   Stage directions and physical descriptions in a screenplay.

book, the   Actors' name for the script.

boom   Mobile support pole so microphone can follow speakers and stay out of shot.

boxcar cutting   Assembly of scenes in which sound and picture are cut level for speed and convenience. *See* **overlap cut.**

breakaway properties   Disposable properties needing replacements for multiple takes.

breakdown   *See* crossplot.

broad lighting   Lighting that produces a broad band of highlight on a three-dimensional object.

business   Activities generated by actors to fill out their characters' behavior.

butt splice   Taped film splice made without the overlap necessary for cement splicing.

buzz track   *See* **presence.**

callback   Second round of auditioning for actors passing the first round.

call sheet   Document detailing the who, what, when, and where of upcoming shooting.

camera left, camera right   Method of specifying movement or placement in relation to the camera: "Davy walks away camera left." Also expressed as screen right or left.

camera motivation   Whatever subject movement or story logic justifies a camera movement.

camera-to-subject axis   The invisible line drawn between the camera and the subject in the composition. *See also* **scene axis.**

capturing   *See* **digitizing.**

cardioid microphone   A directional microphone with a heart-shaped pickup pattern.

cattle call   The call for a number of actors or dancers to audition for parts.

cel   Clear cellulose sheet used as a base for title lettering or painted animation cel.

cement splice   Splice made by cementing two overlapping portions of film together.

CG   Character generator. Electronic device for titling or visual effects. Nowadays, it's usually a resident program rather than a separate machine.

chalk marks   Temporary floor marks made for actors or camera during their movements.

character biography   Background circumstances an actor invents for his character.

character generator   *See* **CG.**

checkerboarding   The practice, during film conforming, of alternating scenes with black leader in each A & B roll of camera original. Sound tracks prior to mixing are likewise alternated between two channels, with silence separating sound segments. This allows a grace period in which to adjust printer or sound channel settings before the next segment.

chippy   Carpenter.

cinéma verité   Observational documentary method that, although it makes camera subservient to an actuality, allows action to be catalyzed by the director. *See also* **direct cinema.**

clapper board   Identifying board also called the slate or clapsticks. Its bar closing facilitates synchronizing sound to action.

clapsticks *See* **clapper board.**

climax The dramatic apex of a scene.

coincidence Event forced into being. Used at the dramatist's peril.

color bars Standard electronic video color test, usually generated by the camera.

color chart Chart attached to film slate board as a color reference for the laboratory.

color temperature Light color quality as measured in degrees Kelvin (K).

comm Commentary.

communion The principle by which actors closely react to the nuances in each other's performances and regain the spontaneity of real life.

complementary shot A shot compositionally designed to intercut with another.

composite print A film print combining sound and picture.

compression When sound has a wide dynamic range, it can be proportionately compressed so that loudest and softest sounds are closer in volume. All TV transmissions and most radio transmissions are compressed, with the exception of classical-fidelity music stations. Cinemas usually give you the authentic range between whispers and the roar of battle.

concept The dramatic raison d'être underlying the whole screenplay.

conforming The process by which the film-camera original is edited in conformity with the fine-cut work print prior to making release prints.

confrontation The collision between the people or forces that represent a piece's main conflict.

contingency percentage Percentage added to a budget to provide for the unforeseeable.

contingency planning Alternative shooting lined up in case weather or other imponderables stymie the planned shooting.

continuity Consistency of physical detail between shots intended to match.

continuity script Script made from finished film as record of its contents. Useful in proving piracy or censorship.

continuity supervisor *See* **script supervisor.**

contrast Difference in brightness between highlight and deep shadow areas in an image.

contrast ratio Ratio of lightest to darkest areas in an image.

controlling point of view The psychological perspective (a character's or the Storyteller's) from which a particular scene is shown.

counterpoint The juxtaposing of antithetical elements, perhaps between sound and picture, to create a conflict of impressions for the audience to resolve.

coverage The different camera angles covering a scene that allow it to be flexibly edited.

crab dolly Wheeled camera-support platform that can roll in any direction.

crane A boom supporting the camera that can be raised or lowered during the shot.

crash zoom Very fast zoom in or zoom out.

crib notes Director's notes listing intentions and *don't forgets* for a scene.

crossing the line Moving the camera across the scene axis. Can be problematic.

cross-plot or **scene breakdown** A chart displaying the locations, characters, and script pages necessary to each scene.

CS Close shot.

CU Close-up.

cutaway A shot, often from a character's physical point of view, that allows us to cut away momentarily from the main action.

dailies The film unit's daily output, processed and ready to be viewed. Also called rushes because of the rush involved in readying them.

DAT recorder Digital audiotape recorder.

day for night Special photography that allows a sunlit day shot to pass as moonlit night.

decay The tapering away of a concluding sound.

deep focus Photography that holds objects both near and far in sharp focus.

degradation   Deterioration of a picture, either video or photo, often when it passes through multiple generations of copying.

depth of field   How much depth in the image is in acceptably sharp focus. Varies widely according to lens and f-stop (lens iris) in use.

deus ex machina   The improbable event imported into a story to make it turn out right.

diegetic sound   Sound that characters can hear and that belongs naturally with the situation we see in picture.

diffused light   Light composed of disorganized rays that cast an indistinct shadow.

digital intermediate (DI)   Digital copy, usually of motion picture film, that allows extremely fine color and image manipulation prior to making film release copies.

digitizing or **capturing**   The process of turning an analog signal, whether audio or video, into a digital record. This involves applying an algorithmic formula that compresses the information and avoids recording duplicate information from one frame to the next.

direct cinema   Low-profile observational style of shooting documentary that disallows any directorial intrusion to shape or instigate incidents. Also known as observational cinema. *See also* **cinéma verite.**

discontinuity   Form of storytelling in which time progression is deliberately confused or abridged.

dissolve or **lap dissolve**   Transitional device in which one sound or image melts into another.

DOF   Depth of field; that is, how much in the depth of an image is in acceptable focus.

Dolby   A proprietary electronic recording system that produces low-noise sound recording; that is, having a lowered systemic hiss.

dolly shot   Any shot from a wheeled camera support.

double-system recording   Camera and sound recorder are separate instruments.

DP   Director of photography.

dramatic dynamics   The variations of dramatic pressure during a scene or piece.

dramatic interpretation   Dominant meaning that someone finds in a text.

drop frame   Periodic and automatic adjustment in NTSC timecode to make it correspond with elapsed clock time. Nondrop frame is unadjusted NTSC code.

dry run   A camera rehearsal that is not filmed.

dry sound   Sound that is free of reverberant additions.

dub   To copy from one electronic medium to another. Can be sound or video picture.

dupe   Duplicate.

dutch angle   Shot made with camera deliberately tilted out of horizontal.

DVD   Digital video disc.

dynamic character definition   Defining a dramatic character by what he or she wants and is trying to accomplish.

dynamic composition   Pictorial composition that changes as its subject changes.

echo   Sound reflections that return after a constant delay time.

ECU   Extra, or extreme, close-up (also BCU, big close-up).

edge numbers   Code numbers imprinted on the edge of camera original film and printing through to the work print.

edit decision list (EDL)   Sound and picture edit decisions defined in the form of a timecode or Keykode list.

effects (FX)   Sounds specially laid to augment the sound track of a film.

elision   Omission of unnecessary narrative elements to make a long process short.

emotional memory   Actors who carefully devise specific actions to fit a particular character mood find, when they perform, that they spontaneously experience the characters' emotions.

emotional transition   A character's emotional change during a scene. Scripts often challenge actors by calling for leaps from one mood to another in record time.

energy level   Scenes and performances each have their own energy levels. A director may call for a different energy level when a scene is failing or the actors are getting tired.

epic hero   Larger-than-life main character with superhuman attributes.

equalizing (EQ)   Using sound filters to reduce the discrepancy between sound tracks that are supposed to match and appear seamless.

establishing shot   A shot establishing a scene's geographic and human contents. *See also* **master shot.**

exposition   The phase in a narrative when basic information is relayed to the audience. Good exposition is buried within action and goes unnoticed.

expressionism   A mode in art evoking disturbed or subjective vision.

ext   Exterior.

external composition   Compositional relationship at cutting point between two images.

eye light   Low-wattage light mounted on camera to put a liquid sparkle in actors' eyes.

eye line   A character's visual trajectory.

fade down   To lower sound level or fade picture.

fade in   To fade up an image from (usually) black.

fade out   To fade an image to black.

fade to white   To fade an image to white instead of black.

fade up   To raise sound level.

falling action   *See* **resolution.**

FG   Foreground.

FI   Fade in.

fill light   Diffused light used to raise light level in shadows cast by key light.

film-to-tape transfer   Video copy, usually made on a telecine machine in a film lab—from film of perhaps 16 fps, 18 fps, 24 fps, or 25 fps—without the strobing you get when you shoot a projected image with a 25 fps or 30 fps video camera. *See* **tape-to-film transfer.**

fishpole   A handheld microphone boom.

flash-forward Moving temporarily forward in time, the cinematic equivalent of the future tense. This quickly becomes a new form of present.

flashback   Temporary move backward in time. Sustained, it becomes a new present.

floor plan   *See* **ground/floor plan.**

fluff or **flub**   Result when an actor misspeaks a word or line.

FO   Fade out.

focal distance   Distance between camera and subject.

focus (acting)   Seeing, hearing, thinking in character. When an actor loses focus, he or she becomes self-consciously aware of participating in a make-believe world.

focus (lens)   Lens setting in which the edges of the composition's subject are in the sharpest possible focus.

Foley   Generic name for a stage where sound effects are re-created to picture.

foregrounding   Practice of placing one sound track in the auditory foreground while other sound tracks are in the background.

foreshadowing   A rather fatalistic narrative technique hinting at a particular outcome later. Helps raise expectant tensions in the audience.

form   The means and arrangement chosen to present a story's content.

freeze-frame A single frame arrested and held as a still picture.

frontal lighting   Key light coming from the direction of the camera and showing the subject virtually without shadows.

FTs   Footsteps. Often must be re-created.

FX   Sound effects.

gaffer   Works closely with the director of photography. Sets lights and arranges their power supply.

generation   Camera or sound recorder original is the first generation, and copies are subsequent generations, with each analog copy showing some degradation in fidelity to the original. In contrast, it is said that up to 40 generations of digital copies can be made before degradation ensues.

genre A kind or type of film (horror, sitcom, cowboy, domestic drama, etc.).

givens Whatever is nonnegotiably specified in a text.

gofer Junior production team member who has to *go for* this and *go for* that. Known as *runner* or *dogsbody* in England.

grab shooting Action shot as it happens, with no rehearsal or other preparation.

grading *See* **timing.**

graduated tonality An image lacking extremes of highlight or shadow illumination.

gray scale Camera test chart showing range of gray tones between black and white.

grip Location technician expert in handling lighting and set construction equipment.

ground/floor plan. Diagram showing objects and actor's movements on a set or location.

hand properties Those props an actor handles.

hard light *See* **specular light.**

headroom Compositional space left above heads.

high-concept film One easily understood and whose plot can be summarized in a single-sentence premise, or "concept."

high contrast Image with large range of brightnesses.

high definition (HD) Name for higher-resolution images than standard NTSC is capable of delivering. There are currently two competing standards. The 720p (p = progressive) format creates an image with 720 lines, each with 1,280 pixels (picture elements), so it has a resolution of 1,280 × 720 pixels. The 1080i (i = interlaced) format creates an image with 1,080 lines, each with 1,920 pixels, so its resolution is a higher 1,920 × 1,080. The more pixels, the more highly defined an image is.

high down/high angle Camera mounted high, looking down.

high-key picture Image that is overall bright, with few areas of shadow.

highlight Brightest areas in picture.

hi-hat Metal, ultralow camera support shaped like a top hat.

hypercardioid microphone One that is superdirectional in its pickup pattern.

hyphenate Anyone who combines crafts, such as an actor-director, director-editor, writer-director.

ideation Process of finding and developing the foundational idea for a narrative.

improv Improvisation. A dramatic interaction that encourages both process and outcome to emerge spontaneously. Improvs may set a goal to be reached by an undetermined path.

indicating What actors do when they demonstrate a thought or feeling intellectually rather than organically and in character.

insert A shot of detail inserted into a shot containing more comprehensive action.

int Interior.

interior action Any inner change, such as a decision or rejection, that may lead to physical action. *See also* **physical action.**

interior monologue The interior *"thoughts voice"* an actor sustains to stay in character and in focus.

internal composition Composition internal to a frame. *External composition* refers to relationship between adjacent shots at a cut.

irony The revelation of a reality different from that which was initially apparent.

juicer Electrician.

jump cut Transitional device whereby two similar images taken at different times are cut together so the elision of intervening time is apparent. The audience infers that time has passed. An unintended jump cut, such as you find in family films, can be a disruptive mistake.

juxtaposition The placing of different pictorial or sound elements together so the spectator draws comparison, inference, and heightened thematic awareness.

Keykode Kodak's proprietary system for bar coding each camera original film frame with its own timecode. After editing, the coding permits negative cutting (conforming) from a digitally produced edit decision list (EDL).

key light A scene's apparent source of illumination, and the one creating the intended shadow pattern.

key numbers *See* **edge numbers.**

keystone distortion The distortion of parallel lines that results from photographing an object from an off-axis position.

knowing narrator Literary term for a narrator exhibiting superior knowledge and intelligence.

LA Low angle.

L Cut *See* **overlap cut.**

lap cut *See* **overlap cut.**

lap dissolve *See* **dissolve.**

lavaliere mic Any neck or chest microphone.

lead space The additional compositional space allowed in front of a figure or moving object photographed in profile.

legal release A legally binding release form, signed by a participant in a film, that gives permission to use footage taken.

leitmotif Intentionally repeated element (sound, shot, dialogue, music, etc.) that helps unify a film by reminding the viewer of its earlier appearance. May represent a particular character or event.

lens speed How *fast* a lens is depends on how much light it transmits at its maximum aperture.

level Sound volume.

limbo lighting Photography that isolates a character in space, and that uses a featureless background, usually of plain, seamless paper, to achieve a limbo effect.

lighting ratio The ratio of highlight brightness to shadow illumination.

limiter Electronically applied upper sound limit, useful for preventing momentary transient sounds—such as a door slamming—from distortion through overrecording.

line of tension Invisible dramatic axis, or line of awareness, that can be drawn between protagonists and important elements in a scene.

lipsync Re-created speech that is in complete sync with the speaker. Singers often lipsync to their recordings and fake a singing performance on television.

looping *See* **postsynchronization.**

lose focus *See* **focus (acting).**

low angle Camera looking up at subject.

low-contrast image Small differences of brightness between highlight areas and shadow.

low-key picture An image or scene that is predominantly dark, but that may have bright highlights.

LS Long shot.

M&E track *See* **music and effects track.**

magazine Removable lightproof film container for a film camera.

mannerisms An actor's idiosyncratic and repeated details of behavior. Very hard to change or suppress.

master mix Final mixed sound, first generation.

master shot Shot that shows most or all of the scene and most or all of the characters.

matchback The process of conforming a film negative from numbers generated by a video-editing process.

match cut *See* **action match cut.**

MCS Medium close shot.

memory stick A removable solid-state memory for a digital video camera that records setup or other information. Useful for standardizing setup parameters from shot to shot.

metaphor A verbal or visually implied analogy that ascribes to one thing the qualities associated with another.

MIDI　Musical Instrument Digital Interface, a connection system that enables computers to control musical instruments.

midtones　The intermediate shades of gray lying between absolute black and absolute white.

mimesis　Action that imitates the actuality of life.

mise-en-scéne　The totality of lighting, blocking, camera use, and composition that produces the dramatic image on film.

mix　The combining together of sound tracks.

mix chart　Cue chart functioning like a musician's score to assist in a film sound mix.

MLS　Medium long shot.

montage　Originally meant editing in general, but now limited to the kind of sequence showing a process or the passage of time.

montage sequence　*See* **montage.**

MOS　Short for "Mit out sound." Apocryphally, this is what German directors in Hollywood called for when they intended to shoot picture without sound. Such a shot in Britain is called a *mute* shot. *See also* **sync.**

motif　Any formal element repeated from film history or from the film itself whose repetition draws attention to an unfolding thematic statement. *See also* **leitmotif.**

motivating light source　Apparent source of light in a lighted setup that simulates light coming from the scene's window, skylight, fluorescent fixture, candle, etc.

motivation　Whatever plot logic impels a character to act or react in a particular way, usually a combination of psychological makeup and external events.

MS　Medium shot.

Murphy's Law　Anything that can go wrong will go wrong. Applies to people, not just things.

mus　Music.

music and effects track　A mix of nondialogue tracks to provide all background sound for a foreign version dub. Often called an *M&E track.*

music cues　The beginnings and endings, in feet or in timecode, of music segments. *See also* **spotting notes.**

music editor　Music specialist whose responsibility is to closely fit music to film and who works with the composer and the production's editor.

music sync points　Places in a film's action where music must exactly fit. Also called *picture pointing,* it can easily be overdone.

mute shot　*See* **MOS.**

naive narrator　Literary term for a character (for example, Forrest Gump) whom the audience is made to see as less sophisticated than themselves.

narr　Narration.

narrating point of view　Literary term for first-person point of view telling the story.

narrow lighting　Lighting in portraiture that produces a narrow band of highlight on a face.

negative cutting　*See* **conforming.**

NLE　Digital nonlinear editing.

noise　Unwanted interference inherent in either a sound or video recording system.

noise reduction　Recording and playback techniques that minimize system noise. *See also* **Dolby.**

nondiagetic sound　Anything in a film's sound track that the characters cannot logically hear.

normal lens　A lens of a focal length that, in the format being used, renders perspective in the proportions that the human eye is used to seeing.

NTSC (National Television Standards Committee) video　Signal standard used in American broadcasting. Also known as *composite video* or *RS-170A.*

obligatory moment　The moment of maximum dramatic intensity in a scene and for which the whole scene exists.

observational cinema　*See* **direct cinema.**

offline edit   Low-resolution video editing. *See also* **online edit.**

omnidirectional microphone   One whose pickup pattern favors all directions equally.

omniscient point of view   A storytelling mode in which the audience is exposed to the author's capacity to see or know anything going on in the story, to move at will in time and space, and to freely comment upon meanings or themes.

online edit   Completion process that uses the offline edit's EDL to make a final version at the highest possible resolution, complete with opticals and titles.

on the nose   Writing that is literal and overly explicit.

open call   *See* **cattle call.**

optical   Any visual special effect, including a fade, dissolve, wipe, iris wipe, ripple dissolve, matte, superimposition, etc.

optical house   A company specializing in visual special effects.

optical track   A photographic sound track like that on the edge of 35 mm film.

OS   Can mean offscreen or overshoulder, depending on context.

over the top   A performance carried out with an excess of signified emotion.

overlap cut   Any cut where picture and sound cuts are staggered instead of level.

pan   Short for *panoramic*. Horizontal camera movement.

parallel storytelling   Two separate stories proceeding through time in parallel. Useful for abridging each and suggesting ironic contrasts.

personalizing   An actor personalizes when he or she enters completely into becoming their character and discusses the character's issues and problems in the first, not the third, person.

perspective   The size differential between foreground and background objects that causes us to infer receding space. Obviously distorted perspective makes us attribute subjective distortion in the point of view being expressed.

physical action   An externally visible action such as closing a door, starting a car, or asking someone for a telephone number. Unless physical actions are automatic responses, they are preceded by interior action. *See also* **interior action.**

picture pointing   Making music fit picture events. Walt Disney films used the device so much that its overuse is called *Mickey Mousing.*

picture texture   This can be hard or soft. A hard image has large areas in sharp focus and tends to be high contrast, whereas a soft image has areas out of focus and lacks contrast.

playwriting   One actor's tendency to take control of a scene, particularly in improv work, and manipulate other actors into becoming compliant.

plot   The arrangement of incidents and the logic of causality in a story. Plot should create a sense of momentum and credibility, and act as a vehicle for the thematic intention of the piece.

plot-driven narrative   Story mode in which events tend to shape main characters' actions rather than vice versa. Plot-driven narrative sets out to entertain by generating tension.

PM   Production manager.

point of view   Sometimes literally what a character sees (a clock approaching midnight, say), but more usually signifies the outlook and sensations of a character within a particular environment. Can be the momentary consciousness of an unimportant character or the ruling consciousness of a main character (*see* **controlling point of view**). It can also be the Storyteller's point of view (*see* **omniscient point of view**).

postsynchronization   Dialogue or effects shot to sync with existing action.

POV   Point of view. When abbreviated thus in a screenplay, it nearly always means a shot reproducing a character's eye-line view.

practical   Any light source visible in the frame as part of the set.

premise   *See* **concept.**

premix   A preliminary pass in which subsidiary sound elements are mixed together in preparation for the final mix.

preroll   The amount of time a video-editing rig needs to get up to speed before it can safely make a cut.

presence   Specially recorded location atmosphere to authentically augment "silent" portions of track. Every space has its own unique presence. Also called *room tone* and *buzz track*.

progressive scan   The drawing of a complete video frame from top to bottom in one scan instead of the conventional interlace method in which odd lines and even lines are drawn in two separate passes.

prop   Property or object used for set dressing or by actors. *See also* **breakaway properties; hand properties; stage properties.**

property   Physical object handled by actors or present for authenticity in a set. A term also used for a script to which someone has secured the rights.

psychoacoustics   Human perception and evaluation of sounds in contrast to their scientific evaluation.

rack focus   Altering focus between foreground and background during a shot. Prompts or accommodates an attention shift (a figure enters a door at the back of the room, for instance).

radio frequency interference   Sound system intrusions that have their origins in radio transmissions. Also called *RF.*

radio microphone   A microphone system that transmits its signal by radio to the recorder and is therefore wireless. Famous for picking up taxis and CB enthusiasts at inopportune moments.

reader's script   Transcript of a finished film presented in a publisher's format that makes maximum use of the page.

recall   The faculty of selective memory that is useful to writers because memory tends to drop what is unnecessary or uninteresting.

reconnaissance   Careful examination of locations prior to shooting. *See also* **scouting.**

reflected sound   Sound thrown back by sound-reflective surfaces.

release print   Final print destined for audience consumption.

research   Library work and observation of real life in search of authentic detail to fill out fictional characters and situations.

resistance   Human evasion mechanisms that show up in actors under different kinds of stress.

resolution   The wind-down events following the plot's climax that form the final phase of the plot's development. Also called *falling action.*

reverberation   Sound reflections returning in a disorganized pattern of delay.

RF   *See* **radio frequency interference.**

rising action   The plot developments, including complication and conflict, that lead to a plot's climax.

rolling off   Practice of reducing the level of a band of frequencies

room tone   *See* **presence.**

running lines   The action of actors rehearsing lines before a take, usually done with the script supervisor.

rushes   Unedited raw footage as it appears after shooting. Also called *dailies.*

rushes book   Log of important first reactions to performances in rushes footage.

scene axis   The invisible line in a scene representing the scene's dramatic polarization. In a labor dispute scene, this might be drawn between the main protagonists: the plant manager and the union negotiator. Coverage is shot from one side of this line to preserve consistent screen directions for all participants. Complex scenes involving multiple characters and physical regrouping generally have multiple axes. *See also* **crossing the line.**

scene breakdown or **cross-plot**   A chart displaying the locations, characters, and script pages necessary for each scene.

scene dialectics   The forces in opposition in a scene that usually require externalizing through acting, blocking, composition, visual and aural metaphors, etc.

scene geography   The physical layout of the location and the placing of the characters when they are first encountered. *See also* **master shot.**

scouting   Careful examination of locations prior to shooting. Also called *reconnaissance.*

scratch music   Trial music added as an illustration during editing. Later, it gets replaced by the final music choice.

screen direction   The orientation or movement of characters and objects relative to the screen (screen left, screen right, upscreen, downscreen).

screen left, screen right   Movement or direction specifications. *See also* **screen direction.**

screenplay   Standard script format showing dialogue and stage direction but no camera or editing instructions.

script supervisor   Also called *continuity supervisor,* this person notes the physical details of each scene and the actual dialogue used so that complementary shots, designed to cut together, will match.

SDTV   Standard Definition Television; that is, the original American NTSC television standard of 480 lines with 640 pixels per line. *See also* **high definition (HD).**

segue (pronounced *SEG-way*)   Sound transition, often a dissolve.

set light   A light whose function is to illuminate the set.

setup   The combination of particular lens, camera placement, and composition to produce a particular shot.

SFX   Sound effects.

shooting ratio   The ratio of material shot in relation to its eventual edited screen time. For dramatic film, 8:1 or higher is usual.

shooting script   Screenplay with scenes numbered and amended to show intended camera coverage and editing.

shotgun/rifle mic   Ultradirectional microphone good for minimizing ambient noise.

side coaching   During breaks in a scene's dialogue, the director can quietly feed directions to the actors, who incorporate these instructions without breaking character. Most often used when shooting reaction shots.

sides   Scenes read by actors at an audition or supplied to actors playing minor parts.

sight lines   Lines that can be drawn along each character's main lines of vision and that influence the pattern of coverage in order to reproduce the feeling of each main character's consciousness.

silhouette lighting   Lighting in which the subject is a dark outline against a light background.

simple narrative   Primarily functional, and supplies an exposition of events, usually in chronological order. Simple narrative exists to inform.

single shot   A shot containing only one character.

single-system recording   Sound recording made on film or video that also carries the picture. *See* **double-system recording.**

slate   *See* **clapper board.** Stage actors understand "slate" to mean a two- or three-sentence self-introduction for the benefit of those watching the audition.

slate number   Setup and take number shown on the slate, or clapper, which identifies a particular take.

soft light   Light that does not produce hard-edged shadows.

sound axis   The direct line between the microphone and the source of sound, such as speech. Directional microphones favor sound that is *on axis,* and discriminate against sound that is *off axis.*

sound dissolve   One sound track dissolving into another.

sound effects   Nondialogue recordings of sounds intended either to intensify a scene's realism or to give it a subjective heightening.

sound mix   The mixing together of elements into a composition that becomes the film's sound track.

sound perspective   Apparent distance of sound source from the microphone. Lavaliere mics, for instance, give no change of perspective when characters move or turn because these microphones remain in a fixed relationship to the wearer.

soundscape   The aural picture built in the audience's imagination by skillfully deployed sound tracks.

sparks   Electrician.

specular light   Light composed of parallel rays that cast a comparatively hard-edged shadow.

split-page format   *See* **AV format.**

spot effects   Featured sounds such as a door closing, dog barking, hammer on nails, or other sound effects that are more than general background.

spotting notes   Notes that may refer to spot sound effects or music segments.

stage directions   Nondialogue screenplay instructions, also known as *body copy*.

stage properties   Those properties that are used to dress the stage but are not handled by characters.

stand-in   Someone who takes the place of an actor during setup time or for shots that involve special skills, such as horse riding, fights, etc.

static character definition   Giving a character static attributes instead of defining him in terms of dynamic volition.

static composition   The composition elements in a static image.

Steadicam   Proprietary body-brace camera support that uses counterbalance and gimbal technology so the camera can float while the operator walks.

step outline   Synopsis of a screenplay expressed as a series of numbered steps, preferably including a definition of each step's function in the whole.

sting   Musical accent to heighten a dramatic moment.

storyboard   Series of key images sketched to suggest what a series of shots will look like.

strobing   The unnatural result on-screen resulting from the interaction of camera shutter speed with a patterned subject such as the rotating spokes of a wheel or panning across a picket fence.

structure   The formal organization of the elements of a story, principally the handling of time, and their arrangement into a dramatically satisfying development that includes a climax and resolution.

style   An individual stamp on a film; the elements in a film that issue from its makers' own artistic identity.

subjective camera angle   An angle that implies the physical point of view of one of the characters.

subtext   The hidden, underlying meaning to the text. It is supremely important, and actors and director must often search for it.

superobjective   The overarching thematic purpose of the work as it is interpreted by a director and his or her cast.

surrealism   A movement in art and literature. Concerned with the free movement of the imagination, particularly as expressed in dreams, where the dreamer has no conscious control over events. Often associated with helplessness.

sweetening   *See* **audio sweetening.**

sync   Any sound that is synchronous with picture, or vice versa. *See* **MOS**

sync coding   Code marks to help an editor keep sound and action in sync.

synecdoche   A literary figure of speech in which a part stands for a whole. In film, you might use a revolving blue light to stand for the police.

tag   An irreducibly brief description useful for its focus upon essentials.

take   One filmed attempt from one setup. Each setup may have several takes.

tape-to-film transfer   Laboratory transfer of 25 fps or 30 fps video to 24 fps film. Requires timebase correction to even out motion. *See* **film-to-tape transfer.**

telecine   Machine used to convert film to video. *See* **film-to-tape transfer.**

telephoto lens   Long or telescopic lens that foreshortens the apparent distance between foreground and background objects.

tense, change of   Temporary change from present to either past, future, or conditional tenses in a film's narrative flow. Whatever tense a film invokes speedily becomes a new, ongoing present. For this reason, screenwriting is always in the present tense.

thematic purpose   The overall interpretation of a complete work that is ultimately decided by the director. *See* **superobjective.**

theme   A dominant idea made concrete through its representation by the characters, action, and imagery of the film.

three-shot (3S)   Shot containing three people.

through-line   Spine or superobjective of a role; that is, what drive connects all the character's actions—past, present, and likely future. The through-line in each scene fits logically with the character's through-line for the whole script.

thumbnail character sketch   Brief character description useful either in screenwriting or for recruiting actors.

tilt   Camera swiveling in a vertical arc—tilting up and down to show the height of a flagpole, for instance.

time-base correction   Electronic stabilization of the video image, particularly necessary to make it compatible with the sensitive circuitry used in transmission over the air.

timecode   Electronic code number unique to each video frame.

timing   The process of examining and grading a negative for color quality and exposure prior to printing. Also called *grading*.

tracking shot   Moving camera shot in which the camera dolly often runs on tracks like a miniature railroad.

transitional device   Any visual, sound, or dramatic screen element that signals a jump to another time or place.

treatment   Usually a synopsis in present-tense, short-story form of a screenplay that summarizes dialogue and describes only what an audience would see and hear. Can also be used to refer to a puff piece designed to sell the script rather than give comprehensive information about content.

trucking shot   Moving camera shot that was originally shot from a truck. The term is used interchangeably with *tracking shot*.

two-shot (2S)   Shot containing two people.

ultradirectional microphone   *See* **hypercardioid microphone.**

unit   The whole group of people shooting a film.

VCR   Videocassette recorder.

verbal action   Words conceived and delivered so as to act upon the listener and instigate a result.

video assist or **video feed**   Video taken from the film camera's viewfinder and displayed on a monitor, usually for the director to watch during film shooting.

visual rhythm   Each image according to its action and compositional complexity requires a different duration on-screen to look right and to occupy the same audience concentration as its predecessor. A succession of images, when sensitively edited, exhibit a rhythmic constancy that can be slowed or accelerated like any other kind of rhythm.

VO   Voice-over.

volition   The will of a character to accomplish something. This leads to constant struggle of one form or another, a concept vital in making dramatic characters come to life.

VT   Videotape.

VTR   Videotape recorder.

WA   Wide angle.

walk-through   The stage during lighting setup when actors or stand-ins are asked to walk through their physical movements.

whip pan   Very fast panning movement.

white balance   Video camera setup procedure in which circuitry is adjusted to the color temperature of the lighting source so a white object is rendered as white on-screen.

wide-angle lens   A lens with a wide angle of acceptance. Its effect is to increase the apparent distance between foreground and background objects.

wild   Not in sync.

wild track   A sound track shot alone, with no synchronous picture.

window dub   A transfer made from a timecoded, video camera original that displays each frame's timecode number in a window near the bottom of frame.

wipe   Optical transition between two scenes that appears on-screen as a line moving across the screen. An iris wipe makes the new scene appear as a dot that enlarges to fill the screen. These effects are overused on the TV screen.

wireless mic   *See* **radio microphone.**

work print   A film print made for the express purpose of editing.

wrap   End of shooting.

WS   Wide shot.

WT   Wild track.

XLS   Extralong shot.

zoom lens   A lens whose focal length is infinitely variable between two extremes.

zoom ratio   The ratio of the longest to the widest focal lengths. A 10 mm to 100 mm zoom would have a 10:1 zoom ratio.

BIBLIOGRAPHY AND USEFUL WEB SITES

The bibliography is laid out in approximate order of the production phases. Asterisked works are ones I've found particularly useful. You can get kindly used books of all kinds at very reasonable prices via AbeBooks (www.abebooks.com).

BIBLIOGRAPHY

SCREENWRITING

Atchity, Kenneth, and Chi-Li Wong. *Writing Treatments That Sell: How to Create and Market Your Story Ideas to the Motion Picture and TV Industry,* 2nd ed. Owl Books, 2003.

*Bergman, Ingmar. *Four Stories by Ingmar Bergman*. Doubleday, 1977.

Biro, Yvette, and Marie-Geneviéve Ripeau. *To Dress a Nude: Exercises in Imagination*. Kendall/Hunt, 1998.

Blacker, Irwin R. *The Elements of Screenwriting*. Hungry Minds, 1996.

Blum, Richard A. *Television and Screen Writing from Concept to Contract,* 4th ed. Focal Press, 2000.

*Cooper, Pat, and Ken Dancyger. *Writing the Short Film,* 2nd ed. Focal Press, 1999.

*Dancyger, Ken. *Global Scriptwriting*. Focal Press, 2001.

*Dancyger, Ken, and Jeff Rush. *Alternative Scriptwriting: Writing Beyond the Rules,* 4th ed. Focal Press, 2006.

*Dannenbaum, Jed, Carroll Hodge, and Doe Meyer. *Creative Filmmaking from the Inside Out: Five Keys to Making Inspired Movies and Television*. Fireside, 2003.

Field, Syd. *Screenplay: The Foundations of Screenwriting*. Delta, 2005.

———. *The Screenwriter's Workbook*. Dell, 1988.

Horton, Andrew. *Writing the Character-Centered Screenplay*. University of California Press, 1994.

Howard, David. *The Tools of Screenwriting*. St. Martin's Press, 1995.

Rabiger, Michael. *Developing Story Ideas 2ed*. Focal Press, 2006.

Rosenthal, Alan. *Writing Docudrama: Dramatizing Reality for Film and Television*. Focal Press, 1994.

Seger, Linda. *Creating Unforgettable Characters*. Owl Books, 1990.

———. *Making a Good Script Great*. Samuel French, 1994.

*Vale, Eugene. *Vale's Technique of Screen and TV Writing*. Focal Press, 1998.

*Vogler, Christopher. *The Writer's Journey*. Pan, 1999.

ADAPTATION

*Bluestone, George. *Novels into Film*. University of California Press, 1957.

Boyum, Joy Gould. *Double Exposure: Fiction into Film*. Signet, 1989.

Brady, Ben. *Principles of Adaptation for Film and Television*. University of Texas Press, 1994.

Halperin, Michael. *Writing for the Second Act: Building Conflict and Tension*. Michael Wiese Productions, 2003.

————. *Writing the Killer Treatment: Selling Your Story Without a Script*. Michael Wiese Productions, 2003.

Horton, Andrew. *Writing the Character-Centered Screenplay*, 2nd ed. University of California Press, 2000.

*McDougal, Stuart Y. *Made into Movies: From Literature to Film*. Harcourt Brace Jovanovich, 1997.

Portnoy, Kenneth. *Screen Adaptation: A Scriptwriting Handbook*, 2nd ed. Focal Press, 1998.

*Richardson, Robert. *Literature and Film*. Garland, 1985.

*Seger, Linda. *The Art of Adaptation: Turning Fact and Fiction into Film*. Owl Books, 1992.

ACTING

Barr, Tony. *Acting for the Camera*, rev. ed. Harper Paperbacks, 1997.

Benedetti, Robert. *The Actor at Work*, 8th ed. Allyn & Bacon, 2001.

*————. *The Actor in You: Sixteen Simple Steps to Understanding the Art of Acting*, 2nd ed. Allyn & Bacon, 2003.

Caine, Michael. *Acting in Film: An Actor's Take on Moviemaking*. Applause Theatre Book Publishers, 2000.

*Hagen, Uta, and Haskel Frankel. *Respect for Acting*. Wiley, 1973.

Hodgson, John, and Ernest Richards. *Improvisation*. Grove Press, 1979.

*Marowitz, Charles. *The Art of Being: Towards a Theory of Acting*. Taplinger, 1978.

*Moore, Sonia. *The Stanislavski System*. Viking Press, 1965.

————. *Stanislavski Revealed*. Applause Books, 2000.

*Morris, Eric, Joan Hotchkis, and Jack Nicholson. *No Acting Please*. Ermor Enterprises, 1995.

*Spolin, Viola. *Improvisation for the Theatre*, 3rd ed. Northwestern University Press, 1999.

DIRECTING

*Ball, William. *A Sense of Directing: Some Observations on the Art of Directing*. Drama Publishers, 1984. (Theatrical directing, but much good advice that applies to film.)

*Bresson, Robert. *Notes on the Cinematographer*. Green Integer Books, 1997.

*Clurman, Harold. *On Directing*. Fireside, 1997. (Theatrical directing, but much good advice that applies to film.)

Crisp, Mike. *The Practical Director*, 2nd ed. Focal Press, 1996.

————. *Directing Single Camera Drama*, 2nd ed. Focal Press, 2004.

*DeKoven, Lenore. *Changing Direction: A Practical Approach to Directing Actors in Film and Theatre*. Focal Press, 2006.

Kagan, Jeremy. *Directors Close Up*. Scarecrow Press, 2006.

*Katz, Steven D. *Film Directing Shot by Shot*. Focal Press in association with Michael Wiese Productions, 1991.

*Lumet, Sidney. *Making Movies*. Knopf/Random House, 1996.

*Mamet, David. *On Directing Film*. Penguin, 1991.

Proferes, Nicholas. *Film Directing Fundamentals: See Your Film Before Shooting*, 2nd ed. Focal Press, 2004.

Rabiger, Michael. *Directing the Documentary*, 4th ed. Focal Press, 2004.

Rea, Peter, and David Irving. *Producing and Directing the Short Film and Video*, 3rd ed. Focal Press, 2006.

Sherman, Eric. *Directing the Film: Film Directors on Their Art*. Acrobat Books, 1988.

*Weston, Judith. *Directing Actors: Creating Memorable Performances for Film and Television*. Michael Wiese Productions, 1996.

———. *The Film Director's Intuition: Script Analysis and Rehearsal Techniques*. Michael Wiese Productions, 2003.

PRODUCTION MANAGEMENT

Cleve, Bastian. *Film Production Management*, 3rd ed. Focal Press, 2005.

Gates, Richard. *Production Management for Film and Video*, 3rd ed. Elsevier, 1999.

Hofhaner, Eve. *The Complete Film Production Handbook*, 3rd ed. Focal Press, 2001. (Book and CD-ROM.)

Maier, Robert G. *Location Scouting and Management Handbook*. Focal Press, 1994.

Patz, Deborah S. *Film Production Management: The Ultimate Guide for Film and Television Production Management and Coordination*. Michael Wiese Productions, 2002.

ART DIRECTION

Affron, Charles, and Mirella Affron. *Sets in Motion*. Rutgers University Press, 1995.

Ettedgui, Peter. *Production Design and Art Direction*. Focal Press, 2000.

Lobrutto, Vincent. *The Filmmaker's Guide to Production Design*. Allworth Press, 2002.

Olson, Robert. *Art Direction for Film and Video*, 2nd ed. Focal Press, 1998.

Preston, Ward. *What an Art Director Does*. Silman-James, 1994.

Sennett, Richard S. *Setting the Scene: The Great Hollywood Art Directors*. Harry N. Abrams, 1994.

COSTUMING AND MAKEUP

Delamar, Penny. *The Complete Makeup Artist: Working in Film, Television, and Theatre*. Northwestern University Press, 2002.

Ingham, Rosemary, and Liz Covey. *The Costume Designer's Handbook: A Complete Guide for Amateur and Professional Costume Designers*, 3rd ed. Heinemann, 2003.

Timpone, Anthony. *Men, Makeup, and Monsters: Hollywood's Masters of Illusion and FX*. St. Martin's Press, 1996.

LIGHTING

Box, Harry. *The Set Lighting Technician's Handbook: Film Lighting Equipment, Practice, and Electrical Distribution*, 3rd ed. Focal Press, 2003.

*Carlson, Verne, and Sylvia Carlson. *Professional Lighting Handbook*, 4th ed. Focal Press, 1993.

Ferncase, Richard K. *Basic Lighting Worktext for Film and Video*. Focal Press, 1992.

———. *Film and Video Lighting Terms and Concepts*. Focal Press, 1995.

Fitt, Brian, and Joe Thornley. *A–Z of Lighting Technology*, 2nd ed. Focal Press, 2001.

Gloman, Chuck, and Tom LeTourneau. *Placing Shadows: Lighting Techniques of Video Production*, 3rd ed. Focal Press, 2005.

Malkiewicz, J. Kris. *Film Lighting: Talks with Hollywood's Cinematographers and Gaffers.* Fireside, 1986.

Millerson, Gerald. *Lighting for TV and Film,* 3rd ed. Focal Press, 1999.

Uva, Michael G. *The Grip Book,* 3rd ed. Focal Press, 2006.

Viera, Dave, and Maria Viera. *Lighting for Film and Electronic Cinematography,* 2nd ed. Wadsworth, 2004.

CINEMATOGRAPHY AND MOTION PICTURE TECHNIQUES

Arijon, Daniel. *Grammar of the Film Language.* Silman-James, 1991.

Ascher, Steven, and Edward Pincus. *The Filmmaker's Handbook, Completely Revised and Updated.* Plume, 2007.

Brown, Blain. *Cinematography: Theory and Practice.* Focal Press, 2002.

*Detmers, Fred, ed. *American Cinematographer Handbook.* American Society of Cinematographers, 2004.

Ettedgui, Peter. *Cinematography.* Focal Press, 1999.

Groticelli, Michael, ed. *American Cinematographer Video Manual.* American Cinematographer, 2004.

Hines, William E. *Operating Cinematography for Film and Video: A Professional and Practical Guide.* Ed-Venture Films/Books, 1997.

Hirschfeld, Gerald, and Julia Tucker. *Image Control: Motion Picture and Video Camera Filters and Lab Techniques.* ASC Press, 2005.

*Hurbis-Cherrier, Mick. *Voice and Vision: A Creative Approach to Narrative Film and DV Production.* Focal Press, 2007.

Laszlo, Andrew, and Andrew Quicke. *Every Frame a Rembrandt: Art and Practice of Cinematography.* Focal Press, 2000.

Lobrutto, Vincent. *Principal Photography: Interviews with Feature Film Cinematographers.* Greenwood, 1999.

*Malkiewicz, J. Kris, and M. David Mullen. *Cinematography.* Fireside, 2005.

Mascelli, Joseph. *The Five C's of Cinematography: Motion Picture Filming Technique.* Silman-James, 1998.

MICROPHONES, RECORDING, AND SOUND

Bartlett, Bruce, and Jenny Bartlett. *On Location Recording Techniques.* Focal Press, 1999.

———. *Practical Recording Techniques,* 4th ed. Focal Press, 2005.

Borwick, John. *Sound Recording Practice,* 2nd rev. ed. Oxford University Press, 1995.

Huber, David Miles, and Robert E. Runstein. *Modern Recording Techniques,* 6th ed. Focal Press, 2005.

Lyver, Des, and Graham Swainson. *Basics of Video Sound,* 2nd ed. Focal Press, 1999.

Nisbett, Alec. *The Sound Studio,* 7th ed. Focal Press, 2003.

Rumsey, Francis. *Desktop Audio Technology.* Focal Press, 2003.

Rumsey, Francis, and Tim McCormick. *Sound and Sound Recording: An Introduction,* 5th ed. Focal Press, 2005.

Watkinson, John. *The Art of Digital Recording,* 3rd ed. Focal Press, 2000.

———. *An Introduction to Digital Audio,* 2nd ed. Focal Press, 2002.

White, Glenn D. *The Audio Dictionary,* 3rd ed. University of Washington Press, 2005.

CONTINUITY

*Miller, Pat P. *Script Supervising and Film Continuity,* 3rd ed. Focal Press, 1999.

Rowlands, Avril. *The Continuity Supervisor,* 4th ed. Focal Press, 2000.

POSTPRODUCTION

Bayes, Steve. *The Avid Handbook: Techniques for the Avid Media Composer and Avid Express*, 4th ed. Focal Press, 2003.

Browne, Steven E. *High Definition Postproduction*. Focal Press, 2006.

Collins, Mike. *Pro Tools for Music Production*. Focal Press, 2004.

*Dancyger, Ken. The *Technique of Film and Video Editing: Theory and Practice*, 4th ed. Focal Press, 2006.

*Murch, Walter, and Francis Ford Coppola. *In the Blink of an Eye: A Perspective on Film Editing*. Silman-James, 1995.

Oldham, Gabriella. *First Cut: Conversations with Film Editors*. University of California Press, 1995.

*Rosenblum, Ralph, and Robert Karen. *When the Shooting Stops, the Cutting Begins*. Da Capo, 1986.

MUSIC

Russell, Mark, and James Young. *Film Music*. Focal Press, 2000.

FINANCE, PRODUCTION, AND DISTRIBUTION

Cones, John W. *Film Finance and Distribution: A Dictionary of Terms*. Silman-James, 1992.

*Donaldson, Michael C. *Clearance and Copyright: Everything the Independent Filmmaker Needs to Know*, 2nd rev. ed. Silman-James, 2003.

Erickson, Gunnar, Harris Tulchin, and Mark Halloran. *The Independent Producer's Survival Guide: A Business and Legal Sourcebook*, 2nd ed. Schirmer Trade Books, 2005.

Farber, Donald C. *Producing, Financing, and Distributing Film: A Comprehensive Legal and Business Guide*. Limelight Editions, 2004.

Goodell, Gregory. *Independent Feature Film Production*. St. Martin's Griffin, 1998.

Houghton, Buck. *What a Producer Does: The Art of Moviemaking (Not the Business)*. Silman-James, 1992.

Koster, Robert J. *The Budget Book for Film and Television*, 2nd ed. Focal Press, 2004.

Lazarus, Paul N. III. *The Film Producer*. St. Martin's Press, 1992.

Lee, John J. *The Producer's Business Handbook*, 2nd ed. Focal Press, 2005.

Levison, Louise. *Filmmakers and Financing: Business Plans for Independents*, 5th ed. Focal Press, 2006.

Litwak, Mark. *Dealmaking in the Film and Television Industry from Negotiations to Final Contracts*, 2nd ed. Silman-James, 2002.

———. *Risky Business: Financing and Distributing Independent Films*. Silman-James, 2004.

Ohanian, Thomas A., and Michael E. Phillips. *Digital Filmmaking: The Changing Art and Craft of Making Motion Pictures*, 2nd ed. Focal Press, 2000.

Singleton, Ralph. *Film Budgeting*. Lone Eagle, 2006.

Wiese, Michael. *The Independent Filmmakers' Guide*, 2nd ed. Michael Wiese Productions, 1998.

Wiese, Michael, and Deke Simon. *Film and Video Budgets*, 4th ed. Michael Wiese Productions, 2006.

EDUCATION AND CAREER POSSIBILITIES

Bayer, William. *Breaking Through, Selling Out, Dropping Dead*. Limelight Editions, 2004.

Bone, Jan, and Ana Fernandez. *Opportunities in Film Careers*. McGraw-Hill, 2004.

Edgar, Tom, and Karen Kelly. *Film School Confidential: The Insider's Guide to Film Schools*. Perigee, 2007. (Graduate level only.)

O'Donnell, Gail, and Michele Travolta, eds. *Making It in Hollywood*. Sourcebooks, 1994.

Peterson's Guides to Graduate Programs in the Humanities/Arts/Social Sciences, Book 2. Peterson's, 2007.

Yager, Fred, and Jan Yager. *Career Opportunities in the Film Industry*. Facts on File, 2003.

USEFUL WEB SITES

ORGANIZATIONS

www.afionline.org American Film Institute. A center for archives, film studies, and film education.

www.bfi.org.uk British Film Institute. Archives, publications, and screenings.

www.cilect.org CILECT (Centre International de Liaison des Ecoles de Cinéma et de Télévision) is the Brussels-based organization of international film schools, and it always has an interesting range of special projects going.

www.cinematography.com Professional motion picture camera people, news, and resources.

www.facets.org Facets Cinémathèque has 35,000 films of every kind for sale on tape or DVD. A helpful and knowledgeable organization with a passion for international and minority interest movies. Be sure to check that they have the film you want in the format you can play. (Banish compatibility problems by investing in a zone-free DVD player.)

www.focalpress.com Focal Press. The newest books on media.

www.lcweb.loc.gov Library of Congress.

www.soc.org Society of Camera Operators. Information, book lists, and links to other professional societies around the world.

www.ufva.org University Film and Video Association. An organization for North American screen educators.

www.wga.org Writers Guild of America.

INFORMATIONAL DATABASES

www.allmovie.com A very large movie database.

www.boxofficeguru.com Box office and other statistics.

www.imdb.com Gargantuan movie database that enables every imaginable kind of production research, down to the careers of obscure technicians.

SCREENWRITING RESOURCES

www.cinestory.com Screenwriters' resource.

www.donedealpro.com Columns, books, advice, contests, examples, agencies, links.

www.screenplay.com Screenwriting software downloads.

www.screenstyle.com Screenplay software center.

www.screenwriting.com Screenwriters' resource with many links.

www.screenwritingexpo.com Annual screenwriting exposition.

www.writersstore.com Everything for writers and filmmakers, including software.

PERIODICALS

www.backstage.com *Back Stage* magazine, "the actor's resource."

www.dv.com *Digital Video* magazine. Excellent for software and equipment reviews and for keeping up-to-date with developments in the digital world.

www.filmlinc.com *Film Comment* magazine.

www.theasc.com/magazine American Society of Cinematographers.

www.variety.com *Variety,* the show business oracle. Get ready to learn a whole new vocabulary.

www.videomaker.com *Videomaker* magazine. Lots of good technology reviews and information.

RESOURCES

www.bhphotovideo.com B&H in New York City is simply the biggest supplier of camera, video, and sound equipment in the country. Their inventory is humongous, their information prodigious, and their prices are usually the best.

www.equipmentemporium.com A California sound equipment sales and rental center with a passion for educating people in sound recording. Lots of good advice and even basic procedural information online.

www.kino-eye.com Digital film, media technology, podcasting. Good for bibliographies on particular film subjects.

INDEX